THE VICTORIA HISTORY
OF THE
COUNTIES OF ENGLAND

GENERAL
INTRODUCTION

THE VICTORIA HISTORY
OF THE
COUNTIES OF ENGLAND

EDITED BY R. B. PUGH

THE UNIVERSITY OF LONDON
INSTITUTE OF
HISTORICAL RESEARCH

Oxford University Press, Ely House, 37 Dover Street, London, W.1

GLASGOW   NEW YORK   TORONTO   MELBOURNE   WELLINGTON
CAPE TOWN   SALISBURY   IBADAN   NAIROBI   DAR ES SALAAM   LUSAKA   ADDIS ABABA
BOMBAY   CALCUTTA   MADRAS   KARACHI   LAHORE   DACCA
KUALA LUMPUR   SINGAPORE   HONG KONG   TOKYO

SBN 19 722716 3

PRINTED IN GREAT BRITAIN
AT THE UNIVERSITY PRESS, OXFORD
BY VIVIAN RIDLER
PRINTER TO THE UNIVERSITY

INSCRIBED TO THE

MEMORY OF HER LATE MAJESTY

QUEEN VICTORIA

WHO GRACIOUSLY GAVE THE TITLE TO

AND ACCEPTED THE DEDICATION

OF THIS HISTORY

THE VICTORIA HISTORY
OF THE
COUNTIES OF ENGLAND

GENERAL
INTRODUCTION

EDITED BY R. B. PUGH

942

PUBLISHED FOR

THE INSTITUTE OF HISTORICAL RESEARCH

BY

OXFORD UNIVERSITY PRESS

1970

Distributed by Oxford University Press until 1 January 1974
thereafter by Dawsons of Pall Mall

CONTENTS

		PAGE
Dedication		v
Contents		ix
Classes of documents in the Public Record Office used in this volume		xi
The Victoria History: its Origin and Progress . . .	By Professor R. B. PUGH . .	1
Bibliographical Excursus		28
List of Volumes		30
Lists of Contents		34
Index of Titles of Articles	By PATRICIA A. TATTERSFIELD .	237
Index of Authors		275

LIST OF CLASSES OF DOCUMENTS IN THE PUBLIC RECORD OFFICE
USED IN THIS VOLUME
WITH THEIR CLASS NUMBERS

Board of Trade

    B.T. 31   Files of Dissolved Companies

Supreme Court of Judicature

    J 4   Affidavits, Series I

    J 15   Entry Books of Decrees and Orders (Chancery Division)

    J 57   Reports and Certificates

THE VICTORIA HISTORY: ITS

ORIGIN AND PROGRESS

I T is not precisely known by whom the *Victoria History* was invented.[1] Some credit has always gone to George Laurence (later Sir Laurence) Gomme, folklorist, antiquary, and first Clerk of the London County Council (1853–1916), who, according to one account, conceived the *History* as a monument to the Diamond Jubilee.[2] During the year 1898 Gomme expounded his ideas to Herbert Arthur Doubleday (1867–1941), a partner in the firm of Archibald Constable & Co., and well known in later life as the editor of *The Complete Peerage*.[3] Doubleday, who even at the time was thought to be more interested in historical research than in general publishing,[4] proved a sympathetic listener to Gomme's persuasive words, and the conversations which the two had together resulted in the germination of a *History* of dimensions 'out of all proportion'[5] to those that Gomme had originally proposed. In the spring of 1899 Doubleday drew up a preliminary scheme 'in conjunction with Gomme' and the two participants became joint editors[6] and jointly issued a prospectus.[7] Naturally enough Constables became the publishers.

The partnership was short, for Gomme's civic responsibilities soon forced him to withdraw. How soon this happened is uncertain. Doubleday said it was 'almost immediately after'[8] the publication of the first prospectus. William Page, later sole editor, said it was in 1902.[9] Since Page claimed to be Gomme's direct successor his testimony is weighty. On the other hand Gomme seems to have done little after 1899 and his name is not linked with Doubleday's as editor of any volume. Indeed the first volume in the series, *Hampshire* I (1900), was published under the editorship of Doubleday and Page. The truth seems to be that, as Doubleday himself put it, 'the idea of *a* County History originated with Gomme'[10] but that Doubleday so enlarged the idea as to make it his own. G. J. Turner, Ethel Stokes, and Stenton have united to acclaim Doubleday the founder.[11] More than that it was Doubleday who spent several vigorous

---

[1] The records of the *V.C.H.* are kept in the Institute of Historical Research. Most of the papers up to 1934 were weeded in 1952 and reduced from 200 to 60 boxes. They are here cited as '*V.C.H.* recs.' with the addition of box number, date, and description. Editorial correspondence accumulating between 1934 and 1949 is kept in the Editor's room. It is here referred to by date and description, with '*V.C.H.* recs., B' prefixed. Other correspondence, i.e. that conducted by the Secretary of the Institute, is in the Institute files and is arranged under the names of correspondents. It is here referred to as 'I.H.R. recs.' Since about Nov. 1949 most of the *V.C.H.* records have been segregated from the rest of the Institute records and classed by subject. They are here referred to as '*V.C.H.* files'. The minutes of the *V.C.H.* Committee are referred to as '*V.C.H.* Cttee. Mins.' and those of the Institute Committee as 'I.H.R. Cttee. Mins.'

[2] *Antiq. Jnl.* xiv. 196. For Gomme see *Proc. Soc. Antiq.*, 2nd ser. xxviii, 211–12; *The Times*, 25 Feb. 1916, 5b.

[3] For Doubleday see *Herbert Arthur Doubleday 1867–1941* (London, 1942), hereinafter called *Doubleday*. In-

formation about the origins of the *History* is also to be found in copies of letters to Granville Proby enclosed in a letter, 21 May 1938, from Doubleday to L. F. Salzman, then editor, in *V.C.H.* recs., B. The letters to Proby were prompted by an anonymous booklet distributed to those who attended the dinner in the University of London on 27 April 1938 to signalize the publication of the *History's* 100th volume. The booklet seemed to Doubleday to attribute too little credit to himself as the originator of the *V.C.H.* The chief letter (7 May) was written by Doubleday and is referred to here as 'Doubleday to Proby'. It supports the preceding sentence.

[4] *Doubleday*, 17.

[5] Doubleday to Proby.

[6] Ibid.

[7] *V.C.H.* recs., A37, undated prospectus.

[8] Doubleday to Proby.

[9] *History*, xvii (1933), 331.

[10] Doubleday to Proby.

[11] *Doubleday*, 22, 24–26.

years in mustering support, both financial and literary, and in endowing the *History* with a splendid format.

No records of the firm of Constable survive for this period.[12] Posterity is, therefore, very ill informed about the advantages which the firm hoped to derive from its new venture. Plainly the *History* could not have been published at a loss. Doubleday, ever skilful at attracting subsidies, secured indirectly an initial endowment of £20,000 from (Sir) Osmond E. D'Avigdor-Goldsmid[13] (created a baronet in 1934, d. 1940), equally eminent in Kentish local government and in the affairs of Anglo-Jewry.[14] Presumably there were other, if less magnificent, gifts. Lord Alverstone is remembered as a benefactor as is Hugh Spottiswoode, the publisher.[15] In general, however, the *History* was meant to be self-financing. For many years it was issued, in limited editions, to subscribers only whose names, in order to induce them to pay until completion, were to be printed in the last volume of each county set. The formation of local committees in each county, under the chairmanship in each instance of the Lord Lieutenant, was partly motivated by the desire to attract such subscriptions. But it seems that at first Doubleday hoped for a profit of £250,000, which, he declared in 1903, would, if earned, be given to some work 'of public utility'.[16]

In order that the *History* might enjoy due national and international renown Doubleday approached Lord Lorne, the *literato* of the royal family, with the suggestion that the *History* should bear Queen Victoria's name. Lorne, destined next year to succeed his father as 9th Duke of Argyll, agreed to ask the Queen, and, with the aid of Richard Rivington Holmes (later K.C.V.O.), the librarian at Windsor, induced her to consent. Ever since each volume of the *History* has been dedicated to the Queen or to her memory. Doubleday hoped that he might be allowed to say that the *History* was under the Queen's patronage. This was not sanctioned, but by commanding that a set should be placed in the library at Windsor the Queen was in effect deemed to be patron and in any event became by that command the first subscriber.[17] An attempt made in 1903 to induce Edward VII to become patron met with no better success.[18]

Doubleday, a skilled and persistent negotiator, angled for every benefit. He knew that the official publications of the Public Record Office would prove the life-blood of his enterprise and that they would be needed by contributors living in places inaccessible to libraries. He therefore secured, in 1900, an exchange of publications with the Public Record Office, the Office supplying three copies of each volume in return for volumes of the *History*. In 1902 this arrangement was complemented by another. Doubleday moved Balfour, who was then Prime Minister, to instruct the Stationery Office to supply on loan any official publications asked for by the *History*. Thus by 1922 Page had custody of two sets, one of which he then returned,[19] though the permission granted in 1902 was not rescinded.[20]

By 1899 an Advisory Council,[21] or, as it was called by 1901,[22] a General Advisory Council, had been formed, Argyll, we are told, playing a large part in assembling it.[23] It was a mixture of public men and scholars. In scholarship the Council was eminent.

[12] They were destroyed by enemy action in 1940: *V.C.H.* files, Constable Publishers to the author, 26 Feb. 1968.

[13] Doubleday to Proby.   [14] *Who was Who.*

[15] F. Clarke, 'The Parish Pump', *London Mercury*, xvii. 280; and see below, p. 6.

[16] Royal Archives, Windsor, R.A., Ed. VII, PP 30340, citing 3020 (no longer extant). Extracts herein from the Royal Archives are included by gracious permission of Her Majesty Queen Elizabeth II.

[17] *V.C.H.* recs., A30. For the forms of dedication see below, pp. 28–29.

[18] *V.C.H.* recs., A30, Lord Knollys to Doubleday, 14 Oct. 1903; Lord Kenyon to Doubleday, 18 Oct. 1903.

[19] Ibid. A34, P.R.O. and H.M.S.O. corresp.; A31, Letter Bk. 1922, ff. 28, 39*b*, 48.

[20] Ibid. A33, H.M.S.O. to Page, 25 Feb. 1931.

[21] *V.C.H.* recs., B, 1899 prospectus. Subsequent lists of its members will be found in the first volume of each county set up to *Suffolk* I (1911).

[22] *V.C.H.* recs., B, *Some Particulars concerning the Victoria History of the Counties of England* [1901], 17.

[23] Doubleday to Proby.

Acton, Creighton, and Stubbs were foundation members, and the first list of names also includes Geikie, Sir John Hooker, W. H. (later Sir William) St. John Hope, Lister, Maxwell Lyte, Sir Frederick Pollock, Round, and Maunde Thompson. What part the Council played in planning or management cannot be said. It may be doubted whether it was a large one. The only duty assigned to its members was to certify the destruction of copies of volumes surplus to the number subscribed for.[24] Below the Council were two committees, which may well have been effective. On the Records Committee sat Maitland, Maxwell Lyte, Round, and W. H. Stevenson, and on the Architectural Committee Blomfield, Baldwin Brown, Hope, and Round.[25] As has been said, there were also local committees, which, apart from their money-raising functions, were supposed to seek out local editors and contributors and 'gain access to private collections of MSS.'[26]

From the outset the *History* was planned as a whole. Every geographical county was included, the number of volumes ranging from eight for Yorkshire to two for Rutland. No special provision was made for London, which was included in Middlesex. The volumes for each county were to cover Natural History (including geology), Pre-historic, Roman, and Anglo-Saxon Remains, Ethnography, Domesday Book, Architecture, Ecclesiastical, Political, Maritime, and Economic and Social History, Industries, Arts, and Manufactures, the Feudal Baronage, Sport, 'Persons Eminent in Art, Literature, [and] Science', and Bibliographies. There were also to be 'Topographical Accounts of Parishes and Manors', and, if possible, a 'modern Domesday' listing all owners of estates of five acres or more. The volumes were to be plentifully supplied with maps, including reproductions of Speed's survey of 1610.[27] This plan has not been radically altered. Ethnography, however, was never in practice provided for, perhaps because of Gomme's departure, nor did the 'modern Domesday' appear. The 'Eminent Persons' found their niche not in separate articles but in the several parish histories. Moreover few general articles on architecture were published. The other 'general' articles, though some of them have been reshaped or re-entitled in the last twenty years, have been continued. By 1901 they had been joined by Schools.[28]

The articles on 'feudal baronage' deserve a distinct paragraph. They were to cover the descent of the 'feudal chiefs' up to the 'almost complete extinction of the old families at the end of the feudal period', presumably the Battle of Wakefield. From that point the curious reader must trace 'the family history' 'under the manors in the Topographical Section'. But in addition to this the editors contemplated chart-pedigrees as appendices to volumes. According to the first prospectus (1899) these were to form 'a supplemental volume for each county'. The oversea descendants of those families would be traced and 'feudal coats' would be emblazoned in colour. The arms would also be tricked out in the 'topographical' volumes, a practice which prevailed until after the Second World War. By c. 1901 the editors had designed a genealogical volume for each county to contain 'elaborately drawn pedigrees', with portraits, 'of those county families, titled or untitled, who have held a seat and landed estate in their male line since 1760'. The 'feudal baronage' articles were stopped in 1907[29] after only two of them had appeared and only for Hertfordshire and Northamptonshire were the genealogical volumes published.

The *History* was to run to 160 volumes, apart from the volumes of pedigrees.[30]

[24] e.g. *V.C.H.* recs., B, 1899 prospectus.
[25] Ibid.
[26] Ibid.
[27] Ibid.
[28] *Some Particulars . . .*, 13.

[29] *V.C.H.* recs., A58, memo. of 16 Apr. 1907. It should, however, be noted that an article called 'Feudal Wiltshire' was included in *Wiltshire* V (1957).
[30] *V.C.H.* recs., B, 1899 prospectus.

It could at first be supplied in parts, but the plan to provide them, though later revived, seems to have lapsed by 1901.

Doubleday appointed subject editors to write or organize the writing of topics in which they were specialists. They had a nation-wide responsibility and did not concentrate on particular regions, although they were supposed to keep in touch with local experts. Thus Hercules Read and Reginald Smith were the editors for 'Anglo-Saxon Remains', Haverfield for 'Roman Remains', Round for Domesday. All these had been appointed by 1899.[31] By 1901 A. F. Leach had become the editor for schools.[32] These men, of course, were not salaried employees. They wrote in their leisure for fees. In 1905 their editorial title was abandoned and they are represented in advertisements as contributors and helpers. In some counties at least there were also local editors. Thus R. S. Ferguson was appointed editor for Cumberland as early as 1899 and when he died next year was replaced by the Revd. James Wilson (d. 1923).[33] By 1903 William Farrar seems to have been acting similarly in Lancashire, having agreed to convert a scheme of his own for a Lancashire history into a set of *V.C.H.* volumes.[34] Those curious to trace the editorial structure may do so by examining the 'general advertisements' inserted up to 1911 (*Suffolk* I) in each first volume of a county set and the list of published volumes printed below[35] in which the local editors, where they existed, are named.

The pattern of the *History* is now so familiar and historical investigation has proceeded so far in the last seventy years that it is easy to forget that in origin the *History* was in the forefront of progress. First, it was a co-operative effort in which authorities of national repute were assigned tasks appropriate to them. Secondly, it laid great emphasis on the newly emergent science of archaeology and on economic history, also only just beginning to attract attention. Thirdly, it insisted that official records should be methodically searched and buildings scientifically examined. Fourthly, the narratives were to be illustrated by an abundance of maps. All these things were required by Doubleday and his Advisory Council and are still required. Finally, the *History* was to be systematic and uniform between county and county, such uniformity being achieved by the preparation and circulation of instructions to authors.

At a very early stage in planning Doubleday realized that his 'most troublesome problem' was going to be 'the compiling of the manorial histories'. The first scheme for the 'topographical' volumes seems to have omitted manorial descents. It must soon have been recognized that this would not do, and someone hit on the idea of entrusting the work to the local clergy. It then became apparent that far too few were fit to do it and still fewer free to visit London where the main body of accessible sources was to be found. This led to the conclusion that record searching must be centrally organized, and Doubleday accordingly called for help upon Messrs. Hardy and Page, a leading firm of London record agents. At first Hardy advised and supplied material for use by an unnamed local contributor who was commissioned to write the parish histories of the Hampshire hundred of Alton (*Hampshire* II, 1903). The experiment failed and it then became clear that what was needed was to assemble a team of university women, who had qualified in history or classics, to write the parish histories from extracts from the records supplied by Hardy and Page. If, however, this was to be done, there must be someone to give the training, since many though not all of them had only quite recently finished their courses. Doubleday persuaded Hardy and Page to rearrange their partnership so that Hardy should provide the materials and Page the training. By this means

[31] *V.C.H.* recs., B. 1899 prospectus.
[32] *Some Particulars . . .*, 13.
[33] *V.C.H.* recs., A57, Wilson to Doubleday, 15 Mar. 1900.
[34] *V.C.H.* recs., A37, printed circular to Advisory Council, July 1903.
[35] See pp. 30–33.

William Page (1861–1934), who was already the editor of many texts and author of many articles,[36] was brought into the organization as a permanent official. He gave up what he later called 'a lucrative practice'[37] in order to help Doubleday with this work as well as with the 'general' articles; and he became co-editor.[38] In July 1903 the two submitted the draft of a general *Guide*, founded upon the instructions to contributors already mentioned, to the Advisory Council.[39] The *Guide* appeared soon after. It described the treatment to be accorded to different topics, surveyed the most useful sources, and printed translations of Latin Christian names and surnames and of the titles of bishoprics. A few of its precepts are still adhered to. Its list of cartularies remained the only one available until the publication of *Medieval Cartularies of Great Britain* in 1958 edited by Dr. G. R. C. Davis. The editors also constructed somewhat unconventional rules for heraldic nomenclature and printed them.

The system by which the material for the 'topographical' volumes was accumulated wins the admiration of all who come into contact with it. The workers employed by Hardy and Page or by Page alone examined the indexes of all the Public Record Office publications then in print and likely to be useful and noted the names of all the places occurring in them on small quarto sheets of paper, called 'slips', with page references to those places; they did the same with the reports of the Historical Manuscripts Commission and with certain other large series; they read the whole of the *Dictionary of National Biography* for references to places in which those obituarized had lived or worked; they read through the manuscript indexes to the Notes of Fines and to the Recovery Rolls; they examined very large numbers of inquisitions post mortem, guild and chantry certificates, uncalendared Chancery rolls, proceedings in the prerogative courts; they similarly extracted some of the P.R.O. *Lists and Indexes*; they then sorted the 'slips' according to the parishes of *c.* 1831 and placed the slips for each parish into one or more envelopes. References to hundreds were treated similarly.[40] These 'slips' still exist in large quantities for all unfinished counties and are still the foundation of the 'topographical' narratives. Since their creation, however, there have been losses. It was the custom to send them out to contributors who were supposed to return them with their finished narratives. Not all, however, were recovered when the *History* collapsed after the First World War[41] and later still the collection was probably a little damaged during the evacuation of 1941.

During these first five feverish years an attempt was made to launch a *Victoria History of the Counties of Wales*.[42] The story, which is incomplete, seems to date from June 1901 when Doubleday arranged to meet the 4th Lord Kenyon (d. 1927) evidently to discuss such a project. By February next the Prince of Wales (later George V) had consented to become President and by March the first meeting of the 'General Committee' had been summoned. Kenyon himself was the chairman, Sir John Williams, Bt., and Dr. Henry Owen leading figures, and one Edward Owen, of the India Office,[43] the secretary. Under this body was an Executive Committee and for a while there was also an editorial sub-committee, charged with drawing up a scheme. Appeals for support began to be circulated and subscribers' names recorded. Soon after this a prospectus was issued on behalf of the Welsh Executive Committee outlining the plan, the essence of which was that there should be two 'general' volumes for the whole Principality and a sequence of 48 'topographical' volumes arranged county by county. 'The general supervision and editorial control' were to be in the hands of Doubleday and

[36] See the bibliography in *V.C.H. Rut.* ii, pp. xiv–xv.
[37] *V.C.H.* recs., B, Page to Hambleden, 5 Oct. 1931.
[38] Doubleday to Proby.
[39] In *V.C.H.* recs., A37.

[40] Ibid., undated memo. on work at P.R.O.
[41] *V.C.H.* recs., B, memo. for Mr. Meredith.
[42] *V.C.H.* recs., A19, prospectus.
[43] He was a Staff Clerk: *Whitaker's Almanack*, 1902.

Page but the 'local writers and departmental editors' were to be 'so far as possible . . . Welsh scholars'.

By the autumn of 1903 an attempt was being made to fuse the English and Welsh organizations under the Prince of Wales who, it was hoped, would become President of the *V.C.H.* Advisory Council. Kenyon acted as mediator and the Prince was understood to have consented provided that he was satisfied that the scheme was financially secure. Suitable assurances had not been received by March 1904 and meanwhile the Welsh promoters had grown anxious about the future of the Welsh histories. Edward Owen pressed Doubleday and Page for news but received none that contented him. He was merely asked to be patient. In the end, in July, the Welsh Committee terminated negotiations with the *V.C.H.* Syndicate and in September released the Welsh subscribers from their obligations.[44]

In 1904 Doubleday had a disagreement with his partners in Constables and left the firm. Whatever may have been the cause of the disagreement it had nothing to do with the *V.C.H.* nor with Page with whom Doubleday's relations 'remained most cordial'.[45] Page thereupon became sole editor and so continued until his death in 1934.

The *History* was by now a substantial enterprise. In 1900 a private limited company, called the 'County History Syndicate, Limited' had been formed to manage it.[46] The constituting instrument was in the form of a conveyance by Doubleday, Otto Kyllman, and William Maxse Meredith, all described as 'publishers' and all members of the Constable firm, to the new syndicate. Meredith was the favourite son of George Meredith, whose novels had been published by Constables since 1895.[47] The vendors became the first directors, with the addition of D'Avigdor-Goldsmid a few months after registration. Meredith became managing director in or about 1904. The nominal share capital at flotation was £15,000; the list of shareholders contained twenty names, and remained at approximately that number until the end. By 1907 Doubleday had ceased to be a director and had been replaced by G. E. Nathan. The offices of the *History* were registered at 2 Whitehall Gardens in 1900, whence they were moved to 16 James (later Orange) Street, off the Haymarket, in 1904.

By the articles of association the Directors were authorized to raise loans, particularly by the issue of debentures. They took full, indeed excessive, advantage of this power.[48] By 1906 they had created debentures of the nominal value of £75,000 of which £51,800 had actually been issued. In addition in the same year D'Avigdor-Goldsmid advanced the sum of £50,000 secured by the deposit of 50 £1,000 prior lien debentures at 6 per cent., the holders of ordinary debentures agreeing at about the same time that the prior lien debentures should have priority over their own. The prior lien debentures were issued in the Syndicate's name to the Directors and transferred to nominees of Coutts & Co., the Syndicate's bankers.[49] Soon afterwards they were guaranteed by William Hugh and Cyril Andrew Spottiswoode, D'Avigdor-Goldsmid, and W. F. D. Smith, later 2nd Viscount Hambleden,[50] who became a shareholder next year.[51] To the provision of these different types of loan capital it will be necessary to revert.

By 1903 the general editors were in touch with forty 'sectional editors'.[52] Then or soon after they were employing two full-time sub-editors and a team of more junior women workers. The sub-editors in 1907 were Dr. L. F. Salzman (then Mr. and

[44] *V.C.H.* recs., A30, Kenyon to Doubleday, 18 Oct. 1903; A19, prospectus.
[45] Doubleday to Proby.
[46] Except where otherwise stated this paragraph is drawn from P.R.O., B.T.31/16421/66282.
[47] *D.N.B.*
[48] P.R.O., B.T.31/16421/66282.
[49] P.R.O., J 4/9294/458.
[50] Coutts & Co., file 4640, Waterhouse to Coutts, 14 Dec. 1920.
[51] P.R.O., B.T.31/16421/66282.
[52] *V.C.H.* recs., A37, printed circular to Advisory Council, July 1903.

Salzmann) and C. H. Vellacott.[53] A list of junior workers of 1905 contains 16 names, five of the bearers having secured a title to first class degrees at either Oxford or Cambridge. They included Phyllis Wragge, who left in 1908 to become a Lecturer at Goldsmiths' College. Their salaries were very low and were raised in 1905 on the advice of some Heads of Houses. Page estimated in 1905 that after three months a worker had received 'a training sufficient to make her efficient in the compilation of topography'.[54] A somewhat later estimate and a more sober one declared that it took 'over a year to teach a worker'. At that time there were only about ten 'competent' topographers though there was space to house double that number.[55] Architectural surveying was first entrusted to St. John Hope. In 1903 he was joined or replaced by C. J. (later Sir Charles) Peers who was the salaried architect until 1910. Late in 1907 Peers had six assistants, whom Page, ever willing to adopt new devices, would have liked to mount on motor bicycles.[56]

Over this corps of collaborators and assistants Page presided. Versatile, tactful, energetic, progressive, and scholarly, he was the *History*'s greatest asset.[57] Besides being these things he was a realist, whereas Doubleday seems to have been something of a visionary.[58] One cannot believe that at any time Page would have estimated, as Doubleday did at the beginning,[59] that the whole enterprise would be completed in six years.

The *History*, as has been shown, was planned as a whole, a pre-determined number of volumes being assigned to each county. It was the aim to get all the counties started and running together since it was only by this means that there could be a sufficient return on the capital. Since the 'general' history was published in the earlier volumes of each county 'set' it was the 'general' volumes that most rapidly appeared. All the seven volumes published up to 1902 were 'general' ones. Authors could work fast in those days; the accessible sources were much fewer and the editorial standards laxer. Printers also worked faster than they now can do. Output, therefore, by the standards of today was very large; between 1905 and 1907 27 volumes appeared, making a total by that date of 38 volumes. Sales were fostered by booklets,[60] one of 1905 or 1906 and one of 1906 or 1907, describing the scheme of the *History* at some length. The second was called *A National Memorial*, which shows how valuable the link with the throne remained.

By 1907 the *History* was beginning to get into difficulties. The difficulties first become apparent in a memorandum drawn up by Page in April in which various prospective economies are listed. Further articles on the feudal baronage would be dropped; delays caused by concentrating authorship in the hands of a few experts would be avoided by using more junior workers whose work would be vetted by experts; a new method of numbering the footnotes would reduce the cost of printing.[61] Whether the Syndicate had positively asked for economies is not clear but at a meeting in December they certainly sent Page a minute asking for a report on progress. Obviously if more volumes appeared more sales would result. Page said[62] that he aimed to maintain an output of 16 volumes a year, which meant that he had to have on hand about 22 volumes at a time so that if some volume were delayed by a dilatory contributor another could be put in its place. He pointed out, however, that what really retarded progress was the 'topographical' volumes. He had said in April that they were the most difficult of all to complete because

[53] Ibid. A37, Page to Syndicate, Dec. 1907. Dr. Salzman, however, had joined the staff in 1904: ibid. A18, Salzman corresp.

[54] *V.C.H.* recs., A37, memo. on staff salaries, 14 Mar. 1905.

[55] Ibid. A58, undated note on Mr. Meredith's estimate.

[56] Ibid. A37, Page to Syndicate, Dec. 1907.

[57] For his life see *V.C.H. Rut.* ii; *D.N.B.*

[58] *Doubleday*, 14.

[59] R.A., Ed. VII, PP 30340, citing 2045 (no longer extant).

[60] *V.C.H.* recs., B.

[61] In *V.C.H.* recs., A58.

[62] Ibid. A37, Page to Syndicate, Dec. 1907.

there was a dearth of qualified writers. They were also more expensive than 'general' volumes. Meredith's suggestion, which he commended, was to employ some of the existing staff, presumably in their leisure, at piece rates. He saw little hope in enlarging the corps of local editors. Some of those they had tried had been found wanting; H. E. Malden, the Surrey editor, fell into this class and Page also had his doubts about James Wilson. Brownbill had, however, done good work on Lancashire and the Revd. Thomas Taylor and Stenton were expected to do the like on Cornwall and Nottinghamshire. The Syndicate did not deal very systematically with these suggestions but asked Page[63] to limit the expenses on each volume to a figure named, if necessary amending the requirements of the *Guide*; they questioned whether the architectural descriptions were not too elaborate, and seemed to recommend a somewhat more popular treatment.

It is not known precisely what provoked the crisis and the consequent investigation. It is possible that a crisis had for some time been building up, for it is fairly clear that Doubleday had underestimated the problems presented by 'topographical' volumes. Be this as it may, it becomes clear by early 1909 that 'the great financial prop of the organization'—whoever he may have been—had withdrawn support, as it was said 'apparently for private reasons'.[64]

To meet prospective losses prices had been raised in 1908,[65] a 'bumper' year for publication,[66] but work had to stop in 1909.[67] In the same year, however, efforts were made to promote a guarantee fund by interesting Edward VII in the work. Petitions were presented by the Society of Antiquaries and the Royal Historical Society to the king in the hope of inducing him to express his approval of the *History* and so prevent its abandonment. Despite intervention by Princess Louise and Sir John Fortescue (then Librarian at Windsor) the king was unwilling to do more than allow it to be known privately that he regretted the financial difficulties described and that he would be glad to be kept informed of the progress of the *History*. No open expression of the king's approval and appreciation of the national importance of the work, such as the promoters of the petitions had hoped for, was forthcoming.[68] Later evidence, however, makes it clear that the king was willing to bestow a baronetcy on any suitable person who would endow the *History*. John Rankin (1845–1928), a Liverpool shipowner and benefactor to Liverpool University,[69] was approached accordingly but evidently was unwilling at the time to make an adequate benefaction. The idea was not forgotten.

Nevertheless by means that are only partly known the *History* revived and survived. Prospects had become brighter by May 1909[70] and by April 1910 a new start was made. This was in part achieved through an agreement of March 1910[71] which provided that W. F. D. Smith should guarantee the interest on the loans made by the debenture holders, should finance and print through W. H. Smith & Sons certain specified volumes, should pay outright some of the Syndicate's debts, and should receive the proceeds of the specified volumes until his debt should be discharged. Certain payments to Constables for rent and services and fees due to the Syndicate Directors were to be held in abeyance for three years. By 1912 the President of the Society of Antiquaries of London was able to announce in his address to the Anniversary meeting that the *History* was on its feet again thanks to Smith's liberality.[72]

Although this was to the good, the *History* had naturally been set back. Some of the

[63] *V.C.H.* recs., A37, Syndicate to Page, report of meeting of 31 Dec. 1907.
[64] R.A., G. V, 588.
[65] *V.C.H.* recs., A37, prospectus of Jan. 1908.
[66] 12 vols.
[67] *V.C.H.* recs., B., memo. for Mr. Meredith.
[68] R.A., Ed. VII, PP 30340.

[69] *V.C.H.* recs., A31, Letter Bk. 1922, 1b. For him see *Who was Who* and *The University of Liverpool 1903–1953*, 7.
[70] *V.C.H.* recs., A16, Page to Scott-Holmes, 12 May 1909.
[71] Ibid. A37, agreement of 22 Mar. 1910.
[72] *Proc. Soc. Antiq.* 2nd ser. xxiv. 250.

former staff had had to be laid off. Of these some left for good and had to be replaced, while others could not return until they had fulfilled their interim engagements.[73] The arrangements for architectural surveying had also to be reorganized. By 1909 a relationship had been established with the Historical Monuments Commission, which had been formed in the preceding year. Two employees of the Commission, J. W. Blow and J. M. Kendall, were allowed to work for the *History*. The notes that they took were to belong to the Commission but the *History* was to have the right to use them. By 1912 these two, with C. C. Durston, were using notes already collected by the Commission.[74] In 1911, however, there were still staff architects. John Queckett, with 18 months' service, was the chief of these. He succeeded Peers as chief architect, but was killed in the First World War.[75] E. A. R. Rahbula was another. There were, however, still men whom Page was trying to retain at piece rates: Kaines Smith, a former full-timer, who had left so that he might continue lecturing, Peers, and Harold (later Sir Harold) Brakspear.[76] Constables provided these architects with bicycles.[77]

A new prospectus[78] was issued which reveals certain changes. Eleven counties were divided in two, the divisions consisting of 'general' volumes and two or three 'topographical' 'sections'. In Yorkshire's case the three 'sections' corresponded to the three ridings. A separate history of London had now been planned. The genealogical volumes had been silently abandoned. For the first time mention is made of a distinct volume devoted to the Roman history of the six northern counties. This Roman volume had been devised by 1903 but apparently never advertised. At first it embraced only Cumberland, Durham, Northumberland, and Westmorland.[79] By 1905 the possibility of extending it to Lancashire and Yorkshire was being considered owing to Haverfield's inability 'to deliver the articles . . . to the time required',[80] and these counties were settled additions by 1910.[81] The total number of volumes, advertised in the prospectus, was thus raised to 181 and an 'Empire' edition, procurable on the instalment plan, provided.

Edward VII died in May 1910. Almost exactly a year thereafter an attempt was made to stimulate the *History*'s fortunes by arousing his successor's enthusiasm.[82] The new sovereign was asked to express interest, and to utter the hope that the *History* might be completed at 'an early date' and that he might be kept informed of its progress. He was also asked to grant Page and Meredith an audience, at which the difficulties and achievements of the undertaking might be explained. Such an audience, it was thought, would show 'the general public the importance of the undertaking' and would give pleasure to literary contributors and to the owners of manuscripts who had allowed access to them. Finally Queen Mary, known to be much interested in women's work, was asked to take note that much of the preliminary research and many of the manorial descents had been entrusted to women 'who have taken scholarships at the Universities'. In the event the King and Queen assured the petitioners that they were as interested in the *History* as their predecessors had been and hoped for its completion and that they appreciated the laborious nature of the research; and the king asked to be kept informed of progress. The request for an audience, however, was not conceded. This looks like another attempt to secure a baronetcy for a benefactor.[83]

[73] *V.C.H.* recs., A58, memo. of 6 Dec. 1910.
[74] Ibid. A34, correspondence with Hist. Mon. Com.
[75] *Proc. Soc. Antiq.* 2nd ser. xxx. 191.
[76] *V.C.H.* recs., A58, memo. on architectural staff, 5 Oct. 1911.
[77] Ibid. A31, Page to Rahbula, 21 Nov. 1913.
[78] *V.C.H.* recs., B.
[79] Ibid. A57, Page to Jas. Wilson, 18 Nov. 1903.

[80] Ibid. A37, memo. of 11 Apr. 1905.
[81] Ibid. A58, memo. of 6 June 1910. The statement, however, there made that the six counties were to be divided into two volumes is not supported by later prospectuses.
[82] R.A., G. V., 588.
[83] When corresponding about the baronetcy in 1922 (see p. 11) Page sent Meredith a letter in this series.

By this time the new financial arrangements had begun to produce results. Eight volumes were issued in 1911 and 14 more in the three succeeding years, making by the end of 1914 a grand total, excluding genealogical volumes, of 74. New prospectuses were issued in 1914, one a slightly 'jazzy' one showing portraits of Queen Victoria and her two successors and of various contributors and editors, and a new booklet like those of ten years before called *The Record of a Great National Undertaking*.[84] By this time all editions were procurable by instalment payments and specially designed Globe-Werwicke bookcases, to enclose the *History*, were on the market! It seems too that the policy of limiting purchases to subscribers had been abandoned, for in February 1913 the Caxton Publishing Company was marketing the volumes.[85] The limitation, however, continued to be expressed in the preliminaries.

War naturally put a stop to all activity. No work was done after 1915, nothing was published during the war years, and the staff, said to number 'some four sub-editors, four architects, and over forty research and clerical workers', dispersed.[86] While the situation must have been most mortifying to Page he could nonetheless recall with satisfaction that by this time nine counties had been for all practical purposes finished. In a few instances the volumes could not be published until later and consequently the sets could not be indexed but the promoters had done well in face of their difficulties. Page spent part of the war organizing a series of lives of the kings and queens of England in which Dr. Salzman's *Henry II* (1917) was a contemporary title, and in preparing with some of his former colleagues *Commerce and Industry* (2 volumes, 1919).

By 1920 the Syndicate, hopeful of revival, had worked out a new scheme. In the past only complete county sets could be subscribed for. It was now decided to offer the *History*, both what had already been published and what was yet to come, in wrapper-cased parts.[87] The supply of complete volumes, however, was not discontinued. Presumably there was little bound stock remaining and the provision of parts seemed to offer profits on a 'get rich quick' system. Instead of binding up whole volumes in sheet form, preference was given to binding parts. With characteristic cleverness Page persuaded the Board of Education to allow him to republish two paragraphs from *Suggestions for the consideration of Teachers and others concerned in the Work of Public Elementary Schools* when advertising the parts. These paragraphs, taken from Chapter VI of the *Suggestions* on 'The Teaching of History', commended local studies as a means of interesting children in history in general.[88]

These efforts did not save the *History*. By no device could sales be made to match the greatly increased costs of production. Moreover the *History* had lost by death several of its former supporters.[89] By December 1920 it was necessary to inform Coutts & Co. that almost certainly no interest would be paid in the coming January on the £50,000 long ago advanced by them on the security of prior lien debentures. The Directors, who were now Hambleden, Meredith, Kyllman, and Nathan, with Hambleden as chairman, decided that regular publication must cease and that the Syndicate must be wound up. A winding-up meeting took place on 1 March 1920 at which a liquidator was appointed. The Directors very naturally wished to preserve as much as possible of the fabric and realized this could best be done if a receiver and manager were appointed with the Supreme Court's authority. Accordingly Coutts & Co., acting for the prior lien debenture holders, soon after brought a successful action in the Chancery Division against the Syndicate, which was thereupon liquidated. The surviving guarantors of

84 *V.C.H.* recs., B.
85 Ibid. cutting from *The Times*, 5 Feb. 1913.
86 Ibid. appeal to the Pilgrim Trust, 1931; A58, Page to Hambleden, 19 July 1924.
87 Ibid. B., prospectus.
88 Ibid.
89 Ibid. A33, Page to Rees, 3 Feb. 1930.

the debentures forfeited their guarantees; the Spottiswoodes having meanwhile died, a compromise settlement was reached with their executors. The ordinary debenture holders received only a proportion of their due. The assets, such as they were, were to be sold for a small sum.[90] The authors of unpublished articles had already been notified of the state of affairs and their contributions returned to them. Among the returned articles was Stenton's introduction to the Lincolnshire Domesday, which was published elsewhere.[91]

Page carried on as editor without a salary, for a period which in the end amounted to two years. In these desperate circumstances his thoughts turned again to Rankin and he found him more amenable than he had formerly been. In fact Rankin made it known that if a baronetcy were forthcoming he would endow the *History* with £50,000, the equivalent of the bank loan. The negotiation went far but at the last moment an attempt was made to secure the money for party funds. The attempt failed and Rankin's name did not appear in the New Year's honours' list of 1922. Backed by Lord Crawford and H. A. L. Fisher Page begged him not to withdraw his support. By 23 February he had consented to maintain it. Two days later news came that he had fallen ill. By 1 March the offer had been rescinded and the contract cancelled. Whether Rankin was and remained too ill to conduct further business, or whether his sickness affected his judgement and caused him to change his mind, cannot now be known.[92]

Determined to save the *History* Page now applied to the Delegates of the Oxford University Press, in the hope of persuading the Clarendon Press to accept the *History* as a gift, with a view to its eventual completion. He thought it could be bought from the liquidator rather cheaply and received free from debt. He was persuaded that the Press could make it pay in the end. The project had the powerful support of George McDonald, H. A. L. Fisher, Sir Arthur Evans, and A. C. Headlam, and, among the Delegates, C. R. L. Fletcher and the Bishop of Ripon (Dr. T. B. Strong). The omens were favourable but early in May the Delegates turned the application down.[93]

Throughout the year the 2nd Lord Hambleden (W. F. D. Smith), whose financial interest in the *History* has already been explained, had been kept constantly informed by Page of what had been going on. He it was who would have bought the *History* for the Clarendon Press, had things gone well. To him Page now turned with the following scheme. Hambleden should buy the *History* from the receiver; any saleable assets should be realized; the proceeds of the sale should be paid out over the first three succeeding years, one half to Smiths for printing off and binding those volumes which had been set up in type but could not be completed for lack of capital, and the other half to Page for his work as editor and manager; Page should try to find means to carry on the work after the triennium had elapsed; the stock and notes should be removed from Orange Street, but Constables should continue as sales agents.[94] This scheme was quickly accepted by Hambleden who in July purchased the rights for £2,000 and authorized Page to carry on as best he could. Page had meanwhile built a cottage (Ashmere Croft) at Middleton near Bognor and moved there from Frognal Lodge, Hampstead, in the autumn. In the garden he built a hut to which he

[90] Part of the story will be found in Coutts & Co., file no. 4640. It is complemented by P.R.O., B.T.31/16421/66282; B.T.34/2936/66282; J 4/9294/458, /9295/548, /9298/1183, /9300/1613, /9296/890, /9300/1566; J 15/3575 no. 893, /3582 no. 2346, /3583 no. 2533; J 57/6119, filed 18 Apr., and /6176, filed 1 Aug. The action number is 1921 C. 1216. The syndicate was finally dissolved in 1926: *Lond. Gaz.* 7 Dec. 1926, p. 8029.

[91] *The Lincolnshire Domesday . . .*, ed. C. W. Foster and T. Longley (Lincs. Rec. Soc. xix, 1924).

[92] The story has been pieced together from *V.C.H.* recs., A31, Letter Bk., ff. 1–4A*b*; ibid. B., Page to Hambleden, 5 Oct. 1931; I.H.R. Pollard Corresp. 6/16, note by Pollard of conversation with Page on 22 June 1932. The second source (which in 1969 was mislaid) seems wrongly to imply that Rankin never considered renewing his offer after his name had been dropped.

[93] *V.C.H.* recs., A31, Letter Bk., ff. 3*b*–19*b*.

[94] Ibid. ff. 20*b*–22, 38*b*, 39.

transferred all the materials, weighing 14 tons,[95] needed for continuing the *History*.[96] There they remained until his death.

The parting with Constables was not a happy one[97] and it was perhaps partly in consequence of this that the St. Catherine Press, an outlier of Smiths, undertook publication in 1923. Back stock was then moved from Constables premises to the St. Catherine Press warehouses.[98] Hambleden continued to make the *History* an allowance even after the end of the agreed triennium but this met only the cost of general editorial expenses and other overheads, and there was no margin with which to pay a staff. All the writing had to be done by Page himself or be contracted out. Moreover, once the volumes awaiting publication had been issued, Page had to secure subsidies if he wished to initiate new projects.[99] These in the case of the Huntingdon and Northampton volumes required the benefactors either by direct grant or by guarantee to a bank to provide a sufficient sum to cover any loss on the volumes. Page rendered six-monthly accounts to the guarantors.[1] It is obvious that this was a time-consuming operation and also personally uncongenial to Page.[2] Nor were his attempts to secure guarantors always successful by any means. In 1925 he tried to induce E. C. Grenfell (later Lord St. Just), of the firm of Morgan, Grenfell & Co., bankers, to guarantee the London volumes. His failure was the more regrettable, since, had he succeeded, 'the University of London would have given its co-operation'.[3]

At first Page favoured the sale of the *History* in parts, continuing the earlier policy, and an experiment was made with *Cornwall* II, two sections of which were so issued in 1924. The experiment, however, seems to have been a financial failure and the intention to complete the volume, voiced in 1926, has not yet been fulfilled. In 1927 Hambleden allowed Page to sell nearly all the Northumberland materials to the Northumberland County History Committee, then actively completing Hodgson's history of that county.[4] Hence and henceforth Northumberland was cut out of the *V.C.H.*

The support given by the 2nd Lord Hambleden was continued by his son, the 3rd viscount, for some years after his father's death in 1928. The economic crisis of 1931, however, made it impossible to maintain it. In December 1930, when support was about to be withdrawn, Page made a fruitless appeal for aid to the Pilgrim Trust,[5] a body which had then only very recently been created. The appeal was lodged with the Trustees by F. M. (later Sir Maurice) Powicke, who earlier in the year had tried to ensure the continuance of the Oxfordshire volumes. Powicke's efforts had led Page to approach the Oxford Press again in the hope that they would at least publish those volumes, if no others.[6]

In the end Hambleden conveyed the surviving rights to Page on easy terms and on 3 February 1932 Page became sole owner as well as editor.[7] On the eve of transfer he was privileged to recall that since 1923 he had brought out 16 volumes and two parts almost unaided.

During this depressing period a connexion had been established with the Institute of Historical Research which had been founded in 1921. A complete set of volumes was presented to the Institute in 1922 and as an act of reciprocity Page was allotted

[95] *V.C.H.* recs. A33, Page to Rees, 3 Feb. 1930.
[96] Ibid. A31, Letter Bk., ff. 23*b* sqq.
[97] Ibid. f. 50.
[98] Ibid. A58, Page to Hambleden, 11 Feb. 1924.
[99] Ibid. B, appeal to the Pilgrim Trust, 1931.
[1] I.H.R. Pollard Corresp., 6/16, Page to Morris, 18 Sept. 1928.
[2] *V.C.H.* recs., B, Page to Hambleden, 5 Oct. 1931.

[3] Ibid. A58, Page to Hambleden, 31 July 1925; A32, D. C. Gray and Page correspondence.
[4] Ibid. A58, Page to Hambleden, 23 and 26 May 1927.
[5] Ibid. A33, Powicke and Page correspondence.
[6] Ibid., Cope and Page and Powicke and Page correspondence; undated letter from Page to H. Milford.
[7] Ibid. A33, Harper to Page, 5 Feb. 1932.

a room in the building,[8] which he retained though he did not often use it. He presented new volumes to the Institute as they appeared and supervised a few external Ph.D. students.[9]

From his long association with it Page must naturally have thought of the Institute as a possible adopter.[10] Perhaps this was something that he and A. F. Pollard, then Director, had casually discussed before. At any rate, on 24 May 1932 Page asked Pollard whether, should he fail to secure any other means of support, the Institute would like the *History* on his death as a gift. He did not positively require the Institute to continue the *History*, though that was naturally his wish, but felt that in any case its materials could be used in the Institute. Page was fond of declaring that over the years 'a school of local history' had been founded under him, a 'school of archaeological architecture' under Peers and Queckett, and a school of heraldry under E. E. (later Canon) Dorling. He now looked forward to the establishment of 'a school of local history' in the Institute.[11]

The negotiations proceeded steadily and well. By July 1932 Page was offering to transfer the *History* to the University immediately, subject to certain guarantees. In September the Institute Committee recommended the Senate to accept the gift. The Senate agreed and in November the Court approved the Senate's resolution and the same month news of the transfer was broken to the world.[12]

At Page's suggestion the Pilgrim Trust had been induced to provide an initial endowment, and in March 1933 the Institute Committee were asked by the Principal to produce a scheme of administration. This was ready by the time of the Committee's May meeting and was approved by the Senate in June.[13] The scheme provided that a sub-committee of not more than twelve should be appointed by the Institute Committee, consisting partly of members of that Committee and partly of other persons, expert in the sources of local art, archaeology, history, and architecture, and persons prominently connected with such organizations as the Public Record Office, the British Records Association, the Society of Antiquaries, and the Place Name Society. The objects of the Committee were to be '(i) the collection of material for, and preparation of, new volumes of the Victoria County History, and the revision of the old volumes', and '(ii) the editing and publication of such material, or such volumes, as may be gradually rendered feasible by financial support'. On 28 June the Institute Committee set up the sub-committee 'to conduct the editorial and business management of the History, subject to the authority of the [Institute] Committee in matters of finance; and to examine and report upon the annual estimates of the History'. The sub-committee met first on 19 July 1933 and elected Page for its Chairman. It has been meeting regularly ever since, term by term, except during the years of the Second World War. In October 1950 its number was increased to fifteen.

The advantages of the transfer to the Institute were not immediate. By the deed of gift, dated 15 February 1933, Page had indeed undertaken to complete the seven volumes then in hand without cost to the Institute. At the same time he had reserved for his own and his wife's life the proceeds of sales, subject to the liability to pay off to the guarantors the debt upon the guaranteed volumes. The *History*'s only endowment came from the Pilgrim Trust, which amounted to no more than £1,500 payable over three years. Page himself was over seventy and was known to have a weak heart.

---

[8] *Annual Rep. of I.H.R.* 1921–2; I.H.R. corresp. (Page).

[9] *V.C.H.* recs., A58, Page to Hambleden, 22 Jan. 1926.

[10] This paragraph and the next are based on I.H.R., Pollard corresp. 6/16; I.H.R. Cttee. Mins.; and *V.C.H.* Cttee. Mins.

[11] *History*, xvii. 331.

[12] *The Times*, 15 Nov. 1932 with leading article.

[13] From this point to p. 27 the narrative, except where otherwise stated, rests on the Mins. of the *V.C.H.* Cttee.

Nevertheless the transfer seemed to offer a real hope of continuity and its announcement at once attracted offers of co-operation from outside. The only one to be taken up came from an influential group[14] in Oxfordshire who asked whether with local aid the Oxfordshire volumes might not be continued. A sub-committee of the Victoria County History Committee was formed to negotiate with these sponsors. As a result the sponsors were authorized to appeal for funds and to issue a prospectus announcing that if those funds were forthcoming a volume on the City and University would be given priority. The Committee also appointed a part-time assistant to the Editor, Miss Catherine Jamison, who had been a *V.C.H.* worker in the early years and had written on contract subsequently.[15] She was commissioned to revise the most advanced of the *London* volumes. Later events frustrated this imaginative enterprise.

Before the Committee's third meeting could occur Page had died. There was thus no Editor and emergency arrangements had to be made for completing the four volumes then in hand. The unsold stock, notes, and other materials at Middleton, of which there were no proper inventories and which were enormously bulky, were listed and removed to London. The Committee decided to appeal for a grant from University funds to provide an editor's salary after the Pilgrim Trust money was exhausted and also for a loan as working capital. The Institute Committee approved and in June Charles Johnson and Stenton represented the *V.C.H.* Committee at a discussion with the Finance and General Purposes Committee of the University. In the end the petition was blessed by the Senate on 18 June 1934 and eventually approved by the Court. The loan capital was set at £4,000 payable to the end of 1937–8 and recoverable from sales and any contributions that outside sources might yield, and an outright grant for the Editor became available in 1936–7.[16] Dr. Salzman, who had already consented to complete the two Sussex volumes in hand, accepted the editorship, though initially for one year only, and took up office on 1 January 1935.

Meanwhile Mrs. Page had agreed to accept an annuity out of *V.C.H.* funds in lieu of her rights to the proceeds of sales. This was ratified at the January meeting of the Committee, over which since October Sir Charles Peers had presided. The plan for continuing *London* was dropped, a new and somewhat ambitious programme, drafted by Dr. Salzman, was considered, various economies in the text of future volumes were recommended, and negotiations initiated, which closed successfully in November for appointing the Oxford University Press as publishers on an agency basis and printers of the *History* in place of the St. Catherine Press. This decision was taken partly in the belief that the new contract would produce economies. By June a part-time Assistant to the Editor had been appointed. No other additions were made to the staff before the outbreak of war except that in June 1937 a part-time architect was appointed. After the revival of 1922 the *History*'s contacts with the Historical Monuments Commission had been renewed and were effective by 1926.[17] When the University acquired the *History* the architectural surveying was still being done on contract and Blow was one of the men employed. Having retired from the Commission's service he was now appointed on a yearly basis to fill the post created, the Committee having condemned the contract system in May 1935.

A grave lack of cash continued to embarrass the Committee, and in November 1935 a Finance Sub-Committee of the *V.C.H.* Committee met to consider ways of improving the funds. It was converted into a standing sub-committee and sat until June 1939. It had become clear that sales at least over the first five years or so[18] were not meeting

[14] (Sir) Charles Peers, (Sir) Maurice Powicke, Dr. H. E. Salter, and (Sir) George Clark.
[15] Obit. in *Archives*, vii. 169.
[16] Senate Mins. 18 June 1934, paras. 3031–4.
[17] *V.C.H.* recs., A58, Page to Hambleden, 22 Jan. 1926.
[18] *Genealogists' Mag.* vii (1937), 454.

costs and that there was a deficit on each volume. It was decided that a general appeal would probably fail at that time and that reliance must be placed on local ones. War-wickshire and Cambridgeshire were selected for this treatment and intensive efforts were made to interest Local Authorities in the appeals. Dr. Salzman had suggested in the previous March that *Sussex* VII should be published without guarantees and that the Sussex authorities should be asked for their support. With him, therefore, originates the idea of local government co-operation, although it was some time before anyone tried to interest the authorities in Sussex.

Warwickshire responded well to the application. The County Council offered £500 in annual instalments and later Birmingham, Coventry, Sutton Coldfield, and Nuneaton joined in. Their grants were linked with requests, which were granted, for copies of the published volumes or of offprints. To remove any doubts that District Auditors might entertain about the propriety of such grants the Minister of Health (Sir Kingsley Wood) stated in July 1936 that he would sanction applications by local authorities for leave to make grants to the Committee for the completion of the histories of their areas. This authority governed all future grants until the Local Government (Financial Provisions) Act, 1963,[19] amending Section 136 of the Local Government Act, 1948,[20] made it superfluous. The Warwickshire appeal went well, and from 1 June 1937 Mr. Philip Styles, then Lecturer in Local History at Birmingham University, was appointed part-time Local Editor to complete or superintend the completion of *War-wickshire* III and IV. The Warwickshire subscribers were to receive *Bulletins* reporting progress, of which apparently two were issued. Mr. Styles was able to superintend only Volume III and was released from any further liability in 1942. The Warwickshire volumes have since been completed by other means.

The Cambridgeshire appeal was less successful. In January 1936 the Cambridge Colleges were asked to support it and did so, but the local authorities, though con-sulted, never contributed. The volumes, however, went ahead and the first was issued in 1938. Later on, early in 1939, a Sussex appeal was issued by the Lord Lieutenant (Lord Leconfield) to the Sussex local authorities and others. Considering the difficulties of the time and uncertainties of the future this went reasonably well and the proceeds were spent on Sussex volumes then in production. The Oxfordshire Committee con-tinued to accumulate funds and to supervise work on the history of the City and University. The funds were handed to the *V.C.H.* Committee about June 1937 for custody but the history of the City and University was not finished by the outbreak of war. Plans for issuing a county appeal were postponed in June 1939 until the next September but obviously could not be realized.

During this period the *V.C.H.* Committee must have been encouraged to receive in 1935 a letter of good will from George V's Private Secretary noting the transfer of management to the University and asking for future progress reports. Not less encouraging was the publication of the hundredth volume which was celebrated by a dinner in the University buildings in April 1938 presided over by the Chancellor, Lord Athlone. A booklet surveying progress was distributed to the guests and another royal message read.[21] The dinner was arranged partly in the hope of attracting some large benefaction, perhaps the £50,000 for which the Editor had asked in the preceding year.[22] No such benefactor, however, stepped forward.

War was declared on 3 September 1939. Two meetings of the Committee occurred thereafter, the second in March 1940. They can only have been melancholy occasions.

---

[19] 1963, c. 46.
[20] 11 & 12 Geo. VI, c. 26.

[21] *The Times*, 28 Apr. 1938, 16c.
[22] *Genealogists' Mag.* vii (1937), 454.

True, the publication of *Oxfordshire* I and *Sussex* VII, which were then well advanced, was sanctioned and occurred. Moreover, the Editor was retained and continued to work on the Warwickshire *History* to the extent that circumstances allowed, though his Assistant (renamed Assistant Editor) was released. The future, however, was bleak and it had to be recalled that since 1933 only ten volumes had been published. Several conclusions could have been drawn. First, that financing by means of guarantees was impracticable in the world of the 1930s; secondly, the *History* could not be made self-supporting; thirdly, for the future, if there was to be a future, some help might be expected from local authorities. As to the guarantees it may here be mentioned that the Institute remained responsible for those for *Northamptonshire* III, *Rutland* II and Index, and *Sussex* III and IX, though it compounded for the last four in 1965 and the first in 1966. Granville Proby, who had personally guaranteed the Huntingdonshire volumes and had paid for the index volume outright in 1935, transferred his guarantee together with the copyright in those volumes to the University in 1935 and 1939.

The Committee met next in May 1943 under the chairmanship of Sir Cyril Flower, honorary acting Director of the Institute. The Institute Committee, inspired by the mid-war ardour for reconstruction, had called for a report on post-war plans. From it there emerged a short paper by Flower urging a much enlarged publication programme of four volumes a year with a consequential increase in staff. Little, he thought, was to be expected from local authorities in future, other sources of supply could be ignored, and the University should increase its grant, then running at about £1,000 a year, by a further £5,000 a year. Dr. Salzman thought that there should be closer links with the Historical Monuments Commission and the National Buildings Record and that the Editor should become a professor with a responsibility for teaching local history and training local archivists. Dr. Salzman's suggestions were far sighted. By 1960 the House of Commons had become nervous lest there might be duplication in architectural surveying[23] and by 1962 the Government had somewhat rationalized the system.[24] By 1947 Sir Hilary Jenkinson had perceived the lack of systematic training for archivists and was helping to enlarge the School of Librarianship at University College, London, to embrace archive administration.

Flower's report was considered by the Institute Committee in the same month. In its reaction to it the first signs of friction between the two committees is perceptible. The Institute Committee forwarded the report to the Finance and General Purposes Committee but declined to associate itself with a request for an extra £5,000 if that would prejudice other claims that the Institute might make on University funds. This was reported back to the *V.C.H.* Committee and aroused Peers to seek the concurrence of his fellow-members in a strongly-worded rejoinder. He failed to carry the whole Committee with him, however, and his rejoinder never reached the Institute Committee textually. The next step was for the Institute Committee in February 1944 to set up a special committee 'representing themselves and other bodies to explore the whole question'. The future of the *History* was next debated in the Academic Council, which set up a further committee in April to advise them 'upon the scientific value' of the *History* and the appropriateness of securing its 'completion either upon the present or upon some modified plan'. The committee consisted of Stenton, Professor V. H. Galbraith, who had become Director of the Institute in 1944, and Peers. By October the Council had referred the report to the Institute Committee who set up a *V.C.H.* Policy Sub-Committee. The Sub-Committee's report was approved by the Institute

[23] *5th Rep. from Sel. Cttee. on Estimates 1959–60. Historic Buildings and Ancient Monuments*, H.C. 274 (1959–60), vi. [24] 16 *Parl. Deb.* 6th ser. 31–33.

Committee in March 1945 and forwarded to the Council who considered it in November together with reports received meanwhile by the Board of Studies in History and the Board of the Faculty of Arts. Later in the month the Senate recommended to the Court that the increase in the annual grant should amount not to £5,000 but to £2,000 which the Court ruled should not become payable until 1946–7. Those who were struggling to keep the *History* going may well have been perplexed by this long-drawn-out procedure. Dr. Salzman announced to the March 1946 meeting of the *V.C.H.* Committee that he intended to retire soon and asked whether the *History* was 'to drag on as it has had to do in recent years?' It would be most unfortunate, he said, if 'an appearance of servile somnolence' were displayed at a time when interest in the *History* seemed to be reviving. The delays at all events were now over but at a cost which Flower may have regretted.

The revived interest to which Dr. Salzman had drawn attention was evinced partly by a remarkable sales campaign pinned to a special prospectus. This had been launched in the spring of 1942, at a depressing stage in the war, and had resulted in numerous purchases and orders both at home and abroad. The financial consequences were such that the debt from the *History* to central university funds was greatly reduced and by November 1947 was almost extinguished. The other favourable development needs a fuller explanation.

In 1943 the Borough of Swindon had noticed that no Wiltshire volumes of the *History* had been published, and enquired whether there was any hope that they might be. It was told that nothing fit for publication was available, but that the provision of financial assistance might alter the position. The Corporation had itself hinted at 'co-operation'. Discussions were resumed in 1945 which led to the conclusion that the money then available to the Corporation was not enough to make it possible for the Editor to start on the Wiltshire volumes. Advised by G. M. Young, then living in the county, the corporation next turned its attention to the prospect of publishing a series of monographs and also, at the suggestion of Dr. G. D. Ramsay, then on active service in South East Asia, to encouraging the newly founded Records Branch of the Wiltshire Archaeological Society. Both Young and Dr. Ramsay approached the present writer in March 1945 and by May a scheme had been drafted for the expenditure of the money already voted on the simultaneous publication of sources and also of monographs implicitly tending towards the publication of a Wiltshire *V.C.H.* By December the Corporation had agreed to make a grant to the Records Branch, which, subsequently augmented, has continued. By gradual stages, the scheme for monographs was dropped and the original idea of starting a Wiltshire *V.C.H.* reverted to. To the March 1946 *V.C.H.* Committee the present writer submitted a plan for publishing the proposed monographs within the framework of the *V.C.H.* Further information was asked for and general encouragement given to the formation of local *V.C.H.* funds not only in Wiltshire. Meanwhile the Wiltshire County Council and later the City of Salisbury had joined with Swindon to form a joint fund. In June 1947 the scheme for a Wiltshire *V.C.H.* was approved by the *V.C.H.* Committee, in November the first meeting of the Wiltshire *V.C.H.* Committee occurred, and at a meeting of that Committee in February 1948 an Assistant Local Editor was appointed. Young had become Honorary Editor in November 1947 and in May 1949 the present writer was associated with him in a joint office. Young withdrew in 1953[25] and his colleague in 1955 when the Assistant Editor became Editor.[26]

The arrangements made in 1946–7 between the Institute and the Wiltshire *V.C.H.*

[25] Letter to the present writer, 24 Feb. 1953.   [26] Wilts. *V.C.H.* Cttee. Mins.

Committee have formed a model which has been much imitated in the succeeding twenty years. This justifies the space devoted to the negotiations and must excuse the devotion of still more space to the definition of the relationship. Where a partnership has been formed between a body of local patrons interested in furthering its county history and the Institute, the former have undertaken to provide funds for the salary and expenses of a local editor and his assistants. That editor is to work under the general supervision of the general Editor and produce the texts of volumes which meet with his approval. If that approval is forthcoming,[27] the Institute will meet the costs of printing and publishing without burdening the local fund therewith. The effect of such an arrangement is that the central organization of the *History* is provided with extra staff without cost and that the local patrons are provided with the guarantee of a very high academic standard through the incorporation of the volumes which they have patronized in a series of world-wide reputation. The way in which Wiltshire's initiative was imitated will be told later on.

By 1947 the central staff had begun slowly to expand. A full-time Assistant to the Editor began work in February and at the same time a search began for a new Editor to replace Dr. Salzman. This meant finding more money for a higher salary. A second Assistantship was authorized at the same time and the post filled by February 1949. Mrs. Page died in May 1947 which made it possible to close the annuity account. The Warwickshire County Council, ever disposed to foster history, made a grant in 1946 towards the Warwickshire volumes. Professor Galbraith, who had been Chairman of the Committee since 1944, left the chair on ceasing to be Director of the Institute in 1948 and was succeeded by Professor J. G. (later Sir Goronwy) Edwards, the new Director, in the same year. Finally, all the stock and other materials, which, after some war damage to them, had been removed to the country, were returned to London. The 'slips' and draft narratives, which had been in the disused church of Furtho (Northants.), were repatriated by November 1948. At the ensuing reorganization those of them that related to Wales, accumulated long ago for the abortive Welsh history, were sent to the National Library of Wales. The materials for Monmouthshire went with them,[28] apparently by accident rather than design, and since then the implication has been that Monmouthshire has been excluded from the programme.

Dr. Salzman retired in November 1949 and was succeeded by the present Editor. The ensuing twenty years can be viewed only as a continuum, for, even if in future they may seem divisible into periods, the present perspective forbids it. On the administrative side the most prominent feature has been the multiplication of local patrons. In November 1947 proposals for forming a Leicestershire Committee had been put forward by Dr. (later Professor) W. G. Hoskins, and in the following March similar proposals came from Oxfordshire. The Leicestershire Committee seems to have been inaugurated in December 1948, the Oxfordshire Committee in January 1949. The formation of a Staffordshire Committee was being debated in the following June. It was inaugurated in 1950.

Other such Committees slowly followed. An Essex Committee was formed in 1951, an East Riding of Yorkshire Committee in 1953, a Middlesex Committee in 1955. The Leicestershire Committee ceased to exist in 1958 but its loss was compensated for by the establishment of a Gloucestershire Committee in 1959. Shropshire followed in 1960 and Somerset in 1964. These committees could not always start work at once, partly because they could not at once find staff. The dates for starting work have been as

[27] An exception to this rule was made by the *V.C.H.* Committee in 1955, when a committee of Oxford historians, approved by the Committee, was authorized to give final approval to the text of *Oxfordshire* VI.

[28] *V.C.H.* files, National Library of Wales to the author, 26 July 1969.

follows: Essex 1951; East Riding 1954; Middlesex 1956; Gloucestershire 1960; Shropshire 1961; Somerset 1967. The East Riding Committee has a long pre-history, for in 1933, when the University of London had just assumed responsibility for the *History*, an offer of co-operation had been received from what was then University College, Hull. The offer did not at the time take practical shape.

The committees have been variously constituted. The Wiltshire Committee has always been a partnership between the Wiltshire County Council, the Swindon Borough Council, and the Salisbury City Council, though only for a brief period did Salisbury actually make payments to the fund. The Leicestershire Committee drew its resources from the Leicestershire County Council, the Leicester City Council, and the Leicestershire Archaeological Society. For a while the Leicestershire Literary and Philosophical Society also subscribed, and when it ceased to do so, was replaced by University College, Leicester, now the University of Leicester. The original Oxfordshire Committee drew upon a variety of sources—the County Council, Oxford City Council, some of the District Councils within the County, the University of Oxford, some of the Colleges, and numerous private subscribers. This method of raising money lasted until 1965. To the Essex Committee nearly all the local authorities within the historic county have contributed, apart from the County Council itself. This means, in present terms, the London Boroughs of Barking, Havering, Newham, Redbridge, and Waltham Forest, the County Borough of Southend-on-Sea, and almost all the District Councils. The partnership in the East Riding has been between the County Council itself and the City Councils of Kingston-upon-Hull and York. That in Middlesex was originally between the London County Council and the District Councils in the former Administrative County of Middlesex. Since 1965 it has been between the Greater London Council, the nine London Boroughs which have succeeded former District Councils, and two surviving District Councils.

The funds made available by these committees were at first voted, at the suggestion of the Institute, for periods of five years, though often on the tacit understanding that they would need to be renewed for further quinquennia. None of the committees could hope to complete their tasks in a quinquennium, so such a chronological limitation was unreal. Its unreality had been recognized as early as 1951 when the Committee, with Senate approval, devised means by which all local editorial posts could be made pensionable.[29] Terminable grants, however, continued. Their impermanence naturally caused anxiety to the local editorial staff and also to the 'central' Committee and in 1957 these anxieties were eventually brought formally to the 'central' Committee's notice by the local editors themselves. In consequence the 'central' Committee became convinced that, if future local organizations were to be established, those organizations must be able to draw upon funds for much longer terms than a quinquennium.

It so came about that when the next county, Gloucestershire,[30] sought an alliance, it was told that something in the nature of permanence was essential. This led the Gloucestershire County Council to conclude that the staff which it provided must be local government officers, borne on the Council's strength and housed in its buildings. The 'central' Committee accepted this situation and the staff in Gloucestershire, Shropshire, and Somerset have accordingly been permanent County Council employees. In 1965 the Oxfordshire County Council took over from the former *ad hoc* committee responsibility for the local management of the Oxfordshire project and in the treatment

---

[29] If the Institute Committee, acting on the advice of the *V.C.H.* Committee, approves the appointment of a county editor or of his assistant, that person may, at the request of the county committee, become technically a member of the 'central' *V.C.H.* staff and as such a member of the Federated Superannuation System for Universities.

[30] Attempts to promote a Gloucestershire *History* had been made in 1933 and again in 1950–1.

of its staff followed Gloucestershire's example, though contributions have continued to be received from the City and the University of Oxford.

Since the inception of this system of alliances each local organization has had at least one local editor or assistant local editor. In earlier days the senior of them might be honorary. The situation in Wiltshire has already been explained, while in Leicestershire Dr. (later Professor) W. G. Hoskins, the promoter of the project, was part-time honorary editor until 1952. It very soon became apparent that one person, even with the addition of a part-time honorary colleague, was not enough, and the 'central' Committee has subsequently urged that there must be a minimum of two editors, one senior to the other or others. At the present time the situation is that in Essex there is an editor and a deputy editor, in Middlesex, Staffordshire, and Wiltshire an editor and two assistants, in Oxfordshire an editor, an assistant, and a part-time general assistant, and in the other counties an establishment for an editor and one assistant.

These editors, styled at first Local Editors and since November 1968 County Editors, have been partly concerned to find, negotiate with, and superintend contributors. To an ever increasing extent, however, they have become the authors of the articles in their histories, especially of the unwritten parish histories, of which there is so great a load. In the hope of ensuring that all workers in the same field profited by the experience of their colleagues, meetings of county editors were begun in 1949. They continued somewhat fitfully for some years but were revived as a sequence in 1965 since when they have usually taken place at six-monthly intervals.

While it has seemed prudent by such means to keep the editorial staff in close communication, it has seemed not less desirable that representatives of the 'central' and county committees should meet from time to time. Such meetings began over lunch in the Senate House in July 1956 and have recurred in 1957, 1958, 1961, and 1969. The 1957 meeting was held at Lydiard Park, Wiltshire, at the invitation of the Mayor of Swindon. Resolutions in favour of more permanent funds and of aligning local salaries with academic scales were passed at the 1957 meeting and were reiterated in more formal language at the meetings of 1958 and 1961. Since the meeting of the 'central' Committee of October 1964 efforts to secure this system of 'linkage', as it is often called, have been intensified and have met with a good deal of success. At the meeting with County representatives in 1969 it was resolved to hold such meetings annually and to form a 'working party' to try to frame a general agreement acceptable alike to the Institute and the local organizations.

It will, of course, be clear that by means of the partnership described above it has proved possible to carry out a great deal of work concurrently, which, otherwise, might have had to be done more slowly. An average of over two published volumes a year has been maintained, even though the content of the volumes, as will be explained, has become much richer since 1949. On the other hand the administrative cost to the Institute has been very high in real terms, since a great deal of time has had to be spent in negotiating with local patrons suitable terms of employment for county editors and attending the meetings of county committees.

The older methods of outside assistance were not completely superseded by the system of alliances. In 1953 an appeal was made to some Local Authorities and individuals in Sussex and a small fund formed. When the Sussex guarantee fund was liquidated in 1965 some guarantors allowed their loans to be converted into gifts and transferred to this fund. Secondly the University, Colleges, and City of Cambridge made grants in 1953–4 to enable the Cambridgeshire volume on the city and university to be completed. The money was used to retain the services of a local editor. Thirdly in 1946 and 1951 the Warwickshire County Council made further grants, the second to meet some of the expenses of indexing *Warwickshire* I–VI. In 1963–4 they and the Cities of Birmingham and Coventry gave further sums to help towards the completion of *Warwickshire* VII and VIII.

In addition to the creation of a local staff in the counties the 'central' staff has expanded. After a great deal of discussion the post of Deputy Editor, first suggested in October 1950, was created and filled ten years later. The post of Architect which had been a part-time one since 1937, was made full-time but temporary in 1953 by means of a grant from the Pilgrim Trust, and established as a full-time one in 1957 after that grant had run out. The Pilgrim Trust found the means in 1956 and 1960 to provide the Editor with a third Assistant on a temporary footing and this post was also made permanent in 1965. Secretarial assistance was first provided on a part-time footing in 1950 and made permanent and full-time in 1961.

Finally it must be recorded with thankfulness that the administrative changes of the past twenty years have in no way weakened the interest which the Sovereign has taken in the *History*. A message of good will was conveyed on behalf of Queen Elizabeth II in 1952 and contained the usual request that the Queen might be kept informed of progress. The request was met ten years later by Professor Francis Wormald, then Chairman of the *V.C.H.* Committee and Director of the Institute, and was greeted with an encouraging request for fuller information and an expression of pleasure that Local Authorities had played so large a part in recent developments.

The last twenty years have also been marked by a great deal of editorial activity directed towards reshaping without radically altering the content of the *History* itself. Wiltshire was a virgin field for experiment since there were no existing volumes into which new volumes might need to be 'dovetailed'. Accordingly it was possible to design the 'general' volumes somewhat differently from those which had already appeared for other counties. Apart from an introductory chapter on physique, articles on natural history were dropped—a suggestion which had been made by the Secretary of the *V.C.H.* Committee as long before as March 1934. Pre-history was replanned and a gazetteer of archaeological sites published. The general ecclesiastical history was treated more lengthily and separate chapters devoted to the Established Church, Protestant Nonconformity, and Roman Catholicism. Very much fuller treatment than usual was given to agriculture and the old 'social and economic' chapter reduced to an introduction to a sequence of articles on agriculture and particular industries. The old 'political' chapter was transformed into two sequences of articles on parliamentary and administrative history. 'Forestry' became a discourse on the extent and administration of the medieval forests. Three articles were devoted to communications. These experiments were to some degree imitated in the 'general' volumes for other counties. The Middlesex pre-history articles follow the Wiltshire design and so to a degree does the volume on Roman Essex (*Essex* III). Leicestershire contains similarly lengthy articles on agriculture and communications; Staffordshire similarly divides its ecclesiastical history. Middlesex, however, contains no general treatment of ecclesiastical history although there is a note on the framework of ecclesiastical organization. Leicestershire provided chapters on population history, which, in a more attenuated form, are to be found in Wiltshire, and also a chapter on painters. An experiment of a different kind, not imitated elsewhere, has been to add to the Essex 'set' a volume consisting of a full bibliography for the county. While all these developments represent an enlargement of the original design there have also been two contractions. No general study of local architecture has yet been supplied and no chapter on the maritime history of Essex, the only one of these counties with a seaboard whose 'general' history was left incomplete.

A great deal of effort has also been expended in improving the 'topographical' volumes, on which throughout the period the staff have been ever more extensively engaged. The earliest design for the topography goes back to the days of Doubleday and Gomme. It is somewhat crudely drafted and confusedly presented. It seems, however, that these sections were to contain a brief description of the 'village'—and there is no express reference to the treatment of urban areas—with an indication whether the land was wooded, arable, or pasture. They were to describe the manor-house, the domestic architecture, and the church with its fittings, monuments, bells, plate, and registers, state the patronage of the church, narrate the history of the advowson, and list the incumbents, 'when of great interest'. They were also to supply information about parish guilds, charities, feasts, fairs, archaeological 'finds', customs, tokens, historical events, and industries, past and present. The lists of incumbents were to be included only if a county archaeological society could supply them.[31] This scheme, somewhat altered, was later to be printed in the general *Guide*. It may also be deduced from the early volumes themselves.

What was that scheme? First it must be noted that the arrangement within the volumes was and always has been by hundreds preceded by an article on the history of each hundred considered as an administrative unit. Within the hundred the 'ancient' parishes were taken as they were *c.* 1831 before boundaries began to be extensively changed by Statute.[32]

The features that were to be covered within the 'ancient' parishes were the descent of land, particularly manors and advowsons, descriptions of the more conspicuous earlier buildings, and charities—a scheme of arrangement which owed much to earlier county histories. To each parish history was prefixed a 'General Introduction' which stated the location and area of the parish, enumerated the 'worthies', and made a few general remarks partly about national events connected with the respective places and partly about certain buildings and physical features observable in the parishes at the time of publication. No attempt was made to trace in detail the evolution of the settlement pattern or of the centres of nonconformist worship. Where the place was of greater size than a rural parish, e.g. a borough, a section was devoted to the borough government; where it contained a castle, a section might be devoted to its history. Markets and fairs, where they existed or had existed, might constitute a separate section.

This remained the approximate pattern up to 1950. The articles so designed, composed of what may be called the 'old' standard features, caused dissatisfaction among certain users of the *History* because they seemed to present an incomplete picture of the development of the communities under description. While the treatment was undoubtedly limited, it must at the same time be recalled that it was the intention of the editors that the various 'topographical' articles should be read in conjunction with the 'general' articles and that those wishing to obtain a full picture of any particular place must see what was said about it or about the district in which it lay in the 'general' articles as well. In other words the 'topographical' articles were not meant to be encyclopaedic but rather to deal with those topics which could be examined only, or at least most conveniently, on a parochial basis. This would have been more readily apparent if more counties had been completed and had been complemented on their completion by collective indexes.

[31] *V.C.H.* recs., A37, undated prospectus.

[32] Except where otherwise stated the succeeding fourteen paragraphs are largely drawn from an article by the present writer in *Bull. of Inst. Hist. Res.* xl. 65, and reproduced here by permission of the Editor of the *Bulletin*.

When the special committee appointed by the Academic Council in 1944 and referred to above delivered its report, it defined the *History*, as it had emerged from the hands of its originators, as 'an historical encyclopaedia of the English counties rather than an ordinary "county history"'. It described the character of the 'general' articles but declared that 'the main body of the work' was 'a systematic collection of accurate data for the history of every village, parish, and manor in the country'. The committee pointed out that much less progress had been made with the 'topographical' than with the 'general' volumes but said that it thought that it was through the former that the *History* 'would take its place as a permanent work of reference'. It considered that in those volumes 'a high general level had been maintained', though future ones would need strengthening by giving more attention to the period before 1200 and to economic history from the 17th century onwards. While not without its limitations, the *History*, if continued in a somewhat enlarged form, 'would provide a framework of ascertained facts by which generalisation could be controlled. . . . It would become one of those works . . . which are taken for granted by the ordinary reader, but make possible the books of general interest, which influence opinion'. The committee concluded this part of its report by remarking that the utility of the *History* could in the future be increased by allowing for the 'treatment of commercial and industrial developments' in certain districts and the insertion 'at appropriate points' of 'articles of a general character on changes of industrial process and methods of transport' and 'upon developments in agricultural practice'. 'But work of this kind, however desirable, would always, in the committee's opinion, be subsidiary to the main purpose of the *History*—the accurate registration of the manorial descents which form the central thread of English social history.'

Notwithstanding the somewhat conservative views expressed by the committee of 1944, an enlarged scheme for treating parish histories was laid before the *Victoria County History* Committee in March 1950 and to this the Committee gave its blessing. The main feature of this scheme was the addition of three new standard features, called 'Roman Catholicism', 'Protestant Nonconformity', and 'Schools', to the existing standard features, namely the 'General Introduction', 'Manors', 'Churches', and 'Charities'. Besides this it was agreed that some encouragement should be given to handling the occupational history and the local government of each parish. In fact these last two features, usually called 'Economic History' and 'Local Government', have tended to become standard features also and to form themselves into distinct sections.

In addition to these developments, changes, some of them consequential upon the developments themselves, have been taking place in the form of the 'General Introduction'. This now contains a fuller discussion than ever before of the physical development of the parish, of changes in population, of the extension of external communications, and of the growth of public services. If the place is of a substantial size the remarks about physical growth and about public services are removed and formed into separate sections. Sometimes, to a degree varying with the character of the place, other parts of the 'General Introduction' are similarly detached. The 'Introduction', however, continues to contain, though with an exactness not aimed at in the older volumes, a definition of the area under description and a brief discourse on the history of the boundaries, together with remarks about local customs and national events connected with the parish and an enumeration of the 'worthies'. The section on physical development relies to a much greater extent than ever before on maps of all dates, the evidence of deeds, and field work.

Other changes have taken place in the other 'old' standard features. 'Manors' is now usually supplemented by a section called 'Lesser' or 'Other Estates'. This section is sometimes distinct from 'Manors', sometimes fused with it. It cannot be made so comprehensive as 'Manors' but is designed to ensure that the major freehold and copyhold estates which did not have the status of manors are not overlooked. Monastic property within a parish, not being of manorial status, is systematically included here. The 'Church' sections, which originally contained only the descent of the advowson and a description of the fabric, now extend to the nature and revenues of the benefice, with some information, less systematically collected, on the ecclesiastical policy of the incumbents and the conduct of the services. Formerly no more was recorded about any charity than the date and circumstances of its foundation and its value at the time of publication. Now, in the case of the larger charities, some intermediate history is given. The change in the form of the 'Charities' section was partly caused by the impossibility of continuing to compile the sections on the old lines. In the past they had been supplied on a contract basis by officials of the Charity Commission. It was discovered in 1950 that no such official writer was any longer available. The Commissioners courteously granted *V.C.H.* workers direct access to their files and a more historical treatment of the subject has resulted.

While all the foregoing features have been expanded, the treatment of architecture has conversely become less elaborate. Here it may be useful to digress. As already stated, the original plan provided for chapters on architecture though such were published for two counties only, and architectural descriptions in all the parishes. The scope of the surveying is not defined, but it was largely medieval and it did not extend to the smaller domestic buildings of any age.

As early as March 1934 the Secretary of the *V.C.H.* Committee questioned whether in view of the Commission's work the *History*'s descriptions should not be reduced. On his appointment as Editor Dr. Salzman undertook to do this and since his time reduction has gone still further. This is partly because so much competing architectural surveying is now carried on. To the Commission was added in 1941 the National Buildings (since 1964 Monuments) Record. Under Section 42 of the Town and Country Planning Act, 1944, the Ministry of Town and Country Planning began to list and grade buildings throughout the country, and to the lists since 1949 the *History* has had generous access. Finally in 1951 Professor (later Sir) Nikolaus Pevsner began his *Buildings of England* series. It can no longer be said that on the *History* alone must posterity rely for a proper record of the buildings of the past. Accordingly exact measurements and the descriptions of minuter detail have been eliminated, and the buildings are described historically with more emphasis on their value as evidence than on their aesthetic merits. To compensate, however, for this brevity, many more buildings, in particular 'vernacular' ones, are examined and reported upon. It has been possible to carry this compression to the greatest lengths in those counties where the Commission is concurrently at work. Besides this there have been changes in arrangement. Formerly all secular buildings were described together in the 'General Introduction'. Although many domestic ones still find their place there, it is now the custom to place parsonages under 'Churches', manor-houses under 'Manors', alms-houses under 'Charities', municipal buildings under 'Local Government', and so forth.

This well-nigh exhausts the 'old' standard features. The 'new' ones called 'Roman Catholicism' and 'Protestant Nonconformity' are primarily concerned with the formation and dissolution of organized churches and communities. 'Schools' was originally limited to primary schools. Particulars, however, about private secondary schools have subsequently been added, and in the future certain other teaching establishments, such as rate-supported secondary schools, technical colleges, and mechanics' institutes will also be covered, if they have not already been described in 'general' volumes. Where the section is thus broadened, it will be called 'Education'. Endowed grammar schools and also some of the larger independent schools are reserved for the 'general' volumes. 'Local Government' is meant to describe historically the activities of the manorial courts and of the vestry and parish officers. It may include information about poor relief before 1835 and the history of workhouses. In boroughs it contains an historical description of the deliberative assemblies and courts, the borough officers, the main sources of revenue and objects of expenditure, and the seals and regalia. Comparable treatment is meted out to the government of towns that were not or are not boroughs.

The most difficult section to handle is that called 'Economic History' or 'Economic and Social History'. When first discussed in 1950 this was intended to give a picture of the occupations, mainly the industrial ones, of the inhabitants. In practice, however, it has extended itself to include a discourse on husbandry in the parish, commercial activities, and even the organization of leisure. Into it particulars about mills, which have always been dealt with in the *History* fairly fully, are sometimes inserted, though sometimes they form a separate section. Perhaps the 'Economic History' has not yet reached a fully satisfactory form. This is partly because parish boundaries have little relevance to the story of many economic and social changes. The originators of 1899 perceived this and were no doubt right in reserving the economic history of counties for treatment in 'general' volumes. At the same time there are some pieces of economic (or economic and social) information that can be conveniently assembled by parishes. Inclosure, whether effected by statute or other means, is usually one of them, and so often are the details of manorial tenures, the size of holdings, and the enfranchisement of copyholds. While economic sections must in some form naturally continue, it is important to frame them in such a way that they do not give a spurious impression of comprehensiveness.

There is little doubt that the present pattern for the 'topographical' volumes is one that better suits rural places, whether small towns or villages, than larger towns and cities. In recent years four volumes have each been devoted exclusively to the history of one city and one or two others of this kind are in preparation. These have been arranged as though the city under description was a county in itself, as in the technical sense it sometimes has been, and two have been equipped with articles of a 'general' kind ('Part I') and a long appendix ('Part II') dealing with the minuter facts about landed property, churches, chapels, schools, and charities.

During these two decades the attitude to sources has also been changing. It was often said in the past that the parish histories were based too much upon sources available in London. Recently a great deal more reliance has been placed on manuscripts in local custody, though these are of course regarded as additional to and not substitutes for the centrally-preserved sources. Secondly, since the wealth of material for almost any parish history is enormous, it has become important to define, and indeed to limit, those that are systematically searched. As a means to that end county check-lists have been drawn up on which are entered the minimum sources, both printed and unprinted, which it is expedient to search for each parish in the county. These sources are partly common to almost the whole of England and partly special to a particular county. The check-lists are duplicated. When a county editor or other worker starts to collect the materials for a parish history, he keeps a copy of his county check-list beside him and strikes out each source as he finishes searching it. Thus the county editor (and, in the last resort, the general Editor) can see at a glance what has been examined. This reduces the risk of overlooking important sources and ensures a good national standard for sources. The check-lists are naturally not exhaustive. They have almost always to be supplemented by sources special to a particular place or area. But such sources need not be examined for *every* place in the county in question and therefore need not go into the check-list. It may be pointed out that to the general corpus of sources have been added in this period the riches of the great sequence of Parliamentary Papers.[33]

Some of the new features have demanded the use of sources hitherto insufficiently explored, while some of the fairly familiar sources for the older features have not invariably been perfectly understood. Hence it has been necessary to compile from time to time memoranda or articles upon sources. These have dealt with (i) and (ii) the history of Nonconformity, (iii) and (iv) the history of primary schools, (v) 'Parliamentary Surveys', (vi) 'New Ecclesiastical Parishes', (vii) 'Wesleyan Chapel Committee Reports', (viii) 'Fines and Recoveries', and (ix) the records of the Charity Commission. Of these (i)–(iv) have been published.[34]

An activity no less arduous has been the preparation of memoranda upon the design of particular sections rather than upon the sources for them. Thus the notes on sources for schools have been followed or supplemented by a note on the treatment of the 'Education' section, accompanied by some specimen narratives. There is a similar note on the treatment of 'Charities'. Because it is not always easy to decide what constitutes a 'parish' for the purpose of compiling a *V.C.H.* parish history, a survey, called 'The Parochial Frame', has been prepared, purporting to set out the principles upon which that decision can best be made and entering into a good deal of detail about the different types of parish. There is another survey, hardly less potentially useful, upon designing the 'Church' sections. There are similar 'treatment' notes on the 'General Introductions', 'Endowed Grammar Schools', and 'Seals'. Such notes aim among other things at suggesting what are the leading facts to look for, and emphasize what facts should, owing to the limitations of time and space, be discarded, and in what order it seems best to arrange the information that is to be recorded. Memoranda on later 17th century borough charters and on new ecclesiastical parishes have a somewhat similar purpose. When a few more 'treatment' memoranda shall have been produced, the *Guide* of 1903 can be replaced by something better.

It may not be out of place to take a backward look at the compilation of *V.C.H.* parish histories. It was by these, said Page in 1907, 'that the History will undoubtedly stand or fall',[35] and the Committee of 1944 used much the same words. 'Village' histories, as conceived by Gomme and Doubleday, were to run to 800–900 words.[36] By 1910 the average for each parish had risen to a 'a little over 2,000' and the histories were then thought by Page to be so short that hardly any reduction would be possible; some prospective local patrons of a scheme to revive Lincolnshire were, however, then pressing for a reduction.[37] The present average in a recent rural volume, *Gloucestershire* VIII (1968), is 9,700. The time-table, as calculated by Page about 1907, was three weeks for rural parishes, based on the 'slips' already accumulated and six to eight weeks, on the same basis, for 'large boroughs'.[38] The average time taken for each parish in *Gloucestershire* VIII, which includes a small town, was two months. Some workers, particularly the less experienced, would have taken longer. There has thus been since the early years of the century a very large increase both in wordage and in time,

[33] *Local History from Blue Books*, ed. W. R. Powell (Historical Association, *Helps for Students of History*, no. 64, 1962).

[34] (i) and (ii) in *Bull. of Inst. Hist. Res.* xxv. 213; xxxi. 79; (iii) and (iv) in *Brit. Jnl. of Educational Studies*, i. 43.

[35] *V.C.H.* recs., A58, memo. of 16 Apr. 1907.

[36] Ibid. A37, undated prospectus.

[37] Ibid. A58, schemes for completing Lincs.

[38] Ibid. Note on Mr. Meredith's Estimate.

although there are many who would urge that the former is insufficient, and, by inference, the latter.

Page had once held, as has been shown, that workers, after a year's training, could convert 'slips' into narratives, which required only what was (perhaps euphemistically) called 'revision' to make them fit for publication.[39] Such methods seem to have continued throughout his life, for in March 1934 the Secretary of the *V.C.H.* Committee reported that the 'topographical' articles on the eve of Page's death were written by 'completely inexperienced persons', checked against the 'slips' by Page's secretary, and then often rewritten by Page himself. While all is still by no means perfect it can hardly be denied that today's topographers are better trained and much more competent and that with the aid of central guidance the whole process has been professionalized.

In order to extend some general advice to county editors on the best way to negotiate with contributors and to shape their volumes and present them to the general Editor for approval, a 'Tract on Editing' was drawn up in 1956 and given a limited circulation. Some printed notes for the guidance of contributors on the minuter points of spelling, punctuation, and the like had been available in Page's time. These were revised in 1949 and duplicated. In 1954 a new *Handbook for Contributors* was printed and distributed. It is to be replaced in 1970 by a new *Handbook for Editors and Authors*. This incorporates passages from the old *Guide*, the '*Tract*', and sundry memoranda. Though Page's booklet on heraldry was never revised, some guidance on the treatment of heraldry has been provided in the two editions of the *Handbook*.

In its early days the *History* was abundantly illustrated. In particular it contained numerous plans of buildings, some of them sumptuous and in colour. It also contained sketch-maps of hundreds, half-inch orographical sheets, and maps to illustrate Domesday and to show the distribution of religious houses. The plans of buildings have been much reduced in number to conform with the simpler treatment of architecture. The Domesday, ecclesiastical, and hundred maps have continued. Beginning with Ely in *Cambridgeshire* IV there have been added town plans showing all the important buildings and sites mentioned in the text, plans showing changes in civic boundaries and urban growth, and maps to illustrate the evolution from village to town in areas of rapid recent expansion.

The *History*'s other early illustrations were a mixture. The old volumes contained frontispieces in photogravure, high in quality and often romantic in conception.[40] By decision of the Committee in May 1935 these were abandoned in favour of half-tones, which always contributed the bulk of the pictorial illustrations. The total number of half-tones has been a good deal reduced in number since the Committee examined the question of cost in October 1951. Every effort has, however, been made to make up in quality what has been lost in quantity and to diversify the type. No longer is it the practice to illustrate every ancient church, as seems in early days to have been customary, by the reproduction of post cards. In particular it has become the rule to depict the scenery of a region—a habit imitated by *The Buildings of England* series. Coloured illustrations, often good in earlier days, have had to be restricted, but a few, it is hoped no worse than their predecessors, have been included in recent volumes.

Finally, since 1951 it has become the rule to index every volume as it appears, and, in those instances where a preceding volume or volumes lacked an index, to install a collective one in the next in numerical sequence to be published. This practice was initiated with *Leicestershire* III which indexes that and the two preceding volumes.

August 1969

[39] See p. 7. [40] e.g. Lincoln Minster rising out of the mist: *Lincs.* II.

BIBLIOGRAPHICAL EXCURSUS[1]

UNTIL 1954 the series title page bore the series title, namely 'The Victoria History of the Counties of England' with the words 'Victoria History' printed in red, followed successively by the county name, the publisher's name, and the place of publication (in red until the publication of *Sussex* III in 1935). The half-title page bore the series title, followed successively by the name of the general editor or editors, the volume title, in the form 'A History of the County of . . .', and the volume number. In some of the early volumes the name of the designated editor or editors of the county set, with the predicted number of volumes needed to complete the set, are printed on the back of the half-title page. The volume title-pages were inscribed with the title appropriate to the county set, followed by the volume number, the sub-title (if any) defining that number in red, usually the volume editor's name, the publisher's name and address, and the date of publication. Until the publication of *Sussex* III (1935) the place of publication or at least some part of the publisher's address was printed in red. The county title was usually expressed in the form 'The Victoria History of the County of . . .'. *Hertfordshire* II, however, was inscribed 'The Victoria History of Hertfordshire' and *Somerset* II 'The Victoria History of Somerset'. *Hampshire* I (1900) and II (1903) were inscribed 'A History of Hampshire and the Isle of Wight'. In the case of the Berkshire volumes, *London* I, *Shropshire* I, and *Wiltshire* VII the words 'the county of' were, for obvious reasons, omitted. The two parts of *Cornwall* II are entitled 'A History of the County of Cornwall' with the date of publication, series name, and publisher's name and address at the foot. The parts include no series title-page or half-title page. *Cambridgeshire* I, presumably by accident, is entitled 'A History of the County of Cambridgeshire and the Isle of Ely'.

Since the publication of *Leicestershire* III in 1955 each series title-page has borne the series title, in the traditional style, followed successively by the editor's name, and the publisher's name, without address. The half-title page has borne the series name, followed successively by the county name, in the traditional style, and the volume number. The volume title-page has borne the county name, in the form 'History of the County of . . .', or, in the case of Shropshire and Wiltshire, 'A History of . . .', followed by the other details as they appeared up to 1954. The volume number, or what stands in lieu, has been printed in red and the sub-title (if any) in black.

The *History* has always been dedicated to Queen Victoria or to her memory. The original dedication read 'To Victoria by the Grace of God of the United Kingdom of Great Britain and Ireland Queen Empress of India this History is by gracious privilege dedicated'. This is found in *Hampshire* I, the only volume to appear in the Queen's life-time, the word 'Victoria' being printed in red. After her death the dedication at first read 'Inscribed to the memory of her late Majesty Queen Victoria who in her lifetime graciously gave the title to and accepted the dedication of this History'. This form of words will be found in *Cumberland* I, *Norfolk* I, and *Worcestershire* I, all published in 1901, and in *Hertfordshire* I, *Northamptonshire* I, and *Surrey* I, published

---

[1] Mr. William Kellaway has given valuable advice in the preparation of this Excursus and the ensuing List of Volumes.

in 1902. With *Essex* I and *Hampshire* II, published in 1903, the words 'in her lifetime' were omitted. The formula then settled has remained in use. Since the publication of *Leicestershire* III in 1955 the words 'Queen Victoria' have been printed in red. *Rutland* II contains a supplementary dedication in the following form: 'Dedicated by Owen Hugh Smith to the memory of Maud wife of John Gretton. She loved and was loved by Rutland.'

In each first volume of each county set up to *Huntingdonshire* I (1926) there was included a table of abbreviations and in every such volume up to *Suffolk* I (1911) a 'general advertisement' explaining the nature of the series and a list of the members of the Advisory Council. All such volumes up to *Suffolk* I also included a list of members of the local committee except in the case of London where presumably no such committee existed. Since 1953 the names of the members of local committees have been printed in those volumes which have been produced with the co-operation of local authorities except for *Gloucestershire* VI and VIII, *Oxfordshire* IX, and *Shropshire* VIII. *Oxfordshire* V–VIII include lists of private contributors.

As explained above, the *History* was at first published by Archibald Constable and Company and was, in form at least, issued to subscribers only. All volumes appearing up to 1914 are so inscribed apart from the *Indexes* to Bedfordshire, Hampshire, and Surrey, which print lists of subscribers at the end, and the volume of Hertfordshire genealogies which records the limited imprint. Between 1923 and 1935 the *History* was published by the St. Catherine Press, and since 1935 has been published by the Oxford University Press as agents for the Institute of Historical Research of the University of London. Both publishers were used in 1935.

The first printers to the *History* were the firm of Butler and Tanner, of Frome, and it was they who printed *Bedfordshire* I, *Berkshire* I, *Buckinghamshire* I, *Cumberland* I and II, *Derbyshire* I, *Essex* I, *Gloucestershire* II, *Hampshire* I and II, *Hertfordshire* I, *Kent* I, *Norfolk* I, *Northamptonshire* I, *Somerset* I and II, *Surrey* I and II, *Sussex* I, *Warwickshire* I, and *Worcestershire* I. The last of these to appear was *Somerset* II (1911). A little later the firm of Eyre and Spottiswoode began to be employed and it was they who printed *Bedfordshire* II, *Berkshire* II, *Buckinghamshire* II, *Cornwall* I, *Derbyshire* II, *Devon* I, *Dorset* II, *Durham* I and II, *Essex* II, *Gloucestershire* II, *Hampshire* III, *Herefordshire* I, *Hertfordshire* II, *Kent* II and III, *Lancashire* I–V, *Leicestershire* I, *Lincolnshire* II, *London* I, *Middlesex* II, *Norfolk* II, *Northamptonshire* II, *Nottinghamshire* I and II, *Oxfordshire* II, *Rutland* I, *Shropshire* I, *Staffordshire* I, *Suffolk* I and II, *Surrey* III, *Sussex* II, *Warwickshire* II, *Worcestershire* II, and *Yorkshire* I–III. The first of their volumes, *Durham* I, came out in 1905. The last under the Constable regime was *Yorkshire* III (1913), but they also printed *Kent* II and III for the St. Catherine Press. The third printer was the firm of W. H. Smith & Son. Under the Constable regime they printed the *Bedfordshire Index*, *Hampshire* IV, V, and the *Index*, *Hertfordshire* III and IV, *Lancashire* VI–VIII, *Surrey* IV, *Worcestershire* III, and *Yorkshire* I, and completed the work in 1914. The volumes, however, were not published until 1923–5, after Constable had been replaced by the St. Catherine Press. They also printed *Berkshire* III and IV, *Buckinghamshire* III, *Worcestershire* IV, and *Yorkshire, North Riding*, II for Constable. They also probably printed the *Surrey Index*, although it bears no imprint. After the St. Catherine Press took over, Smiths printed all the volumes up to and including *Huntingdonshire* III (1936). From 1936, and beginning with the *Rutland Index*, the Oxford University Press have printed all the volumes apart from *Essex* V (1966), *Oxfordshire* IX (1969), *Staffordshire* III (1970), *Warwickshire* VII (1964) and VIII (1969), and *Wiltshire* VI (1962), VIII (1965), and IX (1971). Of these excepted volumes *Wiltshire* VIII was printed by the firm of E. J. Brill, of Leiden, and the rest by the firm of Robert MacLehose & Co., of Glasgow.

Apart from the two genealogical volumes, the format of the *History* has always been medium quarto. It was originally set in Caslon fourteen point, eleven point, and ten point. Beginning with *Oxfordshire* V, published in 1957, the type was changed to Imprint twelve on fourteen point, eleven point, and ten point severally. With the same reservation the standard edition has always been bound in red cloth with the arms of England in gold leaf on the front cover. Except for index volumes a representation of St. George and the Dragon also in gold leaf was impressed upon the spine until 1963, when, with the publication of *Staffordshire* VIII, it was omitted. An edition in brown half-morocco, originally bound by Zaehnsdorf, was available, apparently from the outset until 1964. Between 1910 and 1914 this was called the 'Empire' edition. An edition in full morocco was available from *c.* 1905 until 1914 and in three-quarters morocco between 1910 and 1914.

The fore-edges and bottom edges of volumes were uncut until the publication of *Shropshire* VIII in 1968. Since then those edges have been cut except in the case of *Dorset* III and *Warwickshire* VIII.

A photographic facsimile of *Warwickshire* III, then out of print, was put on sale in 1962. The edition was soon sold out. In 1965 Messrs. William Dawson, of Pall Mall, London, began to reproduce a sequence of out-of-print volumes, beginning with Warwickshire and including Volume III. Their work continues.

The two genealogical volumes are large folio and bound in blue cloth. About 1905 they were also being supplied in full and half-morocco.

LIST OF VOLUMES

The table below lists all the volumes in the series, including the genealogical volumes, that have appeared or are planned to appear before the end of 1970, together with the names of their editors, the year of publication, the number of pages, and the extent of the impression. Roman figures indicate the number of the last page of the preliminaries to bear a number, Arabic figures in non-italic type the last page of the text to bear a number. Arabic figures in italic type indicate the number of copies printed, where known. The word 'Index', unless more narrowly defined, implies that the index covers all the volumes in that set.

According to the heads of an arrangement made in 1910, to which the *V.C.H.* Syndicate was a party, the number of copies of each volume to be printed by W. H. Smith & Sons was set at 1,000. An estimate preserved among the records of the Institute suggests that from 1935, when the Oxford University Press became the publishing agents, the number of copies printed was 650. This was the size of the impression in 1946 and so remained for a while.

The county names are expressed in their most condensed form. Thus it is to be assumed that the volume title page of *Cumberland* I reads 'The Victoria History of the County of Cumberland', *Derbyshire* I 'The Victoria History of the County of Derby', and *Wiltshire* III 'A History of Wiltshire'. Editors' names that appear only on the back of the half-title page and not on the series title page are enclosed in square brackets.

The list excludes all details of photographic facsimiles.

Introduction to the History

ed. R. B. Pugh. 1970. ix, 282. *1,400*

Bedfordshire

I [ed. H. Arthur Doubleday and William Page]. 1904. xxii, 412
II, ed. William Page. 1908. xvii, 387
III, ed. William Page. 1912. xix, 462
Index [no editor named]. 1914. iii (recte [vii]), 61

Berkshire

I, ed. P. H. Ditchfield and William Page. 1906. xxv, 422
II, ed. the Revd. P. H. Ditchfield and William Page. 1907. xv, 353
III, ed. the Revd. P. H. Ditchfield and William Page, assisted by John Hautenville Cope. 1923.[1] xxii, 549
IV, ed. the Revd. P. H. Ditchfield and William Page, assisted by John Hautenville Cope. 1924.[1] xxi, 551
Index [no editor named]. 1927. [iv], 124

Buckinghamshire

I, ed. William Page. 1905. xxiii, 414
II, ed. William Page. 1908. xv, 372
III, ed. William Page. 1925.[1] xx, 489
IV, ed. William Page. 1927.[2] xxi, 552
Index [no editor named]. 1928. [iv], 107

Cambridgeshire and the Isle of Ely

I, ed. L. F. Salzman. 1938. xiii, 436
II, ed. L. F. Salzman. 1948. xiii, 419. *650*
III (the City and University of Cambridge), ed. J. P. C. Roach. 1959. xx, 504. *1,000*
IV, ed. R. B. Pugh. 1953. xvi, 280. *650*
Index to Volumes I–IV, ed. R. B. Pugh. 1960. [xii], 77. *750*

Cornwall

I, ed. William Page. 1906. xxv, 586
[II], Part 5, ed. William Page. 1924. 43
    Part 8, ed. William Page. 1924. 113

Cumberland

I [no editor named]. 1901. xxvi, 425
II, ed. James Wilson. 1905. xvii, 507

Derbyshire

I, ed. William Page. 1905. xxxii, 435
II, ed. William Page. 1907. xiii, 376

Devonshire

I, ed. William Page. 1906. xxv, 630

Dorset

II, ed. William Page. 1908. xiii, 370
III, ed. R. B. Pugh. 1968. xiii, 189. With index to II and III. *1,000*

Durham

I, ed. William Page. 1905. xxiii, 422
II, ed. William Page. 1907. xi, 429
III, ed. William Page. 1928. xiv, 376

Essex

I [no editor named]. 1903. xix, 598
II, ed. William Page and J. Horace Round. 1907. xxi, 628
III (Roman Essex with index to I–III), ed. W. R. Powell. 1963. xx, 258. *750*
IV (Ongar Hundred), ed. W. R. Powell. 1956. xix, 337. Indexed. *750*
V, ed. W. R. Powell. 1966. xxi, 319. Indexed. *1,200*
Bibliography, ed. W. R. Powell. 1959. xxiii, 352. *750*

Gloucestershire

II, ed. William Page. 1907. xv, 448
VI, ed. C. R. Elrington. 1965. xxii, 273. Indexed. *850*
VIII, ed. C. R. Elrington. 1968. xxiii, 311. Indexed. *850*. 2nd impression 1969. *300*

Hampshire and the Isle of Wight

I [ed. H. Arthur Doubleday and William Page]. 1900. xx, 537
II [ed. H. Arthur Doubleday and William Page]. 1903. xvii, 527
III [ed. William Page]. 1908. xvii, 537
IV [ed. William Page]. 1911. xxii, 658
V [ed. William Page]. 1912. xix, 576
Index [no editor named]. 1914. [vii], 135

Herefordshire

I, ed. William Page. 1908. xxiii, 428

Hertfordshire

I, ed. William Page. 1902. xx, 393
II, ed. William Page. 1908. xxi, 515
III, ed. William Page. 1912. xxi, 511
IV, ed. William Page. 1914. xvii, 467
Index [no editor named]. 1923. [iv], 116
Hertfordshire Families, ed. Duncan Warrand. 1907. 325, xxi. Indexed. *500*

Huntingdonshire

I, ed. William Page and Granville Proby, assisted by H. E. Norris. 1926. xxi, 410
II, ed. William Page, Granville Proby, and S. Inskip Ladds. 1932. xviii, 383
III, ed. the late William Page, Granville Proby, and S. Inskip Ladds. 1936. xxv, 306
Index [no editor named]. 1938. 52

Kent

I, ed. William Page. 1908. xxv, 518
II, ed. William Page. 1926. xv, 388
III, ed. William Page. 1932. xv, 452

Lancashire

I, ed. William Farrer and J. Brownbill. 1906. xxv, 381
II, ed. William Farrer and J. Brownbill. 1908. xv, 668. With index to I and II
III, ed. William Farrer and J. Brownbill. 1907. xv, 449
IV, ed. William Farrer and J. Brownbill. 1911. xv, 406

---

[1] Volume completed in 1914 but publication delayed owing to the war and other reasons.

[2] Volume completed in 1915 but publication delayed owing to the war and other reasons.

V, ed. William Farrer and J. Brownbill. 1911. xiii, 409. With index to III–V

VI, ed. William Farrer and J. Brownbill. 1911. xxi, 560

VII, ed. William Farrer and J. Brownbill. 1912. xiii, 435. With index to VI and VII

VIII, ed. William Farrer and J. Brownbill. 1914. xviii, 457. Indexed

Leicestershire

I, ed. William Page. 1907. xxi, 401

II, ed. W. G. Hoskins assisted by R. A. McKinley. 1954. xvii, 270. *650*

III, ed. W. G. Hoskins and R. A. McKinley. 1955. xxi, 338. With index to I–III. *650*

IV, ed. R. A. McKinley. 1958. xx, 484. Indexed. *750*

V, ed. J. M. Lee and R. A. McKinley. 1964. xvii, 367. Indexed. *750*

Lincolnshire

II, ed. William Page. 1906. xv, 528

London, including London within the Bars, Westminster, and Southwark

I, ed. William Page. 1909. xxvii, 588

Middlesex

I, ed. J. S. Cockburn, H. P. F. King, and K. G. T. McDonnell. 1969. xxiv, 385. Indexed. *1,400*

II, ed. William Page. 1911. xi, 406

III, ed. Susan Reynolds. 1962. xx, 325. With index to II and III. *750*

Norfolk

I [ed. H. Arthur Doubleday]. 1901. xx, 351

II, ed. William Page. 1906. xix, 563

Northamptonshire

I, ed. W. Ryland D. Adkins and R. M. Serjeantson. 1902. xx, 436

II, ed. the Revd. R. M. Serjeantson and W. Ryland D. Adkins. 1906. xxi, 603

III, ed. William Page. 1930. xviii, 280

IV, ed. L. F. Salzman. 1937. xv, 300

Northamptonshire Families, ed. O. Barron. 1906. xxi, 380

Nottinghamshire

I, ed. William Page. 1906. xxix, 381

II, ed. William Page. 1910. xv, 422

Oxfordshire

I, ed. L. F. Salzman. 1939. xiv, 497

II, ed. William Page. 1907. xv, 372

III (The University of Oxford), ed. the Revd. H. E. Salter and Mary D. Lobel. 1954. xix, 382. Indexed. *1,000*

V (Bullingdon Hundred), ed. Mary D. Lobel. 1957. xxvi, 344. Indexed. *750*

VI (Ploughley Hundred), ed. Mary D. Lobel. 1959. xxviii, 389. Indexed. *750*

VII (Dorchester and Thame Hundreds), ed. Mary Lobel. 1962. xxviii, 248. Indexed. *750*

VIII (Lewknor and Pyrton Hundreds), ed. Mary D. Lobel. 1964. xxix, 298. Indexed. *750*

IX (Bloxham Hundred), ed. Mary D. Lobel and Alan Crossley. 1969. xxiv, 205. Indexed. *1,000*

Rutland

I, ed. William Page. 1908. xxi, 307

II, ed. William Page. 1935. xliv, 284

Index [no editor named]. 1936. [31]

Shropshire

I, ed. William Page. 1908. xxv, 497

VIII, ed. A. T. Gaydon. 1968. [xx], 356. Indexed. *850*. 2nd impression 1969. *300*

Somerset

I, ed. William Page. 1906. xxv, 537

II, ed. William Page. 1911. xv, 649

Staffordshire

I, ed. William Page. 1908. xxi, 379

II, ed. M. W. Greenslade and J. G. Jenkins. 1967. xxiv, 416. With index to I and II. *1,200*

III, ed. M. W. Greenslade. 1970. xx, 379. Indexed. *1,400*

IV (Staffordshire Domesday and West Cuttlestone Hundred), ed. L. Margaret Midgley. 1958. xxiii, 197. Indexed. *750*

V (East Cuttlestone Hundred), ed. L. Margaret Midgley. 1959. xxiii, 199. Indexed. *750*

VIII, ed. J. G. Jenkins. 1963. xxiv, 348. Indexed. *750*. 2nd impression 1964. *400*

Suffolk

I, ed. William Page. 1911. xxv, 695

II, ed. William Page. 1907. xv, 409

Surrey

I, ed. H. E. Malden. 1902. xix, 449

II, ed. H. E. Malden. 1905. xvii, 626

III, ed. H. E. Malden. 1911. xix, 570

IV, ed. H. E. Malden. 1912. xvii, 464

Index [no editor named]. 1914. 104

Sussex

I ed. William Page. 1905. xxiii, 554

II, ed. William Page. 1907. xv, 481

III, ed. L. F. Salzman. 1935. xiii, 169

IV (The Rape of Chichester), ed. L. F. Salzman. 1953. xv, 239. *650*

VII (The Rape of Lewes), ed. L. F. Salzman. 1940. xv, 286

IX (The Rape of Hastings), ed. L. F. Salzman. 1937. xv, 279

Warwickshire

I [ed. H. Arthur Doubleday and William Page]. 1904. xxii, 415

II, ed. William Page. 1908. xv, 468

III (Barlichway Hundred), general editor: L. F. Salzman; local editor: Philip Styles. 1945. xv, 288. *650*

IV (Hemlingford Hundred), ed. L. F. Salzman. 1947. xiii, 263. *650*

V (Kington Hundred), ed. L. F. Salzman. 1949. xiii, 224. *650*

VI (Knightlow Hundred), ed. L. F. Salzman. 1951. xiii, 287. *650*

Index to Volumes I–VI, ed. R. B. Pugh. 1955. xii, 142. *750*

VII (The City of Birmingham), ed. W. B. Stephens. 1964. xviii, 598. Indexed. *1,000*. 2nd impression 1965. *300*

VIII (The City of Coventry and The Borough of Warwick), ed. W. B. Stephens. 1969. xxiv, 583. Indexed. *1,400*

Wiltshire

I, Part I, ed. R. B. Pugh and Elizabeth Crittall. 1957. xxi, 279. *750*

II, ed. R. B. Pugh and Elizabeth Crittall. 1955. xvii, 245. Indexed. *750*

III, ed. R. B. Pugh and Elizabeth Crittall. 1956. xix, 424. Indexed. *750*

IV, ed. Elizabeth Crittall. 1959. xx, 486. Indexed. *750*

V, ed. R. B. Pugh and Elizabeth Crittall. 1957. xxi, 383. Indexed. *750*

VI, ed. Elizabeth Crittall. 1962. xx, 239. Indexed. *750*

VII, ed. R. B. Pugh, assisted by Elizabeth Crittall. 1953. xix, 241. Indexed. *650*

VIII, ed. Elizabeth Crittall. 1965. xx, 285. Indexed. *850*

IX, ed. Elizabeth Crittall. 1970. xx, 220. Indexed. *1,000*

Worcestershire

I [ed. J. W. Willis-Bund and H. Arthur Doubleday]. 1901. xx, 340

II, ed. J. W. Willis-Bund and William Page. 1906. xvii, 429

III, general editor: William Page; local editor: J. W. Willis-Bund. 1913. xxi, 573

IV, general editor: William Page; local editor: J. W. Willis-Bund. 1924.[1] xix, 540

Index [no editor named]. 1926. [iv], 114

Yorkshire, [General]

I, ed. William Page. 1907. xxiii, 523

II, ed. William Page. 1912. xv, 550

III, ed. William Page. 1913. xviii, 548

Index [no editor named]. 1925. 102

Yorkshire, East Riding

I (The City of Kingston-upon-Hull), ed. K. J. Allison. 1969. xx, 498. Indexed. *1,200*

Yorkshire, North Riding

I, ed. William Page. 1914. xxii, 566

II, ed. William Page. 1923.[1] xxii, 560

Index [no editor named]. 1925. 90

Yorkshire, The City of York

ed. P. M. Tillott. 1961. xx, 577. Indexed. *1,000*

Volume completed in 1914 but publication delayed owing to the war and other reasons.

LISTS OF CONTENTS

Below are reprinted the lists of contents of all the volumes of the *History* published by 1970, excluding Index Volumes and the *General Introduction*. A few changes have been made, either to correct errors that have been discovered in the original lists or to remove minor inconsistencies. No attempt has been made, however, to achieve uniformity, and in particular it has been thought best neither to augment nor to curtail the information given about authors in the lists as originally published.

BEDFORDSHIRE

VOLUME ONE

PAGE

Dedication .	v
The Advisory Council of the Victoria History	vii
General Advertisement	vii
The Bedfordshire County Committee	xiii
Contents	xv
List of Illustrations .	xvii
Preface	xix
Table of Abbreviations	xx

Natural History

Geology .	By John Hopkinson, F.L.S., F.G.S., and James Saunders, A.L.S.	1
Palaeontology	By R. Lydekker, F.R.S., F.G.S., F.L.S.	33
Botany	By John Hamson and G. Claridge Druce, M.A., F.L.S.; assisted by James Saunders, A.L.S. and E. M. Holmes, F.L.S.	37

Zoology

Mollusca (*Snails, etc.*) .	By B. B. Woodward, F.G.S., F.R.M.S.	69
Insecta (*Insects*)		
Coleoptera (*Beetles*) .	By the Revd. Canon Fowler, M.A., F.L.S.	71
Lepidoptera (*Butterflies*)	By Charles G. Barrett, F.E.S.	78
Arachnida (*Spiders*) .	By F. O. Pickard-Cambridge, M.A.	88
Crustacea (*Crabs, etc.*) .	By the Revd. T. R. R. Stebbing, M.A., F.R.S., F.L.S.	91
Pisces (*Fishes*) .	By Arthur R. Thompson .	98
Reptilia (*Reptiles*) and Batrachia (*Batrachians*)	By J. Lacey Fishwick	102
Aves (*Birds*) .	By J. Steele-Elliott	104
Mammalia (*Mammals*) .	,, ,,	138
Early Man .	By Worthington G. Smith, F.L.S., F.A.I.	145
Anglo-Saxon Remains	By Reginald A. Smith, B.A., F.S.A.	175
Introduction to the Bedfordshire Domesday .	By J. Horace Round, M.A.	191
Text of the Bedfordshire Domesday	By the Revd. F. W. Ragg, M.A.	221
Ancient Earthworks	By A. R. Goddard, B.A.	267
Ecclesiastical History	By the Sister Elspeth of the Community of All Saints	309
Religious Houses	,, ,, ,, ,, ,, ,,	
Introduction		349
Priory of Beaulieu		351
Abbey of Elstow .		353
Priory of Markyate		358
Abbey of Warden		361
,, ,, Woburn		366

CONTENTS OF VOLUMES: BEDS. I

		PAGE
Priory of Dunstable	. . . .	371
,, ,, Newnham	. . . .	377
,, ,, Caldwell	. . . .	382
,, ,, Bushmead	. . . .	385
,, ,, Harrold	. . . .	387
,, ,, Chicksand	. . . .	390
Preceptory of Melchbourne	. . . .	394
Franciscans of Bedford	. . . .	395
Dominicans of Dunstable	. . . .	395
Hospital of St. John, Bedford	. . . .	396
,, ,, St. Leonard, Bedford	. . . .	398
,, ,, St. Mary Magdalene, Luton	. . . .	399
,, ,, St. John Baptist, Luton	. . . .	400
,, ,, Farley near Luton	. . . .	400
,, ,, St. Mary Magdalene, Dunstable	. . . . . .	400
,, ,, St. John Baptist, Hockliffe	. . . . . .	401
,, ,, St. John Baptist, Toddington	. . . . .	402
College of Northill	. . . .	403
Priory of La Grave or Grovebury	. . . .	403
Index to the Bedfordshire Domesday	By the Revd. F. W. RAGG, M.A. . .	405

VOLUME TWO

		PAGE
Dedication .	. . . .	v
Contents	. . . .	ix
List of Illustrations and Maps	. . . .	xiii
Editorial Note	. . . .	xvii
Romano-British Bedfordshire	By the General Editor and Miss KEATE	1
Political History	By C. GORE CHAMBERS, M.A. . .	17
Social and Economic History	By ARTHUR RANSOM . .	73
Table of Population, 1801–1901 .	By GEORGE S. MINCHIN . . .	111
Industries	By ARTHUR RANSOM	
Introduction	. . . .	117
Straw Plait, Hat, and Bonnet Industry	. . . . . .	118
Pillow-Lace Making	. . . .	122
Pavenham Rush-Matting and Wicker Basket Industries	. . . . . .	124
Engineering Works	. . . .	125
Agriculture	By ARTHUR RANSOM . .	129
Forestry	By the Revd. J. C. COX, LL.D., F.S.A. .	143
Schools	By A. F. LEACH, M.A., F.S.A.	
Introduction	. . . .	149
Bedford Grammar School	. . . .	152
Modern School for Boys	. . . .	177
Girls' Schools .	. . . .	177
Bedford County School, now Elstow School	. . . .	177
Dunstable Schools	. . . .	178
Biggleswade Free School .	. . . .	179
Houghton Conquest School	. . . .	180
Luton School	. . . .	180
Public Elementary Schools	. . . .	181

CONTENTS OF VOLUMES: BEDS. II

PAGE

Sport Ancient and Modern . . . Edited by E. D. Cuming
  Hunting . . . . . By Arthur Ransom 187
  Foxhounds . . . . . ,, ,, ... 187
    The Oakley Hunt . . . ,, ,, . . . 187
  Harriers and Beagles . . . ,, ,, . . . 190
  Racing . . . . By E. D. Cuming 190
    Flat Racing . . . . ,, ,, ... 190
    Steeplechasing . . . ,, ,, ... 194
  Polo . . . . . ,, ,, ... 195
  Shooting . . . . By C. Alington 195
  Golf . . . . . By A. J. Robertson 198
  Cricket . . . . By Arthur Ransom 199
  Football . . . . . ,, ,, ... 200
  Aquatics . . . . . ,, ,, ... 200
Topography . . . . General descriptions and manorial descents compiled under the superintendence of the General Editor; Architectural descriptions under the superintendence of C. R. Peers, M.A., F.S.A., by J. W. Bloe, J. Murray Kendall, and S. F. Beeke Lane; Heraldic drawings and blazon by the Revd. E. E. Dorling, M.A.; Charities from information supplied by J. W. Owsley, I.S.O., late Official Trustee of Charitable Funds
  Biggleswade Hundred . . . General descriptions and descents of manors and advowsons by Miss A. V. Rickards, Hist. Tripos (Honours)
    Introduction 201
    Astwick 203
    Little Barford 206
    Biggleswade with Stratton and Holme 209
    Cockayne Hatley 215
    Dunton with Millo 218
    Edworth 223
    Everton 226
    Eyworth 230
    Langford 234
    Potton 237
    Sandy with Girtford 242
    Sutton 246
    Tempsford 251
    Wrestlingworth 255
  Clifton Hundred . . . . General descriptions and descents of manors and advowsons, by Miss A. V. Rickards, Hist. Tripos (Honours)
    Introduction . . . . ,, ,, ,, 260
    Arlesey . . . . ,, ,, ,, 261
    Campton cum Shefford and Chicksands By Miss M. R. Manfield, Hist. Tripos (Honours) . 266
    (Architectural description of Chicksands Priory by C. R. Peers, M.A., F.S.A.)
    Clifton . . . . By Miss M. R. Manfield, Hist. Tripos (Honours) . 276
    Henlow . . . . By Miss A. V. Rickards ,, ,, . 280
    Holwell . . . . ,, ,, ,, ,, ,, . 286
    Meppershall . . . . By Miss M. R. Manfield ,, ,, . 288
    Shillington with Lower Stondon and
      Little Holwell . . . By Miss A. V. Rickards ,, ,, . 293
    Stotfold . . . . ,, ,, ,, ,, ,, . 300
    Upper Stondon . . . ,, ,, ,, ,, ,, . 304
  Flitt Hundred . . . . General descriptions and descents of manors and advowsons, by Miss M. R. Manfield, Hist. Tripos (Honours)

		PAGE
Introduction	By Miss M. R. MANFIELD, Hist. Tripos (Honours)	306
Barton in the Clay	,, ,, ,, ,, ,,	308
Caddington	By Miss O. M. MOGER	314
(Architectural description of church by C. R. PEERS, M.A., F.S.A.)		
Clophill	By Miss M. R. MANFIELD, Hist. Tripos (Honours)	320
Flitton cum Silsoe	,, ,, ,, ,, ,,	325
Upper Gravenhurst	,, ,, ,, ,, ,,	333
Lower Gravenhurst	,, ,, ,, ,, ,,	336
Hawnes or Haynes	,, ,, ,, ,, ,,	338
Higham Gobion	,, ,, ,, ,, ,,	344
Luton with East and West Hyde, Stopsley, Limbury cum Biscott, and Leagrave	By Miss A. V. RICKARDS ,, ,,	348
Pulloxhill	By Miss M. R. MANFIELD ,, ,,	376
Streatley with Sharpenhoe	By Miss A. V. RICKARDS ,, ,,	381
Sundon	,, ,, ,, ,, ,,	384

VOLUME THREE

		PAGE
Dedication		v
Contents		ix
List of Illustrations		xiii
List of Maps		xvii
Editorial Note		xix
Topography	General descriptions and manorial descents compiled under the superintendence of the General Editor; Architectural descriptions by R. W. ATKEY, T. F. INGRAM, and ERNEST A. R. RAHBULA, under the superintendence of C. R. PEERS, M.A., F.S.A., and S. C. KAINES-SMITH, M.A.; Heraldic drawings and blazon by the Revd. E. E. DORLING, M.A., F.S.A.; Charities from information supplied by J. W. OWSLEY, I.S.O., late Official Trustee of Charitable Funds	
Bedford Borough	History of Borough and manorial descents by VIOLET RICKARDS, Hist. Tripos (Honours)	1
Willey Hundred	General descriptions and manorial descents by VIOLET RICKARDS, Hist. Tripos (Honours)	
Introduction		34
Biddenham		36
Bletsoe		40
Bromham		44
Carlton		49
Chellington		54
Farndish		57
Felmersham with Radwell		59
Harrold		63
Odell		69
Pavenham		76
Podington with Hinwick		80
Sharnbrook		88
Souldrop		94
Stagsden		96
Stevington		100
Thurleigh		104
Turvey		109
Wymington or Wimington		117

CONTENTS OF VOLUMES: BEDS. III

PAGE

Stodden Hundred . . . General descriptions and manorial descents by
H. S. F. LEA

Introduction 123
Bolnhurst 124
Clapham 128
Dean 132
Keysoe 136
Knotting 139
Melchbourne 142
Milton Ernest 143
Oakley 149
Pertenhall 153
Riseley or Risley 157
Shelton 161
Little Staughton 165
Swineshead 168
Tilbrook 171
Yelden . . . [General descriptions and manorial descents by
VIOLET RICKARDS, Hist. Tripos (Honours)] . 175

Barford Hundred
Introduction . . . . By VIOLET RICKARDS, Hist. Tripos (Honours) . 180
Great Barford . . . . General descriptions and manorial descents by
STANLEY WILLIAMS, B.A. . . . 181
Colmworth . . . . ,, ,, ,, . 186
Eaton Socon . . . . General descriptions and manorial descents by
VIOLET RICKARDS, Hist. Tripos (Honours) . 189
Goldington . . . . General descriptions and manorial descents by
MURIEL R. MANFIELD, Hist. Tripos (Honours) . 202
Ravensden . . . . ,, ,, ,, . 209
Renhold . . . . General descriptions and manorial descents by
STANLEY WILLIAMS, B.A. . . . 214
Roxton . . . . ,, ,, ,, . 218
Wilden . . . . General descriptions and manorial descents by
VIOLET RICKARDS, Hist. Tripos (Honours) . 223

Wixamtree Hundred . . . General descriptions and manorial descents by
GRACE A. ELLIS, B.A. (Lond.)

Introduction 227
Blunham with Moggerhanger and
Chalton 228
Cardington with Eastcotts 233
Cople 238
Northill 242
Old Warden 251
Southill with Rowney 256
Willington 262

Redbornestoke Hundred
Introduction . . . . By VIOLET RICKARDS, Hist. Tripos (Honours) . 267
Ampthill . . . . General descriptions and manorial descents by
H. S. F. LEA 268
Cranfield . . . . General descriptions and manorial descents by
J. HAUTENVILLE COPE . . . 275
Elstow . . . . General descriptions and manorial descents by
H. S. F. LEA 279
Flitwick . . . . General descriptions and manorial descents by
VIOLET RICKARDS, Hist. Tripos (Honours), and
CATHERINE BEVERIDGE, M.A. (Aberdeen) . . 284
Houghton Conquest . . . General descriptions and manorial descents by
H. S. F. LEA 288
Kempston . . . . General descriptions and manorial descents by
MURIEL R. MANFIELD, Hist. Tripos (Honours) . 296

CONTENTS OF VOLUMES: BEDS. III

PAGE

Lidlington	General descriptions and manorial descents by STANLEY WILLIAMS, B.A.	305
Marston Moretaine	,,　　　　,,　　　　,,	307
Maulden	General descriptions and manorial descents by VIOLET RICKARDS, Hist. Tripos (Honours), and CATHERINE BEVERIDGE, M.A. (Aberdeen)	313
Millbrook	General descriptions and manorial descents by J. HAUTENVILLE COPE	316
Ridgmont	General descriptions and manorial descents by STANLEY WILLIAMS, B.A.	320
Steppingley	General descriptions and manorial descents by VIOLET RICKARDS, Hist. Tripos (Honours), and CATHERINE BEVERIDGE, M.A. (Aberdeen)	324
Wilshamstead	General descriptions and manorial descents by STANLEY WILLIAMS, B.A.	325
Wootton	General descriptions and manorial descents by MURIEL R. MANFIELD, Hist. Tripos (Honours)	328
Manshead Hundred		
Introduction	By VIOLET RICKARDS, Hist. Tripos (Honours)	336
Aspley Guise	General descriptions and manorial descents by ANNIE R. GRUNDY	338
Battlesden	General descriptions and manorial descents by VIOLET RICKARDS, Hist. Tripos (Honours), and CLARE THUNDER	343
Chalgrave with Tebworth & Wingfield	General descriptions and manorial descents by MURIEL R. MANFIELD, Hist. Tripos (Honours)	345
Dunstable	,,　　　　,,　　　　,,	349
Eaton Bray	General descriptions and manorial descents by ANNIE R. GRUNDY	369
Eversholt	,,　　　　,,　　　　,,	375
Harlington	,,　　　　,,　　　　,,	379
Hockliffe	General descriptions and manorial descents by VIOLET RICKARDS, Hist. Tripos (Honours)	383
Holcot	General descriptions and manorial descents by VIOLET RICKARDS, Hist. Tripos (Honours), and CLARE THUNDER	386
Houghton Regis	General descriptions and manorial descents by H. S. F. LEA	389
Husborne Crawley	General descriptions and manorial descents by ANNIE R. GRUNDY	394
Leighton Buzzard with Billington, Eggington, Heath and Reach, and Stanbridge	General descriptions and manorial descents by MURIEL R. MANFIELD, Hist. Tripos (Honours)	399
Milton Bryant or Bryan	General descriptions and manorial descents by ANNIE R. GRUNDY	417
Potsgrove	General descriptions and manorial descents by VIOLET RICKARDS, Hist. Tripos (Honours), and CLARE THUNDER	421
Salford	General descriptions and manorial descents by VIOLET RICKARDS, Hist. Tripos (Honours)	424
Studham	General descriptions and manorial descents by OLIVE M. MOGER	426
Tilsworth	General descriptions and manorial descents by VIOLET RICKARDS, Hist. Tripos (Honours), and CLARE THUNDER	432
Tingrith	General descriptions and manorial descents by VIOLET RICKARDS, Hist. Tripos (Honours)	435
Toddington	General descriptions and manorial descents by ANNIE R. GRUNDY	438
Totternhoe	,,　　　　,,　　　　,,	447
Westoning	,,　　　　,,	451

PAGE

Whipsnade . . . . General descriptions and manorial descents by
ANNIE R. GRUNDY 455
Woburn . . . . General descriptions and manorial descents by
H. S. F. LEA 457
(Architectural description of Woburn Abbey by S. C. KAINES-SMITH, M.A.)

BERKSHIRE

VOLUME ONE

PAGE

Dedication v
The Advisory Council of the Victoria History vii
General Advertisement vii
The Berkshire County Committee xiii
Contents xv
List of Illustrations xvii
Preface xxi
Table of Abbreviations xxiii
Natural History
Geology . . . . . By HORACE W. MONCKTON, F.G.S., F.L.S. . . 1
Palaeontology . . . . By R. LYDEKKER, F.R.S., F.G.S., F.L.S. . . 25
Botany . . . . . By G. CLARIDGE DRUCE, Hon. M.A. Oxon., F.L.S. . 27
Zoology
Molluscs . . . . By B. B. WOODWARD, F.G.S., F.R.M.S. . . 69
Insects . . . . Edited by the Revd. Canon W. W. FOWLER, M.A.,
F.L.S., F.E.S. 71
Orthoptera (*Earwigs, Grasshoppers,
Crickets, etc.*) . . By W. J. LUCAS, B.A., F.E.S. . . . 72
Neuroptera (*Dragonflies, Lace-wings,
etc.*) . . . . ,, ,, ,, . . . 73
Hymenoptera Phytophaga (*Sawflies,
Gall-flies, etc.*) . . By A. H. HAMM 74
Hymenoptera Aculeata (*Ants, Wasps,
and Bees*) . . . ,, ,, ... 76
Coleoptera (*Beetles*) . . By W. HOLLAND and Dr. NORMAN H. JOY . 79
Lepidoptera (*Butterflies and Moths*) . By A. H. HAMM and W. HOLLAND . . 100
Hemiptera (*Bugs*) . . By W. HOLLAND 117
Spiders . . . By the late F. O. PICKARD-CAMBRIDGE, M.A. . 120
Crustaceans . . . By the Revd. T. R. R. STEBBING, M.A., F.R.S.
F.Z.S. 123
Fishes . . . . By C. H. COOK, M.A. . . . 132
Reptiles and Batrachians . . By the late CHARLES J. CORNISH, M.A. . 138
Birds . . . . By HEATLEY NOBLE . . . 140
Mammals . . . By the late CHARLES J. CORNISH, M.A. . 167
Early Man 173
The Palaeolithic Age: Neolithic Age:
Bronze Age . . . By O. A. SHRUBSOLE, F.G.S.
The Prehistoric Iron Age: The White
Horse at Uffington: Ancient British
Coins: Ancient Roads: Pile Dwell-
ings . . . . By GEORGE CLINCH, F.G.S.
Romano-British Berkshire . . By the General Editor and Miss C. M. CALTHROP,
First Class Classical Tripos . . 197
Anglo-Saxon Remains . . By REGINALD A. SMITH, B.A., F.S.A. . 229
Ancient Earthworks . . By HAROLD J. E. PEAKE . . 251
Introduction to the Berkshire Domesday . By J. HORACE ROUND, M.A., LL.D. . 285

PAGE

Translation of the Berkshire Domesday . By the Revd. F. W. Ragg, M.A. . . . 324
Industries . . . . . By the Revd. P. H. Ditchfield, M.A., F.S.A.
   Introduction 371
   Ironworks 383
   Boat Building 385
   Cloth Making 387
   Silk Manufacture 395
   Tanning 397
   Printing 400
   Brewing 404
   Biscuit Making 411
   Bell Foundries . . . . By Alfred Heneage Cocks, M.A., F.S.A. . . 412

VOLUME TWO

PAGE

Dedication v
Contents ix
List of Illustrations xiii
Editorial Note xv
Ecclesiastical History . . . By the Revd. J. C. Cox, LL.D., F.S.A. . . 1
Religious Houses . . . . ,, ,, ,,
   Introduction 49
   Abbey of Abingdon 51
   ,, ,, Reading 62
   Priory of Hurley 73
   ,, ,, Wallingford 77
   ,, ,, Bromhall 80
   Cell or Grange of Faringdon 81
   Priory of Bisham 82
   ,, ,, Poughley 85
   ,, ,, Sandleford 86
   Preceptory of Greenham 88
   Grey Friars of Reading 89
   Crouched Friars of Donnington 91
   Hospital of St. Helen, Abingdon 92
   ,, ,, St. John, Abingdon 92
   ,, ,, St. Mary Magdalen, Abingdon 93
   ,, ,, Childrey 93
   ,, ,, Donnington 93
   ,, ,, Fyfield 94
   ,, ,, St. John Baptist, Hungerford 94
   ,, ,, St. Laurence, Hungerford 95
   ,, ,, Lambourn 95
   ,, ,, St. Bartholomew, Newbury 95
   ,, ,, Mary Magdalen, Newbury 97
   ,, ,, St. John, Reading 97
   ,, ,, St. Mary Magdalen, Reading 98
   Barnes Hospital, Reading 99
   Hospital of St. John Baptist, Wallingford 99
   ,, ,, St. Mary Magdalen, Wallingford 101
   ,, ,, St. Peter, Windsor 101
   ,, ,, St. John, Windsor 102
   College of Shottesbrook 102
   ,, ,, Wallingford 103

PAGE

Collegiate Church of Windsor 106
Alien Priory of Steventon 112
    ,,   ,, Stratfield Saye 113
Political History . . . . By Miss Alice Sergeant, Oxford Honours School of
    Modern History 115
Social and Economic History . By Miss E. C. Lodge, Oxford Honours School of
    Modern History 167
Table of Population, 1801–1901 . By George S. Minchin . . . 234
Schools . . . . . By A. F. Leach, M.A., F.S.A.
  Introduction 245
  Reading Grammar School 245
  Abingdon School 259
  St. Bartholomew's School, Newbury 272
  Childrey School 275
  Wantage Grammar School 276
  Hungerford Grammar School 277
  Wallingford Grammar School 277
  Radley College 277
  Bradfield College 279
  Wellington College 281
  Elementary Schools founded before 1750 281
Sport Ancient and Modern . . Edited by the Revd. P. H. Ditchfield, M.A., F.S.A.
  Hunting . . . . By the Revd. P. H. Ditchfield, M.A., F.S.A. . 285
    Staghounds 285
      The Royal Buckhounds 285
      Berks and Bucks Farmers' Staghounds 287
      Lord Barrymore's Staghounds 287
      Mr. Seymour Dubourg's Harriers 287
    Fox-hunting 287
      South Berks Hunt 289
      The Garth Hunt 290
      The Craven Hunt 291
      The Old Berkshire Hunt 294
    Harriers 295
      Berkshire Vale Harriers 295
    Draghounds 296
    Basset Hounds 296
  Bull-Baiting . . . By the Revd. P. H. Ditchfield, M.A., F.S.A. . 296
  Cock-Fighting . . . .   ,,   ,,   ,, 297
  Coursing . . . .   ,,   ,,   ,, 298
  Shooting . . . By the late Charles John Cornish, M.A. . 300
  Angling . . . . By C. H. Cook, M.A. . . . 302
  Racing . . . . By the Revd. P. H. Ditchfield, M.A., F.S.A. . 305
    Flat-Racing 305
      Royal Ascot 305
    Steeplechasing 309
  Rowing . . . . By the Revd. P. H. Ditchfield, M.A., F.S.A., and
    Walter B. Woodgate 310
    Radley 310
    Thames Regattas 311
  Archery . . . . By the Revd. P. H. Ditchfield, M.A., F.S.A. . 311
  Pugilism . . . .   ,,   ,,   ,, 313
    Cudgel Play and the Revels 314
    Cut-legs and Kick-shins 315
  Golf . . . . By the Revd. E. E. Dorling, M.A. . 316
  Cricket . . . . By the Revd. P. H. Ditchfield, M.A., F.S.A.,
    assisted by P. J. de Paravicini, H. W. Brougham,
    and A. C. M. Croome 317

PAGE

Wellington 324
Radley 324
Bradfield 325
Sandhurst 326
Football . . . . . By the Revd. P. H. DITCHFIELD, M.A., F.S.A.,
      assisted by J. L. BEVIR and A. C. M. CROOME . 327

Wellington 327
Radley 328
Bradfield 328
Sandhurst 329
Town and Village Clubs 329
Agriculture . . . . . By the Revd. P. H. DITCHFIELD, M.A., F.S.A., and
      W. ANKER SIMMONS, F.S.I. . . . 331
Forestry . . . . . By the Revd. J. C. COX, LL.D., F.S.A. . . 341

VOLUME THREE

PAGE

Dedication v
Contents ix
List of Illustrations xiii
List of Maps and Plans xix
Editorial Note xxi
Topography . . . . . General descriptions and manorial descents compiled
      under the superintendence of WILLIAM PAGE,
      F.S.A.; Architectural descriptions under the super-
      intendence of the late JOHN QUEKETT, M.A.,
      F.S.A., by ERNEST A. R. RAHBULA, A.R.I.B.A.,
      F.S.A., J. W. BLOE, F.S.A., C. C. DURSTON;
      Heraldic drawings and blazon by the Revd. E. E.
      DORLING, M.A., F.S.A.; Charities from informa-
      tion supplied by J. W. OWSLEY, I.S.O., late
      Official Trustee of Charitable Funds

Royal Borough of Windsor . . By the late GLADYS TEMPERLEY, M.B.E., Fellow of
      Newnham College, Cambridge. Architectural
      description of Castle by the late Sir W. H.
      ST. JOHN HOPE, M.A., Litt.D., D.C.L. . . I

Ripplesmere Hundred
  Introduction . . . . By NORA ALEXANDER 71
  Clewer . . . . By J. HAUTENVILLE COPE and N. ALEXANDER . 72
  Easthampstead . . . By J. HAUTENVILLE COPE 77
  Old Windsor . . . By J. HAUTENVILLE COPE and N. ALEXANDER . 80
  Winkfield . . . .   ,,   ,,   ,, . 85
Bray Hundred
  Introduction . . . . By MARJORY HOLLINGS, Oxford Honours School of
      Modern History 92
  Bray with the Borough of Maidenhead .   ,,   ,,   ,,   ,, . 93
Cookham Hundred . . . By NORA ALEXANDER
  Introduction 117
  Binfield 119
  Cookham 124
  Sunninghill 134
Beynhurst Hundred . . . By NORA ALEXANDER
  Introduction 137
  Bisham 139
  Hurley 152
  Remenham 160
  Shottesbrook 164

CONTENTS OF VOLUMES: BERKS. III

		PAGE
White Waltham		171
Wargrave Hundred . . .	By CATHERINE JAMISON, Oxford Honours School of Modern History	
Introduction	. . . . . .	178
Waltham St. Lawrence .	. . . . . .	179
Warfield . . .	. . . . . .	184
Wargrave . . .	. . . . . .	191
Sonning Hundred		
Introduction . . .	By NORA ALEXANDER . . .	198
Arborfield . . .	,, ,, . . .	200
Ruscombe . . .	,, ,, . . .	203
Sandhurst . . .	By N. ALEXANDER, LEONARD A. MAGNUS, and ALICE RAVEN	206
Sonning with Earley, Woodley, and Sandford . . .	By N. ALEXANDER, ALICE RAVEN, and Revd. P. H. DITCHFIELD, M.A., F.S.A. . .	210
Wokingham . .	By N. ALEXANDER and ALICE RAVEN .	225
Charlton Hundred . .	By the Revd. P. H. DITCHFIELD, M.A., F.S.A.	
Introduction . . .	. . . . . .	237
Barkham . . .	. . . . . .	238
Finchampstead . .	. . . . . .	241
Hurst . . .	. . . . . .	247
Shinfield . . .	. . . . . .	261
Swallowfield . .	. . . . . .	267
Reading Hundred		
Introduction . . .	By MARJORY HOLLINGS, Oxford Honours School of Modern History	275
Beenham . . .	By CATHERINE JAMISON, Oxford Honours School of Modern History	277
Blewbury with Upton and Aston Upthorpe . . .	,, ,, ,,	280
Bucklebury . . .	,, ,, ,,	291
Cholsey . . .	,, ,, ,,	296
Pangbourne . . .	,, ,, ,,	303
Sulhampstead Abbots with Grazeley .	,, ,, ,,	306
Thatcham . . .	,, ,, ,,	311
Tilehurst . . .	,, ,, ,,	329
Reading Borough with St. Giles with Whitley and St. Mary with Southcot	History of Borough to 1638 by HENRIETTA HAYNES, from 1638 by CATHERINE JAMISON. History of the Advowson by HENRIETTA HAYNES . .	336
Theale Hundred		
Introduction . . .	By MARJORY HOLLINGS, Oxford Honours School of Modern History	385
Aldermaston . . .	By CATHERINE JAMISON, Oxford Honours School of Modern History	386
Bradfield . . .	,, ,, ,,	395
Burghfield . . .	,, ,, ,,	399
Englefield . . .	,, ,, ,,	405
Padworth . . .	By MARJORY HOLLINGS . . .	413
Purley . . .	,, ,, . . .	417
Stratfield Mortimer . .	,, ,, . . .	422
Sulham . . .	,, ,, . . .	428
Sulhamstead Bannister .	By CATHERINE JAMISON . . .	430
Tidmarsh . . .	By MARJORY HOLLINGS . . .	433
Ufton Nervet . . .	By NORA ALEXANDER . . .	437
Woolhampton . . .	By MARJORY HOLLINGS . . .	444
Moreton Hundred		
Introduction . . .	. . . . . .	447
Ashampstead . . .	By the Revd. J. E. FIELD, M.A. . .	449

CONTENTS OF VOLUMES: BERKS. III

			PAGE
Aston Tirrold	. . .	By Lilian J. Redstone, M.B.E., B.A. . .	452
Basildon	. . . .	By the Revd. J. E. Field, M.A. . . .	457
Brightwell	. . . .	,, ,, . .	464
Didcot	. . . .	By Lilian J. Redstone, M.B.E., B.A. .	471
Hagbourne	. . . .	,, ,, ,, .	475
Harwell	. . . .	,, ,, ,, .	484
North Moreton	. . .	By the Revd. J. E. Field, M.A. . .	492
South Moreton	. . .	,, ,, . .	498
Moulsford	. . . .	By Lilian J. Redstone, M.B.E., B.A. .	504
Sotwell	. . . .	By the Revd. J. E. Field, M.A. . .	507
Streatley	. . . .	By Lilian J. Redstone, M.B.E., B.A. .	511
Wallingford Borough .	. .	By the late Gladys Temperley, M.B.E., and Revd. J. E. Field, M.A.	517
The Liberty of Clapcot	. .	,, ,, ,, .	546

VOLUME FOUR

		PAGE
Dedication	. . . .	v
Contents	. . . .	ix
List of Illustrations . .	. . . .	xiii
List of Maps and Plans .	. . . .	xix
Editorial Note . . .	. . . .	xxi
Topography	General descriptions and manorial descents compiled under the superintendence of William Page, F.S.A.; Architectural descriptions under the superintendence of the late John Quekett, M.A., F.S.A.; Heraldic drawings and blazon by the Revd. E. E. Dorling, M.A., F.S.A.; Charities from information supplied by J. W. Owsley, I.S.O., late Official Trustee of Charitable Funds	
Hundred of Compton . .	By Nora Alexander; Architectural descriptions by Ernest A. R. Rahbula, A.R.I.B.A., F.S.A.	
Introduction . . .	. . . .	1
Aldworth . . .	. . . .	3
Catmore . . .	. . . .	9
Chilton . . .	. . . .	11
Compton . . .	. . . .	15
Farnborough . .	. . . .	21
East Ilsley . .	. . . .	24
West Ilsley . .	. . . .	32
Hundred of Faircross . .	By Harold J. E. Peake, F.S.A.; Architectural descriptions by the late John Quekett, M.A., F.S.A., J. W. Bloe, F.S.A., and C. C. Durston	
Introduction . . .	. . . .	38
Beedon . . .	. . . .	40
Boxford with Westbrook	. . . .	44
Brightwalton . .	. . . .	48
Brimpton . . .	. . . .	51
Chieveley with Leckhampstead and Winterbourne . .	. . . .	55
Frilsham . . .	. . . .	70
Hampstead Norris .	. . . .	73
Peasemore . . .	. . . .	81
Sandleford . . .	. . . .	84
Shaw-cum-Donnington	. . . .	87
Speen with Speenhamland, Wood Speen, and Bagnor .	. . . .	97

CONTENTS OF VOLUMES: BERKS. IV

PAGE

Stanford Dingley 110
Wasing 114
Welford 116
Yattendon and Speenham 125
Borough of Newbury . . . By the late Anne B. Wallis Chapman, D.Sc. (Oec.), F.R.H.S. 130
Hundred of Kintbury Eagle . . By Harold J. E. Peake, F.S.A.; Architectural descriptions by F. H. Cheetham, F.S.A.

Introduction 156
Avington 158
Chaddleworth with Woolley 162
Enborne 168
Fawley with Whatcombe 174
Hampstead Marshall 178
Hungerford with Eddington, Hidden, and Sandon Fee 183
Inkpen 200
Kintbury 205
Letcombe Bassett 217
Letcombe Regis with East Challow and West Challow 222
Shalbourne 228
East Shefford or Little Shefford 234
West or Great Shefford 238
West Woodhay 242
Hundred of Lambourn . . . By Myra Curtis, Classical Tripos; Architectural descriptions by F. H. Cheetham, F.S.A., and J. W. Bloe, F.S.A.

Introduction 246
East Garston 247
Lambourn 251
Hundred of Wantage . . . By Myra Curtis, Classical Tripos; Architectural descriptions by A. W. Clapham, O.B.E., F.S.A.

Introduction 267
Ardington 269
Childrey 272
Denchworth 280
Hanney 285
East Hendred 294
West Hendred 302
East and West Lockinge 307
Sparsholt 311
Wantage 319
Hundred of Ock . . . By Ada Russell, M.A.; Architectural descriptions by A. W. Clapham, O.B.E., F.S.A.

Introduction 333
Appleton 335
Drayton 341
Fyfield 344
Kingston Bagpuize 349
Marcham 354
Milton 361
Steventon 365
Sutton Courtenay 369
Tubney 379
Little Wittenham 380
Long Wittenham 384
Hundred of Hormer . . . By Myra Curtis, Classical Tripos; Architectural descriptions by A. W. Clapham, O.B.E., F.S.A.

PAGE

Introduction 391
Bagley Wood 393
Bessels Leigh 393
Cumnor 398
North Hinksey 405
South Hinksey 408
Radley 410
St. Helen's 416
Seacourt 421
Sunningwell 423
Wytham 427
Borough of Abingdon 430
Hundred of Ganfield . . . By Frances Brough, M.A.; Architectural
                        descriptions by A. W. Clapham, O.B.E., F.S.A.
Introduction 452
Buckland 453
Hatford 461
Hinton Waldrist 463
Longworth 466
Pusey 471
Shellingford 475
Stanford in the Vale 478
Hundred of Faringdon . . . By Henrietta L. E. Garbett; Architectural
                        descriptions by A. W. Clapham, O.B.E., F.S.A.
Introduction 486
Great Coxwell 487
Great Faringdon 489
Hundred of Shrivenham . . . Architectural descriptions by F. H. Cheetham,
                        F.S.A.
Introduction . . . . By Alice Raven 500
Ashbury . . . . . ,, ,, ... 503
Buscot . . . . . By Marjory Hollings, Oxford Honours School of
                        Modern History, and Nora Alexander . . 512
Coleshill . . . . . ,, ,, ,, . 517
Compton Beauchamp . . . By Henrietta L. E. Garbett and Nora Alexander 523
Eaton Hastings . . . . By Nora Alexander 528
Shrivenham . . . . By Alice Raven and Nora Alexander . . 531
Uffington . . . . By Henrietta L. E. Garbett and Nora Alexander 543

BUCKINGHAMSHIRE

VOLUME ONE

PAGE

Dedication v
The Advisory Council of the Victoria History vii
General Advertisement vii
The Buckinghamshire County Committee xiii
Contents xv
List of Illustrations xvii
Table of Abbreviations xix
Preface xxiii
Natural History
  Geology . . . . . By H. B. Woodward, F.R.S., F.G.S. . . I

CONTENTS OF VOLUMES: BUCKS. I

PAGE

Palaeontology . . . . By R. Lydekker, F.R.S., F.G.S., F.L.S. . . 25
Botany . . . . . By G. C. Druce, Hon. M.A. Oxon., F.L.S. . . 27
Zoology
  Molluscs . . . . By B. B. Woodward, F.G.S., F.R.M.S. . . 69
  Insects . . . . By the Revd. Canon Fowler, M.A., F.L.S., and
    the late Charles G. Barrett, F.E.S. . . 71
  Spiders . . . By the late F. O. Pickard-Cambridge, M.A. . 107
  Crustaceans . . . By the Revd. T. R. R. Stebbing, M.A., F.R.S.,
    F.Z.S. 110
  Fishes . . . . By C. H. Cook 120
  Reptiles and Batrachians . . By A. E. Gibbs, F.L.S. . . . 125
  Birds . . . . . By Ernst Hartert, assisted by the Hon. Walter
    Rothschild 128
  Mammals . . . By A. Heneage Cocks, M.A., F.S.A. . 153
Early Man . . . . . By George Clinch, F.G.S. . . 177
Anglo-Saxon Remains . . . By Reginald A. Smith, B.A., F.S.A. . 195
Introduction to the Buckinghamshire
  Domesday . . . By J. Horace Round, M.A., LL.D. . 207
Text of the Buckinghamshire Domesday . By the Revd. F. W. Ragg, M.A. . . 230
Ecclesiastical History . . . By the Sister Elspeth of the Community of All
  Saints 279
Religious Houses . . . . ,, ,, ,,
  Introduction 346
  Priory of Luffield 347
  ,, ,, Bradwell 350
  ,, ,, Snelshall 352
  ,, ,, Ivinghoe 353
  ,, ,, Ankerwick 355
  ,, ,, Little Marlow 357
  ,, ,, Tickford or Newport Pagnel 360
  Abbey of Biddlesden 365
  ,, ,, Missenden 369
  ,, ,, Medmenham 376
  ,, ,, Nutley 377
  Priory of Chetwode 380
  ,, ,, Ravenstone 381
  Abbey of Burnham 382
  ,, ,, Lavendon 384
  College of Ashridge 386
  Commandery of Hogshaw 390
  Preceptory of Bulstrode 391
  House of Franciscan Friars, Aylesbury 391
  Hospital of St. John Baptist, Aylesbury 392
  ,, ,, St. Leonard, Aylesbury 392
  ,, ,, St. John Baptist, Buckingham 392
  ,, ,, St. Laurence, Buckingham 392
  ,, ,, St. John Baptist and St. John
    Evangelist, Newport Pagnel 393
  Hospital of St. Margaret, Newport Pagnel 393
  ,, ,, St. John Baptist, Stony
    Stratford 394
  Hospital of St. John Baptist, Wendover 394
  ,, ,, St. Margaret, High Wycombe 394
  ,, ,, St. Giles, High Wycombe 394
  ,, ,, St. John Baptist, High
    Wycombe 394
  Hospital of Ludgershall 395

		PAGE
Priory of Newton Longville	. . . .	395
,, ,, Wing	. . . .	396
Agriculture	By J. H. Donald	397
Index to the Buckinghamshire Domesday	. . . . . .	405

VOLUME TWO

		PAGE
Dedication	. . . .	v
Contents	. . . .	ix
List of Illustrations and Maps	. . . .	xiii
Editorial Note . . .	. . . .	xv
Romano-British Buckinghamshire .	By Miss S. S. Smith, Oxford Honours School of English Literature	1
Ancient Earthworks . .	By George Clinch, F.S.A. Scot., F.G.S. .	21
Social and Economic History .	By Miss C. Jamison, Oxford Honours School of Modern History	37
Table of Population, 1801–1901 .	By George S. Minchin . . .	94
Industries	By Miss C. Jamison, Oxford Honours School of Modern History	
Introduction . . .	. . . .	103
Lace-making . . .	. . . .	106
Wooden Ware and Chair-making	. . . .	109
Paper-making . . .	. . . .	111
Tanning and Shoe-making .	. . . .	112
Straw-plaiting . . .	. . . .	113
Bricks, Tiles, and Pottery .	. . . .	114
Bell-Foundries . . .	(By Alfred Heneage Cocks, M.A., F.S.A.)	116
Iron-Foundries, Shipbuilding, and Railway Works . . .	. . . .	126
Needle-making . . .	. . . .	127
Textile Industries . .	. . . .	128
Forestry	By the Revd. J. C. Cox, LL.D., F.S.A. .	131
Schools	By A. F. Leach, M.A., F.S.A.	
Introduction . . .	. . . .	145
Eton College . . .	. . . .	147
The Royal Latin School, Buckingham	. . . .	207
Royal Grammar School, High Wycombe .	. . . .	210
Stony Stratford Grammar School .	. . . .	212
Amersham Grammar School .	. . . .	213
Sir William Borlase's School, Marlow	. . . .	214
Aylesbury Grammar School .	. . . .	215
Wycombe Abbey School .	. . . .	216
The County High School for Girls, High Wycombe . . .	. . . .	217
Wolverton County School .	. . . .	218
Elementary Schools founded before 1800 .	. . . .	218
Sport Ancient and Modern .	Edited by E. D. Cuming	
Foxhounds . . .	. . . .	223
The Old Berkeley Hunt .	By O. P. Serocold . . .	223
The Whaddon Chase .	By E. D. Cuming . . .	227
Stag Hunting . . .	,, ,, . . .	228
The Royal Buckhounds .	. . . .	228
Lord Rothschild's Staghounds .	. . . .	228
Earl Carrington's Bloodhounds .	. . . .	229
Harriers	By E. D. Cuming . . .	229

PAGE

Beagles	By E. D. Cuming	.	230
Otterhounds	,, ,, ...	.	230
Coursing	By J. W. Bourne	.	230
Racing	By E. D. Cuming	.	230
Flat Racing	. . . . .	.	230
Steeplechasing	. . . . .	.	232
Shooting	By Col. Alfred Gilbey, J.P. .	.	233
Angling	By C. H. Cook, M.A. . . .	.	236
Cricket	By Sir Home Gordon, Bart. . .	.	239
Golf	By A. J. Robertson . . .	.	240
Rowing (Henley Regatta) . . .	By Theodore A. Cook, M.A., F.S.A. .	.	240
Athletics	By J. E. Fowler-Dixon . . .	.	243
Topography	General descriptions and manorial descents compiled under the superintendence of the General Editor; Architectural descriptions by J. Murray Kendall and S. F. Beeke Lane, under the superintendence of C. R. Peers, M.A., F.S.A.; Heraldic drawings and blazon by the Revd. E. E. Dorling, M.A.; Charities, from information supplied by J. W. Owsley, I.S.O., late Official Trustee of Charitable Funds		
The Three Hundreds of Aylesbury (Risborough, Stone, Aylesbury)	General descriptions and manorial descents by Miss C. Jamison, Oxford Honours School of Modern History		
Introduction	. . . . . .	.	245
Risborough Hundred . . .	. . . . . .	.	247
Bledlow with Bledlow Ridge .	. . . . . .	.	247
Horsenden . . .	. . . . . .	.	253
Monks Risborough . .	. . . . . .	.	256
Princes Risborough . .	. . . . . .	.	260
Stone Hundred . . .	. . . . . .	.	267
Cuddington . . .	. . . . . .	.	267
Dinton with Ford and Upton .	. . . . . .	.	271
Haddenham . . .	. . . . . .	.	281
Great Hampden . . .	. . . . . .	.	287
Little Hampden . . .	. . . . . .	.	291
Hartwell	. . . . . .	.	293
Great Kimble . . .	. . . . . .	.	298
Little Kimble . . .	. . . . . .	.	303
Stone	. . . . . .	.	307
Aylesbury Hundred . . .	. . . . . .	.	312
Aston Clinton . . .	. . . . . .	.	312
Bierton (with Broughton) . .	. . . . . .	.	320
Buckland	. . . . . .	.	327
Ellesborough . . .	. . . . . .	.	331
Halton	. . . . . .	.	339
Hulcott	. . . . . .	.	342
Lee	. . . . . .	.	345
Great Missenden . . .	(By Miss M. E. Seebohm, Hist. Tripos) .	.	347
Little Missenden . . .	(,, ,, ,,) .	.	354
Stoke Mandeville . . .	. . . . . .	.	360
Weston Turville . . .	. . . . . .	.	365

VOLUME THREE

PAGE

Dedication	. . . .	v
Contents	. . . .	ix
List of Illustrations . .	. . . .	xiii

CONTENTS OF VOLUMES: BUCKS. III

		PAGE
List of Maps	. . . .	xvii
Editorial Note	. . . .	xix
Topography	. . . . General descriptions and manorial descents compiled under the superintendence of WILLIAM PAGE, F.S.A.; Architectural descriptions by the late JOHN QUEKETT, M.A., F.S.A., the late C. E. LOVELL, and SIDNEY TOY, A.R.I.B.A., F.S.A., with access by permission to the notes, plans, and cards of the Royal Commission on Historical Monuments (England); Heraldic drawings and blazon by the Revd. E. E. DORLING, M.A., F.S.A.; Charities from information supplied by J. W. OWSLEY, I.S.O., late Official Trustee of Charitable Funds	
Aylesbury Borough with Walton	. . . .	1
Wendover Borough	. . . .	20
The Chiltern Hundreds of Chiltern		
Introduction . . .	. . . .	33
Desborough Hundred		
Bradenham . . .	By ALICE V. JENKINSON, Hist. Tripos . .	35
Fawley . . .	By the GRACE A. ELLIS, B.A.; Architectural descriptions of Fawley Court by the late JOHN QUEKETT, M.A., F.S.A.	37
Fingest . . .	By ALICE V. JENKINSON, Hist. Tripos .	42
Hambleden . . .	By the late GRACE A. ELLIS, B.A. . . .	45
Hedsor . . .	,, ,, ,, . . .	45
Hughenden . . .	By the late GRACE A. ELLIS, B.A., and CATHERINE JAMISON, Oxford Honours School of Modern History	57
Ibstone . . .	By the late GRACE A. ELLIS, B.A. . . .	62
Great Marlow . . .	By MURIEL R. MANFIELD, Hist. Tripos . .	65
Little Marlow . . .	,, ,, ,, . .	77
Medmenham . .	By the late GRACE A. ELLIS, B.A. . . .	84
Radnage . . .	By ALICE V. JENKINSON, Hist. Tripos . .	89
Saunderton . . .	By the late GRACE A. ELLIS, B.A. . . .	92
Stokenchurch . . .	,, ,, ,, . . .	96
Turville . . .	,, ,, ,, . . .	101
Wooburn . . .	,, ,, ,, . . .	105
High Wycombe . .	By ALICE V. JENKINSON, Hist. Tripos . .	112
West Wycombe . .	,, ,, ,, . .	135
Burnham Hundred . .	By MURIEL R. MANFIELD, Hist. Tripos	
Amersham Borough . .	. . . .	141
Beaconsfield . . .	. . . .	155
Burnham with Lower Boveney	. . . .	165
Chalfont St. Giles . .	. . . .	184
Chalfont St. Peter . .	. . . .	193
Chenies . . .	. . . .	199
Chesham . . .	. . . .	203
Chesham Bois . .	. . . .	218
Dorney . . .	. . . .	221
Farnham Royal with Hedgerley Dean and Seer Green . .	. . . .	225
Hitcham . . .	. . . .	231
Penn . . .	. . . .	235
Taplow . . .	. . . .	240
Stoke Hundred		
Colnbrook . . .	By the late GRACE A. ELLIS, B.A. . .	246
Datchet . . .	,, ,, ,, . . .	249
Denham . . .	By MURIEL R. MANFIELD, Hist. Tripos .	255

		PAGE
Eton	By DOROTHY L. POWELL, Mod. Lang. Tripos	261
Fulmer	By the late GRACE A. ELLIS, B.A. . .	275
Hedgerley	,, ,, ,, . .	278
Horton	,, ,, ,, . .	281
Iver	By MURIEL R. MANFIELD, Hist. Tripos .	286
Langley Marish . . .	By the late GRACE A. ELLIS, B.A. . .	294
Slough . . .	By DOROTHY L. POWELL, Mod. Lang. Tripos	301
Stoke Poges . . .	By the late GRACE A. ELLIS, B.A. . .	302
Upton-cum-Chalvey . .	By DOROTHY L. POWELL, Mod. Lang. Tripos	314
Wexham . . .	By the late GRACE A. ELLIS, B.A. . .	318
Wyrardisbury or Wraysbury . .	,, ,, ,, . .	320
Cottesloe Hundred		
Introduction		326
Aston Abbots . . .	By DOROTHY M. JENNINGS, M.A. . .	328
Cheddington . . .	,, ,, ,, . .	331
Cholesbury . . .	,, ,, ,, . .	334
Creslow . . .	,, ,, ,, . .	335
Cublington . . .	,, ,, ,, . .	338
Drayton Beauchamp . .	,, ,, ,, . .	341
Drayton Parslow . .	,, ,, ,, . .	345
Dunton . . .	,, ,, ,, . .	348
Edlesborough . . .	,, ,, ,, . .	350
Grove	,, ,, ,, . .	361
Hardwick with Weedon .	,, ,, ,, . .	363
Hawridge . . .	,, ,, ,, . .	367
Hoggeston . . .	,, ,, ,, . .	369
Great Horwood . .	,, ,, ,, . .	372
Little Horwood . .	,, ,, ,, . .	376
Ivinghoe . . .	By DOROTHY L. POWELL, Mod. Lang. Tripos	379
Linslade . . .	,, ,, ,,	387
Marsworth . . .	By DOROTHY M. JENNINGS, M.A. . .	391
Mentmore . . .	By DOROTHY L. POWELL, Mod. Lang. Tripos	397
Mursley . . .	,, ,, ,,	401
Pitstone . . .	,, ,, ,,	406
Slapton . . .	,, ,, ,,	412
Soulbury . . .	,, ,, ,,	414
Stewkley . . .	,, ,, ,,	420
Swanbourne . . .	,, ,, ,,	427
Tattenhoe . . .	,, ,, ,,	432
Whaddon with Nash . .	,, ,, ,,	435
Whitchurch . . .	By the late GRACE A. ELLIS, B.A. . .	442
Wing	,, ,, ,, . .	449
Wingrave . . .	,, ,, ,, . .	458
Winslow . . .	By DOROTHY M. JENNINGS, M.A. . .	465
Buckingham Borough, containing the Hamlet of Bourton and the Ecclesiastical Parish of Gawcott with Lenborough . .	By ALICE V. JENKINSON, Hist. Tripos	471

VOLUME FOUR

	PAGE
Dedication	v
Contents	ix
List of Illustrations	xiii
List of Maps	xix

CONTENTS OF VOLUMES: BUCKS. IV

		PAGE
Editorial Note	. . . .	xxi
Topography	General descriptions and manorial descents compiled under the superintendence of WILLIAM PAGE, F.S.A.; Architectural descriptions by the late JOHN QUEKETT, M.A., F.S.A., the late C. E. LOVELL, and SIDNEY TOY, A.R.I.B.A., F.S.A., with access by permission to the notes, plans, and cards of the Royal Commission on Historical Monuments (England); Heraldic drawings and blazon by the Revd. E. E. DORLING, M.A., F.S.A.; Charities from information supplied by J. W. OWSLEY, I.S.O., late Official Trustee of Charitable Funds	
Ashendon Hundred		
Introduction	By CHARLOTTE M. CALTHROP, first class Classical Tripos	1
Ashendon	,, ,, ,,	3
Aston Sanford . . .	By the late GRACE A. ELLIS, B.A. . . .	8
Boarstall	By CHARLOTTE M. CALTHROP, Classical Tripos	9
Brill	,, ,, ,,	14
Chearsley	By DOROTHY L. POWELL, Mod. Lang. Tripos	19
Chilton	By CHARLOTTE M. CALTHROP, Classical Tripos	22
East Claydon	By the late GRACE A. ELLIS, B.A. . .	28
Middle Claydon . . .	,, ,, ,,	32
Long Crendon . . .	By CHARLOTTE M. CALTHROP, Classical Tripos	36
Dorton	,, ,, ,,	45
Grandborough . . .	By DOROTHY L. POWELL, Mod. Lang. Tripos	48
Grendon Underwood . . .	,, ,, ,,	50
Hogshaw	By the late GRACE A. ELLIS, B.A. . .	54
Ickford	By DOROTHY L. POWELL, Mod. Lang. Tripos	56
Ilmer	,, ,, ,,	61
Kingsey	By the late GRACE A. ELLIS, B.A. . .	63
Ludgershall with Kingswood . .	,, ,, ,,	68
Fleet Marston	,, ,, ,,	74
North Marston . . .	,, ,, ,,	76
Oakley	By CHARLOTTE M. CALTHROP, Classical Tripos	80
Oving	By DOROTHY L. POWELL, Mod. Lang. Tripos	85
Pitchcott	By the late GRACE A. ELLIS, B.A. . .	89
Quainton with Shipton Lee . .	,, ,, ,,	92
Quarrendon	,, ,, ,,	100
Shabbington	,, ,, ,,	102
Towersey	,, ,, ,,	105
Waddesdon with Westcott and Woodham	,, ,, ,,	107
Lower or Nether Winchendon . .	By CHARLOTTE M. CALTHROP, Classical Tripos	118
Upper Winchendon . . .	,, ,, ,,	122
Worminghall . . .	By the late GRACE A. ELLIS, B.A. . .	125
Wotton Underwood . . .	By CHARLOTTE M. CALTHROP, Classical Tripos	130
Buckingham Hundred		
Introduction . . .	By the late GRACE A. ELLIS, B.A. . .	135
Addington	By ALICE V. JENKINSON, Hist. Tripos .	137
Adstock	,, ,, ,,	140
Akeley	By MAUD E. SIMKINS . . .	144
Barton Hartshorn . . .	By DOROTHY L. POWELL, Mod. Lang. Tripos	147
Beachampton	,, ,, ,,	149
Biddlesden	,, ,, ,,	153
Caversfield	,, ,, ,,	157
Chetwode	,, ,, ,,	163
Edgcott	,, ,, ,,	168

CONTENTS OF VOLUMES: BUCKS. IV

PAGE

Foscott	By Dorothy L. Powell, Mod. Lang. Tripos	170
Hillesden	,, ,, ,,	173
Leckhampstead	By Maud E. Simkins	180
Lillingstone Dayrell	By Dorothy L. Powell, Mod. Lang. Tripos	187
Lillingstone Lovell	By the late Grace A. Ellis, B.A.	191
Luffield Abbey	By Alice V. Jenkinson, Hist. Tripos	197
Maids Moreton	By Maud E. Simkins	198
Marsh Gibbon	By Alice V. Jenkinson, Hist. Tripos	205
Padbury	By Lilian J. Redstone, B.A.	209
Preston Bissett	By Alice V. Jenkinson, Hist. Tripos	215
Radclive	,, ,, ,,	220
Shalstone	,, ,, ,,	223
Steeple Claydon	By the late Grace A. Ellis, B.A.	226
Stowe	By Alice V. Jenkinson, Hist. Tripos; Architectural description of Stowe House by the late John Quekett, M.A.	229
Thornborough	By Muriel R. Manfield, Hist. Tripos, and Myra Curtis, Classical Tripos	237
Thornton	By Muriel R. Manfield, Hist. Tripos	243
Tingewick	,, ,, ,,	249
Turweston	,, ,, ,,	251
Twyford with Charndon and Poundon	By the late Grace A. Ellis, B.A.	254
Water Stratford	By Nancy Spilman, M.A.	260
Westbury	By Alice V. Jenkinson, Hist. Tripos	263
Newport Hundred		
Introduction	By the late Grace A. Ellis, B.A.	268
Astwood	By Alice V. Jenkinson, Hist. Tripos	270
Bletchley with Fenny Stratford and Water Eaton	By Nancy Spilman, M.A.	274
Bradwell	By Maud E. Simkins	283
Bow Brickhill	By Charlotte M. Calthrop, Classical Tripos	289
Great Brickhill	,, ,, ,,	293
Little Brickhill	,, ,, ,,	298
Broughton	By Maud E. Simkins	303
Calverton	,, ,,	308
Chicheley	By Alice V. Jenkinson, Hist. Tripos	311
Clifton Reynes	By Maud E. Simkins	316
Cold Brayfield	By Nancy Spilman, M.A.	323
North Crawley	By Maud E. Simkins	327
Emberton	,, ,,	338
Gayhurst	By the late Grace A. Ellis, B.A.	343
Hanslope with Castle Thorpe	,, ,, ,,	348
Hardmead	By Dorothy L. Powell, Mod. Lang. Tripos	362
Haversham	,, ,, ,,	366
Lathbury	By the late Grace A. Ellis, B.A.	372
Lavendon	By Henrietta L. E. Garbett	379
Great Linford	By Dorothy M. Jennings, M.A.	387
Little Linford	,, ,, ,,	392
Loughton	By Maud E. Simkins	395
Milton Keynes	,, ,,	401
Moulsoe	By Alice V. Jenkinson, Hist. Tripos	406
Newport Pagnell	By Myra Curtis, Classical Tripos	409
Newton Blossomville	By Maud E. Simkins	422
Newton Longville	,, ,,	425
Olney with Warrington	By Henrietta L. E. Garbett	429
Ravenstone	,, ,,	439

		PAGE
Shenley	By MAUD E. SIMKINS	445
Sherington	,, ,,	451
Simpson	,, ,,	458
Stantonbury	By ALICE V. JENKINSON, Hist. Tripos	462
Stoke Goldington	By the late GRACE A. ELLIS, B.A.	466
Stoke Hammond	,, ,, ,,	471
Stony Stratford	By NANCY SPILMAN, M.A.	476
Tyringham with Filgrave	By the late GRACE A. ELLIS, B.A.	482
Walton	By ALICE V. JENKINSON, Hist. Tripos	485
Wavendon	By DOROTHY L. POWELL, Mod. Lang. Tripos	489
Weston Underwood	By MAUD E. SIMKINS	497
Willen	,, ,,	502
Wolverton	By MYRA CURTIS, Classical Tripos	505
Great Woolstone	By MAUD E. SIMKINS	509
Little Woolstone	,, ,,	512
Woughton-on-the-Green	By ALICE V. JENKINSON, Hist. Tripos	515
Political History	By the Revd. F. W. RAGG, M.A.	521

CAMBRIDGESHIRE AND THE ISLE OF ELY

VOLUME ONE

		PAGE
Dedication		v
Contents		ix
List of Illustrations		xi
List of Maps		xii
Editorial Note		xiii
Natural History		
Geology	By the late Professor J. E. MARR, Sc.D., F.R.S. revised by H. DIGHTON THOMAS, Ph.D., F.G.S.	1
Botany	By H. GODWIN, Ph.D.	35
Zoology	Edited by A. D. IMMS, D.Sc., F.R.S.	
Turbellaria	By P. ULLYOTT, M.A.	77
Hirudinea	By W. A. HARDING, M.A.	78
Crustacea	By A. G. LOWNDES, M.A.	80
Myriapoda	By E. B. WORTHINGTON, Ph.D.	87
Insecta		
Introduction	By A. D. IMMS, D.Sc., F.R.S.	89
Collembola	By C. H. N. JACKSON, D.Sc., Ph.D.	90
Orthoptera and Dermaptera	By E. B. WORTHINGTON, Ph.D.	91
Odonata	By A. D. IMMS, D.Sc., F.R.S.	92
Psocoptera	By R. M. GAMBLES, M.A.	94
Hemiptera—Heteroptera	By E. C. BEDWELL, F.R.E.S.	96
Neuroptera and Mecoptera	By A. D. IMMS, D.Sc., F.R.S.	103
Coleoptera	By H. J. K. DONISTHORPE, F.R.E.S.	104
Trichoptera	By A. D. IMMS, D.Sc., F.R.S.	137
Lepidoptera	By J. C. F. FRYER, M.A., O.B.E.	139
Hymenoptera: Symphyta	By R. B. BENSON, M.A.	162
Apocrita	By G. J. KERRICH, M.A.	165
Diptera	By J. E. COLLIN, F.R.E.S.	189
Ephemeroptera	By A. D. IMMS, D.Sc., F.R.S.	205
Arachnida	By W. S. BRISTOWE, Sc.D.	206
Mollusca	By H. H. BRINDLEY, M.A.	213

CONTENTS OF VOLUMES: CAMBS. I

		PAGE
Fishes	By W. H. Whiting, B.A.	218
Reptiles and Batrachians	By W. A. Harding, M.A.	221
Birds	By A. H. Evans, Sc.D.	224
Mammals	By E. N. Barclay	243
Early Man	By J. Grahame Clark, Ph.D., F.S.A.	247
Anglo-Saxon Remains	By T. C. Lethbridge, M.A., F.S.A.	305
Introduction to the Cambridgeshire Domesday	By L. F. Salzman, M.A., F.S.A.	335
Translation of the Text of Cambridgeshire Domesday	By Jocelyn Otway-Ruthven	358
Translation of the *Inquisitio Comitatus Cantabrigiensis*	,, ,, ,,	400
Index to Domesday and the *Inquisitio*		429

VOLUME TWO

		PAGE
Dedication		v
Contents		ix
List of Illustrations		xi
List of Maps		xii
Editorial Note		xiii
Ancient Earthworks	By C. W. Phillips, M.A., F.S.A.	1
Social and Economic History		
Introduction	By Professor H. C. Darby, M.A., Ph.D.	48
Domesday Cambridgeshire	,, ,, ,,	49
Medieval Cambridgeshire	By L. F. Salzman, M.A., F.S.A.	58
Economic Affairs, 1500–1800:		
(i) Agriculture	By Professor H. C. Darby, M.A., Ph.D.	72
(ii) Draining the Fens	,, ,, ,,	76
(iii) Communications and Trade	By Ethel M. Hampson, M.A., Ph.D.	83
Social History, 1500–1900:		
(i) Poor Relief	,, ,, ,,	90
(ii) Vagrancy	,, ,, ,,	100
(iii) Prisons and Crime	,, ,, ,,	105
The Nineteenth Century	By Professor H. C. Darby, M.A., Ph.D.	111
Modern Agriculture	By R. McG. Carslaw, M.A., Ph.D.	123
Railway Construction	By Professor H. C. Darby, M.A., Ph.D.	131
Table of Population	By George S. Minchin	133
Ecclesiastical History	By Kathleen L. Wood-Legh, B.Litt., Ph.D.	141
Religious Houses	By Dorothy M. B. Ellis and L. F. Salzman, M.A., F.S.A.	
Introduction		197
Abbey and Cathedral Priory of Ely		199
Abbey of Thorney		210
Priory of St. Radegund, Cambridge		218
Abbey of Chatteris		220
Priory of Ickleton		223
,, ,, Swaffham Bulbeck		226
,, ,, Anglesey		229
,, ,, Barnwell		234
,, ,, Spinney		249
,, ,, St. Edmund, Cambridge		254
,, ,, Fordham		256
,, ,, Marmont		258

PAGE

Preceptory of Denney 259
   ,,   ,,   Duxford 262
   ,,   ,,   Great Wilbraham 263
   ,,   ,,   Chippenham 264
   ,,   ,,   Shingay 266
Dominican Friars of Cambridge 269
Franciscan   ,,   ,, ... 276
Carmelite   ,,   ,, ... 282
Friars of St. Mary   ,, ... 286
Austin Friars of Cambridge 287
Friars of the Sack of Cambridge 290
Crutched Friars of Barham 291
Abbey of Waterbeach 292
   ,,   ,,   Denney 295
Brigettines at Cherry Hinton 303
Hospital of St. John, Cambridge 303
   ,,   ,,   St. Anthony and St. Eloy,
     Cambridge 307
Hospital of Sturbridge 307
Hospitals of St. Mary Magdalene and
     St. John Baptist, Ely 308
Hospital of Longstow 310
   ,,   ,,   St. Nicholas, Royston 310
   ,,   ,,   Wisbech 311
Buckingham College 312
College of St. Mary-on-the-Sea, Newton 312
Priory of Linton 314
   ,,   ,,   Swavesey 315
Schools . . . . By ETHEL M. HAMPSON, M.A., Ph.D.
   Introduction 319
   Grammar Schools: Ely 321
     The Perse, Cambridge 324
     Wisbech 327
     Leys School, Cambridge 330
   Semi-classical Schools: Cheveley 331
     Soham 331
     Dullingham 332
     March 333
     Haddenham 334
   Choir Schools: Ely 335
     King's College, Cambridge 336
     St. John's and Trinity Colleges,
     Cambridge 337
   Elementary Education: Before 1660 338
     Charity and Endowed Elementary
     Schools, 1660–1800 339
   The Sunday School Movement 345
   Elementary Education, 1800–33 347
   Modern Developments 352
     Village Colleges 353
     Training Colleges 353
Industries . . . . . By FRANCES M. PAGE, M.A., Ph.D.
   Introduction 357
   Industries derived from Agriculture 359
     ,,   ,,   Geology 365
     ,,   ,,   the University 368
   Miscellaneous Industries 374
   Occupational Statistics 376

PAGE

Political History . . . . By Professor H. C. DARBY, M.A., Ph.D., and
E. MILLER, M.A.

   Anglo-Saxon Settlement and Danish
     Invasion 377
   The Anglo-Norman Settlement 381
   The Disinherited 389
   Parliamentary Representation and the
     Peasant Revolt 397
   The Tudor Period and the Civil War . By D. COOK, M.A., Ph.D. 402
   Parliamentary Representation after 1660 . ,, ,, ... 410

VOLUME THREE

PAGE

Dedication v
Contents ix
List of Illustrations xi
List of Maps and Plans xiii
Editorial Note xv
Classes of Public Records used xvii
Notes on Abbreviations xix
The City of Cambridge . . . By Professor HELEN M. CAM, C.B.E., Litt.D., F.B.A.
Schools, almshouses, and other charities by SUSAN
REYNOLDS 1

   Medieval History 2
   Modern History 15
   Constitutional History 29
   Parliamentary Representation 68
   Town and Gown 76
   Economic History 86
   Public Health 101
     Addenbrooke's Hospital 106
   Topography 109
     Growth of the City 109
     Wards 111
     Crosses 113
     Bridges 114
     Inns 115
     Public Buildings 116
     Manor Houses 122
     Churches 123
     Medieval Chapels 132
     Religious Guilds 133
     Protestant Nonconformity 135
     Roman Catholicism 138
     Synagogues 138
     Theological Colleges 139
     Schools 141
     Almshouses 146
     Other Charities 147
     Distinguished Natives and Residents 148
The University of Cambridge . . By J. P. C. ROACH 150
   The Middle Ages 150
   The Sixteenth Century 166
   The Early Stuarts and Civil War
     (1603–60) 191

PAGE

The Age of Newton and Bentley
(1660–1800) 210
The Age of Reforms (1800–82) 235
The Modern University (1882–1939) 266
Epilogue (1939–56) 307
The Schools and the University Library . By J. P. C. ROACH 312
The University Press . . . By Sir SYDNEY ROBERTS, LL.D., sometime
Secretary to the Press Syndicate . . . 321
The University Botanic Garden . . By J. S. L. GILMOUR, Director . . . 324
The Fitzwilliam Museum . . By C. R. ELRINGTON 326
The University Archives . . . ,, ,, . . . 327
The University Seals and Insignia . . ,, ,, . . . 330
List of Chancellors of the University 331
The Colleges and Halls of the University
Peterhouse . . . . By Professor H. BUTTERFIELD, LL.D., Litt.D.,
Lit.D., Master 334
Clare College . . . . By W. J. HARRISON, M.B.E. . . 340
Pembroke College . . . By the late Sir ELLIS MINNS, Litt.D., F.B.A., and
J. P. C. ROACH 346
Gonville and Caius College . . By P. GRIERSON 356
Trinity Hall . . . . By C. W. CRAWLEY 362
Corpus Christi College . . . By J. P. T. BURY 371
King's College . . . . By J. SALTMARSH 376
Queens' College . . . . By R. G. D. LAFFAN 408
St. Catharine's College . . . By W. H. S. JONES, Litt.D., F.B.A. . 415
Jesus College . . . . By the late J. G. SIKES and FREDA JONES . 421
Christ's College . . . . By the late H. RACKHAM . . . 429
St. John's College . . . By E. MILLER 437
Magdalene College . . . By F. R. SALTER, O.B.E. . . . 450
Trinity College . . . . By P. A. BEZODIS 456
Emmanuel College . . . By the Revd. J. C. DICKINSON . . 474
Sidney Sussex College . . . By the late R. H. D. MAYALL . . 481
Downing College . . . By the late W. L. CUTTLE . . . 487
Girton College . . . . By JEAN LINDSAY 490
Newnham College . . . By DOROTHY BRODIE . . . 493
Selwyn College . . . . By the late L. A. BORRADAILE . . 495
Fitzwilliam House . . . By the late C. J. B. GASKOIN and J. L. KIRBY . 497
Cambridge University and Borough Hearth
Tax Assessments . . . By C. A. F. MEEKINGS . . . 500

VOLUME FOUR

PAGE

Dedication v
Contents ix
List of Illustrations xi
Editorial Note xiii
Classes of Public Records used and Note on
Manuscript Sources xv
Topography . . . . Where not otherwise stated, by H. B. WELLS, M.A.;
Architectural Descriptions by E. T. LONG, F.S.A.
The Liberty of Ely . . . By EDWARD MILLER, M.A. . . . I
City of Ely . . . . General Description, Manors, Churches, and
Charities, by ETHEL M. HAMPSON, M.A., Ph.D.;
Architectural Description of Cathedral and Precincts
by the late T. D. ATKINSON, F.R.I.B.A. . . 28

PAGE

Ely Hundred
  Downham 90
  Littleport 95
North Witchford Hundred
  Chatteris 103
  Doddington 110
  March 116
  North Stanground 123
  Whittlesey 123
South Witchford Hundred
  Coveney with Manea 136
  Haddenham 140
  Mepal 149
  Stretham and Thetford 151
  Sutton 159
  Welches Dam 164
  Wentworth 165
  Wilburton 168
  Witcham 172
  Witchford 176
Wisbech Hundred
  Elm 180
  Leverington .   .   . General Description, Manors, Churches,
                         Nonconformity, and Charities by
                         G. M. G. WOODGATE, F.S.A. .   . 186
  Chapelry of Parson Drove .   .   ,,   ,,   .   . 197
  Newton .   .   .   ,,   ,,   .   . 201
  Outwell and Upwell 206
  Thorney 219
  Tydd St. Giles .   .   . General Description, Manors, Churches,
                         Nonconformity, and Charities by
                         G. M. G. WOODGATE, F.S.A. .   . 224
  Wisbech St. Mary 232
  Wisbech 238
Analysis of Hearth Tax Assessments . By C. A. F. MEEKINGS, M.A. .   . 272

CORNWALL

VOLUME ONE

PAGE

Dedication v
The Advisory Council of the Victoria History vii
General Advertisement vii
The Cornwall County Committee xiii
Contents xv
List of Illustrations xvii
Preface xxi
Table of Abbreviations xxiii
Natural History
  Geology .   .   .   . By J. B. HILL, F.G.S. 1
  Palaeontology .   .   . By R. LYDEKKER, F.R.S., F.G.S., F.L.S. . 47
  Botany .   .   .   . Edited by F. HAMILTON DAVEY, F.L.S.
    Introduction .   .   . By F. HAMILTON DAVEY, F.L.S. .   . 49
    Summary of Orders .   .   .   ,,   ,,   .   . 55

PAGE

Botanical Districts	By F. Hamilton Davey, F.L.S.	56
Brambles (*Rubi*)	By the Revd. W. Moyle Rogers, F.L.S.	71
Menthae	By F. Hamilton Davey, F.L.S.	72
Filices, *etc.*	,, ,,	73
Mosses (*Musci*)	By E. M. Holmes, F.L.S.	74
Liverworts (*Hepaticae*)	,, ,,	79
Marine Algae	,, ,,	81
Freshwater Algae	,, ,,	90
Lichens (*Lichenes*)	,, ,,	98
Fungi	,, ,,	106
Zoology		
Marine	By Professor Jas. Clark, M.A., D.Sc., A.R.C.S.	113
Non-Marine Molluscs	By B. B. Woodward, F.L.S., F.G.S., F.R.M.S.	160
Insects	By Professor Jas. Clark, M.A., D.Sc., A.R.C.S.	
Introduction	,, ,, ,,	163
Aptera (*Spring-tails and Bristle-tails*)	,, ,, ,,	166
Orthoptera (*Earwigs, Grasshoppers, etc.*)	,, ,, ,,	166
Neuroptera (*Dragon-flies, Lace-wings, etc.*)	,, ,, ,,	169
Hymenoptera Phytophaga (*Saw-flies, etc.*)	,, ,, ,,	173
Cynipidae (*Gall-flies*)	,, ,, ,,	176
Entomophaga (*Ichneumon-flies*)	,, ,, ,,	176
Braconidae	,, ,, ,,	180
Chrysididae (*Ruby-wasps*)	,, ,, ,,	181
Hymenoptera Aculeata (*Ants, Wasps, and Bees*)	,, ,, ,,	181
Coleoptera (*Beetles*)	,, ,, ,,	186
Lepidoptera Rhopalocera (*Butterflies*)	,, ,, ,,	203
Lepidoptera Heterocera (*Moths*)	,, ,, ,,	207
Diptera (*Flies*)	,, ,, ,,	227
Hemiptera Heteroptera (*Bugs*)	,, ,, ,,	238
Hemiptera Homoptera	,, ,, ,,	241
Aphides	,, ,, ,,	243
Spiders	By the late F. O. Pickard-Cambridge, M.A., revised and corrected by the Revd. O. Pickard-Cambridge, M.A., F.R.S.	245
Crustaceans	By the Revd. T. R. R. Stebbing, M.A., F.R.S., F.Z.S.	255
Fishes	By J. T. Cunningham, M.A.	291
Reptiles and Batrachians	By Professor Jas. Clark, M.A., D.Sc., A.R.C.S.	307
Birds	,, ,, ,,	309
Mammals	,, ,, ,,	348
Early Man	By J. B. Cornish	353
Anglo-Saxon Remains	By Reginald A. Smith, B.A., F.S.A.	375
Stone Circles	By G. F. Tregelles	379
Early Christian Monuments	By Arthur G. Langdon, F.S.A.	407
Ancient Earthworks	By J. B. Cornish	451
Maritime History	By M. Oppenheim	475
Industries		
Introduction	By the Revd. Thos. Taylor, M.A., F.S.A.	513
Granite Quarrying		517
Slate Quarrying	By J. Hockaday	519
Tin Mining	By George R. Lewis	522
Copper Mining	,, ,,	563
Foundries and Engineering Works	By Stephen Michell	570
China Clay	By the Revd. Thos. Taylor, M.A., F.S.A.	577
Horticulture	,, ,, ,,	578
The Fisheries	By J. B. Cornish	582

VOLUME TWO

PAGE

Romano-British Cornwall . . . By the late F. HAVERFIELD, M.A., LL.D., D.Litt., F.S.A.,Camden Professor of Ancient History, Oxford, revised and edited by M. V. TAYLOR, M.A., with a note on the Milestones and Roads of Cornwall by R. G. COLLINGWOOD, M.A., F.S.A. . 1

The Domesday Survey for Cornwall
   Introduction . . . . By L. F. SALZMANN, B.A., F.S.A., and others . 45
   Translation of the Text . . . By the Revd. Canon THOMAS TAYLOR, M.A., B.D., F.S.A. 60
   Index 104

[*Note.* The two chapters specified above are all of Volume Two that has been printed. They were published as two separate parts, numbered 5 and 8 respectively. No list of contents was printed: the details above are taken from the title-pages of the two parts.]

CUMBERLAND

VOLUME ONE

PAGE

Dedication v
The Advisory Council of the Victoria History vii
General Advertisement vii
The Cumberland County Committee xiii
List of Errata xiv
Contents xv
List of Illustrations xvii
Preface xix
Natural History
   Introduction to Natural History . . By the Revd. H. A. MACPHERSON, M.A., M.B.O.U. . xxiii
   Geology . . . . . By J. G. GOODCHILD, F.G.S., F.Z.S., H.M. Geol. Survey 1
   Climate . . . . By the late WILLIAM HODGSON, A.L.S. . . 65
   Palaeontology . . . By RICHARD L. LYDEKKER, B.A., F.R.S., F.G.S. . 71
   Botany
      Introduction . . . By the late WILLIAM HODGSON, A.L.S. . . 73
      Summary of Orders . . ,, ,, ,, . 76
      The Botanical Districts . . ,, ,, ,, . 78
      Musci (*Mosses*) . . . By the Revd. C. H. BINSTEAD, M.A. . . 94
   Zoology
      Mollusca (*Snails, etc.*) . . By B. B. WOODWARD, F.G.S., R.F.M.S. . 99
      Insecta (*Insects*)
         Orthoptera (*Earwigs, etc.*) . . By F. H. DAY 101
         Neuroptera (*Dragonflies*) . . ,, ... 102
         Hymenoptera (*Bees, etc.*) . . ,, ... 103
         Coleoptera (*Beetles*) . . . ,, ... 105
         Lepidoptera (*Butterflies and Moths*) . ,, ... 117
         Diptera (*Flies*) . . . ,, ... 140
         Hemiptera (*Bugs, etc.*) . . ,, ... 141
      Myriapoda (*Centipedes*) . . By R. I. POCOCK 143
      Arachnida (*Spiders*) . . By F. O. PICKARD-CAMBRIDGE, M.A. . 144
      Crustacea (*Crabs, etc.*) . . By the Revd. T. R. R. STEBBING, M.A., F.R.S., F.L.S. 158
      Pisces (*Fishes*) . . . By the Revd. H. A. MACPHERSON, M.A., M.B.O.U. 169

PAGE

Reptilia (*Reptiles*) and Batrachia
  (*Batrachians*) . . . By the Revd. H. A. MACPHERSON, M.A., M.B.O.U. 177
Aves (*Birds*) . . . . ,, ,, ,, . 179
Mammalia (*Mammals*) . . . ,, ,, ,, . 218
Early Man . . . . . By the late R. S. FERGUSON, M.A., LL.M., F.S.A. 225
Pre-Norman Remains . . . By W. G. COLLINGWOOD, M.A. . . . 253
Introduction to the Cumberland Domesday,
  Early Pipe Rolls, and Testa de Nevill . By the Revd. JAMES WILSON, M.A. . 295
The Text of the Cumberland Domesday . ,, ,, . . . 336
The Text of the Early Pipe Rolls . . ,, ,, . . . 338
The Text of the Testa de Nevill . . ,, ,, . . . 419

VOLUME TWO

PAGE

Dedication v
Contents ix
List of Illustrations xi
Editorial Note xiii
Table of Abbreviations xv
Ecclesiastical History . . . By the Revd. JAMES WILSON, M.A. . . 1
Religious Houses . . . . ,, ,,
  Introduction 127
  Priory of Carlisle 131
  ,, ,, Lanercost 152
  Abbey of Holmcultram 162
  ,, ,, Calder 174
  Priory of St. Bees 178
  ,, ,, Wetheral 184
  Nunnery of Armathwaite 189
  ,, ,, Seton or Lekeley 192
  Four Houses of Friars 194
  Hospital of St. Nicholas, Carlisle 199
  ,, ,, St. Sepulchre, Carlisle 203
  ,, ,, St. Leonard, Wigton 204
  ,, ,, Lennh', Bewcastle 204
  ,, House of Caldbeck 204
  House of St. John, Keswick 204
  College of Greystoke 204
  ,, ,, Kirkoswald 208
Monumental Effigies . . . By the Revd. Canon BOWER, M.A. . . 211
Political History . . . By the Revd. JAMES WILSON, M.A., and R. A.
    ALLISON 221
Industries
  Introduction . . . By the Revd. JAMES WILSON, M.A. . 331
  Coal Mining . . . By R. W. MOORE 348
  Haematite Mining . . . By JOHN MACKELLAR MAIN . . 385
  Eden and Esk Fisheries . . By THOMAS ROBINSON . . . 407
  Derwent Fisheries . . By H. P. SENHOUSE, M.A. . . 411
  Ravenglass Fisheries . . By FREDERICK REYNOLDS . . 415
  Solway Fisheries . . . By GEORGE HOLMES . . . 416
Sport Ancient and Modern
  Introduction . . . By G. W. HARTLEY . . . 419
  Fox Hunting . . . By the Lady MABEL HOWARD . . 422
  Shooting . . . By G. W. HARTLEY . . . 428
  Horse Racing . . . By the Revd. JAMES WILSON, M.A. . 440

		PAGE
Wildfowling	By William Nicol . . .	. 446
Foulmart Hunting . . .	By the Revd. James Wilson, M.A. .	. 452
Sweetmart Hunting . . .	„ „ . .	. 455
North Country Trail Hounds and Trails	By Francis Nicholson, F.Z.S. . .	. 457
Otter Hunting	By William Steel . .	. 461
Angling	By Fraser Sandeman . .	. 464
Coursing	By W. F. Lamonby . .	. 469
Game Cockfighting . . .	By Francis Nicholson, F.Z.S. .	. 475
Wrestling	„ „ .	. 482
Football	By C. W. Alcock, assisted by R. Westray and R. S. Wilson	. 491
Forestry	By J. Nisbet, D.Oec. . .	. 497

DERBYSHIRE

VOLUME ONE

		PAGE
Dedication		. v
The Advisory Council of the Victoria History		. vii
General Advertisement		. vii
The Derbyshire County Committee		. xiii
Contents		. xv
List of Illustrations		. xvii
Preface		. xix
Table of Abbreviations		. xxi
Natural History		
Introduction . . .	By the Revd. F. C. R. Jourdain, M.A., M.B.O.U.	. xxvii
Addenda and Corrigenda . .	„ „ „	. xxix
Geology	By H. Arnold Bemrose, M.A., F.G.S. .	. 1
Palaeontology . . .	By R. Lydekker, F.R.S., F.L.S., F.G.S. .	. 35
Botany	By the Revd. W. R. Linton, M.A. .	. 39
Zoology		
Molluscs . . .	By B. B. Woodward, F.G.S., F.R.M.S., and Lionel Adams, B.A. . . .	. 51
Insects		
Orthoptera . . .	By the Revd. F. C. R. Jourdain, M.A., M.B.O.U. .	. 54
Neuroptera . . .	By the Revd. A. E. Eaton, M.A., F.E.S. .	. 55
Trichoptera . . .	. . . . .	. 57
Hymenoptera . .	By the Revd. F. C. R. Jourdain, M.A., M.B.O.U. .	. 57
Coleoptera . . .	By J. le B. Tomlin, M.A., F.E.S. . .	. 61
Lepidoptera . . .	By the Revd. F. C. R. Jourdain, M.A., M.B.O.U. .	. 77
Diptera . . .	„ „ „	. 94
Hemiptera . . .	„ „ „	. 99
Aphides . . .	„ „ „	. 100
Spiders . . .	By the late F. O. Pickard-Cambridge, M.A.	. 100
Crustaceans . . .	By the Revd. T. R. R. Stebbing, M.A., F.R.S., F.Z.S.	. 102
Fishes . . .	By the Revd. F. C. R. Jourdain, M.A., M.B.O.U. .	. 110
Reptiles and Batrachians .	By G. H. Storer, F.Z.S. . .	. 117
Birds	By the Revd. F. C. R. Jourdain, M.A., M.B.O.U. .	. 119
Mammals . . .	„ „ „	. 150
Early Man	By John Ward, F.S.A. . .	. 159
Romano-British Remains . .	By F. Haverfield, M.A., LL.D., F.S.A. .	. 191
Anglo-Saxon Remains . .	By John Ward, F.S.A. . .	. 265

PAGE

Early Christian Art . . . By J. ROMILLY ALLEN, F.S.A. . . . 279
Introduction to the Derbyshire Domesday . By F. M. STENTON, B.A. 293
Text of the Derbyshire Domesday . . ,, ,, ... 327
Ancient Earthworks . . . By the Revd. J. C. Cox, LL.D., F.S.A. . . 357
Forestry . . . . . ,, ,, ,, . 397
Index to the Derbyshire Domesday 427

VOLUME TWO

PAGE

Dedication v
Contents ix
List of Illustrations and Maps xi
Editorial Note xiii
Ecclesiastical History . . . By the Revd. J. C. Cox, LL.D., F.S.A. . I
Religious Houses . . . . ,, ,, ,,
 Introduction 41
 Priory of King's Mead 43
 ,, ,, St. James, Derby 45
 Abbey of Darley 46
 Priory of Breadsall 54
 ,, ,, Gresley 56
 ,, ,, Repton with the Cell of Calke 58
 Abbey of Beauchief 63
 ,, ,, Dale 69
 Preceptory of Yeaveley and Barrow 75
 ,, ,, Locko 77
 Dominican Friars of Derby 78
 Hospital of Alkmonton 80
 ,, ,, St. Leonard, Chesterfield 81
 ,, ,, St. Helen, Derby 83
 ,, ,, St. James, Derby 83
 ,, ,, St. Leonard, Derby 84
 ,, ,, St. Mary in the Peak 86
 Collegiate Church of All Saints, Derby 87
Political History . . . . By the Revd. J. C. Cox, LL.D., F.S.A. . 93
Social and Economic History . . By Mrs. J. H. LANDER, B.Sc. (Lond.) . 161
 Table of Population, 1801–1901 . By GEORGE S. MINCHIN . . . 192
Schools . . . . . By A. F. LEACH, M.A., F.S.A.
 Introduction 207
 Derby Grammar School 208
 Chesterfield Grammar School 223
 Repton School 226
 Tideswell Grammar School 247
 Dronfield Grammar School 250
 Wirksworth Grammar School 253
 Ashbourne Grammar School 254
 Staveley or Netherthorpe Grammar
  School 266
 Risley Grammar School 267
 Lady Manners School, Bakewell 269
 Buxton Grammar School 271
 Grammar Schools now Elementary 272
 Elementary Schools founded before 1800 274
Sport Ancient and Modern . . . Edited by E. D. CUMING
 Hunting 283

PAGE

The Meynell Hunt . . . By J. L. RANDALL 284
The Barlow Hunt . . . By E. D. CUMING 287
Harriers . . . . ,, ,, ... 288
Coursing . . . . . By J. W. BOURNE 288
Racing . . . . . By H. A. BRYDEN and E. D. CUMING . . 289
Shooting . . . . By H. A. BRYDEN 293
Angling . . . . By WALTER M. GALLICHAN . . . 295
Cricket . . . . By Sir HOME GORDON, Bart. . . . 298
Golf . . . . . By H. A. BRYDEN 301
Old Sports and Games . . By the Revd. J. C. COX, LL.D., F.S.A. . 304
Agriculture . . . . . By CHARLES E. B. BOWLES . . . 305
Industries
Introduction . . . . By Mrs. J. H. LANDER, B.Sc. (Lond.) . 321
Lead Mining . . . . By Mrs. J. H. LANDER, B.Sc. (Lond.) and C. H.
VELLACOTT, B.A. 323
Coal Mining . . . By Mrs. J. H. LANDER, B.Sc. (Lond.) and C. H.
VELLACOTT, B.A. . . . 349
Iron . . . . . By Mrs. J. H. LANDER, B.Sc. (Lond.) and C. H.
VELLACOTT, B.A. . . . 356
Hardware 362
Silver and other Minerals . . By C. H. VELLACOTT, B.A. . . . 363
Silver 363
Zinc 363
Manganese 363
Pyrites and Ochre 364
Copper 364
Barytes 364
Fluor and Calc Spar 364
Chert 364
Marble, Stone, and Slate 364
Fireclay 365
Gypsum or Alabaster 366
Hosiery . . . . By Mrs. J. H. LANDER, B.Sc. (Lond.) . 367
Lace . . . . . ,, ,, . 370
Textile Trades . . . . ,, ,, . 370
Flax and Hemp . . . ,, ,, . 372
Silk . . . . . ,, ,, . 372
Cotton . . . . . ,, ,, . 372
Pottery . . . . . ,, ,, . 374
China . . . . . ,, ,, . 375

DEVONSHIRE

VOLUME ONE

PAGE

Dedication v
The Advisory Council of the Victoria History vii
General Advertisement vii
The Devonshire County Committee xiii
Contents xv
List of Illustrations xvii
Preface xxi
Table of Abbreviations xxiii

CONTENTS OF VOLUMES: DEVON I

PAGE

Natural History

Geology . . . . . By W. A. E. Ussher . . . .

Palaeontology . . . . By R. Lydekker, F.R.S., F.G.S., F.L.S. . . 49

Botany

　Introduction . . . By W. P. Hiern, M.A. 55

　Summary of Orders . . . ,, ,, ... 59

　Botanical Districts . . . ,, ,, ... 64

　Brambles (*Rubi*) . . . By the Revd. W. Moyle Rogers, F.L.S. . . 94

　Roses (*Rosae*) . . . . ,, ,, . . 95

　Vascular Cryptogams . . . By W. P. Hiern, M.A. 96

　Mosses (*Musci*) . . . By E. M. Holmes, F.L.S. 101

　Liverworts (*Hepaticae*) . . . ,, ,, ... 106

　Freshwater Algae . . . . ,, ,, ... 108

　Marine Algae . . . . . ,, ,, ... 110

　Lichens (*Lichenes*) . . . . ,, ,, ... 117

　Fungi . . . . . . ,, ,, ... 123

Zoology

　Marine . . . . . By Reginald Austen Todd, B.Sc. (Vic.) . . 131

　Non-Marine Molluscs . . . By B. B. Woodward, F.L.S., F.G.S., F.R.M.S. . 159

　Insects . . . . Edited by Herbert Goss, F.L.S., late Secretary to the Entomological Society

　　Orthoptera (*Earwigs, Grasshoppers, Crickets, etc.*) . . . By George C. Bignell, F.E.S. . . . 163

　　Neuroptera (*Dragon-flies, Lace-wings, etc.*) . . . . By Charles A. Briggs, F.E.S. . . . 164

　　Hymenoptera Phytophaga (*Saw-flies, etc.*) . . . . By George C. Bignell, F.E.S. . . . 166

　　　Cynipidae (*Gall-flies*) . . ,, ,, . . . 169

　　　Ichneumonidae (*Ichneumon-flies*) . ,, ,, . . . 171

　　　Braconidae . . . . ,, ,, . . . 181

　　　Oxyura . . . . . ,, ,, . . . 186

　　　Chalcididae . . . . ,, ,, . . . 187

　　Hymenoptera Aculeata (*Ants, Wasps, and Bees*) . . . ,, ,, . . . 187

　　　Chrysididae . . . . ,, ,, . . . 190

　　Coleoptera (*Beetles*) . . By the Revd. Canon Fowler, M.A., D.Sc., F.L.S. . 190

　　Lepidoptera Rhopalocera (*Butterflies*) By the late Chas. G. Barrett, F.E.S. . 208

　　Lepidoptera Heterocera (*Moths*) ,, ,, . 211

　　Diptera (*Flies*) . . . By Ernest E. Austen . . . 230

　　Hemiptera Heteroptera (*Bugs*) . By George C. Bignell, F.E.S. . . 239

　　Hemiptera Homoptera . . ,, ,, . . 242

　　Aphididae . . . . ,, ,, . . 243

　Spiders . . . . By the late F. O. Pickard-Cambridge, M.A. . 245

　Crustaceans . . . . By the Revd. T. R. R. Stebbing, M.A., F.R.S., F.Z.S. 253

　Fishes . . . . . By J. T. Cunningham, M.A. . . 277

　Reptiles and Batrachians . . By E. Ernest Lowe, F.L.S. . . 288

　Birds . . . . . By William S. M. D'Urban . . 291

　Mammals . . . . By J. Brooking Rowe, F.S.A., F.L.S. . 335

Early Man . . . . . By R. Burnard, F.S.A. . . . 341

Anglo-Saxon Remains . . . By Reginald A. Smith, B.A., F.S.A. . 373

Introduction to the Devonshire Domesday . By the Revd. Oswald J. Reichel, M.A., B.C.L., F.S.A. 375

Translation of the Devonshire Domesday . ,, ,, ,, . 403

Feudal Baronage . . . . ,, ,, ,, . 551

Ancient Earthworks . . . By J. Charles Wall . . . 573

67

DORSET

VOLUME TWO

			PAGE
Dedication			v
Contents			ix
List of Illustrations and Maps			xi
Editorial Note			xiii
Ecclesiastical History . . .	By Miss M. M. C. Calthrop	. . .	1
Religious Houses			
Introduction	,, ,,	. .	47
Abbey of Abbotsbury . . .	,, ,,	. .	48
,, ,, Cerne	,, ,,	. .	53
,, ,, Milton	,, ,,	. .	58
,, ,, Sherborne . .	,, ,,	. .	62
Priory of Cranborne . . .	,, ,,	. .	70
,, ,, Horton . . .	,, ,,	. .	71
Abbey of Shaftesbury . .	,, ,,	. .	73
Priory of Holne or East Holme . .	,, ,,	. .	80
Abbey of Bindon . . .	,, ,,	. .	82
,, ,, Tarrant Kaines .	,, ,,	. .	87
Preceptory of Friar Mayne . .	,, ,,	. .	90
Dominican Friars of Gillingham .	By A. G. Little, M.A.	. .	92
,, ,, Melcombe Regis .	,, ,,	. .	92
Franciscan Friars of Dorchester .	,, ,,	. .	93
Carmelite Friars of Bridport .	,, ,,	. .	95
,, ,, Lyme .	,, ,,	. .	96
Austin Friars of Sherborne .	,, ,,	. .	96
'Priory Hermitage' of Blackmoor .	By Miss M. M. C. Calthrop	. .	96
Wilcheswood	,, ,,	. .	98
Hospital of St. Mary Magdalen, Allington	,, ,,	. .	98
,, ,, Long Blandford . .	,, ,,	. .	100
Hospital of St. Mary and the Holy Spirit, Lyme . . .	,, ,,	. .	100
Hospital of St. John the Baptist, Bridport	,, ,,	. .	100
,, ,, St. John the Baptist, Dorchester	,, ,,	. .	101
Hospital or Lazar-House, Dorchester .	,, ,,	. .	103
Hospital of St. John the Baptist, Shaftesbury	,, ,,	. .	103
Hospital of St. John the Baptist and St. John the Evangelist, Sherborne .	,, ,,	. .	104
Hospital of St. Thomas, Sherborne .	,, ,,	. .	105
,, ,, St. Leonard, Tarrant Rushton	,, ,,	. .	105
,, ,, St. Margaret and St. Anthony, Wimborne . . .	,, ,,	. .	106
Hospital of Wareham . . .	,, ,,	. .	107
Wimborne Minster . . .	,, ,,	. .	107
Priory of Frampton . . .	,, ,,	. .	113
,, ,, Loders . . .	,, ,,	. .	116
,, ,, Povington . . .	,, ,,	. .	118
,, ,, Spettisbury . . .	,, ,,	. .	119
,, ,, Wareham . . .	,, ,,	. .	121
Political History . . .	By Mrs. Edward Fripp, Oxford Honours School of Modern History		123
Maritime History . . .	By M. Oppenheim		175

		PAGE
Social and Economic History . .	By Miss MADELEINE C. FRIPP and Miss PHYLLIS WRAGGE, Oxford Honours School of Modern History	229
Table of Population, 1801–1901 .	By GEORGE S. MINCHIN . . .	264
Agriculture	By A. J. BUCKLE	275
Forestry	By the Revd. J. C. COX, LL.D., F.S.A. .	287
Sport, Ancient and Modern . .	Edited by the Revd. E. E. DORLING, M.A.	
Introduction	By the Revd. PIERCE A. BUTLER ('Purbeck Pilgrim') .	299
Hunting	,, ,, ,, .	300
Foxhounds	,, ,, ,, .	300
Blackmore Vale Hounds . .	,, ,, ,, .	304
The Cattistock . . .	,, ,, ,, .	308
The South Dorset . .	,, ,, ,, .	310
Lord Portman's Hounds . .	,, ,, ,, .	312
Point-to-Point Races . .	,, ,, ,, .	313
Stag-Hunting . . .	,, ,, ,, .	313
The Ranston Bloodhounds . .	,, ,, ,, .	313
Roe-Deer Hunting . .	,, ,, ,, .	314
Harriers and Beagles . .	,, ,, ,, .	315
Otter-Hunting . . .	,, ,, ,, .	315
Racing	,, ,, ,, .	316
Racing Celebrities . . .	,, ,, ,, .	317
Training Establishments and Stud Farms	,, ,, ,, .	317
Polo	,, ,, ,, .	318
Shooting	,, ,, ,, .	318
Falconry	By Capt. EUSTACE RADCLYFFE, J.P. . .	319
Angling	By the Revd. PIERCE A. BUTLER ('Purbeck Pilgrim') .	320
Golf	By the Revd. E. E. DORLING, M.A. .	322
Industries		
Introduction . . .	By Miss M. M. CRICK, B.A. (Dublin), Oxford Honours School of Modern History .	325
Quarrying . . .	By C. H. VELLACOTT, B.A. . .	331
The Hemp Industry . .	By Miss M. M. CRICK, B.A. (Dublin), Oxford Honours School of Modern History .	344
Fisheries	,, ,, ,, .	353
Cloth	,, ,, ,, .	360
Silk	,, ,, ,, .	362
Pottery and Tiles . . .	,, ,, ,, .	363
Brewing	,, ,, ,, .	366
Cider	By Miss M. M. CRICK, B.A. (Dublin), Oxford Honours School of Modern History, and C. H. VELLACOTT, B.A. . . .	369

VOLUME THREE

		PAGE
Dedication . . .		v
Contents . . .		ix
List of Illustrations . .		xi
Editorial Note . . .		xiii
Introduction to the Dorset Domesday	By ANN WILLIAMS	1
Translation of the Text of the Dorset Domesday . . .	,, ,,	61
Introduction to the Dorset Geld Rolls .	,, ,,	115
Text and Translation of the Dorset Geld Rolls	,, ,,	124
Summaries of Fiefs in Exon Domesday	,, ,,	148

PAGE

Index to the Dorset Domesday and Geld
    Rolls . . . . .   By Ann Williams 150
Index to Volumes II and III . .   By P. A. Spalding and Ann Williams . . 161
Corrigenda to Volume II 190

DURHAM
VOLUME ONE

PAGE

Dedication v
The Advisory Council of the Victoria History vii
General Advertisement vii
The Durham County Committee xiii
Contents xv
List of Illustrations xvii
Preface xix
Table of Abbreviations xxi
Natural History
  Geology . . . .   By G. A. Lebour, M.A. 1
  Palaeontology . . .   By R. Lydekker, F.R.S., F.G.S., F.L.S. . 31
  Botany . . . .   By M. C. Potter, M.A. . . . 35
  Zoology
    Marine . . .   By the Revd. A. M. Norman, D.C.L., LL.D.,
            F.R.S., Hon. Canon of Durham . . 83
    Marine Molluscs . . .   ,,   ,,   ,, 87
    Non-Marine Molluscs . .   By B. B. Woodward, F.G.S., F.R.M.S. . 90
    Insects . . .   By the Revd. W. J. Wingate, and J. E. Robson,
            F.E.S. (*Lepidoptera*) . . . 93
    Spiders . . .   By the late F. O. Pickard-Cambridge, M.A. . 141
    Crustaceans . . .   By the Revd. T. R. R. Stebbing, M.A., F.R.S.,
            F.Z.S. 150
    Fishes . . . .   By Alexander Meek, M.Sc., F.Z.S. . 168
    Reptiles and Batrachians .   By E. Leonard Gill, B.Sc. . 174
    Birds . . . .   By the Revd. H. B. Tristram, LL.D., F.R.S.,
            Canon of Durham . . . 175
    Mammals . . .   By E. Leonard Gill, B.Sc. . . 192
Early Man . . . .   By the Revd. Wm. Greenwell, D.C.L., F.R.S.,
            F.S.A., Minor Canon of Durham, and Geo.
            Clinch, F.G.S. 199
Anglo-Saxon Remains . .   By Charles C. Hodges . . . 211
The Contents of St. Cuthbert's Shrine .   By the Very Revd. G. W. Kitchin, D.D., F.S.A.,
            Dean of Durham . . . 241
Introduction to the Boldon Book .   By G. T. Lapsley, M.A., Ph.D. (Harvard) . 259
Text of the Boldon Book . .   ,,   ,,   ,, 327
Ancient Earthworks . .   By I. Chalkley Gould . . . 343
History of Schools . .   By A. F. Leach, M.A., F.S.A. . . 365
Index to the Boldon Book 415

VOLUME TWO

PAGE

Dedication v
Contents ix
List of Illustrations and Maps xi
Ecclesiastical History . . .   By the Revd. Henry Gee, D.D., F.S.A. . 1
Religious Houses . . .   By Miss Margaret E. Cornford
  Introduction 78

PAGE

Monastery of Hartlepool 79
St. Hilda's First Monastery 80
Gateshead House 80
Nunnery of Ebchester 81
Monasteries of Wearmouth and
   Jarrow 81
Priory of St. Cuthbert, Durham 86
   ,, ,, St. John the Baptist and
     St. Godric, Finchale 103
Priory of St. Mary, Neasham 106
   ,, ,, Baxterwood 109
Franciscan Friars of Hartlepool 109
   ,, ,, Durham 110
Friars Preachers of Hartlepool 110
   ,, ,, Jarrow 110
Austin Friars of Barnard Castle 111
Hospital of St. Giles, Kepier 111
   ,, ,, St. Mary Magdalen,
     Witton Gilbert 114
Hospital of Bathel 114
   ,, ,, SS. Lazarus, Martha, and
     Mary, Sherburn 115
Hospital of the Holy Trinity,
   Gateshead 117
Hospital of St. John the Baptist,
   Barnard Castle 117
Hospital of St. Edmund, Bishop and
   Confessor, Gateshead 118
Hospital of St. Mary Magdalen,
   Durham 119
Hospital of St. Stephen, Pelaw 120
   ,, ,, SS. Mary and Cuthbert,
     Greatham 121
Hospital of St. Leonard, Durham 123
   ,, ,, Friarside 123
   ,, ,, St. Edmund, King and
     Martyr, Gateshead 124
Hospital of Gainford 125
   ,, ,, Werhale 125
College of Darlington 125
   ,, ,, Auckland St. Andrew 126
   ,, ,, Norton 127
   ,, ,, Lanchester 127
   ,, ,, Chester-le-Street 128
   ,, ,, Staindrop 129
   ,, ,, Barnard Castle 129
Hermitages 130
Political History . . . . By KENNETT C. BAYLEY, F.S.A. . . 133
Social and Economic History . . By FREDERICK BRADSHAW, M.A. (Oxon.), D.Sc.
     (Lond.) 175

Table of Population, 1801–1901 . . By GEORGE S. MINCHIN . . . 261
Industries
   Introduction . . . . By Miss MAUD SELLERS, Hist. Tripos Cantab. . 275
   Iron and Steel . . . . . ,, ,, ,, 278
   The Chemical Works . . . . ,, ,, ,, 293
   Shipbuilding . . . . . ,, ,, ,, 302
   Glass Works . . . . . ,, ,, ,, 309
   Potteries . . . . . . ,, ,, ,, 312
   Textile Industries. . . . . ,, ,, ,, 314

PAGE

Mining	By Professor HENRY LOUIS, M.A. (Dur.), Assoc. R.S.M., M. Inst. C.E., &c., and C. H. VELLACOTT, B.A.	319
Coal	,, ,, ,,	320
Lead	,, ,, ,,	348
Iron	,, ,, ,,	353
Barytes	,, ,, ,,	356
Fluorspar	,, ,, ,,	356
Agriculture	By DOUGLAS A. GILCHRIST, M.Sc. (Dur.), B.Sc. (Edin.), F.R.S.E.	357
Forestry	By the Revd. J. C. COX, LL.D., F.S.A., and ARTHUR CHAS. FORBES, F.H.A.S.	373
Sport Ancient and Modern		
Introduction	By PERCY S. T. STEPHENS	385
Fox-hunting	,, ,,	388
The Raby, Mr. Cradock's, and Lord Zetland's Foxhounds	,, ,,	388
The Lambton, the Durham County, and the South Durham Foxhounds	,, ,,	393
The Durham County Hounds	,, ,,	395
The North Durham Foxhounds	,, ,,	397
The Hurworth Hunt	,, ,,	398
The Braes of Derwent	,, ,,	399
The Grove	,, ,,	400
Hare-Hunting	,, ,,	401
Otter-Hunting	,, ,,	403
Coursing	By J. B. RADCLIFFE	404
Shooting	By PERCY S. T. STEPHENS	409
Angling	,, ,,	414
Horse-Racing	,, ,,	417
Rowing	By R. H. J. POOLE	420
Golf	By the Revd. E. E. DORLING, M.A.	426
Football	By C. J. BRUCE MARRIOTT, M.A.	427

VOLUME THREE

PAGE

Dedication		v
Contents		ix
List of Illustrations		xi
List of Maps		xii
Editorial Note		xiii
Topography	General descriptions and manorial descents compiled under the superintendence of WILLIAM PAGE, F.S.A.; Heraldic drawings and blazon by the Revd. E. E. DORLING, M.A., F.S.A.; Charities from information supplied by J. W. OWSLEY, I.S.O., late Official Trustee of Charitable Funds	
City of Durham		
General History of the City	By the Very Revd. HENRY GEE, D.D., F.S.A., Dean of Gloucester	I
City Jurisdictions	By K. C. BAYLEY, F.S.A.	53
The Castle	By W. T. JONES, F.S.A.	64
The Cathedral:		
Historical Description	By C. R. PEERS, C.B.E., M.A., F.B.A., F.S.A., Chief Inspector of Ancient Monuments	93
Architectural Description	By the late JOHN QUEKETT, M.A., F.S.A., and F. H. CHEETHAM, F.S.A.	96
Monastic Buildings	By F. H. CHEETHAM, F.S.A.	123

PAGE

Parish of St. Oswald . . .	General descriptions and manorial descents by HENRIETTA L. E. GARBETT; Architectural descriptions by F. H. CHEETHAM, F.S.A. .	. 144
Parish of St. Giles . . .	General descriptions and manorial descents by HENRIETTA L. E. GARBETT; Architectural descriptions by F. H. CHEETHAM, F.S.A. .	. 182
Stockton Ward	General descriptions and manorial descents compiled under the superintendence of WILLIAM PAGE, F.S.A.; Heraldic drawings and blazon by the Revd. E. E. DORLING, M.A., F.S.A.; Charities from information supplied by J. W. OWSLEY, I.S.O., late Official Trustee of Charitable Funds	
Introduction	By MYRA CURTIS, Classical Tripos . .	. 191
Billingham	,, ,, ,, . .	. 195
Bishop Middleham . . .	,, ,, ,, . .	. 204
Bishopton . . .	By JOHN BROWNBILL, M.A. . .	. 213
Crayke	. . . . .	. 216
Low Dinsdale . . .	By JOHN BROWNBILL, M.A. . .	. 217
Egglescliffe . . .	,, ,, . .	. 222
Elton	,, ,, . .	. 232
Elwick Hall . . .	By MADELEINE HOPE DODDS, Historical Tripos	. 235
Greatham . . .	By MYRA CURTIS, Classical Tripos . .	. 242
Grindon	,, ,, ,, . .	. 247
Hart	By MADELEINE HOPE DODDS, Historical Tripos	. 254
Hartlepool . . .	,, ,, ,,	. 263
Hurworth . . .	By JOHN BROWNBILL, M.A. . .	. 285
Middleton St. George . .	,, ,, . .	. 293
Long Newton . . .	,, ,, . .	. 299
Norton	,, ,, . .	. 304
Redmarshall . . .	,, ,, . .	. 315
Sedgefield . . .	By MYRA CURTIS, Classical Tripos . .	. 321
Sockburn	. . . . .	. 343
Stainton . . .	By MYRA CURTIS, Classical Tripos . .	. 344
Stockton-on-Tees . . .	By JOHN BROWNBILL, M.A. . .	. 348
Stranton . . .	By MADELEINE HOPE DODDS, Historical Tripos	. 365

ESSEX

VOLUME ONE

PAGE

Dedication		v
The Advisory Council of the Victoria History		vii
General Advertisement		vii
The Essex County Committee		xiii
Contents		xv
List of Illustrations		xvii
Preface		xix
Natural History		
Geology	By H. B. WOODWARD, F.G.S. . .	1
Palaeontology . . .	By RICHARD LYDEKKER, B.A., F.R.S., F.G.S.	25
Botany	By J. C. SHENSTONE, F.L.S. . .	31
Zoology		
Marine . . .	By WALTER GARSTANG, assisted by H. C. SORBY, LL.D., F.R.S., F.S.A. . . .	69
Mollusca (Snails, etc.) . .	By B. B. WOODWARD, F.G.S., F.R.M.S. .	89
Insecta (Insects) . .	By W. HARWOOD . . .	91

PAGE

Myriapoda (*Centipedes*) . . By R. I. Pocock 193
Arachnida (*Spiders*) . . . By F. O. Pickard-Cambridge, M.A. . . 196
Crustacea (*Crabs, etc.*) . . . By the Revd. T. R. R. Stebbing, M.A., F.R.S.,
F.S.A., F.L.S. 204
Pisces (*Fishes*) . . . . By H. Laver, J.P., F.S.A., F.L.S., M.R.C.S. . 220
Reptilia (*Reptiles*) and Batrachia
(*Batrachians*) . . . . ,, ,, ,, . 230
Aves (*Birds*) . . . . By Miller Christy, F.L.S. . . . 232
Mammalia (*Mammals*) . . By H. Laver, J.P., F.S.A., F.L.S., M.R.C.S. . 254
Early Man . . . . By Geo. F. Beaumont, F.S.A., and I. Chalkley
Gould 261
Ancient Earthworks . . . By I. Chalkley Gould . . . 275
Anglo-Saxon Remains . . . By Reginald A. Smith, B.A. . . 315
Introduction to the Essex Domesday . By J. Horace Round, M.A. . . 333
Text of the Essex Domesday . . . ,, ,, . . 427
Index to the Essex Domesday 579

VOLUME TWO

PAGE

Dedication v
Contents ix
List of Illustrations xv
Editorial Note xvii
Table of Abbreviations xix
Ecclesiastical History . . . By the Revd. J. C. Cox, LL.D., F.S.A., and
J. Horace Round, M.A., LL.D. . . . 1
Religious Houses . . . By R. C. Fowler, M.A.
Introduction . . . . ,, ,, . . . 84
Abbey of Colchester . . . ,, ,, . . . 93
Priory of Earl's Colne . . . ,, ,, . . . 102
,, ,, Hatfield Peverel . . ,, ,, . . . 105
,, ,, Hatfield Regis or Broadoak . ,, ,, . . . 107
Abbey of Walden . . . ,, ,, . . . 110
,, ,, Barking . . . ,, ,, . . . 115
Priory of Castle Hedingham . . ,, ,, . . . 122
,, ,, Wix . . . ,, ,, . . . 123
Abbey of Coggeshall . . . ,, ,, . . . 125
,, ,, Stratford Langthorne . . ,, ,, . . . 129
,, ,, Tilty . . . ,, ,, . . . 134
Priory of Little Horkesley . . ,, ,, . . . 137
,, ,, Prittlewell . . . ,, ,, . . . 138
,, ,, Stanesgate . . . ,, ,, . . . 141
,, ,, Berden . . . ,, ,, . . . 143
,, ,, Bicknacre or Woodham Ferrers . ,, ,, . . . 144
,, ,, Blackmore . . . ,, ,, . . . 146
,, ,, St. Botolph, Colchester . . ,, ,, . . . 148
,, ,, Little Dunmow . . . ,, ,, . . . 150
,, ,, Latton . . . ,, ,, . . . 154
,, ,, Little Leighs . . . ,, ,, . . . 155
Abbey of Chich or St. Osyth's . . ,, ,, . . . 157
Priory of Thoby . . . ,, ,, . . . 162
,, ,, Thremhall . . . ,, ,, . . . 163
,, ,, Tiptree . . . ,, ,, . . . 164
Abbey of Waltham Holy Cross . . ,, ,, . . . 166
,, ,, Beeleigh by Maldon . . ,, ,, . . . 172

CONTENTS OF VOLUMES: ESSEX II

PAGE

Preceptory of Cressing . . . By R. C. Fowler, M.A. 177
,, ,, Little Maplestead . . ,, ,, . . . 178
Black Friars of Chelmsford . . . ,, ,, . . . 179
Grey Friars of Colchester . . . ,, ,, . . . 180
Crossed Friars of Colchester . . . ,, ,, . . . 181
White Friars of Maldon . . . ,, ,, . . . 182
Hospital of Bocking . . . . ,, ,, . . . 183
,, ,, Braintree . . . ,, ,, . . . 184
,, ,, Castle Hedingham . . ,, ,, . . . 184
,, ,, St. Mary Magdalen, Colchester ,, ,, . . . 184
,, ,, Ilford . . . ,, ,, . . . 186
,, ,, Little Maldon . . . ,, ,, . . . 188
,, ,, Newport . . . ,, ,, . . . 190
,, ,, East Tilbury . . . ,, ,, . . . 191
,, ,, Brook Street in South Weald . ,, ,, . . . 192
College of Halstead . . . ,, ,, . . . 192
,, ,, Pleshey . . . . ,, ,, . . . 193
Hospital or Priory of Hornchurch . ,, ,, . . . 195
Priory of West Mersea . . . . ,, ,, . . . 196
,, ,, Panfield . . . . ,, ,, . . . 197
,, ,, Takeley . . . . ,, ,, . . . 199
Hospital of Writtle . . . . ,, ,, . . . 200
Political History . . . . By Miss Ethel Stokes and J. Horace Round, LL.D. 203
Maritime History . . . . By M. Oppenheim 259
Social and Economic History . . By Miss Nora E. MacMunn . . . 313
    Table of Population 1801–1901 . . By G. S. Minchin 342
Industries . . . . . Edited by Miller Christy, F.L.S.
    Introduction . . . . By Miller Christy, F.L.S. . . 355
    Saffron-Culture . . . . ,, ,, . . . 359
    Cultivation of Weld or Dyer's Weed . . ,, ,, . . . 366
    Cyder-Making . . . . ,, ,, . . . 366
    Making of Mead . . . . ,, ,, . . . 366
    Hop-Growing . . . . ,, ,, . . . 366
    Hop Poles . . . . ,, ,, . . . 369
    Cheese-Making . . . . ,, ,, . . . 369
    Candied Eryngo . . . By J. C. Shenstone, F.L.S. . . 371
    Making of Potash . . . By Henry Laver, F.S.A., M.R.C.S. . 372
    Straw-Plaiting . . . . By Miller Christy, F.L.S. . . 375
    Making of Straw Hats and Bonnets . ,, ,, . . . 378
    Making of Artificial Flowers . . ,, ,, . . . 379
    Flock-Making . . . . ,, ,, . . . 379
    Jute-Spinning . . . . ,, ,, . . . 379
    Sack-Making . . . . ,, ,, . . . 380
    Woollen Industry . . . . ,, ,, . . . 380
    Calico-Printing and Silk-Printing . ,, ,, . . . 404
    Making of Leather Breeches and Gloves . ,, ,, . . . 408
    Roman Cement . . . . By Henry Laver, F.S.A., M.R.C.S. . 408
    Copperas Industry . . . By J. C. Shenstone, F.L.S. . . 411
    Tobacco-Pipe Making . . . By Miller Christy, F.L.S. . . 413
    Flint-Working . . . . ,, ,, . . . 413
    Manufacture of Pottery . . . ,, ,, . . . 413
    Manufacture of 'Art' Pottery . . By Miss C. Fell-Smith . . 414
    Glass-Making . . . . By Miller Christy, F.L.S. . . 415
    China-Manufacturing . . . ,, ,, . . . 415
    Making of 'Artificial Slate' . . ,, ,, . . . 417
    Making of Pattens . . . ,, ,, . . . 418

CONTENTS OF VOLUMES: ESSEX II

		PAGE
Cutting and Preparing of Cork	By MILLER CHRISTY, F.L.S.	418
Making of Wooden Chairs	,, ,,	418
Manufacture of Congreve War-Rockets	,, ,,	418
Vinegar-Making	,, ,,	419
Manufacture of Starch	,, ,,	419
Manufacture of Linseed Oil	,, ,,	419
Manufacture of Emery-Cloth	,, ,,	419
Pin-Making	,, ,,	419
Clock-Making	,, ,,	420
Manufacture of Cutlery	,, ,,	421
Manufacture of Steel Pens	,, ,,	421
Manufacture of Sheet Lead	,, ,,	421
Working of Copper	,, ,,	422
Flax-Growing	,, ,,	422
Cultivation of Coriander, Caraway, and Teazel	,, ,,	423
Oyster Fisheries	By J. C. SHENSTONE, F.L.S.	425
Gathering of Shell-Fish	By MILLER CHRISTY, F.L.S.	439
Sea Fisheries	By W. W. GLENNY	439
Salt-Making	By MILLER CHRISTY, F.L.S.	445
Malting and Brewing	,, ,,	445
Distilling of Spirits	,, ,,	445
Corn-Milling	By WILSON MARRIAGE	446
Charcoal-Burning	By T. S. DYMOND, F.C.S., F.I.C.	447
Quarrying of Chalk	By MILLER CHRISTY, F.L.S.	450
Lime-Burning	,, ,,	450
Manufacture of Whiting	,, ,,	451
Making of Gunpowder	By Lieut.-Col. Sir FREDERICK L. NATHAN, R.A.	451
Brick-Making and Tile-Making	By MILLER CHRISTY, F.L.S.	455
Candle-Making	,, ,,	457
Soap-Making	,, ,,	458
Leather Industries	,, ,,	458
Paper-Making	,, ,,	460
Manufacture of Rope and Twine	,, ,,	461
Silk Industry	By Miss C. FELL-SMITH and MILLER CHRISTY, F.L.S.	462
Making of Baskets and Sieves	By MILLER CHRISTY, F.L.S.	469
Brass-Founding	,, ,,	469
Bell-Founding	,, ,,	470
Building of Trading Ships	,, ,,	470
Printing	,, ,,	470
Newspaper-Publishing	,, ,,	472
Supplying Hay and Straw to the London Markets	,, ,,	473
Market-Gardening	By W. W. GLENNY	474
Fruit-Growing	By MILLER CHRISTY, F.L.S.	477
Seed-Growing	,, ,,	478
Nursery-Gardening	,, ,,	480
Rose-Growing	By J. C. SHENSTONE, F.L.S.	481
Jam-Making and Fruit-Preserving	By MILLER CHRISTY, F.L.S.	482
Isinglass and Gelatine-Making	,, ,,	482
Glue-Making	,, ,,	483
Yeast Industry	,, ,,	483
Manufacture of Mats and Matting	,, ,,	483
Manufacture of Clothing (wholesale)	,, ,,	483
Lace-Making	By Miss C. FELL-SMITH	484
Manufacture of Boots and Shoes	By MILLER CHRISTY, F.L.S.	487
Brush-Making	,, ,,	488

PAGE

Building of Pleasure Yachts	By MILLER CHRISTY, F.L.S.	488
Portland Cement	By JOHN AVERY, F.S.S.	492
Manufacture of Chemicals	By MILLER CHRISTY, F.L.S.	493
Manufacture of Photographic Dry Plates	,, ,,	495
Manufacture of Gutta-percha and India-rubber Goods	,, ,,	495
Sugar-Refining	,, ,,	496
Manufacture of Ammunition	,, ,,	496
Manufacture of Explosives	,, ,,	496
Iron-Founding	,, ,,	496
Manufacture of Agricultural Implements	,, ,,	497
Engine-Building and General Engineering	,, ,,	498
Gun-Making	,, ,,	499
Stove-Making	,, ,,	499
Manufacture of Steel Balls	,, ,,	499
Building of Steam Motor Omnibuses	,, ,,	499
Electrical Engineering	,, ,,	499
Schools	By Miss C. FELL-SMITH	501
Sport Ancient and Modern	Edited by E. D. CUMING	
Hunting:		
Foxhounds	By R. F. BALL	565
Harriers	,, ,,	579
Beagles	,, ,,	580
Otter Hounds	,, ,,	580
Staghounds	,, ,,	581
Shooting	By A. W. RUGGLES-BRISE	584
Racing	By R. F. BALL	586
Wild Fowling	By J. H. SALTER	587
Angling	By F. ANDERSON	590
Golf	By A. J. R. ROBERTSON	592
Athletics	By CHARLES HERBERT	594
Polo	By E. D. CUMING	595
Coursing	By HORACE LEDGER	595
Cricket	By HOME GORDON, assisted by O. R. BORRODAILE and the Revd. R. C. GUY, M.A.	599
Football	By C. W. ALCOCK	612
Forestry	By J. NISBET, D.Oec.	615

VOLUME THREE

PAGE

Dedication		v
Contents		ix
List of Plates		xi
List of Figures in the Text		xiii
Editorial Note		xv
Essex Victoria County History Committee		xvii
Notes on Abbreviations		xix
Roman Essex	By Professor I. A. RICHMOND, C.B.E., F.B.A.	1
Roman Roads	By M. R. HULL	24
The Red Hills	,, ,,	32
Roman Gazetteer	By M. R. HULL. Sections on Chelmsford, Great Chesterford, Harlow, and Rivenhall by Major J. G. S. BRINSON	35
Index to Volumes I–III	By AVRIL H. POWELL and D. W. HUTCHINGS	205
Corrigenda to Volumes I and II		256

VOLUME FOUR

	PAGE
Dedication	v
Contents	ix
List of Illustrations and Maps	xi
Editorial Note	xiii
Essex V.C.H. Committee	xv
Classes of Public Records used	xvii
Classes of Documents in the Essex Record Office used	xviii
Note on Abbreviations	xix

Topography — *Where not otherwise stated*, Architectural descriptions by MARGARET TOMLINSON; bridges, roads, postal services, and public services (except in Chigwell) by GLADYS A. WARD; Roman Catholicism from information supplied by the Revd. B. C. FOLEY; Methodist Churches (except in Lambourne) by G. HARRINGTON; all other Nonconformist Churches by W. R. POWELL; Primary Schools by A. F. J. BROWN; Charities by SUSAN REYNOLDS

		PAGE
Ongar Hundred	By W. R. POWELL	1
Bobbingworth	By AUDREY M. TAYLOR	9
Chigwell	By E. J. ERITH. Architectural descriptions from information supplied by the Ministry of Housing and Local Government	18
Fyfield	By AUDREY M. TAYLOR	43
Greenstead	By W. R. POWELL	58
Kelvedon Hatch	By E. E. BARKER, W. R. POWELL, and AUDREY M. TAYLOR	63
Lambourne	By W. R. POWELL. Parish Government and Poor Relief by D. M. M. SHORROCKS	72
High Laver	By AUDREY M. TAYLOR	87
Little Laver	By AUDREY M. TAYLOR. Parish Government and Poor Relief by J. H. HOLMES	97
Magdalen Laver	,, ,, ,,	103
Loughton	By W. R. POWELL. Architectural descriptions from information supplied by the Ministry of Housing and Local Government	110
Moreton	By AUDREY M. TAYLOR. Parish Government and Poor Relief by D. M. M. SHORROCKS	129
Navestock	By E. E. BARKER, W. R. POWELL, and AUDREY M. TAYLOR	139
Norton Mandeville	By W. R. POWELL	150
Chipping Ongar	,, ,,	155
High Ongar	,, ,,	171
Abbess Roding	By W. R. POWELL. Parish Government and Poor Relief by D. M. M. SHORROCKS	188
Beauchamp Roding	,, ,, ,,	197
Shelley	By AUDREY M. TAYLOR	203
Stanford Rivers	By W. R. POWELL. Parish Government and Poor Relief by J. H. HOLMES	208
Stapleford Abbots	By AUDREY M. TAYLOR	222
Stapleford Tawney	By AUDREY M. TAYLOR. Parish Government and Poor Relief by D. M. M. SHORROCKS	233
Stondon Massey	By E. E. BARKER, W. R. POWELL, and AUDREY M. TAYLOR. Architectural descriptions by J. H. FARRER and CYNTHIA E. BOOTH. Parish Government and Poor Relief by D. M. M. SHORROCKS	240
Theydon Bois	By A. A. DIBBEN	249
Theydon Garnon	,, ,,	258
Theydon Mount	,, ,,	275

PAGE

North West Bassett . . . By W. R. POWELL. Parish Government and Poor
Relief by D. M. M. SHORROCKS . . . 284

Analysis of Some Medieval Tax Assess-
ments: Ongar Hundred . . By M. W. BERESFORD 296

Analysis of Hearth Tax Assessments for
Ongar Hundred, 1662, 1670, and 1674 By K. H. BURLEY 303

Analysis of Bishop Compton's Census of
1676: Ongar Hundred . . ,, ,, ... 311

Index . . . . . By W. R. POWELL 313

VOLUME FIVE

PAGE

Dedication v
Contents ix
List of Illustrations xi
List of Maps and Plans xiii
Editorial Note xv
Essex Victoria History Committee xvii
Classes of Documents in the Public Record
Office used xix
Classes of Documents in the Essex Record
Office used xx
Note on Abbreviations xxi
Metropolitan Essex since 1850 . . By Professor W. ASHWORTH . . . I
Topography . . . . Architectural descriptions partly based on informa-
tion supplied by the Ministry of Housing and
Local Government; and revised by MARGARET
TOMLINSON. Local Government (except in Barking
and Ilford) by ANNE V. WORSLEY; Protestant
Nonconformity (except in Barking and Ilford) by
W. R. POWELL; Schools by A. F. J. BROWN and
ANNE V. WORSLEY; Charities by ANNE V. WORSLEY;
Manors revised by W. R. POWELL, with assistance
(in Barking and Ilford) from H. H. LOCKWOOD

Waltham Hundred . . . By the Revd. Canon J. L. FISHER . . . 93
Chingford . . . . ,, ,, . . 97
Epping . . . . By the Revd. Canon J. L. FISHER. Architecture of
Copped Hall by NANCY BRIGGS . . . 114
Nazeing . . . . By the Revd. Canon J. L. FISHER . . . 140
Waltham Holy Cross . . . ,, ,, . . . 151
Becontree Hundred . . . By W. R. POWELL 181
Barking and Ilford . . . By J. E. OXLEY 184
Barking 235
Ilford 249
Dagenham . . . . By J. G. O'LEARY 267
Index . . . . . By AVRIL H. POWELL 303

BIBLIOGRAPHY

PAGE

Dedication v
Contents ix
List of Illustrations x
Editorial Note xi
Essex V.C.H. Committee xii
Introduction to the Bibliography xv

		PAGE
Note on Abbreviations		xix
List of Periodicals Searched		xxi
Periodicals: Dates and Volume Numbers		xxiii
Essex Bibliography		1
Part I: The County		1
Part II: Biography and Family History		59
Part III: Individual Places and Regions		143
Voluntary Public Libraries	By A. F. J. BROWN	311
Rate-supported Public Libraries	By E. R. GAMESTER and W. R. POWELL	324
Bibliography: Author Index	By W. R. POWELL	333
Bibliography: Miscellaneous Index	,, ,,	350

GLOUCESTERSHIRE

VOLUME TWO

		PAGE
Dedication		v
Contents		ix
List of Illustrations		xiii
Editorial Note		xv
Ecclesiastical History	By Miss ROSE GRAHAM, F.R. Hist.S.	1
Religious Houses	,, ,,	
Introduction		52
Abbey of St. Peter at Gloucester		53
,, ,, Tewkesbury		61
,, ,, Winchcombe		66
Priory of Stanley St. Leonard		72
,, ,, St. James, Bristol		74
Abbey of St. Augustine, at Bristol		75
,, ,, Cirencester		79
Priory of St. Oswald, Gloucester		84
,, ,, Lanthony by Gloucester		87
,, ,, Horsley		91
,, ,, St. Mary Magdalen, Bristol		93
Abbey of Flaxley		93
,, ,, Hayles		96
,, ,, Kingswood		99
Priory of Beckford		102
,, ,, Brimpsfield		102
,, ,, Deerhurst		103
,, ,, Newent		105
College of Westbury-on-Trym		106
Black Friars, Bristol		109
Grey Friars, Bristol		110
Augustinian Friars, Bristol		110
Carmelite Friars, Bristol		110
Friars of the Penance of Jesus Christ, or Friars of the Sack, Bristol		111
Black Friars, Gloucester		111
Grey Friars, Gloucester		111
Carmelite or White Friars, Gloucester		112
Crutched Friars of Wotton-under-Edge		112

CONTENTS OF VOLUMES: GLOS. II

PAGE

Preceptory of Guiting	. . . .	113
,, ,, Quenington	. . . .	113
Hospital of St. Mark, Billeswick, called Gaunt's Hospital	. . . .	114
Hospital of St. Bartholomew, Bristol	. . . .	118
,, ,, St. Lawrence, Bristol	. . . .	119
,, ,, St. Mary Magdalen, Bristol	. . . .	119
,, ,, St. Bartholomew, Gloucester	. . . . . .	119
,, ,, St. Margaret, Gloucester	. . . .	121
,, ,, St. Mary Magdalen, Gloucester	. . . . .	122
,, ,, St. John, Cirencester	. . . .	122
,, ,, St. Lawrence, Cirencester	. . . . . .	123
,, ,, St. Thomas, Cirencester	. . . . . .	123
,, ,, Longbridge, by Berkeley	. . . . . .	123
,, ,, Lorwing	. . . .	124
,, ,, St. John the Baptist, Lechlade	. . . . . .	125
,, ,, Winchcombe	. . . .	126
,, ,, Tewkesbury	. . . .	126
,, ,, Holy Trinity, Stow-on-the-Wold	. . . .	126
Social and Economic History . .	By Miss RUTH F. BUTLER, Oxford Honour School of Modern History . . .	127
Table of Population, 1801–1901 . .	By GEORGE S. MINCHIN	173
Industries		
Introduction	By Miss R. F. BUTLER and Miss C. VIOLET BUTLER, Oxford Honour School of Modern History	189
Wool	By Miss R. F. BUTLER . . .	193
Waterproofs, Ropes, and other Textiles .	,, ,, . . .	199
Timber, etc.	By Miss C. V. BUTLER . . .	199
Engineering and Metal Industries .	By Miss R. F. BUTLER . . .	202
Bell-Founding	,, ,, . . .	204
Pins	By Miss C. V. BUTLER . . .	206
Printing and Paper . . .	By Miss R. F. BUTLER . . .	208
Leather	,, ,, . . .	209
Soap and Chemicals . . .	,, ,, . . .	210
Milling, Malting, and Brewing . .	,, ,, . . .	211
Sugar and Chocolate . . .	,, ,, . . .	212
Glass, Pottery, Bricks, and Building Materials	,, ,, . . .	213
Handicrafts	,, ,, . . .	215
Mining	By GEORGE R. LEWIS, Ph.D., and C. H. VELLACOTT, B.A.	215
Agriculture	By ROBERT ANDERSON, F.S.I. . .	239
Forestry	By J. NISBET, D.Oec., and C. H. VELLACOTT, B.A. .	263
Sport, Ancient and Modern . .	Edited by E. D. CUMING	
Stag-Hunting	By H. S. KENNEDY SKIPTON . .	287
Fox-Hunting .		
The Berkeley Hunt . .	By H. O. LLOYD BAKER . .	288
The Cotteswold . .	By H. S. KENNEDY SKIPTON . .	290
The North Cotteswold .	,, ,, . .	292
The Vale of White Horse (Cirencester)	,, ,, . .	293
Harriers	,, ,, . .	295
Coursing	By J. W. BOURNE . . .	295
Racing	By T. J. LONGWORTH . . .	296
Falconry	By CHARLES A. WITCHELL . .	299
Shooting	By the Revd. A. R. WINNINGTON INGRAM, M.A.	299
Wild-fowling	By W. LOCK MELLERSH . . .	301
Angling	By J. W. WILLIS-BUND, M.A., LL.B., F.S.A.	303

PAGE

Golf . . . . . By A. Hoare 304
Athletics . . . . By J. E. Fowler Dixon . . . 306
    The Cotteswold Games . By E. D. Cuming 306
Cricket . . . . By Sir Home Gordon, Bart. . . 306
Schools . . . . By A. F. Leach, M.A., F.S.A. . . 313

VOLUME SIX

PAGE

Dedication v
Contents ix
List of Illustrations xi
List of Maps and Plans xiii
Editorial Note xv
Classes of Documents in the Public Record
    Office used xvii
Gloucestershire Records Office Accumulations xix
Note on Abbreviations xxi
Topography . . . . *Where not otherwise stated by* C. R. Elrington and
    Kathleen Morgan. *Architectural descriptions*
    compiled or revised by Margaret Tomlinson

  Slaughter Hundred 1
    Adlestrop 8
    Great and Little Barrington 16
    Bledington 27
    Bourton-on-the-Water . . By C. R. Elrington and Helen O'Neil . 33
    Broadwell 49
    Clapton 59
    Condicote 63
    Eyford 72
    Naunton 76
    Oddington 87
    Great Rissington 98
    Little Rissington 106
    Wick Rissington 114
    Sherborne 120
    Lower Slaughter 128
    Upper Slaughter 134
    Stow-on-the-Wold 142
    Lower Swell 165
    Westcote 172
    Windrush 178
  Tewkesbury Hundred, upper division 185
    Alderton with Dixton 189
    Bourton-on-the-Hill 197
    Clifford Chambers 207
    Lower Lemington 216
    Prescott 220
    Stanway 223
    Great Washbourne 232
  Westminster Hundred, upper division 238
    Moreton-in-Marsh 240
    Todenham 250
Index 259

VOLUME EIGHT

	PAGE
Dedication	v
Contents	ix
List of Illustrations	xi
List of Maps and Plans	xiii
Editorial Note	xv
Classes of Documents in the Public Record Office used	xvii
Gloucestershire Records Office Accumulations	xix
Note on Abbreviations	xxi
Topography *Where not otherwise stated by* C. R. ELRINGTON, KATHLEEN MORGAN, and N. M. HERBERT; architectural descriptions compiled or revised by MARGARET TOMLINSON	
Cleeve Hundred	1
Bishop's Cleeve	2
Deerhurst Hundred	26
Coln St. Dennis	28
Deerhurst	34
Elmstone Hardwicke	50
Leigh	60
Prestbury	67
Preston on Stour	81
Staverton	89
Tirley	95
Woolstone	105
Tewkesbury Borough *Domestic buildings by* S. R. JONES	110
Tewkesbury Hundred, lower division	170
Ashchurch	172
Boddington	188
Forthampton	196
Kemerton	209
Oxenton	220
Tredington	228
Walton Cardiff	236
Tibblestone Hundred	243
Ashton under Hill	245
Beckford *By* A. CROSSLEY	250
Hinton on the Green	262
Westminster Hundred, lower division	269
Corse	271
Hasfield	282
Index	291
Corrigenda to Volume VI	311

HAMPSHIRE
AND THE ISLE OF WIGHT

VOLUME ONE

	PAGE
Dedication	v
The Advisory Council of the Victoria History	vii
General Advertisement	vii
The Hampshire and Isle of Wight County Committee	xiii

CONTENTS OF VOLUMES: HANTS I

		PAGE
Contents		xv
List of Illustrations		xvii
Preface		xix
Natural History	Edited by AUBYN TREVOR-BATTYE, M.A., F.L.S.	
Introduction to Natural History .	By A. TREVOR-BATTYE, M.A., F.L.S. . .	1
Geology	By CLEMENT REID, F.R.S., F.L.S., F.G.S. .	11
Palaeontology	By RICHARD L. LYDEKKER, B.A., F.R.S., F.G.S. .	41
Botany	Edited by FREDERICK TOWNSEND, M.A., F.L.S. .	47
Rubi and Rosae (*Brambles and Roses*) .	By the Revd. W. MOYLE ROGERS, F.L.S. . .	69
Musci and Hepaticae (*Mosses and Liverworts*) . .	By H. N. DIXON, F.L.S.	71
Lichenes (*Lichens*) . . .	By W. H. WILKINSON, F.L.S. . . .	75
Algae	By E. M. HOLMES, F.L.S. . . .	79
Fungi	By the Revd. W. L. W. EYRE . . .	82
Marine Zoology	By WALTER GARSTANG, M.A., F.L.S. . .	89
Mollusca (*Whelks, Oysters, Snails, etc.*) .	By B. B. WOODWARD, F.G.S., F.R.M.S., and L. E. ADAMS, B.A.	103
Insecta (*Insects*) . . .	Edited by HERBERT GOSS, F.L.S., F.E.S. .	109
Orthoptera (*Grasshoppers, etc.*) .	By MALCOLM BURR, F.Z.S., F.E.S. . .	109
Neuroptera (*Dragonflies*) and Trichoptera (*Caddis-flies*) . . .	By ROBERT MCLACHLAN, F.R.S., F.L.S., J. J. F. X. KING, F.E.S., and KENNETH MORTON, F.E.S. .	112
Hymenoptera, Aculeata (*Bees, etc.*) .	By EDWARD SAUNDERS, F.L.S. . .	114
Hymenoptera, Phytophaga .	By ETHEL F. CHAWNER, F.E.S. . .	118
Coleoptera (*Beetles*) . .	By the Revd. Canon FOWLER, M.A., F.L.S., and JAMES J. WALKER, R.N., F.L.S. . .	121
Lepidoptera, Rhopalocera (*Butterflies*) .	By HERBERT GOSS, F.L.S., F.E.S., assisted by W. H. B. FLETCHER, M.A., F.E.S., and Capt. SAVILE REID, F.E.S., late R.E. . .	130
Lepidoptera, Heterocera (*Moths*)	By PERCY M. BRIGHT, F.E.S., assisted by EUSTACE R. BANKES, M.A., F.E.S., CHAS. G. BARRETT, F.E.S., and W. H. B. FLETCHER, M.A., F.E.S. .	134
Diptera (*Flies*) . . .	By FREDERICK C. ADAMS, F.E.S. . .	154
Hemiptera Heteroptera (*Bugs*) .	By EDWARD SAUNDERS, F.L.S. . .	160
Hemiptera Homoptera (*Cicadas*) .	By JAMES EDWARDS, F.E.S. . . .	162
Myriapoda (*Centipedes, etc.*) .	By R. I. POCOCK	163
Arachnida (*Spiders, Scorpions, etc.*) .	By F. O. PICKARD-CAMBRIDGE, M.A. .	165
Crustacea (*Crabs, Lobsters, etc.*) .	By the Revd. T. R. R. STEBBING, M.A., F.R.S. F.L.S.	185
Pisces (*Fishes*) . . .	By G. A. BOULENGER, F.R.S., F.Z.S. .	197
Amphibia (*Amphibians*) and Reptilia (*Reptiles*) . . .	,, ,, .	204
Aves (*Birds*) . . .	By EDMUND G. B. MEADE-WALDO, F.Z.S., M.B.O.U.	208
Mammalia (*Mammals*) .	By A. TREVOR-BATTYE, M.A., F.L.S., assisted by the Hon. GERALD LASCELLES, B.A., F.Z.S. .	239
Early Man	By W. BOYD DAWKINS, M.A., F.R.S., F.S.A. .	253
Romano-British Remains . .	By F. HAVERFIELD, M.A., F.S.A. . .	265
Silchester	By GEORGE E. FOX, M.A., F.S.A., and W. H. ST. JOHN HOPE, M.A. . .	350
Anglo-Saxon Remains . .	By REGINALD A. SMITH, B.A. . .	373
Introduction to the Hampshire Domesday .	By J. HORACE ROUND, M.A. . .	399
The Text of the Hampshire Domesday .	,, ,, . . .	448
The Winchester Survey . . .	,, ,, . . .	527

VOLUME TWO

		PAGE
Dedication		v
Contents		ix
List of Illustrations		xi

CONTENTS OF VOLUMES: HANTS II

	PAGE
Preface	xiii
List of Abbreviations	xv
Ecclesiastical History . . . By the Revd. J. C. Cox, LL.D., F.S.A. . .	1
Religious Houses . . . . ,, ,,	
Introduction	104
Priory of St. Swithun, Winchester	108
New Minster, or the Abbey of Hyde	116
Nunnaminster, or the Abbey of St. Mary, Winchester	122
Abbey of Romsey	126
,, ,, Wherwell	132
,, ,, Quarr	137
,, ,, Beaulieu	140
,, ,, Netley	146
Priory of Wintney	149
,, ,, Christchurch Twyneham	152
,, ,, St. Denis, Southampton	160
,, ,, Southwick	164
,, ,, Breamore	168
,, ,, Mottisfont	172
,, ,, Selborne	175
Oratory of Barton	180
Abbey of Titchfield	181
Preceptory of Baddesley or Godsfield	187
Dominicans of Winchester	189
Franciscans of Winchester	191
Austin Friars of Winchester	192
Carmelites of Winchester	193
Franciscans of Southampton	193
Hospital of St. Cross, near Winchester	193
,, ,, St. Mary Magdalene, Winchester	197
Hospital of St. John Baptist, Winchester	200
,, ,, St. Julian or God's House, Southampton	202
Hospital of St. Mary Magdalene, Southampton	205
God's House, Portsmouth	206
Hospital of St. John Baptist, Basingstoke	208
,, ,, Fordingbridge	211
College of Marwell	211
,, ,, St. Elizabeth, Winchester	212
Chapel and Gild of the Holy Ghost, Basingstoke	214
Priory of St. Helen	215
,, ,, Hayling	216
,, ,, Hamble	221
,, ,, Andwell	223
,, ,, St. Cross, I. of Wight	225
,, ,, Monk Sherborne	226
,, ,, Ellingham	229
,, ,, Carisbrooke	230
,, ,, Appledurcombe	231
Early Christian Art and Inscriptions . By J. Romilly Allen, F.S.A. . .	233
History of Schools . . . By A. F. Leach, M.A., F.S.A. . .	250
Forestry and the New Forest . . By J. Nisbet, D.Oec., and The Hon. Gerald W. Lascelles	409

CONTENTS OF VOLUMES: HANTS II

		PAGE
Topography: Alton Hundred	Compiled by W. J. HARDY, F.S.A.	
Alton Hundred		471
Alton	Architectural description of Church, by W. H. ST. JOHN HOPE, M.A.	473
Binsted	,, ,, ,,	483
Bramshott	Architectural description of Church, by C. R. PEERS, M.A., F.S.A.	491
Chawton	Architectural description of Church, by W. H. ST. JOHN HOPE, M.A.	496
,,	Architectural description of Manor House, by C. R. PEERS, M.A., F.S.A.	496
Froyle	Architectural description of Church, by W. H. ST. JOHN HOPE, M.A.	501
Greatham	Architectural description of Church, by C. R. PEERS, M.A., F.S.A.	506
Hartley Mauditt	Architectural description of Church, by W. H. ST. JOHN HOPE, M.A.	508
Holybourne and Neatham	Architectural description of Church, by C. R. PEERS, M.A., F.S.A.	511
Kingsley	Architectural description of Church, by W. H. ST. JOHN HOPE, M.A.	515
East Worldham	,, ,, ,,	518
West Worldham	,, ,, ,,	521
Index of Parishes in Topographical Maps		524

VOLUME THREE

		PAGE
Dedication		v
Contents		ix
List of Illustrations and Maps		xiii
Editorial Note		xvii
Topography	General descriptions and manorial descents compiled under the superintendence of the General Editor; Architectural descriptions by C. R. PEERS, M.A., F.S.A.; Heraldic drawings and blazon by the Revd. E. E. DORLING, M.A.; Charities from information supplied by J. W. OWSLEY, I.S.O., late Official Trustee of Charitable Funds	
Selborne Hundred	General descriptions and manorial descents by Miss A. A. LOCKE, Oxford Honours School of Modern History	
Introduction		3
Selborne		4
Empshott		17
Faringdon		20
Hawkley		23
Newton Valence		24
East Tisted		30
Bishop's Sutton Hundred	General descriptions and manorial descents by Miss F. BROUGH, M.A. (Lond.)	
Introduction		37
Bighton		38
Bishop's Sutton		41
Bramdean		45
Headley		51
Ropley		55
West Tisted		58

CONTENTS OF VOLUMES: HANTS III

PAGE

East Meon Hundred . . . General descriptions and manorial descents by Miss
F. Brough, M.A. (Lond.)

Introduction 63
East Meon 64
Froxfield 76
Steep with North and South Ambersham 77
Finchdean Hundred . . . General descriptions and manorial descents by Miss
F. Brough, M.A. (Lond.)

Introduction 82
Blendworth 84
Buriton 85
Catherington 94
Chalton with Idsworth 102
Clanfield 110
Petersfield Borough with Sheet 111
Havant Parish and Liberty . . General descriptions and manorial descents by Miss
L. J. Redstone 122

Bosmere Hundred . . . ,, ,, ,, . . . 128
Introduction 128
Hayling Island, including North and
South Hayling 129
Warblington with Emsworth 134
Portsdown Hundred with the Liberties of General descriptions and manorial descents by Miss
Portsmouth and Alverstoke . . L. J. Redstone, Miss G. A. Laughton, and Miss
E. M. Hartland

Introduction 140
Bedhampton 142
Boarhunt 144
Farlington with Drayton 148
Portchester 151
Southwick 161
Wymering with Cosham and Hilsea 165
Widley 171
Liberty of Portsmouth and Portsea
Island 172
Liberty of Alverstoke with Gosport 202
Fareham Hundred . . . General descriptions and manorial descents by Miss
A. M. Hendy

Introduction 209
Fareham 210
Titchfield Hundred . . . General descriptions and manorial descents by Miss
A. M. Hendy

Introduction 217
Rowner 218
Titchfield 220
Wickham 233
Hambledon Hundred . . . General descriptions and manorial descents by Miss
G. A. Laughton

Introduction 237
Hambledon with Denmead, Chidden,
Glidden, and Ervill's Exton 238
Meonstoke Hundred . . . General descriptions and manorial descents by Miss
F. Brough, M.A. (Lond.)

Introduction 245
Corhampton 246
Meonstoke 254
Soberton 257
Warnford 268

CONTENTS OF VOLUMES: HANTS III

PAGE

Bishop's Waltham Hundred . . General descriptions and manorial descents by Miss CICELY WILMOT, Oxford Honours School of Modern History

Introduction 274
Bishop's Waltham 276
Bursledon 283
Droxford 284
Durley 288
Exbury with Lepe 290
Fawley 292
St. Mary Extra, otherwise Weston 297
Upham 299

Fawley Hundred with the Liberty of Alresford . . . . General descriptions and manorial descents by Miss G. A. LAUGHTON and Miss A. A. LOCKE, Oxford Honours School of Modern History

Introduction 302
Old Alresford 304
Avington 306
Bishopstoke 308
Cheriton with Beauworth 311
Chilcomb 314
Easton 317
Exton 319
Hinton Ampner 321
Kilmeston 323
Martyr Worthy with Chilland 325
Medsted 327
Morestead 329
Ovington 331
Owslebury with Baybridge 332
Privett 336
Tichborne 336
Twyford 339
West Meon 342
Wield 345
Winnall 348
Liberty of Alresford . . . By Miss F. BROUGH, M.A. (Lond.) . . . 348

Bermondspit Hundred . . . General descriptions and manorial descents by Miss E. G. BRODIE and Miss A. M. HENDY

Introduction 355
Dummer with Kempshot 357
Ellisfield 360
Farleigh Wallop 364
Herriard 366
Nutley 369
Preston Candover 371
South Warnborough 378
Upton Grey 382
Weston Corbett 386

Micheldever Hundred . . . General descriptions and manorial descents by Miss L. J. REDSTONE

Introduction 389
Micheldever 390
Northington 394
Popham 397
East Stratton 399

PAGE

Buddlesgate Hundred . . . General descriptions and manorial descents by Miss A. A. LOCKE, Oxford Honours School of Modern History, and Miss F. BROUGH, M.A. (Lond.)

Introduction 401
Chilbolton 403
Compton 406
Crawley with Hunton 408
Houghton 413
Hursley 417
Littleton 422
Michelmersh 423
Millbrook 427
Nursling 433
Otterbourne 440
Sparsholt with Lainston 444
Stoke Charity 447
Weeke or Wyke 451
Wonston 453

Mainsbridge Hundred . . . General descriptions and manorial descents by Miss A. R. GRUNDY

Introduction 462
North Baddesley 463
Botley 465
Chilworth 468
Hamble-le-Rice 469
Hound with Netley . . . (Plan of Netley Abbey by HAROLD BRAKSPEAR, F.S.A.) 472
North Stoneham 478
South Stoneham 481

Borough of Southampton . . . History of borough by the Revd. J. SILVESTER DAVIES, M.A., F.S.A., architectural descriptions by C. R. PEERS, M.A., F.S.A., and the Revd. J. SILVESTER DAVIES, M.A., F.S.A. . . . 490

VOLUME FOUR

PAGE

Dedication v
Contents ix
List of Illustrations xv
List of Maps xx
Editorial Note xxi

Topography . . . . General descriptions and manorial descents compiled under the superintendence of the General Editor; Architectural descriptions by J. W. BLOE, J. MURRAY KENDALL and S. F. BEEKE LANE, under the superintendence of C. R. PEERS, M.A., F.S.A.; Heraldic drawings and blazon by the Revd. E. E. DORLING, M.A., F.S.A.; Charities from information supplied by J. W. OWSLEY, I.S.O., late Official Trustee of Charitable Funds

Crondall Hundred . . . General descriptions and manorial descents by Miss A. M. McKILLIAM, M.A. (St. Andrews)

Introduction 1
Aldershot 2
Crondall 5
Farnborough 15
Long Sutton 18
Yateley 20

CONTENTS OF VOLUMES: HANTS IV

PAGE

Bentley Liberty and Parish . . General descriptions and manorial descents by Miss
M. Perry, B.A. (R.U.I.) . . . 27

Holdshot Hundred . . . General descriptions and manorial descents by Miss
F. Brough, M.A. (Lond.)

Introduction 31
Eversley 32
Hartley Wespall 42
Heckfield 44
Silchester 51
Stratfieldsaye 57
Stratfield Turgis 63

Odiham Hundred . . . General descriptions and manorial descents by Miss
O. M. Moger, Miss F. Kennedy, and Miss K. M.
Upcott

Introduction 66
Bentworth 68
Dogmersfield 72
Elvetham 74
Greywell or Grewell 76
Hartley Wintney 79
Lasham 81
Liss 84
Odiham 87
Rotherwick 99
Shalden 101
Sherfield-upon-Loddon 103
Weston Patrick 108
Winchfield 109

Basingstoke Hundred . . . General descriptions and manorial descents by Miss
F. Brough, M.A. (Lond.)

Introduction 113
Basing or Old Basing 115
Basingstoke . . . (By Miss M. Curtis, Classical Tripos) . . 127
Bramley 140
Cliddesden 145
Eastrop 147
Maplederwell 149
Nately Scures 153
Newnham 156
Sherborne St. John 158
Steventon 171
Tunworth 174
Up Nately 176
Winslade with Kempshott 179

Mainsborough Hundred . . . General descriptions and manorial descents by Miss
F. Kennedy

Introduction 182
Brown Candover 183
Chilton Candover 184
Woodmancott 186

Bountisborough Hundred . . General descriptions and manorial descents by Miss
A. M. McKilliam, M.A. (St. Andrews)

Introduction 188
Godsfield 189
Itchen Abbas 191
Itchen Stoke with Abbotstone 192
Swarraton 195

CONTENTS OF VOLUMES: HANTS IV

PAGE

Overton Hundred . . . General descriptions and manorial descents by Miss F. BROUGH, M.A. (Lond.)

Introduction 197
Ashe 198
Bradley 202
Deane 205
Laverstoke 208
Overton 210
Tadley 219
North Waltham 221
Chuteley Hundred . . . General descriptions and manorial descents by Miss M. HOLLINGS, Oxford Honours School of Modern History

Introduction 223
Church Oakley 224
Hannington 229
Monk Sherborne 231
Wootton St. Lawrence 239
Worting 243
Kingsclere Hundred . . . General descriptions and manorial descents by Miss F. BROUGH, M.A. (Lond.)

Introduction 245
Ewhurst 247
Kingsclere 249
Litchfield 267
Wolverton 270
Evingar Hundred . . . General descriptions and manorial descents by Miss K. M. UPCOTT

Introduction 273
Ashmansworth 274
Baughurst 275
Burghclere 277
Freefolk 282
Highclere 285
Hurstbourne Priors 287
Newtown . . . . History of the Borough by CHARLES H. VELLACOTT, B.A. 292
St. Mary Bourne 295
Whitchurch 299
East Woodhay 305
Pastrow Hundred . . . General descriptions and manorial descents by Miss F. BROUGH, M.A. (Lond.)

Introduction 308
Combe 310
Crux Easton 311
Faccombe 314
Hurstbourne Tarrant 319
Linkenholt 324
Tangley 326
Vernhams Dean 329
Woodcott 331
Andover Hundred . . . General descriptions and manorial descents by FRANCIS L. BICKLEY

Introduction 333
Abbotts Ann 334
Amport 337

CONTENTS OF VOLUMES: HANTS IV

PAGE

Andover with Foxcott 345
Appleshaw 358
Upper Clatford 359
Fyfield 366
Grateley 369
Kimpton 372
Knight's Enham 377
Monxton 379
Penton Mewsey 381
Quarley 385
Thruxton 387
Tidworth, South 391
Weyhill with Penton Grafton 394
Wherwell Hundred . . . General descriptions and manorial descents by
FRANCIS L. BICKLEY

Introduction 400
Bullington 402
Goodworth Clatford 403
Longparish 406
Tufton or Tuckington 409
Wherwell with Westover 411
Barton Stacey Hundred . . . General descriptions and manorial descents by Miss
M. HOLLINGS, Oxford Honours School of Modern
History

Introduction 415
Barton Stacey 417
Colemore 423
Headbourne Worthy 426
Kings Worthy 430
Pamber 433
Priors Dean 436
King's Somborne Hundred . . . General descriptions and manorial descents by Miss
M. PERRY, B.A. (R.U.I.)

Introduction 438
Ashley 440
Farley Chamberlayne 443
Leckford 446
Longstock 449
Romsey Extra and Infra 452
King's Somborne 469
Little Somborne 480
Stockbridge 483
Timsbury 486
Thorngate Hundred . . . General descriptions and manorial descents by Miss
M. HOLLINGS, Miss O. M. MOGER, and Miss M.
PERRY

Introduction 489
Bossington 491
Broughton with Frenchmoor 493
East Dean 498
Lockerley 500
Mottisfont 503
Sherfield English 510
Shipton Bellinger 512
East Tytherley 515
West Tytherley with Buckholt 519
Nether Wallop 525

PAGE

Over Wallop 530
East Wellow with Dunwood and Embley 535
Melchet Park 540
Plaitford 542
Redbridge Hundred . . . General descriptions and manorial descents by Miss
O. M. MOGER

Introduction 544
Eling 546
Fordingbridge Hundred . . . General descriptions and manorial descents by Miss
O. M. MOGER and Miss H. M. POWELL

Introduction 559
North Charford with South Charford 560
Ellingham 563
Fordingbridge with Godshill, Broomy
Lodge, Linford, Picked Post, and
Shobley 567
Hale 577
Ibsley 579
Rockbourne 581
South Damerham 586
Martin 592
Whitsbury 594
Breamore Liberty . . . General descriptions and manorial descents by Miss
O. M. MOGER

Introduction 596
Breamore 596
Ringwood Hundred . . . General descriptions and manorial descents by
FRANCIS L. BICKLEY

Introduction 603
Harbridge 604
Ringwood 606
New Forest Hundred . . . General descriptions and manorial descents by Miss
A. M. HENDY

Introduction 615
Boldre 616
Bramshaw 623
Brockenhurst 626
Linwood 629
Lyndhurst 630
Minstead . . . . (By Miss A. A. LOCKE, Oxford Honours School of
Modern History) 635
Lymington Borough . . . By Miss H. L. E. GARBETT 639
Beaulieu Liberty . . . By FRANCIS L. BICKLEY 650
(Description and plan of Beaulieu Abbey by HAROLD
BRAKSPEAR, F.S.A.)
Dibden Liberty . . . By FRANCIS L. BICKLEY 655

VOLUME FIVE

PAGE

Dedication v
Contents ix
List of Illustrations xiii
List of Maps xvii
Editorial Note xix

CONTENTS OF VOLUMES: HANTS V

PAGE

Topography . . . . General descriptions and manorial descents compiled under the superintendence of WILLIAM PAGE, F.S.A., the General Editor. Architectural descriptions of Winchester, Christchurch, and Westover by C. C. DURSTON, J. MURRAY KENDALL, S. F. BEEKE LANE, and JOHN QUEKETT, B.A., under the superintendence of C. R. PEERS, M.A., F.S.A., H.M. Inspector of Ancient Monuments. Architectural descriptions of the Isle of Wight by P. G. STONE, F.S.A. Heraldic drawings and blazon by the Revd. E. E. DORLING, M.A., F.S.A. Charities from information supplied by J. W. OWSLEY, I.S.O., late Official Trustee of Charitable Funds

Winchester . . . . History of Borough and manorial descents by A. AUDREY LOCKE, Oxford Honours School of Modern History. History of St. Giles' Fair and the Ancient Custom and Soke of Winchester by C. H. VELLACOTT, B.A. Architectural descriptions of Wolvesey Castle, and Winchester Monastic Buildings by C. R. PEERS, M.A., F.S.A. Architectural description of Winchester Cathedral by C. R. PEERS, M.A., F.S.A., and HAROLD BRAKSPEAR, F.S.A. Architectural description of Winchester College by A. F. LEACH, M.A., F.S.A. . . 1

Christchurch Hundred . . . General descriptions and manorial descents by JOHN HARLEY, M.A., and A. AUDREY LOCKE, Oxford Honours School of Modern History

Introduction 81
Christchurch . . . . Architectural descriptions of Town, Castle, and Priory Church by C. R. PEERS, M.A., F.S.A. . 83
Hordle 110
Milford 115
Milton 124
Sopley 127
Westover Liberty with parishes of Holdenhurst and Bournemouth . General descriptions and manorial descents by JOHN HARLEY, M.A. 133
East Medine Liberty or Hundred . General descriptions and manorial descents by P. G. STONE, F.S.A.

Introduction 138
Arreton 139
Binstead . . . . Architectural description of Quarr Abbey by S. C. KAINES-SMITH, M.A. . . . 151
Bonchurch 155
Brading 156
Godshill 170
Newchurch 177
Niton 187
St. Helens 189
St. Lawrence 193
Shanklin 195
Whippingham 197
Whitwell 202
Wootton 204
Yaverland 206
West Medine Liberty or Hundred . General descriptions and manorial descents by P. G. STONE, F.S.A., MARJORY HOLLINGS, Oxford Honours School of Modern History, HILDA M. LIGHT, OLIVE M. MOGER, and KATHLEEN UPCOTT

Introduction 209
Brighstone or Brixton 211
Brook 215

CONTENTS OF VOLUMES: HANTS V

			PAGE
Calbourne	. . . .		217
Carisbrooke	. . . .		221
Chale .	. . . .		235
Freshwater	. . . .		240
Gatcombe	. . . .		246
Kingston	. . . .		249
Mottistone	. . . .		251
Newport	. . . .	History of the Borough by OLIVE M. MOGER	253
Newtown	. . . .	,, ,, ,,	265
Northwood	. . . .		268
Shalfleet	. . . .		272
Shorwell	. . . .		278
Thorley	. . . .		284
Yarmouth	. . . .	History of the Borough by OLIVE M. MOGER	286
Political History	. . . .	By A. AUDREY LOCKE, Oxford Honour School of Modern History	293
Maritime History	. . .	By L. G. CARR LAUGHTON	359
Social and Economic History	. .	By VIOLET M. SHILLINGTON, Hist. Tripos, D.Sc. (Econ.)	409
Table of Population, 1801–1901	.	By G. S. MINCHIN	435
Industries			
Introduction	. . .	By ETHEL M. HEWITT . . .	451
Quarrying	. . .	By ETHEL M. HEWITT and C. H. VELLACOTT, B.A.	462
Iron and Ironworks	. .	By ETHEL M. HEWITT . . .	463
Brickmaking	. . .	,, ,, . . .	465
Fisheries	. . .	,, ,, . . .	466
Salt	. . .	By C. H. VELLACOTT, B.A. . . .	469
Malting and Brewing	. .	By ETHEL M. HEWITT . . .	472
Cider	. . . .	By C. H. VELLACOTT, B.A. . . .	474
Textiles .	. . .	,, ,, . . .	475
Paper-making	. .	By ETHEL M. HEWITT . . .	489
Glass-making and Pottery	.	,, ,, . . .	490
Agriculture .	. . .	By W. H. R. CURTLER . . .	493
Sport, Ancient and Modern	.	Edited by the Revd. E. E. DORLING, M.A., F.S.A.	
Fox-hunting	. .	By FRANK BONNETT . . .	513
The Hampshire Hunt .	. . . .		514
The Vine	. . . .		520
The Hambledon	. . . .		523
The Hursley .	. . . .		528
The Tedworth .	. . . .		531
The Garth	. . . .		533
The Isle of Wight	. . . .		535
Harriers .	. . .	By FRANK BONNETT . . .	536
Beagles .	. . .	,, ,, . . .	542
Racing .	. . .	,, ,, . . .	543
Shooting	. . .	,, ,, . . .	556
Angling .	. . .	By the late WALTER H. POPE . . .	560
Sport in the New Forest .	.	By the Hon. GERALD LASCELLES . . .	565
Cricket .	. . .	By A. R. MALDEN, M.A., F.S.A. . . .	574

HEREFORDSHIRE
VOLUME ONE

PAGE

Dedication v
The Advisory Council of the Victoria History vii
General Advertisement vii
Contents xiii
List of Illustrations and Maps xv
Preface xix
Table of Abbreviations xxi
Natural History
  Geology . . . . . By Linsdall Richardson, F.G.S. . . 1
  Palaeontology . . . . By R. Lydekker, F.R.S., F.L.S., F.G.S. . . 35
  Botany
    Introduction . . . . By the Revd. Augustin Ley, M.A. . . . 39
    Botanical Districts . . . ,, ,, . . 42
    Cryptogamia Vascularia
      Filices (*Ferns and Fern Allies*) . ,, ,, . 53
      Equisetaceae and Lycopodiaceae . ,, ,, . . 54
    Musci (*Mosses*) . . . By the Revd. C. H. Binstead, M.A. . 54
    Fungi . . . . . By Carleton Rea, B.C.L., M.A. . . 56
  Zoology
    Molluscs . . . . By B. B. Woodward, F.L.S., F.G.S., F.R.M.S. . 77
    Insects . . . . Edited by the Revd. Canon W. W. Fowler, M.A., D.Sc., F.L.S., F.E.S. . . . 80

      Orthoptera (*Earwigs, Grasshoppers, etc.*) and Neuroptera (*Dragon-flies, Lace-wings, etc.*) . By W. J. Lucas, B.A., F.E.S. . . 80
      Coleoptera (*Beetles*) . . By the Revd. Canon W. W. Fowler, M.A., D.Sc., F.L.S., F.E.S. 80
      Lepidoptera (*Butterflies and Moths*) . By J. H. Wood, M.B. . . . 85
      Diptera (*Flies*) . . . ,, ,, . . . 96
    Spiders . . . . By the Revd. O. Pickard-Cambridge, M.A., F.R.S. 109
    Crustaceans . . . By the Revd. T. R. R. Stebbing, M.A., F.R.S., F.Z.S. 112
    Fishes . . . . By J. F. Symonds 122
    Reptiles and Batrachians . . By Gerald R. Leighton, M.D., F.R.S.E. . 127
    Birds . . . . By E. Cambridge Phillips, M.B.O.U., M.P.I.O.C. 130
    Mammals . . . By Miss B. Lindsay . . . 149
Early Man . . . . By George Clinch, F.G.S., F.S.A. Scot. . 157
Romano-British Herefordshire . . By H. B. Walters, M.A., F.S.A. . . 167
Ancient Earthworks . . . Compiled by the late I. Chalkley Gould, F.S.A., principally from plans and notes by the Revd. E. A. Downman 199
  Offa's Dike in Herefordshire . By James G. Wood, M.A., F.G.S., F.S.A. . 258
Introduction to the Herefordshire Domesday By J. Horace Round, M.A., LL.D. . 263
Translation of the Herefordshire Domesday 309
Political History . . . By E. I. Carlyle, M.A. . . 347
Agriculture . . . . By W. H. R. Curtler . . . 407

HERTFORDSHIRE
VOLUME ONE

		PAGE
Dedication		v
The Advisory Council of the Victoria History		vii
General Advertisement		vii
The Hertfordshire County Committee		xiii
Contents		xv
List of Illustrations		xvii
Preface		xix
Natural History		
Geology	By John Hopkinson, F.L.S., F.G.S., Assoc. Inst. C.E.	1
Climate	,, ,, ,, ,,	33
Palaeontology	By Richard Lydekker, B.A., F.R.S., F.G.S.	41
Botany	Edited by John Hopkinson, F.L.S., F.G.S.	
Introduction	By John Hopkinson, F.L.S., F.G.S.	43
Phanerogamia (*Flowering plants*)	,, ,,	44
Notes on the Botanical Districts	,, ,,	51
Cryptogamia (*Non-flowering plants*)	,, ,,	60
Filices (*Ferns*)	,, ,,	61
Equisetaceae (*Horsetails*)	,, ,,	62
Lycopodiaceae (*Clubmosses*)	,, ,,	62
Musci and Hepaticae (*Mosses and Liverworts*)	By A. E. Gibbs, F.L.S., F.R.H.S.	62
Characeae (*Stoneworts*)	By John Hopkinson, F.L.S., F.G.S.	65
Algae	,, ,,	66
Lichenes (*Lichens*)	,, ,,	69
Fungi	,, ,,	70
Mycetozoa	By James Saunders, A.L.S.	80
Zoology		
Mollusca (*Snails, etc.*)	By B. B. Woodward, F.G.S., F.R.M.S.	81
Insecta (*Insects*)	Edited by A. E. Gibbs, F.L.S., F.R.H.S.	
Introduction	By A. E. Gibbs, F.L.S., F.R.H.S.	83
Coleoptera (*Beetles*)	By E. G. Elliman	83
Lepidoptera (*Butterflies and Moths*)	By A. E. Gibbs, F.L.S., F.R.H.S.	110
Orthoptera (*Grasshoppers*) and Neuroptera (*Dragonflies*)	,, ,,	168
Trichoptera (*Caddisflies*) and Hymenoptera (*Bees, etc.*)	By A. E. Gibbs, F.L.S., F.R.H.S.	169
Diptera (*Flies*)	,, ,,	170
Hemiptera (*Bugs, etc.*) and Aphides	,, ,,	171
Arachnida (*Spiders, etc.*)	By F. O. Pickard-Cambridge, M.A.	171
Crustacea (*Crabs, etc.*)	By the Revd. T. R. R. Stebbing, M.A., F.R.S., F.L.S.	181
Pisces (*Fishes*)	By G. A. Boulenger, F.R.S., F.Z.S.	189
Reptilia and Batrachia (*Reptiles and Batrachians*)	By A. F. Crossman, F.L.S.	191
Aves (*Birds*)	,, ,,	193
Mammalia (*Mammals*)	,, ,,	217
Early Man	By Sir John Evans, K.C.B., F.R.S., etc.	223
Anglo-Saxon Remains	By Reginald A. Smith, B.A.	251
Introduction to the Hertfordshire Domesday	By J. Horace Round, M.A., D.L.	263
Text of the Hertfordshire Domesday	By the Revd. F. W. Ragg, M.A.	300
Sport, Ancient and Modern		
Introduction	By Charles T. Part, M.A., D.L., J.P.	345

H

			PAGE
Foxhunting	By Charles T. Part, M.A., D.L., J.P.	.	. 349
Hertfordshire Hounds . . .	,, ,,	.	. 350
Puckeridge Hounds . . .	,, ,,	.	. 352
Old Berkeley Hounds . . .	,, ,,	.	. 355
Harriers	,, ,,	.	. 357
Staghounds	,, ,,	.	. 358
Shooting	,, ,,	.	. 359
Fishing	,, ,,	.	. 361
Hawking	,, ,,	.	. 363
Steeplechasing	,, ,,	.	. 364
Racing	,, ,,	.	. 366
Coursing	,, ,,	.	. 368
Pugilism	,, ,,	.	. 369
Cockfighting	,, ,,	.	. 370
Bullbaiting	,, ,,	.	. 371
'Bob Grimston'	,, ,,	.	. 371
Cricket	By Home Gordon, assisted by J. Earl Norman, M.A., LL.D., C. J. Reid, M.A., P. H. Latham, M.A., and A. J. Garton .	.	. 372
Football	Edited by C. W. Alcock .	.	.
Association . . .	By A. J. Millar . .	.	. 381
Rugby . . .	By C. J. B. Marriott .	.	. 383
Index of the Hertfordshire Domesday		.	. 387

VOLUME TWO

		PAGE
Dedication		. v
Contents		. ix
List of Illustrations and Maps		. xiii
Editorial Note		. xvii
Table of Abbreviations		. xix
Political History . . .	By Miss M. E. Simkins . .	. I
Schools	By A. F. Leach, M.A., F.S.A.	
Introduction		. 47
St. Albans School		. 47
Stevenage School		. 69
Berkhampstead School		. 71
Chipping Barnet Free Grammar School		. 79
Bishop's Stortford Grammar School		. 81
Bishop's Stortford Nonconformist School		. 82
Aldenham Grammar School		. 82
Ware Free School		. 88
The Ware Side School		. 88
Hertford School		. 89
Buntingford Grammar School		. 94
Hitchin Free School		. 94
Stanstead Abbots Free Grammar School		. 95
Watford Endowed Schools		. 95
Christ's Hospital, Hertford		. 96
Cheshunt College		. 97
Haileybury East India College		. 97
Haileybury College		. 98
Elementary Schools founded before 1800		. 99

CONTENTS OF VOLUMES: HERTS. II

PAGE

Ancient Earthworks . . . By D. H. Montgomerie 103
Agriculture . . . . . By A. D. Hall, M.A. 129
Topography
Dacorum Hundred . . . General descriptions and manorial descents by W.
                          Page, F.S.A., Miss O. M. Moger, and Miss H.
                          Douglas-Irvine, M.A. (St. Andrews); Architectural
                          descriptions of churches by C. R. Peers, M.A.,
                          F.S.A., and architectural descriptions of houses by
                          A. Whitford Anderson, A.R.I.B.A.; Heraldic
                          drawings and blazon by the Revd. E. E. Dorling,
                          M.A.; Charities from information supplied by
                          J. W. Owsley, I.S.O.

   Introduction 141
   Aldbury 143
   Aldenham 149
   Berkhampstead St. Peter or Great
      Berkhampstead . . . (Plan and architectural description of Berkhampstead
                          Castle by C. R. Peers, M.A., F.S.A., and D. H.
                          Montgomerie) 162
   Bushey 179
   Caddington 187
   Flamstead 193
   Great Gaddesden 201
   Little Gaddesden . . . (Architectural description of Ashridge by C. R.
                          Peers, M.A., F.S.A.) 208
   Hemel Hempstead with Bovingdon and
      Flaunden 215
   Kensworth 231
   King's Langley . . . (Architectural description of remains of Friary by
                          A. Whitford Anderson, A.R.I.B.A.) . . 234
   Northchurch or Berkhampstead St. Mary 245
   North Mimms 251
   Puttenham 261
   Shenley . . . (Architectural descriptions by W. Page, F.S.A.) . 264
   Studham 274
   Tring with Long Marston 281
   Wheathampstead with Harpenden . (Architectural descriptions by W. Page, F.S.A.) . 294
   Wigginton 314
   Nettleden . . . (Architectural description by J. Murray Kendall) . 317
Cashio Hundred . . . General descriptions and manorial descents by W.
                          Page, F.S.A., Miss O. M. Moger, and Miss L. M.
                          Sanderson; Architectural descriptions of churches
                          by C. R. Peers, M.A., F.S.A., and architectural
                          descriptions of houses by A. Whitford Anderson,
                          A.R.I.B.A.; Heraldic drawings and blazon by the
                          Revd. E. E. Dorling, M.A.; Charities from
                          information supplied by J. W. Owsley, I.S.O.

   Introduction 319
   Abbot's Langley 323
   Barnet 329
   East Barnet 337
   Bramfield 343
   Codicote 345
   Elstree 349
   Hexton 352
   Newnham 355
   Northaw 357
   Norton 361
   Redbourn . . . (Architectural descriptions by W. Page, F.S.A.) . 364

PAGE

Rickmansworth . . . (Architectural descriptions of Moor Park and the
Bury by J. MURRAY KENDALL) . . . 371

Ridge . . . . (Architectural description by J. MURRAY KENDALL) . 386

St. Michael's . . . (Plan and architectural description of Gorhambury by
C. R. PEERS, M.A., F.S.A.) . . . 392

St. Paul's Walden 405

St. Peter's 412

St. Stephen's 424

Sandridge 432

Sarratt 438

Shephall 443

Watford 446

City of St. Alban 469

St. Albans Cathedral . . (Architectural descriptions by C. R. PEERS, M.A.,
F.S.A., and W. PAGE, F.S.A.) . . . 483

VOLUME THREE

PAGE

Dedication v

Contents ix

List of Illustrations xiii

List of Maps xx

Editorial Note xxi

Topography . . . . General descriptions and manorial descents compiled
under the superintendence of WILLIAM PAGE,
F.S.A., the General Editor; Heraldic drawings and
blazon by the Revd. E. E. DORLING, M.A., F.S.A.;
Charities from information supplied by J. W.
OWSLEY, I.S.O., late Official Trustee of Charitable
Funds

Hitchin Hundred . . . Architectural descriptions (Domestic) by A. WHITFORD
ANDERSON, A.R.I.B.A. (except Hitchin Priory
by S. C. KAINES-SMITH, M.A.). Architectural
descriptions (Ecclesiastical) by S. C. KAINES-SMITH,
M.A.

Introduction . . . . By LUCY M. SANDERSON I

Hitchin . . . . General descriptions and manorial descents by LUCY
M. SANDERSON 3

Ickleford . . . . ,, ,, ,, . 21

Ippollitts . . . . ,, ,, ,, . 25

Kimpton . . . . ,, ,, ,, . 29

King's Walden . . . . ,, ,, ,, . 33

Lilley . . . . ,, ,, ,, . 37

Offley . . . . ,, ,, ,, . 39

Pirton . . . . ,, ,, ,, . 44

Broadwater Hundred . . . Architectural descriptions (Domestic) by A. WHITFORD
ANDERSON, A.R.I.B.A. (except Hatfield House
by S. C. KAINES-SMITH, M.A.). Architectural
descriptions (Ecclesiastical) by S. C. KAINES-SMITH,
M.A.

Introduction . . . . By MABEL E. CHRISTIE, Hist. Tripos . . 52

Aston . . . . General descriptions and manorial descents by
MABEL E. CHRISTIE . . . 54

Ayot St. Lawrence or Great Ayot . ,, ,, ,, . 59

Ayot St. Peter . . . . ,, ,, ,, . 63

Baldock . . . . ,, ,, ,, . 65

Benington . . . . ,, ,, ,, . 73

CONTENTS OF VOLUMES: HERTS. III

PAGE

Datchworth	General descriptions and manorial descents by MABEL E. CHRISTIE	78
Digswell	,, ,, ,,	81
Graveley	,, ,, ,,	85
Hatfield or Bishop's Hatfield	,, ,, ,,	91
Knebworth	,, ,, ,,	111
Letchworth	,, ,, ,,	118
Great Munden	,, ,, ,,	124
Little Munden	,, ,, ,,	129
Sacombe	,, ,, ,,	136
Stevenage	,, ,, ,,	139
Totteridge	,, ,, ,,	148
Walkern	,, ,, ,,	151
Watton-at-Stone	,, ,, ,,	158
Welwyn	,, ,, ,,	165
Weston	,, ,, ,,	171
Willian	,, ,, ,,	177
Great or Much Wymondley	,, ,, ,,	181
Little Wymondley	,, ,, ,,	186
Odsey Hundred	Architectural descriptions (Domestic and Ecclesiastical) by A. WHITFORD ANDERSON, A.R.I.B.A. (except Ardeley Church by S. C. KAINES-SMITH, M.A.)	
Introduction	By LILIAN J. REDSTONE, B.A.	192
Ardeley	General descriptions and manorial descents by LILIAN J. REDSTONE, B.A.	194
Ashwell	General descriptions and manorial descents by CICELY WILMOT, Oxford Honours School of Modern History	199
Broadfield	General descriptions and manorial descents by MAUD F. EDWARDS, Oxford Honours School of Modern History	209
Bygrave	General descriptions and manorial descents by LILIAN J. REDSTONE, B.A.	211
Caldecote	General descriptions and manorial descents by LUCY M. SANDERSON	217
Clothall	General descriptions and manorial descents by LILIAN J. REDSTONE, B.A.	220
Cottered	General descriptions and manorial descents by MAUD F. EDWARDS	226
Hinxworth	,, ,, ,,	232
Kelshall	,, ,, ,,	240
Radwell	,, ,, ,,	244
Reed	,, ,, ,,	247
Royston	General descriptions and manorial descents by LILIAN J. REDSTONE, B.A.	253
Rushden	General descriptions and manorial descents by MAUD F. EDWARDS	265
Sandon	General descriptions and manorial descents by LUCY M. SANDERSON	270
Therfield	,, ,, ,,	276
Wallington	General descriptions and manorial descents by LILIAN J. REDSTONE, B.A.	284
Braughing Hundred	Architectural descriptions by A. WHITFORD ANDERSON, A.R.I.B.A.	
Introduction	By ALICE RAVEN	289
Bishop's Stortford	General descriptions and manorial descents by ALICE RAVEN	292
Braughing	,, ,, ,,	306

PAGE

Eastwick . . . . General descriptions and manorial descents by CICELY WILMOT, Oxford Honours School of Modern History 317

Gilston . . . General descriptions and manorial descents by ALICE RAVEN 319

Hunsdon . . . General descriptions and manorial descents by CICELY WILMOT 323

Sawbridgeworth . . . General descriptions and manorial descents by ALICE RAVEN 332

Standon . . . . ,, ,, ,, . 347
Stanstead Abbots . . . ,, ,, ,, . 366
Thorley . . . . ,, ,, ,, . 373
Thundridge . . . ,, ,, ,, . 377
Ware . . . . . ,, ,, ,, . 380
Westmill . . . . ,, ,, ,, . 397
Widford . . . . ,, ,, ,, . 402

Hertford Hundred . . . Architectural descriptions except where otherwise stated by A. WHITFORD ANDERSON, A.R.I.B.A.

Introduction . . . By LILIAN J. REDSTONE, B.A. . . . 407

Parts of All Saints' and St. John's, Hertford, including the liberties of Brickendon and Little Amwell . General descriptions and manorial descents by LILIAN J. REDSTONE, B.A. . . . 409

Great Amwell . . . . ,, ,, ,, . 414

Bayford . . . . General descriptions and manorial descents by MABEL E. CHRISTIE, Hist. Tripos . . 419

Bengeo . . . . General descriptions and manorial descents by ELEANOR J. B. REID, B.A. . . . 423

Little Berkhampstead . . . ,, ,, ,, . 427

Broxbourne with Hoddesdon . . General descriptions and manorial descents by MABEL E. CHRISTIE 430

Cheshunt St. Mary . . . General descriptions and manorial descents by ELEANOR J. B. REID, B.A. Architectural descriptions of Waltham Cross and Theobalds by S. C. KAINES-SMITH, M.A. 441

Essendon . . . . General descriptions and manorial descents by ELEANOR J. B. REID, B.A. . . 458

Hertingfordbury . . . General descriptions and manorial descents by MABEL E. CHRISTIE 462

St. Andrew Rural . . . General descriptions and manorial descents by HELEN DOUGLAS-IRVINE, M.A. Architectural description of Panshanger by Revd. E. E. DORLING, M.A., F.S.A. 468

Stanstead St. Margaret's . . General descriptions and manorial descents by MAUD F. EDWARDS, Oxford Honours School of Modern History 472

Stapleford . . . . ,, ,, ,, . 476

Tewin . . . . General descriptions and manorial descents by MABEL E. CHRISTIE 480

Wormley . . . . General descriptions and manorial descents by ELEANOR J. B. REID, B.A. . . 487

Hertford Borough . . . History of Borough and manorial descents by A. F. H. NIEMEYER, Oxford Honours School of Modern History. Architectural description of Hertford Castle by A. W. CLAPHAM. Domestic Architecture by JOHN QUEKETT, B.A. . . 490

VOLUME FOUR

PAGE

Dedication v
Contents ix
List of Illustrations xiii

CONTENTS OF VOLUMES: HERTS. IV

		PAGE
List of Maps		xvi
Editorial Note		xvii
Topography	General descriptions and manorial descents compiled under the superintendence of WILLIAM PAGE, F.S.A.; Architectural descriptions by A. WHITFORD ANDERSON, A.R.I.B.A.; Heraldic drawings and blazon by the Revd. E. E. DORLING, M.A., F.S.A.; Charities from information supplied by J. W. OWSLEY, I.S.O., late Official Trustee of Charitable Funds	
Edwinstree Hundred		
Introduction	By ALICE RAVEN	1
Albury	By MAUD F. EDWARDS, Oxford Honours School of Modern History . . .	4
Anstey	By HELEN DOUGLAS-IRVINE, M.A. . . .	11
Aspenden *alias* Aspeden with Wakeley .	By MAUD F. EDWARDS	17
Barkway	By LILIAN J. REDSTONE, B.A. . . .	25
Barley	,, ,, . . .	36
Buckland	,, ,, . . .	42
Little Hadham . . .	By MAUD F. EDWARDS and ALICE RAVEN . .	49
Much Hadham . . .	,, ,, ,, . .	58
Great Hormead . . .	By ELEANOR J. B. REID, B.A. . . .	68
Little Hormead . . .	,, ,, . . .	74
Layston	By MAUD F. EDWARDS	77
Meesden	By ALICE RAVEN	88
Brent Pelham . . .	By HELEN DOUGLAS-IRVINE, M.A. . . .	91
Furneux Pelham . . .	,, ,, . . .	100
Stocking Pelham . . .	,, ,, . . .	108
Throcking . . .	By MAUD F. EDWARDS . . .	111
Wyddial	,, ,, . . .	114
Celtic and Romano-British Hertfordshire .	By WILLIAM PAGE, F.S.A. . . .	119
Topographical Index of Romano-British Remains	By M. V. TAYLOR, M.A., Oxford Honours School of Modern History	147
Social and Economic History .	By A. F. H. NIEMEYER, Oxford Honours School of Modern History	173
Table of Population 1801–1901 .	By G. S. MINCHIN	233
Industries		
Introduction . . .	By C. H. VELLACOTT, B.A. . .	239
Textiles	By L. F. SALZMANN, B.A., F.S.A. . .	248
The Straw Plait, Hat, and Bonnet Industry	By ETHEL M. HEWITT . . .	251
Paper-making . . .	By LEWIS EVANS, J.P., F.S.A. . .	256
Printing . . .	By H. R. PLOMER	258
Pottery, Tiles, and Bricks .	By L. F. SALZMANN, B.A., F.S.A. . .	264
Plaster Work . . .	By J. MURRAY KENDALL, F.S.A. . .	266
Bell Founding . . .	By H. B. WALTERS, M.A., F.S.A. . .	268
Water-cress Growing . .	By G. EBSWORTH BULLEN . . .	272
Forestry	By the Revd. J. C. COX, LL.D., F.S.A. .	275
Ecclesiastical History		
Before the Conquest . .	By WILLIAM PAGE, F.S.A. . .	281
After the Conquest . .	By HENRIETTA L. E. GARBETT . .	294
Religious Houses		
Introduction . . .	By MINNIE REDDAN, Hist. Tripos . .	365
Abbey of St. Albans		
Before the Conquest .	By WILLIAM PAGE, F.S.A. . .	367
After the Conquest .	By MINNIE REDDAN, Hist. Tripos, with the assistance of notes supplied by NOWELL SIEVERS, B.A. .	372
Priory of Redbourn . .	By MINNIE REDDAN, Hist. Tripos . .	416
,, ,, Hertford . .	,, ,, . .	419

		PAGE
Priory of Salburn in Standon	By MINNIE REDDAN, Hist. Tripos	421
,, ,, Sopwell	,, ,,	422
,, ,, Cheshunt	,, ,,	426
,, ,, St. Mary de Pré, St. Albans	,, ,,	428
,, ,, St. Giles in the Wood, Flamstead	,, ,,	432
,, ,, Rowney, Great Munden	,, ,,	434
,, ,, Royston	,, ,,	436
,, ,, Wymondley	,, ,,	440
,, ,, New Bigging, Hitchin	,, ,,	443
Preceptory of Standon	,, ,,	444
,, ,, Temple Dinsley	,, ,,	445
Priory of King's Langley	,, ,,	446
Friars Minor of Ware	,, ,,	451
Carmelite Friars of Hitchin	,, ,,	451
Trinitarian Friars of Hertford	,, ,,	452
College of Thele or Stanstead St. Margaret's	,, ,,	454
Priory of Ware	,, ,,	455
Hospital of St. Mary Bigging, Anstey	,, ,,	457
,, ,, St. John Baptist, Berkhampstead	,, ,,	458
Hospital of St. John the Evangelist, Berkhampstead	,, ,,	459
Hospital of St. Erasmus and St. Mary Magdalene, Cheshunt	,, ,,	460
Hospital of St. Mary Magdalene, Clothall	,, ,,	460
,, ,, St. Laud and St. Anthony, Hoddesdon	,, ,,	461
Hospital of St. John and St. James, Royston	,, ,,	462
Hospital of St. Nicholas, Royston	,, ,,	464
,, ,, St. Julian by St. Albans	,, ,,	464

HERTFORDSHIRE FAMILIES

		PAGE
Dedication		v
The Advisory Council of the Victoria History		vii
Contents		ix
List of Illustrations		xiii
Table of Abbreviations		xv
General Introduction	By OSWALD BARRON, F.S.A.	xvii
Preface		xxi
The Landed Houses of Hertfordshire	By the Editor [DUNCAN WARRAND, M.A.]. Introductory portion (pp. 3 and 4), J. HORACE ROUND, M.A., LL.D. Arms, the Revd. E. E. DORLING, M.A.	1
Baker of Bayfordbury		19
Arms	By the Revd. E. E. DORLING, M.A.	
Introduction	By the Editor	21
Genealogy of Baker of Bayfordbury	,,	23
Chart Pedigree		between 32 and 33
Alliances		33
Brand, Viscount Hampden and Lord Dacre		35
Arms	By the Revd. E. E. DORLING, M.A.	
Introduction	,, ,,	37
Genealogy of Brand of Great Hormead	By OSWALD BARRON, F.S.A.	39

CONTENTS OF VOLUMES: HERTS. FAMILIES

PAGE

Genealogy of Brand, Viscount Hampden and Lord Dacre . . .	By Oswald Barron, F.S.A. . . .	42
Chart Pedigree	. . . . .	*between* 48 *and* 49
Alliances . .	. . . . . .	49
Calvert of Furneaux Pelham . .	. . . . . .	51
Arms	By the Revd. E. E. Dorling, M.A.	
Introduction	By the Editor	53
Genealogy of Calvert of Furneaux Pelham	By the Editor and F. L. Bickley .	55
Genealogy of Calvert of Nine Ashes .	,, ,, .	62
Genealogy of Calvert of Albury . .	,, ,, •	65
Genealogy of Calvert of Ockley Court .	,, ,, .	68
Genealogy of Calvert (now Verney), Baronet	,, ,, .	70
Chart Pedigree	. . . . .	*between* 74 *and* 75
Alliances	. . . . . .	75
Capell, Earl of Essex . . .	. . . . . .	77
Arms	By the Revd. E. E. Dorling, M.A.	
Introduction	By J. Horace Round, M.A., LL.D.	79
Genealogy of Capell, Earl of Essex .	By the Editor . . .	83
Chart Pedigree	. . . .	*between* 106 *and* 107
Alliances	. . . . .	107
Cecil, Marquess of Salisbury . .	. . . . .	109
Arms	By the Revd. E. E. Dorling, M.A.	
Introduction	,, ,, .	111
Genealogy of Cecil, Marquess of Salisbury	By Oswald Barron, F.S.A. .	113
Chart Pedigree	. . . .	*between* 126 *and* 127
Alliances	. . . . .	127
Cowper, Earl Cowper . . .	. . . . .	129
Arms	By the Revd. E. E. Dorling, M.A.	
Introduction	By the Editor . . .	131
Genealogy of Cowper, Earl Cowper .	,, .	133
Genealogy of Cowper of Hertingfordbury and Tewin Water . . .	,, .	145
Chart Pedigree	. . . .	*between* 150 *and* 151
Alliances	. . . . .	151
Gape of St. Michael's . . .	. . . . .	153
Arms	By the Revd. E. E. Dorling, M.A.	
Introduction	By the Editor . . .	155
Genealogy of Gape of St. Michael's .	,, .	157
Chart Pedigree	. . . .	*between* 166 *and* 167
Alliances	. . . . .	167
Grimston, Earl of Verulam . .	. . . . .	169
Arms	By the Revd. E. E. Dorling, M.A.	
Introduction	By the Editor . . .	171
Genealogy of Luckyn, Baronet, now Grimston, Earl of Verulam . .	,, .	175
Genealogy of Luckyn of Little Waltham, Baronet	,, .	191
Chart Pedigree	. . . .	*between* 192 *and* 193
Alliances	. . . . .	193
Lytton, Earl of Lytton . . .	. . . . .	195
Arms	By the Revd. E. E. Dorling, M.A.	
Introduction	By the Editor . . .	197
Genealogy of Lytton, Earl of Lytton .	By the Editor and F. L. Bickley .	199
Chart Pedigree	. . . .	*between* 202 *and* 203
Alliances	. . . . .	203

PAGE

Sebright of Beechwood, Baronet 205
    Arms . . . . . By the Revd. E. E. Dorling, M.A.
    Introduction . . . . By J. Horace Round, M.A., LL.D. and the Editor . 207
    Genealogy of Sebright, Baronet . . By the Editor and the Revd. E. E. Dorling, M.A. . 211
    Chart Pedigree . . . . *between* 220 *and* 221
    Alliances 221
Villiers, Earl of Clarendon 223
    Arms . . . . . By the Revd. E. E. Dorling, M.A.
    Introduction . . . . By the Editor 225
    Genealogy of Villiers, Earl of Clarendon .   ,, ... 229
    Chart Pedigree . . . . *between* 238 *and* 239
    Alliances 239
Wilshere of the Frythe 241
    Arms . . . . . By the Revd. E. E. Dorling, M.A.
    Introduction . . . . By the Editor 243
    Genealogy of Wilshere, of the Frythe .   ,, ... 245
    Chart Pedigree . . . . *between* 252 *and* 253
    Alliances 253
Arms of Hertfordshire Families . . By the Revd. E. E. Dorling, M.A. . . 255
List of Copyholders and Freeholders in 1699 269
List of Sheriffs of Hertfordshire 279
List of Members of Parliament elected for the County 289
    ,,   ,,   ,,   Hertford 292
    ,,   ,,   ,,   St. Albans 293
    ,,   ,,   ,,   Bishop's Stortford 295
    ,,   ,,   ,,   Great Berkhampstead 295
Index 297

HUNTINGDONSHIRE
VOLUME ONE

PAGE

Dedication v
Contents ix
List of Illustrations xi
Maps and Plans xiii
Preface xv
Table of Abbreviations xix
Natural History
    Geology . . . . . By the late Horace B. Woodward, F.R.S., F.G.S.;
                revised by H. Dewey, F.G.S. . . . 1
    Palaeontology . . . . By the late Richard Lydekker, F.R.S., F.L.S.,
                F.G.S.; revised by E. Thurlow Leeds, M.A.,
                F.S.A. 21
    Botany . . . . By G. Claridge Druce, M.A., D.Sc., LL.D. . 29
    Zoology
        Mollusca . . . By J. Omer-Cooper, B.A., F.L.S. . . 81
        Insecta . . .   ,,   ,, . . 85
            Coleoptera . . .   ,,   ,, . . 95
            Lepidoptera . . .   ,,   ,, . . 118
            Arachnida . . .   ,,   ,, . . 137
        Crustaceans . . . By the Revd. T. R. R. Stebbing, M.A., F.R.S.,
                F.L.S. 140
        Fishes . . . . By Ambrose Harding, M.A., F.Z.S. . . 156
        Reptiles and Batrachians . .   ,,   ,, . . 159

PAGE

Birds	By the Revd. E. Peake, M.A.	161
Mammals	By Ambrose Harding, M.A., F.Z.S.	188
Early Man	By Cyril Fox, Ph.D., F.S.A., and Miles C. Burkitt, M.A., F.S.A., assisted by G. Wyman Abbott, F.S.A.	193
Romano-British Remains	By Margerie V. Taylor, M.A., F.S.A.	219
Anglo-Saxon Remains	By Reginald A. Smith, B.A., F.S.A.	271
Ancient Earthworks	By S. Inskip Ladds, A.R.I.B.A.	281
Introduction to the Huntingdonshire Domesday	By Professor F. M. Stenton, M.A.	315
Text of the Huntingdonshire Domesday	,, ,,	337
Ecclesiastical History	By the Sister Elspeth of the Community of All Saints, Oxford School of Modern History.	357
Religious Houses	,, ,, ,,	377
Introduction		377
Abbey of Ramsey		377
Priory of St. Neots		385
,, ,, St. Ives		388
,, ,, Hinchinbrook		389
Abbey of Sawtry		391
Priory of St. Mary, Huntingdon		393
,, ,, Stonely		395
Austin Friary, Huntingdon		396
Hospital of St. Margaret, Huntingdon		397
,, ,, St. John Baptist, Huntingdon		397
,, ,, St. Giles, Huntingdon		398
Appendix:—Little Gidding	By William Page, F.S.A.	399
Index to the Huntingdonshire Domesday Introduction and Text		407

VOLUME TWO

PAGE

Dedication		v
Contents		ix
List of Illustrations		xi
List of Maps		xv
Editorial Note		xvii
Political History		
To 1660	By the Revd. R. H. Murray, M.A., Litt.D., and William Page, F.S.A.	1
Parliamentary History	By William Page, F.S.A., and Granville Proby, M.A., F.S.A.	22
Montagu Pedigree	By the late John Brownbill, M.A.	62
Cromwell Pedigree	,, ,,	67
Social and Economic History	By Mrs. C. S. B. Buckland, M.A. Oxon.	73
Table of Population	By George S. Minchin	101
Schools		
Huntingdon Grammar School	By C. Guy Parsloe, M.A.	107
Godmanchester Grammar School	,, ,,	111
Kimbolton Grammar School	,, ,,	113
Ramsey Free School	,, ,,	114
Elementary Schools founded before 1800	,, ,,	115

CONTENTS OF VOLUMES: HUNTS. II

PAGE

Topography . . . . General descriptions and manorial descents compiled under the editorship of WILLIAM PAGE, F.S.A.; Architectural descriptions, except where otherwise stated, by S. INSKIP LADDS, A.R.I.B.A.; Heraldic drawings and blazon by the Revd. E. E. DORLING, M.A., F.S.A.; Charities from information supplied by J. R. SMITH of the Charity Commission

Huntingdon Borough . . . By WILLIAM PAGE, F.S.A., S. INSKIP LADDS, A.R.I.B.A., and others; History of Early Mint by G. C. BROOKE, Litt.D., F.S.A. . . . 121

Hurstingstone Hundred

Introduction . . . . By WILLIAM PAGE, F.S.A. . . . 149
Bluntisham cum Earith . . By the Revd. E. PEAKE, M.A. . . 153
Broughton . . . By WILLIAM PAGE, F.S.A., and MAUD E. SIMKINS; Architectural descriptions by WILLIAM PAGE, F.S.A. 158
Bury cum Hepmangrove . . By the late Canon W. M. NOBLE, B.A., and WILLIAM PAGE, F.S.A.; Architectural descriptions by WILLIAM PAGE, F.S.A. . . 164
Colne . . . . By MAUD E. SIMKINS . . . 167
Hartford cum Sapley . . ,, ,, . . . 171
Holywell with Needingworth . . By LILIAN J. REDSTONE, B.A. . . 175
Houghton . . . . ,, ,, . . 179
Old Hurst . . . By MAUD E. SIMKINS . . . 181
Pidley with Fenton . . . ,, ,, . . . 185
Ramsey . . . By WILLIAM PAGE, F.S.A.; Architectural descriptions by WILLIAM PAGE, F.S.A. . . . 187
Great Raveley . . . By MAUD E. SIMKINS . . . 198
Little Raveley . . . By WILLIAM PAGE, F.S.A. . . . 201
Abbots Ripton . . . By DOROTHY L. POWELL, Mod. Lang. Tripos; Architectural descriptions by WILLIAM PAGE, F.S.A. 202
King's Ripton . . . By DOROTHY L. POWELL, Mod. Lang. Tripos . 207
St. Ives . . . By LILIAN J. REDSTONE, B.A. . . 210
Somersham . . . By MAUD E. SIMKINS; Architectural descriptions by WILLIAM PAGE, F.S.A. . . . 223
Great Stukeley . . . By DOROTHY L. POWELL, Mod. Lang. Tripos 230
Little Stukeley . . . ,, ,, ,, . 234
Upwood . . . By MAUD E. SIMKINS . . . 238
Warboys . . . ,, ,, . 242
Wistow . . . By the late Canon W. M. NOBLE, B.A.; Architectural descriptions by WILLIAM PAGE, F.S.A. . 246
Woodhurst . . . By MAUD E. SIMKINS . . . 250
Wyton . . . . By LILIAN J. REDSTONE, B.A. . . 253

Toseland Hundred

Introduction . . . By WILLIAM PAGE, F.S.A. . . 255
Abbotsley . . . By CATHERINE M. JAMISON, Oxford Hon. School of Mod. Hist. 257
Buckden . . . By MAUD E. SIMKINS . . . 260
Diddington . . . By CATHERINE M. JAMISON, Oxford Hon. School of Mod. Hist. 269
Eynesbury . . . . ,, ,, ,, . 272
Fen Stanton . . . By MAUD E. SIMKINS . . . 280
Godmanchester . . . By CATHERINE M. JAMISON, Oxford Hon. School of Mod. Hist. 286
Great Gransden . . . ,, ,, ,, . 296
Hail Weston . . . ,, ,, ,, . 302
Hemingford Abbots . . By MAUD E. SIMKINS . . . 304
Hemingford Grey . . . ,, ,, . . . 309

		PAGE
Hilton	By MAUD E. SIMKINS	315
Midloe	,, ,, ...	318
Offord Cluny	,, ,, ...	319
Offord Darcy	,, ,, ...	322
Great Paxton . . .	By CATHERINE M. JAMISON, Oxford Hon. School of Mod. Hist.	328
Little Paxton	,, ,, ,,	332
St. Neots	,, ,, ,,	337
Southoe	By MAUD E. SIMKINS	346
Great Staughton . . .	,, ,, ...	354
Tetworth	,, ,, ...	370
Toseland	By CATHERINE M. JAMISON, Oxford Hon. School of Mod. Hist.	374
Waresley	,, ,, ,,	376
Yelling	By MAUD E. SIMKINS	379

VOLUME THREE

		PAGE
Dedication	. . . .	v
Contents	. . . .	ix
List of Illustrations . . .	. . . . . .	xi
List of Maps and Plans . . .	. . . . . .	xvi
Editorial Note	. . . . . .	xvii
Notices relating to Huntingdonshire published since 1926 . . .	. . . . . .	xxi
Corrigenda	. . . .	xxiii
Topography	General descriptions and manorial descents compiled under the editorship of S. INSKIP LADDS, A.R.I.B.A.; Architectural descriptions by S. INSKIP LADDS; Heraldic drawings and blazon by the Revd. E. E. DORLING, M.A., F.S.A.; Charities from information supplied by J. R. SMITH, late of the Charity Commission	
Leightonstone Hundred		
Introduction . . .	By CATHERINE JAMISON, Oxford Hon. School of Mod. Hist.	I
Alconbury-cum-Weston .	By ADA RUSSELL, M.A. . . .	4
Barham	,, ,, . . .	10
Brampton	,, ,, . . .	12
Brington	,, ,, . . .	20
Buckworth . . .	By MAUD E. SIMKINS . . .	22
Bythorn	By ADA RUSSELL, M.A. . . .	26
Catworth	By MAUD E. SIMKINS . . .	28
Copmanford . . .	By ADA RUSSELL, M.A. . . .	35
Covington	By MAUD E. SIMKINS . . .	38
Easton	By ADA RUSSELL, M.A. . . .	41
Ellington	,, ,, . . .	44
Great Gidding . . .	By S. INSKIP LADDS, A.R.I.B.A. . .	48
Little Gidding . . .	,, ,, . .	53
Steeple Gidding . .	By MARJORY HOLLINGS, Oxford Hon. School of Mod. Hist.	57
Grafham with East Perry .	By ADA RUSSELL, M.A. . . .	60
Hamerton	,, ,, . . .	66
Keyston	By MARJORY HOLLINGS, Oxford Hon. School of Mod. Hist.	69
Kimbolton	By ADA RUSSELL, M.A. . . .	75
Leighton Bromswold . .	By MARJORY HOLLINGS, Oxford Hon. School of Mod. Hist.	86

		PAGE
Molesworth	By MAUD E. SIMKINS	92
Spaldwick	By ADA RUSSELL, M.A.	97
Stow Longa	,, ,,	100
Swineshead	By S. INSKIP LADDS, A.R.I.B.A.	104
Thurning	,, ,,	108
Tilbrook	,, ,,	112
Upton	By ADA RUSSELL, M.A.	113
Old Weston	,, ,,	116
Winwick	By MAUD E. SIMKINS	120
Woolley	,, ,,	125
Norman Cross Hundred		
Introduction	By CATHERINE JAMISON, Oxford Hon. School of Mod. Hist.	129
Alwalton	,, ,, ,,	133
Caldecote	By MAUD E. SIMKINS	136
Chesterton	By CATHERINE JAMISON, Oxford Hon. School of Mod. Hist.	139
Conington	By the late WILLIAM PAGE, Hon. D.Litt., F.S.A.	144
Denton	By MAUD E. SIMKINS	151
Elton	By CATHERINE JAMISON, Oxford Hon. School of Mod. Hist.	154
Farcet	,, ,, ,,	166
Fletton	,, ,, ,,	169
Folksworth	By MAUD E. SIMKINS	173
Glatton	By VALERIE CUNNINGHAM	177
Haddon	By MAUD E. SIMKINS	182
Holme	,, ,,	184
Morborne	By MAUD E. SIMKINS	188
Orton Longueville with Botolphbridge	By CATHERINE JAMISON, Oxford Hon. School of Mod. Hist.	190
Orton Waterville	,, ,, ,,	198
Sawtry	,, ,, ,,	203
Stanground	,, ,, ,,	212
Stibbington	By MAUD E. SIMKINS	217
Stilton	By CATHERINE JAMISON, Oxford Hon. School of Mod. Hist.	222
Washingley	By MAUD E. SIMKINS	227
Water Newton	,, ,,	230
Woodston	By CATHERINE JAMISON, Oxford Hon. School of Mod. Hist.	233
Wood Walton	,, ,, ,,	236
Yaxley	,, ,, ,,	241
The Middle Level of the Fens and its Reclamation	By H. C. DARBY, M.A., Ph.D.; with the collaboration of PHYLLIS M. RAMSDEN, B.A., Ph.D.	249
Maps of the Fenland	By EDWARD LYNAM, B.A.	291

KENT

VOLUME ONE

	PAGE
Dedication	v
The Advisory Council of the Victoria History	vii
General Advertisement	vii
The Kent County Committee	xiii
Contents	xv

CONTENTS OF VOLUMES: KENT I

		PAGE
List of Illustrations	. . . .	xvii
Preface	. . . .	xxi
Table of Abbreviations	. . . .	xxiii
Natural History		
Geology	By G. W. Lamplugh, F.G.S. . . .	1
Palaeontology . . .	By R. Lydekker, F.R.S., F.L.S., F.G.S. . .	31
Botany		
Introduction . . .	By the Revd. E. S. Marshall, M.A. . .	45
Mosses (*Musci*) . .	By E. M. Holmes, F.L.S. . . .	68
Scale-Mosses (*Hepaticae*) . .	,, ,, ,, . . .	72
Freshwater Algae . .	,, ,, ,, . . .	73
Marine Algae . . .	,, ,, ,, . . .	74
Characeae . . .	By the Revd. E. S. Marshall, M.A. . .	76
Lichens (*Lichenes*) . .	By E. M. Holmes, F.L.S. . . .	77
Fungi	,, ,, ,, . . .	79
Zoology		
Marine . . .	By H. C. Sorby, LL.D., F.R.S., F.S.A. .	91
Molluscs . . .	By B. B. Woodward, F.L.S., F.G.S., F.R.M.S.	99
Insects	Edited by Herbert Goss, F.E.S. (late Secretary of the Entomological Society) . .	103
Orthoptera (*Earwigs, Grasshoppers, Crickets, etc.*) . .	By Malcolm Burr, B.A., F.L.S., F.Z.S., etc.	103
Neuroptera (*Dragon-flies, Stone-flies, Lace-wings, etc.*) . .	By Wm. J. Lucas, B.A., with notes by the late Robert McLachlan, F.R.S., F.L.S., etc.	106
Hymenoptera Phytophaga (*Saw-flies, etc.*) . . .	By Frederick W. L. Sladen, F.E.S.	108
Hymenoptera Entomophaga (*Ichneumon-flies, etc.*) .	,, ,, ,,	112
Hymenoptera Tubulifera (*Ruby-tailed flies*) . . .	,, ,, ,,	113
Hymenoptera Aculeata (*Ants, Wasps, and Bees*) . .	,, ,, ,,	114
Coleoptera (*Beetles*) . .	By the Revd. Canon Fowler, M.A., D.Sc., F.L.S., with notes by Geo. C. Champion, F.Z.S., and Arthur John Chitty, M.A., F.E.S.	122
Lepidoptera (*Butterflies and Moths*)	. . . . . .	178
Rhopalocera . .	By Herbert Goss, F.E.S., with notes by Chas. Fenn, F.E.S., and Capt. Savile G. Reid, late R.E., F.Z.S., etc. . . .	179
Heterocera . . .	,, ,, ,, ,,	184
Micro-Lepidoptera .	By Benjamin A. Bower, F.E.S. . .	198
Diptera (*Flies*) . .	By Col. John W. Yerbury, late R.A., F.Z.S., F.E.S., with notes by H. Elgar .	209
Hemiptera Heteroptera (*Bugs*)	By Edward Saunders, F.R.S., F.L.S., etc. .	214
Hemiptera Homoptera (*Cicadas, Fiend-flies, Lantern-flies, etc.*)	By Wm. West, with notes by Edward A. Butler, B.A., B.Sc., F.E.S. . . .	222
Spiders . . .	By the late F. O. Pickard-Cambridge, M.A.	226
Crustaceans . . .	By the Revd. T. R. R. Stebbing, M.A., F.R.S., F.Z.S.	237
Fishes	By G. A. Boulenger, F.R.S., F.Z.S. .	263
Reptiles and Batrachians	,, ,, ,, . .	266
Birds	By Boyd Alexander, F.Z.S. . .	267
Mammals . . .	By F. J. Baker, A.R.C.Sc. (Lond.), F.R.H.S.	302
Early Man . . .	By George Clinch, F.G.S. . .	307
Anglo-Saxon Remains . .	By Reginald A. Smith, B.A., F.S.A. .	339

CONTENTS OF VOLUMES: KENT I

		PAGE
Ancient Earthworks	Compiled by the late I. CHALKLEY GOULD, F.S.A., principally from plans and descriptions by the Revd. E. A. DOWNMAN	389
Appendix I. The Deneholes of Kent	By T. V. HOLMES, F.G.S., F. Anthrop. Inst.	446
Appendix II. On the Embankments of the Thames in Kent	By F. C. J. SPURRELL, F.S.A.	454
Agriculture	By C. W. SABIN	457
Forestry	By the Revd. J. C. Cox, LL.D., F.S.A.	471
Sport, Ancient and Modern	Edited by the Revd. E. E. DORLING, M.A.	479
Hunting	By FRANK BONNETT ('East Sussex')	479
Fox-Hunting	,, ,, ,,	479
Staghounds	,, ,, ,,	485
The Mid-Kent Staghounds	,, ,, ,,	485
Harriers	,, ,, ,,	486
Point-to-Point Racing	,, ,, ,,	488
Draghounds	,, ,, ,,	489
Foot Harriers and Beagles	,, ,, ,,	490
Otter-Hunting	,, ,, ,,	490
Coursing	,, ,, ,,	491
Racing	,, ,, ,,	492
Flat Racing	,, ,, ,,	493
Steeplechasing	,, ,, ,,	496
Famous Owners, Trainers, and Horses	,, ,, ,,	498
Polo	,, ,, ,,	500
Shooting	,, ,, ,,	501
Angling	,, ,, ,,	504
Cricket	By Sir HOME GORDON, Bart.	509
Golf	By the Revd. E. E. DORLING, M.A.	513
Athletics	By FRANK BONNETT ('East Sussex')	516

VOLUME TWO

		PAGE
Dedication		v
Contents		ix
List of Illustrations and Maps		xiii
Editorial Note		xv
Ecclesiastical History		
Part I (to death of Lanfranc)	By Revd. Canon G. M. LIVETT, B.A., F.S.A.	I
Part II	By M. E. SIMKINS	25
Religious Houses		
Introduction	By R. C. FOWLER, O.B.E., B.A., F.S.A.	112
Cathedral Priory of Holy Trinity or Christchurch, Canterbury	,, ,, ,,	113
Cathedral Priory of St. Andrew, Rochester	,, ,, ,,	121
Abbey of St. Augustine, Canterbury	,, ,, ,,	126
Priory of Dover	,, ,, ,,	133
Abbey of Faversham	,, ,, ,,	137
,, ,, Reculver	,, ,, ,,	141
Priory of St. Sepulchre, Canterbury	,, ,, ,,	142
,, ,, Davington	,, ,, ,,	144
,, ,, Higham or Lillechurch	,, ,, ,,	145
Abbey of Lyminge	,, ,, ,,	146
,, ,, Malling	,, ,, ,,	146

CONTENTS OF VOLUMES: KENT II

		PAGE
Priory of Minster in Sheppey	By R. C. Fowler, O.B.E., B.A., F.S.A.	149
Abbey of Minster in Thanet	,, ,, ,,	151
Priory of Monks Horton	,, ,, ,,	151
Abbey of Boxley	,, ,, ,,	153
Priory of Bilsington	,, ,, ,,	156
,, ,, St. Gregory, Canterbury	,, ,, ,,	157
,, ,, Combwell	,, ,, ,,	160
,, ,, Leeds	,, ,, ,,	162
Abbey of Lesnes or Westwood	,, ,, ,,	165
Priory of Tonbridge	,, ,, ,,	167
Abbey of West Langdon	,, ,, ,,	169
,, ,, Bradsole or St. Radegund	,, ,, ,,	172
Preceptory of Ewell	,, ,, ,,	175
,, ,, West Peckham	,, ,, ,,	175
,, ,, Sutton at Hone	,, ,, ,,	175
,, ,, Swingfield	,, ,, ,,	176
Dominican Friars of Canterbury	By A. G. Little, M.A., F.B.A.	177
,, ,, Nuns of Dartford	,, ,,	181
Franciscan Friars of Canterbury	,, ,,	190
Observant Friars of Greenwich	,, ,,	194
Franciscan Friars of Maidstone	,, ,,	198
,, ,, Romney	,, ,,	199
Austin Friars of Canterbury	,, ,,	199
Carmelite Friars of Aylesford	,, ,,	201
,, ,, Lossenham	,, ,,	203
,, ,, Sandwich	,, ,,	204
Friars of the Sack of Canterbury	,, ,,	205
Trinitarian Friars of Mottenden	,, ,,	205
Hospital of Boughton under Blean	By R. C. Fowler, O.B.E., B.A., F.S.A.	208
,, ,, Buckland by Dover	,, ,, ,,	208
,, ,, St. James by Canterbury	,, ,, ,,	209
,, ,, St. John Baptist, Northgate, Canterbury	,, ,, ,,	211
Hospital of St. Laurence, Canterbury	,, ,, ,,	212
,, ,, St. Mary of the Poor Priests, Canterbury	,, ,, ,,	212
Hospital of St. Nicholas and St. Catherine, Canterbury	,, ,, ,,	213
Hospital of St. Thomas the Martyr, Eastbridge, Canterbury	,, ,, ,,	214
Hospital of Chatham	,, ,, ,,	216
,, ,, Holy Trinity, Dartford	,, ,, ,,	217
,, ,, St. Mary Magdalene, Dartford	,, ,, ,,	217
,, ,, St. Mary, Dover	,, ,, ,,	217
,, ,, Harbledown	,, ,, ,,	219
,, ,, Hythe	,, ,, ,,	220
,, ,, Maidstone	,, ,, ,,	221
,, ,, Milton by Gravesend	,, ,, ,,	221
,, ,, Ospringe	,, ,, ,,	222
,, ,, Puckeshall or Tonge	,, ,, ,,	224
,, ,, St. John Baptist, Romney	,, ,, ,,	225
,, ,, St. Stephen and St. Thomas	,, ,, ,,	225
,, ,, St. Bartholomew, Sandwich	,, ,, ,,	226
,, ,, St. John, Sandwich	,, ,, ,,	226
,, ,, St. Thomas, Sandwich	,, ,, ,,	227
,, ,, Sevenoaks	,, ,, ,,	227
,, ,, Sittingbourne	,, ,, ,,	227
,, ,, Strood	,, ,, ,,	228

CONTENTS OF VOLUMES: KENT II

		PAGE
College of Bredgar	By R. C. Fowler, O.B.E., B.A., F.S.A.	230
,, ,, Cobham	,, ,, ,,	231
,, ,, Maidstone	,, ,, ,,	232
,, ,, Wingham	,, ,, ,,	233
,, ,, Wye	,, ,, ,,	235
Priory of Folkestone	,, ,, ,,	236
,, ,, Lewisham	,, ,, ,,	238
,, ,, Patrixbourne	,, ,, ,,	239
,, ,, New Romney	,, ,, ,,	239
,, ,, Throwley	,, ,, ,,	239
Hospital of St. Mary, Canterbury	,, ,, ,,	241
,, ,, St. Katherine, Rochester	,, ,, ,,	241
,, ,, St. Anthony, Sandwich	,, ,, ,,	241
,, ,, Holy Cross, Swainestrey in Murston	,, ,, ,,	241
Hospital of St. Leonard, Swainestrey in Murston	,, ,, ,,	241
Hospital of St. Nicholas by the White Ditch, Strood	,, ,, ,,	241
Additional Heads of Houses	,, ,, ,,	242
Maritime History	By M. Oppenheim, M.R.C.S.	243
The Royal Dockyards	,, ,,	336

VOLUME THREE

		PAGE
Dedication		v
Contents		ix
List of Illustrations and Maps		xi
Editorial Note		xv
Romano-British Remains	Originally undertaken and partly written by the late Professor F. J. Haverfield, M.A., LL.D., F.S.A., and Margerie V. Taylor, M.A., F.S.A., revised, brought up to date, and completed by R. E. Mortimer Wheeler, M.A., D.Litt., F.S.A.	
Introduction	By the late Professor F. J. Haverfield, M.A., LL.D., F.S.A., and R. E. Mortimer Wheeler, M.A., D.Litt., F.S.A.	1
Military History	,, ,, ,, ,,	13
Towns	By R. E. Mortimer Wheeler, M.A., D.Litt., F.S.A.	60
Country Houses	By Margerie V. Taylor, M.A., F.S.A.	102
Industries	By R. F. Jessup	127
Roads	,, ,,	134
Topographical Index	By Margerie V. Taylor, M.A., F.S.A., R. F. Jessup, and C. F. C. Hawkes, B.A.	144
Introduction to the Kent Domesday	By Professor Nellie Neilson, M.A., Ph.D.	177
Text of the Kent Domesday	By the late Revd. F. W. Ragg, M.A.	203
The Domesday Monachorum	By Professor Nellie Neilson, M.A., Ph.D.	253
Political History	By Maud E. Simkins	271
Social and Economic History	By Gilbert Slater, M.A., D.Sc.	319
Table of Population	By George S. Minchin	356
Industries	By Ethel M. Hewitt	
Introduction		371
Coal		380
Iron		384
Bell-Founding		389
Quarries, Stone, etc.		391

	PAGE
Brick-Making	393
Chalk	396
Fuller's Earth	396
Copperas	397
Portland Cement	398
Gunpowder, Ammunition, etc.	399
Glass-Making	400
Pottery	402
Cloth-Making	403
Silk-Weaving	412
Paper-Making	416
Printing	420
Fruit Growing and Market Gardening	420
Brewing	424
Cider	426
Fisheries	427
Shellfish	431
Index to the Kent Domesday and Domesday Monachorum . . By EDITH M. KIRKE	437

LANCASHIRE
VOLUME ONE

		PAGE
Dedication		v
The Advisory Council of the Victoria History		vii
General Advertisement		vii
The Lancashire County Committee		xiii
Contents		xv
List of Illustrations		xvii
Preface		xix
Table of Abbreviations		xxiii
Natural History		
Geology	By H. BOLTON, F.R.S.E.	1
Palaeontology	By R. LYDEKKER, F.R.S., F.G.S., F.L.S. .	31
Botany	By HARRY FISHER	37
Zoology		
Marine	By JAMES JOHNSTONE, B.Sc. (Lond.) .	87
Non-Marine Molluscs . . .	By B. B. WOODWARD, F.G.S., F.R.M.S. .	97
Insects	By W. E. SHARP, F.E.S. . . .	101
Spiders	By the late F. O. PICKARD-CAMBRIDGE, M.A., revised and corrected by the Revd. O. PICKARD-CAMBRIDGE, M.A. . .	145
Crustaceans	By the Revd. T. R. R. STEBBING, M.A., F.R.S., F.Z.S.	157
Fishes	By JAMES JOHNSTONE, B.Sc. (Lond.) .	179
Reptiles and Batrachians . .	,, ,, ,, . .	188
Birds	By H. O. FORBES, LL.D. . . .	189
Mammals	,, ,, . . .	206
Early Man	By JOHN GARSTANG, B.Litt., M.A., F.S.A. .	211
Anglo-Saxon Remains . . .	,, ,, ,, .	257
Introduction to the Lancashire Domesday .	By WILLIAM FARRER . . .	269
Text of the Lancashire Domesday .	,, ,, . .	283
Feudal Baronage	,, ,, . .	291
Index to the Lancashire Domesday .	,, ,, . .	377

VOLUME TWO

	PAGE
Dedication	v
Contents	ix
List of Illustrations and Maps	xiii
Editorial Note	xv
Ecclesiastical History	
To the Reformation By Professor JAMES TAIT, M.A.	1
From the Reformation By W. A. SHAW, D.Litt.	40
Religious Houses	
Introduction By Professor JAMES TAIT, M.A.	102
Priory of Penwortham ,, ,, ,,	104
,, ,, Lytham ,, ,, ,,	107
,, ,, Upholland ,, ,, ,,	111
Cell of Kersal ,, ,, ,,	113
Abbey of Furness By Professor JAMES TAIT, M.A.	114
,, ,, Wyresdale ,, ,, ,,	131
,, ,, Whalley ,, ,, ,,	131
Priory of Conishead ,, ,, ,,	140
,, ,, Cartmel ,, ,, ,,	143
,, ,, Burscough By F. M. POWICKE, M.A.	148
,, ,, Cockerham ,, ,, ,,	152
Abbey of Cockersand ,, ,, ,,	154
Priory of Hornby ,, ,, ,,	160
House of Dominican Friars, Lancaster ,, ,, ,,	161
,, ,, Franciscan Friars, Preston ,, ,, ,,	162
,, ,, Austin Friars, Warrington ,, ,, ,,	162
Hospital of St. Mary Magdalen, Preston ,, ,, ,,	163
,, ,, St. Leonard, Lancaster ,, ,, ,,	165
Gardiner's Hospital, Lancaster ,, ,, ,,	166
Lathom Almshouse ,, ,, ,,	166
Hospital of St. Saviour, Stidd under Longridge ,, ,, ,,	166
College of Upholland ,, ,, ,,	166
,, ,, Manchester ,, ,, ,,	167
Priory of Lancaster ,, ,, ,,	167
Political History	
To the end of the Reign of Henry VIII By Professor JAMES TAIT, M.A.	175
From the Reign of Henry VIII By Miss ALICE LAW, First Class Honours Hist. Tripos	218
Social and Economic History ,, ,, ,, ,,	261
Table of Population, 1801–1901 By GEORGE S. MINCHIN	330
Industries	
Introduction By Professor S. J. CHAPMAN, M.A., M.Com., and DOUGLAS KNOOP, M.A.	351
Natural Products By DOUGLAS KNOOP, M.A.	354
Copper Smelting ,, ,, ,,	355
Coal Mining ,, ,, ,,	356
Iron ,, ,, ,,	360
Hardware and Allied Trades ,, ,, ,,	364
Watch-Making ,, ,, ,,	366
Engineering ,, ,, ,,	367
Ordnance and Armaments ,, ,, ,,	374
Shipbuilding ,, ,, ,,	375
Textile Industries	376
The Woollen Industry By DOUGLAS KNOOP, M.A.	376
The Linen Industry ,, ,, ,,	378

CONTENTS OF VOLUMES: LANCS. II

PAGE

The Cotton Industry	By Professor S. J. CHAPMAN, M.A., M.Com.	379
Felt-Hat Making	By DOUGLAS KNOOP, M.A.	393
The Silk Industry	,, ,, ,,	394
Calico Printing	,, ,, ,,	395
Bleaching, Finishing, and Dyeing	,, ,, ,,	398
Chemical Industries	,, ,, ,,	399
India-rubber	,, ,, ,,	401
Soap Industry	,, ,, ,,	402
Potteries and Glass	,, ,, ,,	403
Potteries		403
Glass		404
The Sugar Industry	By DOUGLAS KNOOP, M.A.	406
The Paper Industry	,, ,, ,,	407
Asbestos	,, ,, ,,	408
Miscellaneous Industries	,, ,, ,,	408
Sea Fisheries	By JAMES JOHNSTONE, B.Sc. (Lond.)	409
Agriculture	By W. H. R. CURTLER	419
Forestry	By WILLIAM FARRER	437
Sport Ancient and Modern	Edited by the Revd. E. E. DORLING, M.A.	
Introduction	By Major ARTHUR WILLOUGHBY-OSBORNE	467
Hunting	,, ,, ,,	469
Staghounds		470
Harriers		470
Beagles		471
Otter Hounds		472
Coursing	By HAROLD BROCKLEBANK	472
Racing	By Major ARTHUR WILLOUGHBY-OSBORNE	479
Flat Racing		479
Steeplechasing		480
Polo	By Major ARTHUR WILLOUGHBY-OSBORNE	481
Shooting	,, ,, ,,	482
Duck Decoys		485
Angling	By Major ARTHUR WILLOUGHBY-OSBORNE	487
Cricket	By Sir HOME GORDON, Bart.	489
Rugby Football	By C. J. BRUCE MARRIOTT, M.A.	493
Golf	By the Revd. E. E. DORLING, M.A.	495
Wrestling	By Major ARTHUR WILLOUGHBY-OSBORNE	499
Bowls	,, ,, ,,	500
Tennis	,, ,, ,,	501
Cock-Fighting	,, ,, ,,	502
Whippet Racing	,, ,, ,,	504
Ancient Earthworks		
Lancashire South of the Sands	By WILLOUGHBY GARDNER, F.L.S.	507
Lancashire North of the Sands	By H. SWAINSON COWPER, F.S.A.	555
Schools		
Introduction	By A. F. LEACH, M.A., F.S.A.	561
The Royal Grammar School, Lancaster	,, ,, ,,	561
Preston Grammar School	,, ,, ,,	569
The Harris Institute, Preston	,, ,, ,,	574
Middleton Grammar School	,, ,, ,,	574
Prescot Grammar School	By the Revd. H. J. CHAYTOR, M.A.	578
Manchester Schools		578
The Grammar School	By A. F. LEACH, M.A., F.S.A.	578
Hulme Grammar Schools	,, ,, ,,	589
The Municipal Secondary School	,, ,, ,,	589
Farnworth Grammar School, Widnes		589

PAGE

Blackburn Grammar School . . By A. F. LEACH, M.A., F.S.A. . . . 590
Stonyhurst College, Blackburn 591
Liverpool Schools 593
   The Grammar School . . By A. F. LEACH, M.A., F.S.A. . . 593
   Liverpool Institution, Liverpool Institute,
     and Liverpool College . ,, ,, ,, . 595
Bolton-le-Moors Grammar School . ,, ,, ,, . . 596
The Church Institute School, Bolton-le-
   Moors . . . . ,, ,, ,, . 600
Leyland Grammar School . . ,, ,, ,, . . 600
The Boteler Grammar School,
   Warrington . . . By the Revd. H. J. CHAYTOR, M.A. . 601
St. Michaels-upon-Wyre Grammar School By A. F. LEACH, M.A., F.S.A. . . 603
Winwick School 603
Whalley Grammar School . . By the Revd. H. J. CHAYTOR, M.A. . 604
Kirkham Grammar School . . ,, ,, ,, . 604
Penwortham Endowed School . . ,, ,, ,, . 605
Clitheroe Grammar School . . ,, ,, ,, . 605
Rochdale Grammar School . . ,, ,, ,, . 606
Rivington and Blackrod Grammar School . ,, ,, ,, . 606
Blackrod School . . . ,, ,, ,, . 607
Burnley School . . . . ,, ,, ,, . 607
Urswick Grammar School . . ,, ,, ,, . 608
Hawkshead Grammar School . . ,, ,, ,, . 608
Halsall Endowed School 608
Warton School . . . By the Revd. H. J. CHAYTOR, M.A. . 609
Wigan Grammar School . . . ,, ,, ,, . 609
Heskin Endowed School 609
Churchtown (or Kirkland) Free School,
   Garstang . . . By the Revd. H. J. CHAYTOR, M.A. . 609
Standish Grammar School . . ,, ,, ,, . 609
Ormskirk Grammar School . . ,, ,, ,, . 610
Oldham Grammar School . . ,, ,, ,, . 610
Chorley Grammar School . . ,, ,, ,, . 610
Leigh Grammar School . . ,, ,, ,, . 610
Cartmel Grammar School . . ,, ,, ,, . 611
Merchant Taylors' School, Crosby . ,, ,, ,, . 611
Bispham Free School . . . ,, ,, ,, . 612
Bury Grammar School . . . ,, ,, ,, . 612
Bolton le Sands School . . . ,, ,, ,, . 613
Upholland School . . . ,, ,, ,, . 613
Over Kellet School . . . By WILLIAM FARRER . . 613
Cockerham School (Garstang) . . By the Revd. H. J. CHAYTOR, M.A. . 613
Newchurch Grammar School . . ,, ,, ,, . 613
Ulverston Grammar School . . ,, ,, ,, . 614
Tunstall School . . . ,, ,, ,, . 614
Rossall School . . . By A. F. LEACH, M.A., F.S.A. . 614
Elementary Schools, founded before 1800 . ,, ,, ,, . 615
Index to Volumes I and II 625
Corrigenda 669

VOLUME THREE

PAGE

Dedication v
Contents ix
Index of Parishes, Townships, and Manors xi

CONTENTS OF VOLUMES: LANCS. III

	PAGE
List of Illustrations	xiii
Editorial Note	xv
Topography — General description and manorial descents by WILLIAM FARRER and J. BROWNBILL, M.A. Architectural descriptions by C. R. PEERS, M.A., F.S.A. Heraldic drawings and blazon by the Revd. E. E. DORLING, M.A.	
West Derby Hundred	
Introduction	1
Walton on the Hill	5
Sefton	58
Childwall	102
Huyton	151
Halsall	183
Altcar	221
North Meols	226
Ormskirk	238
Aughton	284
Warrington	304
Prescot	341
Leigh	414

VOLUME FOUR

	PAGE
Dedication	v
Contents	ix
Index of Parishes, Townships, and Manors	xi
List of Illustrations	xiii
Editorial Note	xv
Topography — Architectural descriptions by C. R. PEERS, M.A., F.S.A., and F. H. CHEETHAM. Heraldic drawings and blazon by the Revd. E. E. DORLING, M.A., F.S.A.	
West Derby Hundred (*cont.*)	
Liverpool — Historical description by Professor RAMSAY MUIR, M.A.	1
Wigan — Historical description by W. FARRER, D.Litt., and J. BROWNBILL, M.A.	57
Winwick — ,, ,, ,, ,,	122
Salford Hundred	
Introduction — Historical descriptions by W. FARRER, D.Litt., and J. BROWNBILL, M.A.	171
Manchester — ,, ,, ,, ,,	174
Ashton-under-Lyne — ,, ,, ,, ,,	338
Eccles — ,, ,, ,, ,,	352

VOLUME FIVE

	PAGE
Dedication	v
Contents	ix
List of Illustrations	xi
Editorial Note	xiii

PAGE

Topography   .   .   .   .   General description and manorial descents by
W. FARRER, D.Litt., and J. BROWNBILL, M.A.
Architectural descriptions by C. R. PEERS, M.A.,
F.S.A., and F. H. CHEETHAM. Heraldic
drawings and blazon by the Revd. E. E.
DORLING, M.A., F.S.A.

Salford Hundred (*cont.*)
  Deane 1
  Flixton 42
  Radcliffe 56
  Prestwich-with-Oldham 67
  Bury 122
  Middleton 151
  Rochdale 187
  Bolton-le-Moors 235
Index to Volumes III, IV, and V 305
Corrigenda 409

VOLUME SIX

PAGE

Dedication v
Contents ix
Index of Parishes, Townships, and Manors xi
List of Illustrations xv
List of Maps xix
Editorial Note xxi
Topography   .   .   .   .   General descriptions and manorial descents by
W. FARRER, D.Litt., and J. BROWNBILL, M.A.
Architectural descriptions by F. H. CHEETHAM.
Heraldic drawings and blazon by the Revd.
E. E. DORLING, M.A., F.S.A.

Leyland Hundred
  Introduction 1
  Leyland 3
  Penwortham 52
  Brindle 75
  Croston 81
  Hesketh-with-Becconsall 111
  Tarleton 115
  Rufford 119
  Chorley 129
  Hoole 149
  Eccleston 155
  Standish 182
Blackburn Hundred
  Introduction 230
  Blackburn 235
  Whalley . . . . . . (Architectural description of Abbey by S. C. K.
SMITH) 349

VOLUME SEVEN

PAGE

Dedication v
Contents ix
List of Illustrations xi

CONTENTS OF VOLUMES: LANCS. VII

		PAGE
List of Maps	. . . .	xii
Editorial Note	. . . .	xiii
Topography	. . . . General descriptions and manorial descents by W. FARRER, D.Litt., and J. BROWNBILL, M.A. Architectural descriptions by F. H. CHEETHAM. Heraldic drawings and blazon by the Revd. E. E. DORLING, M.A., F.S.A.	
Blackburn Hundred (*cont.*)		
Mitton (Part of)	. . . .	I
Chipping	. . . .	20
Ribchester	. . . .	36
Amounderness Hundred		
Introduction	. . . .	68
Preston	. . . .	72
Kirkham	. . . .	143
Lytham	. . . .	213
Poulton-le-Fylde	. . . .	219
Bispham	. . . .	242
Lancaster (Part of)	. . . .	251
St. Michael-on-Wyre	. . . .	260
Garstang	. . . .	291
Index to Volumes VI and VII	. . . .	337
Corrigenda	. . . .	435

VOLUME EIGHT

		PAGE
Dedication	. . . .	v
Contents	. . . .	ix
List of Illustrations	. . . .	xi
List of Maps	. . . .	xiv
Editorial Note	. . . .	xv
General Note	. . . .	xviii
Topography	. . . General descriptions and manorial descents by W. FARRER, D.Litt., and J. BROWNBILL, M.A. Architectural descriptions by F. H. CHEETHAM. Heraldic drawings and blazon by the Revd. E. E. DORLING, M.A., F.S.A.	
Lonsdale Hundred (South and North)		
Introduction	. . . .	I
Lonsdale Hundred (South of the Sands)		
Lancaster (Part of)	. . . .	4
Cockerham	. . . .	89
Heysham	. . . .	109
Halton	. . . .	118
Bolton-le-Sands	. . . .	126
Warton	. . . .	151
Burton-in-Kendal (Part of)	. . . .	183
Melling	. . . .	186
Claughton	. . . .	210
Tatham	. . . .	217
Tunstall	. . . .	225
Whittington	. . . .	241
Thornton (Part of)	. . . .	252
Lonsdale Hundred (North of the Sands)		
Cartmel	. . . . (Architectural description of Cartmel Priory by S. C. KAINES-SMITH, M.A.) . .	254

PAGE

Furness . . . . (Architectural description of Furness Abbey by
S. C. KAINES-SMITH, M.A.) . . . 285

Dalton 304
Aldingham 320
Urswick 328
Pennington 338
Ulverston 342
Hawkshead 370
Colton 383
Kirkby Ireleth 387
Index to Volume VIII 411
Corrigenda 453
List of Original Subscribers . . . . *at end of volume*

LEICESTERSHIRE
VOLUME ONE

PAGE

Dedication v
The Advisory Council of the Victoria History vii
General Advertisement vii
Contents xiii
List of Illustrations xv
Preface xvii
Table of Abbreviations xix
Natural History
Geology . . . . . By C. FOX-STRANGWAYS, F.G.S., late of H.M.
Geological Survey 1
Palaeontology . . . . By R. LYDEKKER, F.R.S., F.L.S., F.G.S. . . 19
Botany . . . . By HARRY FISHER
Introduction 27
Botanical Divisions 31
Phaenogamia 35
Cryptogamia Vascularia 47
Cryptogamia Cellularia 47
Musci (*Mosses*) 47
Hepaticae (*Liverworts and Scale Mosses*) 50
Characeae 50
Algae 50
Lichenes (*Lichens*) 53
Fungi 55
Zoology
Molluscs . . . . By B. B. WOODWARD, F.L.S., F.G.S., F.R.M.S. . 61
Insects . . . . By FRANK BOUSKELL, F.E.S., F.R.H.S. . . 64
Hymenoptera (*Ants, Wasps, Bees, etc.*) 64
Aculeata 65
Coleoptera (*Beetles*) 66
Lepidoptera (*Butterflies and Moths*) 78
Rhopalocera 79
Heterocera 79
Diptera (*Flies*) 89
Hemiptera Heteroptera (*Bugs*) 92
Spiders . . . . By FRANK BOUSKELL, F.E.S., F.R.H.S. . . 94

PAGE

Crustaceans	By the Revd. T. R. R. Stebbing, M.A., F.R.S., F.Z.S.	96
Fishes	By Montagu Browne, F.Z.S.	108
Reptiles and Batrachians	,, ,,	112
Birds	,, ,,	114
Mammals	,, ,,	158
Early Man	By George Clinch, F.G.S.	167
Romano-British Leicestershire	By The General Editor and Miss Keate	179
Descriptions of the West Gate and Mosaic Pavements, Leicester	By G. E. Fox, Hon. M.A. Oxon., F.S.A.	
Anglo-Saxon Remains	By Reginald A. Smith, B.A., F.S.A.	221
Ancient Earthworks	By J. Charles Wall	243
Introduction to the Leicestershire Domesday	By F. M. Stenton, M.A.	277
Translation of the Leicestershire Domesday	,, ,,	306
The Leicestershire Survey	,, ,,	339
Ecclesiastical History	By the Sister Elspeth of the Community of All Saints	355

VOLUME TWO

PAGE

Dedication		v
Contents		ix
List of Maps and Illustrations		xi
Editorial Note		xiii
Classes of Public Records used and Note on abbreviations		xvii
Religious Houses	By R. A. McKinley, M.A.	
Introduction		1
Priory of Langley		3
Abbey of Garendon		5
Priory of Breedon		8
,, Launde		10
Leicester Abbey		13
Priory of Ulverscroft		19
Abbey of Owston		21
Priory of Charley		23
,, Bradley		24
Kirby Bellairs		25
Priory of Grace Dieu		27
Abbey of Croxton Kerrial		28
Preceptory of Rothley		31
,, Dalby and Heather		32
Franciscan Friars of Leicester		33
Dominican Friars of Leicester		34
Augustinian Hermits of Leicester		35
Friars of the Sack, Leicester		35
Hospital of Burton Lazars		36
,, Castle Donington		39
,, St. John, Leicester		40
,, St. Leonard, Leicester		41
,, Lutterworth		42
,, St. Mary Magdalene, Leicester		44
,, St. Edmund, Leicester		45
,, St. Bartholomew, Leicester		45
,, Loughborough		45
,, Stockerston		45

		PAGE
College of St. Mary *De Castro*		45
,, Noseley		46
,, the Annunciation, Leicester		48
,, Sapcote		51
Priory of Hinckley		52
Cistercian Abbey of Mount Saint Bernard .		53
Roman Catholicism .	By Brigadier T. B. Trappes-Lomax, C.B.E.	55
Medieval Political History .	By R. A. McKinley, M.A.	74
Political History, 1530–1885 .	By J. H. Plumb, M.A., Ph.D.	102
Political History, 1885–1950 .	By R. A. McKinley, M.A.	135
Medieval Agrarian History .	By R. H. Hilton, M.A., Ph.D.	145
Agrarian History, 1540–1950	By Joan Thirsk, M.A., Ph.D.	199
Appendix I. Table of Inclosures without Parliamentary Acts		254
Appendix II. Table of Parliamentary Inclosure Acts and Awards		260
The Forests of Leicestershire	By R. A. McKinley, M.A.	265

VOLUME THREE

		PAGE
Dedication .		vii
Contents .		ix
List of Illustrations		xi
List of Maps		xiii
Editorial Note		xv
Members of Committee		xvii
Classes of Public Records used		xix
Note on Abbreviations		xxi
Industries		
Introduction	By R. A. McKinley, M.A.	1
Hosiery .	By L. A. Parker, B.Sc., Ph.D.	2
Appendix: Evidence for Framework-Knitters, Stocking-Frames, Bag-Hosiers and Manufacturers in the County of Leicester .		20
Footwear .	By W. G. Hoskins, M.A., Ph.D.	23
Engineering and Metal Working .	By P. Russell, F.S.A.	25
Mining .	By R. A. McKinley, M.A.	30
Quarrying	,, ,,	43
Bell-Founding .	By E. Morris	47
Appendix I: Leicester Bell-Founders .		48
Appendix II: Leicestershire Bells		49
Banking .	By R. A. McKinley, M.A.	50
Roads	By P. Russell, F.S.A.	57
Appendix I: The Principal Road Bridges of Leicestershire		85
Appendix II: A Schedule of Turnpike Roads in Leicestershire		91
Canals	By A. T. Patterson, M.A.	92
Railways .	By Professor J. Simmons, M.A.	108
Population .	By C. T. Smith, M.A.	129
Table I: Domesday: Recorded Population, excluding landholders		156
Table II: 1377 Poll Tax .		163
Table III: Diocesan Population Return, 1563 .		166

PAGE

Table IV: *Liber Cleri*, 1603: Communicants and Recusants 168

Table V: Hearth Tax, Michaelmas 1670 170

Table VI: Ecclesiastical Census, 1676 173

Table VII: Parish Register Statistics, 1700–1800 175

Table VIII: Rickman's Estimates of Population 175

Table of Population 1801–1951 . . By SUSAN M. G. REYNOLDS, M.A. . . . 176

Leicestershire Artists . . . By A. C. SEWTER, B.Sc., M.A. . . . 218

Education

Charity Schools . . . By R. A. McKINLEY, M.A. . . . 243

Elementary Education in the Nineteenth and Twentieth Centuries . . By R. A. McKINLEY, M.A. . . . 247

Adult and Further Education . . By Professor A. J. ALLAWAY, M.A. . . 252

Sport

Hunting . . . . By C. D. B. ELLIS, C.B.E., M.C., M.A., F.S.A., and the late Major T. G. F. PAGET, D.L. . . 269

Cricket . . . . By E. E. SNOW 282

Rugby Football . . . . ,, ,, . . . 286

Association Football . . . ,, ,, ... 288

Index to Volumes I–III . . . By JANET D. MARTIN, B.A., and L. H. IRVINE, M.B.E., M.A. 291

Corrigenda to Volume II 338

VOLUME FOUR

PAGE

Dedication v

Contents ix

List of Illustrations xi

List of Maps and Plans xiii

Editorial Note xv

Leicestershire Victoria County History Committee xvii

Classes of Public Records used xix

Note on Abbreviations xx

The City of Leicester

Political and Administrative History, 1066–1509 . . . By AUDREY M. ERSKINE 1

Social and Economic History, 1066–1509 . By MARIAN K. DALE . . . 31

Political and Administrative History, 1509–1660 . . . By DOREEN SLATTER . . . 55

Social and Economic History, 1509–1660 . By E. W. J. KERRIDGE . . . 76

Parliamentary History, 1660–1835 . By R. W. GREAVES 110

Social and Administrative History, 1660–1835 . . . By W. A. JENKINS and C. T. SMITH . . 153

Parliamentary History since 1835 . By R. H. EVANS 201

Social and Administrative History since 1835 . . . . By R. A. McKINLEY and C. T. SMITH . 251

Hosiery manufacture . . By C. ASHWORTH 303

Footwear manufacture . . By V. W. HOGG 314

Elastic Web manufacture . By JANET D. MARTIN . . . 326

Primary and Secondary Education . ,, ,, . . . 328

Schedule of Schools 335

The Ancient Borough

Topography . . . By R. A. McKINLEY and JANET D. MARTIN; the section on Wyggeston's Hospital in 'Almshouses and Hospitals' by R. M. GARD . . 338

CONTENTS OF VOLUMES: LEICS. IV

		PAGE
All Saints'	.	338
Black Friars .	.	343
Castle View .	.	344
The Newarke	.	346
St. Leonard's	.	348
St. Margaret's	.	350
St. Martin's .	.	361
St. Mary's .	.	369
Bromkinsthorpe	.	380
St. Nicholas's	.	383
White Friars .	.	387
Lost Churches .	.	388
Roman Catholicism	.	389
Protestant Nonconformity	.	390
Mills .	.	395
Hospitals and Almshouses	.	398
Municipal Charities	.	410
Parishes added to Leicester since 1892		
Topography		
Aylestone	By Janet D. Martin and Pauline Wilson .	415
Belgrave	By R. A. McKinley and Janet D. Martin .	420
Braunstone	,, ,, ,,	428
Evington	By Janet D. Martin and Dorothy Pidgeon	434
Humberstone	By Janet D. Martin and Ruth Bird	439
Knighton	,, ,, ,,	443
North-West Leicester .	By R. A. McKinley	447
The Seals, Insignia, and Corporate Offices of Leicester	,, ,,	457
Indexes to Volume IV	By Patricia M. Barnes	459
General Index	.	459
Leicester Index	.	473
Corrigenda to Volumes I–III	.	484

VOLUME FIVE

		PAGE
Dedication .	.	v
Contents .	.	ix
List of Illustrations	.	xi
List of Maps and Plans	.	xiii
Editorial Note	.	xv
Classes of Documents in the Public Record Office used	.	xvi
Note on Abbreviations	.	xvii
Topography	Descriptions of buildings in the first 22 parish articles by Margaret Tomlinson, in the remainder by S. R. Jones and Margaret Tomlinson	
Gartree Hundred .	By J. M. Lee .	1
Billesdon	By Janet D. Martin	6
Blaston	,, ,,	22
Husbands Bosworth	By J. M. Lee .	28
Great Bowden .	By R. A. McKinley	38
Bringhurst	By J. M. Lee .	49
Burrough on the Hill	By Janet D. Martin	61
Burton Overy .	By R. A. McKinley	68
Carlton Curlieu	By Janet D. Martin	77

PAGE

Cranoe	By JANET D. MARTIN		81
Fleckney	,, ,,		84
Foxton	By R. A. McKINLEY		90
Galby and Frisby	By JANET D. MARTIN		96
Great Glen	By R. A. McKINLEY		102
Glooston	By JANET D. MARTIN		112
Gumley	By J. M. LEE		116
Hallaton	By JANET D. MARTIN		121
Market Harborough	By R. A. McKINLEY		133
Horninghold	By JANET D. MARTIN		153
Houghton on the Hill	,, ,,		157
Illston on the Hill	,, ,,		163
Kibworth	By R. A. McKINLEY		167
Knossington	By JANET D. MARTIN		187
Church Langton	By J. M. LEE		193
Laughton	,, ,,		213
Lubenham	,, ,,		220
Medbourne	,, ,,		229
Mowsley	,, ,,		248
King's Norton	By R. A. McKINLEY		256
Noseley	By JANET D. MARTIN		264
Owston	,, ,,		270
Pickwell	By R. A. McKINLEY		275
Saddington	By JANET D. MARTIN		282
Scraptoft	,, ,,		287
Shangton	,, ,,		293
Slawston	,, ,,		297
Stockerston	,, ,,		303
Stonton Wyville	,, ,,		308
Theddingworth	By J. M. LEE		312
Thurnby	By JANET D. MARTIN		321
Welham	By J. M. LEE		330
Wistow	By JANET D. MARTIN		336
Index	By P. A. SPALDING		347
Corrigenda to Volumes I–IV			367

LINCOLNSHIRE
VOLUME TWO

PAGE

Dedication		v
Contents		ix
List of Illustrations		xiii
Editorial Note		xv
Ecclesiastical History (To A.D. 1600)	By Miss M. M. C. CALTHROP	1
,, ,, (From A.D. 1600)	By Miss S. MELHUISH	
Religious Houses		
Introduction	By the Sister ELSPETH of All Saints' Community	78
Lincoln Cathedral	By Miss PHYLLIS WRAGGE, Oxford Honours School of Modern History	80
Monastery of Ikanho	By the Sister ELSPETH of All Saints' Community	96
,, ,, Barrow	,, ,, ,,	97
Abbey of Bardney	,, ,, ,,	97
,, ,, Partney	,, ,, ,,	104
,, ,, Crowland	By Miss ROSE GRAHAM, F.R.Hist.S.	105

		PAGE
Cell of St. Pega	By the Sister ELSPETH of All Saints' Community .	118
Abbey of Stow	,, ,, ,, .	118
Priory of Spalding . . .	,, ,, ,, .	118
,, ,, Belvoir	,, ,, ,, .	124
,, ,, St. Leonard, Stamford . .	,, ,, ,, .	127
,, ,, Freiston . . .	,, ,, ,, .	128
,, ,, Deeping . . .	,, ,, ,, .	129
,, ,, St. Mary Magdalene, Lincoln .	,, ,, ,, .	129
Cell of Sandtoft	,, ,, ,, .	130
,, ,, 'Henes' . . .	,, ,, ,, .	130
Priory of Stainfield . . .	,, ,, ,, .	131
Abbey of Humberston . . .	,, ,, ,, .	133
,, ,, Kirkstead . . .	,, ,, ,, .	135
,, ,, Louth Park . . .	,, ,, ,, .	138
,, ,, Revesby . . .	,, ,, ,, .	141
,, ,, Vaudey	,, ,, ,, .	143
,, ,, Swineshead . . .	,, ,, ,, .	145
Priory of Stixwould . . .	,, ,, ,, .	146
,, ,, Heynings . . .	,, ,, ,, .	149
,, ,, Nuncotham . . .	,, ,, ,, .	151
,, ,, Legbourne . . .	,, ,, ,, .	153
,, ,, Greenfield . . .	,, ,, ,, .	155
,, ,, Gokewell . . .	,, ,, ,, .	156
,, ,, Fosse	,, ,, ,, .	157
,, ,, Axholme . . .	By Miss ROSE GRAHAM, F.R.Hist.S. .	158
Abbey of Grimsby or Wellow . .	By the Sister ELSPETH of All Saints' Community .	161
Priory of Hyrst . . .	,, ,, ,, .	163
Abbey of Thornton . . .	,, ,, ,, .	163
Priory of Thornholm . . .	,, ,, ,, .	166
,, ,, Nocton Park . . .	,, ,, ,, .	168
,, ,, Torksey . . .	,, ,, ,, .	170
,, ,, Elsham . . .	,, ,, ,, .	171
,, ,, Kyme . . .	,, ,, ,, .	172
,, ,, Markby . . .	,, ,, ,, .	174
,, ,, Newstead by Stamford . .	,, ,, ,, .	176
Abbey of Bourne	,, ,, ,, .	177
Priory of St. Leonard, Grimsby . .	,, ,, ,, .	179
,, ,, Sempringham . . .	By Miss ROSE GRAHAM, F.R.Hist.S. .	179
,, ,, Haverholme . . .	,, ,, . .	187
,, ,, St. Catherine outside Lincoln .	,, ,, . .	188
,, ,, Bullington . . .	,, ,, . .	191
,, ,, Alvingham . . .	,, ,, . .	192
,, ,, Sixhills . . .	,, ,, . .	194
,, ,, North Ormsby, or Nun Ormsby	,, ,, . .	195
,, ,, Catley	,, ,, . .	196
,, ,, Tunstall . . .	,, ,, . .	197
,, ,, Newstead-on-Ancholme .	,, ,, . .	197
,, ,, St. Saviour, Bridgend in Horbling	,, ,, . .	198
Abbey of Newhouse of Newsham . .	By the Sister ELSPETH of All Saints' Community .	199
,, ,, Barlings . . .	,, ,, ,, .	202
,, ,, Hagnaby . . .	,, ,, ,, .	205
,, ,, Tupholme . . .	,, ,, ,, .	206
,, ,, Newbo . . .	,, ,, ,, .	207
Priory of Orford . . .	,, ,, ,, .	209
Commandery of Maltby by Louth .	,, ,, ,, .	209
,, ,, Skirbeck . . .	,, ,, ,, .	210
,, ,, Lincoln . . .	,, ,, ,, .	210

CONTENTS OF VOLUMES: LINCS. II

PAGE

Preceptory of Willoughton	By the Sister ELSPETH of All Saints' Community	210
,, ,, Eagle	,, ,, ,,	211
,, ,, Aslackby	,, ,, ,,	211
,, ,, South Witham	,, ,, ,,	212
,, ,, Temple Bruer	,, ,, ,,	212
Austin Friars of Boston	By A. G. LITTLE, M.A.	213
Black Friars of Boston	,, ,,	214
Grey Friars of Boston	,, ,,	215
White Friars of Boston	,, ,,	216
Grey Friars of Grantham	,, ,,	217
Austin Friars of Grimsby	,, ,,	218
Grey Friars of Grimsby	,, ,,	219
Austin Friars of Lincoln	,, ,,	219
Black Friars of Lincoln	,, ,,	220
Grey Friars of Lincoln	,, ,,	222
White Friars of Lincoln	,, ,,	224
Friars of the Sack, of Lincoln	,, ,,	225
Austin Friars of Stamford	,, ,,	225
Black Friars of Stamford	,, ,,	226
Grey Friars of Stamford	,, ,,	227
White Friars of Stamford	,, ,,	229
Friars of the Sack, of Stamford	,, ,,	230
Hospital of Holy Innocents without Lincoln	By the Sister ELSPETH of All Saints' Community	230
Hospital of St. Mary Magdalene, Partney	,, ,, ,,	232
,, ,, Boothby Pagnell	,, ,, ,,	232
,, ,, Glanford Bridge, or Wrawby	,, ,, ,,	232
,, ,, St. Giles without Lincoln	,, ,, ,,	233
,, ,, Mere	,, ,, ,,	233
,, ,, St. John Baptist without Boston	,, ,, ,,	233
,, ,, St. Leonard without the Castle of Lincoln	,, ,, ,,	233
Hospital of St. Mary Magdalene, Lincoln	,, ,, ,,	234
,, ,, Grimsby	,, ,, ,,	234
,, ,, Louth	,, ,, ,,	234
,, ,, Spalding	,, ,, ,,	234
,, ,, St. Bartholomew without Lincoln	,, ,, ,,	234
Hospital of St. John Baptist and St. Thomas the Martyr on Stamford Bridge	,, ,, ,,	234
Hospital of St. Giles, Stamford	,, ,, ,,	234
,, ,, All Saints', Stamford	,, ,, ,,	234
,, ,, Walcot	,, ,, ,,	235
,, ,, Langworth	,, ,, ,,	235
,, ,, Thornton	,, ,, ,,	235
,, ,, Holbeach	,, ,, ,,	235
Hospital called Spittal on the Street	,, ,, ,,	235
Hospital of Grantham	,, ,, ,,	235
College of Spilsby	,, ,, ,,	236
Cantilupe College	,, ,, ,,	236
College of Tattershall	,, ,, ,,	237
,, ,, Thornton	,, ,, ,,	237
Priory of Covenham	,, ,, ,,	238
,, ,, Burwell	,, ,, ,,	238
,, ,, Minting	,, ,, ,,	239
,, ,, Wilsford	,, ,, ,,	240
,, ,, Haugham	,, ,, ,,	240

PAGE

Priory of Willoughton	By the Sister Elspeth of All Saints' Community	241
„ „ Bonby	„ „ „	241
„ „ Wenghale	„ „ „	241
„ „ Great Limber	„ „ „	242
„ „ Long Bennington	„ „ „	242
„ „ Hough	„ „ „	242
„ „ Cammeringham	„ „ „	243
„ „ West Ravendale	„ „ „	243
„ „ North Hykeham	„ „ „	244
Political History	By C. H. Vellacott, B.A.	245
Social and Economic History	By the Revd. W. O. Massingberd, M.A.	293
Table of Population, 1801–1901	By Geo. S. Minchin	356
Industries		
Introduction	By the Revd. W. O. Massingberd, M.A.	381
Deep Sea Fisheries and Fish Docks	By Miss Ethel M. Hewitt	388
Mines and Quarries	„ „	393
Agricultural Implement Manufacturers	„ „	394
Agriculture	By G. E. Collins	397
Forestry	By the Revd. J. C. Cox, LL.D., F.S.A.	417
Schools	By A. F. Leach, M.A., F.S.A.	421
Sport Ancient and Modern	Edited by E. D. Cuming	
Fox Hunting	By G. E. Collins	493
The Brocklesby Hunt	„ „	493
The Burton Hunt	By the Rt. Hon. Lord Monson and G. E. Collins	499
The Blankney Hunt	By G. E. Collins	502
The Southwold Hunt	„ „	503
Mr. Ewbank's Hunt	„ „	505
The Belvoir Hunt	„ „	505
The Marquess of Exeter's Hunt	„ „	505
Harriers and Beagles	„ „	506
Otter Hounds	„ „	506
Racing	By Cuthbert Bradley	506
Polo	„ „	511
Shooting	By the Revd. J. F. Quirk, M.A.	511
Wild Fowling	By Henry Sharp	514
Coursing	By J. W. Bourne	518
Angling	By R. Mason	519
Golf	By W. T. Warrener	525
Athletics	By J. E. Fowler Dixon	528

LONDON

VOLUME ONE

PAGE

Dedication		v
The Advisory Council of the Victoria History		vii
General Advertisement		vii
Contents		xiii
List of Illustrations and Maps		xvii
Preface		xxi
Table of Abbreviations		xxv
Romano-British London		
Introduction: Burials and Roads	By R. A. Smith, B.A., F.S.A.	1
The Roman City Wall	By F. W. Reader	43

PAGE

Note on Roman Pottery found in London	By H. B. WALTERS, M.A., F.S.A.	83
List of Roman Emperors	,, ,, ,,	84
Topographical Index:		
City of London	,, ,, ,,	86
,, Westminster	,, ,, ,,	135
Borough of Southwark (with Bermondsey, Lambeth, and Newington)	,, ,, ,,	136
References to Plan C	,, ,, ,,	142
,, ,, D	,, ,, ,,	145
,, ,, A	By R. A. SMITH, B.A., F.S.A.	146
Anglo-Saxon Remains	,, ,,	147
Ecclesiastical History		
Part I, to 1348	By Miss JOYCE JEFFRIES DAVIS, Oxford Honours School of Modern History	171
Part II, 1348–1521	By Miss JOYCE JEFFRIES DAVIS, Miss E. JEFFRIES DAVIS, B.A. Lond., and Miss M. E. CORNFORD	207
Part III, 1521–1547	By Miss E. JEFFRIES DAVIS, B.A. Lond.	245
Part IV, 1547–1563	By Miss M. E. CORNFORD	287
Part V, 1563–1666	,, ,,	309
Part VI, 1666–1907	By Miss H. L. E. GARBETT	339
Part VII, Nonconformity in London	By the Revd. T. G. CRIPPEN	374
Ecclesiastical Divisions	By J. M. RAMSAY, M.A.	400
Parochial Records	By Miss E. JEFFRIES DAVIS, B.A. Lond.	404
Religious Houses		
Introduction	By Miss M. REDDAN, Hist. Tripos	407
Cathedral of St. Paul	By Miss H. DOUGLAS-IRVINE, M.A. St. Andrews	409
St. Peter's Abbey, Westminster	By Miss PHYLLIS WRAGGE, Oxford Honours School of Modern History	433
St. Helen's Bishopsgate	By Miss M. REDDAN, Hist. Tripos	457
Eastminster, New Abbey, or the Abbey of St. Mary de Graciis	,, ,, ,,	461
Priory of Holy Trinity Aldgate	,, ,, ,,	465
,, ,, St. Bartholomew Smithfield	,, ,, ,,	475
,, ,, Southwark	By the Revd. J. C. COX, LL.D., F.S.A.	480
The Temple	By Miss M. REDDAN, Hist. Tripos	485
Hospital of St. Thomas of Acon	,, ,, ,,	491
,, St. Mary of Bethlehem	,, ,, ,,	495
The Black Friars	,, ,, ,,	498
The Grey Friars	,, ,, ,,	502
The White Friars	,, ,, ,,	507
The Austin Friars	,, ,, ,,	510
The Friars of the Sack	,, ,, ,,	513
The Crossed Friars	,, ,, ,,	514
The Pied Friars, or Friars de Pica	,, ,, ,,	516
The Friars de Areno	,, ,, ,,	516
The Minoresses Without Aldgate	,, ,, ,,	516
Hospital of St. Bartholomew	,, ,, ,,	520
,, ,, St. Katharine by the Tower	,, ,, ,,	525
,, ,, St. Mary Without Bishopsgate	,, ,, ,,	530
,, ,, St. Mary Within Cripplegate	,, ,, ,,	535
,, ,, St. Thomas Southwark	By the Revd. J. C. COX, LL.D., F.S.A.	538
Leper Hospital of Southwark	,, ,, ,,	542
Hospital of St. James Westminster	By Miss M. REDDAN, Hist. Tripos	542
,, ,, the Savoy	,, ,, ,,	546
Whittington's Hospital	,, ,, ,,	549
Milbourne's Almshouses	,, ,, ,,	549

		PAGE
Hospital of St. Augustine Pappey . .	By Miss M. REDDAN, Hist. Tripos . . .	550
Jesus Commons	,, ,, ,, . .	551
Domus Conversorum . . .	,, ,, ,, . .	551
Collegiate Church of St. Martin le Grand	,, ,, ,, . .	555
The Royal Free Chapel of St. Stephen Westminster	,, ,, ,, . .	566
The Chapel of St. Peter ad Vincula in the Tower of London . . .	,, ,, ,, . .	571
The Chapel of St. Thomas on London Bridge	,, ,, ,, . .	572
The College of St. Laurence Pountney .	,, ,, ,, . .	574
The College in the Guildhall Chapel .	,, ,, ,, . .	576
Walworth's College in St. Michael Crooked Lane . . .	,, ,, ,, . .	577
The Fraternity of the Holy Trinity and of the Sixty Priests in Leadenhall Chapel	,, ,, ,, . .	578
Whittington's College . . .	,, ,, ,, . .	578
The College in Allhallows Barking .	,, ,, ,, . .	580
The Hospital of St. Anthony . .	,, ,, ,, . .	581
,, ,, St. Mary Rouncivall .	,, ,, ,, . .	584
,, ,, St. Giles Without Cripplegate . . .	,, ,, ,, . .	585
The Hermits and Anchorites of London .	,, ,, ,, . .	585

MIDDLESEX

VOLUME ONE

		PAGE
Dedication	. . . . .	v
Contents	. . . .	ix
List of Illustrations . .	. . . . .	xi
List of Maps . . .	. . . . .	xiii
Editorial Note . . .	. . . . .	xv
Middlesex Victoria County History Council .	. . . .	xvii
Classes of Documents in the Public Record Office used . . .	. . . . .	xix
Classes of Documents in the Greater London Record Office (Middlesex Records) used	. . . .	xxi
Note on Abbreviations . .	. . . .	xxiii
The Physique of Middlesex . .	By the late Professor S. W. WOOLDRIDGE, C.B.E., F.R.S. . . .	I
Archaeology		
The Lower Palaeolithic Age .	By J. d'A. WAECHTER with additions and notes by J. J. WYMER . . .	II
The Mesolithic Age . .	By A. D. LACAILLE . .	21
The Neolithic Age . .	By F. S. C. CELORIA and JEAN MACDONALD .	29
The Beaker Period . .	,, ,, ,, .	36
The Bronze Age . . .	,, ,, ,, .	42
The Iron Age . . .	,, ,, ,, .	50
The Romano-British Period .	,, ,, ,, .	64
The Pagan Saxon Period . .	,, ,, ,, .	74
Domesday Survey		
Introduction . . .	By T. G. PINDER . .	80
Translation of the Text . .	,, ,, . .	119

CONTENTS OF VOLUMES: MIDDX. I

PAGE

Ecclesiastical Organization . . .	By H. P. F. KING, K. G. T. McDONNELL, and D. C. YAXLEY	. 139
The Jews	By DIANE K. BOLTON . . .	. 149
Religious Houses		
Introduction	By J. S. COCKBURN	. 153
The Priory of Stratford at Bow .	By H. P. F. KING	. 156
The London Charterhouse .	By Professor the Revd. D. C. KNOWLES, Litt.D., F.B.A. . . .	. 159
Bentley Priory . . .	By J. L. KIRBY	. 169
The Priory of St. Mary, Clerkenwell .	,, ,, ...	. 170
,, ,, Haliwell . .	,, ,, ...	. 174
,, ,, Kilburn . .	,, ,, ...	. 178
Syon Abbey . . .	By F. R. JOHNSTON . . .	. 182
The Priory of Hounslow . .	By J. L. KIRBY . . .	. 191
,, ,, St. John of Jerusalem, Clerkenwell . . .	By HELENA M. CHEW . . .	. 193
The Priory of Harmondsworth .	By J. L. KIRBY . . .	. 200
,, ,, Ruislip . .	By MARJORIE M. CHIBNALL . .	. 202
Aldersgate Hospital . . .	By MARJORIE B. HONEYBOURNE .	. 204
The Hospital of the Virgin Mary and the Nine Orders of Holy Angels, Brentford	,, ,, .	. 204
Hammersmith Hospital . .	,, ,, .	. 205
The Hospital of St. Anthony, Highgate .	,, ,, .	. 205
The Hospital of St. Giles-in-the-Fields, Holborn . . .	,, ,, .	. 206
Kingsland (or Hackney) Hospital .	,, ,, .	. 210
Knightsbridge Hospital . .	,, ,, .	. 211
Mile End Hospital . . .	,, ,, .	. 212
The Education of the Working Classes to 1870	By Professor A. M. ROSS . .	. 213
Private Education from the Sixteenth Century	By MARGARET E. BRYANT . .	. 241
Schools	By J. D. MELLOR; Highgate School by H. P. F. KING	
Christ's College, Finchley .	. . . . .	. 290
Coborn School . . .	. . . . .	. 290
The Coopers' Company's School .	. . . . .	. 291
Davenant Foundation Grammar School .	. . . . .	. 293
Enfield Grammar School . .	. . . . .	. 294
Haberdashers' Aske's Schools .	. . . . .	. 296
Hampton Grammar School .	. . . . .	. 298
Harrow School . . .	. . . . .	. 299
Highgate School . . .	. . . . .	. 302
Latymer and Godolphin Schools .	. . . . .	. 305
St. Marylebone Grammar School .	. . . . .	. 306
Mill Hill School . . .	. . . . .	. 307
The North London Collegiate School .	. . . . .	. 308
Owen's School . . .	. . . . .	. 310
Queen's College, Harley Street .	. . . . .	. 311
Raine's Foundation Schools .	. . . . .	. 312
Tottenham Grammar School .	. . . . .	. 314
The University of London		
The University . . .	By Professor H. H. BELLOT, LL.D.	. 315
The Constituent Colleges . .	By J. S. COCKBURN . . .	. 345
Index of Persons and Places in the Domesday Survey . . .	By T. G. PINDER . . .	. 361
General Index . . .	By D. C. YAXLEY . . .	. 363
Corrigenda to Volumes II and III .	. . . . .	. 385

VOLUME TWO

		PAGE
Dedication		v
Contents		ix
List of Illustrations and Maps		xi
Editorial Note		xiii
Ancient Earthworks	By J. C. WALL	1
Political History	By J. VIVIEN MELLOR	15
Social and Economic History	By MARY E. TANNER	65
Table of Population, 1801–1901	By GEORGE S. MINCHIN	112
Industries	By CHARLES WELCH, F.S.A.	
Introduction		121
Silk-weaving		132
Tapestry		138
Cabinet-making and Wood-carving		139
Pottery		141
Fulham Stoneware		142
Bow Porcelain		146
Chelsea Porcelain		150
Glass		155
Clock and Watch-making		158
Bell-founders		165
Brewing		168
Tobacco		179
Musical Instruments		180
Coach-making		193
Paper		195
Printing		197
Bookbinding		201
Agriculture	By CHARLES KAINS JACKSON	205
Forestry	By the Revd. J. C. COX, LL.D., F.S.A.	223
Sport, Ancient and Modern		
Introduction	By URQUHART A. FORBES	253
Hunting	,, ,,	259
Foxhounds	,, ,,	259
Staghounds	,, ,,	260
Harriers	,, ,,	262
Coursing	,, ,,	262
Racing	,, ,,	263
Polo	,, ,,	265
Shooting	,, ,,	266
Angling	,, ,,	267
Cricket	By Sir HOME GORDON, Bart.	
Middlesex County		270
The Marylebone Cricket Club		273
The University Match		274
The Australians at Lord's		274
Harrow School Cricket		275
Football	By C. J. B. MARRIOTT, M.A.	276
Golf	By URQUHART A. FORBES	278
Pastimes	,, ,,	
Archery		283
Rowing		286
Tennis		290
Boxing	By C. J. B. MARRIOTT, M.A.	292
Olympic Games of London (1908)	By URQUHART A. FORBES	295

PAGE

Athletics . . . . . . By W. BIRKETT 301
Topography . . . . General descriptions and manorial descents compiled
under the superintendence of the General Editor;
Architectural descriptions by J. MURRAY KENDALL,
R. W. ATKEY, and C. C. DURSTON, under the
superintendence of C. R. PEERS, M.A., F.S.A.;
Heraldic drawings and blazon by the Revd.
E. E. DORLING, M.A., F.S.A.; Charities from
information supplied by J. W. OWSLEY, I.S.O.,
late Official Trustee of Charitable Funds.

Spelthorne Hundred
Introduction . . . . By J. VIVIEN MELLOR 305
Ashford . . . . ,, ,, . . . 306
East Bedfont with Hatton . . ,, ,, . . . 309
Feltham . . . . ,, ,, . . . 314
Hampton with Hampton Wick . . By EDITH M. KEATE . . . 319
(Description of Hampton Court by C. R. PEERS,
M.A., F.S.A.)
Hanworth . . . . By J. VIVIEN MELLOR . . . 391
Laleham . . . . . ,, ,, . . . 396
Littleton . . . . . ,, ,, . . . 401

VOLUME THREE

PAGE

Dedication v
Contents ix
List of Illustrations xi
List of Maps and Plans xiii
Editorial Note xv
Middlesex Victoria County History Council xvii
Classes of Public Records used xviii
Classes of Documents in the Middlesex
Record Office used xix
Note on Abbreviations xx
Spelthorne Hundred (cont.)
Shepperton . . . . By D. F. A. KIDDLE . . . 1
Staines . . . . By SUSAN REYNOLDS . . . 13
Stanwell . . . . ,, ,, . . . 33
Sunbury . . . . By D. F. A. KIDDLE . . . 51
Teddington . . . . By SUSAN REYNOLDS . . . 66
Isleworth Hundred . . . ,, ,, . . . 83
Heston and Isleworth . . . ,, ,, . . . 85
Twickenham . . . . ,, ,, . . . 139
Elthorne Hundred . . . By GILLIAN WYLD . . . 167
Cowley . . . . By SUSAN REYNOLDS . . . 170
Cranford . . . . By GILLIAN WYLD . . . 177
West Drayton . . . . By R. B. ROSE . . . 187
Greenford . . . . By GILLIAN WYLD . . . 206
Hanwell . . . . By SUSAN REYNOLDS . . . 220
Harefield . . . . By GILLIAN WYLD . . . 237
Harlington . . . . By SUSAN REYNOLDS . . . 258
Index to Volumes II and III . . . By GILLIAN WYLD . . . 277
Corrigenda to Volume II 325

NORFOLK
VOLUME ONE

		PAGE
Dedication	. . . .	v
The Advisory Council of the Victoria History	. . . . . .	vii
General Advertisement	. . . .	vii
The Norfolk County Committee	. . . .	xiii
Contents	. . . .	xv
List of Illustrations	. . . .	xvii
Preface	. . . .	xix
Natural History		
Geology	By H. B. WOODWARD, F.R.S., F.G.S. .	1
Palaeontology	By RICHARD L. LYDEKKER, B.A., F.R.S., F.G.S. .	31
Botany	Edited by HERBERT D. GELDART . .	39
Rubi and Rosae (*Brambles and Roses*)	By HERBERT D. GELDART . . .	55
Menthae	,, ,, .	56
Naiadaceae	,, ,, .	57
Filices (*Ferns, etc.*)	,, ,, .	57
Characeae	By the Revd. G. R. BULLOCK-WEBSTER, M.A. .	58
Musci (*Mosses*) and Hepaticae (*Liverworts*)	By H. N. DIXON, M.A., F.L.S. .	62
Marine Algae	By HERBERT D. GELDART . . .	67
Diatomaceae	,, ,, . . .	69
Lichenes (*Lichens*)	By the Revd. J. CROMBIE, M.A., F.L.S., F.G.S. .	70
Fungi	By C. B. PLOWRIGHT, M.D., L.R.C.P., F.R.C.S. .	72
Zoology		
Marine Zoology	By WALTER GARSTANG, M.A., F.L.S. .	77
Mollusca (*Snails, etc.*)	By B. B. WOODWARD, F.G.S., F.R.M.S. .	87
Insecta (*Insects*)		
Orthoptera (*Grasshoppers, etc.*)	By J. EDWARDS, F.E.S. . .	89
Neuroptera (*Dragonflies*) and Trichoptera (*Caddis-flies*)	,, ,, . . .	91
Hymenoptera (*Bees, etc.*)	By CHARLES G. BARRETT, F.E.S. .	94
Coleoptera (*Beetles*)	By J. EDWARDS, F.E.S. . .	110
Lepidoptera (*Butterflies and Moths*)	By CHARLES G. BARRETT, F.E.S. .	135
Hemiptera (*Bugs and Cicadas*)	By J. EDWARDS, F.E.S. . .	162
Myriapoda (*Centipedes, etc.*)	By R. I. POCOCK . .	171
Arachnida (*Spiders, etc.*)	By F. O. PICKARD-CAMBRIDGE, M.A. .	173
Crustacea (*Crabs, Lobsters, etc.*)	By the Revd. T. R. R. STEBBING, M.A., F.R.S., F.L.S. . . .	183
Pisces (*Fishes*)	By JOHN LOWE, M.D., F.L.S. .	200
Reptilia (*Reptiles*) and Batrachia (*Batrachians*)	By THOMAS SOUTHWELL, F.Z.S. .	217
Aves (*Birds*)	,, ,, .	220
Mammalia (*Mammals*)	,, ,, .	246
Early Man	By GEORGE CLINCH, F.G.S. .	253
Romano-British Remains	By F. HAVERFIELD, M.A., F.S.A. .	279
Anglo-Saxon Remains	By REGINALD A. SMITH, B.A. .	325

VOLUME TWO

		PAGE
Dedication	. . . .	v
Contents	. . . .	ix
List of Illustrations	. . . .	xiii

CONTENTS OF VOLUMES: NORF. II

PAGE

Editorial Note xv
Table of Abbreviations xvii
Introduction to the Norfolk Domesday . By CHARLES JOHNSON, M.A. . . . I
Translation of the Norfolk Domesday . By CHARLES JOHNSON, M.A., and E. SALISBURY, B.A. 39
The Danegeld in Norfolk . . . By CHARLES JOHNSON, M.A. . . . 204
Ecclesiastical History (To A.D. 1279) . By the Revd. Canon JESSOP, D.D., F.S.A. . . 213
    ,,   ,,   (From A.D. 1279) . By Miss M. E. SIMKINS
Religious Houses . . . . . By the Revd. J. C. COX, LL.D., F.S.A.
    Introduction . . . . . . ,, ,, . . 315
    Cathedral Priory of the Holy Trinity of
        Norwich . . . . . ,, ,, . . 317
    Priory of Aldeby . . . . . ,, ,, . . 328
        ,, ,, Lynn . . . . . ,, ,, . . 328
        ,, ,, St. Leonard, Norwich . . ,, ,, . . 329
        ,, ,, Yarmouth . . . . ,, ,, . . 330
    Abbey of St. Benet of Holm . . . ,, ,, . . 330
        ,, ,, Wymondham . . . . ,, ,, . . 336
    Priory of Binham . . . . ,, ,, . . 343
        ,, ,, St. Faith, Horsham . . ,, ,, . . 346
        ,, ,, Modeney . . . . ,, ,, . . 349
        ,, ,, Molycourt . . . . ,, ,, . . 349
        ,, ,, Blackborough . . . ,, ,, . . 350
        ,, ,, Carrow . . . . ,, ,, . . 351
    Nunnery of St. George, Thetford . . ,, ,, . . 354
    Priory of Castle Acre . . . ,, ,, . . 356
        ,, ,, Normansburgh . . . ,, ,, . . 358
    Cell of Slevesholm . . . . ,, ,, . . 359
    Priory of Bromholm . . . . ,, ,, . . 359
        ,, ,, St. Mary, Thetford . . ,, ,, . . 363
    Abbey of Marham . . . . ,, ,, . . 369
        ,, ,, Creake . . . . ,, ,, . . 370
    Priory of Beeston . . . . ,, ,, . . 372
        ,, ,, Bromehill . . . . ,, ,, . . 374
        ,, ,, Old Buckenham . . . ,, ,, . . 376
        ,, ,, Coxford . . . . ,, ,, . . 378
        ,, ,, Flitcham . . . . ,, ,, . . 380
        ,, ,, Hempton . . . . ,, ,, . . 381
        ,, ,, Hickling . . . . ,, ,, . . 383
        ,, ,, Great Massingham . . . ,, ,, . . 386
        ,, ,, Mountjoy . . . . ,, ,, . . 387
        ,, ,, Pentney . . . . ,, ,, . . 388
        ,, ,, Peterstone . . . . ,, ,, . . 391
        ,, ,, the Holy Sepulchre, Thetford . ,, ,, . . 391
        ,, ,, Walsingham . . . . ,, ,, . . 394
        ,, ,, West Acre . . . . ,, ,, . . 402
        ,, ,, Weybourne . . . . ,, ,, . . 404
        ,, ,, Weybridge . . . . ,, ,, . . 406
        ,, ,, Wormegay . . . . ,, ,, . . 407
        ,, ,, Crabhouse . . . . ,, ,, . . 408
        ,, ,, Ingham . . . . ,, ,, . . 410
        ,, ,, Shouldham . . . . ,, ,, . . 412
    Abbey of West Dereham . . . ,, ,, . . 414
        ,, ,, Langley . . . . ,, ,, . . 418
        ,, ,, Wendling . . . . ,, ,, . . 421
    Preceptory of Carbrooke . . . ,, ,, . . 423
    Carmelite Friars of Blakeney . . . ,, ,, . . 425
        ,,   ,,   Burnham Norton . ,, ,, . . 425

		PAGE
Dominican Friars of Lynn . .	By the Revd. J. C. Cox, LL.D., F.S.A. .	. 426
Franciscan Friars of Lynn . . .	,, ,, .	. 427
Carmelite Friars of Lynn	,, ,, .	. 427
Austin Friars of Lynn	,, ,, .	. 427
Friars of the Sack, Lynn	,, ,, .	. 428
Dominican Friars of Norwich . .	,, ,, .	. 428
Franciscan Friars of Norwich . .	,, ,, .	. 430
Carmelite Friars of Norwich . .	,, ,, .	. 431
Austin Friars of Norwich . . .	,, ,, .	. 432
Friars of the Lesser Orders, Norwich .	,, ,, .	. 433
Dominican Friars of Thetford . .	,, ,, .	. 433
Austin Friars of Thetford . . .	,, ,, .	. 434
Franciscan Friars of Walsingham . .	,, ,, .	. 435
Dominican Friars of Yarmouth . .	,, ,, .	. 435
Franciscan Friars of Yarmouth . .	,, ,, .	. 436
Carmelite Friars of Yarmouth . .	,, ,, .	. 437
Austin Friars of Yarmouth . .	,, ,, .	. 437
Hospital of Beck	,, ,, .	. 438
,, ,, Boycodeswade, Coxford .	,, ,, .	. 439
,, ,, Hardwick . . .	,, ,, .	. 439
,, ,, Hautbois . . .	,, ,, .	. 439
,, ,, Herringby . . .	,, ,, .	. 439
,, ,, Horning . . .	,, ,, .	. 440
,, ,, Ickburgh . . .	,, ,, .	. 440
,, ,, Langwade . . .	,, ,, .	. 440
,, ,, St. John Baptist, Lynn .	,, ,, .	. 441
,, ,, St. Mary Magdalen, Lynn .	,, ,, .	. 441
Lazar Houses, Lynn . . .	,, ,, .	. 442
Hospital of St. Giles, Norwich . .	,, ,, .	. 442
,, ,, Hildebrond, Norwich . .	,, ,, .	. 446
,, ,, St. Paul, Norwich . .	,, ,, .	. 447
,, ,, St. Mary Magdalen, Norwich .	,, ,, .	. 448
Lazar Houses at the Norwich Gates .	,, ,, .	. 449
Hospital of St. Saviour, Norwich . .	,, ,, .	. 449
Other Small Hospitals at Norwich .	,, ,, .	. 449
Hospital of Racheness . . .	,, ,, .	. 450
,, ,, West Somerton . .	,, ,, .	. 450
Hospitals of Thetford		
God's House or Domus Dei . .	,, ,, .	. 450
St. Mary and St. Julian . .	,, ,, .	. 451
St. Mary Magdalen . . .	,, ,, .	. 451
St. John Baptist . . .	,, ,, .	. 452
St. John	,, ,, .	. 452
St. Margaret	,, ,, .	. 452
Lazar House of Walsingham . .	,, ,, .	. 452
Hospital of Walsoken . . .	,, ,, .	. 452
,, ,, Wymondham . .	,, ,, .	. 453
,, ,, St. Mary, Yarmouth .	,, ,, .	. 453
Lazar Houses of Yarmouth . .	,, ,, .	. 453
College of Attleborough . . .	,, ,, .	. 453
,, ,, Holy Trinity or Thoresby, Lynn	,, ,, .	. 454
,, ,, the Chapel-in-the-Fields, Norwich	,, ,, .	. 455
College of Raveningham . . .	,, ,, .	. 457
,, ,, Rushworth . . .	,, ,, .	. 458
,, ,, Baily End, or Gild of St. Mary, Thetford	,, ,, .	. 460

PAGE

College of Thompson	By the Revd. J. C. Cox, LL.D., F.S.A.	461
Priory of Docking	,, ,,	462
,, ,, Field Dalling	,, ,,	462
,, ,, Horstead	,, ,,	463
,, ,, Lessingham	,, ,,	463
,, ,, Sporle	,, ,,	463
,, ,, Toft Monks	,, ,,	464
,, ,, Welle, or Well Hall in Gayton	,, ,,	465
,, ,, St. Winwaloe, Wereham	,, ,,	465
,, ,, Witchingham	,, ,,	466
Political History	Compiled upon information supplied by WALTER RYE	467
Medieval Painting	By GEORGE E. FOX, Hon. M.A., Oxon., F.S.A.	529
Early Christian Art	By J. ROMILLY ALLEN, F.S.A.	555

NORTHAMPTONSHIRE

VOLUME ONE

PAGE

Dedication		v
The Advisory Council of the Victoria History		vii
General Advertisement		vii
The Northamptonshire County Committee		xiii
Contents		xv
List of Illustrations		xvi
Preface		xix
Natural History		
Geology	By BEEBY THOMPSON, F.G.S.	I
Palaeontology	By RICHARD L. LYDEKKER, B.A., F.R.S., F.G.S.	41
Botany		
Introduction	By GEORGE CLARIDGE DRUCE, M.A., F.L.S.	47
The Botanical Districts	,, ,, ,,	57
Musci (*Mosses*)	By H. N. DIXON, M.A., F.L.S.	80
Hepaticae (*Liverworts*)	,, ,, ,,	84
Lichenes (*Lichens*)	,, ,, ,,	84
Fungi	,, ,, ,,	84
Zoology		
Mollusca (*Snails, etc.*)	By B. B. WOODWARD, F.G.S., F.R.M.S., and LIONEL E. ADAMS, B.A.	87
Insecta (*Insects*)	Edited by HERBERT GOSS, F.L.S., F.E.S.	89
Hymenoptera (*Bees, etc.*)	By GEORGE B. DIXON, F.E.S.	89
Coleoptera (*Beetles*)	By the Revd. Canon FOWLER, M.A., F.L.S., assisted by FRANK BOUSKELL, F.E.S., and WILLIAM HULL	90
Lepidoptera, Rhopalocera (*Butterflies*)	By HERBERT GOSS, F.L.S., F.E.S.	94
Lepidoptera, Heterocera (*Moths*)		
Nocturni, Geometrae, Drepanulidae, Pseudo-Bombyces, and Noctuae	By HERBERT GOSS, F.L.S., F.E.S., assisted by THOMAS HENRY BRIGGS, M.A., F.E.S., and Capt. J. A. M. VIPAN	97
Deltoides, Pyralides, Crambites, Tortrices, Tineae, and Pterophori	By EUSTACE R. BANKES, M.A., F.E.S.	100
Crustacea (*Crabs, etc.*)	By the Revd. T. R. R. STEBBING, M.A., F.R.S., F.L.S.	101

		PAGE
Pisces (*Fishes*)	By G. A. Boulenger, F.R.S., F.Z.S. .	108
Reptilia (*Reptiles*) and Batrachia (*Batrachians*) . . .	,, ,, ,, .	110
Aves (*Birds*)	By the Revd. H. H. Slater, M.A. . .	111
Mammalia (*Mammals*) . . .	By Lionel E. Adams, B.A. . . .	129
Early Man	By T. J. George, F.G.S. . . .	135
Romano-British Remains . . .	By F. Haverfield, M.A., F.S.A. .	157
Anglo-Saxon Remains . . .	By Reginald A. Smith, B.A. . .	223
Introduction to the Northamptonshire Domesday	By J. Horace Round, M.A. . .	257
Text of the Northamptonshire Domesday	,, ,, . . .	301
The Northamptonshire Survey . .	,, ,, . . .	357
Monumental Effigies . . .	By Albert Hartshorne, F.S.A. . .	393
Domesday Index	. . . . .	423

VOLUME TWO

		PAGE
Dedication	. . . .	v
Contents	. . . .	ix
List of Illustrations . . .	. . . . . .	xiii
Editorial Note . . .	. . . . . .	xvii
Table of Abbreviations . .	. . . . . .	xix
Ecclesiastical History . .	By the Revd. R. M. Serjeantson, M.A., and W. Ryland D. Adkins, B.A. . . .	1
Religious Houses . . .	By the Revd. J. C. Cox, LL.D., F.S.A.	
Introduction . . .	,, ,, ,, . .	79
Abbey of Peterborough . .	,, ,, ,, . .	83
Priory of Luffield . . .	,, ,, ,, . .	95
,, ,, St. Michael, Stamford .	,, ,, ,, . .	98
,, ,, Wothorpe . .	,, ,, ,, . .	101
,, ,, St. Andrew, Northampton	,, ,, ,, . .	102
,, ,, St. Augustine, Daventry	,, ,, ,, . .	109
Abbey of Delapré . . .	,, ,, ,, . .	114
,, ,, Pipewell . .	,, ,, ,, . .	116
Priory of Catesby . . .	,, ,, ,, . .	121
,, ,, Sewardsley . .	,, ,, ,, . .	125
Abbey of St. James, Northampton	,, ,, ,, . .	127
Priory of Canons Ashby . .	,, ,, ,, . .	130
,, ,, Chalcombe . .	,, ,, ,, . .	133
,, ,, Fineshade or Castle Hymel	,, ,, ,, . .	135
Hermitage of Grafton Regis .	,, ,, ,, . .	137
Nunnery of Rothwell . .	,, ,, ,, . .	137
Abbey of Sulby . . .	,, ,, ,, . .	138
Preceptory of Dingley . .	,, ,, ,, . .	142
Black Friars of Northampton .	,, ,, ,, . .	144
Franciscans of Northampton .	,, ,, ,, . .	146
Austin Friars of Northampton .	,, ,, ,, . .	147
Carmelite Friars of Northampton .	,, ,, ,, . .	148
Hospital of Armston . .	,, ,, ,, . .	149
,, ,, Aynho . .	,, ,, ,, . .	150
,, ,, St. James and St. John, Brackley . . .	,, ,, ,, . .	151
Hospital of St. Leonard, Brackley .	,, ,, ,, . .	153
,, ,, Cotes . .	,, ,, ,, . .	154
,, ,, St. David and the Holy Trinity, Kingsthorpe .	,, ,, ,, . .	154

PAGE

Hospital of St. John Baptist and St. John Evangelist, Northampton . .	By the Revd. J. C. Cox, LL.D., F.S.A. . .	156
Hospital of St. Leonard, Northampton .	,, ,, ,, .	159
,, ,, St. Thomas, Northampton .	,, ,, ,, .	161
,, ,, Walbeck, Northampton .	,, ,, ,, .	162
,, ,, St. Leonard, Peterborough .	,, ,, ,, .	162
,, ,, St. Thomas the Martyr, Peterborough . . .	,, ,, ,, .	162
Hospital of Pirho . . .	,, ,, ,, .	163
,, ,, St. Giles, Stamford .	,, ,, ,, .	163
,, ,, St. John Baptist and St. Thomas the Martyr, Stamford .	,, ,, ,,	164
House of St. Sepulchre, Stamford .	,, ,, ,, .	165
Hospital of St. Leonard, Towcester .	,, ,, ,, .	165
,, ,, St. Leonard, Thrapston .	,, ,, ,, .	166
College of Cotterstock . .	,, ,, ,, .	166
,, ,, Fotheringhay . .	,, ,, ,, .	170
,, ,, Higham Ferrers . .	,, ,, ,, .	177
,, ,, Irthlingborough . .	,, ,, ,, .	179
,, ,, All Saints, Northampton .	,, ,, ,, .	180
,, ,, Towcester . .	,, ,, ,, .	181
Priory of Everdon . . .	,, ,, ,, .	182
,, ,, Weedon Beck . .	,, ,, ,, .	182
,, ,, Weedon Pinkney or Weedon Louis	,, ,, ,, .	183
Early Christian Art . . .	By J. Romilly Allen, F.S.A. . .	187
Schools	By A. F. Leach, M.A., F.S.A. .	201
Industries		
Introduction . .	By C. H. Vellacott, B.A. . .	289
Quarries (Historical) . .	,, ,, . .	293
Quarries and Mines (Technical) .	By Beeby Thompson, F.C.S., F.G.S. .	298
Bell Founding . .	By T. J. George, F.G.S. . .	307
Pipe Making . .	By Bruce B. Muscott . .	308
Leather . . .	,, ,, . .	310
Boots and Shoes . .	,, ,, . .	317
Gloves . . .	By T. J. George, F.G.S. . .	331
Whips . . .	By Bruce B. Muscott . .	331
Textiles and Allied Trades .	By T. J. George, F.G.S. . .	332
Lace . . .	,, ,, . .	336
Paper . . .	By Bruce B. Muscott . .	339
Forestry . . .	By J. Nisbet, D. Oec. . .	341
Sport Ancient and Modern .	Edited by E. D. Cuming	
The Royal Buckhounds .	By Christopher A. Markham, F.S.A. .	353
Stag Hunting . .	,, ,, ,, .	354
Early Foxhounds . .	,, ,, ,, .	355
The Pytchley Hounds .	,, ,, ,, .	356
The Woodland Pytchley .	,, ,, ,, .	367
The Pytchley Country .	,, ,, ,, .	368
The Grafton Hounds .	,, ,, ,, .	369
The Grafton Country .	,, ,, ,, .	372
The Fitzwilliam Hounds .	,, ,, ,, .	373
Harriers and Beagles .	,, ,, ,, .	375
Otter Hunting . .	,, ,, ,, .	376
Coursing . . .	,, ,, ,, .	376
Falconry . . .	,, ,, ,, .	377
Shooting . . .	By the Rt. Hon. Lord Lilford .	377
Angling . . .	By M. R. L. White . .	380
Flat Racing . .	By Christopher A. Markham, F.S.A. .	382

CONTENTS OF VOLUMES: NORTHANTS. II

PAGE

Steeplechasing	By CHRISTOPHER A. MARKHAM, F.S.A.	383
Golf	By A. G. BRADLEY	386
Athletics	By CHARLES HERBERT	388
Cricket	By HOME GORDON, assisted by J. P. KINGSTON, B.A., P. H. FRYER, M.A., and the late W. G. GRACE, Jun., M.A.	388
Football	By C. M. PURVIS and C. W. ALCOCK	393
Polo	By CHRISTOPHER A. MARKHAM, F.S.A.	396
Ancient Earthworks	Compiled from notes and plans supplied by the Revd. E. A. DOWNMAN	397
Topography	General descriptions and manorial descents prepared by the General Editor, the Editors for the County, and Miss JOYCE JEFFRIES DAVIS, Oxford Honours School of Modern History; Architectural descriptions by C. R. PEERS, M.A., F.S.A., and J. A. GOTCH, F.S.A.; Heraldic drawings and blazon by the Revd. E. E. DORLING, M.A.	

Soke of Peterborough

Introduction	421
Borough of Peterborough (By Miss MARY BATESON)	424
Bainton	460
Barnack	463
Borough Fen	472
Castor	472
Sutton	481
Upton	483
Etton	486
Eye	490
Glinton	492
Helpston	495
Marholm	499
Maxey	502
Newborough	507
Northborough	508
Paston	512
Peakirk	519
St. Martin's, Stamford Baron	522
Thornhaugh	529
Ufford	533
Wansford	537
Wittering	539

Willybrook Hundred

Introduction	542
Apethorpe	543
Collyweston	550
Cotterstock	555
Duddington	560
Easton on the Hill	564
Fotheringhay	569
Glapthorn	576
King's Cliffe	579
Lutton	584
Nassington	586
Southwick	591
Tansor	595
Woodnewton	599
Yarwell	602

VOLUME THREE

	PAGE
Dedication	v
Contents	ix
List of Illustrations	xi
List of Maps	xv
Editorial Note	xvii
Topography — General descriptions and manorial descents compiled under the superintendence of WILLIAM PAGE, F.S.A.; Architectural descriptions, except where otherwise stated, by F. H. CHEETHAM, F.S.A.; Heraldic drawings and blazon by the Revd. E. E. DORLING, M.A., F.S.A.; Charities from information supplied by J. R. SMITH, of the Charity Commission	
Northampton Borough — By HELEN M. CAM, M.A.; Architectural descriptions by F. H. CHEETHAM, F.S.A., and Professor A. HAMILTON THOMPSON, M.A., D.Litt., F.S.A.	1
Polebrook Hundred	
Introduction — By JOHN BROWNBILL, M.A.	68
Barnwell St. Andrew — By CHARLOTTE M. CALTHROP, Class. Tripos	71
Benefield — ,, ,, ,,	76
Hemington — ,, ,, ,,	80
Luddington — ,, ,, ,,	83
Oundle — By JOHN BROWNBILL, M.A.; Architectural descriptions by F. H. CHEETHAM, F.S.A., and Professor A. HAMILTON THOMPSON, M.A., D.Litt., F.S.A.	85
Polebrook — By CHARLOTTE M. CALTHROP, Class. Tripos; Architectural descriptions by Professor A. HAMILTON THOMPSON, M.A., D.Litt., F.S.A., and F. H. CHEETHAM, F.S.A.	101
Thurning — By JOHN BROWNBILL, M.A.	109
Warmington — By JOHN BROWNBILL, M.A.; Architectural descriptions by F. H. CHEETHAM, F.S.A., and Professor A. HAMILTON THOMPSON, M.A., D.Litt., F.S.A.	113
Navisford Hundred	
Introduction — By CATHERINE M. JAMISON, Oxford Hon. School of Mod. Hist.	123
Clapton — ,, ,, ,,	125
Pilton — ,, ,, ,, Architectural descriptions by Professor A. HAMILTON THOMPSON, M.A., D.Litt., F.S.A., and F. H. CHEETHAM, F.S.A.	129
Stoke Doyle — By CATHERINE M. JAMISON, Oxford Hon. School of Mod. Hist.	132
Thorpe Achurch — ,, ,, ,,	135
Thrapston — ,, ,, ,, Architectural descriptions by Professor A. HAMILTON THOMPSON, M.A., D.Litt., F.S.A., and F. H. CHEETHAM, F.S.A.	139
Titchmarsh — By CATHERINE JAMISON, Oxford Hon. School of Mod. Hist.	142
Wadenhoe — ,, ,, ,,	149
Huxloe Hundred	
Introduction — ,, ,, ,,	153
Addington, Great — By MAUD E. SIMKINS; Architectural descriptions by Professor A. HAMILTON THOMPSON, M.A., D.Litt., F.S.A., and F. H. CHEETHAM, F.S.A.	155
Addington, Little — ,, ,, ,,	160

PAGE

Aldwinkle All Saints	By HELEN DOUGLAS IRVINE, M.A.	164
Aldwinkle St. Peter	By HELEN DOUGLAS IRVINE, M.A.; Description of Lyveden Old and New Buildings by J. A. GOTCH, M.A., F.S.A.	168
Barnwell All Saints	By CHARLOTTE M. CALTHROP, Class. Tripos	173
Barton Seagrave	By CATHERINE JAMISON, Oxford Hon. School of Mod. Hist.	176
Burton Latimer	,, ,, ,,	180
Cranford St. Andrew	,, ,, ,,	186
Cranford St. John	,, ,, ,,	189
Denford	,, ,, ,, Architectural descriptions by Professor A. HAMILTON THOMPSON, M.A., D.Litt., F.S.A., and F. H. CHEETHAM, F.S.A.	192
Finedon	By CATHERINE JAMISON, Oxford. Hon. School of Mod. Hist.	196
Grafton Underwood	,, ,, ,,	203
Irthlingborough	By HELEN DOUGLAS IRVINE, M.A.	207
Islip	By MAUD E. SIMKINS	215
Kettering	By F. W. BULL, F.S.A., and WILLIAM PAGE, F.S.A.; Architectural descriptions by F. H. CHEETHAM, F.S.A., and Professor A. HAMILTON THOMPSON, M.A., D.Litt., F.S.A.	218
Lilford-with-Wigsthorpe	By MAUD E. SIMKINS; Description of Lilford Hall by J. A. GOTCH, M.A., F.S.A.	227
Lowick	By MAUD E. SIMKINS; Architectural descriptions by F. H. CHEETHAM, F.S.A., and Professor A. HAMILTON THOMPSON, M.A., D.Litt., F.S.A.; Description of Drayton House by Professor A. HAMILTON THOMPSON	231
Slipton	By MAUD E. SIMKINS	243
Sudborough	By MAUD E. SIMKINS; Architectural descriptions by Professor A. HAMILTON THOMPSON, M.A., D.Litt., F.S.A., and F. H. CHEETHAM, F.S.A.	245
Twywell	By CATHERINE JAMISON, Oxford Hon. School of Mod. Hist.	248
Warkton	By MAUD E. SIMKINS; Architectural descriptions by F. H. CHEETHAM, F.S.A., and Professor A. HAMILTON THOMPSON, M.A., D.Litt., F.S.A.	252
Woodford	By CATHERINE JAMISON, Oxford Hon. School of Mod. Hist.; Architectural descriptions by F. H. CHEETHAM, F.S.A., and Professor A. HAMILTON THOMPSON, M.A., D.Litt., F.S.A.	255
Borough of Higham Ferrers	By CHARLOTTE M. CALTHROP, Class. Tripos	263
Higham Park	,, ,, ,,	279

VOLUME FOUR

PAGE

Dedication	v
Contents	ix
List of Illustrations	xi
List of Maps	xiv
Editorial Note	xv

CONTENTS OF VOLUMES: NORTHANTS. IV

Topography . . . . . General descriptions and manorial descents in the hundreds of Higham Ferrers, Spelhoe, Hamfordshoe, and Orlingbury, originally compiled by the staff of the late WILLIAM PAGE, Hon. D.Litt., F.S.A., revised by L. F. SALZMAN, M.A., F.S.A.; Architectural descriptions by F. H. CHEETHAM, F.S.A.; Heraldic drawings and blazon by the Revd. E. E. DORLING, M.A., F.S.A.; Charities from information supplied by J. R. SMITH and E. W. PERKINS, of the Charity Commission

Higham Ferrers Hundred
   Introduction I
   Bozeat 3
   Chelveston-cum-Caldecott 8
   Easton Maudit 11
   Hargrave 17
   Irchester with Knuston and Chester-on-the-Water 21
   Newton Bromswold 27
   Raunds 29
   Ringstead 39
   Rushden 44
   Stanwick 51
   Strixton 54
   Wollaston 57
Spelhoe Hundred
   Introduction 63
   Abington 65
   Great Billing 69
   Little Billing 74
   Boughton 76
   Kingsthorpe 81
   Moulton 88
   Moulton Park 94
   Overstone 95
   Pitsford 98
   Spratton with Little Creaton 100
   Weston Favell 107
Hamfordshoe Hundred
   Introduction 112
   Great Doddington 113
   Earls Barton 116
   Ecton 122
   Holcot 127
   Mears Ashby 129
   Sywell 133
   Wellingborough 135
   Wilby 146
Orlingbury Hundred
   Introduction 149
   Brixworth . . . By MARGERY FLETCHER, M.A. . . . 150
   Broughton 158
   Cransley 162
   Faxton 167
   Hannington 172
   Hardwick 175
   Great Harrowden 178
   Little Harrowden 185

		PAGE
Isham		188
Lamport with Hanging Houghton		195
Old *alias* Wold	By MARGERY FLETCHER, M.A.	200
Orlingbury		204
Pytchley		208
Scaldwell		213
Walgrave		217
Wymersley Hundred		
Introduction	By L. F. SALZMAN, M.A., F.S.A.	223
Blisworth	By MARGERY FLETCHER, M.A.	224
Brafield-on-the-Green	By ADA RUSSELL, M.A.	228
Castle Ashby	By MARIAN K. DALE, M.A.; Description of the Castle by J. A. GOTCH, M.A., F.R.I.B.A., F.S.A.	230
Cogenhoe	By ADA RUSSELL, M.A.	236
Collingtree	By MARGERY FLETCHER, M.A.	240
Courteenhall	,, ,,	242
Denton	By MARIAN K. DALE, M.A.	246
Grendon	,, ,,	249
Hardingstone	By ADA RUSSELL, M.A.	252
Horton	By MARIAN K. DALE, M.A.	259
Great Houghton	By ADA RUSSELL, M.A.	262
Little Houghton	,, ,,	266
Milton Malzor	By MARGERY FLETCHER, M.A.	271
Piddington with Hackleton	By MARIAN K. DALE, M.A.	276
Preston Deanery	,, ,,	279
Quinton	By MARGERY FLETCHER, M.A.	282
Rothersthorpe	By ADA RUSSELL, M.A.	285
Whiston	,, ,,	288
Wootton	,, ,,	292
Yardley Hastings	By MARIAN K. DALE, M.A.; Description of the Manor House by J. A. GOTCH, M.A., F.R.I.B.A., F.S.A.	296

NORTHAMPTONSHIRE FAMILIES

	PAGE
Dedication	v
The Advisory Council of the Victoria History	vii
Contents	ix
List of Illustrations	xiii
Table of Abbreviations	xv
General Introduction	xvii
Preface	xxi
The Landed Houses of Northamptonshire	3
Cartwright of Aynhoe	
Introduction	9
Genealogy of Cartwright of Aynhoe	11
,, ,, Cartwright of Edgcote	17
Chart Pedigree	between 18 *and* 19
Arms and Alliances	19
Cecil, Marquess of Exeter	
Introduction	21
Genealogy of Cecil, Lord Burghley, Earl and Marquess of Exeter	25
Chart Pedigree	between 40 *and* 41
Arms and Alliances	41

CONTENTS OF VOLUMES: NORTHANTS. FAMILIES

PAGE

Dryden of Canons Ashby

Introduction 43

Genealogy of Turner of Sutton Coldfield and Bramcote 47

,, ,, Turner and Page-Turner of London and Ambrosden 50

,, ,, Dryden of Canons Ashby 55

Chart Pedigree . . . . *between* 56 *and* 57

Arms and Alliances 57

Elwes (now Cary-Elwes) of Billing Hall

Introduction 59

Genealogy of Elwes of Askham and Saundby 61

,, ,, the Elwes family in London 63

,, ,, the Elwes family of Stoke in Suffolk, baronets 66

,, ,, the Berkshire family of Elwes 72

,, ,, the family of Elwes, now Cary-Elwes, formerly of Throcking in Hertfordshire, and now of Great Billing in Northamptonshire, and of Roxby and Brigg in Lincolnshire . . 74

Chart Pedigree . . . . *between* 80 *and* 81

Arms and Alliances 81

Fane, Earl of Westmorland

Introduction 83

Genealogy of Fane, Earl of Westmorland 89

,, ,, Fane of Fulbeck, afterwards Earl of Westmorland 104

,, ,, Fane of Basildon, Viscount Fane 112

,, ,, Fane of Combe Bank in Sundridge, co. Kent 115

,, ,, Fane of Fulbeck 117

Chart Pedigree . . . . *between* 122 *and* 123

Arms and Alliances 123

Fitz Roy, Duke of Grafton

Introduction 125

Genealogy of Fitz Roy, Duke of Grafton 127

,, ,, Fitz Roy of Salcey Lawn and Frogmore Park 135

Chart Pedigrees . . . . *between* 138 *and* 139

Arms and Alliances 139

Isham of Lamport

Introduction 141

Genealogy of Isham of Pytchley 143

,, ,, Isham of Barby, Willey and Barwell 150

,, ,, Isham of Lamport 155

Chart Pedigrees . . . . *between* 166 *and* 167

Arms and Alliances 167

Knightley of Fawsley

Introduction 169

Genealogy of Knightley of Knightley 173

,, ,, Knightley of Gnosall 177

,, ,, Knightley of Fawsley 180

,, ,, Knightley of Burgh Hall, afterwards of Fawsley 186

,, ,, Knightley of Hackney, afterwards of Fawsley 191

,, ,, Knightley of Norton and Cottesbrook 197

,, ,, Knightley of Offchurch 200

,, ,, Knightley of Byfield and Charwelton 204

Chart Pedigree . . . . *between* 206 *and* 207

Arms and Alliances 207

Langham of Cottesbrooke

Introduction 209

Genealogy of Langham of Cold Ashby 211

,, ,, Langham of Guilsborough, afterwards of London and Cottesbrooke . . . 215

Chart Pedigree . . . . *between* 224 *and* 225

Arms and Alliances 225

CONTENTS OF VOLUMES: NORTHANTS. FAMILIES

PAGE

Maunsell of Thorpe Malsor
    Introduction 227
    Genealogy of Maunsell of Chicheley and Thorpe Malsor 229
    ,, ,, Maunsell of Ireland, afterwards of Thorpe Malsor 232
    Chart Pedigree . . . . *between* 236 *and* 237
    Arms and Alliances 237
Palmer of Carlton
    Introduction 239
    Genealogy of Palmer of Carlton 241
    ,, ,, Palmer of Withcote Hall 250
    Chart Pedigree . . . . *between* 252 *and* 253
    Arms and Alliances 253
Powys, Lord Lilford
    Introduction 255
    Genealogy of Powys, Lord Lilford 257
    ,, ,, the Powys family at Montacute in Somerset 267
    Chart Pedigree . . . . *between* 268 *and* 269
    Arms and Alliances 269
Robinson of Cranford
    Introduction 271
    Genealogy of Robinson of Cranford 273
    Chart Pedigree . . . . *between* 280 *and* 281
    Arms and Alliances 281
Rokeby of Arthingworth
    Introduction 283
    Genealogy of Rokeby of Arthingworth 287
    Chart Pedigree . . . . *between* 290 *and* 291
    Arms and Alliances 291
Spencer, Earl Spencer
    Introduction 293
    Genealogy of Spencer of Althorp 295
    Chart Pedigree . . . . *between* 298 *and* 299
    Arms and Alliances 299
Thornton of Brockhall
    Introduction 301
    Genealogy of Thornton of Brockhall 303
    Chart Pedigree . . . . *between* 310 *and* 311
    Arms and Alliances 311
Wake of Courteenhall
    Introduction 313
    Genealogy of Wake of Bourne, Lord Wake of Liddell 315
    ,, ,, Blisworth and Deeping, afterwards of Clevedon, and now of Courteenhall . 319
    ,, ,, London and Antwerp 336
    Chart Pedigree . . . . *between* 338 *and* 339
    Arms and Alliances 330
Willes of Astrop
    Introduction 341
    Genealogy of Willes of Astrop 343
    Chart Pedigree . . . . *between* 352 *and* 353
    Arms and Alliances 353
Young of Orlingbury
    Introduction 355
    Genealogy of Young of Hanley Castle 357
    ,, ,, Evesham, now of Orlingbury 359
    Chart Pedigree . . . . *between* 364 *and* 365
    Arms and Alliances 365

PAGE

List of Sheriffs of Northamptonshire 369
List of Members of Parliament elected for the County 374
    ,,   ,,   Northampton 376
    ,,   ,,   Peterborough 378
    ,,   ,,   Brackley 379
    ,,   ,,   Higham Ferrers 380

NOTTINGHAMSHIRE
VOLUME ONE

PAGE

Dedication v
The Advisory Council of the Victoria History vii
General Advertisement vii
The Nottinghamshire County Committee xiii
Contents xv
List of Illustrations xvii
Preface xix
Table of Abbreviations xxi
Natural History
  Introduction . . . . By Professor J. W. CARR, M.A., F.L.S., F.G.S. xxvii
  Geology . . . . By Professor J. F. BLAKE, M.A., F.G.S. . . I
  Palaeontology . . . By R. LYDEKKER, F.R.S., F.L.S., F.G.S. . . 37
  Botany . . . . By Professor J. W. CARR, M.A., F.L.S., F.G.S.
    Introduction 41
    Botanical Districts 48
    Vascular Plants 51
    Musci (*Mosses*) 61
    Hepaticae (*Liverworts and Scale Mosses*) 65
    Algae 66
    Lichens 67
    Fungi 68
  Zoology
    Molluscs . . . . By B. STURGES DODD and B. B. WOODWARD, F.L.S.,
        F.G.S., F.R.M.S. 75
    Insects . . . . By Professor J. W. CARR, M.A., F.L.S., F.G.S.
      Aptera (*Spring-tails and Bristle-tails*) 79
      Orthoptera (*Earwigs, Grasshoppers, etc.*) 80
      Neuroptera (*Dragon-flies, May-flies,*
        Caddis-flies, etc.) 81
      Hymenoptera (*Ants, Bees, Saw-flies,*
        Ichneumons, etc.) 83
      Coleoptera (*Beetles*) 93
      Lepidoptera (*Butterflies and Moths*) 108
      Diptera (*Flies*) 123
      Hemiptera (*Bugs, etc.*) 128
    Myriapoda (*Centipedes and Millipedes*) . By Professor J. W. CARR, M.A., F.L.S., F.G.S. 131
    Spiders . . . .   ,,   ,,   ,, 132
    Crustaceans . . . By the Revd. T. R. R. STEBBING, M.A., F.R.S.,
        F.L.S. 141
    Fishes . . . . By Professor J. W. CARR, M.A., F.L.S., F.G.S. 152
    Reptiles and Batrachians . .   ,,   ,,   ,, 155
    Birds . . . . By J. WHITAKER, F.Z.S., etc. . . 156
    Mammals . . . . By Professor J. W. CARR, M.A., F.L.S., F.G.S. 177

PAGE

Early Man . . . . . By Professor Frank Granger, D.Litt. . . 183

Anglo-Saxon Remains . . . By Reginald A. Smith, B.A., F.S.A. . . 193

Introduction to the Nottinghamshire
    Domesday . . . . By F. M. Stenton, B.A. . . . 207

Text of the Nottinghamshire Domesday . ,, ,, ... 247

Ancient Earthworks . . . By W. Stevenson . . . 289

Political History . . . . By Miss A. A. Locke, Honours School of Modern
    History, Oxford 317

Forestry . . . . By the Revd. J. C. Cox, LL.D., F.S.A., and the
    Revd. R. H. Whitworth . . . 365

VOLUME TWO

PAGE

Dedication v

Contents ix

List of Illustrations and Maps xiii

Editorial Note xv

Romano-British Nottinghamshire . . By H. B. Walters, M.A., F.S.A. . . . 1

Ecclesiastical History . . . By the Revd. J. C. Cox, LL.D., F.S.A. . . 37

Religious Houses . . . . ,, ,,

  Introduction 79

  Priory of Blyth 83

  ,, ,, Wallingwells 89

  ,, ,, Lenton 91

  Abbey of Rufford 101

  Priory of Beauvale 105

  ,, ,, Felley 109

  ,, ,, Newstead 112

  ,, ,, Shelford 117

  ,, ,, Thurgarton 120

  ,, ,, Worksop 125

  Abbey of Welbeck 129

  Priory of Broadholme 138

  ,, ,, Mattersey 140

  Preceptory of Ossington 142

  Franciscan Friars of Nottingham 144

  Carmelite Friars of Nottingham 145

  Observant Friars of Newark 147

  College of Clifton 148

  Chantries or College of Newark 148

  College of Ruddington 149

  ,, ,, Sibthorpe 150

  Collegiate Church of Southwell 152

  College of Tuxford 161

  Hospital of Bawtry 162

  ,, ,, St. Edmund, Blyth 164

  ,, ,, St. John the Evangelist, Blyth 164

  ,, ,, Bradebusk 166

  ,, ,, St. Anthony, Lenton 167

  ,, ,, St. Leonard, Newark 167

  ,, ,, the Holy Sepulchre,
  Nottingham 168

  Hospital of St. John Baptist, Nottingham 168

  ,, ,, St. Leonard, Nottingham 173

  ,, ,, St. Mary at West Bar,
  Nottingham 174

PAGE

Plumtree's Hospital, Nottingham 174
Hospital of St. Mary Magdalen, Southwell 175
,, ,, St. Leonard, Stoke 176
Schools
Introduction . . . By A. F. LEACH, M.A., F.S.A. . . 179
Southwell Minster Grammar School . ,, ,, . . 183
The Magnus Grammar School, Newark . ,, ,, . . 199
The Newark Girls' School . . ,, ,, . . 215
Nottingham Grammar School . . ,, ,, . . 216
Nottingham University College . . ,, ,, . . 238
East Retford Grammar School . . ,, ,, . . 239
Mansfield Grammar School . . ,, ,, . . 245
Brunts' Technical School, Mansfield . ,, ,, . . 249
The Girls' Grammar School . . ,, ,, . . 250
Tuxford Grammar School . . ,, ,, . . 250
Elementary Schools founded before 1800 . By F. FLETCHER, M.A. . . 252
Social and Economic History . . By Miss A. B. WALLIS CHAPMAN, D.Sc. (Oec.) . 265
Table of Population, 1801–1901 . . By GEORGE S. MINCHIN . . 307
Industries
Introduction . . . By Miss E. M. HEWITT . . 319
Coal . . . . By C. H. VELLACOTT, B.A. . . 324
Building Stone . . . By Miss E. M. HEWITT . . 330
Gypsum or Alabaster . . . ,, ,, . . 331
Glass and Pottery . . . ,, ,, . . 333
Fisheries . . . . ,, ,, . . 335
Tanning . . . . ,, ,, . . 337
Shoe-making . . . ,, ,, . . 339
Glove-making . . . ,, ,, . . 340
Wool . . . . ,, ,, . . 340
Cloth . . . . ,, ,, . . 344
Dyeing and Bleaching . . ,, ,, . . 347
Silk and Velvet . . . ,, ,, . . 350
Flax and Linen . . . ,, ,, . . 351
Cotton . . . . ,, ,, . . 351
Hosiery . . . . ,, ,, . . 352
Worsted . . . . ,, ,, . . 358
Lace . . . . ,, ,, . . 358
Malting and Brewing . . . ,, ,, . . 363
Ironwork, Foundries, Motors, Cycles, and
    Machine Building . . . ,, ,, . . 366
Bell-Founding . . . . ,, ,, . . 367
Agriculture . . . . By W. H. R. CURTLER . . 371
Sport Ancient and Modern . . Edited by the Revd. E. E. DORLING, M.A., F.S.A.
Hunting . . . . By F. BONNETT . . 383
    Foxhounds . . . ,, ,, . . 383
        The Rufford . . . ,, ,, . . 383
        The South Notts . . ,, ,, . . 385
        The Grove . . . ,, ,, . . 386
Racing . . . . ,, ,, . . 388
Shooting . . . . ,, ,, . . 398
    Decoys . . . ,, ,, . . 401
Angling . . . . ,, ,, . . 402
Cricket . . . . By Sir HOME GORDON, Bart. . . 405
Old Time Sports . . . By F. BONNETT . . 410
Rowing . . . . ,, ,, . . 413
Swimming . . . . ,, ,, . . 416
Athletics . . . . ,, ,, . . 418

OXFORDSHIRE
VOLUME ONE

		PAGE
Dedication		v
Contents		ix
List of Illustrations		xi
List of Maps		xiii
Editorial Note		xiv
Geology	By W. J. ARKELL, M.A., D.Sc., F.G.S. . .	1
Botany	By the late G. CLARIDGE DRUCE, M.A., D.Sc., F.R.S., revised by Professor A. G. TANSLEY, M.A., F.R.S.	27
Zoology	Edited by B. M. HOBBY, M.A., D.Phil., F.R.E.S.	
Crustacea (Aquatic) . .	By A. G. LOWNDES, M.A., C.M.Z.S. . .	57
,, (Land) . . .	By E. TAYLOR	60
Insecta:		
Introduction . . .	By B. M. HOBBY, M.A., D.Phil., F.R.E.S. . .	62
Apterygota . . .	By J. FORD, B.A.	64
Orthoptera . . .	By F. J. KILLINGTON, D.Sc., A.L.S., F.R.E.S. .	65
Dermaptera	,, ,, ,, .	66
Plecoptera	,, ,, ,, .	66
Psocoptera	,, ,, ,, .	67
Ephemeroptera . . .	,, ,, ,, .	68
Odonata	,, ,, ,, .	68
Hemiptera	By W. E. CHINA, M.A.	69
Megaloptera . . .	By F. J. KILLINGTON, D.Sc., A.L.S., F.R.E.S. .	77
Neuroptera	,, ,, ,, .	78
Mecoptera	,, ,, ,, .	79
Trichoptera . . .	By the Revd. Professor L. W. GRENSTED, M.A., D.D., F.R.E.S. . . .	80
Lepidoptera . . .	By the late Commander J. J. WALKER, R.N., M.A., F.L.S., F.R.E.S., and B. M. HOBBY, M.A., D.Phil., F.R.E.S. . . .	82
Coleoptera . . .	By E. W. AUBROOK . . .	107
Strepsiptera . . .	By A. H. HAMM, A.L.S., F.R.E.S. . .	135
Hymenoptera		
Symphyta . . .	By R. B. BENSON, M.A., F.R.E.S. . .	136
Ichneumonoidea . .	By J. F. PERKINS, B.Sc., F.R.E.S. . .	139
Braconidae . . .	By G. E. J. NIXON, B.A. . . .	143
Proctotrupoidea . . .	,, ,, . .	144
Chalcidoidea . . .	By A. H. HAMM, A.L.S., F.R.E.S. .	145
Cynipoidea . . .	By G. J. KERRICH, M.A., F.R.E.S. . .	145
Aculeata . . .	By O. W. RICHARDS, M.A., D.Sc., F.R.E.S.	147
Diptera . . .	By A. H. HAMM, A.L.S., F.R.E.S. . .	156
Siphonaptera . . .	,, ,, . .	178
Arachnida . . .	By W. FALCONER, F.R.E.S. . .	179
Mollusca	By the Revd. Professor L. W. GRENSTED, M.A., D.D., F.R.E.S. . . .	187
Fishes . . .	By J. E. DUFFIELD, B.A. . . .	192
Reptiles and Amphibians .	By B. W. TUCKER, M.A., M.B.O.U. .	199
Birds	By W. B. ALEXANDER, M.A., M.B.O.U. .	201
Mammals . . .	By C. ELTON, M.A. . . .	217
Early Man		
I. Quaternary Geology and Palaeolithic Man . . .	By K. S. SANDFORD, M.A., D.Phil. .	223
II. Mesolithic and Neolithic .	By E. THURLOW LEEDS, M.A., F.S.A. .	238
III. Bronze Age . . .	,, ,, .	241

CONTENTS OF VOLUMES: OXON. I

		PAGE
IV. Early Iron Age . . .	By H. N. Savory, B.A., D.Phil. . . .	251
Romano-British Remains		
A. Introduction . . .	By Margerie V. Taylor, M.A., F.S.A. . .	267
B. Roads . . .	By D. B. Harden, M.A. . . .	271
C. Settlement-sites		
1. Towns . . .	,, ,, . . .	281
2. Villages, etc. . . .	,, ,, . . .	296
D. Industries . . .	,, ,, . . .	303
E. Country Houses . .	By Margerie V. Taylor, M.A., F.S.A. .	306
F. Coins . . .	By C. H. V. Sutherland, M.A. . .	324
G. Topographical Index . .	By Margerie V. Taylor, M.A., F.S.A. .	330
Anglo-Saxon Remains . .	By E. Thurlow Leeds, M.A., F.S.A. .	346
Domesday Survey		
Introduction . . .	By Professor F. M. Stenton, D.Litt., Litt.D., F.B.A.	373
Text	,, ,, ,,	396
Political History . . .	By the late Sir Robert S. Rait, C.B.E., LL.D., revised by J. M. Ramsay, O.B.E., M.A. .	429
Schools	By Mary D. Lobel, B.A. . . .	457
Elementary Schools founded before 1800 .	By Margaret Midgley . . .	483
Domesday Index . . .	. . . . .	491

VOLUME TWO

		PAGE
Dedication . . .	. . . . .	v
Contents . . .	. . . . .	ix
List of Illustrations . .	. . . . .	xiii
Editorial Note . .	. . . . .	xv
Ecclesiastical History . .	By the Revd. H. E. Salter, M.A. . .	1
Religious Houses . .	,, ,,	
Introduction . .	,, ,, . .	64
Abbey of Eynsham . .	,, ,, . .	65
Priory of Pheleley . .	,, ,, . .	67
Canterbury College, Oxford .	,, ,, .	68
Durham College, Oxford .	,, ,, .	68
Gloucester College, Oxford .	,, ,, .	70
Abbey of Godstow . .	,, ,, . .	71
Priory of Littlemore . .	,, ,, . .	75
,, ,, Studley . .	,, ,, . .	77
Abbey of Bruern . .	,, ,, . .	79
,, ,, Rewley . .	,, ,, . .	81
,, ,, Thame . .	,, ,, . .	83
College of St. Bernard, Oxford .	,, ,, .	86
Abbey of Dorchester .	,, ,, .	87
,, ,, Oseney . .	,, ,, .	90
Priory of Bicester . .	,, ,, .	93
,, ,, Cold Norton .	,, ,, .	95
,, ,, St. Frideswide, Oxford .	,, ,, .	97
,, ,, Wroxton .	,, ,, .	101
St. Mary's College, Oxford .	,, ,, .	102
Priory of Goring . .	,, ,, .	103
,, ,, Clattercote .	,, ,, .	105
Preceptory of Clanfield .	,, ,, .	105
,, ,, Sandford .	,, ,, .	106

CONTENTS OF VOLUMES: OXON. II

PAGE

House of Black Friars	By A. G. LITTLE, M.A.	107
,, ,, Grey Friars	,, ,,	122
,, ,, White Friars	,, ,,	137
,, ,, Austin Friars	,, ,,	143
,, ,, Crutched Friars	,, ,,	148
,, ,, Friars of the Sack	,, ,,	149
,, ,, Trinitarian Friars	,, ,,	150
Hospital of St. John the Baptist, Banbury	By the Revd. H. E. SALTER, M.A.	152
,, ,, St. Leonard, Banbury	,, ,,	154
,, ,, Bicester	,, ,,	154
,, ,, St. John the Evangelist, Burford	,, ,,	154
Hospital of Cold Norton	,, ,,	155
,, ,, Crowmarsh	,, ,,	155
,, ,, Ewelme	,, ,,	156
,, ,, Eynsham	,, ,,	156
,, ,, St. Bartholomew, Oxford	,, ,,	157
,, ,, St. Clement, Oxford	,, ,,	158
,, ,, St. Giles, Oxford	,, ,,	158
,, ,, St. John the Baptist, Oxford	,, ,,	158
,, ,, St. Peter, Oxford	,, ,,	160
,, ,, Holy Cross, Woodstock	,, ,,	160
,, ,, St. Mary, Woodstock	,, ,,	160
,, ,, Woodstock	,, ,,	160
Canons of the Church of St. George, Oxford	,, ,,	160
College of St. George, Oxford	,, ,,	161
Priory of Cogges	,, ,,	161
,, ,, Minster Lovell	,, ,,	162
Social and Economic History	By Miss BEATRICE A. LEES, Oxford Honours School of Modern History	165
Table of Population, 1801–1901	By GEORGE S. MINCHIN	213
Industries	By REGINALD W. JEFFERY, M.A.	
Introduction		225
The Oxford Press		229
Bookbinding		235
Parchment and Paper-Making		240
Textile Industries		242
Blanket-Making		247
Silk Weaving and Winding		252
Lace-Making		252
Leather		253
Glove-Making		255
Malting and Brewing		259
Quarries		265
Iron Ore Industry		268
Agricultural Machine-Making and Iron-Founding		268
Bell-Founding		270
Steel-Work		271
The Oxford Mint		272
Tiles and Bricks		273
Glass-Making		274
Boat-Building		274
Chair-Making		275
Banbury Cakes		276
Banbury Cheese		277

		PAGE
Agriculture	By R. L. ANGAS	279
Forestry	By the Revd. J. C. Cox, LL.D., F.S.A.	293
Ancient Earthworks	By WILLIAM POTTS	303
Sport Ancient and Modern	Edited by E. D. CUMING	
Fox-Hunting	By Capt. H. L. RUCK KEENE, D.S.O.	351
The South Oxfordshire	,, ,,	351
The Heythrop	,, ,,	354
The Bicester and Warden Hill	,, ,,	356
Stag-Hunting	,, ,,	359
Harriers	,, ,,	359
Beagles	,, ,,	359
Coursing	By J. W. BOURNE	359
Shooting	By Capt. H. L. RUCK KEENE, D.S.O.	360
Angling	By Dr. W. J. TURRELL	362
Racing	By Capt. P. H. M. WYNTER	364
Rowing	By T. A. COOK, M.A., F.S.A.	369
Golf	By A. J. ROBERTSON	371

VOLUME THREE

		PAGE
Dedication		v
Contents		ix
List of Plans and Illustrations		xi
Editorial Note		xv
List of Chief Printed Sources		xix
The University of Oxford	By STRICKLAND GIBSON, M.A.	1
The Grammar Schools of the Medieval University	By MARY D. LOBEL, B.A., F.S.A.	40
The Buildings of the University		
The Bodleian Library	By the late Professor D. KNOOP, M.A., and Professor G. P. JONES, M.A., Litt.D.	44
The Old Ashmolean Museum	,, ,, ,,	47
The Physic Garden	,, ,, ,,	49
The Sheldonian Theatre	By MARY D. LOBEL, B.A., F.S.A.	50
The Clarendon Building	By H. M. COLVIN, M.A.	54
The Radcliffe Camera	By S. G. GILLIAM, B.Litt., M.A.	55
The University Press and other Modern Buildings	By P. S. SPOKES, B.Sc., M.A., F.S.A.	56
The Colleges and Halls		
University College	By ARTHUR OSWALD, M.A.	61
Balliol College, History	By R. W. HUNT, M.A., D.Phil.	82
,, Buildings	By R. H. C. DAVIS, M.A., F.S.A.	90
Merton College	By H. W. GARROD, C.B.E., M.A., D.Litt., F.B.A.	95
Exeter College	By R. W. SOUTHERN, M.A.	107
Oriel College and St. Mary Hall	By W. A. PANTIN, M.A., F.B.A., F.S.A.	119
The Queen's College	By the late R. H. HODGKIN, M.A., formerly Provost	132
New College	By Professor A. H. M. JONES, M.A., F.B.A.	144
Lincoln College	By MARGARET R. TOYNBEE, M.A., Ph.D., F.S.A.	163
All Souls College, History	By Professor E. F. JACOB, M.A., D.Phil., F.B.A., F.S.A.	173
,, Buildings	By Professor A. H. M. JONES, M.A., F.B.A.	183
Magdalen College, History	By N. DENHOLM-YOUNG, M.A.	193
,, Buildings	By the late Professor D. KNOOP, M.A., adn Professor G. P. JONES, M.A., Litt.D.	202
Brasenose College	By LADY DE VILLIERS, O.B.E., B.Litt., M.A.	207
Corpus Christi College	By W. O. HASSALL, M.A., D.Phil., F.S.A.	219

		PAGE
Christ Church	By M. MACLAGAN, M.A., F.S.A. . . .	228
Trinity College	By the late Revd. H. E. D. BLAKISTON, D.D., formerly President	238
St. John's College . . .	By the late Revd. H. E. SALTER, M.A., D.Litt., F.B.A.	251
Jesus College	By J. N. L. BAKER, B.Litt., M.A. . . .	264
Wadham College . . .	By H. B. WELLS, M.A.	279
Pembroke College . . .	By LUCY S. SUTHERLAND, C.B.E., M.A., Principal of Lady Margaret Hall . . .	288
Gloucester Hall and Worcester College		
History	By H. V. F. SOMERSET, M.A., and the late Revd. H. E. SALTER, M.A., D.Litt., F.B.A. .	298
Buildings	By Professor A. H. M. JONES, M.A., F.B.A. .	301
Hertford College . . .	By FREDA K. JONES, B.A. . . .	309
St. Edmund Hall . . .	By A. B. EMDEN, M.A., formerly Principal .	319
Keble College	By the Revd. H. J. CARPENTER, M.A., Warden	335
St. Peter's Hall . . .	By the Rt. Revd. C. M. CHAVASSE, O.B.E., M.C., D.D., Bishop of Rochester and formerly Master	336
St. Catherine's Society . .	By the Revd. V. J. K. BROOK, M.A., formerly Censor	338
Campion Hall . . .	By the Revd. J. F. ROGERS, S.J., M.A. . .	339
St. Benet's Hall . . .	By the Very Revd. P. J. McCANN, O.S.B., M.A., formerly Master	340
Lady Margaret Hall . .	By MADELINE B. SOUTHERN, B.A., B.Litt. .	341
Somerville College . . .	By LUCY S. SUTHERLAND, C.B.E., M.A., Principal of Lady Margaret Hall. Buildings by LADY DE VILLIERS, O.B.E., B.Litt., M.A. . .	343
St. Hugh's College . . .	By BEATRICE M. JALLAND, B.Litt., M.A. .	347
St. Hilda's College . . .	By CHRISTINE M. E. BURROWS, M.A., formerly Principal	348
St. Anne's College . . .	By RUTH F. BUTLER, M.A. . .	351
Nuffield College . . .	By A. LOVEDAY, M.A., D.Litt., Warden .	354
Index	By S. G. GILLAM, B.Litt., M.A. . .	355

VOLUME FIVE

	PAGE
Dedication	v
Contents	ix
List of Illustrations	xi
List of Maps and Plans	xiii
Editorial Note	xv
Oxfordshire V.C.H. Committee	xvii
List of Subscribers	xix
Classes of Public Records used	xxii
Principal Bodleian Manuscripts used	xxiii
Note on Abbreviations	xxiv
Topography	Where not otherwise stated either in this table or in the footnotes to the articles concerned, by MARY D. LOBEL, assisted by JOYCELYNE G. DICKINSON, HESTER JENKINS, and FRANCES RIDDELL BLOUNT. All school histories by H. LOUKES and FRANCES RIDDELL BLOUNT
Bullingdon Hundred . .	By MARY D. LOBEL . . .	1
Albury (with Tiddington)	8
Ambrosden	15
Marsh Baldon . . .	By MARY D. LOBEL . . .	30
Toot Baldon . . .	,, ,, . . .	47

PAGE

Beckley	By B. P. WOLFFE	56
Cowley	Before the Dissolution, by SUSAN WOOD; after the Dissolution, by B. P. WOLFFE	76
Cuddesdon	By W. O. HASSALL and the Oxfordshire Editorial Staff	96
Cuddesdon		100
Denton and Chippinghurst		106
Wheatley and Littleworth		108
Old Wheatley and Coombe		115
The Vent		116
Elsfield	By Sir GEORGE N. CLARK, D.Litt., F.B.A.	116
Forest Hill		122
Garsington	By MARY D. LOBEL	134
Headington	By LADY DE VILLIERS, O.B.E.	157
Holton		168
Horspath	By W. O. HASSALL and the Oxfordshire Editorial Staff	177
Iffley	Before the Dissolution, by SUSAN WOOD; after the Dissolution, by J. CATHERINE COLE	189
Littlemore	,, ,, ,,	206
Marston	By Sir GEORGE N. CLARK, D.Litt., F.B.A.	214
Merton	By MARY D. LOBEL	221
Nuneham Courtenay	,, ,,	234
Piddington	By JOYCELYNE G. DICKINSON	249
St. Clement's	By LADY DE VILLIERS, O.B.E.	258
Sandford on Thames	By JOHN HALE	267
Shotover	By W. O. HASSALL and the Oxfordshire Editorial Staff	275
Stanton St. John	By H. E. BELL	282
Stowood	By W. O. HASSALL and JOYCELYNE G. DICKINSON	293
Waterperry		295
Wood Eaton		309
Tax Assessments of Villages and Hamlets in the Hundred, 1306–1523	By R. F. WALKER	318
Index	By HESTER JENKINS, R. M. HAINES, and other members of the Oxfordshire Editorial Staff	321
Addenda and Corrigenda to Volumes I and III		344

VOLUME SIX

PAGE

Dedication		v
Contents		ix
List of Illustrations		xi
List of Maps and Plans		xiii
Editorial Note		xv
Oxfordshire V.C.H. Committee		xvii
List of Subscribers		xix
Classes of Public Records used		xxii
Principal Bodleian Manuscripts used		xxiii
Note on Abbreviations		xxiv
Topography	Where not otherwise stated either in this table or in the footnotes to the articles concerned, by MARY D. LOBEL, assisted by R. F. WALKER, HESTER JENKINS, and FRANCES RIDDELL BLOUNT	
Ploughley Hundred	By MARY D. LOBEL	1
Ardley	By the Oxfordshire Editorial Staff	7

CONTENTS OF VOLUMES: OXON. VI

		PAGE
The Market-town of Bicester . .	By MARY D. LOBEL and GWENDOLINE H. DANNATT	14
Bletchingdon	By the Oxfordshire Editorial Staff . . .	56
Bucknell	,, ,, . . .	71
Charlton-on-Otmoor . .	,, ,, . . .	80
Chesterton	,, ,, . . .	92
Cottisford . . .	By MARGARET TOYNBEE and the Oxfordshire Editorial Staff	103
Finmere	,, ,, ,, .	116
Fringford	By the Oxfordshire Editorial Staff . .	125
Fritwell . . .	,, ,, . .	134
Godington	,, ,, . .	146
Hampton Gay . . .	By R. P. BECKINSALE and the Oxfordshire Editorial Staff	152
Hampton Poyle . . .	,, ,, ,, .	160
Hardwick . . .	By MARGARET TOYNBEE and the Oxfordshire Editorial Staff	168
Hethe	,, ,, ,, .	174
Lower Heyford . .	By R. F. WALKER and the Oxfordshire Editorial Staff	182
Upper Heyford . .	By the Revd. E. P. BAKER, MOIRA LONG, and the Oxfordshire Editorial Staff . .	196
Islip	By BARBARA HARVEY . . .	205
Kirtlington . . .	By A. D. M. COX	219
Launton	By BARBARA HARVEY . . .	232
Middleton Stoney . .	By H. M. COLVIN . . .	243
Mixbury	By MARGARET TOYNBEE and the Oxfordshire Editorial Staff	251
Newton Purcell . . .	,, ,, ,,	262
Noke	By R. F. WALKER and the Oxfordshire Editorial Staff	268
Oddington . . .	By MOIRA LONG (Economic History) and the Oxfordshire Editorial Staff .	276
Shelswell . . .	By MARGARET TOYNBEE and the Oxfordshire Editorial Staff	285
Somerton . . .	By ALEC GAYDON (Manorial History) and the Oxfordshire Editorial Staff . .	290
Souldern	By the Oxfordshire Editorial Staff . .	301
Stoke Lyne . . .	By HESTER JENKINS and the Oxfordshire Editorial Staff	312
Stratton Audley . . .	By the Oxfordshire Editorial Staff . .	324
Tusmore	By MARGARET TOYNBEE and the Oxfordshire Editorial Staff	333
Wendlebury . . .	By JANET MARTIN and the Oxfordshire Editorial Staff	338
Weston-on-the-Green . .	By PATRICIA PUGH and the Oxfordshire Editorial Staff	346
Statistical Material for the Villages and Hamlets of Ploughley Hundred, 1086–1768 . . .	By MARY D. LOBEL, R. F. WALKER, and MARY BARRAN	353
Index	By MARY SAVILL, ETHEL SAVILL, and others under the Supervision of MARY D. LOBEL	363
Addenda and Corrigenda to Volume V		389

VOLUME SEVEN

	PAGE
Dedication	v
Contents	ix
List of Illustrations	xi

CONTENTS OF VOLUMES: OXON. VII

		PAGE
List of Maps and Plans		xiii
Editorial Note		xv
Oxfordshire V.C.H. Committee		xvii
List of Subscribers		xix
Classes of Public Records used		xxii
Principal Bodleian Manuscripts used		xxiii
Note on Abbreviations		xxv
Topography	Where not otherwise stated, by the Oxfordshire Editorial Staff, namely, MARY LOBEL, HESTER JENKINS, and MARJORIE JONES, assisted by FRANCES RIDDELL BLOUNT, R. M. HAINES, and MARY BARRAN	
Dorchester Hundred	By P. H. SAWYER	1
Chislehampton		5
Clifton Hampden	By L. G. R. NAYLOR and the Oxfordshire Editorial Staff	16
Culham	,, ,, ,,	27
Dorchester	By P. H. SAWYER (Introduction and Manors), H. M. COLVIN (Church Building), and the Oxfordshire Editorial Staff	39
Burcot	By L. G. R. NAYLOR and the Oxfordshire Editorial Staff	65
Drayton St. Leonard	By P. H. SAWYER	71
Stadhampton	By R. M. HAINES and other members of the Oxfordshire Editorial Staff	81
South Stoke	By HESTER JENKINS and other members of the Oxfordshire Editorial Staff	93
Thame Hundred	By MARY LOBEL	113
Great Milton	By MARJORIE JONES and other members of the Oxfordshire Editorial Staff	117
Tetsworth		147
Thame	By W. GUEST, MARY LOBEL, and HESTER JENKINS	160
Waterstock		220
Tax Assessments of the Villages and Hamlets of Dorchester and Thame Hundreds, 1306–1523		231
Index	By ETHEL SAVILL, MARY SAVILL, and others under the direction of MARY LOBEL	233
Addenda and Corrigenda to Volumes III, V, and VI		248

VOLUME EIGHT

		PAGE
Dedication		v
Contents		ix
List of Illustrations		xi
List of Maps and Plans		xiii
Editorial Note		xv
Oxfordshire V.C.H. Committee		xvii
List of Subscribers		xix
Classes of Public Records in the Public Record Office used		xxii
Principal Bodleian Manuscripts used		xxiii
Note on Abbreviations		xxv
Topography	Where not otherwise stated, by MARY LOBEL and HESTER JENKINS, assisted by MARJORIE JONES	

CONTENTS OF VOLUMES: OXON. VIII

PAGE

Lewknor Hundred 1
  Adwell 7
  Aston Rowant 16
  Britwell Salome 43
  Chinnor 55
  Crowell 80
  Emmington 91
  Lewknor . . . By the late Sir EDMUND CRASTER . . . 98
  Sydenham 116
Pyrton Hundred 128
  Pishill 131
  Pyrton 138
  Shirburn 178
  Stoke Talmage 198
  Watlington 210
  South Weston 253
  Wheatfield 263
Village Tax Assessments and Numbers
  of contributors, 1306–1523 274
Index . . . . . By ETHEL SAVILL and others under the direction of
      MARY LOBEL 277
Corrigenda to Volumes V, VI, and VII 298

VOLUME NINE

PAGE

Dedication v
Contents ix
List of Illustrations xi
List of Maps and Plans xiii
Editorial Note xv
Classes of documents in the Public Record Office used xvii
Principal Bodleian Manuscripts used xix
Note on Abbreviations xxi
Topography . . . . Where not otherwise stated, by MARY D. LOBEL and the
      Oxfordshire Editorial Staff, namely, HESTER
      JENKINS, MARJORIE JONES, and R. F. WALKER,
      assisted by J. L. BOLTON, A. CROSSLEY, and JUDITH
      HOOK
  Bloxham Hundred . . By J. F. A. MASON 1
    Adderbury 5
    Alkerton 44
    Bloxham 53
    Broughton 85
    Drayton 103
    Hanwell 112
    Horley and Hornton 123
    Shenington 139
    Tadmarton 150
    Wigginton 159
    Wroxton . . . By Professor LAWRENCE STONE and the Oxfordshire
      Editorial Staff 171
Index 190

RUTLAND
VOLUME ONE

		PAGE
Dedication		v
The Advisory Council of the Victoria History		vii
General Advertisement		vii
Contents		xiii
List of Illustrations and Maps		xv
Preface		xvii
Table of Abbreviations		xix
Natural History		
Geology	By A. Jukes-Browne, B.A., F.G.S.	1
Palaeontology	By R. Lydekker, F.R.S., F.L.S., F.G.S.	17
Botany	By Howard Candler, M.A.	19
Zoology		
Molluscs	By B. B. Woodward, F.L.S., F.G.S., F.R.M.S., and C. E. Wright	35
Insects	By Robert N. Douglas, M.A.	38
Orthoptera (*Earwigs, Cockroaches, Grasshoppers, and Crickets*)		38
Neuroptera (*Psocids, Stone-flies, May-flies, Dragon-flies, etc.*)		38
Hymenoptera (*Ants, Wasps, Bees, etc.*)		39
Coleoptera (*Beetles*)		39
Lepidoptera (*Butterflies and Moths*)		40
Rhopalocera		41
Heterocera		42
Diptera (*Flies*)		45
Hemiptera (*Bugs, Plant-lice, etc.*)		45
Heteroptera		45
Homoptera		45
Crustaceans	By the Revd. T. R. R. Stebbing, M.A., F.R.S., F.Z.S.	46
Fishes	By C. Reginald Haines, M.A., F.S.A., F.R. Hist. Soc., M.B.O.U.	51
Reptiles and Batrachians	,, ,, ,,	54
Birds	,, ,, ,,	55
Mammals	,, ,, ,,	77
Early Man	By Vernon B. Crowther-Benyon, M.A., F.S.A.	81
Romano-British Rutland	By H. B. Walters, M.A., F.S.A., and Miss Keate	85
Anglo-Saxon Remains	By Reginald A. Smith, B.A., F.S.A.	95
Ancient Earthworks	By J. Charles Wall	107
Introduction to the Rutland Domesday	By F. M. Stenton, M.A.	121
Translation of the Rutland Domesday	,, ,,	138
Ecclesiastical History	By the Sister Elspeth of the Community of All Saints	143
Religious Houses	,, ,, ,,	
Introduction		159
Priory of Brooke		159
Hospital of Tolethorpe		161
,, St. Margaret, Great Casterton		162
,, St. John Evangelist and St. Anne at Oakham		162
College of Blessed Mary at Manton		163
Priory of Edith Weston		163

PAGE

Political History
    To 1625 . . . . . By J. M. Ramsay, M.A. 165
    From 1625 . . . . By Urquhart A. Forbes 184
Social and Economic History . . By Miss S. E. Moffat 211
    Table of Population, 1801–1901 . By G. S. Minchin 229
Industries . . . . By Miss E. M. Hewitt
    Introduction 233
    Quarrying 235
    Wool and Textiles 236
Agriculture . . . . . By W. H. R. Curtler . . . 239
Forestry . . . . By the Revd. J. C. Cox, LL.D., F.S.A. . . 251
Schools . . . . By F. Fletcher, M.A.
    Introduction 259
    The Grammar Schools of Oakham and
      Uppingham 261
      Their Foundation 261
      Subsequent History of Oakham
        Grammar School 269
      Subsequent History of Uppingham
        Grammar School 281
    Elementary Schools founded before 1800 298
Sport Ancient and Modern . . Edited by the Revd. E. E. Dorling, M.A.
    Fox-hunting . . . . By Cuthbert Bradley . . . 301
      The Cottesmore 301
    Racing . . . . By Major Hughes Onslow . . 306
    Shooting . . . . ,, ,, . . 306
    Angling . . . . . ,, ,, . . 307

VOLUME TWO

PAGE

Dedication vii
William Page, D.Litt., F.S.A. . . By Sir Charles Peers, C.B.E., Litt.D., F.B.A.,
      F.R.I.B.A. ix
A List of the Writings of Dr. William Page . By Agnes E. Roberts, M.A. . . . xiii
Contents xix
List of Illustrations xxi
Editorial Note xxv
Topography . . . General descriptions and manorial descents compiled
    under the editorship of the late William Page,
    Hon. D.Litt., F.S.A.; Architectural descriptions,
    except where otherwise stated, by F. H.
    Cheetham, F.S.A.; Heraldic drawings and blazon
    by the Revd. E. E. Dorling, M.A., F.S.A.;
    Charities from information supplied by J. R.
    Smith, of the Charity Commission
    Introduction . . . By Catherine M. Jamison, Oxford Hon. School of
      Mod. Hist., and F. H. Cheetham, F.S.A. . xxvii
    County of Rutland . . By the late William Page, Hon. D.Litt., F.S.A. . 1
    Oakham Soke
      Introduction . . . By the late William Page, Hon. D.Litt., F.S.A. . 4
      Oakham . . . By Catherine M. Jamison, Oxford Hon. School of
        Mod. Hist. 5
        Belton . . . . ,, ,, ,, . 27
        Braunston . . . . ,, ,, ,, . 32
        Brooke . . . . ,, ,, ,, . 37
        Clipsham . . . . ,, ,, ,, . 41
        Egleton . . . . ,, ,, ,, . 45

CONTENTS OF VOLUMES: RUT. II

PAGE

Langham	By Catherine M. Jamison, Oxford Hon. School of Mod. Hist.	48
Wardley	,, ,, ,, .	53
Martinsley Hundred		
Introduction . . .	By the late William Page, Hon. D.Litt., F.S.A. .	58
Ayston	By Ada Russell, M.A.	59
Beaumont Chase . . .	By the late William Page, Hon. D.Litt., F.S.A. .	61
Edith Weston . . .	By Olive M. Moger, Oxford Hon. Math. . .	62
Hambleton . . .	By Ada Russell, M.A.; Description of Hambleton Old Hall by J. A. Gotch, M.A., F.R.I.B.A., F.S.A.	66
Lyndon . . .	By Ada Russell, M.A.; Description of Lyndon Hall by J. A. Gotch, M.A., F.R.I.B.A., F.S.A. .	72
Manton . . .	By Olive M. Moger, Oxford Hon. Math. . .	77
Martinsthorpe . . .	,, ,, ,, . .	84
Normanton . . .	,, ,, ,, Description of Normanton Park by J. A. Gotch, M.A., F.R.I.B.A., F.S.A. . . .	86
Preston . . .	By Ada Russell, M.A. . . .	88
Ridlington . . .	,, ,, ...	91
Uppingham . . .	By Catherine M. Jamison, Oxford Hon. School of Mod. Hist.	95
Wing	By Ada Russell, M.A.	103
Alstoe Hundred		
Introduction . . .	By the late William Page, Hon. D.Litt., F.S.A. .	107
Ashwell . . .	By Olive M. Moger, Oxford Hon. Math. . .	108
Burley . . .	,, ,, ,, Description of Burley-on-the-Hill by J. A. Gotch, M.A., F.R.I.B.A., F.S.A. . .	112
Cottesmore with Barrow . .	Ada Russell, M.A. . . .	120
Exton . . .	By the late Charlotte M. Calthrop, Class. Tripos; Description of Exton Old Hall by J. A. Gotch, M.A., F.R.I.B.A., F.S.A. . .	127
Greetham . . .	By Ada Russell, M.A. . . .	134
Horn . . .	By the late Charlotte M. Calthrop, Class. Tripos	138
Market Overton . .	By Ada Russell, M.A. . . .	141
Stretton . . .	,, ,, . . .	145
Teigh . . .	By Olive M. Moger, Oxford Hon. Math. . .	151
Thistleton . . .	By Ada Russell, M.A. . . .	155
Whissendine . . .	,, ,, . . .	157
Whitwell . . .	By the late Charlotte M. Calthrop, Class. Tripos	165
Wrandike Hundred		
Introduction . . .	By the late William Page, Hon. D.Litt., F.S.A. .	169
Barrowden . . .	By Olive M. Moger, Oxford Hon. Math. . .	170
Bisbrooke . . .	By Marjory Hollings, Oxford Hon. School of Mod. Hist.	175
Caldecott . . .	By Maud E. Simkins . . .	179
Glaston . . .	By Olive M. Moger, Oxford Hon. Math. . .	182
Liddington . . .	By Maud E. Simkins . . .	188
Luffenham, North . .	By Olive M. Moger, Oxford Hon. Math. .	195
Luffenham, South . .	,, ,, ,, .	203
Morcott . . .	,, ,, ,, .	207
Pilton . . .	,, ,, ,, .	211
Seaton with Thorpe-by-Water .	By Marjory Hollings, Oxford Hon. School of Mod. Hist.	213
Stoke Dry . . .	By Maud E. Simkins . . .	221
Tixover . . .	By Olive M. Moger, Oxford Hon. Math. .	227

PAGE

East Hundred

Introduction	By the late WILLIAM PAGE, Hon. D.Litt., F.S.A. .	231
Casterton, Great . . .	By VALERIE CUNNINGHAM	232
Casterton, Little . . .	By the late WILLIAM PAGE, Hon. D.Litt., F.S.A.; Description of Tolthorpe Hall by J. A. GOTCH, M.A., F.R.I.B.A., F.S.A. . .	236
Empingham	By OLIVE M. MOGER, Oxford Hon. Math. .	242
Essendine	,, ,, ,, .	250
Ketton	By MAUD E. SIMKINS . . .	254
Pickworth	By OLIVE M. MOGER, Oxford Hon. Math. .	265
Ryhall	,, ,, ,, .	268
Tickencote	By ST. JOHN O. GAMLEN, M.A. . .	275
Tinwell with Ingthorpe . .	,, ,, . .	281

SHROPSHIRE

VOLUME ONE

PAGE

Dedication		v
The Advisory Council of the Victoria History		vii
General Advertisement		vii
The Shropshire County Committee		xiii
Contents		xv
List of Illustrations and Maps		xvii
Preface		xxi
Table of Abbreviations		xxiii

Natural History

Geology	By T. C. CANTRILL, B.Sc. (Lond.) . .	I
Palaeontology	By R. LYDEKKER, F.R.S., F.L.S., F.G.S. .	47
Botany	Edited by WM. P. HAMILTON	
Introduction . . .	By the late WM. PHILLIPS, F.L.S. . .	51
Notes on the Geology of Shropshire in relation to its Flora .	By E. S. COBBOLD, M.Inst.C.E., F.G.S. .	55
Botanical Districts . .	By the late WM. PHILLIPS, F.L.S., and E. S. COBBOLD, M.Inst.C.E., F.G.S. . .	57
Phanerogamia and Pteridophyta (*Flowering Plants and Vascular Cryptogams*) . .	By the late R. de G. BENSON . .	61
Musci (*Mosses*) . . .	By WM. P. HAMILTON . . .	73
Hepaticae (*Liverworts and Scale Mosses*)	,, ,, . .	78
Algae	,, ,, . .	78
Lichenes (*Lichens*) . .	By the late WM. PHILLIPS, F.L.S. . .	80
Fungi	By the late WM. PHILLIPS, F.L.S. and WM. B. ALLEN	84

Zoology

Molluscs	By B. B. WOODWARD, F.L.S., F.G.S., F.R.M.S. .	99
Insects		
Introduction . . .	By F. B. NEWNHAM, M.A. . . .	101
Neuroptera (*Dragon Flies*) .	By W. J. LUCAS, B.A., F.E.S. . .	102
Coleoptera (*Beetles*) . .	By the Revd. Canon W. W. FOWLER, M.A., D.Sc., F.L.S., F.E.S. . . .	102
Lepidoptera (*Butterflies and Moths*) .	By F. B. NEWNHAM, M.A. . .	108
Rhopalocera . .		109
Heterocera . .		115
Spiders	By the Revd. O. PICKARD-CAMBRIDGE, M.A., F.R.S.	135
Crustaceans . . .	By the Revd. T. R. R. STEBBING, M.A., F.R.S., F.Z.S. . . .	141
Fishes	By H. E. FORREST . . .	152

PAGE

Reptiles and Batrachians . . By H. E. FORREST 157
Birds . . . . . ,, ,, ... 159
Mammals . . . . ,, ,, . . . 187
Early Man . . . . . By the Revd. Preb. T. AUDEN, M.A., F.S.A. . 195
Romano-British Shropshire . By Professor F. HAVERFIELD, M.A., LL.D., F.S.A.,
and Miss M. V. TAYLOR, M.A. (Dublin), Oxford
Honours School of Modern History . . 205
Introduction to the Shropshire Domesday . By Professor JAMES TAIT, M.A. . . . 279
Translation of the Shropshire Domesday . By the Revd. C. H. DRINKWATER, B.A. . . 309
Ancient Earthworks . . . Compiled by J. CHAS. WALL, principally from plans
and descriptions by the Revd. E. A. DOWNMAN . 351
Industries . . . . . By JOHN RANDALL
Introduction 415
River and Canal Industries 425
Clothmaking 428
Tanning 433
Pottery 434
Porcelain 435
Broseley Tobacco-Pipes 440
Brick and Tile Manufacture 442
Encaustic and Tesselated Tile Works 444
Quarries 447
Coal and Iron 449
Ironworks 460
Machinery 476
Chain-Making 479
Forestry . . . . . By the Revd. J. C. COX, LL.D., F.S.A. . . 483

VOLUME EIGHT

PAGE

Dedication v
Contents ix
List of Illustrations xi
List of Maps xiii
Editorial Note xv
Classes of Documents in the Public Record
Office used xvii
Select List of Collections in the Shropshire
County Record Office used xviii
Note on Abbreviations xix
Topography . . . . By A. T. GAYDON and J. B. LAWSON. Architectural
descriptions compiled or revised by MARGARET
TOMLINSON
Condover Hundred 1
Acton Burnell 3
Berrington 13
Condover 27
Cound 58
Cressage 73
Frodesley 79
Harley 85
Kenley 93
Leebotwood 98
Longnor 107
Pitchford 115

PAGE

Church Preen 124
Church Pulverbatch 129
Ruckley and Langley 141
Smethcott 146
Stapleton 161
Woolstaston 170
Ford Hundred 178
Alderbury-with-Cardeston 181
Ford 223
Habberley 238
Pontesbury 244
Westbury 295
Index 333

SOMERSET

VOLUME ONE

PAGE

Dedication v
The Advisory Council of the Victoria History vii
General Advertisement vii
The Somerset County Committee xiii
Contents xv
List of Illustrations xvii
Preface xxi
Table of Abbreviations xxiii
Natural History
  Geology . . . . . By H. B. WOODWARD, F.R.S., F.G.S. . . 1
  Palaeontology . . . . By R. LYDEKKER, F.R.S., F.G.S., F.L.S. . 35
  Botany
    Introduction . . . . By the Revd. R. P. MURRAY, M.A., F.L.S. . . 41
    Summary of Orders . . . ,, ,, ,, . 43
    The Botanical Districts . . ,, ,, ,, . 44
    Brambles (*Rubi*) . . . ,, ,, ,, . 49
    Vascular Cryptogams . . ,, ,, ,, . 49
    Mosses (*Musci*) . . . By the Revd. C. H. BINSTEAD, M.A. . 51
    Scale Mosses (*Hepaticae*) . . By E. M. HOLMES, F.L.S. . . 53
    Freshwater Algae . . . ,, ,, ,, . 53
    Marine Algae . . . ,, ,, ,, . 54
    Lichens (*Lichenes*) . . . ,, ,, ,, . 56
    Fungi . . . . By CEDRIC BUCKNALL, Mus. Bac. . . 59
    Mycetozoa . . . . ,, ,, ,, . 66
  Zoology
    Molluscs . . . By B. B. WOODWARD, F.L.S., F.G.S., F.R.M.S. . 71
    Insects . . . By Lt.-Col. LINLEY BLATHWAYT, F.L.S., F.E.S. . 73
      Orthoptera . . . ,, ,, ,, ,, . 74
      Neuroptera . . . ,, ,, ,, ,, . 74
      Hymenoptera . . ,, ,, ,, ,, . 74
      Coleoptera . . . ,, ,, ,, ,, . 76
      Lepidoptera . . . By ALFRED E. HUDD, F.E.S., F.S.A. . 87
      Diptera . . . By Lt.-Col. LINLEY BLATHWAYT, F.L.S., F.E.S. . 115
      Hemiptera . . . ,, ,, ,, ,, . 118
    Myriapods . . . By R. I. POCOCK 121
    Spiders . . . By the late F. O. PICKARD-CAMBRIDGE, M.A. . 124

PAGE

Crustaceans . . . . By the Revd. T. R. R. Stebbing, M.A., F.R.S.,
F.Z.S. 126

Fishes . . . . . By G. A. Boulenger, F.R.S., F.Z.S. . . 135

Reptiles and Batrachians . . ,, ,, ,, ,, . 139

Birds . . . . . By the Revd. F. L. Blathwayt, M.A. . . 140

Mammals . . . . By H. J. Charbonnier 163

Early Man . . . . . By W. Boyd Dawkins, M.A., D.Sc., F.R.S., F.S.A. 167

Romano-British Somerset . . . By F. J. Haverfield, M.A., LL.D., F.S.A. . 207

Anglo-Saxon Remains . . . By Reginald A. Smith, B.A., F.S.A. . . 373

Introduction to the Somerset Domesday . By J. Horace Round, M.A., LL.D. . . 383

Text of the Somerset Domesday . . By the Revd. E. H. Bates, M.A. . . 434

Geld Inquest . . . . . ,, ,, ,, . . 527

VOLUME TWO

PAGE

Dedication v

Contents ix

List of Illustrations xiii

Editorial Note xv

Ecclesiastical History . . . By the Revd. Chancellor T. Scott Holmes, M.A. . 1

Religious Houses . . . . ,, ,, ,, ,,

Introduction 68

Cathedral Priory of Bath 69

Priory of Dunster 81

Abbey of Glastonbury 82

,, ,, Athelney 99

,, ,, Muchelney 103

Priory of Barrow Gurney 107

,, ,, Cannington 109

,, ,, Montacute 111

Abbey of Cleeve 115

Priory of Hinton 118

,, ,, Witham 123

Abbey of Keynsham 129

Priory of Barlynch 132

,, ,, Bruton 134

,, ,, Burtle Moor 139

,, ,, Stavordale 139

,, ,, Taunton 141

,, ,, Worspring 144

Preceptory of Templecombe 146

Commandery of Templecombe 147

Preceptory of Minchin Buckland 148

Dominicans at Ilchester 150

Franciscans at Bridgwater 151

Carmelites at Taunton 152

Hospital of St. John the Baptist, Bath 152

,, ,, St. Mary Magdalen, Bath 153

,, ,, St. Katherine, Bedminster 153

,, ,, St. John the Baptist, Bridgwater 154

,, ,, Bruton 156

,, ,, Ilchester 156

,, ,, Priory at White Hall, Ilchester 156

,, ,, Langport 158

,, ,, Taunton 158

,, ,, St. John the Baptist, Wells 158

,, ,, St. John the Baptist, Redcliffe 160

CONTENTS OF VOLUMES: SOM. II

		PAGE
Almshouse of Yeovil		161
College of North Cadbury		161
,, ,, Stoke-under-Hamdon		161
Cathedral of Wells		162
Priory of Stogursey		169
Political History	By MARY A. WILLS SANDFORD	173
Maritime History	By M. OPPENHEIM	245
Social and Economic History	By GLADYS BRADFORD, Fellow of Newnham College, Cambridge	267
Table of Population, 1801–1901	By GEORGE S. MINCHIN	338
Industries		
Introduction	By ETHEL M. HEWITT	353
Lead Mining	By C. H. VELLACOTT, B.A.	362
Coal	By C. H. VELLACOTT, B.A. and ETHEL M. HEWITT	379
Zinc	By C. H. VELLACOTT, B.A.	388
Iron	By C. H. VELLACOTT, B.A. and ETHEL M. HEWITT	392
Building Stone	,, ,, ,, ,,	393
Sea Fisheries	By ETHEL M. HEWITT	398
Brewing	,, ,,	401
Cider and Wine	,, ,,	403
Textiles	,, ,,	405
Card-making	,, ,,	425
Lace, Net and Thread	,, ,,	426
Glove-making	,, ,,	427
Pottery and Glass	,, ,,	429
Bell Founding	,, ,,	431
Schools	By the Revd. Chancellor T. SCOTT HOLMES, M.A.	
Introduction		435
Cathedral Grammar School, Wells	(By A. F. LEACH, M.A., F.S.A.)	435
Song School		440
Free Grammar School, Bath		443
,, ,, Taunton		444
,, ,, Bridgwater		446
Bruton Grammar School		448
Free Grammar School, Ilminster		451
Free School, Crewkerne		453
Grammar School, Mells		455
Free Grammar School, Frome		455
Grammar School, Yeovil		455
Free School, Langport Eastover		456
Free Grammar School, Shepton Mallet		457
,, ,, Martock		458
Grammar School, Chard		459
St. Gregory's, Downside		460
United Charity School, or Blue School, Wells		461
Blue Coat School, Bath		462
Kingswood School, Bath		463
Huish Secondary School		463
Bishop Fox's Girls' School		463
Queen's College, Taunton		464
Taunton School, Staplegrove		464
Sexey School Foundations, Bruton		464
Blue or Charity School, Frome		465
Ancient Earthworks	By C. H. BOTHAMLEY	467
Agriculture	By ELDRED G. F. WALKER	533

PAGE

Forestry . . . . . . By the Revd. J. C. Cox, LL.D., F.S.A., and the
        Revd. W. H. P. Greswell, M.A. . . 547

Sport Ancient and Modern . . . Edited by the Revd. E. E. Dorling, M.A., F.S.A.
  Hunting . . . . . By Arthur B. Heinemann, M.A. . . . 573
    Staghounds 573
      Devon and Somerset and the Quantock 573
      Huntsmen, Whips and Harbourers 583
    Hunting of the Stag 585
    Hunting the Hind 586
    Harbouring 587
    Fox-hunting 588
      The Exmoor 588
      The Dulverton 589
      The West Somerset 589
      The Taunton Vale 590
    Harriers 590
      The Bath and County 590
      The Cotley 590
      The Minehead 590
      The Nettlecombe 591
      The Quarme 591
      The Seavington 591
      The Sparkford Vale 591
      The Stanton Drew 591
      The Taunton Vale 591
      The Wells Subscription 591
      The Weston 591
    Otter Hunting 592
    Badger Digging 593
  Coursing . . . . . By Arthur Heinemann, M.A. . . . 594
  Racing . . . . . ,, ,, . . . 595
  Polo . . . . . ,, ,, . . . 595
  Shooting . . . . . ,, ,, . . . 596
  Angling . . . . . ,, ,, . . . 596
  Cricket . . . . . By Sir Home Gordon, Bart. . . 597
  Golf . . . . . By the Revd. E. E. Dorling, M.A., F.S.A. . 600
Index to the Somerset Domesday 603
Index to Volumes I and II 617

STAFFORDSHIRE

VOLUME ONE

PAGE

Dedication v
The Advisory Council of the Victoria History vii
General Advertisement vii
Contents xiii
List of Illustrations and Maps xv
Preface xvii
Table of Abbreviations xix
Natural History
  Geology . . . . . By Walcot Gibson, D.Sc., F.G.S. . . 1
  Palaeontology . . . . . By R. Lydekker, F.R.S., F.L.S., F.G.S. . . 33

CONTENTS OF VOLUMES: STAFFS. I

PAGE

Botany . . . . . By J. E. Bagnall, A.L.S.
  Introduction 41
  Botanical Districts 46
  Summary of Orders, etc. 49
    Mosses (*Musci*) 60
    Liverworts (*Hepaticae*) 64
    Lichens (*Lichenes*) 65
    Freshwater Algae (*Algae*) 68
    Fungi 70
Zoology
  Molluscs . . . By B. B. Woodward, F.L.S., F.G.S., F.R.M.S.,
        and J. R. B. Masefield, M.A. . . . 77
  Insects . . . . . Edited by the Revd. F. C. R. Jourdain, M.A., etc.
    Orthoptera (*Earwigs, Cockroaches,*
      Grasshoppers, etc.) . . By the Revd. F. C. R. Jourdain, M.A., etc. . 80
    Neuroptera (*Psocids, Stone-flies,*
      Dragon-flies, etc.) . . By the Revd. F. C. R. Jourdain, M.A., etc. and
        the Revd. A. E. Eaton, M.A., F.E.S. . . 80
    Trichoptera (*Caddis-flies*) . By the Revd. F. C. R. Jourdain, M.A., etc., and
        the Revd. A. E. Eaton, M.A., F.E.S. . . 82
    Hymenoptera . . . By the Revd. F. C. R. Jourdain, M.A., etc. . 82
      Aculeata (*Ants, Wasps, and Bees*) . ,, ,, ,, ,, . 83
      Phytophaga (*Saw-flies and Gall-flies*) . ,, ,, ,, ,, . 85
      Entomophaga (*Chrysids, Ichneumons,*
       etc.) . . . . ,, ,, ,, ,, . 86
    Coleoptera (*Beetles*) . . By J. R. le B. Tomlin, M.A., F.E.S. . 87
    Lepidoptera (*Butterflies and Moths*) . By J. R. B. Masefield, M.A., and the Revd.
        F. C. R. Jourdain, M.A., etc. . . 96
      Rhopalocera 98
      Heterocera 99
    Diptera (*Flies*) . . By the Revd. F. C. R. Jourdain, M.A., etc. 113
    Hemiptera Heteroptera (*Bugs*) . ,, ,, ,, ,, . 118
    Hemiptera Homoptera . ,, ,, ,, ,, . 118
    Aphides, etc. . . . ,, ,, ,, ,, . 119
    Spiders . . . By the late F. O. Pickard-Cambridge, M.A. . 120
    Acarina (*Mites*) . . By the Revd. F. C. R. Jourdain, M.A., etc. . 124
  Crustaceans . . . By the Revd. T. R. R. Stebbing, M.A., F.R.S.
        F.Z.S. 125
  Fishes . . . . By G. H. Storer, F.Z.S. . . . 133
  Reptiles and Batrachians . . ,, ,, . . . 137
  Birds . . . . By J. R. B. Masefield, M.A. . . 139
  Mammals . . . By G. H. Storer, F.Z.S. . . . 162
Early Man . . . . By George Clinch, F.G.S. . . 169
Romano-British Staffordshire . . By W. Page, F.S.A. and Miss Keate . 183
Anglo-Saxon Remains . . By Reginald A. Smith, B.A., F.S.A. . 199
Political History . . . By W. H. R. Curtler . . . 217
Social and Economic History . By Miss Mildred Spencer . . . 275
  Table of Population, 1801–1901 . By George S. Minchin . . 318
Ancient Earthworks . . . By Charles Lynam, F.S.A. . . 331

VOLUME TWO

PAGE

Dedication v
Contents ix
List of Illustrations xi
List of Maps and Plans xiii
Editorial Note xv

PAGE

Staffordshire Victoria History Committee xvii

Classes of Documents in the Public Record
    Office used xviii

Classes of Official Documents in the
    Staffordshire Record Office used xix

Note on Abbreviations xxi

Analysis of sources in *Staffordshire Historical
    Collections* used xxiii

Pottery . . . . . By R. G. HAGGAR; Early and medieval pottery by
    A. R. MOUNTFORD; Labour organizations by
    J. THOMAS 1

Coal . . . . . By Professor A. J. TAYLOR 68

Iron to 1750 . . . . By Professor B. L. C. JOHNSON . . . 108

Iron and Steel from 1750 . . . By A. BIRCH 121

Engineering . . . . By J. G. JENKINS 134

Tinplate and Allied Products . . By Professor W. E. MINCHINTON . . . 173

Stone . . . . . By D. A. JOHNSON; Gypsum by G. T. WARWICK . 185

Textiles . . . . . By J. G. JENKINS 206

Other Industries

    Glass . . . . By J. G. JENKINS 224

    Footwear . . . . ,, ,, ... 230

    Saddlery and Allied Trades . . ,, ,, ... 235

    Nails . . . . By ANN J. KETTLE (Mrs. D. A. JOHNSON) and
    W. K. V. GALE 239

    Beer . . . . By C. H. UNDERHILL and J. G. JENKINS . . 242

    Salt . . . . By ANN J. KETTLE 246

    Locks and Keys . . . By N. W. TILDESLEY 251

    Bricks and Tiles . . . By J. THOMAS 255

    Edge Tools . . . By the late E. J. HOMESHAW . . . 259

    Chains and Chain Cables . . By D. A. JOHNSON and W. K. V. GALE . 262

    Copper and Brass . . By J. R. HARRIS 266

    Fireclay . . . . By Professor B. L. C. JOHNSON . . . 269

    Metal Tubes . . . By ANN J. KETTLE 272

Roads . . . . . By S. A. H. BURNE 275

Canals . . . . . By Professor M. J. WISE, M.C. . . . 285

Railways . . . . By P. L. CLARK 305

Forests . . . . By M. W. GREENSLADE; Needwood by ANN
    J. KETTLE 335

    Brewood 337

    Cannock 338

    Kinver 343

    The New Forest 348

    Needwood Forest 349

Sport

    Foxhunting . . . By D. A. JOHNSON 359

    Horseracing . . . By ANN J. KETTLE 364

    Cricket . . . . By S. A. H. BURNE 368

    Association Football . . By the late W. E. JEPHCOTT . . . 371

Index to Volumes I and II . . By G. C. BAUGH and M. W. GREENSLADE . 375

Corrigenda to Volume I 415

VOLUME THREE

PAGE

Dedication v

Contents ix

List of Illustrations xi

CONTENTS OF VOLUMES: STAFFS. III

		PAGE
Editorial Note	. . . .	xiii
Staffordshire Victoria History Committee	. . . .	xv
Classes of Documents in the Public Record Office used	. . . .	xvi
Classes of Official Documents in the Staffordshire Record Office used	. . . . . .	xvii
Classes of Documents in the Lichfield Joint Record Office used	. . . .	xvii
Note on Abbreviations	. . . .	xviii
Analysis of sources in *Collections for a History of Staffordshire* used	. . . . . .	xix
The Medieval Church	By P. HEATH . . .	1
The Church of England since the Reformation	By the Revd. L. W. COWIE . . .	44
Deaneries	By G. C. BAUGH and M. W. GREENSLADE .	92
Roman Catholicism	By M. W. GREENSLADE . . .	99
Protestant Nonconformity	By the Revd. R. MANSFIELD . .	116
Religious Houses		
Introduction	By M. W. GREENSLADE . . .	135
House of Secular Canons		
1. The Cathedral of Lichfield	By ANN J. KETTLE and D. A. JOHNSON .	140
Houses of Benedictine Monks		
2. The Abbey of Burton	By UNA C. HANNAM and M. W. GREENSLADE	199
3. The Priory of Canwell	By Professor A. SALTMAN . . .	213
4. The Priory of Sandwell	,, ,, ,, . . .	216
Houses of Benedictine Nuns	By J. L. KIRBY	
5. The Priory of Blithbury	. . . . .	220
6. The Priory of Brewood (Black Ladies)	. . . . .	220
7. The Priory of Farewell	. . . . .	222
Houses of Cistercian Monks	By A. P. DUGGAN and M. W. GREENSLADE	
8. The Abbey of Radmore	. . . . . .	225
9. The Abbey of Croxden	. . . . . .	226
10. The Abbey of Dieulacres	. . . . . .	230
11. The Abbey of Hulton	. . . . . .	235
Houses of Augustinian Canons	By the Revd. J. C. DICKINSON	
12. The Priory of Calwich	. . . . . .	237
13. The Priory of Stone	. . . . . .	240
14. The Abbey of Rocester	. . . . . .	247
15. The Priory of Ranton	. . . . . .	251
16. The Priory of Trentham	. . . . . .	255
17. The Priory of St. Thomas near Stafford	. . . . . .	260
House of Knights Templars		
18. The Preceptory of Keele	By M. W. GREENSLADE . .	267
Friaries	By the late Professor HILDA JOHNSTONE	
19. The Franciscan Friars of Lichfield	. . . . . .	268
20. The Franciscan Friars of Stafford	. . . . . .	270
21. The Dominican Friars of Newcastle-under-Lyme	. . . . . .	272
22. The Austin Friars of Stafford	. . . . . .	273
Hospitals	By G. C. BAUGH	
23. Cannock, St. Mary	. . . . . .	274
24. Freeford, St. Leonard	. . . . . .	274
25. Lichfield, Dr. Milley's	. . . . . .	275
26. Lichfield, St. John the Baptist	. . . . . .	279
27. Newcastle-under-Lyme	. . . . . .	289
28. Radford, St. Lazarus or the Holy Sepulchre	. . . . . .	289

PAGE

29. Stafford, Forebridge, St. John the
    Baptist 290
30. Stafford, Forebridge, St. Leonard 293
31. Tamworth, St. James 294
32. Wolverhampton, St. Mary 296
Colleges
33. Burton, Christ and St. Mary . . By UNA C. HANNAM . . . 297
34. Penkridge, St. Michael . . By DOROTHY STYLES . . . 298
35. Stafford, St. Mary . . . By A. K. B. EVANS 303
36. Tamworth, St. Edith . . By D. A. JOHNSON 309
37. Tettenhall, St. Michael . . By A. K. B. EVANS 315
38. Wolverhampton, St. Peter . . By A. K. B. and R. H. EVANS . . 321
Alien Houses
39. The Priory of Tutbury . . By Professor A. SALTMAN . . . 331
40. The Priory of Lapley . . By J. L. KIRBY 340
Index 345

VOLUME FOUR

PAGE

Dedication v
Contents ix
List of Illustrations xi
List of Maps and Plans xiii
Editorial Note xv
Staffordshire Victoria County History
    Committee xvii
Classes of Public Records used xviii
Classes of Documents in the Staffordshire
    Record Office used xix
Note on Abbreviations xx
Analysis of sources in *Staffordshire Historical
    Collections* xxi
Introduction to the Staffordshire Domesday . By C. F. SLADE 1
Translation of the Text of the Staffordshire
    Domesday . . . . . By C. F. SLADE 37
Topography . . . . . Architectural descriptions by MARGARET
                                TOMLINSON in collaboration with G. R. RIGBY
                                (medieval churches) and S. R. JONES (timber-
                                framed buildings); Roman Catholicism by
                                M. W. GREENSLADE; Protestant Nonconformity by
                                BARBARA DONALDSON and the Revd. R.
                                MANSFIELD; Charities by the Staffordshire
                                editorial staff
Cuttlestone Hundred . . . By S. A. H. BURNE 61
    Western Division:
Blymhill . . . . By KATHARINE L. DAVIES . . . 64
Bradley . . . . By L. MARGARET MIDGLEY . . . 73
Church Eaton . . . By KATHARINE L. DAVIES and L. MARGARET
                                MIDGLEY 91
Forton . . . . By S. A. H. BURNE 103
Gnosall . . . . By L. MARGARET MIDGLEY . . . 111
Haughton . . . . By S. A. H. BURNE 136
Lapley . . . . By KATHARINE L. DAVIES . . . 143
Norbury . . . . By S. A. H. BURNE 155
Stretton . . . . By M. W. GREENSLADE . . . 163
Weston under Lizard . . By KATHARINE L. DAVIES . . . 169

			PAGE
Index to the text of the Staffordshire Domesday	By M. W. GREENSLADE		177
General Index	By J. G. JENKINS		183

VOLUME FIVE

		PAGE
Dedication		v
Contents		ix
List of Illustrations		xi
List of Maps and Plans		xiii
Editorial Note		xv
Staffordshire Victoria County History Committee		xvii
Classes of Public Records used		xviii
Classes of Documents in the Staffordshire Record Office used		xix
Note on Abbreviations		xx
Analysis of sources in *Staffordshire Historical Collections*		xxi
Topography	Architectural descriptions by MARGARET TOMLINSON in collaboration with G. R. RIGBY (medieval churches) and S. R. JONES (Brewood and Penkridge, and timber-framed buildings); Roman Catholicism by M. W. GREENSLADE; Protestant Nonconformity by BARBARA DONALDSON and the Revd. R. MANSFIELD; Charities by the Staffordshire editorial staff	
Cuttlestone Hundred (*cont.*)		
Eastern Division:		
Baswich or Berkswich	By S. A. H. BURNE and BARBARA DONALDSON	1
Acton Trussell and Bednall		11
Brewood	By M. W. GREENSLADE and L. MARGARET MIDGLEY	18
Cannock	By M. W. GREENSLADE	49
Huntington		75
Great Wyrley		77
Castle Church	By L. MARGARET MIDGLEY and BARBARA DONALDSON	82
Cheslyn Hay	By M. W. GREENSLADE	100
Penkridge	By L. MARGARET MIDGLEY and M. W. GREENSLADE	103
Coppenhall		138
Dunston		143
Rugeley	By M. W. GREENSLADE	149
Shareshill	By S. A. H. BURNE	173
Teddesley Hay	By M. W. GREENSLADE	182
Index	By A. W. MABBS	185

VOLUME EIGHT

		PAGE
Dedication		v
Contents		ix
List of Illustrations		xi
List of Maps and Plans		xiii
Editorial Note		xv
Staffordshire Victoria County History Committee		xvii

PAGE

Classes of Documents in the Public Record
   Office used   xviii

Classes of Official Documents in the
   Staffordshire Record Office used   xix

Note on Abbreviations   xxi

Analysis of sources in *Staffordshire Historial
   Collections* used   xxiii

The Borough of Newcastle-under-Lyme .   By J. G. JENKINS; Architectural descriptions by
                                        MARGARET TOMLINSON; Roman Catholicism and
                                        Charities for the Poor by M. W. GREENSLADE;
                                        Protestant Nonconformity and Schools by
                                        BARBARA YOUNG   I

Clayton .   .   .   .   .   By M. W. GREENSLADE   75

The City of Stoke-on-Trent   .   *Except where otherwise stated* by M. W. GREENSLADE;
                                          Architectural descriptions by MARGARET
                                          TOMLINSON   80

   Tunstall   81

   Burslem   105

   Hanley   142

   Stoke-upon-Trent   .   .   Manors by J. G. JENKINS .   .   .   173

   Fenton .   .   .   .   By BARBARA YOUNG and J. G. JENKINS; Industries
                                          by M. W. GREENSLADE .   .   .   205

   Longton .   .   .   .   ,,   ,,   ,,   ,,   224

   Botteslow   246

   Hulton   247

   The Federation of the Six Towns   .   By J. G. JENKINS   252

   The County Borough since 1910 .   ,,   ,,   .   .   .   259

   Roman Catholicism   271

   Protestant Nonconformity .   .   By BARBARA YOUNG .   .   .   276

   Jewish Congregations .   .   ,,   ,,   .   .   .   307

   Schools .   .   .   .   ,,   ,,   .   .   .   307

   Charities for the Poor   329

Index .   .   .   .   .   By P. A. SPALDING   333

SUFFOLK

VOLUME ONE

PAGE

Dedication   v

The Advisory Council of the Victoria History   vii

General Advertisement   vii

The Suffolk County Committee   xiii

Contents   xv

List of Illustrations and Maps   xvii

Preface   xxi

Table of Abbreviations   xxiii

Natural History

   Geology .   .   .   .   By H. B. WOODWARD, F.R.S., F.G.S. .   .   I

   Palaeontology .   .   .   By R. LYDEKKER, F.R.S., F.L.S., F.G.S. .   31

   Botany .   .   .   .   Edited by the Revd. E. N. BLOOMFIELD, M.A.,
                                          F.E.S.

      Introduction .   .   .   By C. E. SALMON   47

      Botanical Districts .   .   ,,   ,,   .   .   .   51

      List of Phanerogamia .   .   ,,   ,,   .   .   .   60

      Characeae (*Stoneworts*) .   .   By the Revd. G. R. BULLOCK-WEBSTER, M.A. .   69

      Musci (*Mosses*) .   .   .   By the Revd. E. N. BLOOMFIELD, M.A., F.E.S. .   71

PAGE

Hepaticae (*Liverworts*) . . . By the Revd. E. N. Bloomfield, M.A., F.E.S. . 73
Freshwater Algae and Diatoms . . ,, ,, ,, . 74
Marine Algae . . . . ,, ,, ,, . 77
Lichenes (*Lichens*) . . . ,, ,, ,, . 79
Fungi . . . . . ,, ,, ,, . 81
Zoology
  Marine . . . . By the late H. C. Sorby, LL.D., F.R.S., F.S.A. . 85
  Molluscs (Non-Marine) . . By B. B. Woodward, F.L.S., F.G.S., F.R.M.S.,
      and A. Mayfield 96
  Insects 101
    Orthoptera (*Earwigs, Grasshoppers,
      Crickets, etc.*) . . By Claude Morley, F.E.S. . . . 102
    Neuroptera (*Dragon-flies, Stone-flies,
      Lacewings, etc.*) . . . ,, ,, . . . 104
    Hymenoptera (*Ants, Bees, Wasps,
      Saw-flies, Gall-flies, etc.*) . . ,, ,, . . . 107
    Coleoptera (*Beetles*) . . . ,, ,, . . . 122
    Lepidoptera (*Butterflies and Moths*) . By Claude Morley, F.E.S., and the Revd. E. N.
      Bloomfield, M.A., F.E.S. . . 128
    Diptera (*Flies*) . . . By Claude Morley, F.E.S. . . 135
    Hemiptera (*Bugs*) . . . ,, ,, . . 141
    Spiders . . . . ,, ,, . . 150
    Crustaceans . . . By the Revd. T. R. R. Stebbing, M.A., F.R.S.,
      F.Z.S. 153
  Fishes . . . . By J. T. Cunningham, M.A. . . 163
  Reptiles and Batrachians . . By G. T. Rope 173
  Birds . . . . By the Revd. Julian Tuck, M.A. . . 177
  Mammals . . . . By G. T. Rope 215
Early Man 235
  Palaeolithic Age . . . By W. Allen Sturge, M.V.O., M.D., F.R.C.P. . 235
  Neolithic Age . . . . ,, ,, ,, ,, . 248
  Topographical List of Palaeolithic and
    Neolithic Localities . . By W. A. Dutt . . . 256
  Bronze Age . . . . By George Clinch, F.G.S., F.S.A. (Scot.) . . 263
  Early Iron Age . . . . ,, ,, ,, . 270
  Topographical List of Bronze Age and
    Early Iron Age Antiquities . . ,, ,, ,, . 275
Romano-British Suffolk . . . By the late George E. Fox, M.A., F.S.A. . 279
  Appendix on Santon Downham hoard . By Reginald A. Smith, B.A., F.S.A. . 321
Anglo-Saxon Remains . . . ,, ,, ,, . 325
Introduction to the Suffolk Domesday . By Beatrice A. Lees, Oxford Honours School of
    Modern History 357
Translation of the Suffolk Domesday . Adapted from the Translation by the late Lord
    Hervey 418
Ancient Earthworks . . . By J. C. Wall 583
Social and Economic History 633
  Part I . . . . By Professor George Unwin, B.A. . . 633
  Part II . . . . By Dorothy Kemp, Oxford Honours School of
    Modern History 660
  Table of Population 1801–1901 . By George S. Minchin . . . 683

VOLUME TWO

PAGE

Dedication v
Contents ix
List of Illustrations xiii
Editorial Note xv

CONTENTS OF VOLUMES: SUFF. II

		PAGE
Ecclesiastical History	By the Revd. J. C. Cox, LL.D., F.S.A.	I
Religious Houses	,, ,, ,,	
Introduction		53
Abbey of Bury St. Edmunds		56
Priory of Eye		72
,, ,, Dunwich		76
,, ,, Edwardstone		76
,, ,, Hoxne		76
,, ,, Rumburgh		77
,, ,, Snape		79
,, ,, Felixstowe		80
,, ,, Bungay		81
,, ,, Redlingfield		83
,, ,, St. George, Thetford		85
,, ,, Mendham		86
,, ,, Wangford		88
Abbey of Sibton		89
Priory of Alnesbourn		91
,, ,, Blythburgh		91
,, ,, Bricett		94
,, ,, Butley		95
,, ,, Chipley		99
,, ,, Dodnash		99
,, ,, Herringfleet		100
,, ,, St. Peter and St. Paul, Ipswich		102
,, ,, the Holy Trinity, Ipswich		103
,, ,, Ixworth		105
,, ,, Kersey		107
,, ,, Letheringham		108
,, ,, the Holy Sepulchre, Thetford		109
,, ,, Woodbridge		111
,, ,, Campsey		112
,, ,, Flixton		115
Abbey of Leiston		117
Knights Templars of Dunwich		120
Preceptory of Battisford		120
Dominican Friars of Dunwich		121
,, ,, Ipswich		122
,, ,, Sudbury		123
Franciscan Friars of Bury St. Edmunds		124
,, ,, Dunwich		125
Grey Friars of Ipswich		126
Austin Friars of Clare		127
,, ,, Gorleston		129
,, ,, Orford		130
Carmelite Friars of Ipswich		130
Abbey of Bruisyard		131
Hospital of Beccles		132
,, ,, Domus Dei, Bury St. Edmunds		133
,, ,, St. Nicholas, Bury St. Edmunds		134
,, ,, St. Peter, Bury St. Edmunds		134
,, ,, St. Petronilla, Bury St. Edmunds		135
,, ,, St. Saviour, Bury St. Edmunds		135
,, ,, St. James, Dunwich		137
,, ,, the Holy Trinity, Dunwich		137
,, ,, Eye		138
Leper House of Gorleston		138

CONTENTS OF VOLUMES: SUFF. II

PAGE

		PAGE
Leper Hospitals of St. Mary Magdalen and St. James, Ipswich	. . . .	139
Hospital of St. Leonard, Ipswich .	. . . .	139
Hospitals of Orford . .	. . . .	139
Hospital of Domus Dei, Thetford	. . . .	140
,, ,, St. John, Thetford	. . . .	140
,, ,, Sibton .	. . . .	140
,, ,, St. Leonard, Sudbury	. . . .	140
College of Jesus, Bury St. Edmunds	. . . .	141
,, ,, Denston .	. . . .	142
Cardinal's College, Ipswich .	. . . .	142
College of Mettingham .	. . . .	144
,, ,, Stoke by Clare .	. . . .	145
,, ,, Sudbury .	. . . .	150
,, ,, Wingfield .	. . . .	152
Priory of Blakenham .	. . . .	152
,, ,, Creeting St. Mary	. . . .	153
,, ,, Creeting St. Olave	. . . .	153
,, ,, Stoke by Clare .	. . . .	154
Hospital of Great Thurlow .	. . . .	155
,, ,, Sudbury .	. . . .	155
Political History . . .	By Miss MARY CROOM BROWN, Oxford Honours School of Modern History . .	157
Maritime History . . .	By M. OPPENHEIM	199
Industries	By GEORGE UNWIN, M.A.	
Introduction . . .	,, ,, . . .	247
Woollen Cloth—The Old Draperies .	,, ,, . . .	254
The New Draperies, Woolcombing and Spinning . . .	,, ,, . . .	267
Sailcloth and other Hempen Fabrics .	,, ,, . . .	271
Silk Throwing and Silk Weaving .	,, ,, . . .	273
Mixed Textiles (Drabbet, Horsehair, Cocoa-nut Fibre) and Ready-made Clothing . . .	,, ,, . . .	274
Stay and Corset Making . .	,, ,, . . .	276
Lowestoft China . . .	,, ,, . . .	277
Agricultural Implements, Milling Machinery, Locomotives, etc. .	,, ,, . . .	281
Fertilizers	,, ,, . . .	285
Gun-Cotton . . .	,, ,, . . .	286
Xylonite	,, ,, . . .	287
Malting	,, ,, . . .	288
Printing	,, ,, . . .	288
Fisheries	By Miss E. M. HEWITT . . .	289
Schools	. . . .	301
Introduction, Dunwich, Thetford, Bury St. Edmunds, Ipswich, and Elementary Schools . .	By A. F. LEACH, M.A., F.S.A.	
The remaining Schools . .	By Miss E. P. STEELE HUTTON, M.A. (St. Andrews)	
Sport Ancient and Modern . .	Edited by E. D. CUMING	
Hunting	By EDWARD HUDDLESTON . . .	357
Staghounds . . .	By E. D. CUMING . . .	360
Harriers . . .	,, ,, . . .	361
Coursing	By H. LEDGER . . .	361
Shooting	By NICHOLAS EVERITT . . .	364
Wild-fowling . . .	,, ,, . . .	371
Angling	,, ,, . . .	375
Racing	By CUTHBERT BRADLEY . . .	380

		PAGE
Golf	By F. E. R. Fryer	. 383
Camp Ball	By E. D. Cuming	. 384
Athletics	By J. E. Fowler Dixon . . .	. 384
Agriculture	By Herman Biddell . . .	. 385
Forestry	By the Revd. J. C. Cox, LL.D., F.S.A. .	. 403

SURREY

VOLUME ONE

		PAGE
Dedication	. . . .	v
The Advisory Council of the Victoria History	. . . . . .	vii
General Advertisement . . .	. . . . . .	vii
The Surrey County Committee	. . . .	xiii
Contents	. . . . . .	xv
List of Illustrations . . .	. . . .	xvii
Preface	. . . . . .	xix
Natural History		
Geology	By G. W. Lamplugh, F.G.S. .	1
Palaeontology . . .	By Richard Lydekker, B.A., F.R.S., F.G.S.	29
Botany	Edited by W. H. Beeby, F.L.S.	
Introduction . . .	By W. H. Beeby, F.L.S. . .	35
Phanerogams, Summary of Orders .	,, ,, ,, . .	39
The Botanical Districts .	,, ,, ,, . .	40
Rubi (Brambles) . .	By the Revd. W. Moyle Rogers, F.L.S. .	47
Vascular Cryptogams (Ferns, etc.)	By W. H. Beeby, F.L.S. . .	49
Musci (Mosses) . . .	By Harold W. Monington .	51
Characeae . . .	By W. H. Beeby, F.L.S. . .	56
Freshwater Algae . .	By William West, F.L.S., and G. S. West, B.A., A.R.C.S.	57
Lichenes (Lichens) . .	By E. M. Holmes, F.L.S. . .	60
Fungi	By George Massee, F.L.S. . .	63
Zoology		
Mollusca (Snails, etc.) . .	By B. B. Woodward, F.G.S., F.R.M.S. .	71
Insecta (Insects) . .	Edited by Herbert Goss, F.L.S., F.G.S., Sec. to the Entomological Society .	73
Orthoptera (Grasshoppers, Earwigs, etc.)	By Malcolm Burr, F.L.S., F.Z.S., with notes by William J. Lucas, B.A., F.E.S. .	73
Neuroptera (Dragonflies, etc.) and Trichoptera (Caddisflies, etc.) .	By William J. Lucas, B.A., F.E.S., with notes by Charles A. Briggs, F.E.S., and Robert McLachlan, F.R.S., F.L.S., etc.. .	76
Hymenoptera Aculeata (Bees, etc.) .	By Edward Saunders, F.L.S., Vice-President Entomological Society . .	84
Chrysididae . . .	By the Revd. Francis D. Morice, M.A., F.E.S.	90
Hymenoptera Phytophaga (Saw-flies, etc.)	By Ethel F. Chawner, F.E.S., with notes by Alfred Beaumont, F.E.S., and the Revd. Francis D. Morice, M.A., F.E.S. .	91
Coleoptera (Beetles) . .	By George C. Champion, F.Z.S., F.E.S., with notes by Horace St. J. K. Donisthorpe, F.Z.S., F.E.S., and Robert Wyllie Lloyd, F.E.S. .	94
Lepidoptera Rhopalocera (Butterflies) .	By Herbert Goss, F.L.S., F.G.S., F.E.S., with notes by Thomas H. Briggs, M.A., F.E.S., and Sydney Webb	109

PAGE

Lepidoptera Heterocera (*Moths*),
    Nocturni, Geometrae,
    Drepanulidae, Pseudo-Bombyces,
    Noctuae, Deltoides, Pyralides,
    Crambites . . . By HERBERT GOSS, F.L.S., F.G.S., etc., with notes
                        by CHARLES G. BARRETT, Vice-President
                        Entomological Society, THOMAS H. BRIGGS, M.A.,
                        F.E.S., and SYDNEY WEBB . . . 116

Tortrices, Tineae, Pterophori . By CHARLES G. BARRETT, Vice-President Entomo-
                        logical Society, with notes by THOMAS H. BRIGGS,
                        M.A., F.E.S., and SYDNEY WEBB . . 137

Diptera (*Flies*) . . . By ERNEST E. AUSTEN 151

Hemiptera Heteroptera (*Bugs*) . By EDWARD SAUNDERS, F.L.S., Vice-President
                        Entomological Society 161

Hemiptera Homoptera (*Cicadas,*
    Aphides, etc.) . . . By GEORGE BOWDLER BUCKTON, F.R.S., F.L.S., etc. 168

Myriapoda (*Centipedes, etc.*) . . By R. I. POCOCK 176

Arachnida (*Spiders*) . . . By F. O. PICKARD-CAMBRIDGE, M.A. . 178

Crustacea (*Crabs, etc.*) . . By the Revd. T. R. R. STEBBING, M.A., F.R.S.,
                        F.L.S. 187

Pisces (*Fishes*) . . . By G. A. BOULENGER, F.R.S., F.Z.S. . 198

Reptilia (*Reptiles*) and Batrachia
    (*Batrachians*) . . . „ „ „ . . 200

Aves (*Birds*) . . . By J. A. BUCKNILL, M.A. . . . 202

Mammalia (*Mammals*) . . By J. A. BUCKNILL, M.A. and H. W. MURRAY,
                        F.Z.S. 219

Early Man . . . . By GEORGE CLINCH, F.G.S. . . 227

Anglo-Saxon Remains . . By REGINALD A. SMITH, B.A. . . 255

Introduction to the Surrey Domesday . By J. HORACE ROUND, M.A. . . 275

The Text of the Surrey Domesday . By H. E. MALDEN, M.A. . . . 295

Political History . . . „ „ „ . . . 329

Index to the Surrey Domesday 445

VOLUME TWO

PAGE

Dedication v

Contents ix

List of Illustrations xi

Editorial Note xiii

Table of Abbreviations xv

Ecclesiastical History . . By H. E. MALDEN, M.A. . . . I

Religious Houses . . . By the Revd. J. C. COX, LL.D., F.S.A.

    Introduction 54

    Abbey of Chertsey 55

        „ „ Bermondsey 64

        „ „ Waverley 77

    Priory of Sheen 89

        „ „ St. Mary of Merton 94

        „ „ Newark 102

        „ „ Reigate 105

        „ „ Southwark 107

        „ „ Tandridge 112

    Dominican Friars of Guildford 114

    Friars Observant of Richmond 116

    Hospital of Newington 118

        „ „ Sandon 118

        „ „ St. Thomas, Southwark 119

CONTENTS OF VOLUMES: SURR. II

		PAGE
Leper Hospital of Southwark		124
Collegiate Chapel of St. Mary Magdalen, Kingston		125
College of Lambeth		127
,, ,, Lingfield		127
,, ,, Malden		128
Priory of Tooting		129
Military History	By H. E. MALDEN, M.A. . . .	131
History of Schools	By A. F. LEACH, M.A., F.S.A. . . .	155
Industries	By MONTAGUE S. GIUSEPPI, F.S.A.	
Introduction		243
Iron		263
Stone Quarries, Lime Burning, Fullers' Earth, etc.		277
Pottery		281
Glass		295
Battersea Enamels		305
Gunpowder		306
Leather		329
Cloth		342
Miscellaneous Textile and Allied Industries		349
Tapestry		354
Felt and Hat Making		359
Dyeing, Bleaching, Calico Printing		363
Brewing		378
Distilling		394
Vinegar and British Wines		397
Aerated and Mineral Waters		401
Soap and Candle Making		402
Metal and Machinery Works		410
Paper		418
Printing and Printing Machinery		421
Ecclesiastical Architecture . . .	By PHILIP JOHNSTON . . .	425
Domestic Architecture . . .	By RALPH NEVILL, F.S.A., F.R.I.B.A. .	461
Sport Ancient and Modern . . .	Edited by E. D. CUMING	
Foxhounds	By CHARLES RICHARDSON . . .	483
Staghounds	,, ,, . . .	490
Harriers and Beagles . . .	,, ,, . . .	490
Racing	,, ,, . . .	491
Polo		513
Shooting	By YALDEN H. KNOWLES . . .	514
Angling	By C. H. COOK	517
Athletics	By CHARLES HERBERT . . .	520
Golf	By A. J. ROBERTSON . . .	521
Cricket	By HOME GORDON, assisted by C. W. ALCOCK, J. DOUGLAS, and the Revd. A. J. TAIT .	526
Football	By C. W. ALCOCK, assisted by H. E. STEED, W. R. M. LEAKE, and others . .	549
Forestry	By J. NISBET, D.Oec. . .	561
Topography: Farnham Hundred .	By H. E. MALDEN, M.A.	
Farnham Hundred		579
Farnham	Architectural description of Castle by C. R. PEERS, M.A., F.S.A.	581
,, ...	Architectural description of Church by C. R. PEERS, M.A., F.S.A.	
Elsted		605

		PAGE
Frensham	Architectural description of Church by C. R. Peers, M.A., F.S.A.	. 608
Seale	. . . . . .	. 616
Waverley	Architectural description of Abbey by Harold Brakspear, F.S.A., A.R.I.B.A. . .	. 620

VOLUME THREE

		PAGE
Dedication		. v
Contents		. ix
List of Illustrations		. xiii
List of Maps		. xviii
Editorial Note		. xix
Topography	General descriptions by H. E. Malden, M.A.; Manorial descents compiled under the superintendence of William Page, F.S.A., and H. E. Malden, M.A.; Architectural descriptions except where otherwise stated compiled under the superintendence of C. R. Peers, M.A., F.S.A., by J. Murray Kendall, J. W. Bloe, and C. C. Durston of the Architectural Staff; Heraldic drawings and blazon by Revd. E. E. Dorling, M.A., F.S.A.	
Godalming Hundred . .	Architectural descriptions by Philip M. Johnston, F.S.A.	
Introduction . . .	By Lilian J. Redstone, B.A. . .	. 1
Artington . . .	Manorial descents by Lilian J. Redstone .	. 3
Chiddingfold . . .	,, ,, ,, .	. 10
Compton . . .	,, ,, ,, .	. 16
Godalming . . .	History of borough and manorial descents by Lilian J. Redstone . . .	. 24
Hambledon . . .	Manorial descents by Lilian J. Redstone .	. 42
Haslemere . . .	History of borough and manorial descents by Lilian J. Redstone . . .	. 45
Peper Harow . . .	Manorial descents by Lilian J. Redstone .	. 49
Puttenham . . .	,, ,, ,, .	. 52
Thursley . . .	,, ,, ,, .	. 59
Witley . . .	,, ,, ,, .	. 61
Blackheath Hundred . .	Architectural descriptions by Philip M. Johnston, F.S.A., except Ewhurst, by Architectural Staff	
Introduction . . .	By Lilian J. Redstone, B.A. . .	. 70
Albury . . .	Manorial descents by Lilian J. Redstone .	. 72
Alfold . . .	,, ,, ,, .	. 77
Bramley . . .	,, ,, ,, .	. 80
Cranleigh . . .	,, ,, ,, .	. 86
Dunsfold . . .	,, ,, ,, .	. 92
Ewhurst . . .	,, ,, ,, .	. 97
Hascombe . . .	,, ,, ,, .	. 102
St. Martha's or Chilworth .	,, ,, ,, .	. 104
Shalford . . .	,, ,, ,, .	. 107
Shere . . .	,, ,, ,, .	. 111
Wonersh . . .	,, ,, ,, .	. 121
Wotton Hundred . .	Architectural descriptions by Philip M. Johnston, F.S.A., except Abinger, by Architectural Staff	
Introduction . . .	By Dorothy W. Sprules, Oxford Honours School of Modern History . . .	. 128
Abinger . . .	Manorial descents by Dorothy W. Sprules .	. 129

CONTENTS OF VOLUMES: SURR. III

							PAGE
Capel .	.	.	.	.	Manorial descents by DOROTHY W. SPRULES	.	134
Dorking	.	.	.	.	,, ,, ,, ,, .	.	141
Ockley .	.	.	.	.	,, ,, ,, ,, .	.	150
Wotton	.	.	.	.	,, ,, ,, ,, .	.	154
Reigate Hundred .	.	.	.	Architectural descriptions by Architectural Staff, except Betchworth, Horley, Merstham, and Reigate by PHILIP M. JOHNSTON, F.S.A.		
Introduction	.	.	.	.	By DOROTHY L. POWELL, Modern Language Tripos		165
Betchworth	.	.	.	.	Manorial descents by DOROTHY L. POWELL .	.	166
Buckland	.	.	.	.	,, ,, ,, .	.	173
Burstow	.	.	.	.	,, ,, ,, .	.	176
Charlwood	.	.	.	.	,, ,, ,, .	.	182
Chipstead	.	.	.	.	,, ,, ,, .	.	189
Gatton	.	.	.	.	History of borough and manorial descents by LILIAN J. REDSTONE, B.A. . .	.	196
Horley .	.	.	.	.	Manorial descents by DOROTHY L. POWELL .	.	200
Leigh .	.	.	.	.	,, ,, VALENTINA HAWTREY .	.	208
Merstham	.	.	.	.	,, ,, ,, ,, .	.	213
Nutfield	.	.	.	.	,, ,, DOROTHY L. POWELL .	.	222
Reigate	.	.	.	.	History of borough and manorial descents by LILIAN J. REDSTONE, B.A. . .	.	229
Copthorne Hundred	.	.	.	Architectural descriptions by Architectural Staff		
Introduction	.	.	.	.	By HENRIETTA L. E. GARBETT . .	.	246
Ashtead	.	.	.	.	Manorial descents by ELIZA B. MILLER .	.	247
Banstead	.	.	.	.	,, ,, DOROTHY L. POWELL, Modern Language Tripos . . .	.	252
Chessington	.	.	.	Manorial descents by WINIFRED RAY, B.A. .	.	263
Cuddington	.	.	.	.	,, ,, ,, ,, .	.	266
Epsom .	.	.	.	.	,, ,, ELIZA B. MILLER .	.	271
Ewell .	.	.	.	.	,, ,, ,, ,, .	.	278
Fetcham	.	.	.	.	,, ,, WINIFRED RAY, B.A. .	.	284
Headley	.	.	.	.	,, ,, VALENTINA HAWTREY .	.	290
Letherhead	.	.	.	.	,, ,, EMILY G. ALLINGHAM	.	293
Mickleham	.	.	.	.	,, ,, ,, ,,	.	301
Newdigate (part of)	.	.	.	,, ,, VALENTINA HAWTREY .	.	310
Walton-on-the-Hill	.	.	.	,, ,, ,, ,, .	.	315
Effingham Hundred	.	.	.	Architectural descriptions by Architectural Staff		
Introduction	.	.	.	.	By WINIFRED RAY, B.A. . .	.	320
Effingham	.	.	.	.	Manorial descents by WINIFRED RAY, B.A. .	.	321
Great Bookham	.	.	.	,, ,, ,, ,, .	.	326
Little Bookham	.	.	.	,, ,, ,, ,, .	.	335
Woking Hundred	.	.	.	Architectural descriptions by Architectural Staff		
Introduction	.	.	.	.	By DOROTHY W. SPRULES, Oxford Honours School of Modern History . . .	.	339
Ash .	.	.	.	.	Manorial descents by DOROTHY W. SPRULES	.	340
East Clandon .	.	.	.	,, ,, ,, ,,	.	344
West Clandon .	.	.	.	,, ,, ,, ,,	.	346
East Horsley .	.	.	.	,, ,, ,, ,,	.	349
West Horsley .	.	.	.	,, ,, ,, ,,	.	353
Merrow	.	.	.	.	,, ,, ,, ,,	.	357
Ockham	.	.	.	.	,, ,, ,, ,,	.	359
Pirbright	.	.	.	.	,, ,, ,, ,,	.	363
Send with Ripley	.	.	.	,, ,, ,, ,,	.	365
Stoke next Guildford	.	.	.	,, ,, ,, ,,	.	371
Wanborough	.	.	.	.	,, ,, ,, ,,	.	374
Windlesham	.	.	.	.	,, ,, ,, ,,	.	376
Wisley .	.	.	.	.	,, ,, ,, ,,	.	378

CONTENTS OF VOLUMES: SURR. III

					PAGE
Woking	.	.	.	.	Manorial descents by DOROTHY W. SPRULES	. 381
Worplesdon	.	.	.	.	,, ,, ,, ,,	. 390
Godley Hundred	.	.	.	Architectural descriptions by Architectural Staff, except Pyrford by PHILIP M. JOHNSTON, F.S.A.	
Introduction	.	.	.	.	By DOROTHY L. POWELL, Modern Language Tripos	396
Bisley	.	.	.	.	Manorial descents by DOROTHY L. POWELL .	398
Byfleet	.	.	.	.	,, ,, ,, ,, .	. 399
Chertsey	.	.	.	.	,, ,, ,, ,, .	. 403
Chobham	.	.	.	.	,, ,, ,, ,, .	. 413
Egham	.	.	.	.	,, ,, ,, ,, .	. 419
Horsell	.	.	.	.	,, ,, ,, ,, .	. 427
Pyrford	.	.	.	.	,, ,, ,, ,, .	. 431
Thorpe	.	.	.	.	,, ,, ,, ,, .	. 437
Elmbridge Hundred	.	.	.	Architectural descriptions by Architectural Staff	
Introduction	.	.	.	.	By HENRIETTA L. E. GARBETT . .	. 441
Cobham	.	.	.	.	Manorial descents by MARGARET E. CORNFORD	. 442
Esher	.	.	.	.	,, ,, ,, ,, .	. 447
East and West Molesey	.	.	.	,, ,, ,, ,, .	. 451
Stoke D'Abernon	.	.	.	,, ,, ,, ,, .	. 457
Thames Ditton	.	.	.	,, ,, ,, ,, .	. 462
Walton-on-Thames	.	.	.	,, ,, ,, ,, .	. 467
Weybridge	.	.	.	,, ,, ,, ,, .	. 475
Kingston Hundred	.	.	.	Architectural descriptions by Architectural Staff	
Introduction	.	.	.	.	By HENRIETTA L. E. GARBETT . .	. 481
Kew	.	.	.	.	General description and manorial descents by VALENTINA HAWTREY . . .	. 482
Kingston-upon-Thames	.	.	History of borough and manorial descents by HENRIETTA L. E. GARBETT . .	. 487
Long Ditton	.	.	.	Manorial descents by EMILY G. ALLINGHAM	. 516
Malden	.	.	.	.	,, ,, ,, ,, .	. 523
Petersham	.	.	.	.	,, ,, WINIFRED RAY, B.A. .	. 525
Richmond, anciently Sheen	.	.	General description and manorial descents by MARION WESTON, History Tripos .	. 533
Guildford Borough	.	.	.	Architectural descriptions by Architectural Staff, except Guildford Castle by L. F. SALZMANN, B.A.; History of the borough by DOROTHY W. SPRULES, Oxford Honours School of Modern History	. 547

VOLUME FOUR

									PAGE
Dedication	.	.	.	.	.	.	.	.	. v
Contents	.	.	.	.	.	.	.	.	. ix
List of Illustrations	.	.	.	.	.	.	.	. xi
List of Maps	.	.	.	.	.	.	.	.	. xv
Editorial Note	.	.	.	.	.	.	.	.	. xvii
Topography	.	.	.	General descriptions by H. E. MALDEN, M.A., except for Brixton Hundred and Croydon, which are by the authors of the manorial descents; Manorial descents compiled under the superintendence of WILLIAM PAGE, F.S.A., and H. E. MALDEN, M.A.; Architectural descriptions, except where otherwise stated, under the superintendence of C. R. PEERS, M.A., F.S.A., and S. C. KAINES-SMITH, M.A., by J. MURRAY KENDALL, S. F. BEEKE LANE, J. W. BLOE, JOHN QUEKETT, B.A., and ERNEST A. R. RAHBULA; Heraldic drawings and blazon by the Revd. E. E. DORLING, M.A., F.S.A.			

		PAGE
Brixton Hundred	Architectural descriptions by Architectural Staff	
Introduction	By HELEN DOUGLAS-IRVINE, M.A. . . .	1
Barnes	Manorial descents by MAUD F. EDWARDS, Oxford Honours School of Modern History . .	3
Battersea with Penge . . .	Manorial descents by LILIAN J. REDSTONE, B.A. .	8
	Charities from information supplied by J. W. OWSLEY, I.S.O., late Official Trustee of Charitable Funds.	
Bermondsey	Manorial descents by HELEN DOUGLAS-IRVINE, M.A.	17
Camberwell	,, ,, LEONARD A. MAGNUS, LL.B. .	24
Clapham	,, ,, LILIAN J. REDSTONE, B.A. .	36
Deptford St. Paul (Hamlet of Hatcham)	,, ,, LEONARD A. MAGNUS, LL.B. .	42
Lambeth	,, ,, VALENTINA HAWTREY . .	44
	Architectural description of Lambeth Palace by W. D. CARÖE, M.A., F.S.A.	
Merton	Manorial descents by LEONARD A. MAGNUS, LL.B. .	64
Mortlake	,, ,, MAUD F. EDWARDS . .	69
Newington	,, ,, LEONARD A. MAGNUS, LL.B. .	74
Putney	,, ,, MARION WESTON, History Tripos	78
Rotherhithe	Manorial descents by HELEN DOUGLAS-IRVINE, M.A.	83
Streatham	,, ,, CHARLOTTE M. CALTHROP, Classical Tripos	92
	Charities from information supplied by J. W. OWSLEY, I.S.O.	
Tooting Graveney . . .	Manorial descents by CHARLOTTE M. CALTHROP, Classical Tripos	103
	Charities from information supplied by J. W. OWSLEY, I.S.O.	
Wandsworth	Manorial descents by CHARLOTTE M. CALTHROP, Classical Tripos	108
	Charities from information supplied by J. W. OWSLEY, I.S.O.	
Wimbledon	Manorial descents by MARION WESTON, Hist. Tripos	120
Southwark Borough with Christchurch .	History of Borough and manorial descents by HELEN DOUGLAS-IRVINE, M.A. . . .	125
	Southwark Cathedral by S. C. KAINES-SMITH, M.A. ,, Domestic Architecture and St. Thomas's Church by A. W. CLAPHAM	
Wallington Hundred . . .	Architectural descriptions by Architectural Staff, except Addington, Chaldon, Coulsdon, and Sanderstead, by PHILIP M. JOHNSTON, F.S.A.	
Introduction	By HELEN DOUGLAS-IRVINE, M.A. . .	163
Addington	Manorial descents by LEONARD A. MAGNUS, LL.B. .	164
Beddington	,, ,, ,, ,,	168
Carshalton	,, ,, EMILY G. ALLINGHAM .	178
Chaldon	,, ,, ELIZA B. MILLER .	188
Cheam	,, ,, LEONARD A. MAGNUS, LL.B. .	194
Coulsdon	,, ,, ELIZA B. MILLER .	199
Croydon	,, ,, DOROTHY HUDDLESTONE .	205
Mitcham	,, ,, LEONARD A. MAGNUS, LL.B. .	229
Morden	,, ,, ,, ,,	235
Sanderstead	,, ,, ELIZA B. MILLER .	237
Sutton	,, ,, LEONARD A. MAGNUS, LL.B. .	243
Woodmansterne . . .	,, ,, ELIZA B. MILLER .	246
Tandridge Hundred . . .	Architectural descriptions by Architectural Staff, except Caterham, Chelsham, Farley, Tandridge, Tatsfield, Warlingham, and Woldingham, by PHILIP M. JOHNSTON, F.S.A., and Lingfield by S. C. KAINES-SMITH, M.A.	

			PAGE
Introduction	By DOROTHY L. POWELL, Modern Language Tripos		251
Blechingley	Manorial descents by DOROTHY L. POWELL . .		253
Caterham	,, ,, ,, ,, .		265
Chelsham	,, ,, LUCY DRUCKER .		270
Crowhurst	,, ,, DOROTHY L. POWELL .		274
Farley	,, ,, ELIZA B. MILLER .		281
Godstone	,, ,, DOROTHY L. POWELL .		283
Horne	,, ,, ,, ,, .		291
Limpsfield	,, ,, LUCY DRUCKER .		297
Lingfield	,, ,, DOROTHY L. POWELL .		302
Oxted	,, ,, ELIZA B. MILLER .		312
Tandridge	,, ,, DOROTHY L. POWELL .		321
Tatsfield	,, ,, LUCY DRUCKER .		326
Titsey	,, ,, ,, ,, .		330
Warlingham	,, ,, ,, ,, .		334
Woldingham	,, ,, ELIZA B. MILLER .		339
Romano-British Surrey . . .	By WILLIAM PAGE, F.S.A., and EDITH M. KEATE		343
	(Noviomagus. By Professor F. HAVERFIELD, M.A., LL.D., F.S.A.)		
Ancient Earthworks	By GEORGE CLINCH, F.G.S., F.S.A. (Scot.), and DUNCAN MONTGOMERIE, F.S.A. . .		379
Social and Economic History . .	By H. E. MALDEN, M.A. . . .		407
Table of Population 1801–1901 .	By GEORGE S. MINCHIN . . .		445
Agriculture	By AUBREY J. SPENCER, M.A. . .		455

SUSSEX

VOLUME ONE

		PAGE
Dedication		v
The Advisory Council of the Victoria History		vii
General Advertisement		vii
The Sussex County Committee		xiii
Contents		xv
List of Illustrations		xvii
Preface		xix
Table of Abbreviations		xxi
Natural History		
Geology	By CLEMENT REID, F.R.S., F.L.S., F.G.S. .	1
Palaeontology	By R. LYDEKKER, F.R.S., F.L.S., F.G.S. .	27
Botany	By the Revd. FREDERICK H. ARNOLD, M.A., LL.D. .	41
Brambles	By the Revd. W. MOYLE ROGERS . .	67
Marine Zoology . . .	By the late PHILIP J. RUFFORD, F.G.S. .	71
Non-Marine Molluscs . . .	By B. B. WOODWARD, F.G.S., F.R.M.S. .	108
Insects	Edited by HERBERT GOSS, F.L.S., late Secretary to the Entomological Society	
Orthoptera (*Earwigs, Grasshoppers, Crickets, etc.*) . .	By MALCOLM BURR, M.A., F.L.S., F.Z.S., with Notes by WILLIAM J. LUCAS, B.A., F.E.S. .	110
Neuroptera (*Dragonflies, Lacewings, etc.*)	By WILLIAM J. LUCAS, B.A., F.E.S., with Notes by the Revd. E. N. BLOOMFIELD, M.A., F.L.S. .	113
Hymenoptera Phytophaga, Tenthre- dinidae (*Sawflies*) .	By the Revd. EDWIN BLOOMFIELD, M.A., F.L.S., etc.	118
Cynipidae (*Gallflies*) . .	,, ,, ,, ,, ,,	122
Entomophaga (*Ichneumon Flies*) .	By CLAUDE MORLEY, F.E.S. . .	124

PAGE

Braconidae . . . . . By the Revd. EDWIN N. BLOOMFIELD, M.A., F.L.S.,
etc. 129

Chrysididae . . . . . ,, ,, ,, ,, ,, 129

Hymenoptera Aculeata (*Ants, Wasps
and Bees*) . . . By EDWARD SAUNDERS, F.R.S., F.L.S. . . 130

Coleoptera (*Beetles*) . . . By the Revd. Canon FOWLER, M.A., D.Sc., F.L.S. . 136

Lepidoptera Rhopalocera (*Butterflies*) . By HERBERT GOSS, F.L.S., with Notes by WILLIAM
H. B. FLETCHER, M.A., F.Z.S., etc. . . 164

Lepidoptera Heterocera (*Moths*) . By WILLIAM H. B. FLETCHER, M.A., F.Z.S., with
Notes by HERBERT GOSS, F.L.S., JAMES HERBERT
A. JENNER, F.E.S., and A. C. VINE . . 170

Diptera (*Flies*) . . . . By JAMES HERBERT A. JENNER, F.E.S., with Notes by
the Revd. EDWIN N. BLOOMFIELD, M.A., F.L.S. . 210

Hemiptera Heteroptera (*Bugs*) . . By EDWARD A. BUTLER, B.A., B.Sc., F.E.S. . . 226

Hemiptera Homoptera . . . By EDWARD A. BUTLER, B.A., B.Sc., F.E.S., and the
Revd. EDWIN N. BLOOMFIELD, M.A., F.L.S. . 234

Spiders . . . . . By the late F. O. PICKARD-CAMBRIDGE, M.A. . 238

Crustaceans . . . . By the Revd. T. R. R. STEBBING, M.A., F.R.S.,
F.Z.S. 245

Fishes . . . . . By CHARLES E. WALKER, F.L.S. . . 267

Reptiles and Batrachians . . . By W. C. J. RUSKIN BUTTERFIELD . . 271

Birds . . . . . By JOHN GUILLE MILLAIS, F.Z.S. . . 273

Mammals . . . . By W. C. J. RUSKIN BUTTERFIELD . . 299

Early Man . . . . . By GEORGE CLINCH, F.G.S. . . 309

Anglo-Saxon Remains . . . By REGINALD A. SMITH, B.A., F.S.A. . . 333

Introduction to the Sussex Domesday . By J. HORACE ROUND, M.A., LL.D., and L. F.
SALZMANN, B.A. 351

Translation of the Sussex Domesday . By L. F. SALZMANN, B.A. 387

Ancient Earthworks . . . By GEORGE CLINCH, F.G.S. . . . 453

Political History . . . . By L. F. SALZMANN, B.A. 481

Index to the Sussex Domesday 541

VOLUME TWO

PAGE

Dedication v

Contents ix

List of Illustrations and Maps xiii

Editorial Note xv

Ecclesiastical History . . . By L. F. SALZMANN, B.A. 1

Religious Houses . . . . ,, ,, ,,

Introduction 45

Cathedral of Chichester 47

Abbey of Battle 52

Priory of Boxgrove 56

,, ,, Sele 60

Nunnery of 'Ramestede' 63

Priory of Rusper 63

,, ,, Lewes 64

Abbey of Robertsbridge 71

Priory of Hardham 74

,, ,, Hastings 75

,, ,, Michelham 77

,, ,, Pynham 80

,, ,, Shulbred 81

,, ,, Tortington 82

,, ,, Easebourne 84

CONTENTS OF VOLUMES: SUSS. II

PAGE

Abbey of Otham 86
,, ,, Bayham 86
,, ,, Dureford 89
Preceptory of Saddlescombe 92
,, ,, Shipley 92
,, ,, Poling 93
House of Dominican Friars, Arundel 93
,, ,, ,, Chichester 94
,, ,, ,, Winchelsea 94
House of Franciscan Friars, Chichester 95
,, ,, ,, Lewes 95
,, ,, ,, Winchelsea 96
House of Austin Friars, Rye 96
,, ,, Carmelite Friars, Shoreham 97
Hospital of St. James, Arundel 97
,, ,, the Holy Trinity, Arundel 97
,, ,, Battle 98
,, ,, Bidlington 98
,, ,, Buxted 99
,, ,, St. James and St. Mary
Magdalen, Chichester 99
Hospital of St. Mary, Chichester 100
,, ,, 'Loddesdown', Chichester 102
,, ,, Rumboldswyke, Chichester 103
,, ,, Stockbridge, Chichester 103
,, ,, Harting 103
,, ,, Hastings 103
,, ,, St. James, Lewes 103
,, ,, St. Nicholas, Lewes 104
,, ,, Playden 104
,, ,, St. James, Seaford 105
,, ,, St. Leonard, Seaford 105
,, ,, St. James, Shoreham 106
,, ,, St. Katherine, Shoreham 106
,, ,, Sompting, or Cokeham 106
,, ,, Westham 106
,, ,, West Tarring 107
,, ,, St. Bartholomew, Winchelsea 107
,, ,, the Holy Cross, Winchelsea 107
,, ,, St. John, Winchelsea 107
,, ,, Windham 108
College of Arundel 108
,, ,, Bosham 109
,, ,, Hastings 112
,, ,, South Malling 117
Priory of Arundel 119
Ballivate of Atherington 120
Priory of Lyminster 121
,, ,, Runcton 121
Collegiate Church of Steyning 121
Priory of Wilmington 122
,, ,, Withyham 123
Ballivate of Warminghurst 124
Maritime History . . . By M. OPPENHEIM 125
Social and Economic History . . By Miss PHYLLIS WRAGGE, Oxford Honours School
of Modern History 169
Table of Population, 1801–1901 . . By GEORGE S. MINCHIN 215

PAGE

Industries . . . . . By L. F. SALZMANN, B.A.
  Introduction 229
  Iron 241
  Bell-Founding 249
  Pottery 251
  Brickmaking 253
  Glass 254
  Textile Industries 255
  Tanning 259
  Brewing 260
  Cider 263
  Fisheries 264
Agriculture . . . . . By WALTER F. INGRAM, F.S.I. . . . 273
Forestry . . . . . By W. HENEAGE LEGGE 291
Architecture . . . . By PHILIP M. JOHNSTON, F.R.I.B.A.
  Ecclesiastical 327
  Civil and Domestic 380
  Military 394
Schools . . . . . By A. F. LEACH, M.A., F.S.A.
  Introduction 397
  Chichester Prebendal School 399
  Hastings Grammar School 409
  Lewes Grammar School 411
  Cuckfield Grammar School 416
  Horsham Grammar School 421
  Steyning Grammar School 424
  Rye Grammar School 425
  Hartfield School 427
  Midhurst Grammar School 427
  East Grinstead School 430
  Brighton College 430
  Brighton Grammar School 431
  The Woodard Schools 431
    Lancing College 432
    Hurstpierpoint College 433
    St. Saviour's School, Ardingly 434
  Eastbourne College 434
  Christ's Hospital, West Horsham 435
  Elementary Schools founded before 1800 437
Sport Ancient and Modern . . . Edited by E. D. CUMING
  Hunting . . . . . By H. A. BRYDEN 441
    Fox-Hunting 441
      The Charlton Hunt 441
      The Goodwood Hounds 443
      The Petworth Hounds 444
      The First East Sussex Hunt 446
      The South Down Foxhounds 446
      The Present East Sussex Hunt 447
      The Crawley and Horsham Hunt 447
      The Eridge Hunt 448
      The Burstow Hunt 448
      The Eastbourne Hunt 448
    Stag-Hunting 448
      The South Coast Staghounds 449
      The Warnham Staghounds 449
    Harriers 449

		PAGE
Point-to-Point Races		452
Beagles		452
Otter-Hunting		453
Coursing	By J. W. BOURNE	453
Racing	By H. A. BRYDEN and E. D. CUMING .	454
Polo	By E. D. CUMING	461
Shooting	By PHILIP CHASMORE . . .	461
Angling	By G. F. SALTER	463
Cricket	By Sir HOME GORDON, Bart., assisted by A. S. HURST, A. J. GASTON, O. R. BORRADAILE, and others	467
Golf	By A. J. ROBERTSON . . .	477
Athletics	By W. BIRKETT	480

VOLUME THREE

		PAGE
Dedication		v
Contents		ix
List of Illustrations and Maps		xi
Editorial Note		xiii
Romano-British Sussex . .	By S. E. WINBOLT, M.A.	
Introduction		1
Pevensey		5
Chichester		9
Country Houses		20
Ironworks		29
Roads and Camps		32
Topographical Index		49
City of Chichester . . .	Architectural descriptions, except where otherwise stated, by the late WILLIAM PAGE, Hon. D.Litt., F.S.A., and HURFORD ROWE; Heraldic drawings and blazon by the Revd. E. E. DORLING, M.A., F.S.A.; Charities from information supplied by J. R. SMITH, of the Charity Commission	
General description of the City . .	By the late WILLIAM PAGE, Hon. D.Litt., F.S.A., and W. D. PECKHAM, M.A. . . .	71
History of the City . . .	By the late Professor ELIZABETH LEVETT, Ph.D., and the late WILLIAM PAGE, Hon. D.Litt., F.S.A. .	82
Port	By A. M. MELVILLE, M.A. . . .	100
Kingsham	By DAVID K. CLARKE, B.A. . .	104
Cathedral . . .	By WALTER H. GODFREY, F.R.I.B.A., F.S.A., and J. W. BLOE, F.S.A. . . .	105

VOLUME FOUR

		PAGE
Dedication		v
Contents		ix
List of Illustrations—Plates		xi
Maps and Plans		xii
Editorial Note		xv
Topography . . .	Where not otherwise stated, by the Editor; Domestic architecture by J. W. BLOE, O.B.E., F.S.A.; Ecclesiastical architecture by W. D. PECKHAM; Charities from information supplied by the Charity Commission	

CONTENTS OF VOLUMES: SUSS. IV

		PAGE
The Rape of Chichester		1
The Hundred of Dumpford	By Olive M. Moger	3
Chithurst	Architectural descriptions by Margaret E. Wood, F.S.A.	4
Didling	,, ,, ,,	6
Elsted		8
Harting		10
Rogate	Architectural descriptions by Margaret E. Wood, F.S.A.	21
Terwick	,, ,, ,,	28
Treyford		30
Trotton	Architectural descriptions by Margaret E. Wood, F.S.A.	32
The Hundred of Easebourne		40
Bepton		41
Cocking	By Helen M. Briggs	43
Easebourne		47
Fernhurst	Architectural descriptions by Margaret E. Wood, F.S.A.	54
Graffham		58
Heyshott	Architectural descriptions by Margaret E. Wood, F.S.A.	60
Iping	,, ,, ,,	63
West Lavington		65
Linch	Architectural descriptions by Margaret E. Wood, F.S.A.	65
Linchmere	,, ,, ,,	67
Lodsworth	,, ,, ,,	71
Midhurst		74
Selham	By Helen M. Briggs	80
Stedham		82
Woolbeding		84
The Hundred of Westbourne and Singleton		88
Binderton		89
Compton		91
East Dean		94
West Dean		97
East Lavant	By Barbara Crook, B.A.	101
Mid Lavant	,, ,,	104
East Marden	,, ,,	107
North Marden	,, ,,	108
Up Marden	,, ,,	110
Racton	,, ,,	113
Singleton		118
Stoughton		121
Westbourne		126
The Hundred of Box and Stockbridge		133
Aldingbourne		134
Appledram		138
Boxgrove		140
Donnington		150
Eartham		152
New Fishbourne		154
Hunston		156
Merston		158
North Mundham		160
Oving		165

	PAGE
Rumboldswyke	171
Up Waltham	174
Westhampnett	175
The Hundred of Bosham	181
Bosham	182
Chidham	188
Funtington	190
West Stoke	192
West Thorney	195
The Hundred of Manhood	198
Birdham	199
Earnley	201
West Itchenor	204
Selsey	205
Sidlesham	210
East Wittering	215
West Wittering	217
The Hundred of Aldwick	222
Bersted	223
Bognor Regis	226
Pagham	227
Slindon	234
Tangmere	237

VOLUME SEVEN

		PAGE
Dedication		v
Contents		ix
List of Illustrations		xi
Editorial Note		xv
Topography	Heraldic drawings and blazon by the Revd. E. E. DORLING, M.A., F.S.A.; Charities from information supplied by Mr. E. W. PERKINS, of the Charity Commission	
The Rape and Honour of Lewes	By MARGARET MIDGLEY, M.A.	I
The Borough of Lewes	By MARGARET SHARP, M.A., Ph.D., and MARGARET MIDGLEY, M.A.; Architectural descriptions by WALTER H. GODFREY, F.R.I.B.A., F.S.A.	7
The Hundred of Southover		44
Southover	By MARGARET MIDGLEY, M.A.; Architectural descriptions by WALTER H. GODFREY, F.R.I.B.A., F.S.A.	45
The Hundred of Swanborough	By GEORGE MOREY, B.A.; Architectural descriptions by HUGH S. BRAUN, F.R.I.B.A., F.S.A.	51
Iford		52
Kingston near Lewes		57
The Hundred of Holmestrow		61
Newhaven		62
Piddinghoe		66
Rodmell		69
Southease		73
Telscombe		76
The Hundred of Barcombe	By the late EILEEN H. FAGAN, M.A.; Architectural descriptions by MARGARET WOOD, M.A.	79
Barcombe		80
Hamsey		83

CONTENTS OF VOLUMES: SUSS. VII

		PAGE
Newick		87
The Hundred of Streat . . .	By M. ELIZABETH CHRISTIE, F.R.Hist.Soc.; Architectural descriptions by MARGARET WOOD, M.A. .	92
Chailey		94
East Chiltington		98
Ditchling		102
Plumpton		109
Streat		113
Westmeston		116
Wivelsfield		119
The Hundred of Buttinghill . .	By M. ELIZABETH CHRISTIE, F.R.Hist.Soc.; Architectural descriptions by J. W. BLOE, O.B.E., F.S.A.	125
Ardingly		127
Balcombe		132
Bolney		136
Clayton		140
Crawley		144
Cuckfield		147
West Hoathly		164
Hurstpierpoint		172
Keymer		179
Slaugham		181
Twineham		186
Worth		192
The Hundred of Poynings . .	By the late EILEEN H. FAGAN, M.A.; Architectural descriptions by HUGH S. BRAUN, F.R.I.B.A., F.S.A.	201
Fulking		202
Newtimber		204
Poynings		208
Pyecombe		212
The Hundred of Dean . .	By OLIVE M. MOGER; Architectural descriptions by HUGH S. BRAUN, F.R.I.B.A., F.S.A. .	215
Patcham		216
The Hundred of Younsmere . . .		221
Falmer		223
Ovingdean		227
Rottingdean		232
Stanmer		238
The Hundred of Whalesbone . . .		241
West Blatchington		242
The Borough of Brighton . .	By CATHERINE JAMISON; Architectural descriptions by HUGH S. BRAUN, F.R.I.B.A., F.S.A.; Modern churches by R. R. SALZMAN . .	244
The Hundred of Preston . . .		264
The Borough of Hove . . .		265
Preston		268
The Half-Hundred of Fishersgate .	By OLIVE M. MOGER; Architectural descriptions by HUGH S. BRAUN, F.R.I.B.A., F.S.A. .	274
Aldrington		275
Hangleton		277
Portslade		282

VOLUME NINE

					PAGE
Dedication	.	.	.	.	v
Contents	.	.	.	.	ix
List of Illustrations	.	.	.	.	xii
Editorial Note	.	.	.	.	xv

Topography . . . . General descriptions and manorial descents, except where otherwise stated, by members of the late Dr. WILLIAM PAGE's staff, revised by M. ELIZABETH CHRISTIE, F.R.Hist.Soc.; Heraldic drawings and blazon by the Revd. E. E. DORLING, M.A., F.S.A.; Charities from information supplied by Mr. J. R. SMITH, of the Charity Commission

The Rape and Honour of Hastings . By the late WILLIAM PAGE, Hon. D.Litt., F.S.A. . 1

The Borough of Hastings, with St. Leonards . . . . By M. ELIZABETH CHRISTIE, F.R.Hist.Soc.; Architectural description of the Town and Castle by J. W. BLOE, O.B.E., F.S.A.; of the Churches by J. E. RAY, F.R.Hist.Soc. . . . 4

The Cinque Ports . . . By the late WILLIAM PAGE, Hon. D.Litt., F.S.A., and L. F. SALZMAN, M.A., F.S.A. . . 34

The Borough of Rye . . . By the late WILLIAM PAGE, Hon. D.Litt., F.S.A.; Architectural description of the Town by J. W. BLOE, O.B.E., F.S.A.; of the Church by SIDNEY TOY, F.R.I.B.A., F.S.A. 39

Winchelsea . . . . By the late WILLIAM PAGE, Hon. D.Litt., F.S.A., and H. B. WALTERS, O.B.E., M.A., F.S.A.; Architectural description of the Town by G. E. CHAMBERS, B.A., F.S.A.; of the Church by SIDNEY TOY, F.R.I.B.A., F.S.A. . . . 62

The Hundred of Baldslow . . Architectural descriptions—domestic by J. W. BLOE, O.B.E., F.S.A.; Churches by J. E. RAY, F.R.Hist.Soc.

Introduction	.	.	.	.	.	.	76
Crowhurst	.	.	.	.	.	.	77
Hollington	.	.	.	.	.	.	81
Ore	.	.	.	.	.	.	87
Westfield	.	.	.	.	.	.	90

The Hundred of Battle

Introduction	.	.	.	.	.	.	95

Battle . . . . Architectural descriptions—domestic by J. W. BLOE, O.B.E., F.S.A.; of the Abbey by the late Sir HAROLD BRAKSPEAR, K.C.V.O., F.R.I.B.A., F.S.A.; of the Church by SIDNEY TOY, F.R.I.B.A., F.S.A. 97

Whatlington . . . . Architectural descriptions by E. T. LONG . . 112

The Hundred of Bexhill

Introduction	.	.	.	.	.	.	115

Bexhill . . . . Architectural descriptions—domestic by J. W. BLOE, O.B.E., F.S.A.; of the Churches by J. E. RAY, F.R.Hist.Soc., W. E. MEADS, and P. L. SALZMAN . 116

The Hundred of Foxearle . . Architectural descriptions—domestic by IAN C. HANNAH, M.P., M.A., F.S.A.; Churches by SIDNEY TOY, F.R.I.B.A., F.S.A.

Introduction	.	.	.	.	.	.	125
Ashburnham	.	.	.	.	.	.	126

Herstmonceux . . . . Architectural description of the Castle by WALTER H. GODFREY, F.R.I.B.A., F.S.A. . . . 131

Wartling 137

The Hundred of Goldspur . . By M. ELIZABETH CHRISTIE, F.R.Hist.Soc.; Architectural descriptions—domestic by J. W. BLOE, O.B.E., F.S.A.; Churches by SIDNEY TOY, F.R.I.B.A., F.S.A.

CONTENTS OF VOLUMES: SUSS. IX

		PAGE
Introduction		142
Beckley		143
Broomhill	By L. F. Salzman, M.A., F.S.A. . . .	148
East Guldeford		150
Iden		152
Peasmarsh		157
Playden		160
The Hundred of Gostrow . .	By Ada Russell, M.A.; Architectural descriptions—domestic by J. W. Bloe, O.B.E., F.S.A.; Churches by Sidney Toy, F.R.I.B.A., F.S.A.	
Introduction		164
Brede		165
Udimore		172
The Hundred of Guestling . .	By M. Elizabeth Christie, F.R.Hist.Soc.; Architectural descriptions—domestic by J. W. Bloe, O.B.E., F.S.A.; Churches by J. E. Ray, F.R.Hist.Soc.	
Introduction		175
Fairlight		176
Guestling		179
Icklesham		184
Pett		190
The Hundred of Hawksborough . .	Architectural descriptions—domestic by G. E. Chambers, B.A., F.S.A.; Churches by E. T. Long	
Introduction		193
Burwash		194
Heathfield		200
Warbleton		204
The Hundred of Henhurst . .	Architectural descriptions—domestic by G. E. Chambers, B.A., F.S.A.; Churches by E. T. Long	
Introduction		210
Etchingham		211
Salehurst		217
The Hundred of Netherfield . .	Architectural descriptions of Churches by E. T. Long	
Introduction		226
Brightling	Architectural descriptions—domestic by G. E. Chambers, B.A., F.S.A. . . .	227
Dallington	,, ,, ,,	232
Mountfield	Architectural descriptions—domestic by Ian C. Hannah, M.P., M.A., F.S.A. . .	234
Penhurst	,, ,, ,,	237
The Hundred of Ninfield . .	Architectural descriptions of Churches by Sidney Toy, F.R.I.B.A., F.S.A.	
Introduction		239
Catsfield	Architectural descriptions—domestic by J. W. Bloe, O.B.E., F.S.A. . . .	240
Hooe	Architectural descriptions—domestic by Ian C. Hannah, M.P., M.A., F.S.A. . .	244
Ninfield	,, ,, ,,	247
The Hundred of Shoyswell		
Introduction		251
Ticehurst	Architectural descriptions—domestic by G. E. Chambers, B.A., F.S.A.; Church by Sidney Toy, F.R.I.B.A., F.S.A. . . .	252
The Hundred of Staple		
Introduction		258
Bodiam	Architectural descriptions of Castle and Church by Sidney Toy, F.R.I.B.A., F.S.A. . .	259

195

PAGE

Ewhurst	Architectural descriptions—domestic by G. E. CHAMBERS, B.A., F.S.A.; Church by E. T. LONG .	265
Northiam	Architectural descriptions—domestic by J. W. BLOE, O.B.E., F.S.A.; Church by SIDNEY TOY, F.R.I.B.A., F.S.A.	268
Sedlescombe	Architectural descriptions—domestic by J. W. BLOE, O.B.E., F.S.A.; Church by SIDNEY TOY, F.R.I.B.A., F.S.A.	276

WARWICKSHIRE

VOLUME ONE

PAGE

Dedication		v
The Advisory Council of the Victoria History		vii
General Advertisement		vii
The Warwickshire County Committee		xiii
Contents		xv
List of Illustrations		xvii
Preface		xix
Table of Abbreviations		xx
Natural History		
Geology	By T. C. CANTRILL	1
Palaeontology	By RICHARD LYDEKKER, F.R.S. . .	29
Botany	By J. E. BAGNALL, A.L.S. . . .	33
Zoology		
Mollusca (*Snails, etc.*) . .	By B. B. WOODWARD, F.G.S., F.R.M.S. .	67
Insecta (*Insects*) . .	Edited by COLBRAN J. WAINWRIGHT, F.E.S.	69
Odonata . . .	By R. C. BRADLEY and COLBRAN J. WAINWRIGHT, F.E.S. . . .	73
Hymenoptera (*Bees, etc.*) .	By A. H. MARTINEAU, F.E.S. . .	73
Coleoptera (*Beetles*) .	By H. WILLOUGHBY ELLIS, F.E.S. .	77
Lepidoptera (*Moths*) .	By COLBRAN J. WAINWRIGHT, F.E.S. .	124
Diptera (*Flies*) . .	,, ,, ,, .	158
Hemiptera Heteroptera (*Bugs, etc.*) .	By H. WILLOUGHBY ELLIS, F.E.S. .	165
Arachnida (*Spiders*) . .	By F. O. PICKARD-CAMBRIDGE, M.A. .	167
Crustacea (*Crabs, etc.*) . .	By the Revd. T. R. R. STEBBING, M.A., F.R.S., F.L.S.	171
Pisces (*Fishes*) . . .	By R. F. TOMES, F.G.S., Corr. Mem. Z.S. .	184
Reptilia (*Reptiles*) and Batrachia (*Batrachians*) . .	,, ,, ,, .	187
Aves (*Birds*) . . .	,, ,, ,, .	189
Mammalia (*Mammals*) .	,, ,, ,, .	208
Early Man	By GEORGE CLINCH, F.G.S. . .	213
Romano-British Remains . .	By F. HAVERFIELD, M.A., F.S.A. .	223
Anglo-Saxon Remains . .	By REGINALD A. SMITH, B.A., F.S.A. .	251
Introduction to the Warwickshire Domesday . . .	By J. HORACE ROUND, M.A. . .	269
Text of the Warwickshire Domesday	By W. F. CARTER, B.A. . . .	299
Ancient Earthworks . .	By WILLOUGHBY GARDNER, F.L.S. . .	345
Index to the Warwickshire Domesday	. . . . . .	407

VOLUME TWO

		PAGE
Dedication .	. . . .	v
Contents .	. . . .	ix
List of Illustrations and Maps	. . . .	xiii
Editorial Note	. . . .	xv
Ecclesiastical History	. . . By the Revd. J. C. Cox, LL.D., F.S.A. .	1
Religious Houses .	. . . ,, ,, ,,	
Introduction	. . . .	51
Priory of Coventry	. . . .	52
Abbey of Alcester	. . . .	59
Priory of Alvecote	. . . .	61
Abbey of Polesworth	. . . .	62
Priory of Henwood	. . . .	65
,, ,, Nuneaton	. . . .	66
,, ,, Wroxall	. . . .	70
Abbey of Combe .	. . . .	73
,, ,, Merevale	. . . .	75
,, ,, Stoneleigh	. . . .	78
Priory of Pinley .	. . . .	82
,, ,, St. Anne, Coventry	. . . .	83
Abbey of Kenilworth	. . . .	86
Priory of Arbury .	. . . .	89
,, ,, Maxstoke	. . . .	91
,, ,, Studley .	. . . .	94
,, ,, St. Sepulchre, Warwick .	. . . . . .	97
Preceptory of Balsall	. . . .	99
,, ,, Balsall and Grafton .	. . . . . .	100
Dominican Friars of Warwick	. . . .	101
Franciscan Friars of Coventry	. . . .	103
Carmelite Friars of Coventry	. . . .	104
Austin Friars of Atherstone	. . . .	106
Trinitarian Friars of Thelsford	. . . .	106
Hospital of St. Thomas, Birmingham	. . . . . .	108
,, ,, Bretford	. . . .	109
,, ,, St. John Baptist, Coventry	. . . . .	109
,, ,, Spon, Coventry	. . . .	111
Bablake or Bond's Hospital, Coventry	. . . . . .	112
Grey Friars Hospital, Coventry .	. . . . . .	112
Hospital of Henley in Arden	. . . .	112
Hospital or Gild of the Holy Cross,		
Stratford-on-Avon .	. . . .	113
Hospital of St. John Baptist, Warwick	. . . . . .	115
,, ,, St. Michael, Warwick .	. . . . . .	116
Collegiate Church of Astley	. . . .	117
College of Bablake, Coventry	. . . .	120
,, ,, Knowle	. . . .	121
,, ,, Stratford-on-Avon	. . . . . .	123
,, ,, St. Mary, Warwick	. . . . . .	124
Priory of Monks Kirby .	. . . .	129
,, ,, Warmington	. . . .	131
,, ,, Wolston	. . . .	132
,, ,, Wootton Wawen	. . . . . .	133
Social and Economic History	. . By Miss Mary Dormer-Harris	137
Table of Population, 1801–1901 .	. By George S. Minchin . . .	182

PAGE

Industries

 Introduction . . . . By Miss E. M. Hewitt 193

 Coal Mining . . . . By Professor R. A. S. Redmayne, M.Sc., and L. F.
              Salzmann, B.A. 217

 The Gun Trade of Birmingham . By Miss E. M. Hewitt 226

 Coinage and Assaying . . . ,, ,, ,, ... 232

 Needles and Pins . . . . ,, ,, ,, ... 234

 Buttons . . . . . ,, ,, ,, ... 237

 Buckles . . . . . ,, ,, ,, ... 240

 Clocks and Watches . . . ,, ,, ,, ... 242

 Glass-Making . . . . ,, ,, ,, ... 244

 Chemicals . . . . ,, ,, ,, ... 249

 Cloth-Making . . . . ,, ,, ,, ... 251

 The Ribbon Trade of Coventry . . ,, ,, ,, ... 257

 The Barcheston Tapestries . . By Miss E. M. Hewitt and Miss M. Jourdain . 263

 Caps and Hats . . . . By Miss E. M. Hewitt 265

 Brewing . . . . . ,, ,, ,, ... 266

Agriculture . . . . . By W. H. R. Curtler 269

Forestry . . . . . By the Revd. J. C. Cox, LL.D., F.S.A. . . 287

Schools . . . . . By A. F. Leach, M.A., F.S.A.

 Introduction 297

 Warwick 299

 Coventry 318

 The Bablake 329

 Stratford-on-Avon 329

 Sutton Coldfield 341

 Nuneaton 342

 King Edward VI's Schools, Birmingham 347

 Birmingham University 356

 Atherstone 356

 Solihull 357

 Rugby 360

 Coleshill 366

 Monks Kirby 367

 Hampton Lucy or Bishops Hampton 367

 Salford Priors 368

 Kingsbury 368

 Elementary Schools, founded before 1750 369

Sport, Ancient and Modern . . Edited by the Revd. E. E. Dorling, M.A.

 Hunting . . . . . By Clifford Cordley 375

  Fox Hunting . . . . ,, ,, ... 375

  Beagles . . . . ,, ,, ... 383

  Otterhounds . . . . ,, ,, ... 383

 Coursing . . . . . ,, ,, ... 384

 Racing . . . . . ,, ,, ... 386

  Flat Racing . . . . ,, ,, ... 386

  Steeplechasing . . . . ,, ,, ... 388

 Shooting . . . . . ,, ,, ... 390

 Angling . . . . . ,, ,, ... 393

 Cricket . . . . By Sir Home Gordon, Bart., assisted by W. Unite
           Jones and H. C. Bradby . . . 395

  Birmingham Local 401

  Rugby 404

  Rugby School 406

  Stratford-on-Avon 409

 Football . . . . By C. J. Bruce Marriott, M.A. . . 410

 Golf . . . . By the Revd. E. E. Dorling, M.A. . . 412

			PAGE
Local Sports and Pastimes	.	By CLIFFORD CORDLEY . . .	414
Cock-Fighting		,, ,, . . .	415
Bull-Baiting		,, ,, . . .	416
Athletics		,, ,, . . .	418
Political History . . .	.	By Miss E. P. STEELE-HUTTON, M.A. (St. Andrews).	421

VOLUME THREE

		PAGE
Dedication		V
Contents		ix
List of Illustrations		xi
Editorial Note		xiii
List of Abbreviations used in References		xv
Topography	Architectural descriptions by Mr. J. W. BLOE, O.B.E., F.S.A.; Heraldic drawings and blazon by the late Revd. E. E. DORLING, M.A., F.S.A.; Charities from information supplied by Mr. E. W. PERKINS, of the Charity Commission	
The Hundreds of Warwickshire .	By BENJAMIN WALKER, F.S.A. . . .	1
Barlichway Hundred . .	,, ,, ,, . . .	5
Alcester . . .	By PHILIP STYLES, M.A., and DOROTHY STYLES, M.A.	8
Great Alne . . .	By MARGARET MIDGLEY, M.A. . . .	22
Arrow	By MARGERY FLETCHER, M.A. . . .	26
Aston Cantlow .	By PHILIP STYLES, M.A.	31
Bearley . . .	By L. F. SALZMAN, M.A., F.S.A. . . .	43
Beaudesert . . .	By WILLIAM COOPER, F.S.A. . . .	45
Bidford . . .	By PHILIP STYLES, M.A.	49
Billesley . . .	By OLIVE M. MOGER	58
Binton	,, ,, ,, ...	62
Budbrooke . . .	By LEVI FOX, M.A.	65
Claverdon . . .	By E. G. TIBBITS, LL.B. . . .	69
Coughton . . .	By MARGARET MIDGLEY, M.A., and EDITH S. SCROGGS	74
Sambourne . .	. . . . . .	86
Exhall	By PHILIP STYLES, M.A. . . .	88
Fulbrook . . .	By LEVI FOX, M.A.	91
Temple Grafton . .	By PHILIP STYLES, M.A. . . .	94
Hampton Lucy . .	,, ,, ,, . . .	100
Haseley . . .	By OLIVE M. MOGER	104
Haselor . . .	,, ,, ,, . . .	108
Hatton . . .	,, ,, ,, . . .	115
Honiley . . .	,, ,, ,, . . .	120
Ipsley	By the late Revd. H. R. HUBAND, M.A., F.S.A. .	123
Kinwarton . . .	By MARGERY FLETCHER, M.A. . . .	126
Loxley	By PHILIP STYLES, M.A. . . .	129
Morton Bagot . .	By DORIS M. BOND, B.A. . . .	134
Norton Lindsey . .	By PHILIP STYLES, M.A. . . .	138
Oldberrow . . .	By L. F. SALZMAN, M.A., F.S.A. . . .	140
Preston Bagot . .	By MARGARET MIDGLEY, M.A. . . .	141
Rowington . . .	By E. G. TIBBITS, LL.B. . . .	146
Salford Priors . .	By PHILIP STYLES, M.A. . . .	155
Sherbourne . . .	By MARGARET MIDGLEY, M.A. . . .	165
Snitterfield . . .	By L. F. SALZMAN, M.A., F.S.A. . . .	167
Spernall . . .	By DORIS M. BOND, B.A. . . .	172

PAGE

Studley . . . By Margery Fletcher, M.A. . . . 175
Weethley . . . „ „ „ . . . 187
Wixford . . . By Philip Styles, M.A. . . . 188
Wolverton . . . By Levi Fox, M.A. . . . 193
Wootton Wawen . . . By William Cooper, F.S.A. . . . 196
 Henley-in-Arden 206
 Ullenhall 212
Wroxall . . . By E. G. Tibbits, LL.B. . . . 215
The Borough of Stratford-upon-Avon . By Philip Styles, M.A. . . . 221
 Alveston 283

VOLUME FOUR

PAGE

Dedication v
Contents ix
List of Illustrations xi
Editorial Note xiii
Topography . . . Architectural descriptions by J. W. Bloe, O.B.E., F.S.A.; Heraldic drawings and blazon by the late Revd. E. E. Dorling, M.A., F.S.A.; Charities from information supplied by Mr. E. W. Perkins, of the Charity Commission

Hemlingford Hundred . . . By the late Benjamin Walker, F.S.A. . . 1
 Ansley . . . . By Olive M. Moger . . . 5
 Austrey . . . By Helen M. Briggs . . . 9
 Baddesley Clinton . . „ „ . . . 13
 Baddesley Ensor . . „ „ . . . 19
 Barston . . . By Olive M. Moger . . . 21
 Baxterley . . . By Gwyneth A. Wise . . . 24
 Berkswell . . . By the late Reginald J. W. Cavill, M.A. . . 27
 Bickenhill . . . By C. E. B. Hubbard, M.A. . . . 34
 Caldecote . . . By Olive M. Moger . . . 40
 Castle Bromwich . . By C. E. B. Hubbard, M.A. . . . 43
 Coleshill . . . By the Revd. Noel Boston, M.A., and Margaret Midgley, M.A. 47
 Corley . . . By Olive M. Moger . . . 57
 Curdworth . . . By John S. G. Simmons, B.A. . . . 60
 Elmdon . . . By Helen M. Briggs . . . 67
 Fillongley . . . By Margaret Midgley, M.A. . . . 69
 Grendon . . . By Gwyneth A. Wise . . . 75
 Hampton-in-Arden . . By L. F. Salzman, M.A., F.S.A. . . . 81
  Balsall 86
  Knowle 91
  Nuthurst 99
 Kingsbury . . . By Margaret Midgley, M.A. . . . 100
 Lea Marston . . . By Helen M. Briggs . . . 114
 Mancetter . . . By Geoffrey Templeman, M.A., and L. F. Salzman, M.A., F.S.A. . . . 116
  Atherstone 126
  Hartshill 131
 Maxstoke . . . By B. A. Fetherston-Dilke, M.B.E., and Margaret Midgley, M.A. 133
 Merevale . . . By L. F. Salzman, M.A., F.S.A. . . . 142
 Meriden . . . By C. E. B. Hubbard, M.A. . . . 147
 Middleton . . . By Margaret Midgley, M.A. . . . 156

		PAGE
Newton Regis	By Gwyneth A. Wise	160
The Borough of Nuneaton . .	By C. E. B. Hubbard, M.A. . . .	165
Chilvers Coton . . .	By Gwyneth A. Wise . . .	173
Weddington	By Olive M. Moger . . .	179
Great Packington . . .	By C. E. B. Hubbard, M.A. . .	180
Little Packington . . .	,, ,, ,, . .	183
Polesworth	By Margaret Midgley, M.A. . .	186
Seckington	By Gwyneth A. Wise . . .	198
Sheldon	By Margaret Midgley, M.A. . .	200
Shustoke	,, ,, ,, . .	205
Bentley	. . . . .	210
Shuttington . . .	By Gwyneth A. Wise . . .	212
Solihull	By Margaret Midgley, M.A. . .	214
The Borough of Sutton Coldfield .	,, ,, ,, . .	230
Tamworth	By L. F. Salzman, M.A., F.S.A. . .	246
Amington and Stonydelph .	. . . . .	246
Bolehall and Glascote .	. . . . .	248
Wilnecote . . .	. . . . .	249
Nether Whitacre . . .	By Margaret Midgley, M.A. . .	251
Over Whitacre . . .	,, ,, ,, . .	256
Wishaw	By C. E. B. Hubbard, M.A. . .	258
Water Orton . . .	By L. F. Salzman, M.A., F.S.A. . .	262

VOLUME FIVE

		PAGE
Dedication		v
Contents		ix
List of Illustrations		xi
Editorial Note		xiii
Topography	Where not otherwise stated, by the Editor; Architectural descriptions by J. W. Bloe, O.B.E., F.S.A.; Charities from information supplied by Mr. E. W. Perkins, of the Charity Commission	
Kington Hundred		1
Atherstone-on-Stour		3
Barcheston		5
Barford		10
Barton-on-the-Heath		13
Brailes		17
Burmington		26
Butlers Marston		28
Chadshunt . . .	By J. S. G. Simmons, B.A. . . .	31
Charlecote . . .	By Bernard W. Smith, B.A. . . .	34
Cherington		38
Chesterton		42
Fenny Compton		47
Little Compton		50
Long Compton		52
Compton Verney		58
Compton Wyniates		60
Avon Dassett		67
Burton Dassett		69
Ettington . . .	By C. E. B. Hubbard, M.A. . . .	77
Farnborough		84
Gaydon . . .	By J. S. G. Simmons, B.A. . . .	88

	PAGE
Halford	89
Honington	92
Idlicote	95
Ilmington	98
Kineton with Combrook	103
Lapworth	108
Lighthorne	117
Moreton Morrell	118
Newbold Pacey	122
Oxhill . . . . By Paul Morgan, B.A.	124
Packwood	129
Pillerton Hersey	133
Pillerton Priors	136
Priors Hardwick	137
Priors Marston	140
Radway	142
Ratley	144
Shotteswell . . . By C. E. B. Hubbard, M.A. . . .	148
Stretton-on-Fosse	153
Sutton-under-Brailes	157
Bishop's Tachbrook	160
Tanworth	165
Tysoe	175
Warmington	182
Wasperton	187
Welford-on-Avon	189
Wellesbourne with Walton	193
Weston-upon-Avon with Milcote	198
Whatcote	202
Whichford	205
Whitchurch	209
Wolford	213
Wormleighton	218

VOLUME SIX

	PAGE
Dedication	v
Contents	ix
List of Illustrations	xi
Editorial Note	xiii
Topography . . . . Where not otherwise stated, by L. F. Salzman, M.A., F.S.A., and H. B. Wells, M.A.; Architectural descriptions by H. A. James, A.R.I.B.A., F.S.A.; Charities from information supplied by Mr. A. J. Walker, of the Charity Commission	
Knightlow Hundred	1
Allesley . . . Architecture by J. H. While, A.R.I.B.A. .	3
Arley . . . . ,, ,, ,, .	8
Ashow	12
Astley . . . Architecture by J. H. While, A.R.I.B.A. .	15
Baginton	22
Bedworth . . . Architecture by J. H. While, A.R.I.B.A. .	26
Bilton . . . . ,, J. T. Smith . .	30
Binley	35
Birdingbury	37

CONTENTS OF VOLUMES: WARWS. VI

		PAGE
Bourton-on-Dunsmore .		39
Brinklow		42
Bubbenhall		46
Bulkington	Architecture by J. H. WHILE, A.R.I.B.A.	48
Burton Hastings	,, ,, ,,	57
Churchover	Architecture by J. T. SMITH	62
Clifton-on-Dunsmore	,, J. H. WHILE, A.R.I.B.A.	65
Combe Fields .		72
Cubbington	Architecture by G. PHILLIPS DALES, F.R.I.B.A.	74
Dunchurch and Thurlaston		78
Exhall .	Architecture by J. H. WHILE, A.R.I.B.A.	86
Frankton		92
Grandborough .		94
Harborough Magna		99
Harbury		103
Hillmorton	Architecture by J. T. SMITH	108
Hodnell		114
Hunningham .		117
Hydes Pastures		120
Bishop's Itchington		121
Long Itchington		125
Kenilworth		132
Ladbroke		143
Church Lawford		147
Leamington Hastings		149
The Borough of Leamington Spa	By the late WILLIAM COOPER, F.S.A.	155
Lillington		161
Milverton		164
Leek Wootton .		167
Marton		170
Monks Kirby .		173
Napton-on-the-Hill		181
Newbold-on-Avon		187
Newnham Regis		193
Offchurch	Architecture by S. PHILLIPS DALES, F.R.I.B.A.	194
Radbourn		198
Radford Semele	Architecture by S. PHILLIPS DALES, F.R.I.B.A.	200
The Borough of Rugby	,, J. T. SMITH	202
Ryton-on-Dunsmore		210
Shilton		213
Upper and Lower Shuckburgh .		215
Southam		219
Stockton		226
Stoneleigh		229
Stretton Baskerville		240
Stretton-upon-Dunsmore and Prince-thorpe		241
Ufton .		245
Wappenbury and Eathorpe		248
Weston-under-Wetherley		251
Whitnash		255
Wibtoft		258
Willey .		259
Willoughby		261
Withybrook		265
Wolfhamcote		269
Wolston		273
Wolvey		281

VOLUME SEVEN

	PAGE
Dedication	v
Contents	ix
List of Illustrations	xi
List of Maps and Plans	xiii
Editorial Note	xv
Classes of Documents in the Public Record Office used	xvii
Note on Abbreviations	xviii
The City of Birmingham	1

The Growth of the City	By C. R. ELRINGTON and P. M. TILLOTT	4
Communications	By C. R. ELRINGTON	26
Secular Architecture	By MARGARET TOMLINSON	43
Manors	By L. F. SALZMAN, C.B.E., and SUSAN REYNOLDS; Architectural descriptions are by MARGARET TOMLINSON	58

Economic and Social History

Medieval Industry and Trade	By P. M. TILLOTT	73
Industry and Trade, 1500–1880	By D. E. C. EVERSLEY	81
Industry and Trade, 1880–1960	By BARBARA M. D. SMITH	140
Social History before 1815	By W. B. STEPHENS	209
Social History since 1815	By Professor ASA BRIGGS	223
Agriculture	By SUSAN REYNOLDS	246
Markets and Fairs	,, ,,	251
Mills	By R. A. PELHAM and D. G. WATTS	253

Political and Administrative History

Political History to 1832	By R. B. ROSE	270
Political History from 1832	By Professor ASA BRIGGS	298
Local Government and Public Services	By C. R. ELRINGTON; the section on Public Health is by D. G. WATTS	318

Religious History

Churches	By C. R. ELRINGTON	354
Roman Catholicism	By SUSAN REYNOLDS; Architectural descriptions are by MARY PARRY	397
Protestant Nonconformity	By R. B. ROSE	411
Other Religious Bodies	,, ,,	483

Public Education

Introduction	By Professor ASA BRIGGS	486
Schools	By SUSAN REYNOLDS	501
King Edward VI Elementary Schools	By J. C. TYSON	549
Charities for the Poor	By D. G. WATTS	556
Arms, Seals, Insignia, Plate, and Officers	By W. B. STEPHENS	568
Index	By ROSEMARY STEPHENS	569

VOLUME EIGHT

	PAGE
Dedication	v
Contents	ix
List of Illustrations	xi
List of Maps and Plans	xv
Editorial Note	xvii
Classes of Documents in the Public Record Office used	xix

CONTENTS OF VOLUMES: WARWS. VIII

PAGE

Documents in the Coventry City Record
   Office used xxi

Classes of Warwick Borough Records in the
   Pageant House, Warwick, used xxii

Classes of Documents in the Warwickshire
   Record Office used xxii

Note on Abbreviations xxiii

The City of Coventry

  Introduction . . . .   By JOAN C. LANCASTER, MARGARET TOMLINSON,
                 and the Editorial Staff . . . 1

  List of Streets . . .   By JOAN C. LANCASTER and the Editorial Staff 24

  Communications . . .   By K. J. ALLISON and R. B. ROSE . . 34

  The Outlying Parts of Coventry .   By D. G. WATTS; Architectural descriptions are
                 by MARGARET TOMLINSON . . 40

    Ansty 43
    Asthill, Horwell, and Whoberley 48
    Coundon 50
    Foleshill 57
    Harnall, Radford, and Whitmore Park 71
    Keresley 77
    Pinley, Shortley, and Whitley 83
    Stivichall 90
    Stoke 96
    Walsgrave-on-Sowe 104
    Willenhall 115
    Wyken and Caludon 119

  Buildings . . .   By MARGARET TOMLINSON . . . 125

  Crafts and Industries . .   By JOAN C. LANCASTER; the sections on cycles,
                 motor-cycles, and motor vehicles are by
                 W. B. STEPHENS . . . 151

  Mills . . . .   By JOAN C. LANCASTER and D. G. WATTS . 190
  The Common Lands . .   By R. B. ROSE 199
  Social History to 1700 . .   By DIANE K. BOLTON . . . 208
  Social History from 1700 . .   By W. B. STEPHENS . . . 222
  The Godiva Legend . .   By DIANE K. BOLTON . . . 242
  Parliamentary Representation .   By K. J. ALLISON 248
  Local Government and Public Services .   By JOAN C. LANCASTER and the Editorial Staff 256
  Public Education . . .   By DIANE K. BOLTON and D. G. WATTS . 299
  Churches . . .   By K. J. ALLISON, CELIA B. CLARKE, JOAN C.
                 LANCASTER, R. B. ROSE, and D. G. WATTS;
                 Architectural descriptions are by MARGARET
                 TOMLINSON 316

  Roman Catholicism . .   By JOAN C. LANCASTER and R. B. ROSE; Archi-
                 tectural descriptions are by MARGARET TOMLINSON 368

  Protestant Nonconformity .   By CELIA B. CLARKE, JOAN C. LANCASTER and
                 R. B. ROSE; Architectural descriptions are by
                 MARGARET TOMLINSON . . . 372

  Other religious groups . .   By R. B. ROSE 396
  Charities for the Poor . .   By CELIA B. CLARKE . . . 398
  Seals, Arms, Insignia, Plate, and Officers .   By R. B. PUGH 415

The Borough of Warwick

  Introduction . . .   By K. J. ALLISON and R. W. DUNNING; Archi-
                 tectural descriptions are based on investigation
                 by S. R. JONES 417

  The Castle and Castle Estate in Warwick .   By M. W. FARR; Architectural descriptions are
                 by MARGARET TOMLINSON. . . 452

  Political and Administrative History to 1545   By K. J. ALLISON 476

  Economic and Social History to 1545 .   „   „ . . . 480

PAGE

Political and Administrative History,
1545–1835 . . . . . By R. W. Dunning 490
Economic and Social History 1545–1835 . ,, ,, ... 504
Warwick from 1835 . . . ,, ,, ... 515
Churches . . . . By K. J. Allison 522
Nonconformity . . . . By K. J. Allison and R. W. Dunning . . 536
Public Education . . . By R. B. Rose 539
Charities for the Poor . . By R. W. Dunning 544
Seals, Arms, Insignia, Plate, and Officers . ,, ,, ... 554
Index . . . . . By P. A. Spalding 557
Corrigenda to Volumes I–VII 582

WILTSHIRE

VOLUME ONE, PART ONE

PAGE

Dedication v
Contents ix
List of Illustrations and Maps xi
Editorial Note xiii
Wiltshire Victoria County History Committee xv
Note on Abbreviations used xvii
The Physique of Wiltshire . . . By Joyce Gifford 1
Archaeological Gazetteer . . . By L. V. Grinsell 21
  Introduction 21
  A General Gazetteer, arranged under
    parishes 21
  B List of Wiltshire barrows 134
    Introduction 134
      I   Long barrows 137
      I a Neolithic bowl-barrows 147
      II Bowl-barrows 147
      III Bowl-barrows with outer bank 205
      IV Bell-barrows 206
      IV a Twin bell-barrows 213
      IV b Triple bell-barrows 214
      IV c Bell-barrows with outer bank 215
      IV d Triple bell-barrow with outer bank 215
      V   Disk-barrows 216
      V a Oval twin disk-barrows 222
      VI Saucer-barrows 222
      VII Pond-barrows 225
      VII a Ditched pond-barrows 226
      VIII Round barrow of exceptional type 226
      IX Analysis of inhumations and cremations from long and round barrows . . 227
      IX a Inhumations of Beaker Period or Early Bronze Age . . . 227
      IX b Unassociated cremations from bowl-barrows 231
      IX c Cremations of Early or Middle Bronze Age from bowl-barrows . . 234
      IX d Cremations of Late Bronze Age from round barrows of all types . . 238
      IX e Cremations with urns presumed of Bronze Age, but of unknown type, from bowl-barrows . 240
      IX f Intrusive Early Iron Age inhumations in barrows of all types . . 242
      IX g Roman inhumations from barrows of all types . . . 242
      IX h Pagan Saxon inhumations from barrows of all types . . . 242
      IX j Undated, but probably Pagan Saxon, inhumations from barrows of all types . . 244

		PAGE
IX *k* Medieval inhumations from barrows of all types	. . . . . .	245
x Evidence of funerary ritual in round barrows	. . . . .	245
C Circles and enclosures of 'Highworth' type	. . . . . .	247
D Ditches	. . . .	249
E Enclosures and hill-forts	. . . .	261
F Field systems	. . . .	272

VOLUME TWO

		PAGE
Dedication	. . . .	vii
Contents	. . . .	ix
List of Maps and Illustrations	. . . .	xi
Editorial Note	. . . .	xiii
Wiltshire Victoria County History Committee	. . . . .	xv
Note on Abbreviations	. . . . . .	xvii
Anglo-Saxon Wiltshire	By Professor R. R. DARLINGTON, B.A., Ph.D., F.B.A., F.S.A.	1
Anglo-Saxon Art	By L. STONE, M.A. . . .	35
Introduction to the Wiltshire Domesday	By Professor R. R. DARLINGTON, B.A., Ph.D., F.B.A., F.S.A. . . .	42
Translation of the Text of the Wiltshire Domesday	,, ,, ,, ,,	113
Introduction to the Wiltshire Geld Rolls	,, ,, ,, ,,	169
Text and Translation of the Wiltshire Geld Rolls	,, ,, ,, ,,	178
Summaries of Fiefs in the Exon Domesday	,, ,, ,, ,,	218
Index of Domesday Survey and the Geld Rolls	,, ,, ,, ,,	223
General Index	By P. A. SPALDING, M.A.	233

VOLUME THREE

		PAGE
Dedication	. . . .	v
Contents	. . . .	ix
List of Illustrations and Map	. . . .	xi
Editorial Note	. . . .	xiii
Wiltshire Victoria County History Committee	. . . . .	xv
Classes of Public Records used	. . . . . .	xvii
Note on Abbreviations	. . . .	xix
Ecclesiastical History 1087–1547	By G. TEMPLEMAN, M.A.	1
The Church of England 1542–1837	By ANNE WHITEMAN, M.A., D.Phil. . .	28
The Church of England since 1837	By the Revd. L. W. COWIE, B.A., Ph.D. .	57
Roman Catholicism	By Brigadier T. B. TRAPPES-LOMAX, C.B.E., D.L. .	87
Protestant Nonconformity	By MARJORIE E. REEVES, M.A., Ph.D. .	99
The Religious Houses of Wiltshire:		
Introduction	By ELIZABETH CRITTALL, M.A. . .	150
1. Cathedral of Salisbury	By KATHLEEN EDWARDS, M.A., Ph.D., F.S.A. .	156
2. Abbey of Malmesbury	By DOM AELRED WATKIN, O.S.B., M.A., F.S.A. .	210
3. Abbey of Wilton	By ELIZABETH CRITTALL . . .	231
4. Abbey, later Priory, of Amesbury	By R. B. PUGH, M.A., F.S.A. . .	242

CONTENTS OF VOLUMES: WILTS. III

PAGE

5. Priory of Kington St. Michael	By J. L. Kirby, M.A., F.S.A.		259
6. Priory of Monkton Farleigh	By H. F. Chettle, C.M.G., O.B.E., M.A., and J. L. Kirby		262
7. Abbey of Stanley	,, ,, ,, ,,		269
8. Priory of Bradenstoke	By Dorothy Styles, M.A.		275
9. Priory of Ivychurch	,, ,,		289
10. Priory of Maiden Bradley	By H. F. Chettle and J. L. Kirby		295
11. Priory of Longleat	By J. L. Kirby		302
12. Abbey of Lacock	By Helena M. Chew, M.A., Ph.D.		303
13. Priory of St. Margaret, Marlborough	By H. F. Chettle and J. L. Kirby		316
14. Priory of St. Mary, Poulton	By H. F. Chettle		319
15. Edington	By J. L. Kirby		320
16. Priory or Hospital of Easton	By H. F. Chettle		324
17. Preceptory of Temple Rockley	By J. L. Kirby		327
18. Preceptory of Ansty	,, ,,		328
19. Franciscan Friars of Salisbury	By Georgina R. Galbraith, M.A., D.Phil.		329
20. Dominican Friars of Wilton	,, ,, ,,		330
21. Dominican Friars of Salisbury	,, ,, ,,		331
22. Carmelite Friars of Marlborough	,, ,, ,,		333
23. Hospital of St. John, Great Bedwyn	By H. F. Chettle and Elizabeth Crittall		334
24. Hospital of St. Margaret, Bradford-on-Avon	,, ,, ,, ,,		334
25. Hospital of St. John and St. Anthony, Calne	By H. F. Chettle		334
26. Hospital of St. John, Cricklade	,, ,,		335
27. Hospital of St. John, Devizes	By H. F. Chettle and Elizabeth Crittall		337
28. Hospital of St. John and St. Katherine, Heytesbury	By J. L. Kirby		337
29. Hospital of St. John, Malmesbury	By H. F. Chettle and Elizabeth Crittall		340
30. Hospital of St. Mary Magdalene, Malmesbury	,, ,, ,, ,,		341
31. Hospital of St. John, Marlborough	By H. F. Chettle		341
32. Hospital of St. Thomas, Marlborough	By H. F. Chettle and Elizabeth Crittall		342
33. Hospital of St. Nicholas, Salisbury	By Kathleen Edwards		343
34. Hospital of the Holy Trinity, Salisbury	By Margaret Parsons, M.A.		357
35. Hospital of St. John and St. Anthony, Salisbury	,, ,, ,,		361
36. Hospital of St. James and St. Denis, Southbroom	By H. F. Chettle and Elizabeth Crittall		362
37. Hospital of St. Giles and St. Anthony, Wilton	By H. F. Chettle		362
38. Hospital of St. John, Wilton	By H. F. Chettle and Elizabeth Crittall		364
39. Hospital of St. Mary Magdalene, Wilton	,, ,, ,, ,,		367
40. Hospital of St. John, Wootton Bassett	,, ,, ,, ,,		368
41. College of De Vaux, Salisbury	By Kathleen Edwards		369
42. College of St. Edmund, Salisbury	By Margaret Parsons		385
43. Collegiate Church of St. Peter and St. Paul, Heytesbury	By J. L. Kirby		389
44. Priory of Avebury	,, ,,		392
45. Priory of Charlton	,, ,,		393
46. Priory of Clatford or Hullavington	By H. N. Blakiston, O.B.E., B.A.		393
47. Priory of Corsham	By J. L. Kirby		394
48. Priory of Ogbourne	By Marjorie M. Chibnall, M.A., D.Phil.		394
49. Priory of Upavon	By J. L. Kirby		396
Index	By P. A. Spalding, M.A.		399

VOLUME FOUR

		PAGE
Dedication .	. . . .	v
Contents .	. . . .	ix
List of Illustrations	. . . .	xi
List of Maps	. . . .	xii
Editorial Note	. . . .	xiii
Wiltshire Victoria County History Committee	. . . . . .	xv
Classes of Public Record used	. . . .	xvii
Note on Abbreviations	. . . .	xix
Economic History .	By W. G. Hoskins	1
Medieval Agriculture	By Richenda Scott . . .	7
Agriculture 1500–1793	By E. Kerridge	43
Agriculture 1793–1870	By R. Molland . . .	65
Agriculture since 1870	By F. M. L. Thompson . .	92
The Woollen Industry before 1550	By Professor Eleanora M. Carus-Wilson .	115
Textile Industries since 1550	By Julia de L. Mann . . .	148
Engineering and Railway Works .	By D. E. C. Eversley . .	183
Other Industries		
Bacon and Associated Products	By Margaret Saunders . .	220
Dairy Products	,, ,, . . .	224
India Rubber .	By Professor W. Woodruff .	229
Tanning	By E. Tonkinson and Margaret Saunders	233
Gloving	,, ,, ,, ,, ,, .	236
Tobacco and Clay Pipes	By W. E. Brown . . .	240
Paper-Making .	By A. H. Shorter . . .	244
Stone-Quarrying	By Margaret Saunders . .	247
Iron-Working .	By the late C. W. Pugh, M.B.E. .	250
Bell-Founding .	By J. E. Buckley . . .	252
Roads	By A. Cossons . . .	254
Canals	By E. C. R. Hadfield, C.M.G. .	272
Railways .	By C. R. Clinker . . .	280
Fifteenths and Tenths: Quotas of 1334	By M. W. Beresford . .	294
Poll-Tax Payers of 1377 .	,, ,, . .	304
Poor Parishes of 1428	,, ,, . .	314
Table of Population, 1801 to 1951	By Margaret Saunders . .	315
Sport	Except where otherwise stated, by Elizabeth Crittall	
Introduction	. . . . . .	362
Fishing .	By Sir John Paskin, K.C.M.G., M.C. .	362
Foxhunting	. . . . . .	369
Cricket .	. . . . . .	377
Racing .	. . . . . .	379
Coursing .	. . . . . .	382
Association Football	. . . . . .	383
Spas and Mineral Springs .	By J. H. P. Pafford . . .	386
Freemasonry	By the late C. W. Pugh . .	389
Royal Forests	By R. Grant	
Introduction	. . . . . .	391
Braydon .	. . . . . .	402
Chippenham and Melksham	. . . . . .	407
Selwood in Wiltshire	. . . . . .	414
Savernake	. . . . . .	417
Chute in Wiltshire	. . . . . .	424
Clarendon and Melchet	. . . . . .	427

PAGE

Grovely 431
    Appendix A: List of Forest Eyres 433
    Appendix B: Wardens of the Forests 434
Cranborne Chase . . . . . By E. H. Lane Poole 458
Index . . . . . By C. R. Elrington 461

VOLUME FIVE

PAGE

Dedication v
Contents ix
List of Illustrations xi
List of Maps xiii
Editorial Note xv
Wiltshire Victoria County History Committee xvii
Classes of Public Records used xix
Note on Abbreviations xxi
The King's Government in the Middle Ages By R. B. Pugh 1
Feudal Wiltshire . . . . . By G. A. J. Hodgett 44
The Commons of Wiltshire in Medieval
    Parliaments . . . . By R. B. Pugh 72
County Government 1530–1660 . . By J. Hurstfield 80
Parliamentary History 1529–1688 . . By Professor S. T. Bindoff . . . 111
County Government 1660–1835 . . By W. R. Ward 170
Parliamentary History 1689–1832 . . By Mary Ransome 195
County Government since 1835 . . By R. A. Lewis 231
Parliamentary History since 1832 . . By Professor F. E. Hyde . . . 296
Public Health and the Medical Services . By Rachel E. Waterhouse . . . 318
Education . . . . . By Emily E. Butcher . . . 348
Index . . . . . By P. A. Spalding 369

VOLUME SIX

PAGE

Dedication v
Contents ix
List of Illustrations xi
List of Maps and Plans xii
Editorial Note xiii
Wiltshire Victoria County History Committee xv
Classes of Public Records used xvii
Note on Abbreviations xix
The Borough of Wilton . . . Except where otherwise stated, by Margery K.
                         James 1

    Early History 7
    Manors and Lesser Estates 8
    Medieval Town Government 9
    Medieval Trade and Industry 12
    Decline 15
    Markets and Fairs 17
    Agriculture 18
    Mills 20
    Modern Town Government and Public
        Services 21
    Poor Relief 23

CONTENTS OF VOLUMES: WILTS. VI

		PAGE
Industry since *c.* 1500		24
Parliamentary Representation		27
Churches		28
Protestant Nonconformity	By MARGARET MORRIS	32
Schools		33
Charities		34
Seals, Insignia, and Officers of the Borough	By ELIZABETH CRITTALL and K. H. ROGERS	36
Fugglestone St. Peter	By MARGARET MORRIS	37
The Borough of Old Salisbury	By Sir FRANCIS HILL, C.B.E., LL.D.	51
Before the Norman Conquest		52
The Castle: Administration and Use		53
The Castle: Buildings		56
The Cathedral		60
The Borough		62
Topography		63
Later History		65
The City of New Salisbury	Except where otherwise stated, by MARIAN K. DALE	
Topography		69
The Liberty of the Close		72
St. Martin's Parish		79
St. Thomas's Parish		81
St. Edmund's Parish		83
The Market Place		85
Bridges, Bars, Gates, and Watercourses		87
Mills		90
The Expansion of the City	By K. H. ROGERS	90
Rural Milford		92
The word 'Sarum'	By R. B. PUGH	93
City Government before 1612		94
Relations with the Bishop before 1612		101
Parliamentary Representation before 1612		103
City Government 1612–1835	By MARY E. RANSOME	105
City Government since 1836	By K. H. ROGERS	113
City Politics and Parliamentary Representation since 1612	By MARY E. RANSOME	117
Economic History before 1612		124
Economic History since 1612	By MARY E. RANSOME	129
The Guild Merchant and Craft Guilds before 1612		132
Trade Companies since 1612	By MARY E. RANSOME	136
Markets and Fairs	By MARIAN K. DALE and MARY E. RANSOME	138
Social Life	By MARY E. RANSOME	141
Churches	By ELIZABETH CRITTALL	144
Roman Catholicism	,, ,,	155
Protestant Nonconformity	By MARGARET MORRIS	156
Schools	By R. J. KNECHT	161
Charities for the Poor	By ELIZABETH CRITTALL	168
Seals, Insignia, Plate, Arms, and Officers of the City	By R. B. PUGH	178
Fisherton Anger	,, ,,	180
The Hundred of Underditch	,, ,,	195
Stratford-sub-Castle	,, ,,	199
Wilsford	By D. G. WATTS	213
Woodford	By C. R. ELRINGTON	221
Index	By P. A. SPALDING	229

VOLUME SEVEN

		PAGE
Dedication .		v
Contents .		ix
List of Illustrations		xi
Editorial Note		xiii
Classes of Public Records used and Note on Abbreviations .		xvii
Topography	Where not otherwise stated, by W. R. POWELL, B.Litt., M.A.; Architectural descriptions by H. A. JAMES, F.S.A., A.R.I.B.A. Schools, except in the case of Trowbridge, from information supplied by DIANA M. GOSCHEN, B.A.	
Bradford Hundred	By R. B. PUGH, M.A., F.S.A.	1
Bradford-on-Avon		5
Broughton Gifford		51
Great Chalfield		59
Monkton Farleigh		66
Wingfield		69
Melksham Hundred	By R. B. PUGH, M.A., F.S.A.	77
Erlestoke	By W. R. POWELL, B.Litt., M.A., and P. M. TILLOTT, B.A.	82
Hilperton	By ELIZABETH CRITTALL, M.A.	86
Melksham	By H. F. CHETTLE, C.M.G., O.B.E., M.A., and P. M. TILLOTT, B.A.	91
Poulshot	By ELIZABETH CRITTALL, M.A.	121
Trowbridge	By R. B. PUGH, M.A., F.S.A.	125
Whaddon	By P. M. TILLOTT, B.A.	171
Potterne and Cannings Hundred .	By R. B. PUGH, M.A., F.S.A.	175
Bromham	By W. R. POWELL, B.Litt., M.A., and ELIZABETH CRITTALL, M.A.	179
Bishop's Cannings	By W. R. POWELL, B.Litt., M.A., and P. M. TILLOTT, B.A.	187
Highway		197
West or Bishop's Lavington	By W. R. POWELL, B.Litt., M.A., and ELIZABETH CRITTALL, M.A.; Schools and Charities by H. B. WELLS, M.A.	198
Potterne		207
Rowde .		217
Index	By P. A. SPALDING, M.A.	225

VOLUME EIGHT

		PAGE
Dedication .		v
Contents .		ix
List of Illustrations		xi
List of Maps and Plans		xii
Editorial Note		xiii
Wiltshire Victoria County History Committee		xv
Classes of Documents in the Public Record Office used		xvii
Note on Abbreviations		xix
Topography	Architectural descriptions prepared in collaboration with MARGARET TOMLINSON	
Warminster Hundred	By K. H. ROGERS .	1
Bishopstrow	,, ,,	6
Corsley	,, ,,	13

PAGE

Dinton . . . . . By Elizabeth Crittall 25
Fisherton de la Mere . . . By R. B. Pugh 34
Norton Bavant . . . . By K. H. Rogers 47
Pertwood . . . . By Elizabeth Crittall 58
Sutton Veny . . . . ,, ,, ... 61
Teffont Magna . . . ,, ,, ... 74
Upton Scudamore . . By K. H. Rogers 78
Warminster . . . . ,, ,, ... 90
Westbury Hundred . . . By Elizabeth Crittall 136
Westbury . . . . ,, ,, ... 139
Whorwellsdown Hundred . . By K. H. Rogers 193
Steeple Ashton . . . ,, ,, ... 198
North Bradley . . . . ,, ,, ... 218
East Coulston . . . ,, ,, ... 234
Edington . . . . ,, ,, ... 239
Keevil . . . . ,, ,, ... 250
Index . . . . . By P. A. Spalding 265
Corrigenda to Volumes I–VII 283

VOLUME NINE

PAGE

Dedication v
Contents xi
List of Illustrations xiii
List of Maps and Plans xv
Editorial Note xvii
Wiltshire Victoria County History Committee xix
Classes of Documents in the Public Record
    Office used xxi
Note on Abbreviations xxiii
Topography . . . . Architectural descriptions prepared in collaboration
        with Margaret Tomlinson

Kingsbridge Hundred . . . By Elizabeth Crittall 1
Chiseldon . . . . By Janet H. Stevenson 6
Clyffe Pypard . . . . By Elizabeth Crittall, Janet H. Stevenson, and
    Colin Shrimpton 23
Draycot Foliat . . . . By Janet H. Stevenson 43
Hilmarton . . . . By Elizabeth Crittall 49
Liddington . . . . By Janet H. Stevenson 65
Lydiard Tregoze . . . . By Elizabeth Crittall 75
Lyneham . . . . By Janet H. Stevenson 90
Swindon . . . . By Elizabeth Crittall and K. H. Rogers; Trade
    and Industry by Colin Shrimpton . . 104
Tockenham . . . . By Janet H. Stevenson 168
Wanborough . . . . By R. W. Dunning 174
Wootton Bassett . . . . By Elizabeth Crittall 186
Index . . . . . By P. A. Spalding 206

WORCESTERSHIRE

VOLUME ONE

PAGE

Dedication v
The Advisory Council of the Victoria History vii
General Advertisement vii
The Worcestershire County Committee xiii
Contents xv

CONTENTS OF VOLUMES: WORCS. I

PAGE

List of Illustrations xvii
Preface xix
Natural History
  Geology . . . . . By H. B. WOODWARD, F.G.S. . . . I
  Palaeontology . . . . By RICHARD L. LYDEKKER, F.R.S., F.G.S., F.L.S. . 27
  Botany . . . . . Edited by JOHN AMPHLETT, M.A., S.C.L. . . 33
    Phanerogamia (*Flowering plants*) . By JOHN AMPHLETT, M.A., S.C.L. . . 45
    Musci (*Mosses*) . . By JAMES E. BAGNALL, A.L.S. . . . 62
    Hepaticae (*Liverworts*) . . .   ,,   ,, . . . 66
    Lichenes (*Lichens*) . . .   ,,   ,, . . . 67
    Algae . . . . .   ,,   ,, . . . 69
    Fungi . . . . By CARLETON REA, M.A., B.C.L. . . 69
  Climate . . . . By J. W. WILLIS-BUND, M.A., F.S.A. . 77
  Zoology
    Mollusca (*Snails, etc.*) . . . By B. B. WOODWARD, F.G.S., F.R.M.S. . 81
    Insecta (*Insects*) . . . Edited by J. E. FLETCHER, F.E.S., and CARLETON REA, M.A., B.C.L. . . . 83
      Introduction to Insecta . By CARLETON REA, M.A., B.C.L. . . 83
      Neuroptera (*Dragonflies*) . . J. E. FLETCHER, F.E.S. . . 84
      Trichoptera (*Caddis-flies*) . .   ,,   ,, . . 85
      Hymenoptera, Aculeata (*Bees*) . By J. E. FLETCHER, F.E.S., and ALFRED H. MARTINEAU, F.E.S. . . 86
      Hymenoptera, Phytophaga (*Sawflies, etc.*) . . . By J. E. FLETCHER, F.E.S. . . 90
      Hymenoptera, Entomophaga .   ,,   ,, . . 93
      Coleoptera (*Beetles*) . .   ,,   ,, . . 96
      Lepidoptera (*Butterflies and Moths*) . By CARLETON REA, M.A., B.C.L., and J. E. FLETCHER, F.E.S. . . 100
    Arachnida (*Spiders*) . . By F. O. PICKARD-CAMBRIDGE, M.A. . 125
    Crustacea (*Crabs, etc.*) . . By the Revd. T. R. R. STEBBING, M.A., F.R.S., F.S.A. . . . 126
    Pisces (*Fishes*) . . . By J. W. WILLIS-BUND, M.A., F.L.S., F.Z.S. . 131
    Reptilia (*Reptiles*) and Batrachia (*Batrachians*) . . By R. F. TOMES, F.G.S., Corr. Mem. Z.S. . 137
    Aves (*Birds*) . . . .   ,,   ,,   ,, . 139
    Mammalia (*Mammals*) . . .   ,,   ,,   ,, . 171
Early Man . . . . By B. C. A. WINDLE, M.D., F.R.S., and J. W. WILLIS-BUND, M.A., F.S.A. . 179
Romano-British Remains . . By F. HAVERFIELD, M.A., F.S.A. . . 199
Anglo-Saxon Remains . . By REGINALD A. SMITH, B.A. . . 223
Introduction to the Worcestershire Domesday . . . By J. HORACE ROUND, M.A. . . 235
The Text of the Worcestershire Domesday .   ,,   ,, . . . 282
Some Early Worcestershire Surveys .   ,,   ,, . . . 324
Index to the Domesday Survey 332

VOLUME TWO

PAGE

Dedication v
Contents ix
List of Illustrations xi
Editorial Note xiii
Table of Abbreviations xv
Ecclesiastical History . . . By J. W. WILLIS-BUND, M.A., LL.B., F.S.A. . I

Religious Houses
Introduction . . . . . By Miss A. A. Locke, Oxford Honours School of
    Modern History 93
Priory of St. Mary of Worcester . . By Miss M. M. C. Calthrop . . . 94
Abbey of Evesham . . . . By Miss A. A. Locke, Oxford Honours School of
    Modern History 112
  ,, ,, Pershore . . . By Miss M. M. C. Calthrop . . . 127
Priory of Great Malvern . . .   ,,   ,, . . . 136
  ,, ,, Little Malvern . . .   ,,   ,, . . . 143
  ,, ,, Westwood . . .   ,,   ,, . . . 148
Abbey of Bordesley . . . By Miss A. A. Locke, Oxford Honours School of
    Modern History 151
Priory of Whistones . . .   ,,   ,,   ,, . 154
  ,, ,, Cookhill . . .   ,,   ,,   ,, . 156
  ,, ,, St. James of Dudley . By Miss M. M. C. Calthrop . . . 158
Abbey of Halesowen . . . By Miss A. A. Locke, Oxford Honours School of
    Modern History 162
Black Friars, Worcester . . . By A. G. Little, M.A. 167
Grey Friars, Worcester . . .   ,,   ,, ... 169
Trinitarian Friars, Worcester . .   ,,   ,, ... 173
Penitent Sisters, Worcester . .   ,,   ,, ... 173
Friars of the Penance of Jesus Christ, or
    Friars of the Sack, Worcester .   ,,   ,, ... 173
Austin Friars, Droitwich . . .   ,,   ,, ... 173
Hospital of St. Wulstan, Worcester . By Miss A. A. Locke, Oxford Honours School of
    Modern History 175
  ,, ,, St. Oswald, Worcester .   ,,   ,,   ,, 177
  ,, ,, St. Mary, Droitwich . .   ,,   ,,   ,, 179
Priory of Astley . . . . By Miss M. M. C. Calthrop . . . 180
Early Christian Art . . . By J. Romilly Allen, F.S.A. . . . 183
Political History . . . . By J. W. Willis-Bund, M.A., LL.B., F.S.A. . 197
Military History . . . . By C. H. Vellacott, B.A. . . . 234
Industries
Introduction . . . . By C. H. Vellacott, B.A. . . . 249
Salt . . . . . By E. B. Pillans, B.A. . . . 256
Coal Mining . . . . By Professor R. A. S. Redmayne, M.Sc. . 264
Iron . . . . . By Miss Margerie V. Taylor, Oxford Honours
    School of Modern History . . . 267
Tools . . . . .   ,,   ,,   ,, . 271
Nails and Chains . . . .   ,,   ,,   ,, . 271
Needles . . . . .   ,,   ,,   ,, . 273
Tiles . . . . .   ,,   ,,   ,, . 274
China . . . . By J. W. Willis-Bund, M.A., LL.B., F.S.A. . 276
Glass . . . . By Miss Margerie V. Taylor, Oxford Honours
    School of Modern History . . . 278
Cloth . . . . .   ,,   ,,   ,, 281
Carpets and Rugs . . . By C. H. Vellacott, B.A. . . . 297
Caps . . . . . By Miss Margerie V. Taylor, Oxford Honours
    School of Modern History . . . 299
Fulling and Dyeing . . .   ,,   ,,   ,, . 301
Leather . . . . .   ,,   ,,   ,, . 302
Gloves . . . . .   ,,   ,,   ,, . 303
Fruit Growing and Market Gardening . By George Jones 305
Agriculture . . . . By J. W. Willis-Bund, M.A., LL.B., F.S.A. 309
Forestry . . . . . By J. Nisbet, D.Oec. . . . 315
Sport, Ancient and Modern . . Edited by E. W. D. Cuming
Hunting . . . . . By Sir Richard Green Price, Bart. . 323
Racing . . . . .   ,,   ,, . . 325

			PAGE
Coursing	. . . .	By J. W. Bourne	. 327
Angling .	. . .	By J. W. Willis-Bund, M.A., LL.B., F.S.A.	. 329
Shooting	. . .	,, ,, ,,	. 332
Athletics	. . .	By Charles Herbert . . .	. 334
Golf	. . .	By the Revd. Percival Ward, M.A. .	. 334
Cricket	. . .	By Home Gordon	. 340
Topography: Blackenhurst Hundred	.	General descriptions and manorial descents prepared under the superintendence of the general editor by Mrs. M. J. Curtis; Architectural descriptions by C. R. Peers, M.A., F.S.A.	
Introduction	. . .	. . . . . .	. 347
Abbot's Morton	. . .	. . . . . .	. 349
Badsey with Aldington	. . .	. . . . . .	. 353
Bretforton	. . .	. . . . . .	. 359
Church Honeybourne	. . .	. . . . . .	. 367
Evesham	. . .	History of Borough by N. M. Trenholme, Ph.D.; Architectural description of Evesham Abbey by C. R. Peers, M.A., F.S.A. . .	. 371
Bengeworth	. . .	. . . . . .	. 396
Great and Little Hampton	. .	. . . . . .	. 404
North and Middle Littleton	.	. . . . . .	. 408
South Littleton	. .	. . . . . .	. 412
Norton	. . .	. . . . . .	. 415
Offenham	. . .	. . . . . .	. 420
Oldberrow	. . .	. . . . . .	. 424
Wickhamford	. . .	. . . . . .	. 427

VOLUME THREE

			PAGE
Dedication .	. . . .	. . . . .	. v
Contents .	. . .	. . . . .	. ix
List of Illustrations	. . .	. . . .	. xiii
List of Maps	. . .	. . . . .	. xx
Editorial Note	. . .	. . . . .	. xxi
Topography	. . .	General descriptions and manorial descents compiled under the superintendence of William Page, F.S.A.; Heraldic drawings and blazon by the Revd. E. E. Dorling, M.A., F.S.A.; Charities from information supplied by J. W. Owsley, I.S.O., late Official Trustee of Charitable Funds	
Halfshire Hundred	. . .	Architectural descriptions by C. R. Peers, M.A., F.S.A., John Quekett, M.A., J. Murray Kendall, F.S.A., J. W. Bloe, Ernest A. R. Rahbula, A.R.I.B.A., Sidney Toy, and S. F. Beeke Lane	
Introduction	. . .	By Olive M. Moger . . .	. 1
Upper Arley	. . .	,, ,, . . .	. 5
Belbroughton	. . .	By M. Campbell-Curtis . . .	. 11
Bromsgrove	. . .	By Olive M. Moger and Ethel M. Hartland	. 19
Broom .	. . .	By Hilda M. Light . . .	. 33
Chaddesley Corbett	. .	,, ,, . . .	. 35
Churchill	. . .	By M. Campbell-Curtis . . .	. 43
Church Lench	. . .	,, ,, . . .	. 45
Clent .	. . .	By Hilda M. Light . . .	. 50
Coston or Cofton Hackett	.	,, ,, . . .	. 54
Crutch	. . .	By Olive M. Moger . . .	. 57
Dodderhill with Elmbridge	.	By M. Campbell-Curtis . . .	. 58
Doverdale	. . .	By Hilda M. Light . . .	. 69

PAGE

Droitwich Borough	.	.	.	By the late MARY BATESON, Fellow of Newnham College, Cambridge 72
Dudley Borough	.	.	.	By HILDA M. LIGHT and M. CAMPBELL-CURTIS	. 90
Elmley Lovett .	.	.	.	By HILDA M. LIGHT	. 106
Feckenham	.	.	.	,, ,, . . .	. 111
Frankley	.	.	.	By HILDA M. LIGHT and M. CAMPBELL-CURTIS	. 120
Grafton Manor	.	.	.	By HILDA M. LIGHT . . .	. 123
Hadzor	.	.	.	,, ,, . . .	. 127
Hagley	.	.	.	By M. CAMPBELL-CURTIS . . .	. 130
Halesowen with Cradley, Lutley, and Warley Wigorn	.		.	By HILDA M. LIGHT . . .	. 136
Hampton Lovett	.	.	.	,, ,, . . .	. 153
Kidderminster Borough with Lower Mitton	.	.	.	By LILIAN J. REDSTONE, B.A. . .	. 158
King's Norton	.	.	.	By HILDA M. LIGHT . . .	. 179
Kington	.	.	.	,, ,, . . .	. 191
Northfield	.	.	.	By M. CAMPBELL-CURTIS . . .	. 194
Pedmore	.	.	.	,, ,, . . .	. 201
Rushock	.	.	.	By HILDA M. LIGHT . . .	. 203
Salwarpe	.	.	.	,, ,, . . .	. 205
Stone .	.	.	.	,, ,, . . .	. 210
Old Swinford with Stourbridge		.	.	By M. CAMPBELL-CURTIS . . .	. 213
Tardebigge	.	.	.	By HILDA M. LIGHT . . .	. 223
Upton Warren	.	.	.	,, ,, . . .	. 231
Westwood Park	.	.	.	,, ,, . . .	. 234
Yardley	.	.	.	,, ,, . . .	. 238
Oswaldslow Hundred	.	.	.	Architectural descriptions by JOHN QUEKETT, M.A., and J. MURRAY KENDALL, F.S.A., assisted by J. W. BLOE, ERNEST A. R. RAHBULA, A.R.I.B.A., SIDNEY TOY, S. F. BEEKE LANE, and other members of the architectural staff	
Introduction	.	.	.	By OLIVE M. MOGER . . .	. 246
Alvechurch	.	.	.	By OLIVE M. MOGER and ALFRED WRAGGE .	. 251
Berrow	.	.	.	By ETHEL M. HARTLAND . . .	. 257
Bishampton	.	.	.	By OLIVE M. MOGER and ALFRED WRAGGE .	. 261
Blockley	.	.	.	By MARJORY HOLLINGS, Oxford Honours School of Modern History	. 265
Bredicot	.	.	.	By ETHEL M. HARTLAND . . .	. 277
Bredon with Cutsdean and Norton by Bredon	.	.	.	By OLIVE M. MOGER . . .	. 279
Broadwas	.	.	.	By ETHEL M. HARTLAND . . .	. 292
Churchill	.	.	.	,, ,, . . .	. 297
Claines with Whistones	.		.	,, ,, . . .	. 300
Cleeve Prior	.	.	.	By MARJORY HOLLINGS and ALFRED WRAGGE	. 308
Croome D'Abitôt	.	.	.	By ETHEL M. HARTLAND . . .	. 313
Earl's Croome .	.	.	.	,, ,, . . .	. 316
Hill Croome .	.	.	.	,, ,, . . .	. 319
Cropthorne with Charlton and Netherton .	.	.	.	By OLIVE M. MOGER and ALFRED WRAGGE .	. 322
Crowle	.	.	.	,, ,, ,,	. 329
Daylesford	.	.	.	By MARJORY HOLLINGS . . .	. 334
Elmley Castle .	.	.	.	By OLIVE M. MOGER and ALFRED WRAGGE .	. 338
Evenlode	.	.	.	By MARJORY HOLLINGS . . .	. 347
Fladbury with Hill and Moor, Ablench, Stock and Bradley, Throckmorton, Wyre Piddle	.	.	.	By OLIVE M. MOGER . . .	. 352
Grimley	.	.	.	By ETHEL M. HARTLAND . . .	. 364
Hallow	.	.	.	,, ,, . . .	. 367

CONTENTS OF VOLUMES: WORCS. III

			PAGE
Hanbury	. . . .	By OLIVE M. MOGER and ALFRED WRAGGE .	. 372
Hartlebury	. . . .	By ETHEL M. HARTLAND . . .	. 380
Harvington	. . . .	By OLIVE M. MOGER and ALFRED WRAGGE .	. 387
Himbleton with Shell	. . .	,, ,, ,,	. 391
Hindlip	. . . .	By MARJORY HOLLINGS . . .	. 398
Holt with Little Witley	. .	,, ,, . .	. 401
Huddington	. . .	By OLIVE M. MOGER and ALFRED WRAGGE .	. 408
Iccomb	. . . .	By MARJORY HOLLINGS . . .	. 412
Inkberrow	. . . .	By OLIVE M. MOGER . . .	. 418
Kempsey	. . . .	,, ,, . . .	. 430
Knightwick with Kenswick	. .	,, ,, . . .	. 437
Lindridge with Knighton on Teme, Newnham, and Pensax	. .	,, ,, . . .	. 442
Little Malvern	. . .	,, ,, . . .	. 449
Norton juxta Kempsey .	. .	,, ,, . . .	. 453
Oddingley	. . . .	,, ,, . . .	. 456
Ombersley	. . . .	,, ,, . . .	. 460
Overbury with Alstone, Conderton, Teddington, and Little Washbourne	.	,, ,, . . .	. 468
Pendock	. . . .	,, ,, . . .	. 478
Redmarley D'Abitôt	. .	By HILDA M. LIGHT . . .	. 481
Ripple with Holdfast	. .	,, ,, . . .	. 486
Rous Lench	. . .	By OLIVE M. MOGER and ALFRED WRAGGE .	. 497
St. John in Bedwardine	.	By MARJORY HOLLINGS; Description of Church by HAROLD BRAKSPEAR, F.S.A., A.R.I.B.A. .	. 501
St. Martin	. . . .	,, ,, ,,	510
St. Peter with Whittington	.	By ALICE RAVEN; Description of Church by HAROLD BRAKSPEAR, F.S.A., A.R.I.B.A. .	. 514
Sedgeberrow	. . .	By OLIVE M. MOGER and ALFRED WRAGGE .	. 518
Shipston on Stour	. .	,, ,, ,, .	. 521
Spetchley	. . .	By HILDA M. LIGHT . . .	. 524
Stoke Prior	. . .	By OLIVE M. MOGER and ALFRED WRAGGE .	. 528
Stoulton	. . .	By HILDA M. LIGHT . . .	. 532
Tibberton	. . .	By OLIVE M. MOGER and ALFRED WRAGGE .	. 537
Tidmington	. . .	,, ,, ,, .	. 539
Tredington with Armscote, Blackwell, Darlingscott, and Newbold on Stour	By OLIVE M. MOGER . . .	. 541
Warndon	. . .	By OLIVE M. MOGER and ALFRED WRAGGE .	. 552
Welland	. . . .	,, ,, ,, .	. 554
White Ladies Aston	. .	,, ,, ,, .	. 557
Wichenford	. . .	,, ,, ,, .	. 561
Wolverley	. . .	By ETHEL M. HARTLAND . . .	. 567

VOLUME FOUR

		PAGE
Dedication .	. . . .	v
Contents .	. . . .	ix
List of Illustrations	. . . .	xiii
List of Maps	. . . .	xviii
Editorial Note	. . . .	xix
Topography	. . . General descriptions and manorial descents compiled under the superintendence of WILLIAM PAGE, F.S.A.; Heraldic drawings and blazon by the Revd. E. E. DORLING, M.A., F.S.A.; Charities from information supplied by J. W. OWSLEY, I.S.O., late Official Trustee of Charitable Funds	

CONTENTS OF VOLUMES: WORCS. IV

PAGE

Pershore Hundred
Introduction I
Abberton . . . . By M. E. SIMKINS and OLIVE M. MOGER; Architectural descriptions by A. W. CLAPHAM, F.S.A. . 4
Alderminster . . . . By M. E. SIMKINS and OLIVE M. MOGER; Architectural descriptions by the late JOHN QUEKETT, M.A., F.S.A., and SIDNEY TOY, F.S.A. . . 7
Beoley . . . . By M. E. SIMKINS; Architectural descriptions by the late JOHN QUEKETT, M.A., F.S.A., and SIDNEY TOY, F.S.A. 12
Besford . . . . By M. E. SIMKINS; Architectural descriptions by A. W. CLAPHAM, F.S.A. 19
Birlingham . . . . By M. E. SIMKINS; Architectural descriptions by A. W. CLAPHAM, F.S.A. 23
Birtsmorton . . . . By ANNE SPILMAN, M.A.; Architectural descriptions by F. H. CHEETHAM, F.S.A. . . . 29
Broadway . . . . By VALENTINA HAWTREY; Architectural descriptions by the late JOHN QUEKETT, M.A., F.S.A., and SIDNEY TOY, F.S.A. 33
Broughton Hackett . . . By M. E. SIMKINS; Architectural descriptions by A. W. CLAPHAM, F.S.A. 43
Bushley . . . . By ANNE SPILMAN, M.A.; Architectural descriptions by F. H. CHEETHAM, F.S.A. . . . 45
Castlemorton . . . . ,, ,, ,, . 49
Chaceley . . . . . ,, ,, ,, . 53
Great Comberton . . . By M. E. SIMKINS; Architectural descriptions by A. W. CLAPHAM, F.S.A. 57
Little Comberton . . . ,, ,, ,, . 60
Dormston . . . . . ,, ,, ,, . 65
Eckington . . . . . ,, ,, ,, . 68
Eldersfield . . . . By ANNE SPILMAN, M.A.; Architectural descriptions by F. H. CHEETHAM, F.S.A. . . . 76
Flyford Flavell . . . . By M. E. SIMKINS; Architectural descriptions by A. W. CLAPHAM, F.S.A. 83
Grafton Flyford . . . . ,, ,, ,, . 85
Hanley Castle . . . By ANNE SPILMAN, M.A.; Architectural descriptions by F. H. CHEETHAM, F.S.A. . . . 89
Leigh with Bransford . . . ,, ,, ,, . 101
Longdon . . . . . ,, ,, ,, . 111
Madresfield . . . . . ,, ,, ,, . 118
Great Malvern with Newland . . By ANNE SPILMAN, M.A.; Architectural descriptions by A. W. CLAPHAM, F.S.A. (except Newland and Guarlford churches by F. H. CHEETHAM, F.S.A.; and glass in Great Malvern church by G. M. RUSHFORTH, M.A., F.S.A.) . . . 123
Martin Hussingtree . . . By M. E. SIMKINS; Architectural descriptions by the late JOHN QUEKETT, M.A., F.S.A., and SYDNEY TOY, F.S.A., A.R.I.B.A. . . . 135
Mathon . . . . . By ANNE SPILMAN, M.A.; Architectural descriptions by F. H. CHEETHAM, F.S.A. . . . 139
Naunton Beauchamp . . . By M. E. SIMKINS; Architectural descriptions by A. W. CLAPHAM, F.S.A. 143
Peopleton . . . . . ,, ,, ,, . 147
Pershore Borough . . . By OLIVE M. MOGER; Architectural descriptions by A. W. CLAPHAM, F.S.A. 151
Pershore Holy Cross with Wadborough and Walcot cum Membris . . ,, ,, ,, . 155
Pershore St. Andrew with Bricklehampton, Defford, Pensham, Pinvin, and Wick . . . . By OLIVE M. MOGER; Architectural descriptions by A. W. CLAPHAM, F.S.A. (except Wick church by F. H. CHEETHAM, F.S.A.) . . . 163

PAGE

North Piddle . . . . . By Valentina Hawtrey; Architectural descriptions
by A. W. Clapham, F.S.A. . . . 177

Pirton . . . . . By M. E. Simkins; Architectural descriptions by
A. W. Clapham, F.S.A. 180

Powick with Clevelode and Woodsfield By Anne Spilman, M.A.; Architectural descriptions
by F. H. Cheetham, F.S.A. . . . 184

Severn Stoke . . . . . ,, ,, ,, 192

Staunton . . . . . By Valentina Hawtrey; Architectural descriptions
by F. H. Cheetham, F.S.A. . . . 197

Strensham . . . . By M. E. Simkins; Architectural descriptions by
A. W. Clapham, F.S.A. 202

Upton Snodsbury . . . By Valentina Hawtrey; Architectural descriptions
by A. W. Clapham, F.S.A. . . . 208

Upton-upon-Severn . . . By Anne Spilman, M.A.; Architectural descriptions
by F. H. Cheetham, F.S.A. . . . 212

Doddingtree Hundred . . . By M. E. Simkins; Architectural descriptions under
the superintendence of the late John Quekett,
M.A., F.S.A., by Sidney Toy, F.S.A., and
Ernest A. R. Rahbula, F.S.A.

Introduction 218
Abberley 220
Acton Beauchamp 224
Areley Kings 227
Astley 230
Bayton 237
Bockleton 241
Clifton-upon-Teme 246
Cotheridge 255
Doddenham 260
Dowles 262
Eastham with Hanley Child and Orleton 265
Edvin Loach 272
Hanley William 275
Kyre Wyard or Kyre Magna 279
Mamble 285
Martley with Hillhampton 289
Ribbesford with the Borough of Bewdley 297
Rochford 317
Rock or Aka 319
Lower Sapey or Sapey Pitchard 328
Shelsley Beauchamp with Shelsley Kings 331
Shelsley Walsh 335
Shrawley 337
Stanford-on-Teme 341
Stockton-on-Teme 345
Stoke Bliss with Kyre Parva 349
Suckley with Alfrick and Lulsley 354
Tenbury 362
Great Witley 372
City of Worcester . . . By Professor F. M. Stenton, M.A.; Architectural
descriptions by Harold Brakspear, F.S.A. . 376

Ancient Earthworks . . . By D. H. Montgomerie, F.S.A. . . . 421
Social and Economic History
Before 1086 . . . . By Professor F. M. Stenton, M.A. . . 435
From 1086 to 1300 . . . By C. H. Vellacott, B.A. . . . 442
From 1300 . . . . By the late A. Audrey Locke, Oxford Honours
School of Modern History . . . 447

Table of Population 1801–1901 . . By G. S. Minchin 464

			PAGE
Schools	By the late A. F. Leach, M.A., F.S.A.		
Introduction			473
Worcester School			475
Worcester Free School, now the Royal Grammar School			491
Prince Henry's Grammar School, Evesham			497
Bromsgrove Grammar School			508
Stourbridge Grammar School			514
Hanley Castle Grammar School			516
Dudley Grammar School			519
Kidderminster Grammar School			523
Hartlebury Grammar School			525
Bewdley Grammar School			527
Powick School			528
Martley School			529
Droitwich Free School			529
Wolverley Free Grammar School			529
Halesowen Grammar School			530
Feckenham Free School			531
Malvern College			531
St. Michael's College, Tenbury			533
Worcester High School for Girls			533
New Secondary Schools			535
Elementary Schools founded before 1800			535

YORKSHIRE [GENERAL]

VOLUME ONE

			PAGE
Dedication			v
The Advisory Council of the Victoria History			vii
General Advertisement			vii
The Yorkshire County Committee			xiii
Contents			xv
List of Illustrations			xvii
Preface			xix
Table of Abbreviations			xxi
Natural History			
Geology	By Professor P. F. Kendall, M.Sc.		1
Palaeontology	By R. Lydekker, F.R.S., F.L.S., F.G.S. .		99
Botany	By J. Gilbert Baker, F.R.S., F.L.S., M.R.I.A., etc., late Keeper of the Herbarium, Kew		
Introduction			111
Botanical Districts			
The North Riding			119
The East Riding			141
The West Riding			145
Mosses (*Musci*)			168
Liverworts (*Hepaticae*)			169
Marine Algae			170
Lichens (*Lichenes*)			171
Fungi			172
Zoology			
Marine	By John Oliver Borley, M.A. . .		173
Non-Marine Molluscs . . .	By B. B. Woodward, F.L.S., F.G.S., F.R.M.S. .		199

PAGE

Insects . . . . . Edited by GEORGE T. PORRITT, F.L.S., F.E.S., etc.

Orthoptera (*Earwigs, Grasshoppers, etc.*) . . . . By GEORGE T. PORRITT, F.L.S., F.E.S. . . 205

Neuroptera and Trichoptera (*Dragon-flies, Caddis-flies, etc.*) . . ,, ,, ,, . . 206

Hymenoptera (*Saw-flies, Gall-flies, Ants, Wasps, Bees, etc.*) . By W. DENISON ROEBUCK, F.L.S. . . 210

Coleoptera (*Beetles*) . . . By E. G. BAYFORD and M. LAWSON THOMPSON, F.E.S. 219

Lepidoptera (*Butterflies and Moths*) . By GEORGE T. PORRITT, F.L.S., F.E.S. . . 245

Diptera (*Flies*) . . . By PERCY H. GRIMSHAW, F.E.S. . . 276

Spiders . . . . By the Revd. O. PICKARD-CAMBRIDGE, M.A. . 286

Crustaceans . . . . By the Revd. T. R. R. STEBBING, M.A., F.R.S., F.Z.S. 294

Fishes . . . . . By OXLEY GRABHAM, M.A., M.B.O.U. . 313

Reptiles and Batrachians . . ,, ,, . 321

Birds . . . . . ,, ,, . 323

Mammals . . . . ,, ,, . 351

Early Man . . . . By GEORGE CLINCH, F.G.S. . . 357

Schools . . . . By A. F. LEACH, M.A., F.S.A. . . 415

Forestry . . . . By the Revd. J. C. COX, LL.D., F.S.A. . 501

VOLUME TWO

PAGE

Dedication v

Contents ix

List of Illustrations xi

List of Maps xiv

Editorial Note xv

Ancient Earthworks . . . By ELLA S. ARMITAGE, Hon. F.S.A. (Scot.) and DUNCAN H. MONTGOMERIE, F.S.A. . . I

Anglo-Saxon Remains . . . By REGINALD A. SMITH, B.A., F.S.A. . 73

Anglo-Saxon Sculptured Stone . By W. G. COLLINGWOOD, M.A., F.S.A. . 109

Introduction to the Yorkshire Domesday . By WILLIAM FARRER, D.Litt. . . 133

Translation of the Yorkshire Domesday . ,, ,, . . 191

Industries

Introduction . . . . By MAUD SELLERS, D.Litt., Fellow of Newnham College, Cambridge . . . 329

Mining and Smelting (Medieval)

Coal . . . . . By C. H. VELLACOTT, B.A. . . 338

Iron . . . . . ,, ,, . 341

Lead . . . . . ,, ,, . 351

Copper . . . . ,, ,, . 354

Modern Mining

Coal Mining . . . . By HERBERT PERKIN, M.I.M.E. . 355

Ironstone Mining . . . ,, ,, . 367

Lead Mining . . . . By JAMES BACKHOUSE . . 368

Quarrying . . . . By C. H. VELLACOTT, B.A. . . 376

Alum . . . . . By MAUD SELLERS, D.Litt. . . 381

Salt . . . . . ,, ,, . 387

Iron and Hardware . . . ,, ,, . 387

Textile Industries . . . ,, ,, . 406

Glass . . . . . ,, ,, . 429

Shipbuilding . . . . ,, ,, . 432

Pottery . . . . . ,, ,, . 436

Bell-Founders . . . . By H. B. WALTERS, M.A., F.S.A. . 449

PAGE

Agriculture . . . . . By JOHN NEWTON 455
Sport Ancient and Modern . . . Edited by the Revd. E. E. DORLING, M.A., F.S.A.
Hunting . . . . . By FRANK BONNETT 481
Foxhounds 481
The Raby 482
The Bedale 483
The Bramham Moor 484
The Badsworth 486
The Bilsdale 488
The Cleveland 489
Earl FitzWilliam's 491
The Goathland 491
The Holderness 492
Mr. Sherbrooke's 493
The Sinnington 494
The Stainton Dale 495
Lord Middleton's 495
The York and Ainsty 495
Mr. Scrope's 496
The Wensleydale 496
Stag Hunting 497
Harriers 498
Beagles 500
Otter Hunting 502
Coursing . . . . . By FRANK BONNETT 503
Racing . . . . . ,, ,, ... 504
Polo . . . . . ,, ,, ... 519
Shooting . . . . . ,, ,, ... 521
Angling . . . . . ,, ,, ... 528
Cricket . . . . . By Sir HOME GORDON, Bart. . . . 537
Football . . . . . By C. J. B. MARRIOTT, M.A. . . . 541
Golf . . . . . By the Revd. E. E. DORLING, M.A., F.S.A. . 543
Athletics . . . . . By FRANK BONNETT 548

VOLUME THREE

PAGE

Dedication v
Contents ix
List of Illustrations and Maps xv
Editorial Note xvii
Ecclesiastical History . . . By A. HAMILTON THOMPSON, M.A., F.S.A. . 1
Religious Houses
Introduction . . . . By L. F. SALZMANN, B.A., F.S.A. . . 89
Priory of Monk Bretton . . . By the late T. M. FALLOW, M.A., F.S.A. . 91
Abbey of Selby . . . . ,, ,, . 95
Priory of Snaith . . . . By the Revd. J. SOLLOWAY, D.D. . . 100
Abbey of Whitby . . . By the late T. M. FALLOW, M.A., F.S.A. . 101
Priory of Middlesbrough . . . ,, ,, . 105
,, ,, All Saints, Fishergate, York . By the Revd. J. SOLLOWAY, D.D. . . 106
Hermitage of Goathland . . . By the late T. M. FALLOW, M.A., F.S.A. . 107
Cell of Hackness . . . . ,, ,, . 107
Abbey of St. Mary, York . . . By the Revd. J. SOLLOWAY, D.D. . . 107

		PAGE
Priory of St. Martin, Richmond .	By the late T. M. Fallow, M.A., F.S.A. .	. 112
,, ,, Arden . . .	,, ,,	. 112
,, ,, St. Stephen, Foukeholm .	,, ,,	. 116
,, ,, Marrick . .	,, ,,	. 117
,, ,, Nunburnholme . .	,, ,,	. 118
,, ,, Nunkeeling . .	,, ,,	. 119
,, ,, Nun Monkton . .	,, ,,	. 122
,, ,, Thicket . .	,, ,,	. 124
,, ,, Wilberfoss . .	,, ,,	. 125
,, ,, Yedingham . .	,, ,,	. 127
,, ,, St. Clement, York .	,, ,,	. 129
Abbey of Byland . . .	,, ,,	. 131
,, ,, Fountains . .	By the Revd. J. Solloway, D.D. .	. 134
,, ,, Jervaulx . .	By the late T. M. Fallow, M.A., F.S.A. .	. 138
,, ,, Kirkstall . .	,, ,,	. 142
,, ,, Meaux . . .	By the Revd. J. Solloway, D.D. .	. 146
,, ,, Rievaulx . .	By the late T. M. Fallow, M.A., F.S.A. .	. 149
,, ,, Roche . . .	,, ,,	. 153
,, ,, Sawley . .	,, ,,	. 156
Priory of Basedale . .	,, ,,	. 158
,, ,, Ellerton in Swaledale .	By the Revd. J. Solloway, D.D. .	. 160
,, ,, Esholt . .	By the late T. M. Fallow, M.A., F.S.A. .	. 161
,, ,, Hampole . .	,, ,,	. 163
,, ,, Handale, otherwise Grendale .	,, ,,	. 165
,, ,, Keldholme . .	,, ,,	. 167
,, ,, Kirklees . .	By Beatrice Barstow . .	. 170
,, ,, Nun Appleton .	By the late T. M. Fallow, M.A., F.S.A. .	. 170
,, ,, Rosedale . .	,, ,,	. 174
,, ,, Sinningthwaite . .	,, ,,	. 176
,, ,, Swine . .	,, ,,	. 178
,, ,, Wykeham . .	,, ,,	. 182
,, ,, Pontefract . .	By the Revd. J. Solloway, D.D. .	. 184
,, ,, Arthington . .	By the late T. M. Fallow, M.A., F.S.A. .	. 187
,, ,, Kingston-upon-Hull .	,, ,,	. 190
,, ,, Mount Grace . .	By Beatrice Barstow . .	. 192
,, ,, Grosmont . .	By the late T. M. Fallow, M.A., F.S.A. .	. 193
,, ,, Bolton . .	,, ,,	. 195
,, ,, Bridlington . .	,, ,,	. 199
,, ,, Drax . . .	,, ,,	. 205
,, ,, Guisborough . .	,, ,,	. 208
,, ,, Haltemprice . .	,, ,,	. 213
,, ,, Healaugh Park .	,, ,,	. 216
,, ,, Kirkham . .	,, ,,	. 219
,, ,, Marton . .	,, ,,	. 223
,, ,, Newburgh . .	,, ,,	. 226
Cell of Hood . . .	,, ,,	. 230
Priory of Nostell . . .	,, ,,	. 231
,, ,, Warter . . .	,, ,,	. 235
,, ,, Moxby . . .	,, ,,	. 239
,, ,, North Ferriby . .	,, ,,	. 241
Abbey of Coverham . .	,, ,,	. 243
,, ,, St. Agatha, Easby .	By the Revd. J. Solloway, D.D. .	. 245
,, ,, Egglestone . .	By Beatrice Barstow . .	. 249
Priory of Ellerton on Spalding Moor .	By the late T. M. Fallow, M.A., F.S.A. .	. 251
,, ,, Malton . .	,, ,,	. 253
,, ,, Watton . .	,, ,,	. 254
,, ,, St. Andrew, York .	,, ,,	. 255

CONTENTS OF VOLUMES: YORKS. GENERAL III

		PAGE
Preceptory of Yorkshire . . .	By L. F. Salzmann, B.A., F.S.A. . .	. 256
,, ,, Copmanthorpe with the Castle Mills, York . . .	,, ,, • •	. 257
Preceptory of Faxfleet . . .	,, ,, • •	. 257
,, ,, Foulbridge . .	,, ,, • •	. 258
,, ,, Penhill . . .	,, ,, • •	. 258
,, ,, Ribston and Wetherby (Knights Templars) . . .	,, ,, • •	. 258
Preceptory of Temple Cowton . .	,, ,, • •	. 259
,, ,, Temple Hirst . .	,, ,, • •	. 259
,, ,, Temple Newsam . .	,, ,, • •	. 259
,, ,, Westerdale . .	,, ,, • •	. 260
,, ,, Whitley . . .	,, ,, • •	. 260
Bailiwick of York . . .	,, ,, • •	. 260
Preceptory of Beverley . . .	,, ,, • •	. 261
,, ,, Mount St. John . .	,, ,, • •	. 261
,, ,, Newland . . .	,, ,, • •	. 261
,, ,, Ribston and Wetherby (Knights Hospitallers) . .	,, ,, • •	. 262
Black Friars of Beverley . . .	By A. G. Little, M.A. . .	. 263
Grey Friars of Beverley . . .	,, ,, • •	. 264
,, ,, of Doncaster . . .	,, ,, • •	. 266
White Friars of Doncaster . .	,, ,, • •	. 267
,, ,, of Hull . .	,, ,, • •	. 269
Austin Friars of Hull . . .	,, ,, • •	. 270
Crutched Friars of Kildale . .	,, ,, • •	. 270
White Friars of Northallerton . .	,, ,, • •	. 270
Black Friars of Pontefract . .	,, ,, • •	. 271
Grey Friars of Richmond . .	,, ,, • •	. 273
,, ,, Scarborough . .	,, ,, • •	. 274
Black Friars of Scarborough . .	,, ,, • •	. 277
White Friars of Scarborough . .	,, ,, • •	. 279
Austin Friars of Tickhill . .	,, ,, • •	. 280
Black Friars of Yarm . . .	,, ,, • •	. 281
,, ,, York . . .	,, ,, • •	. 283
Grey Friars of York . . .	,, ,, • •	. 287
White Friars of York . . .	,, ,, • •	. 291
Austin Friars of York . . .	,, ,, • •	. 294
Friars of the Sack, York . . .	,, ,, • •	. 296
Trinitarian Friars of Knaresborough .	,, ,, • •	. 296
Hospital of Bagby . . .	By the late T. M. Fallow, M.A., F.S.A. .	. 301
,, ,, St. Giles, Beverley . •	,, ,, •	. 301
,, ,, St. Nicholas, Beverley .	,, ,, •	. 302
Trinity Hospital, Beverley . .	,, ,, •	. 303
Hospital of St. Mary without the North Bar, Beverley . . .	,, ,, •	. 303
Hospital of St. John Lairgate, Beverley .	,, ,, •	. 303
Leper House outside the North Bar, Beverley . . .	,, ,, •	. 304
Other Houses, Beverley . . .	,, ,, •	. 304
Hospital of Boroughbridge . .	,, ,, •	. 304
,, ,, St. Helen, Braceford .	,, ,, •	. 304
,, ,, St. Mary, Bridlington .	,, ,, •	. 305
,, ,, St. Giles by Brompton Bridge	,, ,, •	. 305
,, ,, Crayke . . .	,, ,, •	. 306
,, ,, St. James, Doncaster . .	,, ,, •	. 306
,, ,, St. Nicholas, Doncaster .	,, ,, •	. 306

CONTENTS OF VOLUMES: YORKS. GENERAL III

		PAGE
Hospital of Herford . . .	By the late T. M. FALLOW, M.A., F.S.A. .	. 306
,, ,, St. James, Hessle . .	,, ,, .	. 306
,, ,, St. Mary Magdalene, Killingwoldgraves . . .	,, ,, .	. 306
Hospital of St. Mary and St. Andrew, Flixton	,, ,, .	. 307
Hospital of Fangfoss . . .	,, ,, .	. 308
,, ,, St. Mary Magdalene, Newton Garth, Hedon . . .	,, ,, .	. 308
Hospital of St. Sepulchre, Hedon . .	,, ,, .	. 309
,, ,, St. Leonard, Hedon .	,, ,, .	. 310
,, ,, the Gild of the Holy Cross, Hedon	,, ,, .	. 310
Charterhouse Hospital, Hull . .	,, ,, .	. 310
Gregg's Hospital, Hull . . .	,, ,, .	. 312
Riplingham's Hospital, Hull . .	,, ,, .	. 313
Trinity Maison Dieu, Hull . .	,, ,, .	. 313
Trinity House Hospital, Hull . .	,, ,, .	. 313
Selby's Hospital, Hull . . .	,, ,, .	. 313
Hospital of St. Leonard, Lowcross .	,, ,, .	. 314
,, ,, St. Mary Magdalene, Broughton . . .	,, ,, .	. 314
Wheelgate Hospital, Malton . .	,, ,, .	. 314
Hospital of St. Nicholas, Norton . .	,, ,, .	. 315
,, ,, Jesus, Middleham . .	,, ,, .	. 315
,, ,, Mitton . . .	,, ,, .	. 315
,, ,, St. James near Northallerton	,, ,, .	. 315
Maison Dieu, Northallerton . .	,, ,, .	. 317
Hospital of St. Nicholas, Pickering .	,, ,, .	. 318
Knolles Almshouses, Pontefract . .	,, ,, .	. 318
Hospital of St. Nicholas, Pontefract .	,, ,, .	. 320
,, ,, St. Mary Magdalene, Pontefract . . .	,, ,, .	. 321
Hospital of St. Mary the Virgin, Pontefract . . .	,, ,, .	. 321
Hospital of St. Michael, Foulsnape, Pontefract . . .	,, ,, .	. 321
Rerecross Hospital or the Spital on Stainmoor . . .	,, ,, .	. 321
Hospital of St. Nicholas, Richmond .	,, ,, .	. 322
,, ,, St. Mary Magdalene, Ripon .	,, ,, .	. 323
,, ,, St. John the Baptist, Ripon .	,, ,, .	. 327
,, ,, St. Anne or the Maison Dieu, Ripon . . .	,, ,, .	. 329
Hospital of St. Nicholas, Scarborough .	,, ,, .	. 330
,, ,, St. Thomas the Martyr, Scarborough . . .	,, ,, .	. 330
Other Hospitals in Scarborough . .	,, ,, .	. 330
Hospital of Seamer . . .	,, ,, .	. 330
,, ,, St. Leonard, Sheffield .	,, ,, .	. 330
,, ,, St. Mary Magdalene, Sherburn-in-Elmet . .	,, ,, .	. 331
Hospital of St. Mary Magdalene, Skipton	,, ,, .	. 331
,, ,, St. Edmund, Sprotbrough .	,, ,, .	. 331
,, ,, Snaith . . .	,, ,, .	. 332
,, ,, St. Mary, Staxton .	,, ,, .	. 332
,, ,, Tadcaster . .	,, ,, .	. 332
,, ,, St. Leonard, Tickhill .	,, ,, .	. 332

CONTENTS OF VOLUMES: YORKS. GENERAL III

		PAGE
Hospital in the Marsh, Tickhill	By the late T. M. FALLOW, M.A., F.S.A.	332
Maison Dieu, Tickhill	,, ,,	332
Hospital of St. Lawrence, Upsall-in-Cleveland	,, ,,	333
Hospital of St. Michael, Well	,, ,,	333
Leper House of Wentbridge	,, ,,	334
Hospital of St. Michael, Whitby	,, ,,	334
,, ,, St. John the Baptist, Whitby	,, ,,	334
,, ,, St. Nicholas, Yarm	,, ,,	335
,, ,, St. Leonard, York	,, ,,	336
,, ,, St. Mary Bootham, York	,, ,,	345
,, ,, St. Nicholas, York	,, ,,	346
,, ,, St. Thomas the Martyr outside Micklegate Bar, York	,, ,,	349
Trinity Hospital, Fossgate, York	,, ,,	350
Hospital of St. Anthony in Peaseholm, York	,, ,,	350
Hospital of St. Anthony, Gillygate, York	,, ,,	351
St. Andrewgate, Maison Dieu, York	,, ,,	351
Hospital of St. Mary Magdalene, Bootham, York	,, ,,	351
Hertergate or Castle Hill Maison Dieu, York	,, ,,	351
Hospital of St. Helen or Fishergate Hospital, York	,, ,,	351
Hospital of St. Katherine outside Micklegate Bar, York	,, ,,	351
Monk Bridge Maison Dieu, York	,, ,,	352
North Street Maison Dieu, York	,, ,,	352
Ousebridge Maison Dieu, York	,, ,,	352
Peter Lane Little Maison Dieu, York	,, ,,	352
Layerthorpe Hospital, York	,, ,,	352
Whitefriars Lane Maison Dieu, York	,, ,,	352
Collegiate Church of St. John the Evangelist, Beverley	By A. HAMILTON THOMPSON, M.A., F.S.A.	353
Collegiate Church of Hemingbrough	By the Revd. J. SOLLOWAY, D.D.	359
College of Acaster	,, ,,	360
,, ,, Howden	,, ,,	361
Collegiate Church of Kirkby Overblow	,, ,,	362
Hospital or Collegiate Chapel of Lazenby	,, ,,	363
Collegiate Church of Lowthorpe	,, ,,	365
,, ,, Middleham	By the late T. M. FALLOW, M.A., F.S.A.	366
Collegiate Chapel of St. Clement, Pontefract	By the Revd. J. SOLLOWAY, D.D.	366
Collegiate Church of St. Peter and St. Wilfrid, Ripon	By A. HAMILTON THOMPSON, M.A., F.S.A.	367
Jesus College, Rotherham	By the Revd. J. SOLLOWAY, D.D.	372
College of St. James, Sutton-in-Holderness	,, ,,	374
Cathedral Church of St. Peter, York	By A. HAMILTON THOMPSON, M.A., F.S.A.	375
The Bedern, York	By the Revd. J. SOLLOWAY, D.D.	382
College of St. Mary and the Holy Angels, York, alias St. Sepulchre	,, ,,	383
College of St. William, York	By the Revd. J. SOLLOWAY, D.D.	385
Priory of Allerton Mauleverer	By the late T. M. FALLOW, M.A., F.S.A.	387
,, ,, Birstall	,, ,,	387
,, ,, Ecclesfield	,, ,,	388
,, ,, Holy Trinity, York	By the Revd. J. SOLLOWAY, D.D.	389
,, ,, Hedley	,, ,,	390

PAGE

Alien Priory of Begar near Richmond	.	By the late T. M. Fallow, M.A., F.S.A. . . 391
Political History . . .	.	 393
To 1660 . . .	.	By L. F. Salzmann, B.A., F.S.A.
From 1660 . . .	.	By the Revd. D. J. Davies, M.A.
Military History . . .	.	By L. F. Salzmann, B.A., F.S.A.
Social and Economic History	.	By Maud Sellers, D.Litt., sometime Mary Bateson Fellow of Newnham College, Cambridge . 435
Table of Population, 1801–1901 .	.	By G. S. Minchin 485

YORKSHIRE, EAST RIDING

VOLUME ONE

PAGE

Dedication	v
Contents	ix
List of Illustrations	xi
List of Maps and Plans	xii
Editorial Note	xiii
The East Riding of Yorkshire Victoria County History Committee	xv
Classes of Documents in the Public Record Office used	xvii
Note on the Records of Kingston upon Hull Corporation	xix
Note on Abbreviations	xx

PART I

The City of Kingston upon Hull .	. By K. J. Allison and P. M. Tillott . .	1
Medieval Hull . . .	. By K. J. Allison	11
Hull in the 16th and 17th Centuries	. By G. C. F. Forster . . .	90
Hull, 1700–1835 . . .	. By J. E. Williams; the section on Politics is by J. A. Woods	174
Modern Hull . . .	. By Lucy M. Brown; the last three sections are by C. A. McLaren	215

PART II

The Parish Churches . .	. By M. E. Ingram	287
Protestant Nonconformity .	. By K. J. Allison	311
Roman Catholicism . .	. ,, . . .	330
Other Religious Bodies .	. ,, . . .	332
Religious Houses . . .	. By Mary E. Dymond . . .	333
Charities . . .	. By K. J. Allison	335
Education . . .	. By J. Lawson	348
Public Services . . .	. By K. J. Allison	371
Communications . . .	. By M. E. Ingram (Railways) and C. A. McLaren (Ferries, Bridges, Roads, and Air Transport)	387
The Trinity House . .	. By F. W. Brooks	397
Markets and Fairs . .	. By Mary E. Dymond . . .	407
Fortifications . . .	. By K. J. Allison	412
Social Institutions . .	. By Mary Bartlett (Learned Societies, Museums, and Art Gallery), J. B. Nattriss (Libraries), and C. A. McLaren (Places of Entertainment and Newspapers)	418
Civic Institutions . .	. By K. J. Allison (House of Correction; Weighhouse, Exchange, and Custom House; and Workhouses), Mary E. Dymond (Guildhall), and C. A. McLaren (Prison; City Hall; and Seals, Insignia, Plate, and Officers of the City) . .	433

PAGE

Secular Buildings . . . By A. G. CHAMBERLAIN and I. HALL . . 443
Outlying Villages 459
Drypool . . . . . By K. J. ALLISON 460
Marfleet . . . . . By C. A. McLAREN 464
Sculcoates . . . . ,, ... 467
Sutton . . . . By K. J. ALLISON 470
Index . . . . . ,, ... 476

YORKSHIRE, NORTH RIDING

VOLUME ONE

PAGE

Dedication v
Contents ix
List of Illustrations xiii
List of Maps and Plans xix
Editorial Note xxi
Topography . . . . General descriptions and manorial descents compiled
under the superintendence of WILLIAM PAGE,
F.S.A., the General Editor; Heraldic drawings and
blazon by the Revd. E. E. DORLING, M.A., F.S.A.;
Charities from information supplied by J. W.
OWSLEY, I.S.O., late Official Trustee of Charitable
Funds
Honour and Castle of Richmond . . By MABEL MAYNARD, Oxford Honours School of
Modern History; Architectural description of Castle
by C. R. PEERS, M.A., F.S.A. . . . 1
Richmondshire
Introduction . . . . By ADA RUSSELL, M.A. 17
Borough of Richmond . . . By MABEL MAYNARD; Architectural descriptions by
C. R. PEERS, M.A., F.S.A., J. W. BLOE, and A. W.
CLAPHAM, F.S.A. 17
Gilling West Wapentake . . By ADA RUSSELL, M.A.; Architectural descriptions by
C. R. PEERS, M.A., F.S.A., J. W. BLOE, S. F.
BEEKE LANE, A. W. CLAPHAM, F.S.A., R. W.
ATKEY, and T. F. INGRAM
Arkengarthdale 36
Barningham 39
Bowes 42
Brignall 49
Easby . . . . (Architectural description of Abbey by S. C.
KAINES-SMITH, M.A.) 51
Forcett 64
Gilling 71
Hutton Magna or Hutton Longvilliers 84
Kirkby Ravensworth 87
Marrick 97
Marske 100
Melsonby 104
Rokeby with Egglestone Abbey . (Architectural description of Abbey by J. W. BLOE) . 109
Romaldkirk 117
Stanwick St. John 127
Startforth 134
Wycliffe 138
Gilling East Wapentake . . By ADA RUSSELL, M.A.; Architectural descriptions by
C. R. PEERS, M.A., F.S.A., J. W. BLOE, S. F.
BEEKE LANE, A. W. CLAPHAM, F.S.A., R. W.
ATKEY, T. F. INGRAM, and C. C. DURSTON

CONTENTS OF VOLUMES: YORKS. N.R. I

		PAGE
Introduction		143
Ainderby Steeple		144
Barton		150
Bolton-upon-Swale		155
Cleasby		158
East Cowton		160
Croft		162
Danby Wiske		172
Kirkby Wiske		176
Great Langton		184
Manfield		186
Middleton Tyas		190
Great Smeaton		198
Hang West Wapentake	Architectural descriptions by C. R. PEERS, M.A., F.S.A., J. W. BLOE, A. W. CLAPHAM, F.S.A., S. F. BEEKE LANE, ERNEST A. R. RAHBULA, A.R.I.B.A., T. F. INGRAM, and R. W. ATKEY	
Aysgarth	By MYRA CURTIS, Classical Tripos	200
Coverham	By ADA RUSSELL, M.A.; Architectural description of Abbey by ERNEST A. R. RAHBULA, A.R.I.B.A.	214
Downholme	By ADA RUSSELL, M.A.	225
Fingall	By ANNE SPILMAN, M.A., and ADA RUSSELL, M.A.	232
Grinton	By ADA RUSSELL, M.A.	236
Hauxwell	,, ,,	245
Middleham	By MABEL MAYNARD, Oxford Honours School of Modern History; Architectural description of Castle by C. R. PEERS, M.A., F.S.A.	251
Spennithorne	By MYRA CURTIS, Classical Tripos	257
Thornton Steward	By CHARLOTTE M. CALTHROP, Classical Tripos	264
Wensley	By MABEL MAYNARD; Architectural description of Bolton Castle by C. R. PEERS, M.A., F.S.A.	268
East Witton	By ANNE SPILMAN, M.A.; Architectural description of Jervaulx Abbey by HAROLD BRAKSPEAR, F.S.A., A.R.I.B.A.	280
West Witton	By CHARLOTTE M. CALTHROP, Classical Tripos	286
Hang East Wapentake	Architectural descriptions by C. R. PEERS, M.A., F.S.A., JOHN QUEKETT, M.A., J. W. BLOE, A. W. CLAPHAM, F.S.A., S. F. BEEKE LANE, and T. F. INGRAM	
Bedale	By MYRA CURTIS, Classical Tripos	291
Catterick	,, ,,	301
Hornby	,, ,,	313
Kirkby Fleetham	,, ,,	320
Masham	By MARION WESTON, History Tripos	323
Patrick Brompton	By MABEL MAYNARD, Oxford Honours School of Modern History	332
Scruton	By MYRA CURTIS, Classical Tripos	341
Thornton Watlass	By MARION WESTON, History Tripos	344
Well	,, ,,	348
Hallikeld Wapentake	Architectural descriptions by C. R. PEERS, M.A., F.S.A., J. W. BLOE, A. W. CLAPHAM, F.S.A., S. F. BEEKE LANE, and C. C. DURSTON	
Burneston	By MARION WESTON, History Tripos	356
Cundall with Leckby	By MYRA CURTIS, Classical Tripos	363
Kirkby Hill or Kirkby on the Moor	By MARION WESTON, History Tripos	367
Kirklington	,, ,,	371
Pickhill with Roxby	,, ,,	377
West Tanfield	,, ,,	384
Wath	,, ,,	390

PAGE

Allerton Wapentake or Allertonshire   .   Architectural descriptions by C. R. PEERS, M.A., F.S.A., J. W. BLOE, A. W. CLAPHAM, F.S.A., S. F. BEEKE LANE, C. C. DURSTON, T. F. INGRAM, and ERNEST A. R. RAHBULA, A.R.I.B.A.

Introduction	By MYRA CURTIS, Classical Tripos	397
Birkby	By CAROLINE C. MOREWOOD	399
Hutton Conyers	By MYRA CURTIS, Classical Tripos	403
Kirkby Sigston	,, ,,	405
Leake	,, ,,	410
Northallerton	By MARION WESTON, History Tripos	418
Osmotherley	By MYRA CURTIS, Classical Tripos	434
North Otterington	,, ,,	439
West Rounton	,, ,,	444
Sessay	,, ,,	446
Sockburn	,, ,,	449
Thornton le Street	By MARION WESTON, History Tripos	455

Ryedale Wapentake   .   .   Architectural descriptions by JOHN QUEKETT, M.A., assisted by ERNEST A. R. RAHBULA, A.R.I.B.A., J. MURRAY KENDALL, F.S.A., A. W. CLAPHAM, F.S.A., and J. W. BLOE

Introduction	By ADA RUSSELL, M.A.	459
Ampleforth	By CAROLINE C. MOREWOOD	461
Appleton le Street	By ADA RUSSELL, M.A.	464
Barton le Street	,, ,,	472
Great Edston	By CAROLINE C. MOREWOOD	476
Gilling	By ADA RUSSELL, M.A.; Architectural description of Castle by A. W. CLAPHAM, F.S.A.	478
Helmsley	By ADA RUSSELL, M.A.; Architectural description of Castle by J. W. BLOE; Architectural description of Rievaulx Abbey by W. H. ST. JOHN HOPE, M.A., Litt.D., D.C.L.	485
Hovingham	By ADA RUSSELL, M.A.	505
Kirkby Moorside	By MYRA CURTIS, Classical Tripos	511
Kirkdale	By ADA RUSSELL, M.A.	517
Lastingham	,, ,,	524
New Malton, including the parishes of St. Leonard and St. Michael	,, ,,	529
Old Malton	,, ,,	537
Normanby	,, ,,	542
Nunnington	By MYRA CURTIS, Classical Tripos	544
Oswaldkirk	By CAROLINE C. MOREWOOD	549
Salton	By MYRA CURTIS, Classical Tripos	552
Scawton	By CAROLINE C. MOREWOOD	555
Slingsby	By ADA RUSSELL, M.A.	557
Stonegrave	,, ,,	561

VOLUME TWO

PAGE

Dedication	v
Contents	ix
List of Illustrations	xiii
List of Maps and Plans	xix
Editorial Note	xxi

CONTENTS OF VOLUMES: YORKS. N.R. II

PAGE

Topography . . . . General descriptions and manorial descents compiled under the superintendence of WILLIAM PAGE, F.S.A., the General Editor; Heraldic drawings and blazon by the Revd. E. E. DORLING, M.A., F.S.A.; Charities from information supplied by J. W. OWSLEY, I.S.O., late Official Trustee of Charitable Funds

Birdforth Wapentake . . . Architectural descriptions by JOHN QUEKETT, M.A., J. W. BLOE, A. W. CLAPHAM, F.S.A., and C. C. DURSTON

Introduction . . . . By MYRA CURTIS, Classical Tripos . . . 1
Old Byland . . . . ,, ,, . . . 3
Cowesby . . . . ,, ,, . . . 5
Coxwold . . . . By MYRA CURTIS, Classical Tripos; Architectural description of Byland Abbey by J. W. BLOE, F.S.A. 8
East Harlsey . . . . By MYRA CURTIS, Classical Tripos; Architectural description of Mount Grace Priory by A. W. CLAPHAM, F.S.A. 24
Hawnby . . . . By MYRA CURTIS, Classical Tripos . . . 31
Husthwaite . . . . ,, ,, . . . 37
South Kilvington . . . ,, ,, . . . 40
Cold Kirby . . . . ,, ,, . . . 43
Kirkby Knowle . . . . ,, ,, . . . 44
South Otterington . . . ,, ,, . . . 50
Over Silton . . . . By CAROLINE C. MOREWOOD . . . 51
Thirkleby . . . . By MARION WESTON, History Tripos . . 55
Thirsk . . . . . ,, ,, . . 58
Topcliffe . . . . ,, ,, . . 70
Welbury . . . . ,, ,, . . 80
Bulmer Wapentake . . . Architectural descriptions by A. W. CLAPHAM, F.S.A.
Introduction . . . . By MYRA CURTIS, Classical Tripos . . . 83
Alne . . . . . By CAROLINE C. MOREWOOD . . . 85
Bossall . . . . . By CHARLOTTE M. CALTHROP, Classical Tripos . 91
Brafferton . . . . By MARGARET L. MACKAY . . . 98
Brandsby with Stearsby . . By MYRA CURTIS, Classical Tripos . . 103
Bulmer with Henderskelfe . . By CAROLINE C. MOREWOOD . . 107
Crambe . . . . By CHARLOTTE M. CALTHROP, Classical Tripos . 113
Crayke . . . . By HELEN DOUGLAS-IRVINE, M.A. . . . 119
Dalby with Skewsby . . . By MYRA CURTIS, Classical Tripos . . 125
Easingwold . . . . By ANNIE M. McKILLIAM, M.A. . . . 128
Foston with Thornton-le-Clay . . By CHARLOTTE M. CALTHROP, Classical Tripos . 134
Haxby . . . . By MYRA CURTIS, Classical Tripos . . 137
Gate Helmsley . . . . By CHARLOTTE M. CALTHROP, Classical Tripos . 139
Upper Helmsley . . . . ,, ,, ,, . 141
Holtby . . . . ,, ,, ,, . 143
Huntingdon . . . . ,, ,, ,, . 145
Huttons Ambo . . . ,, ,, ,, . 150
Marton with Moxby . . . By MYRA CURTIS, Classical Tripos . . 154
Myton-upon-Swale . . . By ANNE SPILMAN, M.A. . . . 157
Newton-upon-Ouse . . . By CAROLINE C. MOREWOOD . . . 160
Osbaldwick . . . . By ANNE SPILMAN, M.A. . . . 164
Overton . . . . By CAROLINE C. MOREWOOD . . . 167
Sheriff Hutton . . . . By CHARLOTTE M. CALTHROP, Classical Tripos . 172
Stillington . . . . By CAROLINE C. MOREWOOD . . . 187
Stockton-on-the-Forest . . By CHARLOTTE M. CALTHROP, Classical Tripos . 190
Strensall . . . . ,, ,, ,, . 193
Sutton-on-the-Forest . . . By MYRA CURTIS, Classical Tripos . . 196
Terrington . . . . By CAROLINE C. MOREWOOD . . . 202

CONTENTS OF VOLUMES: YORKS. N.R. II

PAGE

Thormanby	By Anne Spilman, M.A.		207
Warthill	By Charlotte M. Calthrop, Classical Tripos		210
Whenby	By Myra Curtis, Classical Tripos		211
Wigginton	,, ,,		214
Langbaurgh Wapentake (West)	Architectural descriptions by F. H. Cheetham		
Introduction	By Ada Russell, M.A.		217
Acklam	By Charlotte M. Calthrop, Classical Tripos		221
Appleton Wiske	,, ,, ,,		223
Great Ayton	By Myra Curtis, Classical Tripos		225
Carlton	,, ,,		232
Crathorne	,, ,,		234
Hilton	By Margaret L. Mackay		237
Ingleby Arncliffe	By Myra Curtis, Classical Tripos		240
Ingleby Greenhow	,, ,,		243
Kildale	,, ,,		249
Kirkby-in-Cleveland	By Charlotte M. Calthrop, Classical Tripos		253
Kirk Leavington	,, ,, ,,		257
Marton	,, ,, ,,		264
Middlesbrough	By Myra Curtis, Classical Tripos		268
Newton	By Charlotte M. Calthrop, Classical Tripos		273
Ormesby	By Margaret L. Mackay		276
Rudby-in-Cleveland	By Myra Curtis, Classical Tripos		283
Seamer	By Margaret L. Mackay		291
Stainton	By Charlotte M. Calthrop, Classical Tripos		293
Stokesley	By Myra Curtis, Classical Tripos		301
Whorlton	,, ,,		309
Yarm	By Margaret L. Mackay		319
Langbaurgh Wapentake (East)	Architectural descriptions except where otherwise stated by F. H. Cheetham		
Brotton	By Margaret L. Mackay; Architectural description of Kilton Castle by A. W. Clapham, F.S.A.		326
Danby	By Ada Russell, M.A.; Architectural description of Danby Castle by A. W. Clapham, F.S.A.		332
Easington	By Ada Russell, M.A.		340
Egton	By Ada Russell, M.A.; Architectural description of Grosmont Priory by John Quekett, M.A.		343
Glaisdale	By Ada Russell, M.A.		348
Guisborough	By Minnie Reddan, History Tripos; Architectural description of Guisborough Priory by A. W. Clapham, F.S.A.		352
Hinderwell	By Ada Russell, M.A.		365
Kirkleatham	By Minnie Reddan, History Tripos		371
Liverton	By Ada Russell, M.A.		383
Loftus	,, ,,		385
Lythe	By Ada Russell, M.A.; Architectural description of Mulgrave Castle by A. W. Clapham, F.S.A.		388
Marske	By Minnie Reddan, History Tripos		399
Skelton	By Margaret L. Mackay		405
Upleatham	By Minnie Reddan, History Tripos		410
Westerdale	By Ada Russell, M.A.; Architectural description of Basedale Priory by John Quekett, M.A.		413
Pickering Lythe Wapentake	By Ada Russell, M.A.; Architectural descriptions by A. W. Clapham, F.S.A.		
Introduction			418
Allerston			421
Brompton			424
Cayton			430
Ebberston			434

PAGE

Ellerburn	.	437
Hutton Bushel	.	441
Kirkby Misperton	.	444
Levisham	.	450
Middleton	.	453
Pickering	.	461
Scalby	.	476
Seamer	.	483
Sinnington	.	489
Thornton Dale	.	492
Wykeham	.	498

Whitby Strand Liberty . . . By ADA RUSSELL, M.A.; Architectural descriptions by A. W. CLAPHAM, F.S.A.

Introduction	.	502
Whitby	.	506
Hackness	.	528
Sneaton	.	532
Fylingdales	.	534

Scarborough Borough . . . By ADA RUSSELL, M.A.; Architectural descriptions of the town and church by A. W. CLAPHAM, F.S.A., and architectural description of castle by JOHN QUEKETT, M.A., with the assistance of notes on the keep from DUNCAN H. MONTGOMERIE, F.S.A. . 538

YORKSHIRE, THE CITY OF YORK

PAGE

Dedication .	v
Contents .	ix
List of Illustrations .	xi
List of Maps and Plans	xiii
Editorial Note	xv
The East Riding of Yorkshire Victoria County History Committee	xvii
Classes of Public Records used	xviii
Note on Abbreviations	xix

PART I

The City of York

York Before the Norman Conquest . By Professor A. G. DICKENS; the section on 'Romano-British York' is by H. G. RAMM . 2

Medieval York . . . . By E. MILLER 25

Tudor York . . . . By Professor A. G. DICKENS . . . 117

York in the 17th Century . . By G. C. F. FORSTER . . . 160

York in the 18th Century . . By K. J. ALLISON and P. M. TILLOTT . 207

Modern York . . . . By E. M. SIGSWORTH; the section 'Religious Life in the 19th and 20th centuries' is by P. M. TILLOTT and 'The City after 1939' by K. J. ALLISON 254

PART II

The Boundaries of the City . . By P. M. TILLOTT; the section on 'The Ridden Boundaries' is by K. J. ALLISON . 311

Romano-British Antiquities . . By H. G. RAMM 322

Anglo-Scandinavian Antiquities . . By Professor A. G. DICKENS . . 332

The Minster and its Precincts . . By P. M. TILLOTT . . . 337

Worship in the Minster . . By the Revd. L. W. COWIE . . 343

CONTENTS OF VOLUMES: YORKS. YORK

PAGE

The Sites and Remains of the Religious
   Houses . . . . By K. J. ALLISON 357
The Parish Churches . . . By P. M. TILLOTT 365
Protestant Nonconformity . . By MARGARET CRAIG 404
Roman Catholicism . . . „ „ 418
The Jews . . . . . „ „ 419
Charities . . . . By R. B. ROSE 420
Schools and Colleges . . . By MARGARET CRAIG 440
Public Services . . . . By K. J. ALLISON 460
Transport . . . . By H. W. PARRIS 472
Guilds . . . . . By K. J. ALLISON 481
Markets and Fairs . . . „ „ 484
Prisons and Gallows . . . By R. B. PUGH 491
Common Lands and Strays . . By K. J. ALLISON 498
Medieval Mills . . . . „ „ 506
The Fishpond of the Foss . . „ „ 509
The City Walls, Bars, and Posterns . By P. M. TILLOTT 510
Bridges . . . . . By K. J. ALLISON 515
The Castle and the Old Baile . . By R. B. PUGH 521
The King's Manor . . . By K. J. ALLISON 529
Places of Entertainment . . The section on the Assembly Rooms is by P. M.
   TILLOTT, that on the Theatre by C. W. SELLARS,
   and the remainder by K. J. ALLISON . . 531
Learned Societies and Museums . By K. J. ALLISON 535
Libraries and Art Gallery . . „ „ 536
Newspapers . . . . „ „ 537
The Barracks . . . . „ „ 541
The Guildhall and Council Chamber . „ „ 542
The Mansion House . . . By P. M. TILLOTT 543
The Seals, Insignia, Plate, and Officers
   of the City . . . The section on Seals is by R. B. PUGH, the remainder
   by K. J. ALLISON . . . 544
Index . . . . . By P. M. TILLOTT 547

INDEX OF TITLES OF ARTICLES

THE following index is of the titles of articles that are printed in the tables of contents. Only limited attempts have been made to penetrate beyond those tables. Thus where the title of an article is insufficient the index is not so constructed as to supply the want. Inevitably there has been much inconsistency in the titling of articles dealing with the same subject. In particular some of the natural history articles are in some counties divided by natural orders and not in others. The titles of subdivisions, where they exist, have been indexed. It must not, however, be imagined that because a subdivision title is absent from the index, the phenomena described thereunder are ignored in the volume in which they should appear; they may be found under a more general or at least another title.

The places named are normally parishes, unless there is an indication to the contrary, and are deemed to lie within the counties whose abbreviated names form part of the reference. If the title of a topographical article is compounded of a major and minor name, e.g. 'Alderton, with Dixton', the lesser name, i.e. Dixton, appears in the index as, e.g., 'Dixton (in Alderton)'. If two places are linked by 'and', e.g. Outwell and Upwell, they will be indexed as 'Outwell and Upwell' and 'Upwell (with Outwell)'. Where there is more than one article on religious houses or schools in a single place the titles of the several articles have not been itemized, and are collectively indexed under the headings 'religious houses' and 'schools'. The names of counties are sometimes included in the titles of articles but with a few exceptions they are not indexed below.

An asterisk (*) indicates that the reference is to more than one article.

Abberley, *Worcs.* iv
Abberton, *Worcs.* iv
Abbotsbury Abbey, *Dors.* ii
Abbotsley, *Hunts.* ii
Abbotstone (in Itchen Stoke), *Hants* iv
Abbreviations (Note on, Table of), *Beds.* i; *Berks.* i; *Bucks.* i; *Cambs.* iii; *Cornw.* i; *Cumb.* ii; *Derb.* i; *Devon* i; *Dur.* i; *Essex* ii, iv–v; *Glos.* vi, viii; *Hants* ii; *Herefs.* i; *Herts.* ii, *Fam.*; *Hunts.* i; *Kent* i; *Lancs.* i; *Leics.* i–v; *Lond.* i; *Mdx.* i, iii; *Norf.* ii; *Northants.* ii, *Fam.*; *Notts.* i; *Oxon.* v–ix; *Rut.* i; *Salop.* i, viii; *Som.* i; *Staffs.* i–v, viii; *Suff.* i; *Surr.* ii; *Suss.* i; *Warws.* i, iii, vii–viii; *Wilts.* i(1), ii–ix; *Worcs.* ii; *Yorks.* i; *Yorks. E.R.* i; *Yorks. York*
Abingdon: Borough, *Berks.* iv; religious houses, *Berks.* ii*; School, *Berks.* ii
Abinger, *Surr.* iii
Abington, *Northants.* iv
Ablench (in Fladbury), *Worcs.* iii
Acarina (Mites), *see* Arachnida
Acaster College, *Yorks.* iii
Acklam, *Yorks. N.R.* ii
Acre, Castle, Priory, *Norf.* ii
Acre, West, Priory, *Norf.* ii
Acton Beauchamp, *Worcs.* iv
Acton Burnell, *Salop.* viii
Acton Trussell and Bednall, *Staffs.* v
Addenda, *see* Corrigenda
Adderbury, *Oxon.* ix
Addington, *Bucks.* iv
Addington, *Surr.* iv
Addington, Great and Little, *Northants.* iii*
Adlestrop, *Glos.* vi
Administrative History, *see* Government; Political History; Social and Administrative History
Adstock, *Bucks.* iv
Advertisement, General, *Beds.* i; *Berks.* i; *Bucks.* i; *Cornw.* i; *Cumb.* i; *Derb.* i; *Devon* i; *Dur.* i; *Essex* i; *Hants* i; *Herefs.* i; *Herts.* i; *Kent* i; *Lancs.* i; *Leics.* i; *Lond.* i; *Norf.* i; *Northants.* i; *Notts.* i; *Rut.* i; *Salop.* i; *Som.* i; *Staffs.* i; *Suff.* i; *Surr.* i; *Suss.* i; *Warws.* i; *Worcs.* i; *Yorks.* i
Advisory Council, *Beds.* i; *Berks.* i; *Bucks.* i; *Cornw.* i; *Cumb.* i; *Derb.* i; *Devon* i; *Dur.* i; *Essex* i; *Hants* i;

Herefs. i; *Herts.* i, *Fam.*; *Kent* i; *Lancs.* i; *Leics.* i; *Lond.* i; *Norf.* i; *Northants.* i, *Fam.*; *Notts.* i; *Rut.* i; *Salop.* i; *Som.* i; *Staffs.* i; *Suff.* i; *Surr.* i; *Suss.* i; *Warws.* i; *Worcs.* i; *Yorks.* i
Adwell, *Oxon.* viii
Aerated and Mineral Waters, *Surr.* ii
Agrarian History, *see* Agriculture
Agricultural Implements (Manufacture, Manufacturers), *Essex* ii; *Lincs.* ii; Machine-Making and Iron-Founding, *Oxon.* ii; Milling Machinery, Locomotives, etc., *Suff.* ii
Agriculture (Agrarian History), *Beds.* ii; *Berks.* ii; *Bucks.* i; *Cambs.* i*; *Derb.* ii; *Dors.* ii; *Dur.* ii; *Glos.* ii; *Hants* v; *Herefs.* i; *Herts.* ii; *Kent* i; *Lancs.* ii; *Leics.* ii*; *Lincs.* ii; *Mdx.* ii; *Notts.* ii; *Oxon.* ii; *Rut.* i; *Som.* ii; *Suff.* ii; *Surr.* iv; *Suss.* ii; *Warws.* ii, vii; *Wilts.* iv*, vi; *Worcs.* ii; *Yorks.* ii
Agriculture, Industries derived from, *Cambs.* ii
Ainderby Steeple, *Yorks. N.R.* i
Aka, *see* Rock
Akeley, *Bucks.* iv
Alabaster, *see* Gypsum
Albury, *Herts.* iv; Calvert of, *see* Genealogy
Albury, *Surr.* iii
Albury, with Tiddington, *Oxon.* v
Alcester, *Warws.* iii; Abbey, *Warws.* ii
Alconbury-cum-Weston, *Hunts.* iii
Aldbury, *Herts.* ii
Aldeby Priory, *Norf.* ii
Aldenham, *Herts.* ii; Grammar School, *Herts.* ii
Alderbury-with-Cardeston, *Salop.* viii
Aldermaston, *Berks.* iii
Alderminster, *Worcs.* iv
Aldersgate Hospital, *Mdx.* i
Aldershot, *Hants* iv
Alderton, with Dixton, *Glos.* vi
Aldingbourne, *Suss.* iv
Aldingham, *Lancs.* viii
Aldington (in Badsey), *Worcs.* ii
Aldrington, *Suss.* vii
Aldwick Hundred, *Suss.* iv
Aldwinkle All Saints and Aldwinckle St. Peter, *Northants.* iii*
Aldworth, *Berks.* iv
Alfold, *Surr.* iii

Alfrick (in Suckley), *Worcs.* iv

Algae, *Cornw.* i*; *Devon* i*; *Hants* i; *Herts.* i; *Kent* i*; *Leics.* i; *Norf.* i; *Notts.* i; *Salop.* i; *Som.* i*; *Staffs.* i; *Suff.* i*; *Surr.* i; *Worcs.* i; *Yorks.* i; *and see* Cryptogams

Alkerton, *Oxon.* ix

Alkmonton Hospital, *Derb.* ii

Allerston, *Yorks. N.R.* ii

Allerton Mauleverer Priory, *Yorks.* iii

Allerton Wapentake or Allertonshire, *Yorks. N.R.* i

Allesley, *Warws.* vi

Alliances, *see* Genealogy

Allington, Hospital of St. Mary Magdalen, *Dors.* ii

Alne, *Yorks. N.R.* ii

Alne, Great, *Warws.* iii

Alnesbourn Priory, *Suff.* ii

Alresford, Old, *Hants* iii

Alresford Liberty, *Hants* iii

Alstoe Hundred, *Rut.* ii

Alstone (in Overbury), *Worcs.* iii

Altcar, *Lancs.* iii

Althorp, Spencer of, *see* Genealogy

Alton, *Hants* ii; Hundred, *Hants* ii

Alum, *Yorks.* ii

Alvechurch, *Worcs.* iii

Alvecote Priory, *Warws.* ii

Alverstoke Liberty, with Gosport, *Hants* iii

Alveston, *Warws.* iii

Alvingham Priory, *Lincs.* ii

Alwalton, *Hunts.* iii

Ambersham, North and South (in Steep), *Hants* iii

Ambrosden (Ambroseden), *Oxon.* v; Turner and Page-Turner of, *see* Genealogy

Amersham: Borough, *Bucks.* iii; Grammar School, *Bucks.* ii

Amesbury Abbey, later Priory, *Wilts.* iii

Amington and Stonydelph, *Warws.* iv

Ammunition, Manufacture of, *Essex* ii; *and see* Gunpowder

Amounderness Hundred, *Lancs.* vii

Amphibia (Amphibians), *see* Reptiles

Ampleforth, *Yorks. N.R.* i

Amport, *Hants* iv

Ampthill, *Beds.* iii

Amwell, Great, *Herts.* iii

Amwell, Little, Liberty (in Hertford), *Herts.* iii

Anchorites, *see* Hermits

Ancient Earthworks, *see* Earthworks

Andover: with Foxcott, *Hants* iv; Hundred, *Hants* iv

Andwell Priory, *Hants* ii

Anglesey Priory, *Cambs.* ii

Angling (Fishing), *Berks.* ii; *Bucks.* ii; *Cumb.* ii; *Derb.* ii; *Dors.* ii; *Dur.* ii; *Essex* ii; *Glos.* ii; *Hants* v; *Herts.* i; *Kent* i; *Lancs.* ii; *Lincs.* ii; *Mdx.* ii; *Northants.* ii; *Notts.* ii; *Oxon.* ii; *Rut.* i; *Som.* ii; *Suff.* ii; *Surr.* ii; *Suss.* ii; *Warws.* ii; *Wilts.* iv; *Worcs.* ii; *Yorks.* ii

Anglo-Norman Settlement, *Cambs.* ii

Anglo-Saxon Art, *see* Art

Anglo-Saxon Remains, *Beds.* i; *Berks.* i; *Bucks.* i; *Cambs.* i; *Cornw.* i; *Derb.* i; *Devon* i; *Dur.* i; *Essex* i; *Hants* i; *Herts.* i; *Hunts.* i; *Kent* i; *Lancs.* i; *Leics.* i; *Lond.* i; *Norf.* i; *Northants.* i; *Notts.* i; *Oxon.* i; *Rut.* i; *Som.* i; *Staffs.* i; *Suff.* i; *Surr.* i; *Suss.* i; *Warws.* i; *Worcs.* i; *Yorks.* ii; *and see* Saxon

Anglo-Saxon Settlement and Danish Invasion, *Cambs.* ii

Anglo-Saxon Wiltshire, *Wilts.* ii

Anglo-Scandinavian Antiquities, *see* Antiquities

Ankerwick Priory, *Bucks.* i

Ann, Abbotts, *Hants* iv

Ansley, *Warws.* iv

Anstey, *Herts.* iv; Hospital of St. Mary Bigging, *Herts.* iv

Ansty, *Warws.* viii

Ansty Preceptory, *Wilts.* iii

Antiquities: Anglo-Scandinavian, *Yorks. York*; Bronze Age and Early Iron Age, Topographical List of, *Suff.* i; Romano-British, *Yorks. York*; *and see* Anglo-Saxon Remains; Earthworks, Ancient; Romano-British Remains

Ants (Hymenoptera Aculeata), *see* Hymenoptera

Antwerp, Wake of, *see* Genealogy

Apethorpe, *Northants.* ii

Appleby, Carmelite Friars, *see* Friars, Four Houses of

Appledram, *Suss.* iv

Appledurcombe Priory, *Hants* ii

Appleshaw, *Hants* iv

Appleton, *Berks.* iv

Appleton, Nun, Priory, *Yorks.* iii

Appleton le Street, *Yorks. N.R.* i

Appleton Wiske, *Yorks. N.R.* ii

Aptera (Apterygota) (Bristle-Tails and Spring-Tails), *Cornw.* i; *Notts.* i; *Oxon.* i; *and see* Collembola

Aquatics, *Beds.* ii

Arachnida (Acarina (Mites), Spiders, Scorpions, etc.), *Beds.* i; *Berks.* i; *Bucks.* i; *Cambs.* i; *Cornw.* i; *Cumb.* i; *Derb.* i; *Devon* i; *Dur.* i; *Essex* i; *Hants* i; *Herefs.* i; *Herts.* i; *Hunts.* i; *Kent* i; *Lancs.* i; *Leics.* i; *Norf.* i; *Notts.* i; *Oxon.* i; *Salop.* i; *Som.* i; *Staffs.* i*; *Suff.* i; *Surr.* i; *Suss.* i; *Warws.* i; *Worcs.* i; *Yorks.* i

Arborfield, *Berks.* iii

Arbury Priory, *Warws.* ii

Archaeological Gazetteer, *see* Gazetteer

Archaeology, *Mdx.* i

Archery, *Berks.* ii; *Mdx.* ii

Architecture: Domestic, *Surr.* ii; Domestic and Civil, *Suss.* ii; Ecclesiastical, *Surr.* ii; *Suss.* ii; Military, *Suss.* ii; Secular, *Warws.* vii

Ardeley, *Herts.* iii

Arden Priory, *Yorks.* iii

Ardingly, *Suss.* vii; St. Saviour's School, *Suss.* ii

Ardington, *Berks.* iv

Ardley, *Oxon.* vi

Areley Kings, *Worcs.* iv

Arkengarthdale, *Yorks. N.R.* i

Arlesey, *Beds.* ii

Arley, *Warws.* vi

Arley, Upper, *Worcs.* iii

Armaments, *see* Ordnance

Armathwaite Nunnery, *Cumb.* ii.

Arms, *see* Genealogy; Seals

Armscote (in Tredington), *Worcs.* iii

Armston Hospital, *Northants.* ii

Arreton, *Hants* v

Arrow, *Warws.* iii

Art: Anglo-Saxon, *Wilts.* ii; Early Christian, *Derb.* i; *Norf.* ii; *Northants.* ii; *Worcs.* ii; and Inscriptions, *Hants.* ii; *and see* Artists; Painting, Medieval

Arthington Priory, *Yorks.* iii

Arthingworth, Rokeby of, *see* Genealogy

Artington, *Surr.* iii

Artists, *Leics.* iii

Arundel, religious houses, *Suss.* ii*

Asbestos, *Lancs.* ii

Ascot, Royal (flat-racing), *Berks.* ii

Ash, *Surr.* iii

Ashampstead, *Berks.* iii

Ashbourne Grammar School, *Derb.* ii

Ashburnham, *Suss.* ix

Ashbury, *Berks.* iv

Ashby, Canons: Dryden of, *see* Genealogy; Priory *Northants.* iv

Ashby, Castle, *Northants.* iv

Ashby, Cold, Langham of, *see* Genealogy

Ashby, Mears, *Northants.* iv

Ashchurch, *Glos.* viii

Ashe, *Hants* iv

Ashendon, *Bucks.* iv; Hundred, *Bucks.* iv

Ashford, *Mdx.* ii

Ashley, *Hants* iv

Ashmansworth, *Hants* iv

Ashow, *Warws.* vi

Ashridge College, *Bucks.* i

Ashtead, *Surr.* iii

Ashton, Steeple, *Wilts.* viii

Ashton under Hill, *Glos.* viii

INDEX OF TITLES OF ARTICLES

Ashton-under-Lyne, *Lancs.* iv
Ashwell, *Herts.* iii
Ashwell, *Rut.* ii
Askham, Elwes of, *see* Genealogy
Aslackby Preceptory, *Lincs.* ii
Aspenden (Aspeden), with Wakeley, *Herts.* iv
Aspley Guise, *Beds.* iii
Assaying, *see* Coinage
Asthill, Horwell, and Whoberley, *Warws.* viii
Astley, *Warws.* vi; Collegiate Church, *Warws.* ii
Astley, *Worcs.* iv; Priory, *Worcs.* ii
Aston, *Herts.* iii
Aston, White Ladies, *Worcs.* iii
Aston Abbots, *Bucks.* iii
Aston Cantlow, *Warws.* iii
Aston Clinton, *Bucks.* ii
Aston Rowant, *Oxon.* viii
Aston Sanford, *Bucks.* iv
Aston Tirrold, *Berks.* iii
Aston Upthorpe (in Blewbury), *Berks.* iii
Astrop, Willes of, *see* Genealogy
Astwick, *Beds.* ii
Astwood, *Bucks.* iv
Athelney Abbey, *Som.* ii
Atherington, Ballivate of, *Suss.* ii
Atherstone, *Warws.* iv; Austin Friars, *Warws.* ii; School, *Warws.* ii
Atherstone-on-Stour, *Warws.* v
Athletics, *Bucks.* ii; *Essex* ii; *Glos.* ii; *Kent* i; *Lincs.* ii; *Mdx.* ii; *Northants.* ii; *Notts.* ii; *Suff.* ii; *Surr.* ii; *Suss.* ii; *Warws.* ii; *Worcs.* ii; *Yorks.* ii
Attleborough College, *Norf.* ii
Auckland St. Andrew College, *Dur.* ii
Aughton, *Lancs.* iii
Australians at Lord's, *Mdx.* ii
Austrey, *Warws.* iv
Avebury Priory, *Wilts.* iii
Aves (Birds), *Beds.* i; *Berks.* i; *Bucks.* i; *Cambs.* i; *Cornw.* i; *Cumb.* i; *Derb.* i; *Devon* i; *Dur.* i; *Essex* i; *Hants* i; *Herefs.* i; *Hunts.* i; *Kent* i; *Lancs.* i; *Leics.* i; *Norf.* i; *Northants.* i; *Notts.* i; *Oxon.* i; *Rut.* i; *Salop.* i; *Staffs.* i; *Som.* i; *Suff.* i; *Surr.* i; *Suss.* i; *Warws.* i; *Worcs.* i; *Yorks.* i
Avington, *Berks.* iv
Avington, *Hants* iv
Axholme Priory, *Lincs.* ii
Aylesbury: Borough, with Walton, *Bucks.* iii; Grammar School, *Bucks.* ii; Hundred, *Bucks.* ii; religious houses, *Bucks.* i*; Three Hundreds of (Risborough, Stone, Aylesbury), *Bucks.* ii
Aylesford, Carmelite Friars, *Kent* ii
Aylestone, *Leics.* iv
Aynho (Aynhoe): Cartwright of, *see* Genealogy; Hospital, *Northants.* ii
Ayot St. Lawrence (Great Ayot) and Ayot St. Peter, *Herts.* iii*
Aysgarth, *Yorks. N.R.* i
Ayston, *Rut.* ii
Ayton, Great, *Yorks. N.R.* ii

Bablake School, *Warws.* ii
Bacon and Associated Products, *Wilts.* iv
Baddesley, North, *Hants* iii
Baddesley Clinton and Baddesley Ensor, *Warws.* iv*
Baddesley (or Godsfield) Preceptory, *Hants* ii
Badger-Digging, *Som.* ii
Badsey, with Aldington, *Worcs.* ii
Badsworth Foxhounds, *see* Foxhounds
Bag-Hosiers, *see* Knitters
Bagby Hospital, *Yorks.* iii
Baginton, *Warws.* vi
Bagley Wood, *Berks.* iv
Bagnor (in Speen), *Berks.* iv
Bainton, *Northants.* ii
Baker Family, *see* Genealogy

Bakewell, Lady Manners School, *Derb.* ii
Balcombe, *Suss.* vii
Baldock, *Herts.* iii
Baldon, Marsh, *Oxon.* v
Baldon, Toot, *Oxon.* v
Baldslow Hundred, *Suss.* ix
Balsall, *Warws.* iv; Preceptory, *Warws.* ii
Balsall and Grafton Preceptory, *Warws.* ii
Banbury, religious houses, *Oxon.* ii*; *and see* Cakes; Cheese
Banking, *Leics.* iii
Banstead, *Surr.* iii
Barby, Isham of, *see* Genealogy
Barcheston, *Warws.* v; Tapestries, *Warws.* ii
Barcombe, *Suss.* vii; Hundred, *Suss.* vii
Bardney Abbey, *Lincs.* ii
Barford, *Warws.* v
Barford, Great, *Beds.* iii
Barford, Little, *Beds.* ii
Barford Hundred, *Beds.* iii
Barham, *Hunts.* iii
Barham, Crutched Friars, *Cambs.* ii
Barkham, *Berks.* iii
Barking, *Essex* v; Abbey, *Essex* ii
Barkway, *Herts.* iv
Barley, *Herts.* iv
Barlichway Hundred, *Warws.* iii
Barlings Abbey, *Lincs.* ii
Barlow Hunt, *see* Hunts
Barlynch Priory, *Som.* ii
Barnack, *Northants.* ii
Barnard Castle, religious houses, *Dur.* ii*
Barnes, *Surr.* iv
Barnet (Chipping Barnet), *Herts.* ii; Free Grammar School, *Herts.* ii
Barnet, East, *Herts.* ii
Barningham, *Yorks. N.R.* i
Barnwell All Saints, *Northants.* iii
Barnwell Priory, *Cambs.* ii
Barnwell St. Andrew, *Northants.* iii
Baronage, Feudal, *Devon* i; *Lancs.* i
Barrington, Great and Little, *Glos.* vi
Barrow, *see* Yeaveley and Barrow Preceptory
Barrow (in Cottesmore), *Rut.* ii
Barrow Gurney Priory, *Som.* ii
Barrow Monastery, *Lincs.* ii
Barrowden, *Rut.* ii
Barrows, *Wilts.* i (1); *and see* Earthworks
Barrymore, Lord, his Staghounds, *see* Staghounds
Barston, *Warws.* iv
Barton, *Yorks. N.R.* i
Barton, Earls, *Northants.* iv
Barton Hartshorn, *Bucks.* iv
Barton in the Clay, *Beds.* ii
Barton le Street, *Yorks. N.R.* i
Barton-on-the-Heath, *Warws.* v
Barton Oratory, *Hants* ii
Barton Seagrave, *Northants.* iii
Barton Stacey, *Hants* iv; Hundred, *Hants* iv
Barwell, Isham of, *see* Genealogy
Barytes (Mining of), *Derb.* ii; *Dur.* ii
Basedale Priory, *Yorks.* iii; *Yorks. N.R.* ii
Basildon, *Berks.* iii; Fane of, *see* Genealogy
Basing (Old Basing), *Hants* iv
Basingstoke, *Hants* iv; Hundred, *Hants* iv; religious houses, *Hants* ii*
Basket, Wicker, Industry, *see* Pavenham
Baskets and Sieves, Making of, *Essex* ii
Basset Hounds, *Berks.* ii
Baswich (Berkswich), *Staffs.* v
Bath: religious houses, *Som.* ii*; schools, *Som.* ii*
Bath and County Harriers, *see* Harriers
Bathel Hospital, *Dur.* ii
Batrachia (Batrachians), *see* Reptiles
Battersea, with Penge, *Surr.* iv
Battersea Enamels, *see* Enamels

Battisford Preceptory, *Suff.* ii
Battle, *Suss.* ix; Abbey, *Suss.* ii, ix; Hospital, *Suss.* ii; Hundred, *Suss.* ix
Battlesden, *Beds.* iii
Baughurst, *Hants* iv
Bawtry Hospital, *Notts.* ii
Baxterley, *Warws.* iv
Baxterwood Priory, *Dur.* ii
Baybridge (in Owslebury), *Hants* iii
Bayford, *Herts.* iii
Bayfordbury, Baker of, *see* Genealogy
Bayham Abbey, *Suss.* ii
Bayton, *Worcs.* iv
Beachampton, *Bucks.* iv
Beaconsfield, *Bucks.* iii
Beagles, *Bucks.* ii; *Essex* ii; *Hants* v; *Lancs.* ii; *Oxon.* ii; *Suss.* ii; *Warws.* ii; *Yorks.* ii; *and see* Harriers
Beaker Period, *Mdx.* i
Bearley, *Warws.* iii
Beauchief Abbey, *Derb.* ii
Beaudesert, *Warws.* iii
Beaulieu: Abbey, *Hants* ii, iv; Liberty, *Hants* iv
Beaulieu Priory, *Beds.* i
Beaumont Chase, *Rut.* ii
Beauvale Priory, *Notts.* ii
Beauworth (in Cheriton), *Hants* iii
Beccles Hospital, *Suff.* ii
Becconsall (in Hesketh), *Lancs.* vi
Beck Hospital, *Norf.* ii
Beckford, *Glos.* viii; Priory, *Glos.* ii
Beckley, *Oxon.* v
Beckley, *Suss.* ix
Becontree Hundred, *Essex* v
Bedale, *Yorks. N.R.* i; Foxhounds, *see* Foxhounds
Beddington, *Surr.* iv
Bedfont, East, with Hatton, *Mdx.* ii
Bedford: Borough, *Beds.* iii; religious houses, *Beds.* i*; schools, *Beds.* ii*
Bedhampton, *Hants* iii
Bedminster, Hospital of St. Katherine, *Som.* ii
Bednall (with Acton Trussell), *Staffs.* v
Bedworth, *Warws.* vi
Bedwyn, Great, Hospital of St. John, *Wilts.* iii
Beechwood, Sebright of, *see* Genealogy
Beedon, *Berks.* iv
Beeleigh Abbey, *see* Maldon
Beenham, *Berks.* iii
Beer, *see* Brewing
Bees (Hymenoptera Aculeata), *see* Hymenoptera
Beeston Priory, *Norf.* ii
Beetles, *see* Coleoptera
Begar Alien Priory, *see* Richmond
Belbroughton, *Worcs.* iii
Belgrave, *Leics.* iv
Bell Founding (Bells, Bell Founders, Bell Foundries), *Berks.* i; *Bucks.* ii; *Essex* ii; *Glos.* ii; *Herts.* iv; *Kent* iii; *Leics.* iii; *Mdx.* ii; *Northants.* ii; *Notts.* ii; *Oxon.* ii; *Som.* ii; *Suss.* ii; *Wilts.* iv; *Yorks.* ii
Belton, *Rut.* ii
Belvoir: Hunt, *see* Hunts; Priory, *Lincs.* ii
Benefield, *Northants.* iii
Bengeo, *Herts.* iii
Bengeworth, *Worcs.* ii
Benington, *Herts.* iii
Bennington, Long, Priory, *Lincs.* ii
Bentley, *Warws.* iv
Bentley Liberty and Parish, *Hants* iv
Bentley Priory, *Mdx.* i
Bentworth, *Hants* iv
Beoley, *Worcs.* iv
Bepton, *Suss.* iv
Berden Priory, *Essex* ii
Berkeley, Hospital at Longbridge by, *Glos.* ii
Berkeley Hounds, Old, *see* Hounds
Berkeley Hunt, *see* Hunts
Berkeley Hunt, Old, *see* Hunts

Berkhampstead, Great (Berkhampstead St. Peter), *Herts.* ii; religious houses, *Herts.* iv*; School, *Herts.* ii; *and see* Parliament, List of Members of
Berkhampstead, Little, *Herts.* iii
Berkhampstead St. Mary, *see* Northchurch
Berkhampstead St. Peter, *see* Berkhampstead, Great
Berks, South, Hunt, *see* Hunts
Berks Farmers' Staghounds, *see* Staghounds
Berkshire Hunt, Old, *see* Hunts
Berkshire Vale Harriers, *see* Harriers
Berkswell, *Warws.* iv
Berkswich, *see* Baswich
Bermondsey, *Surr.* iv; Abbey, *Surr.* ii
Bermondspit Hundred, *Hants* iii
Berrington, *Salop.* viii
Berrow, *Worcs.* iii
Bersted, *Suss.* iv
Besford, *Worcs.* iv
Bessels Leigh, *Berks.* iv
Betchworth, *Surr.* iii
Beverley, religious houses, *Yorks.* iii*
Bewcastle, Hospital of Lennh', *Cumb.* ii
Bewdley: Borough (in Ribbesford), *Worcs.* iv; Grammar School, *Worcs.* iv
Bexhill, *Suss.* ix; Hundred, *Suss.* ix
Beynhurst Hundred, *Berks.* iii
Bibliography, *Essex Bibl.*
Bicester: Market-town, *Oxon.* vi; religious houses, *Oxon.* ii*
Bicester and Warden Hill Hunt, *see* Hunts
Bickenhill, *Warws.* iv
Bicknacre (or Woodham Ferrers) Priory, *Essex* ii
Biddenham, *Beds.* iii
Biddlesden, *Bucks.* iv; Abbey, *Bucks.* i
Bidford, *Warws.* iii
Bidlington Hospital, *Suss.* ii
Bierton, with Broughton, *Bucks.* ii
Biggleswade, with Stratton and Holme, *Beds.* ii; Free School, *Beds.* ii; Hundred, *Beds.* ii
Bighton, *Hants* iii
Billesdon, *Leics.* v
Billesley, *Warws.* iii
Billeswick, Hospital of St. Mark, called Gaunt's Hospital, *Glos.* ii
Billing, Great, *Northants.* iv; Elwes (Cary-Elwes) of, *see* Genealogy
Billing, Little, *Northants.* iv
Billingham, *Dur.* iii
Billington (in Leighton Buzzard), *Beds.* iii
Bilsdale Foxhounds, *see* Foxhounds
Bilsington Priory, *Kent* ii
Bilton, *Warws.* vi
Binderton, *Suss.* iv
Bindon Abbey, *Dors.* ii
Binfield, *Berks.* iii
Binham Priory, *Norf.* ii
Binley, *Warws.* vi
Binstead, *Hants* v
Binsted, *Hants* ii
Binton, *Warws.* iii
Birdforth Wapentake, *Yorks. N.R.* ii
Birdham, *Suss.* iv
Birdingbury, *Warws.* vi
Birds, *see* Aves
Birkby, *Yorks. N.R.* i
Birlingham, *Worcs.* iv
Birmingham: City, *Warws.* vii; Hospital of St. Thomas, *Warws.* ii; King Edward VI's Schools, *Warws.* ii, vii; Local Cricket, *Warws.* ii; University, *Warws.* ii; *and see* Gun Trade
Birstall Priory, *Yorks.* iii
Birtsmorton, *Worcs.* iv
Bisbrooke, *Rut.* ii
Biscott (in Luton), *Beds.* ii
Biscuit-Making, *Berks.* i
Bisham, *Berks.* iii; Priory, *Berks.* ii
Bishampton, *Worcs.* iii

Bishop Compton's Census, *see* Ongar Hundred
Bishop Fox's Girls' School, *Som.* ii
Bishopstoke, *Hants* iii
Bishopstrow, *Wilts.* viii
Bishopton, *Dur.* iii
Bisley, *Surr.* iii
Bispham, *Lancs.* vii; Free School, *Lancs.* ii
Blackborough Priory, *Norf.* ii
Blackburn, *Lancs.* vi; Grammar School, *Lancs.* ii; Hundred, *Lancs.* vi–vii; Stonyhurst College, *Lancs.* ii
Blackenhurst Hundred, *Worcs.* ii
Blackheath Hundred, *Surr.* iii
Blackmoor, 'Priory Hermitage', *Dors.* ii
Blackmore Priory, *Essex* ii
Blackmore Vale Hounds, *see* Hounds
Blackrod School, *Lancs.* ii
Blackwell (in Tredington), *Worcs.* iii
Blakeney, Carmelite Friars, *Norf.* ii
Blakenham Priory, *Suff.* ii
Blandford, Long, Hospital, *Dors.* ii
Blanket-Making, *Oxon.* ii
Blankney Hunt, *see* Hunts
Blaston, *Leics.* v
Blatchington, West, *Suss.* vii
Bleaching and Dyeing, *Notts.* ii; Bleaching, Dyeing, Calico Printing, *Surr.* ii; Bleaching, Finishing, and Dyeing, *Lancs.* ii
Blechingley, *Surr.* iv
Bledington, *Glos.* iv
Bledlow, with Bledlow Ridge, *Bucks.* ii
Bledlow Ridge (in Bledlow), *Bucks.* ii
Blendworth, *Hants* iii
Bletchingdon, *Oxon.* vi
Bletchley, with Fenny Stratford and Water Eaton, *Bucks.* iv
Bletsoe, *Beds.* iii
Blewbury, with Upton and Aston Upthorpe, *Berks.* iii
Blisworth, *Northants.* iv; Wake of, *see* Genealogy
Blithbury Priory, *Staffs.* iii
Blockley, *Worcs.* iii
Bloodhounds: Earl Carrington's, *Bucks.* ii; Ranston, *Dors.* ii
Bloxham, *Oxon.* ix; Hundred, *Oxon.* ix
Blunham, with Moggerhanger and Chalton, *Beds.* iii
Bluntisham cum Earith, *Hunts.* ii
Blymhill, *Staffs.* iv
Blyth, religious houses, *Notts.* ii*
Blythburgh Priory, *Suff.* ii
Boarhunt [village], *Hants* iii
Boarstall, *Bucks.* iv
Boat-Building, *Berks.* i; *Oxon.* ii; *and see* Shipbuilding
Bobbingworth, *Essex* iv
Bocking Hospital, *Essex* ii
Bockleton, *Worcs.* iv
Boddington, *Glos.* viii
Bodiam, *Suss.* ix
Bognor Regis, *Suss.* iv
Boldhurst, *Beds.* iii
Boldon Book, Introduction, Text, and Index, *Dur.* i*
Boldre, *Hants* iv
Bolehall and Glascote, *Warws.* iv
Bolney, *Suss.* vii
Bolton-le-Moors, *Lancs.* v; schools, *Lancs.* ii*
Bolton-le-Sands, *Lancs.* viii; School, *Lancs.* ii
Bolton Priory, *Yorks.* iii
Bolton-upon-Swale, *Yorks. N.R.* i
Bonby Priory, *Lincs.* ii
Bonchurch, *Hants* v
Bonnets (Bonnet Industry), *see* Straw
Bookbinding, *Mdx.* ii; *Oxon.* ii
Bookham, Great and Little, *Surr.* iii
Boothby Pagnell Hospital, *Lincs.* ii
Boots and Shoes (Manufacture of), *Essex* ii; *Northants.* ii; *and see* Footwear
Bordesley Abbey, *Worcs.* ii
Borough Fen, *Northants.* ii

Boroughbridge Hospital, *Yorks.* iii
Bosham, *Suss.* iv; College, *Suss.* ii; Hundred, *Suss.* iv
Bosmere Hundred, *Hants* iii
Bossall, *Yorks. N.R.* ii
Bossington, *Hants* iv
Boston, religious houses, *Lincs.* ii*
Bosworth, Husbands, *Leics.* v
Botanical Districts (Notes on Botanical Districts, Botanical Divisions), *Cornw.* i; *Cumb.* i; *Devon* i; *Herefs.* i; *Herts.* i; *Leics.* i; *Northants.* i; *Notts.* i; *Salop.* i; *Som.* i; *Staffs.* i; *Suff.* i; *Surr.* i; *Yorks.* i*
Botany, *Beds.* i; *Berks.* i; *Bucks.* i; *Cambs.* i; *Cornw.* i; *Cumb.* i; *Derb.* i; *Devon* i; *Dur.* i; *Essex* i; *Hants* i; *Herefs.* i; *Herts.* i; *Hunts.* i; *Kent* i; *Lancs.* i; *Leics.* i; *Norf.* i; *Northants.* i; *Notts.* i; *Oxon.* i; *Rut.* i; *Salop.* i; *Som.* i; *Staffs.* i; *Suff.* i; *Surr.* i; *Suss.* i; *Warws.* i; *Worcs.* i; *Yorks.* i; Summary of Orders, *Cornw.* i; *Cumb.* i; *Devon* i; *Som.* i; *Staffs.* i
Botley, *Hants* iii
Botolphbridge (in Orton Longueville), *Hunts.* iii
Botteslow, *Staffs.* viii
Boughton, *Northants.* iv
Boughton under Blean Hospital, *Kent* ii
Bountisborough Hundred, *Hants* iv
Bourne, Wake of, *see* Genealogy
Bourne Abbey, *Lincs.* ii
Bournemouth (in Westover Liberty), *Hants* v
Bourton (in Buckingham), *Bucks.* iii
Bourton-on-Dunsmore, *Warws.* vi
Bourton-on-the-Hill, *Glos.* vi
Bourton-on-the-Water, *Glos.* vi
Boveney, Lower (in Burnham), *Bucks.* iii
Bovingdean (in Hemel Hempstead), *Herts.* ii
Bow, *see* Stratford at Bow; Porcelain, *see* Porcelain
Bowden, Great, *Leics.* v
Bowes, *Yorks. N.R.* i
Bowls [sport], *Lancs.* ii
Box and Stockbridge Hundred, *Suss.* iv
Boxford, with Westbrook, *Berks.* iv
Boxgrove, *Suss.* iv; Priory, *Suss.* ii
Boxing (Pugilism), *Berks.* iii; *Herts.* i; *Mdx.* ii
Boxley Abbey, *Kent* ii
Bozeat, *Northants.* iv
Braceford, Hospital of St. Helen, *Yorks.* iii
Brackley, religious houses, *Northants.* ii*; *and see* Parliament, List of Members of
Bradebusk Hospital, *Notts.* ii
Bradenham, *Bucks.* iii
Bradenstoke Priory, *Wilts.* iii
Bradfield, *Berks.* iii; College, *Berks.* ii, (cricket), *Berks.* ii, (football), *Berks.* ii
Bradford Hundred, *Wilts.* vii
Bradford-on-Avon, *Wilts.* vii; Hospital of St. Margaret, *Wilts.* iii
Brading, *Hants* v
Bradley, *Hants* iv
Bradley, *Staffs.* iv
Bradley (in Fladbury), *Worcs.* iii
Bradley, Maiden, Priory, *Wilts.* iii
Bradley, North, *Wilts.* viii
Bradley Priory, *Leics.* ii
Bradsole (or St. Radegund's) Abbey, *Kent* ii
Bradwell, *Bucks.* iv; Priory, *Bucks.* i
Brafferton, *Yorks. N.R.* ii
Brafield-on-the-Green, *Northants.* iv
Brailes, *Warws.* v
Braintree Hospital, *Essex* ii
Brambles, *see* Rubi
Bramcote, Turner of, *see* Genealogy
Bramdean, *Hants* iii
Bramfield, *Herts.* ii
Bramham Moor Foxhounds, *see* Foxhounds
Bramley, *Hants* iv
Bramley, *Surr.* iii
Brampton, *Hunts.* iii
Bramshaw, *Hants* iv

Bramshott, *Hants* ii
Brand Family, *see* Genealogy
Brandsby, with Stearsby, *Yorks. N.R.* ii
Bransford (in Leigh), *Worcs.* iv
Brass, *see* Copper; Brass-Founding, *Essex* ii
Braughing, *Herts.* iii; Hundred, *Herts.* iii
Braunston, *Rut.* ii
Braunstone, *Leics.* iv
Bray: with Maidenhead Borough, *Berks.* iii; Hundred, *Berks.* iii
Braydon Forest, *Wilts.* iv
Brayfield, Cold, *Bucks.* iv
Breadsall Priory, *Derb.* ii
Breamore, *Hants* iv; Liberty, *Hants* iv; Priory, *Hants* ii
Brede, *Suss.* ix
Bredgar College, *Kent* ii
Bredicot, *Worcs.* iii
Bredon, with Cutsdean and Norton by Bredon, *Worcs.* iii
Breeches, *see* Leather
Breedon Priory, *Leics.* ii
Brentford, Hospital of the Virgin Mary and the Nine Orders of Holy Angels, *Mdx.* i
Bretford Hospital, *Warws.* ii
Bretforton, *Worcs.* ii
Bretton, Monk, Priory, *Yorks.* iii
Brewing (Beer), *Berks.* i; *Dors.* ii; *Kent* iii; *Mdx.* ii; *Som.* ii; *Staffs.* ii; *Surr.* ii; *Suss.* ii; *Warws.* ii; Brewing and Malting, *Essex* ii; *Hants* v; *Notts.* ii; *Oxon.* ii; Brewing, Milling, and Malting, *Glos.* ii
Brewood, *Staffs.* v; Forest, *Staffs.* ii; Priory (Black Ladies), *Staffs.* iii
Bricett Priory, *Suff.* ii
Brickendon Liberty (in Hertford), *Herts.* iii
Brickhill, Bow, *Bucks.* iv
Brickhill, Great and Little, *Bucks.* iv*
Bricklehampton (in Pershore St. Andrew), *Worcs.* iv
Brick-Making, *Hants* v; *Kent* iii; *Suss.* ii; Brick-Making and Tile-Making (Brick and Tile Manufacture, Bricks and Tiles), *Essex* ii; *Oxon.* ii; *Salop.* i; *Staffs.* ii; Bricks, Building Materials, Glass, and Pottery, *Glos.* ii; Bricks, Tiles, and Pottery, *Bucks.* ii; *Herts.* iv
Bridgend, Priory of St. Saviour, *see* Horbling
Bridges, Principal Road, *Leics.* iii
Bridgwater: Free Grammar School, *Som.* ii; religious houses, *Som.* ii*
Bridlington, religious houses, *Yorks.* iii*
Bridport, religious houses, *Dors.* ii*
Brigg, Elwes (Cary-Elwes) of, *see* Genealogy
Brighstone (Brixton), *Hants* v
Brightling, *Suss.* ix
Brighton: Borough, *Suss.* vii; schools, *Suss.* ii*
Brightwalton, *Berks.* iv
Brightwell, *Berks.* iii
Brignall, *Yorks. N.R.* i
Brill, *Bucks.* iv
Brimpsfield Priory, *Glos.* ii
Brindle, *Lancs.* vi
Bringhurst, *Leics.* v
Brington, *Hunts.* iii
Brinklow, *Warws.* vi
Bristle-Tails, *see* Aptera
Bristol, religious houses, *Glos.* ii*
British Coins, Ancient, *see* Coins
Britwell Salome, *Oxon.* viii
Brixton, *see* Brighstone
Brixton Hundred, *Surr.* iv
Brixworth, *Northants.* iv
Broadfield, *Herts.* iii
Broadholme Priory, *Notts.* ii
Broadwas, *Worcs.* iii
Broadwater Hundred, *Herts.* iii
Broadway, *Worcs.* iv
Broadwell, *Glos.* vi
Brockenhurst, *Hants* iv
Brockhall, Thornton of, *see* Genealogy
Brocklesby Hunt, *see* Hunts

Bromehill Priory, *Norf.* ii
Bromhall Priory, *Berks.* ii
Bromham, *Beds.* iii
Bromham, *Wilts.* vii
Bromholm Priory, *Norf.* ii
Brompton, *Yorks. N.R.* ii
Brompton, Patrick, *Yorks. N.R.* i
Brompton Bridge, Hospital of St. Giles by, *Yorks.* iii
Bromsgrove, *Worcs.* iii; Grammar School, *Worcs.* iv
Bromwich, Castle, *Warws.* iv
Bronze Age, *Berks.* i; *Mdx.* i; *Oxon.* i; *Suff.* i; *and see* Antiquities
Brook, *Hants* v
Brook Street Hospital, *see* Weald, South
Brooke, *Rut.* ii; Priory, *Rut.* i
Broom, *Worcs.* iii
Broomhill, *Suss.* ix
Broomy Lodge (in Fordingbridge), *Hants* iv
Brotton, *Yorks. N.R.* ii
Broughton, *Bucks.* iv
Broughton, *Hunts.* ii
Broughton, *Northants.* iv
Broughton, *Oxon.* ix
Broughton, Hospital of St. Mary Magdalene, *Yorks.* iii
Broughton (in Bierton), *Bucks.* ii
Broughton, with Frenchmoor, *Hants* iv
Broughton Gifford, *Wilts.* vii
Broughton Hackett, *Worcs.* iv
Broxbourne, with Hoddesdon, *Herts.* iii
Bruer, Temple, Preceptory, *Lincs.* ii
Bruern Abbey, *Oxon.* ii
Bruisyard Abbey, *Suff.* ii
Brush-Making, *Essex* ii
Bruton: religious houses, *Som.* ii*; schools, *Som.* ii*
Bubbenhall, *Warws.* vi
Buckden, *Hunts.* ii
Buckenham, Old, Priory, *Norf.* ii
Buckholt (in West Tytherley), *Hants* iv
Buckhounds, Royal, *Berks.* ii; *Bucks.* ii; *Northants.* ii
Buckingham: Borough, with Bourton, and Gawcott with Lenborough, *Bucks.* iii; Hundred, *Bucks.* iv; religious houses, *Bucks.* i*; Royal Latin School, *Bucks.* ii
Buckingham College, *Cambs.* ii
Buckland, *Berks.* iv
Buckland, *Bucks.* ii
Buckland, *Herts.* iv
Buckland, *Surr.* iii
Buckland Hospital, *see* Dover
Bucklebury, *Berks.* iii
Buckles, *Warws.* ii
Bucknell, *Oxon.* vi
Bucks Farmers' Staghounds, *see* Staghounds
Buckworth, *Hunts.* iii
Budbrooke, *Warws.* iii
Buddlesgate Hundred, *Hants* iii
Bugs (Hemiptera Heteroptera), *see* Hemiptera
Building Materials, Glass, Pottery, and Bricks, *Glos.* ii
Bulkington, *Warws.* vi
Bull-Baiting, *Berks.* ii; *Herts.* i; *Warws.* ii
Bullingdon Hundred, *Oxon.* v; *and see* Tax Assessments
Bullington, *Hants* iv
Bullington Priory, *Lincs.* ii
Bulmer: with Henderskelfe, *Yorks. N.R.* ii; Wapentake, *Yorks. N.R.* ii
Bulstrode Preceptory, *Bucks.* i
Bungay Priory, *Suff.* ii
Buntingford Grammar School, *Herts.* ii
Burcot, *Oxon.* vii
Burford, Hospital of St. John the Evangelist, *Oxon.* ii
Burgh Hall, Knightley of, *see* Genealogy
Burghclere, *Hants* iv
Burghfield, *Berks.* iii
Burghley, Lord, *see* Genealogy, Cecil
Burials and Roads [Romano-British], *Lond.* i
Buriton, *Hants* iii
Burley, *Rut.* ii

Burmington, *Warws.* v
Burneston, *Yorks. N.R.* i
Burnham: with Lower Boveney, *Bucks.* iii; Abbey, *Bucks.* i; Hundred, *Bucks.* ii
Burnham Norton, Carmelite Friars, *Norf.* ii
Burnley School, *Lancs.* ii
Burrough on the Hill, *Leics.* v
Burscough Priory, *Lancs.* ii
Bursledon, *Hants* iii
Burslem, *Staffs.* viii
Burstow, *Surr.* iii
Burstow Hunt, *see* Hunts
Burtle Moor Priory, *Som.* ii
Burton Hastings, *Warws.* vi
Burton Hunt, *see* Hunts
Burton-in-Kendal (part of), *Lancs.* viii
Burton Latimer, *Northants.* iii
Burton Lazars Hospital, *Leics.* ii
Burton Overy, *Leics.* v
Burton-upon-Trent, religious houses, *Staffs.* iii*
Burwash, *Suss.* ix
Burwell Priory, *Lincs.* ii
Bury, *Lancs.* v; Grammar School, *Lancs.* ii
Bury cum Hepmangrove, *Hunts.* ii
Bury St. Edmunds: religious houses, *Suff.* ii*; School, *Suff.* ii
Buscot, *Berks.* iv
Bushey, *Herts.* i
Bushley, *Worcs.* iv
Bushmead Priory, *Beds.* i
Butley Priory, *Suff.* ii
Butterflies (Lepidoptera Rhopalocera), *see* Lepidoptera
Buttinghill Hundred, *Suss.* vii
Buttons [manufacture of], *Warws.* ii
Buxted Hospital, *Suss.* ii
Buxton Grammar School, *Derb.* ii
Byfield, Knightley of, *see* Genealogy
Byfleet, *Surr.* iii
Bygrave, *Herts.* iii
Byland, Old, *Yorks. N.R.* ii
Byland Abbey, *Yorks.* iii; *Yorks. N.R.* ii
Bythorn, *Hunts.* iii

Cabinet-Making and Wood-Carving, *Mdx.* ii
Cables, Chain, *see* Chains
Cadbury, North, College, *Som.* ii
Caddington, *Beds.* ii
Caddington, *Herts.* ii
Caddis-flies, *see* Trichoptera
Cakes, Banbury, *Oxon.* ii
Calbourne, *Hants* v
Calc Spar, *see* Fluor Spar
Caldbeck Hospital House, *Cumb.* ii
Caldecote, *Herts.* iii
Caldecote, *Hunts.* iii
Caldecote, *Warws.* iv
Caldecott, *Rut.* ii
Caldecott (in Chelveston), *Northants.* iv
Calder Abbey, *Cumb.* ii
Caldwell Priory, *Beds.* i
Calico-Printing, *Lancs.* ii; Calico-Printing and Silk-Printing, *Essex* ii; Calico-Printing, Dyeing, Bleaching, *Surr.* ii
Calke Cell, *see* Repton Priory
Calne, Hospital of St. John and St. Anthony, *Wilts.* iii
Caludon (with Wyken), *Warws.* viii
Calvert Family, *see* Genealogy
Calverton, *Bucks.* iv
Calwich Priory, *Staffs.* iii
Camberwell, *Surr.* iv
Cambridge: Addenbrooke's Hospital, *Cambs.* iii; City, *Cambs.* iii; Distinguished Natives and Residents, *Cambs.* iii; religious houses, *Cambs.* ii*; schools, *Cambs.* ii*; *and see* Tax Assessments, Hearth
Cambridge University, *Cambs.* iii*; Archives, *Cambs.* iii; Botanic Garden, *Cambs.* iii; Chancellors, List of,

Cambs. iii; Colleges and Halls, *Cambs.* iii*; Fitzwilliam Museum, *Cambs.* iii; Industries Derived from, *Cambs.* ii; Press, *Cambs.* iii; Schools and University Library, *Cambs.* iii
Cammeringham Priory, *Lincs.* ii
Camp Ball, *Suff.* ii
Camps [Romano-British], *see* Roads
Campsey Priory, *Suff.* ii
Campton cum Shefford and Chicksands, *Beds.* ii
Canal Industries, *see* River and Canal Industries
Canals, *Leics.* iii; *Staffs.* ii; *Wilts.* iv
Candle-Making, *Essex* ii; *and see* Soap
Candover, Brown, *Hants* iv
Candover, Chilton, *Hants* iv
Candover, Preston, *Hants* iii
Cannings, Bishop's, *Wilts.* vii
Cannington Priory, *Som.* ii
Cannock, *Staffs.* v; Forest, *Staffs.* ii; Hospital of St. Mary, *Staffs.* iii
Canterbury, Hospital of St. James by, *Kent* ii; religious houses, *Kent* ii*
Cantilupe College, *Lincs.* ii
Canwell Priory, *Staffs.* iii
Capel, *Surr.* iii
Capell Family, *see* Genealogy
Caps, *Worcs.* ii; Caps and Hats, *Warws.* ii
Caraway Cultivation, *see* Coriander
Carbrooke Preceptory, *Norf.* ii
Cardeston (in Alderbury), *Salop.* viii
Cardington, with Eastcotts, *Beds.* iii
Card-Making, *Som.* ii
Carisbrooke, *Hants* v; Priory, *Hants* ii
Carlisle, religious houses, *Cumb.* ii*; *and see* Friars, Four Houses of
Carlton, *Beds.* iii
Carlton, *Yorks. N.R.* ii
Carlton, Palmer of, *see* Genealogy
Carlton Curlieu, *Leics.* v
Carpets and Rugs, *Worcs.* ii
Carrington, Earl, his Bloodhounds, *see* Bloodhounds
Carrow Priory, *Norf.* ii
Carshalton, *Surr.* iv
Cartmel, *Lancs.* viii; Grammar School, *Lancs.* ii; Priory, *Lancs.* ii, viii
Cartwright Family, *see* Genealogy
Cary-Elwes Family, *see* Genealogy, Elwes
Cashio Hundred, *Herts.* ii
Casterton, Great, *Rut.* ii; Hospital of St. Margaret, *Rut.* i
Casterton, Little, *Rut.* ii
Castle Church, *Staffs.* v
Castlemorton, *Worcs.* iv
Castor, *Northants.* ii
Caterham, *Surr.* iv
Catesby Priory, *Northants.* ii
Catherington, *Hants* iii
Catley Priory, *Lincs.* ii
Catmore, *Berks.* iv
Catsfield, *Suss.* ix
Catterick, *Yorks. N.R.* i
Cattistock Hounds, *see* Hounds
Catworth, *Hunts.* iii
Caversfield, *Bucks.* iv
Cayton, *Yorks. N.R.* ii
Cecil Family, *see* Genealogy
Celtic and Romano-British Hertfordshire, *Herts.* i v
Cement: Portland, *Essex* ii; *Kent* iii; Roman, *Essex* ii
Census, Bishop Compton's, *see* Ongar Hundred
Centipedes, *see* Myriapoda
Cerne Abbey, *Dors.* ii
Chaceley, *Worcs.* iv
Chaddesley Corbett, *Worcs.* iii
Chaddleworth, with Woolley, *Berks.* iv
Chadshunt, *Warws.* v
Chailey, *Suss.* vii
Chain-Making, *Salop.* i; Chains and Chain Cables, *Staffs.* ii; *and see* Nails

INDEX OF TITLES OF ARTICLES

Chair-Making (Making of Wooden Chairs), *Essex* ii; *Oxon.* ii; *and see* Wooden Ware
Chalcombe Priory, *Northants.* ii
Chaldon, *Surr.* iv
Chale, *Hants* v
Chalfield, Great, *Wilts.* vii
Chalfont St. Giles and Chalfont St. Peter, *Bucks.* iii*
Chalgrave, with Tebworth and Wingfield, *Beds.* iii
Chalk (Chalk-Quarrying), *Essex* ii; *Kent* iii
Challow, East and West (in Letcombe Regis), *Berks.* iv
Chalton (in Blunham), *Beds.* iii
Chalton, with Idsworth, *Hants* iii
Chalvey (in Upton), *Bucks.* iii
Characeae (Stoneworts), *Herts.* i; *Kent* i; *Leics.* i; *Norf.* i; *Suff.* i; *Surr.* i; *and see* Cryptogams
Charcoal-Burning, *Essex* ii
Chard Grammar School, *Som.* ii
Charford, North, with South Charford, *Hants* iv
Charford, South (in North Charford), *Hants* iv
Charity Schools, *see* Schools
Charlecote, *Warws.* v
Charley Priory, *Leics.* ii
Charlton (in Cropthorne), *Worcs.* iii
Charlton Hundred, *Berks.* iii
Charlton Hunt, *see* Hunts
Charlton-on-Otmoor, *Oxon.* vi
Charlton Priory, *Wilts.* iii
Charlwood, *Surr.* iii
Charndon (in Twyford), *Bucks.* iv
Charwelton, Knightley of, *see* Genealogy
Chatham Hospital, *Kent* ii
Chatteris, *Cambs.* iv; Abbey, *Cambs.* ii
Chawton, *Hants* ii
Cheam, *Surr.* iv
Chearsley, *Bucks.* iv
Cheddington, *Bucks.* iii
Cheese: Banbury, *Oxon.* ii; Cheese-Making, *Essex* ii
Chellington, *Beds.* iii
Chelmsford, Black Friars, *Essex* ii
Chelsea Porcelain, *see* Porcelain
Chelsham, *Surr.* iii
Chelveston-cum-Caldecott, *Northants.* iv
Chemicals (Manufacture, Chemical Industries, Chemical Works), *Dur.* ii; *Essex* ii; *Lancs.* ii; *Warws.* ii; *and see* Soap
Chenies, *Bucks.* iii
Cherington, *Warws.* v
Cheriton, with Beauworth, *Hants* iii
Chert, *Derb.* ii
Chertsey, *Surr.* iii; Abbey, *Surr.* ii
Chesham, *Bucks.* iii
Chesham Bois, *Bucks.* iii
Cheshunt St. Mary, *Herts.* iii; College, *Herts.* ii; religious houses, *Herts.* iv*
Cheslyn Hay, *Staffs.* v
Chessington, *Surr.* iii
Chester-le-Street College, *Dur.* ii
Chester-on-the-Water (in Irchester), *Northants.* iv
Chesterfield: Grammar School, *Derb.* ii; Hospital of St. Leonard, *Derb.* ii
Chesterton, *Hunts.* iii
Chesterton, *Oxon.* vi
Chesterton, *Warws.* v
Chetwode, *Bucks.* iv; Priory, *Bucks.* i
Cheveley School, *Cambs.* ii
Chich, *see* St. Osyth
Chicheley, *Bucks.* iv; Maunsell of, *see* Genealogy
Chichester: Cathedral, *Suss.* ii–iii; City, *Suss.* iii; Port, *Suss.* iii; Prebendal School, *Suss.* ii; Rape, *Suss.* iv; religious houses, *Suss.* ii*; [Romano-British], *Suss.* iii
Chicksands (in Campton), *Beds.* ii; Priory, *Beds.* i–ii
Chidden (in Hambledon), *Hants* iii
Chiddingfold, *Surr.* iii
Chidham, *Suss.* iv
Chieveley, with Leckhampstead and Winterbourne, *Berks.* iv

Chigwell, *Essex* iv
Chilbolton, *Hants* iii
Chilcomb, *Hants* iii
Childrey, *Berks.* iv; Hospital, *Berks.* ii; School, *Berks.* ii
Childwall, *Lancs.* iii
Chilland (in Martyr Worthy), *Hants* iii
Chiltern, Three Hundreds of, *Bucks.* iii
Chiltington, East, *Suss.* vii
Chilton, *Berks.* iv
Chilton, *Bucks.* iv
Chilvers Coton, *Warws.* iv
Chilworth, *Hants* iii
Chilworth, *see* St. Martha's
China (China-Manufacturing), *Derb.* ii; *Essex* ii; *Worcs.* ii; Lowestoft, *Suff.* ii; *and see* Porcelain; Pottery
China Clay, *Cornw.* i
Chingford, *Essex* v
Chinnor, *Oxon.* viii
Chipley Priory, *Suff.* ii
Chippenham and Melksham Forests, *Wilts.* iv
Chippenham Preceptory, *Cambs.* ii
Chipping, *Lancs.* vii
Chippinghurst, with Denton, *Oxon.* v
Chipstead, *Surr.* iii
Chiseldon, *Wilts.* ix
Chislehampton, *Oxon* vii.
Chithurst, *Suss.* iv
Chobham, *Surr.* iii
Chocolate, *see* Sugar
Cholesbury, *Bucks.* iii
Cholsey, *Berks.* iii
Chorley, *Lancs.* vi; Grammar School, *Lancs.* ii
Christchurch, *Hants* v; Hundred, *Hants* v; Priory Church, *Hants* v
Christchurch (in Southwark Borough), *Surr.* iv
Christian Art, Early, *see* Art
Christian Monuments, Early, *see* Monuments
Chrysids (Hymenoptera Entomophaga), *see* Hymenoptera
Church: Medieval, *Staffs.* iii; of England, *Wilts.* iii* of England since the Reformation, *Staffs.* iii
Churchill (Halfshire Hundred), *Worcs.* iii
Churchill (Oswaldslow Hundred), *Worcs.* iii
Churchover, *Warws.* vi
Chute Forest, *Wilts.* iv
Chuteley Hundred, *Hants* iv
Cicadas (Hemiptera Homoptera), *see* Hemiptera
Cider (Cyder-Making), *Dors.* ii; *Essex* ii; *Hants* v; *Kent* iii; *Suss.* ii; Cider and Wine, *Som.* ii
Cinque Ports, *Suss.* ix
Circles and Enclosures of 'Highworth' Type, *Wilts.* i (1); *and see* Stone Circles
Cirencester: Hunt, *see* Hunts; religious houses, *Glos.* ii*
Civil War, *see* Tudor Period and Civil War
Claines, with Whistones, *Worcs.* iii
Clandon, East and West, *Surr.* iii*
Clanfield, *Hants* iii
Clanfield Preceptory, *Oxon.* ii
Clapcot Liberty, *Berks.* iii
Clapham, *Beds.* iii
Clapham, *Surr.* iv
Clapton, *Glos.* vi
Clapton, *Northants.* iii
Clare, Austin Friars, *Suff.* ii
Clarendon, Earl of, *see* Genealogy, Villiers
Clarendon and Melchet Forests, *Wilts.* iv
Clatford, Upper, *Hants* iv
Clatford (or Hullavington) Priory, *Wilts.* iii
Clattercote Priory, *Oxon.* ii
Claughton, *Lancs.* viii
Claverdon, *Warws.* iii
Clay Pipes, *see* Tobacco
Claydon, East and Middle, *Bucks.* iv*
Claydon, Steeple, *Bucks.* iv
Clayton, *Staffs.* viii
Clayton, *Suss.* vii
Cleasby, *Yorks. N.R.* i

Cleeve, Bishop's, *Glos.* viii
Cleeve Abbey, *Som.* ii
Cleeve Hundred, *Glos.* viii
Cleeve Prior, *Worcs.* iii
Clent, *Worcs.* iii
Clerkenwell, religious houses, *Mdx.* i*
Clevedon, Wake of, *see* Genealogy
Cleveland Foxhounds, *see* Foxhounds
Clevelode (in Powick), *Worcs.* iv
Clewer, *Berks.* iii
Cliddesden, *Hants* iv
Cliffe, King's, *Northants.* ii
Clifford Chambers, *Glos.* vi
Clifton, *Beds.* ii; Hundred, *Beds.* ii
Clifton College, *Notts.* ii
Clifton Hampden, *Oxon.* vii
Clifton-on-Dunsmore, *Warws.* vi
Clifton Reynes, *Bucks.* iv
Clifton-upon-Teme, *Worcs.* iv
Climate, *Cumb.* i; *Herts.* i; *Worcs.* i
Clipsham, *Rut.* ii
Clitheroe Grammar School, *Lancs.* ii
Clock- and Watch-Making (Clocks and Watches), *Mdx.*
  ii; *Warws.* ii; Clock-Making, *Essex* ii
Clophill, *Beds.* ii
Cloth (Cloth-Making), *Berks.* i; *Dors.* ii; *Kent* iii; *Notts.* ii;
  Salop. i; *Surr.* ii; *Warws.* ii; *Worcs.* ii; *and see* Wool
Clothall, *Herts.* iii; Hospital of St. Mary Magdalene,
  Herts. iv
Clothing (Wholesale), Manufacture, *Essex* ii; Ready-Made,
  see Textiles, Mixed
Clubmosses, *see* Lycopodiaceae
Clyffe Pypard, *Wilts.* ix
Coach-Making, *Mdx.* ii
Coal (Coal-Mining), *Cumb.* ii; *Derb.* ii; *Dur.* ii; *Kent* iii;
  Lancs. ii; *Notts.* ii; *Som.* ii; *Staffs.* ii; *Warws.* ii; *Worcs.*
  ii; *Yorks.* ii; Coal and Iron, *Salop.* i
Cobham, *Surr.* iii
Cobham College, *Kent* ii
Coborn School, *Mdx.* i
Cock-Fighting, *Berks.* ii; *Cumb.* ii; *Herts.* i; *Lancs.* ii;
  Warws. ii
Cockerham, *Lancs.* viii; Priory, *Lancs.* ii
Cockersand Abbey, *Lancs.* ii
Cocking, *Suss.* iv
Cockroaches, *see* Orthoptera
Cocoa-nut Fibre, *see* Textiles, Mixed
Codicote, *Herts.* ii
Cofton Hackett (Coston Hackett), *Worcs.* iii
Cogenhoe, *Northants.* iv
Cogges Priory, *Oxon.* ii
Coggeshall Abbey, *Essex* ii
Coinage and Assaying, *Warws.* ii; *and see* Oxford, Mint
Coins: Ancient British, *Berks.* i; [Romano-British],
  Oxon. i
Cokeham Hospital, *see* Sompting Hospital
Colchester, religious houses, *Essex* ii*
Colemore, *Hants* iv
Coleoptera (Beetles), *Beds.* i; *Berks.* i; *Cambs.* i; *Cornw.* i;
  Cumb. i; *Derb.* i; *Devon* i; *Hants* i; *Herefs.* i; *Herts.* i;
  Hunts. i; *Kent* i; *Leics.* i; *Norf.* i; *Northants.* i; *Notts.* i;
  Oxon. i; *Rut.* i; *Salop.* i; *Som.* i; *Staffs.* i; *Suff.* i;
  Surr. i; *Suss.* i; *Warws.* i; *Worcs.* i; *Yorks.* i
Coleshill, *Berks.* iv
Coleshill, *Warws.* iv; School, *Warws.* ii
Colleges: Theological, *Cambs.* iii; Training, *Cambs.* ii;
  Village, *Cambs.* ii
Collembola (Spring-Tails), *Cambs.* i; *and see* Aptera
Collingtree, *Northants.* iv
Collyweston, *Northants.* ii
Colmworth, *Beds.* iii
Coln St. Dennis, *Glos.* viii
Colnbrook, *Bucks.* iii
Colne, *Hunts.* ii
Colne, Earl's, Priory, *Essex* ii
Colton, *Lancs.* viii

Combe, *Hants* iv
Combe (with Old Wheatley), *Oxon.* v
Combe Abbey, *Warws.* ii
Combe Fields, *Warws.* vi
Comberton, Great and Little, *Worcs.* iv*
Combrook (in Kineton), *Warws.* v
Combwell Priory, *Kent* ii
Communications, *Warws.* vii–viii; *Yorks. E.R.* i; Com-
  munications and Trade, *Cambs.* ii
Compton, Bishop, his Census, *see* Ongar Hundred
Compton, *Berks.* iv; Hundred, *Berks.* iv
Compton, *Hants* iii
Compton, *Surr.* iii
Compton, *Suss.* iv
Compton, Fenny, *Warws.* v
Compton, Little and Long, *Warws.* v
Compton Beauchamp, *Berks.* iv
Compton Verney, *Warws.* v
Compton Wyniates, *Warws.* v
Conderton (in Overbury), *Worcs.* iii
Condicote, *Glos.* vi
Condover, *Salop.* viii; Hundred, *Salop.* viii
Conington, *Hunts.* iii
Conishead Priory, *Lancs.* ii
Constitutional History, *Cambs.* iii
Cookham, *Berks.* iii; Hundred, *Berks.* iii
Cookhill Priory, *Worcs.* iii
Coombe (with Old Wheatley), *Oxon.* v
Coopers' Company School, *Mdx.* i
Cople, *Beds.* iii
Copmanford, *Hunts.* iii
Coppenhall, *Staffs.* v
Copper, *Derb.* ii; Working of, *Essex* ii; Copper and Brass,
  Staffs. ii; Copper-Mining, *Cornw.* i; *Yorks.* ii; Copper-
  Smelting, *Lancs.* ii
Copperas (Copperas Industry), *Essex* ii; *Kent* iii
Copthorne Hundred, *Surr.* iii
Copyholders and Freeholders in 1699, List, *Herts. Fam.*
Corhampton, *Hants* iii
Coriander, Caraway, and Teazel Cultivation, *Essex* ii
Cork, Cutting and Preparing of, *Essex* ii
Corley, *Warws.* iv
Corn-Milling, *Essex* ii
Corporate Offices, *see* Seals
Corrigenda (and Addenda, Errata), *Beds. Index*; *Berks.
  Index*; *Bucks. Index*; *Cambs. Index*; *Cumb.* i; *Derb.* i
  (Natural History); *Dors.* iii; *Essex Index*; *Glos.* viii;
  Hants Index; *Herts. Index*; *Hunts.* iii; *Lancs.* ii, v,
  vii–viii; *Leics.* iii–v; *Mdx.* i, iii; *Oxon.* v–viii; *Rut. Index*;
  Staffs. ii; *Surr. Index*; *Warws. Index*, viii; *Wilts.* viii;
  Worcs. Index; *Yorks. Index*; *Yorks. N.R. Index*
Corse, *Glos.* viii
Corset-Making, *see* Stay- and Corset-Making
Corsham Priory, *Wilts.* iii
Corsley, *Wilts.* viii
Cosham (in Wymering), *Hants* iii
Coston Hackett, *see* Cofton Hackett
Cotes Hospital, *Northants.* ii
Cotheridge, *Worcs.* iv
Cotley Harriers, *see* Harriers
Cottered, *Herts.* iii
Cotterstock, *Northants.* ii; College, *Northants.* ii
Cottesbrook (Cottesbrooke): Knightley of, *see* Genealogy;
  Langham of, *see* Genealogy
Cottesloe Hundred, *Bucks.* iii
Cottesmore, with Barrow, *Rut.* ii
Cottesmore Hunt, *see* Hunts
Cotteswold and North Cotteswold Hunts, *see* Hunts
Cotteswold Games, *see* Games
Cottisford, *Oxon.* vi
Cotton (Cotton Industry), *Derb.* ii; *Notts.* ii; *Lancs.* ii
Coughton, *Warws.* iii
Coulsdon, *Surr.* iv
Coulston, East, *Wilts.* viii
Cound, *Salop.* viii
Coundon, *Warws.* viii

County Committees, *Beds.* i; *Berks.* i; *Bucks.* i; *Cornw.* i; *Cumb.* i; *Derb.* i; *Devon* i; *Dur.* i; *Essex* i; *Hants* i; *Herts.* i; *Kent* i; *Lancs.* i; *Norf.* i; *Northants.* i; *Notts.* i; *Salop.* i; *Som.* i; *Suff.* i; *Surr.* i; *Suss.* i; *Warws.* i; *Worcs.* i; *Yorks.* i; *and see* Victoria County History Committees; Victoria County History Council

Coursing, *Berks.* ii; *Bucks.* ii; *Cumb.* ii; *Derb.* ii; *Dur.* ii; *Essex* ii; *Glos.* ii; *Herts.* i; *Kent* i; *Lancs.* ii; *Lincs.* ii; *Mdx.* ii; *Northants.* ii; *Oxon.* ii; *Som.* ii; *Suff.* ii; *Suss.* ii; *Warws.* ii; *Wilts.* iv; *Worcs.* ii; *Yorks.* ii

Courteenhall, *Northants.* iv; Wake of, *see* Genealogy

Coveney, with Manea, *Cambs.* iv

Covenham Priory, *Lincs.* ii

Coventry, *Warws.* viii; Outlying Parts, *Warws.* viii; religious houses, *Warws.* ii*; schools, *Warws.* ii*

Coverham, *Yorks. N.R.* i; Abbey, *Yorks.* iii; *Yorks. N.R.* i

Covington, *Hunts.* iii

Cowesby, *Yorks. N.R.* ii

Cowley, *Mdx.* iii

Cowley, *Oxon.* v

Cowper Family, *see* Genealogy

Cowton, East, *Yorks. N.R.* i

Cowton, Temple, Preceptory, *Yorks.* iii

Coxford, religious houses, *Norf.* ii*

Coxwell, Great, *Berks.* iv

Coxwold, *Yorks. N.R.* ii

Crabhouse Priory, *Norf.* ii

Crabs, *see* Crustacea

Cradley (in Halesowen), *Worcs.* iii

Cradock, Mr., his Foxhounds, *see* Foxhounds

Crafts and Industries, *Warws.* viii

Crambe, *Yorks. N.R.* ii

Cranborne Chase, *Wilts.* iv

Cranborne Priory, *Dors.* ii

Cranfield, *Beds.* iii

Cranford, *Mdx.* iii

Cranford St. Andrew, *Northants.* iii; Robinson of, *see* Genealogy

Cranford St. John, *Northants.* iii

Cranleigh, *Surr.* iii

Cranoe, *Leics.* v

Cransley, *Northants.* iv

Crathorne, *Yorks. N.R.* ii

Craven Hunt, *see* Hunts

Crawley, *Suss.* vii

Crawley, North, *Bucks.* iv

Crawley, with Hunton, *Hants* iii

Crawley and Horsham Hunt, *see* Hunts

Crayke, *Dur.* iii

Crayke, *Yorks. N.R.* ii; Hospital, *Yorks.* iii

Creake Abbey, *Norf.* ii

Creaton, Little (in Spratton), *Northants.* iv

Creeting St. Mary Priory, *Suff.* ii

Creeting St. Olave Priory, *Suff.* ii

Crendon, Long, *Bucks.* iv

Creslow, *Bucks.* iii

Cressage, *Salop.* viii

Cressing Preceptory, *Essex* ii

Crewkerne Free School, *Som.* ii

Cricket, *Beds.* ii; *Berks.* ii; *Bucks.* ii; *Derb.* ii; *Essex* ii; *Glos.* ii; *Hants* v; *Herts.* i; *Kent* i; *Lancs.* ii; *Leics.* iii; *Mdx.* ii; *Northants.* ii; *Notts.* ii; *Som.* ii; *Staffs.* ii; *Surr.* ii; *Suss.* ii; *Warws.* ii; *Wilts.* iv; *Worcs.* ii; *Yorks.* ii; University Match, *Mdx.* ii

Crickets, *see* Orthoptera

Cricklade, Hospital of St. John, *Wilts.* iii

Crime, *see* Prisons

Croft, *Yorks. N.R.* i

Cromwell Pedigree, *see* Pedigrees

Crondall, *Hants* iv; Hundred, *Hants* iv

Croome, Earl's, *Worcs.* iii

Croome, Hill, *Worcs.* iii

Croome D'Abitôt, *Worcs.* iii

Cropthorne, with Charlton and Netherton, *Worcs.* iii

Crosby, Merchant Taylors' School, *Lancs.* ii

Croston, *Lancs.* vi

Crowell, *Oxon.* viii

Crowhurst, *Surr.* iv

Crowhurst, *Suss.* ix

Crowland Abbey, *Lincs.* ii

Crowle, *Worcs.* iii

Crowmarsh Hospital, *Oxon.* ii

Croxden Abbey, *Staffs.* iii

Croxton Kerrial Abbey, *Leics.* ii

Croydon, *Surr.* iv

Crustacea (Crustaceans) (Crabs, Lobsters, etc.), *Beds.* i; *Berks.* i; *Bucks.* i; *Cambs.* i; *Cornw.* i; *Cumb.* i; *Derb.* i; *Devon* i; *Dur.* i; *Essex* i; *Hants* i; *Herefs.* i; *Herts.* i; *Hunts.* i; *Kent* i; *Lancs.* i; *Leics.* i; *Norf.* i; *Northants.* i; *Notts.* i; *Oxon.* i*; *Rut.* i; *Salop.* i; *Som.* i; *Staffs.* i; *Suff.* i; *Surr.* i; *Suss.* i; *Warws.* i; *Worcs.* i; *Yorks.* i

Crutch, *Worcs.* iii

Cryptogams (Cryptogamia) (Non-Flowering Plants), *Devon* i; *Herefs.* i; *Herts.* i; *Leics.* i*; *Salop.* i; *Som.* i; *Surr.* i; *and see* Algae; Characeae; Equisetaceae; Filices; Fungi; Hepaticae; Lichenes; Lycopodiaceae; Musci; Mycetozoa

Cubbington, *Warws.* vi

Cublington, *Bucks.* iii

Cuckfield, *Suss.* vii; Grammar School, *Suss.* ii

Cuddesdon, *Oxon.* v

Cuddington, *Bucks.* ii

Cuddington, *Surr.* iii

Cudgel Play and the Revels, *Berks.* ii

Culham, *Oxon.* vii

Cumnor, *Berks.* iv

Cundall, with Leckby, *Yorks. N.R.* i

Curdworth, *Warws.* iv

Cut-legs and Kick-shins, *Berks.* ii

Cutlery Manufacture, *Essex* ii

Cutsdean (in Bredon), *Worcs.* iii

Cuttlestone Hundred: Eastern Division, *Staffs.* v; Western Division, *Staffs.* iv

Cycles, *see* Ironwork

Cyder, *see* Cider

Dacorum Hundred, *Herts.* ii

Dacre, Lord, *see* Genealogy, Brand

Dagenham, *Essex* v

Dairy Products, *Wilts.* iv

Dalby, with Skewsby, *Yorks. N.R.* ii

Dalby and Heather Preceptory, *Leics.* ii

Dale Abbey, *Derb.* ii

Dallington, *Suss.* ix

Dalton, *Lancs.* viii

Damerham, South, *Hants* iv

Danby, *Yorks. N.R.* ii

Danby Wiske, *Yorks. N.R.* i

Danegeld, *Norf.* i

Danish Invasion, *see* Anglo-Saxon Settlement

Darley Abbey, *Derb.* ii

Darlingscott (in Tredington), *Worcs.* iii

Darlington College, *Dur.* ii

Dartford, religious houses, *Kent* ii*

Dassett, Avon, *Warws.* v

Dassett, Burton, *Warws.* v

Datchet, *Bucks.* iii

Datchworth, *Herts.* iii

Davenant Foundation Grammar School, *Mdx.* i

Daventry, Priory of St. Augustine, *Northants.* ii

Davington Priory, *Kent* ii

Daylesford, *Worcs.* iii

Dean, *Beds.* iii

Dean, East, *Hants* iv

Dean, East and West, *Suss.* iv*

Dean, Priors, *Hants* iv

Dean Hundred, *Suss.* vii

Deane, *Hants* iv

Deane, *Lancs.* v

Deaneries, *Staffs.* iii

Decoys (Duck), *Lancs.* ii; *Notts.* ii

Deeping: Priory, *Lincs.* ii; Wake of, *see* Genealogy

Deer, *see* Roe-Deer

Deerhurst, *Glos.* viii; Hundred, *Glos.* viii; Priory, *Glos.* ii

Defford (in Pershore St. Andrew), *Worcs.* iv

Delapré Abbey, *Northants.* ii

Denchworth, *Berks.* iv

Deneholes, *Kent* i; *and see* Earthworks, Ancient

Denford, *Northants.* iii

Denham, *Bucks.* iii

Denmead (in Hambledon), *Hants* iii

Denney, religious houses, *Cambs.* ii*

Denston College, *Suff.* ii

Denton, *Hunts.* iii

Denton, *Northants.* iv

Denton and Chippinghurst, *Oxon.* v

Deptford St. Paul, *Surr.* iv

Derby: Grammar School, *Derb.* ii; religious houses, *Derb.* ii*

Derby, West, Hundred, *Lancs.* iii–iv

Dereham, West, Abbey, *Norf.* ii

Dermaptera (Earwigs), *Oxon.* i; Dermaptera and Orthoptera, *Cambs.* i

Derwent, Braes of, Hounds, *see* Hounds

Desborough Hundred, *Bucks.* iii

Devizes, Hospital of St. John, *Wilts.* iii

Devon and Somerset Staghounds, *see* Staghounds

Diatomaceae (Diatoms), *Norf.* i; Diatomaceae and Freshwater Algae, *Suff.* i; *and see* Cryptogams

Dibden Liberty, *Hants* iv

Didcot, *Berks.* iii

Diddington, *Hunts.* ii

Didling, *Suss.* iv

Dieulacres Abbey, *Staffs.* iii

Digswell, *Herts.* iii

Dingley Preceptory, *Northants.* ii

Dinsdale, Low, *Dur.* iii

Dinsley, Temple, Preceptory, *Herts.* iv

Dinton, *Wilts.* viii

Dinton, with Ford and Upton, *Bucks.* ii

Diptera (Flies), *Cambs.* i; *Cornw.* i; *Cumb.* i; *Derb.* i; *Devon* i; *Hants* i; *Herefs.* i; *Herts.* i; *Kent* i; *Leics.* i; *Notts.* i; *Oxon.* i; *Rut.* i; *Som.* i; *Staffs.* i; *Suff.* i; *Surr.* i; *Suss.* i; *Warws.* i; *Yorks.* i

Disinherited, The, *Cambs.* ii

Distilling, *Surr.* ii; of Spirits, *Essex* ii

Ditches, *Wilts.* i (1)

Ditchling, *Suss.* vii

Ditton, Long, *Surr.* iii

Ditton, Thames, *Surr.* iii

Dixton (in Alderton), *Glos.* vi

Docking Priory, *Norf.* ii

Docks, Fish, *see* Fisheries, Deep Sea

Dockyards, Royal, *Kent* ii

Doddenham, *Worcs.* iv

Dodderhill with Elmbridge, *Worcs.* iii

Doddington, *Cambs.* iv

Doddington, Great, *Northants.* iv

Doddingtree Hundred, *Worcs.* iv

Dodnash Priory, *Suff.* ii

Dogmersfield, *Hants* iv

Domesday Book: Domesday Cambridgeshire, *Cambs.* ii; Exon Domesday, Summaries of Fiefs, *Dors.* iii; *Wilts.* ii; Translations and Introductions, *Beds.* i*; *Berks.* i*; *Bucks.* i*; *Cambs.* i*; *Cornw.* ii (8)*; *Cumb.* i*; *Derb.* i*; *Devon* i*; *Dors.* iii*; *Essex* i*; *Hants* i*; *Herefs.* i*; *Herts.* i*; *Hunts.* i*; *Kent* iii*; *Lancs.* i*; *Leics.* i*; *Mdx.* i*; *Norf.* ii*; *Northants.* i*; *Notts.* i*; *Oxon.* i*; *Rut.* i*; *Salop.* i*; *Som.* i*; *Staffs.* iv*; *Suff.* i*; *Surr.* i*; *Suss.* i*; *Warws.* i*; *Wilts.* ii*; *Worcs.* i*; *Yorks.* ii*; Indexes, *Beds.* i; *Berks. Ind.*; *Bucks.* i; *Cambs.* i; *Cornw.* ii (8); *Derb.* i; *Dors.* iii; *Essex* i; *Hants Ind.*; *Herts.* i; *Hunts.* i; *Kent* iii; *Lancs.* i; *Mdx.* i; *Northants.* i; *Oxon.* i; *Rut. Ind.*; *Som.* ii; *Staffs.* iv; *Surr.* i; *Suss.* i; *Warws.* i; *Wilts.* ii; *Worcs.* i; *Yorks. Ind.*

Domesday Monachorum, and Index, *Kent* iii*

Doncaster, religious houses, *Yorks.* iii*

Donington, Castle, Hospital, *Leics.* ii

Donnington, *Suss.* iv

Donnington (in Shaw), *Berks.* iv; religious houses, *Berks.* ii*

Dorchester, *Oxon.* vii; Abbey, *Oxon.* ii; Hundred, *Oxon.* vii, *and see* Tax Assessments

Dorchester, religious houses, *Dors.* ii*

Dorking, *Surr.* iii

Dormston, *Worcs.* iv

Dorney, *Bucks.* iii

Dorset, South, Hounds, *see* Hounds

Dorton, *Bucks.* iv

Dover: Hospital at Buckland by, *Kent* ii; religious houses, *Kent* ii*

Doverdale, *Worcs.* iii

Dowles, *Worcs.* iv

Downham, *Cambs.* iv

Downholme, *Yorks. N.R.* i

Downside, St. Gregory's [School], *Som.* ii

Drabbet, *see* Textiles, Mixed

Draghounds, *Berks.* ii; *Kent* i

Dragonflies, *see* Odonata

Draperies: New, Woolcombing, and Spinning, *Suff.* ii; Old, *see* Woollen Cloth

Drax Priory, *Yorks.* iii

Draycot Foliat, *Wilts.* ix

Drayton, *Berks.* iv

Drayton, *Oxon.* ix

Drayton, West, *Mdx.* iii

Drayton Beauchamp, *Bucks.* iii

Drayton (in Farlington), *Hants* iii

Drayton Parslow, *Bucks.* iii

Drayton St. Leonard, *Oxon.* vii

Droitwich: Borough, *Worcs.* iii; Free School, *Worcs.* iv; religious houses, *Worcs.* ii*

Dronfield Grammar School, *Derb.* ii

Droxford, *Hants* iii

Dryden Family, *see* Genealogy

Drypool, *Yorks. E.R.* i

Dubourg, Seymour, his Harriers, *see* Harriers

Duck Decoys, *see* Decoys

Duddington, *Northants.* ii

Dudley: Borough, *Worcs.* iii; Grammar School, *Worcs.* iv; Priory of St. James, *Worcs.* ii

Dullingham School, *Cambs.* ii

Dulverton Hunt, *see* Hunts

Dummer, with Kempshot, *Hants* iii

Dumpford Hundred, *Suss.* iv

Dunchurch and Thurlaston, *Warws.* vi

Dunmow, Little, Priory, *Essex* ii

Dunsfold, *Surr.* iii

Dunstable, *Beds.* iii; religious houses, *Beds.* i*; schools, *Beds.* ii*

Dunster Priory, *Som.* ii

Dunston, *Staffs.* v

Dunton, *Bucks.* iii

Dunton, with Millo, *Beds.* ii

Dunwich: religious houses, *Suff.* ii*; School, *Suff.* ii

Dunwood (in East Wellow), *Hants* iv

Dureford Abbey, *Suss.* ii

Durham: Castle, *Dur.* iii; Cathedral, *Dur.* iii*; City, *Dur.* iii; City Jurisdictions, *Dur.* iii; Parishes of St. Oswald and St. Giles, *Dur.* iii; religious houses, *Dur.* ii*

Durham County Foxhounds, *see* Foxhounds

Durham County Hounds, *see* Hounds

Durley, *Hants* iii

Duxford Preceptory, *Cambs.* ii

Dwellings, Pile, *see* Pile Dwellings

Dyeing and Bleaching, *Notts.* ii; Dyeing, Bleaching, and Finishing, *Lancs.* ii; Dyeing, Bleaching, Calico-Printing, *Suss.* ii; Dyeing and Fulling, *Worcs.* ii

Dyers' Weed, *see* Weld

Eagle Preceptory, *Lincs.* ii

Earith (in Bluntisham), *Hunts.* ii

Earley (in Sonning), *Berks.* iii

Early Man, *Beds.* i; *Berks.* i; *Bucks.* i; *Cambs.* i; *Cornw.* i; *Cumb.* i; *Derb.* i; *Devon* i; *Dur.* i; *Essex* i; *Hants* i; *Herefs.* i; *Herts.* i; *Hunts.* i; *Kent* i; *Lancs.* i; *Leics.* i; *Norf.* i; *Northants.* i; *Notts.* i; *Oxon.* i; *Rut.* i; *Salop.* i; *Som.* i; *Staffs.* i; *Suff.* i; *Surr.* i; *Suss.* i; *Warws.* i; *Worcs.* i; *Yorks.* i

Earnley, *Suss.* iv

Eartham, *Suss.* iv

Earthworks, Ancient, *Beds.* i; *Berks.* i; *Bucks.* ii; *Cambs.* ii; *Cornw.* i; *Derb.* i; *Devon* i; *Dur.* i; *Essex* i; *Herefs.* i; *Herts.* ii; *Hunts.* ii; *Kent* i*; *Lancs.* ii*; *Leics.* i; *Mdx.* ii; *Northants.* ii; *Notts.* i; *Oxon.* ii; *Rut.* i; *Salop.* i; *Som.* i; *Staffs.* i; *Suff.* i; *Surr.* iv; *Suss.* i; *Warws.* i; *Worcs.* iv; *Yorks.* ii; *and see* Barrows; Circles; Enclosures; Deneholes; Ditches; Offa's Dike

Earwigs, *see* Dermaptera

Easby, *Yorks. N.R.* i; Abbey of St. Agatha, *Yorks.* iii; *Yorks. N.R.* i

Easebourne, *Suss.* iv; Hundred, *Suss.* iv; Priory, *Suss.* ii

Easington, *Yorks. N.R.* ii

Easingwold, *Yorks. N.R.* ii

East Hundred, *Rut.* ii

East Sussex, First and Present Hunts, *see* Hunts

Eastbourne: College, *Suss.* ii; Hunt, *see* Hunts

Eastcotts (in Cardington), *Beds.* iii

Eastham, with Hanley Child and Orleton, *Worcs.* iv

Easthampstead, *Berks.* iii

Easton, *Hants* iii

Easton, *Hunts.* iii

Easton, Crux, *Hants* iv

Easton Maudit, *Northants.* iv

Easton on the Hill, *Northants.* ii

Easton Priory or Hospital, *Wilts.* iii

Eastrop, *Hants* iv

Eastwick, *Herts.* iii

Eathorpe (with Wappenbury), *Warws.* vi

Eaton, Church, *Staffs.* iv

Eaton, Water (in Bletchley), *Bucks.* iv

Eaton, Wood, *Oxon.* v

Eaton Bray, *Beds.* iii

Eaton Hastings, *Berks.* iv

Eaton Socon, *Beds.* iii

Ebberston, *Yorks. N.R.* ii

Ebchester Nunnery, *Dur.* ii

Eccles, *Lancs.* iv

Ecclesfield Priory, *Yorks.* iii

Ecclesiastical History, *Beds.* i; *Berks.* ii; *Bucks.* i; *Cambs.* ii; *Cumb.* ii; *Derb.* ii; *Dur.* ii; *Essex.* ii; *Glos.* ii; *Hants* ii; *Herts.* iv*; *Hunts.* i; *Kent* ii*; *Lancs.* ii*; *Leics.* i; *Lincs.* ii*; *Lond.* i*; *Norf.* ii*; *Northants.* ii; *Notts.* ii; *Oxon.* ii; *Rut.* i; *Som.* ii; *Suff.* ii; *Surr.* ii; *Suss.* ii; *Warws.* ii; *Wilts.* iii; *Worcs.* ii; *Yorks.* iii; Ecclesiastical Divisions, *Lond.* i; Organization, *Mdx.* i; *and see* Church; Deaneries; Religious History

Eccleston, *Lancs.* vi

Eckington, *Worcs.* iv

Economic History, *Cambs.* iii; *Wilts.* iv, vi*; Economic Affairs, 1500–1800, *Cambs.* ii; *and see* Social and Economic History

Ecton, *Northants.* iv

Eddington (in Hungerford), *Berks.* iv

Edgcote, Cartwright of, *see* Genealogy

Edgcott, *Bucks.* iv

Edge-Tools, *see* Tools

Edington, *Wilts.* viii; [monastery], *Wilts.* iii

Edlesborough, *Bucks.* iii

Edston, Great, *Yorks. N.R.* i

Education, *Leics.* iii; *Wilts.* v; *Yorks. E.R.* i; Adult and Further, *Leics.* iii; Elementary, *Cambs.* ii*; Elementary, in the Nineteenth and Twentieth Centuries, *Leics.* iii; of the Working Classes to 1870, *Mdx.* i; Primary and Secondary, *Leics.* iv; Private, from the Sixteenth Century, *Mdx.* i; Public, *Warws.* vii, viii*; *and see* Colleges; Schools

Edvin Loach, *Worcs.* iv

Edwardstone Priory, *Suff.* ii

Edwinstree Hundred, *Herts.* iii

Edworth, *Beds.* ii

Effigies, *see* Monumental Effigies

Effingham, *Surr.* iii; Hundred, *Surr.* iii

Egginton (in Leighton Buzzard), *Beds.* iii

Egglescliffe, *Dur.* iii

Egglestone Abbey [township] (in Rokeby), *Yorks. N.R.* i; Abbey, *Yorks.* iii; *Yorks. N.R.* i

Egham, *Surr.* iii

Egleton, *Rut.* ii

Egton, *Yorks. N.R.* ii

Elastic Web Manufacture, *Leics.* iv

Eldersfield, *Worcs.* iv

Elementary Education, *see* Education

Elementary Schools, *see* Schools

Eling, *Hants* iv

Ellerburn, *Yorks. N.R.* ii

Ellerton, in Swaledale, Priory, *Yorks.* iii

Ellerton, on Spalding Moor, Priory, *Yorks.* iii

Ellesborough, *Bucks.* ii

Ellingham, *Hants* iv; Priory, *Hants* ii

Ellington, *Hunts.* iii

Ellisfield, *Hants* iii

Elm, *Cambs.* iv

Elmbridge (in Dodderhill), *Worcs.* iii

Elmbridge Hundred, *Surr.* iii

Elmdon, *Warws.* iv

Elmley Castle, *Worcs.* iii

Elmley Lovett, *Worcs.* iii

Elmstone Hardwicke, *Glos.* viii

Elsfield, *Oxon.* v

Elsham Priory, *Lincs.* ii

Elsted, *Surr.* ii

Elsted, *Suss.* iv

Elstow, *Beds.* iii; Abbey, *Beds.* i

Elstree, *Herts.* ii

Elthorne Hundred, *Mdx.* iii

Elton, *Dur.* iii

Elton, *Hunts.* iii

Elvetham, *Hants* iv

Elwes (Cary-Elwes) Family, *see* Genealogy

Elwick Hall, *Dur.* iii

Ely: Abbey and Cathedral Priory, *Cambs.* ii; Cathedral and Precincts (Architectural Description), *Cambs.* iv; City, *Cambs.* iv; Hospitals of St. Mary Magdalene and St. John Baptist, *Cambs.* ii; Hundred, *Cambs.* iv; Liberty, *Cambs.* iv; schools, *Cambs.* ii*

Ely, Isle of, *see* Tax Assessments, Hearth

Emberton, *Bucks.* iv

Embley (in East Wellow), *Hants* iv

Emery-Cloth Manufacture, *Essex* ii

Emmington, *Oxon.* viii

Empingham, *Rut.* ii

Empshott, *Hants* iii

Emsworth (in Warblington), *Hants* iii

Enamels, Battersea, *Surr.* ii

Enborne, *Berks.* iv

Enclosures and Circles of 'Highworth' Type, *Wilts.* i (1)

Enclosures and Hill-Forts, *Wilts.* i (1)

Endowed Elementary Schools, *see* Schools

Enfield Grammar School, *Mdx.* i

Engine-Building and General Engineering, *Essex* ii

Engineering, *Lancs.* ii; *Staffs.* ii; Electrical, *Essex* ii; Engineering and Metal Industries (Metal Working), *Glos.* ii; *Leics.* iii; Engineering and Railway Works, *Wilts.* iv; Engineering Works, *Beds.* ii; *and see* Engine-Building; Foundries

Englefield, *Berks.* iii

Enham, Knight's, *Hants* iv

Ephemeroptera (Mayflies), *Cambs.* i; *Oxon.* i; *and see* Neuroptera

Epping, *Essex* v

Epsom, *Surr.* iii

Equisetaceae (Horsetails), *Herts.* i; *Herefs.* i; *and see* Cryptogams: Plants, Vascular

Eridge Hunt, *see* Hunts

Erlestoke, *Wilts.* vii
Errata, *see* Corrigenda
Eryngo, Candied, *Essex* ii
Esher, *Surr.* iii
Esholt Priory, *Yorks.* iii
Essendine, *Rut.* ii
Essendon, *Herts.* iii
Essex, Earl of, *see* Genealogy, Capell
Essex, Metropolitan, since 1850, *Essex* v
Etchingham, *Suss.* ix
Eton, *Bucks.* iii; College, *Bucks.* ii
Ettington, *Warws.* v
Etton, *Northants.* ii
Evenlode, *Worcs.* iii
Everdon Priory, *Northants.* ii
Eversholt, *Beds.* iii
Eversley, *Hants* iv
Everton, *Beds.* ii
Evesham, *Worcs.* ii; Abbey, *Worcs.* ii; Prince Henry's
   Grammar School, *Worcs.* iv; Young of, *see* Genealogy
Evingar Hundred, *Hants* iv
Evington, *Leics.* iv
Ewbank, Mr., his Hunt, *see* Hunts
Ewell, *Surr.* iii; Preceptory, *Kent* ii
Ewelme Hospital, *Oxon.* ii
Ewhurst, *Hants* iv
Ewhurst, *Surr.* iii
Ewhurst, *Suss.* ix
Exbury, with Lepe, *Hants* iii
Exeter, Earl and Marquess of, *see* Genealogy, Cecil;
   Marquess of, his Hunt, *see* Hunts
Exhall (Barlichway Hundred), *Warws.* iii
Exhall (Knightlow Hundred), *Warws.* vi
Exmoor Hunt, *see* Hunts
Explosives, Manufacture of, *Essex* ii; *and see* Gun-Cotton;
   Gunpowder
Exton, *Hants* iii
Exton, *Rut.* ii
Exton, Ervill's (in Hambledon), *Hants* iii
Eye, *Northants.* ii; religious houses, *Suff.* ii*
Eyford, *Glos.* vi
Eynesbury, *Hunts.* ii
Eynsham, religious houses, *Oxon.* ii*
Eyres, List of Forest, *Wilts.* iv
Eyworth, *Beds.* ii

Faccombe, *Hants* iv
Faircross Hundred, *Berks.* iv
Fairlight, *Suss.* ix
Falconry, *Dors.* ii; *Glos.* ii; *Northants.* ii
Falmer, *Suss.* vii
Fane Family, *see* Genealogy
Fangfoss Hospital, *Yorks.* iii
Farcet, *Hunts.* iii
Fareham Hundred, *Hants* iii
Farewell Priory, *Staffs.* iii
Faringdon, *Hants* iii
Faringdon, Great, *Berks.* iv; Cell or Grange, *Berks.* ii;
   Hundred, *Berks.* iv
Farleigh Wallop, *Hants* iii
Farley, *Surr.* iv
Farley Chamberlayne, *Hants* iv
Farley Hospital, *see* Luton
Farlington, with Drayton, *Hants* iii
Farmers' Staghounds, Berks and Bucks, *see* Staghounds
Farnborough, *Berks.* iv
Farnborough, *Hants* iv
Farnborough, *Warws.* v
Farndish, *Beds.* iii
Farnham, *Surr.* ii; Hundred, *Surr.* ii
Farnham Royal, with Hedgerley Dean and Seer Green,
   Bucks. iii
Faversham Abbey, *Kent* ii
Fawley, *Bucks.* iii
Fawley, *Hants* iii; Hundred, with the Liberty of Alresford,
   Hants iii

Fawley, with Whatcombe, *Berks.* iv
Fawsley, Knightley of, *see* Genealogy
Faxfleet Preceptory, *Yorks.* iii
Faxton, *Northants.* iv
Feckenham, *Worcs.* iii; Free School, *Worcs.* iv
Felixstowe Priory, *Suff.* ii
Felley Priory, *Notts.* ii
Felmersham, with Radwell, *Beds.* iii
Felt- and Hat-Making, *Surr.* ii; Felt-Hat-Making,
   Lancs. ii
Feltham, *Mdx.* ii
Fens: Draining the Fens, *Cambs.* ii; Maps of the Fenland,
   Hunts. iii; Middle Level of the Fens and Its Reclama-
   tion, *Hunts.* iii
Fenton, *Staffs.* viii
Fenton (in Pidley), *Hunts.* ii
Fernhurst, *Suss.* iv
Ferns and Fern Allies, *see* Filices
Ferriby, North, Priory, *Yorks.* iii
Fertilizers, *Suff.* ii
Fetcham, *Surr.* iii
Feudal Baronage, *see* Baronage
Feudal Wiltshire, *Wilts.* v
Field Dalling Priory, *Norf.* ii
Field Systems, *Wilts.* i (1)
Fiend-Flies (Hemiptera Homoptera), *see* Hemiptera
Fifteenths and Tenths: Quotas of 1334, *Wilts.* iv
Filgrave (in Tyringham), *Bucks.* iv
Filices (Ferns and Fern Allies), *Cornw.* i; *Herefs.* i; *Herts.* i;
   Norf. i; *Surr.* i; *and see* Cryptogams; Plants, Vascular
Fillongley, *Warws.* iv
Finchale, Priory of St. John the Baptist and St. Godric,
   Dur. ii
Finchampstead, *Berks.* iii
Finchdean Hundred, *Hants* iii
Finchley, Christ's College, *Mdx.* i
Finedon, *Northants.* iii
Fineshade (Castle Hymel) Priory, *Northants.* ii
Fingall, *Yorks. N.R.* i
Finishing, *see* Bleaching
Finmere, *Oxon.* vi
Fireclay, *Derb.* ii; *Staffs.* ii
Fish Docks, *see* Fisheries, Deep Sea
Fishbourne, New, *Suss.* iv
Fishergate Half-Hundred, *Suss.* vii
Fisheries, *Cornw.* i; *Cumb.* ii*; *Dors.* ii; *Hants* v; *Kent* iii;
   Notts. ii; *Suff.* ii; *Suss.* ii; Deep Sea, and Fish Docks,
   Lincs. ii; Oyster, *Essex* ii; Sea, *Essex* ii; *Lancs.* ii; *Som.* ii
Fisherton Anger, *Wilts.* vi
Fisherton de la Mere, *Wilts.* viii
Fishes, *see* Pisces
Fishing, *see* Angling; Fisheries
Fitz Roy Family, *see* Genealogy
Fitzwilliam, Earl, his Foxhounds, *see* Foxhounds
Fitzwilliam Hounds, *see* Hounds
Fladbury, with Hill and Moor, Ablench, Stock and Bradley,
   Throckmorton, Wyre Piddle, *Worcs.* iii
Flamstead, *Herts.* ii; Priory of St. Giles in the Wood,
   Herts. iv
Flat Racing, *see* Racing
Flaunden (in Hemel Hempstead), *Herts.* ii
Flax and Hemp, *Derb.* ii; Flax and Linen, *Notts.* ii;
   Flax-Growing, *Essex* ii
Flaxley Abbey, *Glos.* ii
Fleckney, *Leics.* v
Fletton, *Hunts.* iii
Flies, *see* Diptera
Flint-Working, *Essex* ii
Flitcham Priory, *Norf.* ii
Flitt Hundred, *Beds.* ii
Flitton cum Silsoe, *Beds.* ii
Flitwick, *Beds.* iii
Flixton, *Lancs.* v
Flixton, Hospital of St. Mary and St. Andrew,
   Yorks. iii
Flixton Priory, *Suff.* ii

Flock-Making, *Essex* ii
Flora, Geology of Shropshire in Relation to, *see* Geology
Flowers, Artificial, Making of, *Essex* ii
Fluor and Calc Spar, *Derb.* ii; Fluorspar-Mining, *Dur.* ii
Flyford, Grafton, *Worcs.* iv
Flyford Flavell, *Worcs.* iv
Foleshill, *Warws.* viii
Folkestone Priory, *Kent* ii
Folksworth, *Hunts.* iii
Football, *Beds.* ii; *Berks.* ii; *Cumb.* ii; *Dur.* ii; *Essex* ii; *Herts.* i; *Mdx.* ii; *Northants.* ii; *Surr.* ii; *Warws.* ii; *Yorks.* ii; Association, *Herts.* i; *Leics.* iii; *Staffs.* ii; *Wilts.* iv; Rugby, *Herts.* i; *Lancs.* ii; *Leics.* iii; Town and Village Clubs, *Berks.* ii
Footwear (Footwear Manufacture), *Leics.* iii–iv; *Staffs.* ii; *and see* Boots and Shoes
Forcett, *Yorks. N.R.* i
Ford, *Salop.* viii; Hundred, *Salop.* viii
Ford (in Dinton), *Bucks.* ii
Fordham Priory, *Cambs.* ii
Fordingbridge: with Godshill, Broomy Lodge, Linford, Picked Post and Shobley, *Hants* iv; Hospital, *Hants* ii; Hundred, *Hants* iv
Forest Hill, *Oxon.* v
Forestry (Forests, Royal Forests), *Beds.* ii; *Berks.* ii; *Bucks.* ii; *Cumb.* ii; *Derb.* i; *Dors.* ii; *Dur.* ii; *Essex* ii; *Glos.* ii; *Hants* ii; *Herts.* iv; *Kent* i; *Lancs.* ii; *Leics.* ii; *Lincs.* ii; *Mdx.* ii; *Northants.* ii; *Notts.* i; *Oxon.* ii; *Rut.* i; *Salop.* i; *Som.* ii; *Staffs.* ii; *Suff.* ii; *Surr.* ii; *Suss.* ii; *Warws.* ii; *Wilts.* iv; *Worcs.* ii; *Yorks.* i; Forest Eyres, *see* Eyres
Forthampton, *Glos.* viii
Forton, *Staffs.* iv
Foscott, *Bucks.* iv
Fosse Priory, *Lincs.* ii
Foston, with Thornton-le-Clay, *Yorks. N.R.* ii
Fotheringhay, *Northants.* ii; College, *Northants.* ii
Foukeholm, Priory of St. Stephen, *Yorks.* iii
Foulbridge Preceptory, *Yorks.* iii
Foulmart-Hunting, *Cumb.* ii
Foundries and Engineering Works, *Cornw.* i; *and see* Iron
Fountains Abbey, *Yorks.* iii
Fox-Hunting, *Berks.* ii; *Cumb.* ii; *Dur.* ii; *Glos.* ii; *Hants* v; *Herts.* i; *Kent* i; *Lincs.* ii; *Oxon.* ii; *Rut.* i; *Staffs.* ii; *Som.* ii; *Suss.* ii; *Warws.* ii; *Wilts.* iv; *and see* Hunting
Foxcott (in Andover), *Hants* iv
Foxearle Hundred, *Suss.* ix
Foxhounds, *Beds.* ii; *Bucks.* ii; *Dors.* ii; *Essex* ii; *Mdx.* ii; *Notts.* ii; *Surr.* ii; *Yorks.* ii; Early, *Northants.* ii; Badsworth, *Yorks.* ii; Bedale, *Yorks.* ii; Bilsdale, *Yorks.* ii; Bramham Moor, *Yorks.* ii; Cleveland, *Yorks.* ii; Cradock's, *Dur.* ii; Durham County, *Dur.* ii; Fitzwilliam, *Yorks.* ii; Goathland, *Yorks.* ii; Grove, *Notts.* ii; Holderness, *Yorks,* ii; Lambton, *Dur.* ii; Middleton, *Yorks.* ii; North Durham, *Dur.* ii; Raby, *Dur.* ii; *Yorks.* ii; Rufford, *Notts.* ii; Scrope's, *Yorks.* ii; Sherbrooke's, *Yorks.* ii; Sinnington, *Yorks.* ii; South Down, *Suss.* ii; South Durham, *Dur.* ii; South Notts, *Notts.* ii; Stainton Dale, *Yorks.* ii; Wensleydale, *Yorks.* ii; York and Ainsty, *Yorks.* ii; Zetland, *Dur.* ii; *and see* Hounds; Hunts
Foxton, *Leics.* v
Frampton Priory, *Dors.* ii
Frankley, *Worcs.* iii
Frankton, *Warws.* vi
Freefolk, *Hants* iv
Freeford, Hospital of St. Leonard, *Staffs.* iii
Freeholders, *see* Copyholders and Freeholders
Freemasonry, *Wilts.* iv
Freiston Priory, *Lincs.* ii
Frenchmoor (in Broughton), *Hants* iv
Frensham, *Surr.* ii
Freshwater, *Hants* v

Friars, Four Houses of [Appleby, Carlisle, and Penrith], *Cumb.* ii
Friarside Hospital, *Dur.* ii
Frilsham, *Berks.* iv
Fringford, *Oxon.* vi
Frisby (with Galby), *Leics.* v
Fritwell, *Oxon.* vi
Frodesley, *Salop.* viii
Frogmore Park, Fitz Roy of, *see* Genealogy
Frome, schools, *Som.* ii*
Froxfield, *Hants* iii
Froyle, *Hants* ii
Fruit-Growing, *Essex* ii; Fruit-Growing and Market-Gardening, *Kent* iii; *Worcs.* ii
Fruit-Preserving, *see* Jam-Making
Frythe, Wilshere of the, *see* Genealogy
Fugglestone St. Peter, *Wilts.* vi
Fulbeck, Fane of, *see* Genealogy
Fulbrook, *Warws.* iii
Fulham Stoneware, *see* Stoneware
Fulking, *Suss.* vii
Fuller's Earth, *Kent* iii; *and see* Stone Quarries
Fulling and Dyeing, *Worcs.* ii
Fulmer, *Bucks.* iii
Fungi, *Cornw.* i; *Devon* i; *Hants* i; *Herefs.* i; *Herts.* i; *Kent* i; *Leics.* i; *Norf.* i; *Northants.* i; *Notts.* i; *Salop.* i; *Som.* i; *Staffs.* i; *Suff.* i; *Surr.* i; *Worcs.* i; *Yorks.* i; *and see* Cryptogams
Funtington, *Suss.* iv
Furness, *Lancs.* viii; Abbey, *Lancs.* ii, viii
Fyfield, *Berks.* iv; Hospital, *Berks.* ii
Fyfield, *Essex* iv
Fyfield, *Hants* iv
Fylingdales, *Yorks. N.R.* ii

Gaddesden, Great and Little, *Herts.* ii*
Gainford Hospital, *Dur.* ii
Galby and Frisby, *Leics.* v
Gall-Flies (Hymenoptera Cynipidae), *see* Hymenoptera
Game Cockfighting, *see* Cock-Fighting
Games: Cotteswold, *Glos.* ii; Olympic, of London (1908), *Mdx.* ii; *and see* Sports
Ganfield Hundred, *Berks.* iv
Gape Family, *see* Genealogy
Garendon Abbey, *Leics.* ii
Garsington, *Oxon.* v
Garstang, *Lancs.* vii; schools, *Lancs.* ii*
Garston, East, *Berks.* iv
Garth Hunt, *see* Hunts
Gartree Hundred, *Leics.* v
Gatcombe, *Hants* v
Gateshead, religious houses, *Dur.* ii*
Gatton, *Surr.* iii
Gawcott (in Buckingham), *Bucks.* iii
Gaydon, *Warws.* v
Gayhurst, *Bucks.* iv
Gazetteer: Archaeological, *Wilts.* i (1); General, Arranged under Parishes, *Wilts.* i (1); Roman, *Essex* iii
Gelatine-Making, *see* Isinglass
Geld Rolls: Introduction, Text, Translation, and Index, *Dors.* iii*; *Wilts.* ii*; Geld Inquest, *Som.* i
Genealogy (Introduction, Chart Pedigree, Arms, and Alliances): Baker of Bayfordbury, *Herts. Fam.*; Brand (of Great Hormead; Viscount Hampden and Lord Dacre), *Herts. Fam.*; Calvert (of Furneaux Pelham; of Nine Ashes; of Albury; of Ockley Court), *Herts. Fam.*; Calvert (Verney), Baronet, *Herts. Fam.*; Capell (Earl of Essex), *Herts. Fam.*; Cartwright (of Aynhoe; of Edgcote), *Northants. Fam.*; Cecil, Lord Burghley, Earl and Marquess of Exeter, *Northants. Fam.*; Cecil, Marquess of Salisbury, *Herts. Fam.*; Cowper (Earl Cowper; of Hertingfordbury and Tewin Water), *Herts. Fam.*; Dryden of Canons Ashby, *Northants. Fam.*; Elwes (of Askham and Saundby; in London; of Stoke in Suffolk, Baronets; in Berkshire), *Northants. Fam.*; Elwes (Cary-Elwes), formerly of Throcking in

Hertfordshire, now of Great Billing in Northampton-shire, and of Roxby and Brigg in Lincolnshire, *Northants. Fam.*; Fane (Earl of Westmorland; of Fulbeck, after-wards Earl of Westmorland; of Basildon, Viscount Fane; of Combe Bank in Sundridge, co. Kent; of Fulbeck), *Northants. Fam.*; Fitz Roy (Duke of Grafton; of Salcey Lawn and Frogmore Park), *Northants. Fam.*; Gape of St. Michael's, *Herts. Fam.*; Grimston (formerly Luckyn) (Earl of Verulam), *Herts. Fam.*; Isham (of Pytchley; of Barby, Willey, and Barwell; of Lamport), *Northants. Fam.*; Knightley (of Knightley; of Gnosall; of Fawsley; of Burgh Hall, afterwards of Fawsley; of Hackney, afterwards of Fawsley; of Norton and Cottesbrook; of Offchurch; of Byfield and Charwelton), *Northants. Fam.*; Langham (of Cold Ashby; of Guils-borough, afterwards of London and Cottesbrooke), *Northants. Fam.*; Luckyn of Little Waltham, Baronet, *Herts. Fam.*; Lytton, Earl of Lytton, *Herts. Fam.*; Maunsell (of Chicheley and Thorpe Malsor; of Ireland, afterwards of Thorpe Malsor), *Northants. Fam.*; Palmer (of Carlton; of Withcote Hall), *Northants. Fam.*; Powys (Lord Lilford; Family at Montacute in Somer-set), *Northants. Fam.*; Rokeby of Arthingworth, *Northants. Fam.*; Robinson of Cranford, *Northants. Fam.*, Sebright, Baronet, *Herts. Fam.*; Spencer (Earl Spencer; of Althorp), *Northants. Fam.*; Thornton of Brockhall, *Northants. Fam.*; Turner of Sutton Coldfield and Bramcote, *Northants. Fam.*; Turner and Page-Turner of London and Ambroseden, *Northants. Fam.*; Villiers, Earl of Clarendon, *Herts. Fam.*; Wake (of Bourne, Lord Wake of Liddell; of Blisworth and Deeping; afterwards of Clevedon, and of Courteenhall; of London and Antwerp), *Northants. Fam.*; Willes of Astrop, *Northants. Fam.*; Wilshere of the Frythe, *Herts. Fam.*; Young (of Hanley Castle; of Evesham, of Orlingbury), *Northants. Fam.*; *and see* Houses, Landed; Pedigrees

Geology, *Beds.* i; *Berks.* i; *Bucks.* i; *Cambs.* i; *Cornw.* i; *Cumb.* i; *Derb.* i; *Devon* i; *Dur.* i; *Essex* i; *Hants* i; *Herefs.* i; *Herts.* i; *Hunts.* i; *Kent* i; *Lancs.* i; *Leics.* i; *Norf.* i; *Northants.* i; *Notts.* i; *Oxon.* i; *Rut.* i; *Salop.* i; *Som.* i; *Staffs.* i; *Suff.* i; *Surr.* i; *Suss.* i; *Warws.* i; *Worcs.* i; *Yorks.* i; in Relation to Flora, *Salop.* i; Industries Derived from, *Cambs.* ii; Quaternary, *Oxon.* i; *and see* Physique

Gibbon, Marsh, *Bucks.* iv
Gidding, Great, *Hunts.* iii
Gidding, Little, *Hunts.* iii; [Ferrar community], *Hunts.* i
Gidding, Steeple, *Hunts.* iii
Gilling (Gilling West Wapentake), *Yorks. N.R.* i
Gilling (Ryedale Wapentake), *Yorks. N.R.* i
Gilling East and West Wapentakes, *Yorks. N.R.* i*
Gillingham, Dominican Friars, *Dors.* ii
Gilston, *Herts.* iii
Girtford (in Sandy), *Beds.* ii
Glaisdale, *Yorks. N.R.* ii
Glanford Bridge (or Wrawby) Hospital, *Lincs.* ii
Glapthorn, *Northants.* ii
Glascote (with Bolehall), *Warws.* iv
Glass (Glass-Making, Glass-Works), *Dur.* ii; *Essex* ii; *Kent* iii; *Lancs.* ii; *Mdx.* ii; *Oxon.* ii; *Staffs.* ii; *Surr.* ii; *Suss.* ii; *Warws.* ii; *Worcs.* ii; *Yorks.* ii; Glass and Pot-tery, *Hants* v; *Notts.* ii; *Som.* ii; Glass, Pottery, Bricks, and Building Materials, *Glos.* ii
Glaston, *Rut.* ii
Glastonbury Abbey, *Som.* ii
Glatton, *Hunts.* iii
Glen, Great, *Leics.* v
Glidden (in Hambledon), *Hants* iii
Glinton, *Northants.* ii
Glooston, *Leics.* v
Gloucester: Priory at Lanthony by, *Glos.* ii; religious houses, *Glos.* ii*
Gloves (Glove-Making, Gloving), *Northants.* ii; *Notts.* ii; *Oxon.* ii; *Som.* ii; *Wilts.* iv; *Worcs.* ii; *and see* Leather Breeches

Glue-Making, *Essex* ii
Gnosall, *Staffs.* iv; Knightley of, *see* Genealogy
Goathland: Foxhounds, *see* Foxhounds; Hermitage, *Yorks.* iii
Godalming, *Surr.* iii; Hundred, *Surr.* iii
Godington, *Oxon.* vi
Godiva Legend, *Warws.* viii
Godley Hundred, *Surr.* iii
Godmanchester, *Hunts.* ii; Grammar School, *Hunts.* ii
Godolphin School, *see* Latymer and Godolphin Schools
Godsfield, *Hants* iv; Preceptory, *see* Baddesley Preceptory
Godshill, *Hants* v
Godshill (in Fordingbridge), *Hants* iv
Godstone, *Surr.* iv
Godstow Abbey, *Oxon.* ii
Gokewell Priory, *Lincs.* ii
Goldington, *Beds.* iii
Goldspur Hundred, *Suss.* ix
Golf, *Beds.* ii; *Berks.* ii; *Bucks.* ii; *Derb.* ii; *Dors.* ii; *Dur.* ii; *Essex* ii; *Glos.* ii; *Kent* ii; *Lancs.* ii; *Lincs.* ii; *Mdx.* ii; *Northants.* ii; *Oxon.* ii; *Som.* ii; *Suff.* ii; *Surr.* ii; *Suss.* ii; *Warws.* ii; *Worcs.* ii; *Yorks.* ii
Goodwood Hounds, *see* Hounds
Goodworth Clatford, *Hants* iv
Goring Priory, *Oxon.* ii
Gorleston, religious houses, *Suff.* ii*
Gosport (in Alverstoke Liberty), *Hants* iii
Gostrow Hundred, *Suss.* ix
Government: City, *Wilts.* vi*; County, *Wilts.* v*; King's, in the Middle Ages, *Wilts.* v
Grace Dieu Priory, *Leics.* ii
Graffham, *Suss.* iv
Grafham, with East Perry, *Hunts.* iii
Grafton, Duke of, *see* Genealogy, Fitz Roy
Grafton, Temple, *Warws.* iii
Grafton [Hunt] Country, *Northants.* ii
Grafton Hounds, *see* Hounds
Grafton Manor, *Worcs.* iii
Grafton Preceptory, *see* Balsall and Grafton Preceptory
Grafton Regis Hermitage, *Northants.* ii
Grafton Underwood, *Northants.* iii
Grammar Schools, *see* Schools
Grandborough, *Bucks.* iv
Grandborough, *Warws.* vi
Granite-Quarrying, *Cornw.* i
Gransden, Great, *Hunts.* ii
Grantham, religious houses, *Lincs.* ii*
Grasshoppers, *see* Orthoptera
Grateley, *Hants* iv
Grave, La, *see* Grovebury
Graveley, *Herts.* iii
Gravenhurst, Upper and Lower, *Beds.* ii*
Gravesend, Hospital at Milton by, *Kent* ii
Grazeley (in Sulhampstead Abbots), *Berks.* iii
Greatham, *Dur.* iii; Hospital of St. Mary and St. Cuthbert, *Dur.* ii
Greatham, *Hants* ii
Greenfield Priory, *Lincs.* ii
Greenford, *Mdx.* iii
Greenham Preceptory, *Berks.* ii
Greenstead, *Essex* iv
Greenwich, Observant Friars, *Kent* ii
Greetham, *Rut.* ii
Grendale, *see* Handale
Grendon, *Northants.* iv
Grendon, *Warws.* iv
Grendon Underwood, *Bucks.* iv
Gresley Priory, *Derb.* ii
Grewell, *see* Greywell
Greystoke College, *Cumb.* ii
Greywell (Grewell), *Hants* iv
Grimley, *Worcs.* iii
Grimsby: Abbey (Wellow Abbey), *Lincs.* ii; religious houses, *Lincs.* ii*
Grimston, Robert ('Bob Grimston'), *Herts.* i; Family (formerly Luckyn), *see* Genealogy

Grindon, *Dur.* iii
Grinstead, East, School, *Suss.* ii
Grinton, *Yorks. N.R.* i
Grosmont Priory, *Yorks.* iii; *Yorks. N.R.* ii
Grove, *Bucks.* iii
Grove Foxhounds, *see* Foxhounds
Grove Hounds, *see* Hounds
Grovebury (La Grave), Priory, *Beds.* i
Grovely Forest, *Wilts.* iv
Guestling, *Suss.* ix; Hundred, *Suss.* ix
Guildford: Borough, *Surr.* iii; Dominican Friars, *Surr.* ii
Guilsborough, Langham of, *see* Genealogy
Guisborough, *Yorks. N.R.* ii; Priory, *Yorks.* iii; *Yorks. N.R.* ii
Guiting Preceptory, *Glos.* ii
Guldeford, East, *Suss.* ix
Gumley, *Leics.* v
Gun-Cotton, *Suff.* ii
Gun-Making, *Essex* ii; Gun Trade of Birmingham, *Warws.* ii
Gunpowder (Gunpowder Manufacture), *Essex* ii; *Surr.* ii; Gunpowder, Ammunition, etc., *Kent* iii
Gutta-Percha and India-Rubber Goods, Manufacture of, *Essex* ii
Gypsum or Alabaster, *Derb.* ii; *Notts.* ii

Habberley, *Salop.* viii
Haberdashers' Aske's Schools, *Mdx.* i
Hackleton (in Piddington), *Northants.* iv
Hackness, *Yorks. N.R.* ii; Cell, *Yorks.* iii
Hackney: Hospital, *see* Kingsland Hospital; Knightley of, *see* Genealogy
Haddenham, *Bucks.* ii
Haddenham, *Cambs.* iv; School, *Cambs.* ii
Haddon, *Hunts.* iii
Hadham, Little and Much, *Herts.* iv*
Hadzor, *Worcs.* iii
Haematite-Mining, *Cumb.* ii
Hagbourne, *Berks.* iii
Hagley, *Worcs.* iii
Hagnaby Abbey, *Lincs.* ii
Haileybury, schools, *Herts.* ii*
Hale, *Hants* iv
Halesowen: with Cradley, Lutley, and Warley Wigorn, *Worcs.* iii; Abbey, *Worcs.* ii; Grammar School, *Worcs.* iv
Halford, *Warws.* v
Halfshire Hundred, *Worcs.* iii
Haliwell Priory, *Mdx.* i
Hallaton, *Leics.* v
Hallikeld Wapentake, *Yorks. N.R.* i
Hallow, *Worcs.* iii
Halsall, *Lancs.* iii; Endowed School, *Lancs.* ii
Halstead College, *Essex* ii
Haltemprice Priory, *Yorks.* iii
Halton, *Bucks.* ii
Halton, *Lancs.* viii
Hamble-le-Rice, *Hants* iii; Hamble Priory, *Hants* ii
Hambledon, *Bucks.* iii
Hambledon, *Surr.* iii
Hambledon: with Denmead, Chidden, Glidden, and Ervill's Exton, *Hants* iii; Hundred, *Hants* iii; Hunt, *see* Hunts
Hambleton, *Rut.* ii
Hamerton, *Hunts.* iii
Hamfordshoe Hundred, *Northants.* iv
Hammersmith Hospital, *Mdx.* i
Hampden, Viscount, *see* Genealogy, Brand
Hampden, Great and Little, *Bucks.* ii*
Hampole Priory, *Yorks.* iii
Hampshire Hunt, *see* Hunts
Hampstead Marshall, *Berks.* iv
Hampstead Norris, *Berks.* iv
Hampton, Bishop's, *see* Hampton Lucy
Hampton, Great and Little, *Worcs.* ii
Hampton, with Hampton Wick, *Mdx.* ii; Hampton Grammar School, *Mdx.* i

Hampton Gay, *Oxon.* vi
Hampton-in-Arden, *Warws.* iv
Hampton Lovett, *Worcs.* iii
Hampton Lucy (Bishop's Hampton), *Warws.* iii; School, *Warws.* ii
Hampton Poyle, *Oxon.* vi
Hampton Wick (in Hampton), *Mdx.* ii
Hamsey, *Suss.* vii
Hanbury, *Worcs.* iii
Handale (Grendale) Priory, *Yorks.* iii
Handicrafts, *Glos.* ii; *and see* Crafts
Hang East and West Wapentakes, *Yorks. N.R.* i*
Hangleton, *Suss.* vii
Hanley, *Staffs.* viii
Hanley Castle, *Worcs.* iv; Grammar School, *Worcs.* iv; Young of, *see* Genealogy
Hanley Child (in Eastham), *Worcs.* iv
Hanley William, *Worcs.* iv
Hanney, *Berks.* iv
Hannington, *Hants* iv
Hannington, *Northants.* iv
Hanslope, with Castle Thorpe, *Bucks.* iv
Hanwell, *Mdx.* iii
Hanwell, *Oxon.* ix
Hanworth, *Mdx.* ii
Harbledown Hospital, *Kent* ii
Harborough, Market, *Leics.* v
Harborough Magna, *Warws.* iv
Harbourers, *see* Huntsmen
Harbouring, *Som.* ii
Harbridge, *Hants* iv
Harbury, *Warws.* vi
Hardham Priory, *Suss.* ii
Hardingstone, *Northants.* iv
Hardmead, *Bucks.* iv
Hardware, *Derb.* ii; and Allied Trades, *Lancs.* ii; *and see* Iron
Hardwick, *Northants.* iv
Hardwick, *Oxon.* vi
Hardwick, Priors, *Warws.* v
Hardwick, with Weedon, *Bucks.* iii
Hardwick Hospital, *Norf.* ii
Hare-Hunting, *Dur.* ii; *and see* Beagles; Harriers
Harefield, *Mdx.* iii
Hargrave, *Northants.* iv
Harley, *Salop.* viii
Harlington, *Beds.* iii
Harlington, *Mdx.* iii
Harlsey, East, *Yorks. N.R.* ii
Harmondsworth Priory, *Mdx.* i
Harnall, Radford, and Whitmore Park, *Warws.* viii
Harpenden (in Wheathampstead), *Herts.* ii
Harriers, *Berks.* ii; *Bucks.* ii; *Derb.* ii; *Essex* ii; *Glos.* ii; *Hants* v; *Herts.* ii; *Kent* i; *Lancs.* ii; *Mdx.* ii; *Oxon.* ii; *Som.* ii; *Suff.* ii; *Suss.* ii; *Yorks.* ii; Bath and County, *Som.* ii; Berkshire Vale, *Berks.* ii; Cotley, *Som.* ii; Dubourg's, *Berks.* ii; Minehead, Nettlecombe, Quarme, Seavington, Sparkford Vale, Stanton Drew, Taunton Vale, Wells Subscription, and Weston, *Som.* ii
Harriers (Foot Harriers) and Beagles, *Beds.* ii; *Dors.* ii; *Kent* i; *Lincs.* ii; *Northants.* ii; *Surr.* ii
Harrold, *Beds.* iii; Priory, *Beds.* i
Harrow School, *Mdx.* i, (cricket), *Mdx.* ii
Harrowden, Great and Little, *Northants.* iv*
Hart, *Dur.* iii
Hartfield School, *Suss.* ii
Hartford cum Sapley, *Hunts.* ii
Harting, *Suss.* iv; Hospital, *Suss.* ii
Hartlebury, *Worcs.* iii; Grammar School, *Worcs.* iv
Hartlepool, *Dur.* iii; religious houses, *Dur.* ii*
Hartley Mauditt, *Hants* ii
Hartley Wespall, *Hants* iv
Hartley Wintney, *Hants* iv
Hartshill, *Warws.* iv
Hartwell, *Bucks.* ii
Harvington, *Worcs.* iii

Harwell, *Berks.* iii
Hascombe, *Surr.* iii
Haseley, *Warws.* iii
Haselor, *Warws.* iii
Hasfield, *Glos.* viii
Haslemere, *Surr.* iii
Hastings: Borough, with St. Leonards, *Suss.* ix; Grammar School, *Suss.* ii; Rape and Honour, *Suss.* ix; religious houses, *Suss.* ii*
Hat Industry (Hat-Making, Hats), *see* Caps; Felt; Straw
Hatcham, Hamlet of (in Deptford St. Paul), *Surr.* iv
Hatfield (Bishop's Hatfield), *Herts.* iii
Hatfield Broadoak (Hatfield Regis) Priory, *Essex* ii
Hatfield Peverel Priory, *Essex* ii
Hatfield Regis, *see* Hatfield Broadoak
Hatford, *Berks.* iv
Hatley, Cockayne, *Beds.* ii
Hatton, *Warws.* iii
Hatton (in East Bedfont), *Mdx.* ii
Haugham Priory, *Lincs.* ii
Haughton, *Staffs.* iv
Hautbois Hospital, *Norf.* ii
Hauxwell, *Yorks. N.R.* i
Havant Parish and Liberty, *Hants* iii
Haverholme Priory, *Lincs.* ii
Haversham, *Bucks.* iv
Hawking, *Herts.* i
Hawkley, *Hants* iii
Hawksborough Hundred, *Suss.* ix
Hawkshead, *Lancs.* viii; Grammar School, *Lancs.* ii
Hawnby, *Yorks. N.R.* ii
Hawnes, *see* Haynes
Hawridge, *Bucks.* iii
Haxby, *Yorks. N.R.* ii
Hay and Straw, Supplying to the London Markets, *Essex* ii
Hayles Abbey, *Glos.* ii
Hayling, North and South (in Hayling Island), *Hants* iii
Hayling Island, including North and South Hayling, *Hants* iii; Hayling Priory, *Hants* ii
Haynes (Hawnes), *Beds.* ii
Headington, *Oxon.* v
Headley, *Hants* iii
Headley, *Surr.* iii
Healaugh Park Priory, *Yorks.* iii
Health, *see* Public Health
Hearth Tax Assessments, *see* Tax Assessments
Heath (in Leighton Buzzard), *Beds.* iii
Heathfield, *Suss.* ix
Heckfield, *Hants* iv
Hedgerley, *Bucks.* iii
Hedgerley Dean (in Farnham Royal), *Bucks.* iii
Hedingham, Castle, religious houses, *Essex* ii*
Hedley Priory, *Yorks.* iii
Hedon, religious houses, *Yorks.* iii*
Hedson, *Bucks.* iii
Helmsley, *Yorks. N.R.* i
Helmsley, Gate, *Yorks. N.R.* ii
Helmsley, Upper, *Yorks. N.R.* ii
Helpston, *Northants.* ii
Hemel Hempstead, with Bovingdon and Flaunden, *Herts.* ii
Hemingbrough Collegiate Church, *Yorks.* iii
Hemingford Abbots, *Hunts.* ii
Hemingford Grey, *Hunts.* ii
Hemington, *Northants.* iii
Hemiptera (Aphides, Bugs, Cicadas, Fiend-Flies, Lantern-Flies, Plant-Lice), *Berks.* i; *Cambs.* i; *Cornw.* i*; *Cumb.* i; *Derb.* i; *Devon* i*; *Hants* i*; *Herts.* i; *Kent* i*; *Leics.* i; *Norf.* i; *Notts.* i; *Oxon.* i; *Rut.* i*; *Som.* i; *Staffs.* i*; *Suff.* i; *Surr.* i*; *Suss.* i*; *Warws.* i; *and see* Aphididae
Hemlingford Hundred, *Warws.* iv
Hemp Industry, *Dors.* ii; *and see* Flax; Rope; Sailcloth
Hempton Priory, *Norf.* ii
Henderskelfe (in Bulmer), *Yorks. N.R.* ii

Hendred, East and West, *Berks.* iv*
'Henes' Cell, *Lincs.* ii
Henhurst Hundred, *Suss.* ix
Henley-in-Arden, *Warws.* iii; Hospital, *Warws.* ii
Henlow, *Beds.* ii
Henwood Priory, *Warws.* ii
Hepaticae (Liverworts, Scale-Mosses), *Cornw.* i; *Devon* i; *Kent* i; *Leics.* i; *Northants.* i; *Notts.* i; *Salop.* i; *Som.* i; *Staffs.* i; *Suff.* i; *Worcs.* i; *Yorks.* i; Hepaticae and Musci, *Hants* i; *Herts.* i; *Norf.* i; *and see* Cryptogams
Hepmangrove (in Bury), *Hunts.* ii
Herford Hospital, *Yorks.* iii
Hermitages, *Dur.* ii
Hermits and Anchorites, *Lond.* i
Herriard, *Hants* iii
Herringby Hospital, *Norf.* ii
Herringfleet Priory, *Suff.* ii
Herstmonceux, *Suss.* ix
Hertford: Borough, *Herts.* iii; Hundred, *Herts.* iii; Parts of All Saints' and St. John's, including the Liberties of Brickendon and Little Amwell, *Herts.* iii; religious houses, *Herts.* iv*; schools, *Herts.* ii*; *and see* Parliament, List of Members of
Hertfordshire Hounds, *see* Hounds
Hertingfordbury, *Herts.* iii; Cowper of, *see* Genealogy
Hesketh-with-Becconsall, *Lancs.* vi
Hesking Endowed School, *Lancs.* ii
Hessle, Hospital of St. James, *Yorks.* iii
Heston and Isleworth, *Mdx.* iii
Hethe, *Oxon.* vi
Hexton, *Herts.* ii
Heyford, Lower and Upper, *Oxon.* vi*
Heynings Priory, *Lincs.* ii
Heysham, *Lancs.* viii
Heyshott, *Suss.* iv
Heytesbury, religious houses, *Wilts.* iii*
Heythrop Hunt, *see* Hunts
Hickling Priory, *Norf.* ii
Hidden (in Hungerford), *Berks.* iv
Higham (or Lillechurch) Priory, *Kent* ii
Higham Ferrers: Borough, *Northants.* iii; College, *Northants.* ii; Hundred, *Northants.* iv; *and see* Parliament, List of Members of
Higham Gobion, *Beds.* ii
Higham Park, *Northants.* iii
Highclere, *Hants* iv
Highgate: Hospital of St. Anthony, *Mdx.* i; School, *Mdx.* i
Highway, *Wilts.* vii
Hill (in Fladbury), *Worcs.* iii
Hill-Forts, *see* Enclosures
Hillesden, *Bucks.* iv
Hillhampton (in Martley), *Worcs.* iv
Hillmorton, *Warws.* vi
Hilmarton, *Wilts.* ix
Hilperton, *Wilts.* vii
Hilsea (in Wymering), *Hants* iii
Hilton, *Hunts.* ii
Hilton, *Yorks. N.R.* ii
Himbleton, with Shell, *Worcs.* iii
Hinchinbrook Priory, *Hunts.* i
Hinckley Priory, *Leics.* ii
Hind, Hunting of the, *Som.* ii
Hinderwell, *Yorks. N.R.* ii
Hindlip, *Worcs.* iii
Hinksey, North and South, *Berks.* iv*
Hinton, Cherry, Brigettines, *Cambs.* ii
Hinton Ampner, *Hants* iii
Hinton on the Green, *Glos.* viii
Hinton Priory, *Som.* ii
Hinton Waldrist, *Berks.* iv
Hinwick (in Podington), *Beds.* iii
Hinxworth, *Herts.* iii
Hirst, Temple, Preceptory, *Yorks.* iii
Hirudinea, *Cambs.* i
Hitcham, *Bucks.* iii

Hitchin, *Herts.* iii; Free School, *Herts.* ii; Hundred, *Herts.* iii; religious houses, *Herts.* iv*

Hoathly, West, *Suss.* vii

Hockliffe, *Beds.* iii; Hospital of St. John Baptist, *Beds.* i

Hoddesdon (in Broxbourne), *Herts.* iii; Hospital of St. Laud and St. Anthony, *Herts.* iv

Hodnell, *Warws.* vi

Hoggeston, *Bucks.* iii

Hogshaw, *Bucks.* iv; Commandery, *Bucks.* i

Holbeach Hospital, *Lincs.* ii

Holborn, Hospital of St. Giles-in-the-Fields, *Mdx.* i

Holcot, *Beds.* iii

Holcot, *Northants.* iv

Holdenhurst (in Westover Liberty), *Hants* v

Holderness Foxhounds, *see* Foxhounds

Holdfast (in Ripple), *Worcs.* iii

Holdshot Hundred, *Hants* iv

Hollington, *Suss.* ix

Holm, St. Benet of, *see* St. Benet of Holm

Holmcultram Abbey, *Cumb.* ii

Holme (in Biggleswade), *Beds.* ii

Holme, *Hunts.* iii

Holme, East, Priory, *see* Holne

Holmestrow Hundred, *Suss.* vii

Holne (East Holme) Priory, *Dors.* ii

Holt, with Little Witley, *Worcs.* iii

Holtby, *Yorks. N.R.* ii

Holton, *Oxon.* v

Holwell, *Beds.* ii

Holwell, Little (in Shillington), *Beds.* ii

Holywell, with Needingworth, *Hunts.* ii

Honeybourne, Church, *Worcs.* ii

Honiley, *Warws.* iii

Honington, *Warws.* v

Hood Cell, *Yorks.* iii

Hooe, *Suss.* ix

Hoole, *Lancs.* vi

Hop-Growing, *Essex* ii

Hop-Poles, *Essex* ii

Horbling, Priory of St. Saviour at Bridgend in, *Lincs.* ii

Hordle, *Hants* v

Horkesley, Little, Priory, *Essex* ii

Horley, *Surr.* iii

Horley and Hornton, *Oxon.* ix

Hornton (with Horley), *Oxon.* ix

Hormead, Great, *Herts.* iv; Brand of, *see* Genealogy

Hormead, Little, *Herts.* iv

Hormer Hundred, *Berks.* iv

Horn, *Rut.* ii

Hornby, *Yorks. N.R.* i

Hornby Priory, *Lancs.* ii

Hornchurch Hospital or Priory, *Essex* ii

Horne, *Surr.* iv

Horning Hospital, *Norf.* ii

Horninghold, *Leics.* v

Horse, White, at Uffington, *see* Uffington

Horse-Racing, *see* Racing

Horsehair, *see* Textiles, Mixed

Horsell, *Surr.* iii

Horsenden, *Bucks.* ii

Horses, Famous, *see* Racing Celebrities

Horsetails, *see* Equisetaceae

Horsham: Grammar School, *Suss.* ii; West, Christ's Hospital, *Suss.* ii

Horsham, Priory of St. Faith, *Norf.* ii

Horsley, East and West, *Surr.* iii*

Horsley Priory, *Glos.* ii

Horspath, *Oxon.* v

Horstead Priory, *Norf.* ii

Horticulture, *Cornw.* i; *and see* Fruit-Growing; Market-Gardening; Nursery-Gardening; Rose-Growing; Seed-Growing

Horton, *Bucks.* iii

Horton, *Northants.* iv

Horton, Monks, Priory, *Kent* ii

Horton Priory, *Dors.* ii

Horwell (with Asthill), *Warws.* viii

Horwood, Great and Little, *Bucks.* iii*

Hosiers, Bag-, *see* Knitters

Hosiery (Hosiery Manufacture), *Derb.* ii; *Leics.* iii–iv; *Notts.* ii

Hough Priory, *Lincs.* ii

Houghton, *Hants* iii

Houghton, *Hunts.* ii

Houghton, Great and Little, *Northants.* iv*

Houghton, Hanging (in Lamport), *Northants.* iv

Houghton Conquest, *Beds.* iii; School, *Beds.* ii

Houghton on the Hill, *Leics.* v

Houghton Regis, *Beds.* iii

Hound, with Netley, *Hants* iii

Hounds: Blackmore Vale, *Dors.* ii; Braes of Derwent, *Dur.* ii; Cattistock, *Dors.* ii; Durham County, *Dur.* ii; Fitzwilliam, *Northants.* ii; Goodwood, *Suss.* ii; Grafton, *Northants.* ii; Grove, *Dur.* ii; Hertfordshire, *Herts.* i; Old Berkeley, *Herts.* i; Petworth, *Suss.* ii; Portman, *Dors.* ii; Puckeridge, *Herts.* i; Pytchley, *Northants.* ii; South Dorset, *Dors.* ii; Woodland Pytchley, *Northants.* ii; *and see* Basset Hounds; Beagles; Bloodhounds; Buckhounds; Draghounds; Foxhounds; Harriers; Otter Hounds; Staghounds; Trail Hounds

Hounslow Priory, *Mdx.* i

Houses, Country [Romano-British], *Kent* iii; *Oxon.* i; *Suss* iii

Houses, Landed, *Herts. Fam.*; *Northants. Fam.*

Hove Borough, *Suss.* vii

Hovingham, *Yorks. N.R.* i

Howden College, *Yorks.* iii

Hoxne Priory, *Suff.* ii

Huddington, *Worcs.* iii

Hughenden, *Bucks.* iii

Huish Secondary School, *Som.* ii

Hulcott, *Bucks.* ii

Hull, *see* Kingston upon Hull

Hullavington Priory, *see* Clatford Priory

Hulton, *Staffs.* viii; Abbey, *Staffs.* iii

Humberston Abbey, *Lincs.* ii

Humberstone, *Leics.* iv

Hungerford, with Eddington, Hidden, and Sandon Fee, *Berks.* iv; Grammar School, *Berks.* ii; religious houses, *Berks.* ii*

Hunnington, *Warws.* vi

Hunsdon, *Herts.* iii

Hunston, *Suss.* iv

Hunting, *Beds.* ii; *Berks.* ii; *Derb.* ii; *Dors.* ii; *Essex* ii; *Kent* i; *Lancs.* ii; *Leics.* iii; *Mdx.* ii; *Notts.* ii; *Som.* ii; *Suff.* ii; *Suss.* ii; *Warws.* ii; *Worcs.* ii; *Yorks.* ii; *and see* Basset Hounds; Beagles; Buckhounds; Draghounds; Foulmart; Foxhounds; Foxhunting; Hare-Hunting; Harriers; Hind; Hounds; Hunts; Otter Hounds; Otter-Hunting; Roe-Deer; Stag-Hunting; Staghounds; Sweetmart

Huntingdon: Borough, *Hunts.* ii; Grammar School, *Hunts.* ii; religious houses, *Hunts.* i*

Huntingdon, *Yorks. N.R.* ii

Huntingdonshire, Notices Relating to, Published since 1926, *Hunts.* iii

Huntington, *Staffs.* v

Hunton (in Crawley), *Hants* iii

Hunts: Barlow, *Derb.* ii; Belvoir, *Lincs.* ii; Berkeley, *Glos.* ii; Bicester and Warden Hill, *Oxon.* ii; Blankney, *Lincs.* ii; Brocklesby, *Lincs.* ii; Burstow, *Suss.* ii; Burton, *Lincs.* ii; Charlton, *Suss.* ii; Cirencester (Vale of White Horse), *Glos.* ii; Cottesmore, *Rut.* i; Cotteswold, *Glos.* ii; Craven, *Berks.* ii; Crawley and Horsham, *Suss.* ii; Dulverton, *Som.* ii; East Sussex, First, *Suss.* ii; East Sussex, Present, *Suss.* ii; Eastbourne, *Suss.* ii; Eridge, *Suss.* ii; Ewbank's, *Lincs.* ii; Exeter, *Lincs.* ii; Exmoor, *Som.* ii; Garth, *Berks.* ii; *Hants* v; Hambledon, *Hants* v; Hampshire, *Hants* v; Heythrop, *Oxon.* ii; Hurworth, *Dur.* ii; Hursley, *Hants* v; Isle of Wight, *Hants* v; Meynell, *Derb.* ii; North Cotteswold, *Glos.* ii;

Oakley, *Beds.* ii; Old Berkeley, *Bucks.* ii; Old Berkshire, *Berks.* ii; South Berks, *Berks.* ii; South Oxfordshire, *Oxon.* ii; Southwold, *Lincs.* ii; Taunton Vale, *Som.* ii; Tedworth, *Hants* v; Vine, *Hants* v; Vale of White Horse (Cirencester), *Glos.* ii; West Somerset, *Som.* ii; Whaddon Chase, *Bucks.* ii; *and see* Hounds

Huntsmen, Whips, and Harbourers, *Som.* ii; *and see* Harbouring

Hurley, *Berks.* iii; Priory, *Berks.* ii

Hursley, *Hants* iii; Hunt, *see* Hunts

Hurst, *Berks.* iii

Hurst, Old, *Hunts.* ii

Hurstbourne Priors, *Hants* iv

Hurstbourne Tarrant, *Hants* iv

Hurstingstone Hundred, *Hunts.* ii

Hurstpierpoint, *Suss.* vii; College, *Suss.* ii

Hurworth, *Dur.* iii; Hunt, *see* Hunts

Husborne Crawley, *Beds.* iii

Husthwaite, *Yorks. N.R.* ii

Hutton, Sheriff, *Yorks. N.R.* ii

Hutton Bushel, *Yorks. N.R.* ii

Hutton Conyers, *Yorks. N.R.* i

Hutton Magna (Hutton Longvilliers), *Yorks. N.R.* i

Huttons Ambo, *Yorks. N.R.* ii

Huxloe Hundred, *Northants.* iii

Huyton, *Lancs.* iii

Hyde, East and West (in Luton), *Beds.* ii

Hyde Abbey, *see* Winchester

Hydes Pastures, *Warws.* vi

Hykeham, North, Priory, *Lincs.* ii

Hymel, Castle, *see* Fineshade

Hymenoptera (Ants, Bees, Chrysids, Gall-Flies, Ichneumons, Ruby-tailed Flies, Ruby-Wasps, Sawflies, Wasps, etc.), *Berks.* i*; *Cambs.* i*; *Cornw.* i*; *Cumb.* i; *Derb.* i; *Devon* i*; *Hants* i*; *Herts.* i; *Kent* i*; *Leics.* i; *Norf.* i; *Northants.* i; *Notts.* i; *Oxon.* i*; *Rut.* i; *Som.* i; *Staffs.* i*; *Suff.* i; *Surr.* i*; *Suss.* i*; *Warws.* i; *Worcs.* i*; *Yorks.* i

Hyrst Priory, *Lincs.* ii

Hythe Hospital, *Kent* ii

Ibsley, *Hants* iv

Ibstone, *Bucks.* iii

Iccomb, *Worcs.* iii

Ichneumon-Flies (Ichneumons) (Hymenoptera Entomophaga or Ichneumonidae), *see* Hymenoptera

Ickburgh Hospital, *Norf.* ii

Ickford, *Bucks.* iv

Ickleford, *Herts.* iii

Icklesham, *Suss.* ix

Ickleton Priory, *Cambs.* ii

Iden, *Suss.* ix

Idlicote, *Warws.* v

Idsworth (in Chalton), *Hants* iii

Iffley, *Oxon.* v

Iford, *Suss.* vii

Ikanho Monastery, *Lincs.* ii

Ilchester, religious houses, *Som.* ii*

Ilford, *Essex* v; Hospital, *Essex* ii

Illston on the Hill, *Leics.* v

Ilmer, *Bucks.* iv

Ilmington, *Warws.* v

Ilminster Free Grammar School, *Som.* ii

Ilsley, East and West, *Berks.* iv*

Implements, *see* Agricultural Implements

Inclosure Acts, Parliamentary, and Awards, Table of, *Leics.* ii; Inclosures without Parliamentary Acts, Table of, *Leics.* ii

India Rubber, *Lancs.* ii; *Wilts.* iv; *and see* Gutta-Percha

Industries, *Beds.* ii; *Berks.* i; *Bucks.* ii; *Cambs.* ii; *Cornw.* i; *Cumb.* ii; *Derb.* ii; *Dors.* ii; *Dur.* ii; *Essex* ii; *Glos.* ii; *Hants* v; *Herts.* iv; *Kent* iii; *Lancs.* ii; *Leics.* iii; *Lincs.* ii; *Mdx.* ii; *Northants.* ii; *Notts.* ii; *Oxon.* ii; *Rut.* i; *Salop.* i; *Som.* ii; *Staffs.* ii; *Suff.* ii; *Surr.* ii; *Suss.* ii; *Warws.* ii; *Wilts.* iv; *Worcs.* ii; *Yorks.* ii; [Romano-British],

Kent iii; *Oxon.* i; Derived from Agriculture, Geology, and the University, *Cambs.* ii*; *and see* Crafts

Ingham Priory, *Norf.* ii

Ingleby Arncliffe, *Yorks. N.R.* ii

Ingleby Greenhow, *Yorks. N.R.* ii

Ingthorpe (in Tinwell), *Rut.* ii

Inkberrow, *Worcs.* iii

Inkpen, *Berks.* iv

Inquisitio Comitatus Cantabrigiensis, Translation and Index, *Cambs.* i*

Inscriptions, *see* Art, Early Christian

Insecta (Insects), *Beds.* i; *Berks.* i; *Bucks.* i; *Cambs.* i; *Cornw.* i; *Cumb.* i; *Derb.* i; *Devon* i; *Dur.* i; *Essex* i; *Hants.* i; *Herefs.* i; *Herts.* i; *Hunts.* i; *Kent* i; *Lancs.* i; *Leics.* i; *Norf.* i; *Northants.* i; *Notts.* i; *Oxon.* i; *Rut.* i; *Salop.* i; *Som.* i; *Staffs.* i; *Suff.* i; *Surr.* i; *Suss.* i; *Warws.* i; *Worcs.* i; *Yorks.* i

Insignia, *see* Seals

Introduction, General [to Genealogy], *Herts. Fam.*; *Northants. Fam.*

Iping, *Suss.* iv

Ippollitts, *Herts.* iii

Ipsley, *Warws.* iii

Ipswich: religious houses, *Suff.* ii*; School, *Suff.* ii

Irchester, with Knuston and Chester-on-the-Water, *Northants.* iv

Iron, *Derb.* ii; *Kent* iii; *Lancs.* ii; *Som.* ii; *Staffs.* ii; *Surr.* ii; *Suss.* ii; *Worcs.* ii; and Coal, *Salop.* i; and Hardware, *Yorks.* ii; and Ironworks, *Hants* v; and Steel, *Dur.* ii; *Staffs.* ii; Iron-Founding, *Essex* ii; Iron-Founding and Agricultural Machine-Making, *Oxon.* ii; Iron-Foundries, Shipbuilding, and Railway Works, *Bucks.* ii; Iron-Mining, *Dur.* ii; *Yorks.* ii; Iron Ore Industry, *Oxon.* ii; Ironstone-Mining, *Yorks.* ii; Ironwork, Foundries, Motors, Cycles, and Machine-Building, *Notts.* ii; Ironworks (Iron-Working), *Berks.* i; *Hants* v; *Salop.* i; *Wilts.* iv; Ironworks [Romano-British], *Suss.* iii; *and see* Foundries

Iron Age, *Mdx.* i; Early, *Oxon.* i; *Suff.* i; *and see* Antiquities; Prehistoric, *Berks.* i

Irthlingborough, *Northants.* iii; College, *Northants.* ii

Isham, *Northants.* iv

Isham Family, *see* Genealogy

Isinglass and Gelatine-Making, *Essex* ii

Isleworth: (with Heston), *Mdx.* iii; Hundred, *Mdx.* iii

Islip, *Northants.* iii

Islip, *Oxon.* vi

Itchen Abbas, *Hants* iv

Itchen Stoke, with Abbotstone, *Hants* iv

Itchenor, West, *Suss.* iv

Itchington, Bishop's, *Warws.* vi

Itchington, Long, *Warws.* vi

Iver, *Bucks.* iii

Ivinghoe, *Bucks.* iii; Priory, *Bucks.* i

Ivychurch Priory, *Wilts.* iii

Ixworth Priory, *Suff.* ii

Jam-Making and Fruit-Preserving, *Essex* ii

Jarrow: Friars Preachers, *Dur.* iii; Monastery, *see* Wearmouth

Jervaulx Abbey, *Yorks.* iii; *Yorks. N.R.* i

Jews (Jewish Congregations), *Mdx.* i; *Staffs.* viii; *Yorks. York*

Jute-Spinning, *Essex* ii

Keele Preceptory, *Staffs.* iii

Keevil, *Wilts.* viii

Keldholme Priory, *Yorks.* iii

Kellet, Over, School, *Lancs.* ii

Kelshall, *Herts.* iii

Kelvedon Hatch, *Essex* iv

Kemerton, *Glos.* viii

Kempsey, *Worcs.* iii

Kempshot (in Dummer), *Hants* iii

Kempshott (in Winslade), *Hants* iv

Kempston, *Beds.* iii

Kenilworth, *Warws.* vi; Abbey, *Warws.* ii
Kenley, *Salop.* viii
Kenswick (in Knightwick), *Worcs.* iii
Kensworth, *Herts.* ii
Kepier, Hospital of St. Giles, *Dur.* ii
Keresley, *Warws.* viii
Kersal Cell, *Lancs.* ii
Kersey Priory, *Suff.* ii
Keswick, House of St. John, *Cumb.* ii
Kettering, *Northants.* iii
Ketton, *Rut.* ii
Kew, *Surr.* iii
Keymer, *Suss.* vii
Keynsham Abbey, *Som.* ii
Keys, *see* Locks
Keysoe, *Beds.* iii
Keyston, *Hunts.* iii
Kibworth, *Leics.* v
Kick-shins, *see* Cut-legs
Kidderminster: Borough, with Lower Mitton, *Worcs.* iii;
    Grammar School, *Worcs.* iv
Kilburn Priory, *Mdx.* i
Kildale, *Yorks. N.R.* ii; Crutched Friars, *Yorks.* iii
Killingwoldgraves, Hospital of St. Mary Magdalene,
    Yorks. iii
Kilmeston, *Hants* iii
Kilvington, South, *Yorks. N.R.* ii
Kimble, Great and Little, *Bucks.* ii*
Kimbolton, *Hunts.* iii; Grammar School, *Hunts.* ii
Kimpton, *Hants* iv
Kimpton, *Herts.* iii
Kineton, with Combrook, *Warws.* v
King's Mead Priory, *Derb.* ii
Kingsbridge Hundred, *Wilts.* ix
Kingsbury, *Warws.* iv; School, *Warws.* ii
Kingsclere, *Hants* iv; Hundred, *Hants* iv
Kingsey, *Bucks.* iv
Kingsham, *Suss.* iii
Kingsland (or Hackney) Hospital, *Mdx.* i
Kingsley, *Hants* ii
Kingsthorpe, *Northants.* iv; Hospital of St. David and the
    Holy Trinity, *Northants.* ii
Kingston, *Hants* v
Kingston, near Lewes, *Suss.* vii
Kingston Bagpuize, *Berks.* iv
Kingston Hundred, *Surr.* iii
Kingston upon Hull (Hull): City, *Yorks. E.R.* i; religious
    houses, *Yorks.* iii*; Trinity House, *Yorks. E.R.* i
Kingston-upon-Thames, *Surr.* iii; Collegiate Chapel of
    St. Mary Magdalen, *Surr.* ii
Kingswood Abbey, *Glos.* ii
Kingswood (in Ludgershall), *Bucks.* iv
Kington, *Worcs.* iii
Kington Hundred, *Warws.* iv
Kington St. Michael Priory, *Wilts.* iii
Kintbury, *Berks.* iv
Kintbury Eagle Hundred, *Berks.* iv
Kinver Forest, *Staffs.* ii
Kinwarton, *Warws.* iii
Kirby, Cold, *Yorks. N.R.* ii
Kirby, Monks, *Warws.* vi; Priory, *Warws.* ii; School,
    Warws. ii
Kirby Bellairs [monastery], *Leics.* ii
Kirkby Fleetham, *Yorks. N.R.* i
Kirkby Hill (Kirkby on the Moor), *Yorks. N.R.* i
Kirkby-in-Cleveland, *Yorks. N.R.* ii
Kirkby Ireleth, *Lancs.* viii
Kirkby Knowle, *Yorks. N.R.* ii
Kirkby Misperton, *Yorks. N.R.* ii
Kirkby Moorside, *Yorks. N.R.* i
Kirkby on the Moor, *see* Kirkby Hill
Kirkby Overblow Collegiate Church, *Yorks.* iii
Kirkby Ravensworth, *Yorks. N.R.* i
Kirkby Sigston, *Yorks. N.R.* i
Kirkby Wiske, *Yorks. N.R.* i
Kirkdale, *Yorks. N.R.* i

Kirkham, *Lancs.* vii; Grammar School, *Lancs.* ii
Kirkham Priory, *Yorks.* iii
Kirkleatham, *Yorks. N.R.* ii
Kirklees Priory, *Yorks.* iii
Kirklington, *Yorks. N.R.* i
Kirkoswald College, *Cumb.* ii
Kirkstall Abbey, *Yorks.* iii
Kirkstead, *Lincs.* ii
Kirtlington, *Oxon.* vi
Knaresborough, Trinitarian Friars, *Yorks.* iii
Knebworth, *Herts.* iii
Knightley, Knightley of, *see* Genealogy
Knightley Family, *see* Genealogy
Knightlow Hundred, *Warws.* vi
Knighton, *Leics.* iv
Knighton on Teme (in Lindridge), *Worcs.* iii
Knightsbridge Hospital, *Mdx.* i
Knightwick, with Kenswick, *Worcs.* iii
Knitters, Framework-, Stocking-Frames, Bag-Hosiers,
    and Manufacturers, *Leics.* iii
Knossington, *Leics.* v
Knotting, *Beds.* iii
Knowle, *Warws.* iv; College, *Warws.* ii
Knuston (in Irchester), *Northants.* iv
Kyme Priory, *Lincs.* ii
Kyre Magna, *see* Kyre Wyard
Kyre Parva (in Stoke Bliss), *Worcs.* iv
Kyre Wyard (Kyre Magna), *Worcs.* iv

Lace (Lace-Making), *Bucks.* ii; *Essex* ii; *Derb.* ii; *Northants.*
    ii; *Notts.* ii; *Oxon.* ii; Lace, Net, and Thread, *Som.* ii;
    Pillow-Lace, *Beds.* ii
Lace-wings, *see* Neuroptera
Lacock Abbey, *Wilts.* iii
Ladbroke, *Warws.* vi
Lainston (in Sparsholt), *Hants* iii
Laleham, *Mdx.* ii
Lambeth, *Surr.* iv; College, *Surr.* ii; Palace, *Surr.* iv
Lambourn, *Berks.* iv; Hospital, *Berks.* ii; Hundred,
    Berks. iv
Lambourne, *Essex* iv
Lambton Foxhounds, *see* Foxhounds
Lamport: with Hanging Houghton, *Northants.* iv; Isham
    of, *see* Genealogy
Lancaster, *Lancs.* vii–viii; religious houses, *Lancs.* ii*;
    Royal Grammar School, *Lancs.* ii
Lanchester College, *Dur.* ii
Lancing College, *Suss.* ii
Landed Houses, *see* Houses, Landed
Lanercost Priory, *Cumb.* ii
Langbaurgh Wapentake (East and West), *Yorks. N.R.* ii
Langdon, West, Abbey, *Kent* ii
Langford, *Beds.* ii
Langham, *Rut.* ii
Langham Family, *see* Genealogy
Langley (with Ruckley), *Salop.* viii
Langley, Abbot's, *Herts.* ii
Langley, King's, *Herts.* ii; Friary or Priory, *Herts.* ii, iv
Langley Abbey, *Norf.* ii
Langley Marish, *Bucks.* iii
Langley Priory, *Leics.* ii
Langport (Langport Eastover): Free School, *Som.* ii;
    Hospital, *Som.* ii
Langton, Church, *Leics.* v
Langton, Great, *Yorks. N.R.* i
Langwade Hospital, *Norf.* ii
Langworth Hospital, *Lincs.* ii
Lantern-Flies (Hemiptera Homoptera), *see* Hemiptera
Lanthony Priory, *see* Gloucester
Lapley, *Staffs.* iv; Priory, *Staffs.* iii
Lapworth, *Warws.* v
Lasham, *Hants* iv
Lastingham, *Yorks. N.R.* i
Lathbury, *Bucks.* iv
Lathom Almshouse, *Lancs.* ii
Latton Priory, *Essex* ii

Latymer and Godolphin Schools, *Mdx.* i
Laughton, *Leics.* v
Launde Priory, *Leics.* ii
Launton, *Oxon.* vi
Lavant, East and Mid, *Suss.* iv*
Lavendon, *Bucks.* iv; Abbey, *Bucks.* i
Laver, High, *Essex* iv
Laver, Little, *Essex* iv
Laver, Magdalen, *Essex* iv
Laverstoke, *Hants* iv
Lavington, Bishop's, *see* Lavington, West
Lavington, West, *Suss.* iv
Lavington, West (Bishop's Lavington), *Wilts.* vii
Lawford, Church, *Warws.* vi
Layston, *Herts.* iv
Lazenby Hospital or Collegiate Church, *Yorks.* iii
Lea Marston, *Warws.* iv
Lead, Sheet, Manufacture, *Essex* ii
Lead-Mining, *Derb.* ii; *Dur.* ii; *Som.* ii; *Yorks.* ii
Leagrave (in Luton), *Beds.* ii
Leake, *Yorks. N.R.* i
Leamington Hastings, *Warws.* vi
Leamington Spa, Borough, *Warws.* vi
Leather (Leather Industries), *Essex* ii; *Glos.* ii; *Northants.* ii; *Oxon.* ii; *Surr.* ii; *Worcs.* ii; Breeches and Gloves, *Essex* ii; *and see* Saddlery; Tanning
Leatherhead, *see* Letherhead
Leavington, Kirk, *Yorks. N.R.* ii
Lechlade, Hospital of St. John the Baptist, *Glos.* ii
Leckby (in Cundall), *Yorks. N.R.* i
Leckford, *Hants* iv
Leckhampstead, *Bucks.* iv
Leckhampstead (in Chieveley), *Berks.* iv
Lee, *Bucks.* ii
Leebotwood, *Salop.* viii
Leeds Priory, *Kent* ii
Legbourne Priory, *Lincs.* ii
Leicester: City, *Leics.* iv; Liberties of Black Friars, Castle View, The Newarke, Bromkinsthorpe, and White Friars, *Leics.* iv*; North-West, *Leics.* iv; Parishes added since 1892, *Leics.* iv; Parishes of All Saints, St. Leonard, St. Margaret, St. Martin, St. Mary, and St. Nicholas, *Leics.* iv*; religious houses, *Leics.* ii*; West Gate and Mosaic Pavements, *Leics.* i
Leicestershire Survey, *Leics.* i
Leigh, *Glos.* viii
Leigh, *Lancs.* iii; Grammar School, *Lancs.* ii
Leigh, *Surr.* iii
Leigh, with Bransford, *Worcs.* iv
Leighs, Little, Priory, *Essex* ii
Leighton Bromswold, *Hunts.* iii
Leighton Buzzard, with Billington, Egginton, Heath and Reach, and Stanbridge, *Beds.* iii
Leightonstone Hundred, *Hunts.* iii
Leiston Abbey, *Suff.* ii
Lekeley, *see* Seton
Lemington, Lower, *Glos.* vi
Lenborough (in Buckingham), *Bucks.* iii
Lench, Church, *Worcs.* iii
Lench, Rous, *Worcs.* iii
Lenton, religious houses, *Notts.* ii*
Lepe (in Exbury), *Hants* iii
Lepidoptera (Micro-Lepidoptera, Butterflies, Moths), *Beds.* i; *Berks.* i; *Cambs.* i; *Cornw.* i*; *Cumb.* i; *Derb.* i; *Devon* i*; *Hants* i*; *Herefs.* i; *Herts.* i; *Hunts.* i; *Kent* i*; *Leics.* i*; *Norf.* i; *Northants.* i*; *Notts.* i; *Oxon.* i; *Rut.* i*; *Salop.* i*; *Som.* i; *Staffs.* i*; *Suff.* i; *Surr.* i*; *Suss.* i*; *Warws.* i; *Worcs.* i; *Yorks.* i
Lesnes (or Westwood) Abbey, *Kent* ii
Lessingham Priory, *Norf.* ii
Letchworth, *Herts.* iii
Letcombe Bassett, *Berks.* iv
Letcombe Regis, with East and West Challow, *Berks.* iv
Letherhead, *Surr.* iii
Letheringham Priory, *Suff.* ii
Leverington, *Cambs.* iv

Levisham, *Yorks. N.R.* ii
Lewes: Borough, *Suss.* vii; Grammar School, *Suss.* ii; Rape and Honour, *Suss.* vii; religious houses, *Suss.* ii*
Lewisham Priory, *Kent* ii
Lewknor, *Oxon.* viii; Hundred, *Oxon.* viii; *and see* Tax Assessments, Village
Leyland, *Lancs.* vi; Grammar School, *Lancs.* ii; Hundred, *Lancs.* vi
Libraries, Public, *Essex Bibl.*
Lichenes (Lichens), *Cornw.* i; *Devon* i; *Hants.* i; *Herts.* i; *Kent* i; *Leics.* i; *Norf.* i; *Northants.* i; *Notts.* i; *Salop.* i; *Som.* i; *Staffs.* i; *Suff.* i; *Surr.* i; *Worcs.* i; *Yorks.* i; *and see* Cryptogams
Lichfield: Cathedral, *Staffs.* iii; religious houses, *Staffs.* iii*
Liddell, Lord Wake of, *see* Genealogy
Liddington, *Rut.* ii
Liddington, *Wilts.* ix
Lidlington, *Beds.* iii
Lighthorne, *Warws.* v
Lilford, Lord, *see* Genealogy, Powys
Lilford-with-Wigsthorpe, *Northants.* iii
Lillechurch Priory, *see* Higham Priory
Lilley, *Herts.* iii
Lillingstone Dayrell, *Bucks.* iv
Lillingstone Lovell, *Bucks.* iv
Lillington, *Warws.* vi
Limber, Great, Priory, *Lincs.* ii
Limbury (in Luton), *Beds.* ii
Lime-Burning, *Essex* ii; *and see* Stone Quarries
Limpsfield, *Surr.* iv
Linch, *Suss.* iv
Linchmere, *Suss.* iv
Lincoln, religious houses, *Lincs.* ii*
Lindridge, with Knighton on Teme, Newnham, and Pensax, *Worcs.* iii
Linen Industry, *Lancs.* ii; *and see* Flax
Linford, Great and Little, *Bucks.* iv*
Linford (in Fordingbridge), *Hants* iv
Lingfield, *Surr.* iv; College, *Surr.* ii
Linkenholt, *Hants* iv
Linseed Oil Manufacture, *Essex* ii
Linslade, *Bucks.* iii
Linton Priory, *Cambs.* ii
Linwood, *Hants* iv
Liss, *Hants* iv
Litchfield, *Hants* iv
Littlemore, *Oxon.* v; Priory, *Oxon.* ii
Littleport, *Cambs.* iv
Littleton, *Hants* iii
Littleton, *Mdx.* ii
Littleton, North, Middle, and South, *Worcs.* ii*
Littleworth (with Wheatley), *Oxon.* v
Liverpool, *Lancs.* iv; schools, *Lancs.* ii*
Liverton, *Yorks. N.R.* ii
Liverworts, *see* Hepaticae
Lobsters, *see* Crustacea
Lockerley, *Hants* iv
Lockinge, East and West, *Berks.* iv
Locko Preceptory, *Derb.* ii
Locks and Keys, *Staffs.* ii
Locomotives, Agricultural Implements, Milling Machinery, etc., *Suff.* i
Loders Priory, *Dors.* ii
Lodsworth, *Suss.* iv
Loftus, *Yorks. N.R.* ii
London: Charterhouse, *Mdx.* i; Elwes of, *see* Genealogy; Hermits and Anchorites, *Lond.* i; Langham of, *see* Genealogy; Markets, *see* Hay; North London Collegiate School, *Mdx.* i; religious houses, *Lond.* i*; Roman City Wall, *Lond.* i; Turner and Page-Turner of, *see* Genealogy; University, *Mdx.* i; University, Constituent Colleges, *Mdx.* i; Wake of, *see* Genealogy; *and see* Games, Olympic
Longbridge Hospital, *see* Berkeley
Longdon, *Worcs.* iv

Longleat Priory, *Wilts.* iii
Longnor, *Salop.* viii
Longparish, *Hants* iv
Longstock, *Hants* iv
Longstow Hospital, *Cambs.* ii
Longton, *Staffs.* viii
Longworth, *Berks.* iv
Lonsdale Hundred (South and North of the Sands), *Lancs.* viii*
Lord's [cricket ground], *see* Australians
Lorwing Hospital, *Glos.* ii
Lossenham, Carmelite Friars, *Kent* ii
Loughborough Hospital, *Leics.* ii
Loughton, *Bucks.* iv
Loughton, *Essex* iv
Louth: Commandery at Maltby by, *Lincs.* ii; Hospital, *Lincs.* ii; Louth Park Abbey, *Lincs.* ii
Lowcross, Hospital of St. Leonard, *Yorks.* iii
Lowestoft China, *see* China
Lowick, *Northants.* iii
Lowthorpe Collegiate Church, *Yorks.* iii
Loxley, *Warws.* iii
Lubenham, *Leics.* v
Luckyn Family, *see* Genealogy
Luddington, *Northants.* iii
Ludgershall: with Kingswood, *Bucks.* iv; Hospital, *Bucks.* i
Luffenham, North and South, *Rut.* ii*
Luffield Abbey [village], *Bucks.* iv; Luffield Priory, *Bucks.* i
Luffield Priory, *Northants.* ii
Lulsley (in Suckley), *Worcs.* iv
Lutley (in Halesowen), *Worcs.* iii
Luton: with East and West Hyde, Stopsley, Limbury cum Biscott, and Leagrave, *Beds.* ii; Hospital of Farley near, *Beds.* i; religious houses, *Beds.* i*; School, *Beds.* ii
Lutterworth Hospital, *Leics.* ii
Lutton, *Northants.* ii
Lycopodiaceae (Clubmosses), *Herts.* i; and Equisetaceae, *Herefs.* i; *and see* Cryptogams; Plants, Vascular
Lydiard Tregoze, *Wilts.* ix
Lyme, religious houses, *Dors.* ii*
Lyminge Abbey, *Kent* ii
Lymington Borough, *Hants* iv
Lyminster Priory, *Suss.* ii
Lyndhurst, *Hants* iv
Lyndon, *Rut.* ii
Lyneham, *Wilts.* ix
Lynn, religious houses, *Norf.* ii*
Lytham, *Lancs.* vii; Priory, *Lancs.* ii
Lythe, *Yorks. N.R.* ii
Lytton Family, *see* Genealogy

Machine-Building, Ironwork, Foundries, Motors, Cycles, *Notts.* ii; Agricultural Machine-Making and Iron-Founding, *Oxon.* ii; Machinery, *Salop.* i; Machinery, Milling, Agricultural Implements, etc., *Suff.* ii; Machinery Works and Metal, *Surr.* ii; *and see* Printing
Madresfield, *Worcs.* iv
Maidenhead Borough (in Bray), *Berks.* iii
Maidstone, religious houses, *Kent* ii*
Mainsborough Hundred, *Hants* iv
Mainsbridge Hundred, *Hants* iii
Malden, *Surr.* iii; College, *Surr.* ii
Maldon, Abbey of Beeleigh by, *Essex* ii
Maldon, Little, Hospital, *Essex* ii
Maldon, White Friars, *Essex* ii
Malling, South, College, *Suss.* ii
Malling Abbey, *Kent* ii
Malmesbury, religious houses, *Wilts.* iii*
Maltby Commandery, *see* Louth
Malting, *Suff.* ii; and Brewing, *Essex* ii; *Hants* v; *Notts.* ii; *Oxon.* ii; Malting, Milling, and Brewing, *Glos.* ii
Malton, New, including the Parishes of St. Leonard and St. Michael, *Yorks. N.R.* i
Malton, Old, *Yorks. N.R.* i; religious houses, *Yorks.* iii*

Malvern, Great, with Newland, *Worcs.* iv; Malvern College, *Worcs.* iv; Priory, *Worcs.* ii
Malvern, Little, *Worcs.* iii; Priory, *Worcs.* ii
Mamble, *Worcs.* iv
Mammalia (Mammals), *Beds.* i; *Berks.* i; *Bucks.* i; *Cambs.* i; *Cornw.* i; *Cumb.* i; *Derb.* i; *Devon* i; *Dur.* i; *Essex* i; *Hants* i; *Herefs.* i; *Herts.* i; *Hunts.* i; *Kent* i; *Lancs.* i; *Leics.* i; *Norf.* i; *Northants.* i; *Notts.* i; *Oxon.* i; *Rut.* i; *Salop.* i; *Som.* i; *Staffs.* i; *Suff.* i; *Surr.* i; *Suss.* i; *Warws.* i; *Worcs.* i; *Yorks.* i
Man, Early, *see* Early Man
Mancetter, *Warws.* iv
Manchester, *Lancs.* iv; College, *Lancs.* ii; schools, *Lancs.* ii*
Manea (in Coveney), *Cambs.* iv
Manfield, *Yorks. N.R.* i
Manganese, *Derb.* ii
Manhood Hundred, *Suss.* iv
Manors, *see* Parishes, Townships, and Manors
Mansfield, schools, *Notts.* ii*
Manshead Hundred, *Beds.* iii
Manton, *Rut.* ii; College of Blessed Mary, *Rut.* i
Maplederwell, *Hants* iv
Maplestead, Little, Preceptory, *Essex* ii
Marble, Stone, and Slate, *Derb.* ii
March, *Cambs.* iv; School, *Cambs.* ii
Marcham, *Berks.* iv
Marden, East, North, and Up, *Suss.* iv*
Marfleet, *Yorks. E.R.* i
Marham Abbey, *Norf.* ii
Marholm, *Northants.* ii
Maritime History, *Cornw.* i; *Dors.* ii; *Essex* ii; *Hants* v; *Kent* ii; *Som.* ii; *Suff.* ii; *Suss.* ii
Markby Priory, *Lincs.* ii
Market-Gardening, *Essex* ii; *and see* Fruit-Growing
Markyate Priory, *Beds.* i
Marlborough, religious houses, *Wilts.* iii*
Marlow, Great, *Bucks.* iii; Sir William Borlase's School, *Bucks.* ii
Marlow, Little, *Bucks.* iii; Priory, *Bucks.* i
Marmont Priory, *Cambs.* ii
Marrick, *Yorks. N.R.* i; Priory, *Yorks.* iii
Marske (East Langbaurgh Wapentake), *Yorks. N.R.* ii
Marske (Gilling West Wapentake), *Yorks. N.R.* i
Marston, *Oxon.* v
Marston, Butlers, *Warws.* v
Marston, Fleet, *Bucks.* iv
Marston, Long (in Tring), *Herts.* ii
Marston, North, *Bucks.* iv
Marston, Priors, *Warws.* v
Marston Mortaine, *Beds.* iii
Marsworth, *Bucks.* iii
Martin, *Hants* iv
Martin Hussingtree, *Worcs.* iv
Martinsley Hundred, *Rut.* ii
Martinsthorpe, *Rut.* ii
Martley: with Hillhampton, *Worcs.* iv; School, *Worcs.* iv
Martock Free Grammar School, *Som.* ii
Marton, *Warws.* vi
Marton, *Yorks. N.R.* ii
Marton, with Moxby, *Yorks. N.R.* ii; Priory, *Yorks.* iii
Marwell College, *Hants* ii
Marylebone Cricket Club, *Mdx.* ii
Masham, *Yorks. N.R.* i
Massingham, Great, Priory, *Norf.* ii
Mathon, *Worcs.* iv
Mats and Matting, Manufacture of, *Essex* ii; Rush-Matting Industry, *see* Pavenham
Mattersey Priory, *Notts.* ii
Maulden, *Beds.* iii
Maunsell Family, *see* Genealogy
Maxey, *Northants.* ii
Maxstoke, *Warws.* iv; Priory, *Warws.* ii
Mayflies, *see* Ephemeroptera
Mayne, Friar, Preceptory, *Dors.* ii
Mead-Making, *Essex* ii

Meaux Abbey, *Yorks.* iii
Mecoptera, *Oxon.* i; and Neuroptera, *Cambs.* i
Medbourne, *Leics.* v
Medical Services, *see* Public Health
Medieval Cambridgeshire, *Cambs.* ii
Medine, East and West, Liberties or Hundreds, *Hants* v*
Medmenham, *Bucks.* iii; Abbey, *Bucks.* i
Medsted, *Hants* iii
Meesden, *Herts.* iv
Megaloptera, *Oxon.* i
Melchbourne, *Beds.* iii; Priory, *Beds.* i
Melchet Forest, *see* Clarendon
Melchet Park, *Hants* iv
Melcombe Regis, Dominican Friars, *Dors.* ii
Melksham, *Wilts.* vii; Forest, *see* Chippenham; Hundred, *Wilts.* vii
Melling, *Lancs.* viii
Mells Grammar School, *Som.* ii
Melsonby, *Yorks. N.R.* i
Members of Parliament, *see* Parliament
Mendham Priory, *Suff.* ii
Menthae, *Cornw.* i; *Norf.* i
Mentmore, *Bucks.* iii
Meols, North, *Lancs.* iii
Meon, East, *Hants* iii; Hundred, *Hants* iii
Meon, West, *Hants* iii
Meonstoke, *Hants* iii; Hundred, *Hants* iii
Mepal, *Cambs.* iv
Meppershall, *Beds.* ii
Mere Hospital, *Lincs.* ii
Merevale, *Warws.* iv; Abbey, *Warws.* ii
Meriden, *Warws.* iv
Merrow, *Surr.* iii
Mersea, West, Priory, *Essex* ii
Merstham, *Surr.* iii
Merston, *Suss.* iv
Merton, *Oxon.* v
Merton, *Surr.* iv; Priory of St. Mary, *Surr.* ii
Mesolithic Age, *Mdx.* i; *Oxon.* i
Metal and Machinery Works, *Surr.* ii; Metal Industries (Working), and Engineering, *Glos.* ii; *Leics.* iii; Metal Tubes, *Staffs.* ii
Mettingham College, *Suff.* ii
Meynell Hunt, *see* Hunts
Micheldever, *Hants* iii; Hundred, *Hants* iii
Michelham Priory, *Suss.* ii
Michelmersh, *Hants* iii
Mickleham, *Surr.* iii
Mid-Kent Staghounds, *see* Staghounds
Middleham, *Yorks. N.R.* i; religious houses, *Yorks.* iii
Middleham, Bishop, *Dur.* iii
Middlesbrough, *Yorks. N.R.* ii; Priory, *Yorks.* iii
Middlesex County Cricket, *Mdx.* ii
Middleton, Lord, his Foxhounds, *see* Foxhounds
Middleton, *Lancs.* v; Grammar School, *Lancs.* ii
Middleton, *Warws.* iv
Middleton, *Yorks. N.R.* ii
Middleton St. George, *Dur.* iii
Middleton Stoney, *Oxon.* vi
Middleton Tyas, *Yorks. N.R.* i
Midhurst, *Suss.* iv; Grammar School, *Suss.* ii
Midloe, *Hunts.* ii
Milcote (in Weston-upon-Avon), *Warws.* v
Mile End Hospital, *Mdx.* i
Milestones and Roads [Romano-British], *Cornw.* ii (5)
Milford, *Hants* v
Milford, Rural, *Wilts.* vi
Military History, *Surr.* ii; *Worcs.* ii; *Yorks.* iii; [Romano-British], *Kent* iii; *and see* Architecture, Military
Mill Hill School, *Mdx.* i
Millbrook, *Beds.* iii
Millbrook, *Hants* iii
Milling, Malting, and Brewing, *Glos.* ii
Milling Machinery, Agricultural Implements, Locomotives, etc., *Suff.* i
Millipedes, *see* Myriapoda

Millo (in Dunton), *Beds.* ii
Milton, *Berks.* iv
Milton, *Hants* v
Milton, Great, *Oxon.* vii
Milton Abbey, *Dors.* ii
Milton Bryant (Milton Bryan), *Beds.* iii
Milton Ernest, *Beds.* iii
Milton Hospital, *see* Gravesend
Milton Keynes, *Bucks.* iv
Milton Malzor, *Northants.* iv
Milverton, *Warws.* vi
Mimms, North, *Herts.* ii
Minchin Buckland Preceptory, *Som.* ii
Minehead Harriers, *see* Harriers
Mineral Springs, *see* Spas
Mineral Waters, *see* Aerated and Mineral Waters
Minerals, *Derb.* ii
Mines and Quarries, *Lincs.* ii; *Northants.* ii
Mining, *Dur.* ii; *Glos.* ii; *Leics.* iii; and Smelting, Medieval, *Yorks.* ii; Modern, *Yorks.* ii; *and see* Barytes; Coal; Copper; Fluorspar; Haematite; Iron; Lead; Tin
Minstead, *Hants* iv
Minster, in Sheppey, Priory, *Kent* ii
Minster, in Thanet, Priory, *Kent* ii
Minster Lovell Priory, *Oxon.* ii
Minting Priory, *Lincs.* ii
Missenden, Great, *Bucks.* ii; Abbey, *Bucks.* i
Missenden, Little, *Bucks.* ii
Mitcham, *Surr.* iv
Mites (Acarina), *see* Arachnida
Mitton (part of), *Lancs.* vii
Mitton, Lower (in Kidderminster Borough), *Worcs.* iii
Mitton Hospital, *Yorks.* iii
Mitton, *Yorks.* iii
Mixbury, *Oxon.* vi
Modeney Priory, *Norf.* ii
Moggerhanger (in Blunham), *Beds.* iii
Molesey, East and West, *Surr.* iii
Molesworth, *Hunts.* iii
Mollusca (Molluscs) (Snails, Oysters, Whelks), *Beds.* i; *Berks.* i; *Bucks.* i; *Cambs.* i; *Cornw.* i; *Cumb.* i; *Derb.* i; *Devon* i; *Dur.* i*; *Essex* i; *Hants* i; *Herefs.* i; *Herts.* i; *Hunts.* i; *Kent* i; *Lancs.* i; *Leics.* i; *Norf.* i; *Northants.* i; *Notts.* i; *Oxon.* i; *Rut.* i; *Salop.* i; *Som.* i; *Staffs.* i; *Suff.* i; *Surr.* i; *Suss.* i; *Warws.* i; *Worcs.* i; *Yorks.* i
Molycourt Priory, *Norf.* ii
Monkton, Nun, Priory, *Yorks.* iii
Monkton Farleigh, *Wilts.* vii; Priory, *Wilts.* iii
Montacute: Powys of, *see* Genealogy; Priory, *Som.* ii
Montagu Pedigree, *see* Pedigrees
Monumental Effigies, *Cumb.* ii; *Northants.* i
Monuments, Early Christian, *Cornw.* i
Monxton, *Hants* iv
Moor (in Fladbury), *Worcs.* iii
Morborne, *Hunts.* iii
Morcott, *Rut.* ii
Morden, *Surr.* iv
Morestead, *Hants* iii
Moreton, *Essex* iv
Moreton, Maids, *Bucks.* iv
Moreton: North and South, *Berks.* iii*; Hundred, *Berks.* iii
Moreton-in-Marsh, *Glos.* vi
Moreton Morrell, *Warws.* v
Mortlake, *Surr.* iv
Morton, Abbot's, *Worcs.* ii
Morton Bagot, *Warws.* iii
Mosses, *see* Musci
Moths (Lepidoptera Heterocera), *see* Lepidoptera
Motor Omnibuses, Steam, Building of, *Essex* ii
Motors, *see* Ironwork
Mottenden, Trinitarian Friars, *Kent* ii
Mottisfont, *Hants* iv; Priory, *Hants* ii
Mottistone, *Hants* v
Moulsford, *Berks.* iii
Moulsoe, *Bucks.* iv
Moulton, *Northants.* iv; Park, *Northants.* iv
Mount Grace Priory, *Yorks.* iii; *Yorks. N.R.* ii

Mount St. Bernard Abbey, *Leics.* ii
Mount St. John Preceptory, *Yorks.* iii
Mountfield, *Suss.* ix
Mountjoy Priory, *Norf.* ii
Mowsley, *Leics.* v
Moxby (in Marton), *Yorks. N.R.* ii; Priory, *Yorks.* iii
Muchelney Abbey, *Som.* ii
Munden, Great, *Herts.* iii; Priory of Rowney, *Herts.* iv
Munden, Little, *Herts.* iii
Mundham, North, *Suss.* iv
Mursley, *Bucks.* iii
Musci (Mosses), *Cornw.* i; *Cumb.* i; *Devon* i; *Hants* i;
    Herefs. i; *Herts.* i; *Kent* i; *Leics.* i; *Norf.* i; *Northants.* i;
    Notts. i; *Salop.* i; *Som.* i; *Staffs.* i; *Suff.* i; *Surr.* i;
    Worcs. i; *Yorks.* i; *and see* Cryptogams
Musical Instruments, *Mdx.* ii
Mycetozoa, *Herts.* i; *Som.* i; *and see* Cryptogams
Myriapoda (Myriapods) (Centipedes and Millipedes),
    Cambs. i; *Cumb.* i; *Essex* i; *Hants* i; *Norf.* i; *Notts.* i;
    Som. i; *Surr.* i
Myton-upon-Swale, *Yorks. N.R.* ii

Naiadaceae, *Norf.* i
Nails, *Staffs.* ii; and Chains, *Worcs.* ii
Napton-on-the-Hill, *Warws.* vi
Nash (in Whaddon), *Bucks.* iii
Nassington, *Northants.* ii
Nately, Up, *Hants* iv
Nately Scures, *Hants* iv
Natural History, *Beds.* i; *Berks.* i; *Bucks.* i; *Cambs.* i;
    Cornw. i; *Cumb.* i; *Derb.* i; *Devon* i; *Dur.* i; *Essex* i;
    Hants i; *Herefs.* i; *Herts.* i; *Hunts.* i; *Kent* i; *Lancs.* i;
    Leics. i; *Norf.* i; *Northants.* i; *Notts.* i; *Rut.* i; *Salop.* i;
    Som. i; *Staffs.* i; *Suff.* i; *Surr.* i; *Suss.* i; *Warws.* i;
    Worcs. i; *Yorks.* i; Addenda and Corrigenda, *Derb.* i
Natural Products, *Lancs.* ii
Naunton, *Glos.* vi
Naunton Beauchamp, *Worcs.* iv
Navestock, *Essex* iv
Navisford Hundred, *Northants.* iii
Nazeing, *Essex* v
Neasham, Priory of St. Mary, *Dur.* ii
Neatham (with Holybourne), *Hants* ii
Needingworth (in Holywell), *Hunts.* ii
Needles (Needle-Making), *Bucks.* ii; *Worcs.* ii; and Pins,
    Warws. ii
Needwood Forest, *Staffs.* ii
Neolithic Age, *Berks.* i; *Mdx.* i; *Oxon.* i; *Suff.* i; Localities,
    see Palaeolithic and Neolithic Localities
Net-Making, *see* Lace
Netherfield Hundred, *Suss.* ix
Netherthorpe Grammar School, *see* Staveley Grammar
    School
Netherton (in Cropthorne), *Worcs.* iii
Netley (in Hound), *Hants* iii; Abbey, *Hants* ii
Nettlecombe Harriers, *see* Harriers
Nettleden, *Herts.* ii
Neuroptera (Caddis-flies, Dragonflies, Mayflies, Lace-
    wings, Psocids, Stone-flies), *Berks.* i; *Cambs.* i;
    Cornw. i; *Cumb.* i; *Derb.* i; *Devon* i; *Hants* i; *Kent* i;
    Norf. i; *Notts.* i; *Oxon.* i; *Rut.* i; *Salop.* i; *Som.* i;
    Staffs. i; *Suff.* i; *Surr.* i; *Suss.* i; *Worcs.* i; *Yorks.* i;
    and Orthoptera, *Herefs.* i; *Herts.* i; *and see* Ephemerop-
    tera; Odonata; Plecoptera; Psocoptera; Trichoptera
New Forest: Forestry and the, *Hants* ii; Hundred, *Hants*
    iv; Sport in the, *Hants* v
New Forest, *Staffs.* ii
New Minster, *see* Winchester
Newark: religious houses, *Notts.* ii*; schools, *Notts.* ii*
Newark Priory, *Surr.* ii
Newbo Abbey, *Lincs.* ii
Newbold-on-Avon, *Warws.* vi
Newbold on Stour (in Tredington), *Worcs.* iii
Newbold Pacey, *Warws.* v
Newborough, *Northants.* ii
Newburgh Priory, *Yorks.* iii

Newbury: Borough, *Berks.* iv; religious houses, *Berks.*
    ii*; St. Bartholomew's School, *Berks.* ii
Newcastle-under-Lyme: Borough, *Staffs.* viii; religious
    houses, *Staffs.* iii*
Newchurch, *Hants* v
Newchurch Grammar School, *Lancs.* ii
Newdigate (Part of), *Surr.* iii
Newent Priory, *Glos.* ii
Newhaven, *Suss.* vii
Newhouse, *see* Newsham
Newick, *Suss.* vii
Newington, *Surr.* iv; Hospital, *Surr.* ii
Newland (in Great Malvern), *Worcs.* iv
Newland Preceptory, *Yorks.* iii
Newnham, *Hants* iv
Newnham, *Herts.* ii
Newnham (in Lindridge), *Worcs.* iii
Newnham Priory, *Beds.* i
Newnham Regis, *Warws.* vi
Newport, *Hants* v
Newport Hospital, *Essex* ii
Newport Hundred, *Bucks.* iv
Newport Pagnell (Newport Pagnel), *Bucks.* iv; Hospital,
    Bucks. i; *and see* Tickford Priory
Newsam, Temple, Preceptory, *Yorks.* iii
Newsham (Newhouse) Abbey, *Lincs.* ii
Newspaper-Publishing, *Essex* ii
Newstead-on-Ancholme Priory, *Lincs.* ii
Newstead Priory, *Notts.* ii
Newstead Priory (Lincs.), *see* Stamford
Newtimber, *Suss.* vii
Newton, *Cambs.* iv; College of St. Mary-on-the-Sea,
    Cambs. ii
Newton, *Yorks. N.R.* ii
Newton, Long, *Dur.* iii
Newton, Water, *Hunts.* iii
Newton Blossomville, *Bucks.* iv
Newton Bromswold, *Northants.* iv
Newton Longville, *Bucks.* iv; Priory, *Bucks.* i
Newton Purcell, *Oxon.* vi
Newton Regis, *Warws.* iv
Newton-upon-Ouse, *Yorks. N.R.* ii
Newton Valence, *Hants* iii
Newtown (Evingar Hundred), *Hants* iv
Newtown (West Medine Liberty), *Hants* v
Nine Ashes, Calvert of, *see* Genealogy
Nineteenth-Century Cambridgeshire, *Cambs.* ii
Ninfield, *Suss.* ix; Hundred, *Suss.* ix
Niton, *Hants* v
Nocton Park Priory, *Lincs.* ii
Noke, *Oxon.* vi
Nonconformity, *Lond.* i; *Warws.* viii; Protestant, *Cambs.*
    iii; *Leics.* iv; *Staffs.* iii, viii; *Warws.* vii, viii*; *Wilts.* iii,
    vi*; *Yorks. E.R.* i; *Yorks.* York
Norbury, *Staffs.* iv
Norman, *see* Anglo-Norman
Norman Cross Hundred, *Hunts.* iii
Normanby, *Yorks. N.R.* i
Normansburgh Priory, *Norf.* ii
Normanton, *Rut.* ii
North Durham Foxhounds, *see* Foxhounds
Northallerton, *Yorks. N.R.* i; Hospital of St. James near,
    Yorks. iii; religious houses, *Yorks.* iii*
Northampton: Borough, *Northants.* iii; religious houses,
    Northants. ii*; *and see* Parliament, List of Members of
Northamptonshire Survey, *Northants.* i
Northaw, *Herts.* ii
Northborough, *Northants.* ii
Northchurch (Berkhampstead St. Mary), *Herts.* ii
Northfield, *Worcs.* iii
Northiam, *Suss.* ix
Northill, *Beds.* iii; College, *Beds.* i
Northington, *Hants* iii
Northwood, *Hants* v
Norton, *Dur.* iii; College, *Dur.* ii
Norton, *Herts.* ii; Knightley of, *see* Genealogy

INDEX OF TITLES OF ARTICLES

Norton, *Worcs.* ii
Norton, Hospital of St. Nicholas, *Yorks.* iii
Norton, Cold, religious houses, *Oxon.* ii*
Norton, King's, *Leics.* v
Norton, King's, *Worcs.* iii
Norton Bavant, *Wilts.* viii
Norton by Bredon (in Bredon), *Worcs.* iii
Norton juxta Kempsey, *Worcs.* iii
Norton Lindsey, *Warws.* iii
Norton Mandeville, *Essex* iv
Norwich, religious houses, *Norf.* ii*
Noseley, *Leics.* v; College, *Leics.* ii
Nostell Priory, *Yorks.* iii
Nottingham: Grammar School, *Notts.* ii; religious houses, *Notts.* ii*; University College, *Notts.* ii
Nunburnholme Priory, *Yorks.* iii
Nuncotham Priory, *Lincs.* ii
Nuneaton: Borough, *Warws.* iv; Priory, *Warws.* ii; School, *Warws.* ii
Nuneham Courtenay, *Oxon.* v
Nunkeeling Priory, *Yorks.* iii
Nunnington, *Yorks. N.R.* i
Nursery-Gardening, *Essex* ii
Nursling, *Hants* iii
Nutfield, *Surr.* iii
Nuthurst, *Warws.* iv
Nutley, *Hants* iii
Nutley Abbey, *Bucks.* i

Oakham, *Rut.* ii; Grammar School, *Rut.* i; Hospital of St. John Evangelist and St. Anne, *Rut.* i; Soke, *Rut.* ii
Oakley, *Beds.* iii
Oakley, *Bucks.* iv
Oakley, Church, *Hants* iv
Oakley Hunt, *see* Hunts
Ochre, *see* Pyrites
Ock Hundred, *Berks.* iv
Ockham, *Surr.* iii
Ockley, *Surr.* iii
Ockley Court, Calvert of, *see* Genealogy
Oddingley, *Worcs.* iii
Oddington, *Glos.* vi
Oddington, *Oxon.* vi
Odell, *Beds.* iii
Odiham, *Hants* iv; Hundred, *Hants* iv
Odonata (Dragonflies), *Cambs.* i; *Oxon.* i; *Warws.* i; *and see* Neuroptera
Odsey Hundred, *Herts.* iii
Offa's Dike, *Herefs.* i
Offchurch, *Warws.* vi; Knightley of, *see* Genealogy
Offenham, *Worcs.* ii
Officers, *see* Seals
Offices, Corporate, *see* Seals
Offley, *Herts.* iii
Offord Cluny, *Hunts.* ii
Offord Darcy, *Hunts.* ii
Ogbourne Priory, *Wilts.* iii
Oil, *see* Linseed Oil
Old (Wold), *Northants.* iv
Oldberrow, *Warws.* iii
Oldberrow, *Worcs.* ii
Oldham (in Prestwich), *Lancs.* v; Grammar School, *Lancs.* ii
Olney, with Warrington, *Bucks.* iv
Olympic Games, *see* Games
Ombersley, *Worcs.* iii
Omnibuses, *see* Motor Omnibuses
Ongar, Chipping, *Essex* iv
Ongar, High, *Essex* iv
Ongar Hundred, *Essex* iv; Analysis of Bishop Compton's Census of 1676, *Essex* iv; *and see* Tax Assessments, Hearth, *and* Medieval
Ordnance and Armaments, *Lancs.* ii; *and see* Gun-Making; War-Rockets
Ore, *Suss.* ix
Orford, religious houses, *Suff.* ii*

Orford Priory, *Lincs.* ii
Orleton (in Eastham), *Worcs.* iv
Orlingbury, *Northants.* iv; Hundred, *Northants.* iv; Young of, *see* Genealogy
Ormesby, *Yorks. N.R.* ii
Ormsby, North, (Nun Ormsby) Priory, *Lincs.* ii
Ormskirk, *Lancs.* iii; Grammar School, *Lancs.* ii
Orthoptera (Crickets, Earwigs, Grasshoppers), *Berks.* i; *Cambs.* i; *Cornw.* i; *Cumb.* i; *Derb.* i; *Devon* i; *Hants* i; *Herefs.* i; *Herts.* i; *Kent* i; *Norf.* i; *Notts.* i; *Oxon.* i; *Rut.* i; *Som.* i; *Staffs.* i; *Suff.* i; *Surr.* i; *Suss.* i; *Yorks.* i; *and see* Dermaptera
Orton, Water, *Warws.* iv
Orton Longueville, with Botolphbridge, *Hunts.* iii
Orton Waterville, *Hunts.* iii
Osbaldwick, *Yorks. N.R.* ii
Oseney Abbey, *Oxon.* ii
Osmotherley, *Yorks. N.R.* i
Ospringe Hospital, *Kent* ii
Ossington Preceptory, *Notts.* ii
Oswaldkirk, *Yorks. N.R.* ii
Oswaldslow Hundred, *Worcs.* iii
Otham Abbey, *Suss.* ii
Otter-Digging, *Som.* ii
Otter Hounds, *Bucks.* ii; *Essex* ii; *Lancs.* ii; *Lincs.* ii; *Warws.* ii
Otter-Hunting, *Cumb.* ii; *Dors.* ii; *Dur.* ii; *Kent* i; *Northants.* ii; *Suss.* ii; *Yorks.* ii
Otterbourne, *Hants* iii
Otterington, North, *Yorks. N.R.* i
Otterington, South, *Yorks. N.R.* ii
Oundle, *Northants.* iii
Outwell and Upwell, *Cambs.* iv
Overbury, with Alstone, Conderton, Teddington, and Little Washbourne, *Worcs.* iii
Overstone, *Northants.* iv
Overton, *Hants* iv; Hundred, *Hants* iv
Overton, *Yorks. N.R.* ii
Overton, Market, *Rut.* ii
Oving, *Bucks.* iv
Oving, *Suss.* iv
Ovingdean, *Suss.* vii
Ovington, *Hants* iii
Owen's School, *Mdx.* i
Owners, Famous, *see* Racing Celebrities
Owslebury, with Baybridge, *Hants* iii
Owston, *Leics.* v; Abbey, *Leics.* ii
Oxenton, *Glos.* viii
Oxford: Mint, *Oxon.* ii; religious houses, *Oxon.* ii*
Oxford University, *Oxon.* iii; Bodleian Library, *Oxon.* iii; Clarendon Building, *Oxon.* iii; Colleges and Halls, *Oxon.* iii; Grammar Schools of the Medieval University, *Oxon.* iii; Old Ashmolean Museum, *Oxon.* iii; Physic Garden, *Oxon.* iii; Press, *Oxon.* ii; Press, and Other Modern Buildings, *Oxon.* iii; Radcliffe Camera, *Oxon.* iii; Sheldonian Theatre, *Oxon.* iii
Oxhill, *Warws.* v
Oxted, *Surr.* iv
Oyster Fisheries, *see* Fisheries
Oysters, *see* Mollusca

Packington, Great and Little, *Warws.* iv*
Packwood, *Warws.* v
Padbury, *Bucks.* iv
Padworth, *Berks.* iii
Page, William, [Obituary] and List of Writings, *Rut.* ii*
Page-Turner Family, *see* Genealogy
Pagham, *Suss.* iv
Painting, Medieval, *Norf.* ii
Palaeolithic Age (Palaeolithic Man), *Berks.* i; *Oxon.* i; *Suff.* i; Lower, *Mdx.* i
Palaeolithic and Neolithic Localities, Topographical List, *Suff.* i
Palaeontology, *Beds.* i; *Berks.* i; *Bucks.* i; *Cornw.* i; *Cumb.* i; *Derb.* i; *Devon* i; *Dur.* i; *Essex* i; *Hants* i; *Herefs.* i; *Herts.* i; *Hunts.* i; *Kent* i; *Lancs.* i; *Leics.* i;

Norf. i; *Northants.* i; *Notts.* i; *Rut.* i; *Salop.* i; *Som.* i; *Staffs.* i; *Suff.* i; *Surr.* i; *Suss.* i; *Warws.* i; *Worcs.* i; *Yorks.* i

Palmer Family, *see* Genealogy

Pamber, *Hants* iv

Panfield Priory, *Essex* ii

Pangbourne, *Berks.* iii

Paper (Paper Industry, Paper-Making), *Bucks.* ii; *Essex* ii; *Hants* v; *Herts.* iv; *Kent* iii; *Lancs.* ii; *Mdx.* ii; *Northants.* ii; *Surr.* ii; *Wilts.* iv; *and see* Parchment; Printing

Parchment and Paper-Making, *Oxon.* ii

Parishes, Poor, of 1428, *Wilts.* iv

Parishes, Townships, and Manors, Index of, *Lancs.* iii–iv, vi

Parishes in Topographical Maps, Index of, *Hants* ii

Parliament, List of Members of, for Great Berkhampstead, *Herts. Fam.*; Brackley, *Northants. Fam.*; Hertford, Hertfordshire, *Herts. Fam.*; Higham Ferrers, Northampton, Northamptonshire, Peterborough, *Northants. Fam.*, St. Albans, Bishop's Stortford, *Herts. Fam.*

Parliamentary History (Parliamentary Representation), *Cambs.* ii*–iii*; *Hunts.* ii; *Leics.* iv*; *Warws.* viii; *Wilts.* v*–vi*

Parochial Records, *Lond.* i

Parson Drove Chapelry, *Cambs.* iv

Partney, religious houses, *Lincs.* ii*

Pastimes, *Mdx.* ii; *and see* Sports

Paston, *Northants.* ii

Pastrow Hundred, *Hants* iv

Patcham, *Suss.* vii

Patrixbourne Priory, *Kent* ii

Pattens, Making of, *Essex* ii

Pavenham, *Beds.* iii; Rush-Matting and Wicker Basket Industries, *Beds.* ii

Paxton, Great and Little, *Hunts.* ii*

Peakirk, *Northants.* ii

Peasant Revolt, and Parliamentary Representation, *Cambs.* ii

Peasemore, *Berks.* iv

Peasmarsh, *Suss.* ix

Peckham, West, Preceptory, *Kent* ii

Pedigrees: Cromwell, *Hunts.* ii; Montagu, *Hunts.* ii; *and see* Genealogy

Pedmore, *Worcs.* iii

Pelaw, Hospital of St. Stephen, *Dur.* ii

Pelham, Brent, *Herts.* iv

Pelham, Furneux (Furneaux), *Herts.* iv; Calvert of, *see* Genealogy

Pelham, Stocking, *Herts.* iv

Pendock, *Worcs.* iii

Penge (in Battersea), *Surr.* iv

Penhill Preceptory, *Yorks.* iii

Penhurst, *Suss.* ix

Penkridge, *Staffs.* v; College of St. Michael, *Staffs.* iii

Penn, *Bucks.* iii

Pennington, *Lancs.* viii

Penrith, Austin Friars, *see* Friars, Four Houses of

Pens, *see* Steel Pens

Pensax (in Lindridge), *Worcs.* iii

Pensham (in Pershore St. Andrew), *Worcs.* iv

Pentney Priory, *Norf.* ii

Penton Grafton (in Weyhill), *Hants* iv

Penton Mewsey, *Hants* iv

Penwortham, *Lancs.* vi; Endowed School, *Lancs.* ii; Priory, *Lancs.* ii

Peopleton, *Worcs.* iv

Peper Harow, *Surr.* iii

Perry, East (in Grafham), *Hunts.* iii

Pershore: Abbey, *Worcs.* ii; Borough, *Worcs.* iv; Hundred, *Worcs.* iv; Holy Cross with Wadborough and Walcot cum Membris, *Worcs.* iv; St. Andrew with Brickle-hampton, Defford, Pensham, Pinvin, and Wick, *Worcs.* iv

Pertenhall, *Beds.* iii

Pertwood, *Wilts.* viii

Peterborough: Borough, *Northants.* ii; religious houses, *Northants.* ii*; Soke of, *Northants.* ii; *and see* Parliament, List of Members of

Petersfield Borough, with Sheet, *Hants* iii

Petersham, *Surr.* iii

Peterstone Priory, *Norf.* ii

Pett, *Suss.* ix

Petworth Hounds, *see* Hounds

Pevensey [Romano-British], *Suss.* iii

Phanerogams (Phanerogamia) (Flowering Plants), *Herts.* i; *Leics.* i; *Salop.* i; *Worcs.* i; List, Summary of Orders, *Suff.* i; *Surr.* i; *and see* Plants, Vascular

Pheleley Priory, *Oxon.* ii

Photographic Dry Plates, Manufacture of, *Essex* ii

Physique, *Mdx.* i; *Wilts.* i (1); *and see* Geology

Picked Post (in Fordingbridge), *Hants* iv

Pickering, *Yorks. N.R.* ii; Hospital of St. Nicholas, *Yorks.* iii; Pickering Lythe Wapentake, *Yorks. N.R.* ii

Pickhill with Roxby, *Yorks. N.R.* i

Pickwell, *Leics.* v

Pickworth, *Rut.* ii

Piddinghoe, *Suss.* vii

Piddington, *Oxon.* v

Piddington, with Hackleton, *Northants.* iv

Piddle, North, *Worcs.* iv

Piddle, Wyre (in Fladbury), *Worcs.* iii

Pidley with Fenton, *Hunts.* ii

Pile Dwellings, *Berks.* i

Pillerton Hersey and Pillerton Priors, *Warws.* v*

Pillow-Lace Making, *see* Lace

Pilton, *Northants.* iii

Pilton, *Rut.* ii

Pinley, Shortley, and Whitley, *Warws.* viii

Pinley Priory, *Warws.* ii

Pins (Pin-Making), *Essex* ii; *Glos.* ii; *and see* Needles

Pinvin (in Pershore St. Andrew), *Worcs.* iv

Pipe-Making (Pipes, Clay), *see* Tobacco Pipes

Pipe Rolls, Early, Introduction and Text, *Cumb.* i

Pipewell Abbey, *Northants.* ii

Pirbright, *Surr.* iii

Pirho Hospital, *Northants.* ii

Pirton, *Herts.* iii

Pirton, *Worcs.* iv

Pisces (Fishes), *Beds.* i; *Berks.* i; *Bucks.* i; *Cambs.* i; *Cornw.* i; *Cumb.* i; *Derb.* i; *Devon* i; *Dur.* i; *Essex* i; *Hants* i; *Herefs.* i; *Herts.* i; *Hunts.* i; *Kent* i; *Lancs.* i; *Leics.* i; *Norf.* i; *Notts.* i; *Northants.* i; *Oxon.* i; *Rut.* i; *Salop.* i; *Som.* i; *Staffs.* i; *Suff.* i; *Surr.* i; *Suss.* i; *Warws.* i; *Worcs.* i; *Yorks.* i

Pishill, *Oxon.* viii

Pitchcott, *Bucks.* iv

Pitchford, *Salop.* viii

Pitsford, *Northants.* iv

Pitstone, *Bucks.* iii

Plaitford, *Hants* iv

Plant-Lice, *see* Hemiptera

Plants: Flowering, *see* Phanerogams; Non-Flowering, *see* Cryptogams; Vascular (Phanerogamia and Pterido-phyta), *Notts.* i; *Salop.* i

Plaster Work, *Herts.* iv

Plate, *see* Seals

Playden, *Suss.* ix; Hospital, *Suss.* ii

Plecoptera (Stone-Flies), *Oxon.* i; *and see* Neuroptera

Pleshey College, *Essex* ii

Ploughley Hundred, *Oxon.* vi; *and see* Statistical Material

Plumpton, *Suss.* vii

Podington, with Hinwick, *Beds.* iii

Point-to-Point Races, *see* Racing

Polebrook, *Northants.* iii; Hundred, *Northants.* iii

Polesworth, *Warws.* iv; Abbey, *Warws.* ii

Poling Preceptory, *Suss.* ii

Political History, *Beds.* ii; *Berks.* ii; *Bucks.* iv; *Cambs.* ii; *Cumb.* ii; *Derb.* ii; *Dors.* ii; *Dur.* ii; *Essex* ii; *Hants* v; *Herefs.* i; *Herts.* ii; *Hunts.* ii; *Kent* iii; *Lancs.* ii*; *Leics.* ii*; *Lincs.* ii; *Mdx.* ii; *Norf.* ii; *Notts.* i; *Oxon.* i; *Rut.* i*; *Som.* ii; *Staffs.* i; *Suff.* ii; *Surr.* i; *Suss.* i; *Warws.* i; *Wilts.* vi; *Worcs.* ii; *Yorks.* iii*; *and* Administrative History, *Leics.* iv*; *Warws.* vii, viii*

Poll Tax, *see* Tax Assessments

INDEX OF TITLES OF ARTICLES

Polo, *Dors.* ii; *Essex* ii; *Kent* i; *Lancs.* ii; *Lincs.* ii; *Mdx.* ii; *Northants.* ii; *Som.* ii; *Surr.* ii; *Suss.* ii; *Yorks.* ii

Pontefract, religious houses, *Yorks.* iii*

Pontesbury, *Salop.* viii

Poor Parishes, *see* Parishes, Poor

Poor Relief, *Cambs.* ii

Popham, *Hants* iii

Population, *Leics.* iii; Tables of, *Beds.* ii, *Berks.* ii; *Bucks.* ii; *Cambs.* ii; *Derb.* ii; *Dors.* ii; *Dur.* ii; *Essex* ii; *Glos.* ii; *Hants* v; *Herts.* iv; *Hunts.* ii; *Kent* iii; *Lancs.* ii; *Leics.* iii; *Lincs.* ii; *Mdx.* ii; *Notts.* ii; *Oxon.* ii; *Rut.* i; *Som.* ii; *Staffs.* i; *Suff.* i; *Surr.* iv; *Suss.* ii; *Warws.* ii; *Wilts.* iv; *Worcs.* iv; *Yorks.* iii

Porcelain, *Salop.* i; Bow and Chelsea, *Mdx.* ii; *and see* China; Pottery

Portchester, *Hants* iii

Portman, Lord, his Hounds, *see* Hounds

Portsdown Hundred with the Liberties of Portsmouth and Alverstoke, *Hants* iii

Portsea Island, *see* Portsmouth

Portslade, *Suss.* vii

Portsmouth, God's House, *Hants* ii

Portsmouth and Portsea Island Liberty, *Hants* iii

Potash-Making, *Essex* ii

Potsgrove, *Beds.* iii

Potterne, *Wilts.* vii

Potterne and Cannings Hundred, *Wilts.* vii

Pottery (Pottery Manufacture, Potteries), *Derb.* ii; *Dur.* ii; *Essex* ii; *Kent* iii; *Lancs.* ii; *Mdx.* ii; *Salop.* i; *Staffs.* ii; *Surr.* ii; *Suss.* ii; *Yorks.* ii; 'Art', Manufacture, *Essex* ii; Roman, Found in London, Note on, *Lond.* i; and Glass, *Hants* v; *Notts.* ii; *Som.* ii; Pottery, Glass, Bricks, and Building Materials, *Glos.* ii; Pottery, Tiles, and Bricks, *Bucks.* ii; *Herts.* iv; *and see* China; Porcelain; Stoneware

Potton, *Beds.* ii

Poughley Priory, *Berks.* ii

Poulshot, *Wilts.* vii

Poulton-le-Fylde, *Lancs.* vii

Poulton Priory, *Wilts.* iii

Poundon (in Twyford), *Bucks.* iv

Povington Priory, *Dors.* ii

Powick: with Clevelode and Woodsfield, *Worcs.* iv; School, *Worcs.* iv

Powys Family, *see* Genealogy

Poynings, *Suss.* vii; Hundred, *Suss.* vii

Preen, Church, *Salop.* viii

Prehistoric Iron Age, *see* Iron Age

Pre-Norman Remains, *Cumb.* i

Prescot, *Lancs.* iii; Grammar School, *Lancs.* ii

Prescott, *Glos.* vi

Prestbury, *Glos.* viii

Preston, *Lancs.* vii; religious houses, *Lancs.* ii; schools, *Lancs.* ii

Preston, *Rut.* ii

Preston, *Suss.* vii; Hundred, *Suss.* vii

Preston Bagot, *Warws.* iii

Preston Bissett, *Bucks.* iv

Preston Candover, *Hants* iii

Preston Deanery, *Northants.* iv

Preston on Stour, *Glos.* viii

Prestwich-with-Oldham, *Lancs.* v

Princethorpe (with Stretton-upon-Dunsmore), *Warws.* vi

Printing, *Berks.* i; *Essex* ii; *Herts.* iv; *Kent* iii; *Mdx.* ii; *Suff.* ii; and Paper, *Glos.* ii; and Printing Machinery, *Surr.* ii; *and see* Cambridge University Press; Oxford University Press

Prisons, *Yorks.* E.R. i; and Crime, *Cambs.* ii

Prittlewell Priory, *Essex* ii

Privett, *Hants* iii

Protestant Nonconformity, *see* Nonconformity

Psocoptera (Psocids), *Cambs.* i; *Oxon.* i; *and see* Neuroptera

Pteridophyta, *see* Equisetaceae; Filices; Lycopodiaceae; *and see* Plants, Vascular

Public Elementary Schools, *see* Schools

Public Health, *Cambs.* iii; and the Medical Services, *Wilts.* v

Puckeridge Hounds, *see* Hounds

Puckeshall (or Tonge) Hospital, *Kent* ii

Pugilism, *see* Boxing

Pulloxhill, *Beds.* ii

Pulverbatch, Castle, *Salop.* viii

Purley, *Berks.* iii

Pusey, *Berks.* iv

Putney, *Surr.* iv

Puttenham, *Herts.* ii

Puttenham, *Surr.* iii

Pyecombe, *Suss.* vii

Pynham Priory, *Suss.* ii

Pyrford, *Surr.* iii

Pyrites and Ochre, *Derb.* ii

Pyrton, *Oxon.* viii; Hundred, *Oxon.* viii; *and see* Tax Assessments

Pytchley, *Northants.* iv; Country, *Northants.* ii; Hounds, *see* Hounds; Isham of, *see* Genealogy; Woodland Pytchley Hounds, *see* Hounds

Quainton, with Shipton Lee, *Bucks.* iv

Quantock Staghounds, *see* Staghounds

Quarley, *Hants* iv

Quarme Harriers, *see* Harriers

Quarr Abbey, *Hants* ii, v

Quarrendon, *Bucks.* iv

Quarries, *Northants.* ii; *Oxon.* ii; *Salop.* i; and Mines, *Lincs.* ii; *Northants.* ii; Quarries, Stone, etc., *Kent* iii; Quarrying, *Dors.* ii; *Leics.* iii; *Hants* v; *Rut.* i; *Yorks.* ii; *and see* Chalk; Granite; Slate; Stone

Queen's College, Harley Street, *Mdx.* i

Quenington Preceptory, *Glos.* ii

Quinton, *Northants.* iv

Raby Foxhounds, *see* Foxhounds

Racheness Hospital, *Norf.* ii

Racing (Races), *Beds.* ii; *Berks.* ii; *Bucks.* ii; *Derb.* ii; *Dors.* ii; *Essex* ii; *Glos.* ii; *Hants* v; *Herts.* i; *Kent* i; *Lancs.* ii; *Lincs.* ii; *Mdx.* ii; *Notts.* ii; *Oxon.* ii; *Rut.* i; *Som.* ii; *Suff.* ii; *Surr.* ii; *Suss.* ii; *Warws.* ii; *Wilts.* iv; *Worcs.* ii; *Yorks.* ii; Flat, *Beds.* ii; *Berks.* ii; *Bucks.* ii; *Kent* i; *Lancs.* ii; *Northants.* ii; *Warws.* ii; Horse-, *Cumb.* ii; *Dur.* ii; *Staffs.* ii; Point-to-Point, *Dors.* ii; *Kent* i; *Suss.* ii; Racing Celebrities (Famous Owners, Trainers, and Horses), *Dors.* ii; *Kent* i; *and see* Steeplechasing; Whippet-Racing

Racton, *Suss.* iv

Radbourn, *Warws.* vi

Radcliffe, *Lancs.* v

Radclive, *Bucks.* iv

Radford, Hospital of St. Lazarus or the Holy Sepulchre, *Staffs.* iii

Radford (with Harnall), *Warws.* viii

Radford Semele, *Warws.* vi

Radley, *Berks.* iv; College, *Berks.* ii, (cricket), *Berks.* ii, (football), *Berks.* ii, (rowing), *Berks.* ii

Radmore Abbey, *Staffs.* iii

Radnage, *Bucks.* iv

Radway, *Warws.* v

Radwell, *Herts.* iii

Radwell (in Felmersham), *Beds.* iii

Railway Construction, *Cambs.* ii

Railway Works, *see* Engineering; Iron-Foundries

Railways, *Leics.* iii; *Staffs.* ii; *Wilts.* iv; *Yorks.* E.R. i

Raine's Foundation Schools, *Mdx.* i

'Ramestede' Nunnery, *Suss.* ii

Ramsey, *Hunts.* ii; Abbey, *Hunts.* i; Free School, *Hunts.* ii

Ranston Bloodhounds, *see* Bloodhounds

Ranton Priory, *Staffs.* iii

Ratley, *Warws.* v

Raunds, *Northants.* iv

Raveley, Great and Little, *Hunts.* ii*

Ravendale, West, Priory, *Lincs.* ii

Raveningham College, *Norf.* ii

Ravensden, *Beds.* iii

Ravenstone, *Bucks.* iv; Priory, *Bucks.*

Reach (in Leighton Buzzard), *Beds.* iii
Reading: Borough, with St. Giles with Whitley and St. Mary with Southcot, *Berks.* iii; Grammar School, *Berks.* ii; Hundred, *Berks.* iii; religious houses, *Berks.* ii*
Reculver Abbey, *Kent* ii
Red Hills, The, *Essex* iii
Redbornestoke Hundred, *Beds.* iii
Redbourn, *Herts.* ii; Priory, *Herts.* iv
Redbridge Hundred, *Hants* iv
Redcliffe, Hospital of St. John the Baptist, *Som.* ii
Redlingfield Priory, *Suff.* ii
Redmarley D'Abitôt, *Worcs.* iii
Redmarshal, *Dur.* iii
Reed, *Herts.* iii
Regattas, Thames, *Berks.* ii
Reigate, *Surr.* iii; Hundred, *Surr.* iii; Priory, *Surr.* ii
Relief, Poor, *see* Poor Relief
Religious History, *Warws.* vii; *and see* Church; Ecclesiastical History; Deaneries; Jews; Nonconformity; Roman Catholicism
Religious Houses, *Beds.* i; *Berks.* ii; *Bucks.* i; *Cambs.* ii; *Cumb.* ii; *Derb.* ii; *Dors.* ii; *Dur.* ii; *Essex* ii; *Glos.* ii; *Hants* ii; *Herts.* iv; *Hunts.* ii; *Kent* ii; *Lancs.* ii; *Leics.* ii; *Lincs.* ii; *Lond.* i; *Mdx.* i; *Norf.* i; *Northants.* ii; *Notts.* ii; *Oxon.* ii; *Rut.* i; *Som.* ii; *Staffs.* iii; *Suff.* ii; *Surr.* ii; *Suss.* ii; *Warws.* ii; *Wilts.* iii; *Worcs.* ii; *Yorks.* iii; Additional Heads of, *Kent* ii; Sites and Remains, *Yorks. E.R.* i; *Yorks.* York
Remenham, *Berks.* iii
Renhold, *Beds.* iii
Reptiles, Batrachians, and Amphibians, *Beds.* i; *Berks.* i; *Bucks.* i; *Cambs.* i; *Cornw.* i; *Cumb.* i; *Derb.* i; *Devon* i; *Dur.* i; *Essex* i; *Hants* i; *Herefs.* i; *Herts.* i; *Hunts.* i; *Kent* i; *Lancs.* i; *Leics.* i; *Norf.* i; *Northants.* i; *Notts.* i; *Oxon.* i; *Rut.* i; *Salop.* i; *Som.* i; *Staffs.* i; *Suff.* i; *Surr.* i; *Suss.* i; *Warws.* i; *Worcs.* i; *Yorks.* i
Repton: Priory with the Cell of Calke, *Derb.* ii; School, *Derb.* ii
Rerecross Hospital, or the Spital on Stainmoor, *Yorks.* iii
Retford, East, Grammar School, *Notts.* ii
Revels, *see* Cudgel Play
Revesby Abbey, *Lincs.* ii
Rewley Abbey, *Oxon.* ii
Ribbesford, with the Borough of Bewdley, *Worcs.* iv
Ribbon Trade of Coventry, *Warws.* ii
Ribchester, *Lancs.* vii
Ribston and Wetherby Preceptories, *Yorks.* iii
Richmond (Sheen), *Surr.* iii; Friars Observant, *Surr.* ii; Sheen Priory, *Surr.* ii
Richmond: Borough, *Yorks. N.R.* i; Alien Priory of Begar near, *Yorks.* iii; Honour and Castle, *Yorks. N.R.* i; religious houses, *Yorks.* iii*
Richmondshire, *Yorks. N.R.* i
Rickmansworth, *Herts.* ii
Ridge, *Herts.* ii
Ridgmont, *Beds.* iii
Ridlington, *Rut.* ii
Rievaulx Abbey, *Yorks.* iii; *Yorks. N.R.* i
Ringstead, *Northants.* iv
Ringwood, *Hants* iv; Hundred, *Hants* iv
Ripley (in Send), *Surr.* iii
Ripon, religious houses, *Yorks.* iii*
Ripple, with Holdfast, *Worcs.* iii
Ripplesmere Hundred, *Berks.* iii
Ripton, Abbots, *Hunts.* ii
Ripton, King's, *Hunts.* ii
Risborough, Monks, *Bucks.* ii
Risborough, Princes, *Bucks.* ii
Risborough Hundred, *Bucks.* ii
Riseley (Risley), *Beds.* iii
Risley Grammar School, *Derb.* ii
Rissington, Great and Little, *Glos.* vi*
Rissington, Wick, *Glos.* vi
River and Canal Industries, *Salop.* i
Rivington and Blackrod Grammar School, *Lancs.* ii
Road Bridges, *see* Bridges

Roads, *Leics.* iii; *Staffs.* ii; *Wilts.* iv; *Yorks. E.R.* i; Ancient, *Berks.* i; and Camps [Romano-British], *Suss.* iii; Roman, *Essex* iii; [Romano-British], *Kent* iii; *Oxon.* i; *and see* Burials; Milestones; Turnpike Roads, Schedule of, *Leics.* iii
Robertsbridge Abbey, *Suss.* ii
Robinson Family, *see* Genealogy
Rocester Abbey, *Staffs.* iii
Rochdale, *Lancs.* v; Grammar School, *Lancs.* ii
Roche Abbey, *Yorks.* iii
Rochester, religious houses, *Kent* ii*
Rochford, *Worcs.* iv
Rock (Aka), *Worcs.* iv
Rockbourne, *Hants* iv
Rockets, *see* War-Rockets
Rockley, Temple, Preceptory, *Wilts.* iii
Roding, Abbess, *Essex* iv
Roding, Beauchamp, *Essex* iv
Rodmell, *Suss.* vii
Roe-Deer Hunting, *Dors.* ii
Rogate, *Suss.* iv
Rokeby Family, *see* Genealogy
Rokeby, with Egglestone Abbey, *Yorks. N.R.*
Romaldkirk, *Yorks. N.R.* i
Roman Catholicism, *Cambs.* iii; *Leics.* ii, iv; *Staffs.* iii, viii; *Warws.* vii–viii; *Wilts.* iii, vi; *Yorks. E.R.* i; *Yorks.* York
Roman Emperors, List of, *Lond.* i
Romano-British Period (Roman, Romano-British Remains), *Beds.* i; *Berks.* i; *Bucks.* ii; *Cornw.* ii (5); *Derb.* i; *Essex* iii; *Hants* i; *Herefs.* i; *Herts.* iv; *Hunts.* i; *Kent* iii; *Leics.* i; *Lond.* i; *Mdx.* i; *Norf.* i; *Northants.* i; *Notts.* i; *Oxon.* i; *Rut.* i; *Salop.* i; *Som.* i; *Staffs.* i; *Suff.* i; *Surr.* iv; *Suss.* iii; *Warws.* i; *Worcs.* i; Topographical Indexes, *Herts.* iv; *Kent* iii; *Lond.* i; *Oxon.* i; *Suss.* iii
Romney, religious houses, *Kent* ii*
Romney, New, Priory, *Kent* ii
Romsey: Abbey, *Hants* ii; Extra and Infra, *Hants* iv
Rope and Twine Manufacture, *Essex* ii; *and see* Water-proofs
Ropley, *Hants* iii
Rosae (Roses), *Devon* i; and Rubi, *Hants* i; *Norf.* i
Rose-Growing, *Essex* ii
Rosedale Priory, *Yorks.* iii
Roses, *see* Rosae
Rossall School, *Lancs.* ii
Rotherham, Jesus College, *Yorks.* iii
Rotherhithe, *Surr.* iv
Rothersthorpe, *Northants.* iv
Rotherwick, *Hants* iv
Rothley Preceptory, *Leics.* ii
Rothschild, Lord, his Staghounds, *see* Staghounds
Rothwell Nunnery, *Northants.* ii
Rottingdean, *Suss.* vii
Rounton, West, *Yorks. N.R.* i
Rowde, *Wilts.* vii
Rowing, *Berks.* ii; *Dur.* ii; *Mdx.* ii; *Notts.* ii; *Oxon.* ii
Rowington, *Warws.* iii
Rowner, *Hants* iii
Rowney (in Southill), *Beds.* iii
Rowney Priory, *see* Munden, Great
Roxby, Elwes (Cary-Elwes) of, *see* Genealogy
Roxby (in Pickhill), *Yorks. N.R.* i
Roxton, *Beds.* iii
Royston, *Herts.* iii; Hospital of St. Nicholas, *Cambs.* ii; *Herts.* iv; religious houses, *Herts.* iv
Rubber, *see* India Rubber
Rubi (Brambles), *Cornw.* i; *Devon* i; *Hants* i; *Norf.* i; *Som.* i; *Surr.* i; *Suss.* i
Ruby-tailed Flies (Hymenoptera Tubulifera), *see* Hymenoptera
Ruby-Wasps (Hymenoptera Chrysididae), *see* Hymenoptera
Ruckley and Langley, *Salop.* viii
Rudby-in-Cleveland, *Yorks. N.R.* ii
Ruddington College, *Notts.* ii

Rufford, *Lancs.* vi
Rufford Abbey, *Notts.* ii
Rufford Foxhounds, *see* Foxhounds
Rugby: Borough, *Warws.* vi; Cricket, *Warws.* ii; School, *Warws.* ii, (cricket), *Warws.* ii
Rugeley, *Staffs.* v
Rugs, *see* Carpets
Ruislip Priory, *Mdx.* i
Rumboldswyke, *Suss.* iv
Rumburgh Priory, *Suff.* ii
Runcton Priory, *Suss.* ii
Ruscombe, *Berks.* iii
Rush-Matting Industry, *see* Pavenham
Rushden, *Herts.* iii
Rushden, *Northants.* iv
Rushock, *Worcs.* iii
Rushworth College, *Norf.* ii
Rusper Priory, *Suss.* ii
Rutland, County of, *Rut.* ii
Rye: Borough, *Suss.* ix; Grammar School, *Suss.* ii; House of Austin Friars, *Suss.* ii
Ryedale Wapentake, *Yorks. N.R.* i
Ryhall, *Rut.* ii
Ryton-on-Dunsmore, *Warws.* vi

Sack-Making, *Essex* ii
Sacombe, *Herts.* iii
Saddington, *Leics.* v
Saddlery and Allied Trades, *Staffs.* ii
Saddlescombe Preceptory, *Suss.* ii
Saffron-Culture, *Essex* ii
Sailcloth and Other Hempen Fabrics, *Suff.* ii
St. Albans: Cathedral, *Herts.* ii; City, *Herts.* ii; religious houses, *Herts.* iv*; School, *Herts.* ii; *and see* Parliament, List of Members of
St. Andrew Rural, *Herts.* iii
St. Bees Priory, *Cumb.* ii
St. Benet of Holm Abbey, *Norf.* ii
St. Clement's, *Oxon.* v
St. Cross Hospital, *see* Winchester
St. Cuthbert's Shrine, Contents, *Dur.* i
St. Giles Hospital, *see* Brompton Bridge
St. Helens, *Hants* v; Priory, *Hants* ii
St. Hilda's First Monastery, *Dur.* ii
St. Ives, *Hunts.* ii; Priory, *Hunts.* i
St. James's Hospital, *see* Canterbury; Northallerton
St. John in Bedwardine, *Worcs.* iii
St. Lawrence, *Hants* v
St. Leonard (in New Malton), *Yorks. N.R.* i
St. Leonards (in Hastings), *Suss.* ix
St. Martha's (Chilworth), *Surr.* iii
St. Martin, *Worcs.* iii
St. Martin's, Stamford Baron, *Northants.* ii
St. Mary Bourne, *Hants* iv
St. Mary *De Castro* College, *Leics.* ii
St. Mary Extra (Weston), *Hants* iii
St. Mary's Hospital in the Peak, *Derb.* ii
St. Marylebone Grammar School, *Mdx.* i
St. Michael (in New Malton), *Yorks. N.R.* i
St. Michael-on-Wyre (St. Michaels-upon-Wyre), *Lancs.* vii; Grammar School, *Lancs.* ii
St. Michael's, *Herts.* ii; Gape of, *see* Genealogy
St. Neots, *Hunts.* ii; Priory, *Hunts.* i
St. Osyth (Chich) Abbey, *Essex* ii
St. Pega's Cell, *Lincs.* ii
St. Peter's, *Herts.* ii
St. Peter with Whittington, *Worcs.* iii
St. Radegund's Abbey, *see* Bradsole Abbey
St. Stephen's, *Herts.* ii
Salcey Lawn, Fitz Roy of, *see* Genealogy
Salehurst, *Suss.* ix
Salford Hundred, *Lancs.* iv–v
Salford Priors, *Warws.* iii; School, *Warws.* ii
Salisbury, Marquess of, *see* Genealogy, Cecil
Salisbury: Cathedral, *Wilts.* iii, vi; New Salisbury, City, *Wilts.* vi; Parishes of St. Edmund, St. Martin, and St.

Thomas, *Wilts.* vi*; Old Salisbury, Borough, *Wilts.* vi; Castle, *Wilts.* vi*; religious houses, *Wilts.* iii*
Salt (Salt-Making), *Essex* ii; *Hants* v; *Staffs.* ii; *Worcs.* ii; *Yorks.* ii
Salton, *Yorks. N.R.* i
Salwarpe, *Worcs.* iii
Sambourne, *Warws.* iii
Sanderstead, *Surr.* iv
Sandford (in Sonning), *Berks.* iii
Sandford on Thames, *Oxon.* v; Preceptory, *Oxon.* ii
Sandhurst, *Berks.* ii–iii, (football), *Berks.* ii
Sandleford, *Berks.* iv; Priory, *Berks.* ii
Sandon, *Herts.* iii
Sandon Fee (in Hungerford), *Berks.* iv
Sandon Hospital, *Surr.* ii
Sandridge, *Herts.* ii
Sandtoft Cell, *Lincs.* ii
Sandwell Priory, *Staffs.* iii
Sandwich, religious houses, *Kent* ii*
Sandy with Girtford, *Beds.* ii
Santon Downham Hoard, Appendix on, *Suff.* i
Sapcote College, *Leics.* ii
Sapey, Lower (Sapey Pitchard), *Worcs.* iv
Sapley (in Hartford), *Hunts.* ii
Sarratt, *Herts.* ii
'Sarum', the word, *Wilts.* vi
Saundby, Elwes of, *see* Genealogy
Saunderton, *Bucks.* iii
Savernake Forest, *Wilts.* iv
Sawbridgeworth, *Herts.* iii
Sawflies (Hymenoptera Phytophaga or Symphata), *see* Hymenoptera
Sawley Abbey, *Yorks.* iii
Sawtrey, *Hunts.* iii; Abbey, *Hunts.* i
Saxon Period, Pagan, *Mdx.* i; *and see* Anglo-Saxon
Scalby, *Yorks. N.R.* ii
Scaldwell, *Northants.* iv
Scale-Mosses, *see* Hepaticae
Scandinavian Antiquities, *see* Antiquities, Anglo-Scandinavian
Scarborough: Borough, *Yorks. N.R.* ii; religious houses, *Yorks.* iii*
Scawton, *Yorks. N.R.* i
Schools (History of Schools), *Beds.* ii; *Berks.* ii; *Bucks.* ii; *Cambs.* ii; *Derb.* ii; *Dur.* i; *Essex* ii; *Glos.* ii; *Hants* ii; *Herts.* ii; *Hunts.* ii; *Lancs.* ii; *Lincs.* ii; *Mdx.* i; *Northants.* ii; *Notts.* ii; *Oxon.* i; *Rut.* i; *Som.* ii; *Suff.* ii; *Surr.* ii; *Suss.* ii; *Warws.* ii; *Worcs.* iv; *Yorks.* i; Charity, *Leics.* iii; Choir, *Cambs.* ii; Elementary, *Suff.* ii; Elementary, Charity, and Endowed, 1600–1800, *Cambs.* ii; Elementary, Founded before 1750, *Berks.* ii; *Warws.* ii; Elementary, Founded before 1800, *Bucks.* ii; *Derb.* ii; *Herts.* ii; *Hunts.* ii; *Lancs.* ii; *Notts.* ii; *Oxon.* i; *Rut.* i; *Suss.* ii; *Worcs.* iv; Grammar, *Cambs.* ii; Grammar, now Elementary, *Derb.* ii; Public Elementary, *Beds.* ii; Secondary, New, *Worcs.* iv; Semi-Classical, *Cambs.* ii; *and see* Education
Scorpions, *see* Arachnida
Scraptoft, *Leics.* v
Scrope, Mr., his Foxhounds, *see* Foxhounds
Scruton, *Yorks. N.R.* i
Sculcoates, *Yorks. E.R.* i
Sculptured Stone, *see* Stone
Seacourt, *Berks.* iv
Seaford, religious houses, *Suss.* ii*
Seale, *Surr.* ii
Seals and Insignia: Cambridge University, *Cambs.* iii; and Arms, Plate, and Officers: Birmingham, *Warws.* vii; Coventry, *Warws.* viii; New Salisbury, *Wilts.* vi; Warwick, *Warws.* viii; and Corporate Offices, Leicester, *Leics.* iv; and Officers, Wilton, *Wilts.* vi; and Plate and Officers: Hull, *Yorks. E.R.* i; York, *Yorks. York.*
Seamer (Pickering Lythe Wapentake), *Yorks. N.R.* ii; Hospital, *Yorks.* iii
Seamer (West Langbaurgh Wapentake), *Yorks. N.R.* ii
Seaton, with Thorpe-by-Water, *Rut.* ii

Seavington Harriers, *see* Harriers
Sebright Family, *see* Genealogy
Seckington, *Warws.* iv
Sedgeberrow, *Worcs.* iii
Sedgefield, *Dur.* iii
Sedlescombe, *Suss.* ix
Seed-Growing, *Essex* ii
Seer Green (in Farnham Royal), *Bucks.* iii
Sefton, *Lancs.* iii
Selborne, *Hants* iii; Hundred, *Hants* iii; Priory, *Hants* ii
Selby Abbey, *Yorks.* iii
Sele Priory, *Suss.* ii
Selham, *Suss.* iv
Selsey, *Suss.* iv
Selwood Forest, *Wilts.* iv
Sempringham Priory, *Lincs.* ii
Send, with Ripley, *Surr.* iii
Sessay, *Yorks. N.R.* i
Seton (Lekeley) Nunnery, *Cumb.* ii
Settlement, Anglo-Norman, *Cambs.* ii; Anglo-Saxon, and Danish Invasion, *Cambs.* ii; Settlement Sites [Romano-British]: Towns and Villages, *Oxon.* i
Sevenoaks Hospital, *Kent* ii
Sewardsley Priory, *Northants.* ii
Shabbington, *Bucks.* iv
Shaftesbury, religious houses, *Dors.* ii*
Shalbourne, *Berks.* iv
Shalden, *Hants* iv
Shalfleet, *Hants* v
Shalford, *Surr.* iii
Shalstone, *Bucks.* iv
Shangton, *Leics.* v
Shanklin, *Hants* v
Shareshill, *Staffs.* v
Sharnbrook, *Beds.* iii
Sharpenhoe (in Streatley), *Beds.* ii
Shaw-cum-Donnington, *Berks.* iv
Sheen, *see* Richmond
Sheet (in Petersfield Borough), *Hants* iii
Sheffield, Hospital of St. Leonard, *Yorks.* iii
Shefford (in Campton), *Beds.* ii
Shefford, East (Little) and West (Great), *Berks.* iv*
Sheldon, *Warws.* iv
Shelford Priory, *Notts.* ii
Shell (in Himbleton), *Worcs.* iii
Shelley, *Essex* iv
Shellfish (Shellfish Gathering), *Essex* ii; *Kent* iii; *and see* Fisheries, Oyster
Shellingford, *Berks.* iv
Shelsley Beauchamp, with Shelsley Kings, *Worcs.* iv
Shelsley Kings (in Shelsley Beauchamp), *Worcs.* iv
Shelsley Walsh, *Worcs.* iv
Shelswell, *Oxon.* vi
Shelton, *Beds.* iii
Shenington, *Oxon.* ix
Shenley, *Bucks.* iv
Shenley, *Herts.* ii
Shephall, *Herts.* ii
Shepperton, *Mdx.* iii
Shepton Mallet Free Grammar School, *Som.* ii
Sherborne, *Glos.* vi
Sherborne, religious houses, *Dors.* ii*
Sherborne, Monk, *Hants* iv; Priory, *Hants* ii
Sherborne St. John, *Hants* iv
Sherbourne, *Warws.* iii
Sherbrooke, Mr., his Foxhounds, *see* Foxhounds
Sherburn, Hospital of St. Lazarus, St. Martha, and St. Mary, *Dur.* ii
Sherburn-in-Elmet, Hospital of St. Mary Magdalene, *Yorks.* iii
Shere, *Surr.* iii
Sherfield English, *Hants* iv
Sherfield-upon-Loddon, *Hants* iv
Sheriffs, Lists of, *Herts. Fam.*; *Northants. Fam.*
Sherington, *Bucks.* iv

Shillington, with Lower Stondon and Little Holwell, *Beds.* ii
Shilton, *Warws.* vi
Shinfield, *Berks.* iii
Shingay Preceptory, *Cambs.* ii
Shipbuilding (Building of Trading Ships), *Dur.* ii; *Essex* ii; *Lancs.* ii; *Yorks.* ii; *and see* Boat-Building; Iron-Foundries
Shipley Preceptory, *Suss.* ii
Shipston on Stour, *Worcs.* iii
Shipton Bellinger, *Hants* iv
Shipton Lee (in Quainton), *Bucks.* iv
Shirburn, *Oxon.* viii
Shobley (in Fordingbridge), *Hants* iv
Shoe-Making, *Notts.* ii; *and see* Boots; Tanning
Shooting, *Beds.* ii; *Berks.* ii; *Bucks.* ii; *Cumb.* ii; *Derb.* ii; *Dors.* ii; *Dur.* ii; *Essex* ii; *Glos.* ii; *Hants* v; *Herts.* i; *Kent* i; *Lancs.* ii; *Lincs.* ii; *Mdx.* ii; *Northants.* ii; *Notts.* ii; *Oxon.* ii; *Rut.* i; *Som.* ii; *Suff.* ii; *Surr.* ii; *Suss.* ii; *Warws.* ii; *Worcs.* ii; *Yorks.* ii
Shoreham, religious houses, *Suss.* ii*
Shortley (with Pinley), *Warws.* viii
Shorwell, *Hants* v
Shotover, *Oxon.* v
Shottesbrook, *Berks.* iii; College, *Berks.* ii
Shotteswell, *Warws.* v
Shouldham Priory, *Norf.* ii
Shoyswell Hundred, *Suss.* ix
Shrawley, *Worcs.* iv
Shrivenham, *Berks.* iv; Hundred, *Berks.* iv
Shuckburgh, Upper and Lower, *Warws.* vi
Shulbred Priory, *Suss.* ii
Shustoke, *Warws.* iv
Shuttington, *Warws.* iv
Sibthorpe College, *Notts.* ii
Sibton, religious houses, *Suff.* ii*
Sidlesham, *Suss.* iv
Sieve-Making, *see* Baskets
Silchester, *Hants* i, iv
Silk (Silk Industry, Silk Manufacture), *Berks.* i; *Derb.* ii; *Dors.* ii; *Essex* ii; *Lancs.* ii; and Velvet, *Notts.* ii; Silk-Weaving (and Throwing and Winding), *Kent* iii; *Mdx.* ii; *Oxon.* ii; *Suff.* ii
Silk-Printing, *see* Calico-Printing
Silsoe (in Flitton), *Beds.* ii
Silver, *Derb.* ii
Simpson, *Bucks.* iv
Singleton, *Suss.* iv; Hundred, *see* Westbourne
Sinningthwaite Priory, *Yorks.* iii
Sinnington, *Yorks. N.R.* ii
Sinnington Foxhounds, *see* Foxhounds
Siphonaptera, *Oxon.* i
Sittingbourne Hospital, *Kent* ii
Six Towns, Federation of the, *Staffs.* viii
Sixhills Priory, *Lincs.* ii
Skelton, *Yorks. N.R.* ii
Skewsby (in Dalby), *Yorks. N.R.* ii
Skipton, Hospital of St. Mary Magdalene, *Yorks.* iii
Skirbeck Commandery, *Lincs.* ii
Slapton, *Bucks.* iii
Slate, Marble, and Stone, *Derb.* ii; 'Artificial Slate', Making of, *Essex* ii; Slate-Quarrying, *Cornw.* i
Slaugham, *Suss.* vii
Slaughter: Upper and Lower, *Glos.* vi*; Hundred, *Glos.* vi
Slawston, *Leics.* v
Slevesholm Cell, *Norf.* ii
Slindon, *Suss.* iv
Slingsby, *Yorks. N.R.* i
Slipton, *Northants.* iii
Slough, *Bucks.* iii
Smeaton, Great, *Yorks. N.R.* i
Smelting, Medieval, *see* Mining
Smethcott, *Salop.* viii
Snails, *see* Mollusca
Snaith, religious houses, *Yorks.* iii*

Snape Priory, *Suff.* ii
Sneaton, *Yorks. N.R.* ii
Snelshall Priory, *Bucks.* i
Snitterfield, *Warws.* iii
Soap Industry (Soap-Making), *Essex* ii; *Lancs.* ii; and Candle-Making, *Surr.* ii; and Chemicals, *Glos.* ii
Soberton, *Hants* iii
Social and Administrative History 1660–1835, *Leics.* iv; Social and Economic History (Economic and Social History), *Beds.* ii; *Berks.* ii; *Bucks.* ii; *Cambs.* ii*; *Derb.* ii; *Dors.* ii; *Dur.* ii; *Essex* ii; *Glos.* ii; *Hants* v; *Herts.* iv; *Hunts.* ii; *Kent* iii; *Lancs.* ii; *Leics.* iv*; *Lincs.* ii; *Mdx.* ii; *Notts.* ii; *Oxon.* ii; *Rut.* i; *Som.* ii; *Staffs.* i; *Suff.* i*; *Surr.* iv; *Suss.* ii; *Warws.* ii, vii, viii*; *Worcs.* iv*; *Yorks.* iii; Social History, *Cambs.* ii; *Warws.* viii*
Sockburn, *Dur.* iii
Sockburn, *Yorks. N.R.* i
Soham School, *Cambs.* ii
Solihull, *Warws.* iv; School, *Warws.* ii
Somborne, King's, *Hants* iv; Hundred, *Hants* iv
Somborne, Little, *Hants* iv
Somersham, *Hunts.* ii
Somerton, *Oxon.* vi
Somerton, West, Hospital, *Norf.* ii
Sompting (or Cokeham) Hospital, *Suss.* ii
Sonning: with Earley, Woodley, and Sandford, *Berks.* iii; Hundred, *Berks.* iii
Sopley, *Hants* v
Sopwell Priory, *Herts.* iv
Sotwell, *Berks.* iii
Soulbury, *Bucks.* iii
Souldern, *Oxon.* vi
Souldrop, *Beds.* iii
South Coast Staghounds, *see* Staghounds
South Down Foxhounds, *see* Foxhounds
South Durham Foxhounds, *see* Foxhounds
South Notts Foxhounds, *see* Foxhounds
South Oxfordshire Hunt, *see* Hunts
Southam, *Warws.* vi
Southampton: Borough, *Hants* iii; religious houses, *Hants* ii*
Southcot (in Reading Borough), *Berks.* iii
Southease, *Suss.* vii
Southill, with Rowney, *Beds.* iii
Southoe, *Hunts.* ii
Southover, *Suss.* vii; Hundred, *Suss.* vii
Southwark: Borough, with Christchurch, *Surr.* iv; Cathedral, *Surr.* iv; religious houses, *Lond.* i*; *Surr.* ii*
Southwell: Minster Grammar School, *Notts.* ii; religious houses, *Notts.* ii*
Southwick, *Hants* iii; Priory, *Hants* ii
Southwick, *Northants.* ii
Southwold Hunt, *see* Hunts
Spalding, religious houses, *Lincs.* ii*
Spaldwick, *Hunts.* iii
Sparkford Vale Harriers, *see* Harriers
Sparsholt, *Berks.* iv
Sparsholt, with Lainston, *Hants* iii
Spas and Mineral Springs, *Wilts.* iv
Speen, with Speenhamland, Wood Speen, and Bagnor, *Berks.* iv
Speen, Wood (in Speen), *Berks.* iv
Speenham (with Yattendon), *Berks.* iv
Speenhamland (in Speen), *Berks.* iv
Spelhoe Hundred, *Northants.* iv
Spelthorne Hundred, *Mdx.* ii–iii
Spencer Family, *see* Genealogy
Spennithorne, *Yorks. N.R.* i
Spernall, *Warws.* iii
Spetchley, *Worcs.* iii
Spettisbury Priory, *Dors.* ii
Spiders, *see* Arachnida
Spilsby College, *Lincs.* ii
Spinney Priory, *Cambs.* ii
Spinning, *see* Draperies, New

Sporle Priory, *Norf.* ii
Sport, *Leics.* iii; *Staffs.* ii; *Wilts.* iv; Ancient and Modern, *Beds.* ii; *Berks.* ii; *Bucks.* ii; *Cumb.* ii; *Derb.* ii; *Dors.* ii; *Dur.* ii; *Essex* ii; *Glos.* ii; *Hants* v; *Herts.* i; *Kent* i; *Lancs.* ii; *Lincs.* ii; *Mdx.* ii; *Northants.* ii; *Notts.* ii; *Oxon.* ii; *Rut.* i; *Som.* ii; *Suff.* ii; *Surr.* ii; *Suss.* ii; *Warws.* ii; *Worcs.* ii; *Yorks.* ii; in the New Forest, *Hants* v
Sports and Games, Old, *Derb.* ii; Local Sports and Pastimes, *Warws.* ii; Old Time Sports, *Notts.* ii
Spring-Tails, *see* Collembola
Stafford: Priory of St. Thomas near, *Staffs.* iii; religious houses, *Staffs.* iii*
Stag Hunting, *Bucks.* ii; *Dors.* ii; *Glos.* ii; *Northants.* ii; *Oxon.* ii; *Som.* ii; *Suss.* ii; *Yorks.* ii
Staghounds, *Berks.* ii; *Essex* ii; *Herts.* i; *Kent* i; *Lancs.* ii; *Mdx.* ii; *Suff.* ii; *Som.* ii; *Surr.* ii; Barrymore, *Berks.* ii; Berks and Bucks Farmers', *Berks.* ii; Devon and Somerset, *Som.* ii; Mid-Kent, *Kent* i; Quantock, *Som.* ii; Rothschild, *Bucks.* ii; South Coast, *Suss.* ii; Warnham, *Suss.* ii
Stagsden, *Beds.* iii
Staindrop College, *Dur.* ii
Staines, *Mdx.* iii
Stainfield Priory, *Lincs.* ii
Stainmoor, the Spital on, *see* Rerecross Hospital
Stainton, *Dur.* iii
Stainton, *Yorks. N.R.* ii
Stainton Dale Foxhounds, *see* Foxhounds
Stamford: religious houses, *Lincs.* ii*; *Northants.* ii*; Priory of Newstead by, *Lincs.* ii
Stanbridge (in Leighton Buzzard), *Beds.* iii
Standish, *Lancs.* vi; Grammar School, *Lancs.* ii
Standon, *Herts.* iii; religious houses, *Herts.* iv*
Stanesgate Priory, *Essex* ii
Stanford Dingley, *Berks.* iv
Stanford in the Vale, *Berks.* iv
Stanford-on-Teme, *Worcs.* iv
Stanford Rivers, *Essex* iv
Stanground, *Hunts.* iii
Stanground, North, *Cambs.* iv
Stanley Abbey, *Wilts.* iii
Stanley St. Leonard Priory, *Glos.* ii
Stanmer, *Suss.* vii
Stanstead Abbots, *Herts.* iii; Free School, *Herts.* ii
Stanstead St. Margarets, *Herts.* iii; (Thele) College, *Herts.* iv
Stanton, Fen, *Hunts.* ii
Stanton Drew Harriers, *see* Harriers
Stanton St. John, *Oxon.* v
Stantonbury, *Bucks.* iv
Stanway, *Glos.* vi
Stanwell, *Mdx.* iii
Stanwick, *Northants.* iv
Stanwick St. John, *Yorks. N.R.* i
Staple Hundred, *Suss.* ix
Stapleford, *Herts.* iii
Stapleford Abbots, *Essex* iv
Stapleford Tawney, *Essex* iv
Staplegrove, Taunton School, *Som.* ii
Stapleton, *Salop.* viii
Starch Manufacture, *Essex* ii
Startforth, *Yorks. N.R.* i
Statistical Material for Ploughley Hundred [including Tax Assessments], *Oxon.* vi
Statistics, Occupational, *Cambs.* ii
Staughton, Great, *Hunts.* ii
Staughton, Little, *Beds.* iii
Staunton, *Worcs.* iv
Staveley (or Netherthorpe) Grammar School, *Derb.* ii
Staverton, *Glos.* viii
Stavordale Priory, *Som.* ii
Staxton, Hospital of St. Mary, *Yorks.* iii
Stay- and Corset-Making, *Suff.* ii
Steam Motor Omnibuses, *see* Motor Omnibuses
Stearsby (in Brandsby), *Yorks. N.R.* ii

Stedham, *Suss.* iv

Steel Balls, Manufacture of, *Essex* ii; Steel Pens, Manufacture of, *Essex* ii; Steel-Work, *Oxon.* ii; *and see* Iron

Steep, with North and South Ambersham, *Hants* iii

Steeplechasing, *Beds.* ii; *Berks.* ii; *Bucks.* ii; *Herts.* i; *Kent* i; *Lancs.* ii; *Northants.* ii; *Warws.* ii

Steppingley, *Beds.* iii

Stevenage, *Herts.* iii; School, *Herts.* ii

Steventon, *Berks.* iv; Alien Priory, *Berks.* ii

Steventon, *Hants* iv

Stevington, *Beds.* iii

Stewkley, *Bucks.* iii

Steyning: Collegiate Church, *Suss.* ii; Grammar School, *Suss.* ii

Stibbington, *Hunts.* iii

Stidd under Longridge, Hospital of St. Saviour, *Lancs.* ii

Stillington, *Yorks. N.R.* ii

Stilton, *Hunts.* iii

Stivichall, *Warws.* viii

Stixwould Priory, *Lincs.* ii

Stock (in Fladbury), *Worcs.* iii

Stockbridge, *Hants* iv

Stockbridge Hundred, *see* Box and Stockbridge Hundred

Stockerston, *Leics.* v; Hospital, *Leics.* ii

Stocking-Frames, *see* Knitters

Stockton, *Warws.* vi

Stockton-on-Tees, *Dur.* iii

Stockton-on-Teme, *Worcs.* iv

Stockton-on-the-Forest, *Yorks. N.R.* ii

Stockton Ward, *Dur.* iii

Stodden Hundred, *Beds.* iii

Stogursey Priory, *Som.* ii

Stoke, *Warws.* viii

Stoke, Elwes of, *see* Genealogy

Stoke, Hospital of St. Leonard, *Notts.* ii

Stoke, Severn, *Worcs.* iv

Stoke, South, *Oxon.* vii

Stoke, West, *Suss.* iv

Stoke Bliss, with Kyre Parva, *Worcs.* iv

Stoke by Clare, religious houses, *Suff.* ii*

Stoke Charity, *Hants* iii

Stoke D'Abernon, *Surr.* iii

Stoke Doyle, *Northants.* iii

Stoke Dry, *Rut.* ii

Stoke Goldington, *Bucks.* iv

Stoke Hammond, *Bucks.* iv

Stoke Hundred, *Bucks.* iii

Stoke Lyne, *Oxon.* vi

Stoke Mandeville, *Bucks.* ii

Stoke next Guildford, *Surr.* iii

Stoke-on-Trent, *Staffs.* viii

Stoke Poges, *Bucks.* iii

Stoke Prior, *Worcs.* iii

Stoke Talmage, *Oxon.* viii

Stoke-under-Hamdon College, *Som.* ii

Stoke-upon-Trent, *Staffs.* viii

Stokenchurch, *Bucks.* iii

Stokesley, *Yorks. N.R.* ii

Stondon, Lower (in Shillington), *Beds.* ii

Stondon, Upper, *Beds.* ii

Stondon Massey, *Essex* iv

Stone, *Bucks.* ii; Hundred, *Bucks.* ii

Stone, *Worcs.* iii

Stone Priory, *Staffs.* iii

Stone [industry], *Staffs.* ii; Building Stone, *Notts.* ii; Stone, Marble, and Slate, *Derb.* ii; Stone, Quarries, etc. (Stone-Quarrying), *Kent* iii; *Wilts.* iv; Stone Quarries, Lime-Burning, Fullers' Earth, etc., *Surr.* ii; *and see* Granite; Quarries; Slate

Stone, Sculptured, Anglo-Saxon, *Yorks.* ii; *and see* Art

Stone Circles, *Cornw.* i

Stone-Flies, *see* Plecoptera

Stonegrave, *Yorks. N.R.* i

Stoneham, North and South, *Hants* iii*

Stoneleigh, *Warws.* vi; Abbey, *Warws.* ii

Stonely Priory, *Hunts.* i

Stoneware, Fulham, *Mdx.* ii

Stoneworts, *see* Characeae

Stonton Wyville, *Leics.* v

Stonydelph (with Amington), *Warws.* iv

Stopsley (in Luton), *Beds.* ii

Stortford, Bishop's, *Herts.* iii; schools, *Herts.* ii*; *and see* Parliament, List of Members of

Stotfold, *Beds.* ii

Stoughton, *Suss.* iv

Stoulton, *Worcs.* iii

Stourbridge (in Old Swinford), *Worcs.* iii; Grammar School, *Worcs.* iv

Stove-Making, *Essex* ii

Stow Abbey, *Lincs.* ii

Stow Longa, *Hunts.* iii

Stow-on-the-Wold, *Glos.* vi; Hospital, *Glos.* ii

Stowe, *Bucks.* iv

Stowood, *Oxon.* v

Stranton, *Dur.* iii

Stratfield Saye, *Hants* iv; Alien Priory, *Berks.* ii

Stratfield Turgis, *Hants* iv

Stratfield Mortimer, *Berks.* iii

Stratford, Fenny (in Bletchley), *Bucks.* iv

Stratford, Stony, *Bucks.* iv; Grammar School, *Bucks.* ii; Hospital of St. John Baptist, *Bucks.* i

Stratford, Water, *Bucks.* iv

Stratford at Bow Priory, *Mdx.* i

Stratford Langthorne Abbey, *Essex* ii

Stratford-upon-Avon: Borough, *Warws.* iii; Cricket, *Warws.* ii; religious houses, *Warws.* ii*; School, *Warws.* ii

Stratford-sub-Castle, *Wilts.* vi

Stratton (in Biggleswade), *Beds.* ii

Stratton, East, *Hants* iii

Stratton Audley, *Oxon.* vi

Straw and Hay, Supplying to the London Markets, *Essex* ii

Straw Hats and Bonnets, Making of, *Essex* ii; Strawplait, Hat, and Bonnet Industry, *Beds.* ii; *Herts.* iv; Straw-Plaiting, *Bucks.* ii; *Essex* ii

Streat, *Suss.* vii; Hundred, *Suss.* vii

Streatham, *Surr.* iv

Streatley, *Berks.* iii

Streatley, with Sharpenhoe, *Beds.* ii

Strensall, *Yorks. N.R.* ii

Strensham, *Worcs.* iv

Strepsiptera, *Oxon.* i

Stretham and Thetford, *Cambs.* iv

Stretton, *Rut.* ii

Stretton, *Staffs.* iv

Stretton Baskerville, *Warws.* vi

Stretton-on-Fosse, *Warws.* v

Stretton-upon-Dunsmore and Princethorpe, *Warws.* vi

Strixton, *Northants.* iii

Strood, religious houses, *Kent* ii*

Stud Farms, *see* Training Establishments

Studham, *Beds.* iii

Studham, *Herts.* ii

Studley, *Warws.* iii; Priory, *Warws.* ii

Studley Priory, *Oxon.* ii

Stukeley, Great and Little, *Hunts.* ii*

Sturbridge Hospital, *Cambs.* ii

Subscribers, Lists of, *Beds. Ind.*; *Hants Ind.*; *Lancs.* viii; *Oxon.* v–viii; *Surr. Ind.*

Suckley, with Alfrick and Lulsley, *Worcs.* iv

Sudborough, *Northants.* iii

Sudbury, religious houses, *Suff.* ii*

Sugar and Chocolate, *Glos.* ii; Sugar Industry, *Lancs.* ii; Sugar-Refining, *Essex* ii

Sulby Abbey, *Northants.* ii

Sulham, *Berks.* iii

Sulhampstead Abbots, with Grazeley, *Berks.* iii

Sulhamstead Bannister, *Berks.* iii

Sunbury, *Mdx.* iii

Sunday School Movement, *Cambs.* ii

Sundon, *Beds.* ii

Sundridge, Fane of Combe Bank in, *see* Genealogy

Sunninghill, *Berks.* iii
Sunningwell, *Berks.* iv
Sutton, *Beds.* ii
Sutton, *Cambs.* iv
Sutton, *Northants.* ii
Sutton, *Surr.* iv
Sutton, *Yorks. E.R.* i
Sutton, Bishop's, *Hants* iii; Hundred, *Hants* iii
Sutton, Long, *Hants* iv
Sutton at Hone Preceptory, *Kent* ii
Sutton Coldfield: Borough, *Warws.* iv; School, *Warws.* ii; Turner of, *see* Genealogy
Sutton Courtenay, *Berks.* iv
Sutton-in-Holderness, College of St. James, *Yorks.* iii
Sutton-on-the-Forest, *Yorks. N.R.* ii
Sutton-under-Brailes, *Warws.* v
Sutton Veny, *Wilts.* viii
Swaffham Bulbeck Priory, *Cambs.* ii
Swainestrey in Murston, religious houses, *Kent* ii*
Swallowfield, *Berks.* iii
Swanborough, *Suss.* vii
Swanbourne, *Bucks.* iii
Swarraton, *Hants* iv
Swavesey Priory, *Cambs.* ii
Sweetmart-Hunting, *Cumb.* ii
Swell, Lower, *Glos.* vi
Swimming [sport], *Notts.* ii
Swindon, *Wilts.* ix
Swine Priory, *Yorks.* iii
Swineshead, *Beds.* iii
Swineshead, *Hunts.* iii
Swineshead Abbey, *Lincs.* ii
Swinford, Old, with Stourbridge, *Worcs.* iii
Swingfield Preceptory, *Kent* ii
Sydenham, *Oxon.* viii
Synagogues, *Cambs.* iii; *and see* Jews
Syon Abbey, *Mdx.* i
Sywell, *Northants.* iv

Tachbrook, Bishop's, *Warws.* v
Tadcaster Hospital, *Yorks.* iii
Tadley, *Hants* iv
Tadmarton, *Oxon.* ix
Takeley Priory, *Essex* ii
Tamworth, *Warws.* iv; religious houses, *Staffs.* iii*
Tandridge, *Surr.* iv; Hundred, *Surr.* iv; Priory, *Surr.* ii
Tanfield, West, *Yorks. N.R.* i
Tangley, *Hants* iv
Tangmere, *Suss.* iv
Tanning, *Berks.* i; *Notts.* ii; *Salop.* i; *Suss.* ii; *Wilts.* iv; and Shoe-Making, *Bucks.* ii
Tansor, *Northants.* ii
Tanworth, *Warws.* v
Tapestry, *Mdx.* ii; *Surr.* ii; *and see* Barcheston
Taplow, *Bucks.* iii
Tardebigge, *Worcs.* iii
Tarleton, *Lancs.* vi
Tarrant Kaines Abbey, *Dors.* ii
Tarrant Rushton, Hospital of St. Leonard, *Dors.* ii
Tarring, West, Hospital, *Suss.* ii
Tatham, *Lancs.* viii
Tatsfield, *Surr.* iv
Tattenhoe, *Bucks.* iii
Tattershall College, *Lincs.* ii
Taunton, religious houses, *Som.* ii*; schools, *Som.* ii*
Taunton Vale Harriers, *see* Harriers; Hunt, *see* Hunts
Tax Assessments: Hearth Tax Analysis [Isle of Ely], *Cambs.* iv; Hearth Tax Analysis, Ongar Hundred, *Essex* iv; Hearth Tax, Cambridge University and Borough, *Cambs.* iii; Medieval, Analysis, Ongar Hundred, *Essex* iv; Poll-Tax Payers of 1377, *Wilts.* iv; Village, and Numbers of Contributors [for Lewknor and Pyrton Hundreds], 1306–1523, *Oxon.* viii; Villages and Hamlets in Bullingdon Hundred, 1306–1523, *Oxon.* v; Villages and Hamlets in Dorchester and Thame Hundreds, 1306–1523, *Oxon.* vii; Villages and Hamlets

in Ploughley Hundred, *see* Statistical Material; *and see* Fifteenths and Tenths
Teazel Cultivation, *see* Coriander
Tebworth (in Chalgrove), *Beds.* iii
Teddesley Hay, *Staffs.* v
Teddington, *Mdx.* iii
Teddington (in Overbury), *Worcs.* iii
Tedworth Hunt, *see* Hunts
Teffont Magna, *Wilts.* viii
Teigh, *Rut.* ii
Telscombe, *Suss.* vii
Templecombe, religious houses, *Som.* ii*
Tempsford, *Beds.* ii
Tenbury, *Worcs.* iv; St. Michael's College, *Worcs.* iv
Tennis, *Lancs.* ii; *Mdx.* ii
Terrington, *Yorks. N.R.* ii
Terwick, *Suss.* iv
Testa de Nevill, Introduction and Text, *Cumb.* i
Tetsworth, *Oxon.* vii
Tettenhall, College of St. Michael, *Staffs.* iii
Tetworth, *Hunts.* ii
Tewin, *Herts.* iii; Tewin Water, Cowper of, *see* Genealogy
Tewkesbury: Borough, *Glos.* viii; Hundred, Lower Division, *Glos.* viii; Hundred, Upper Division, *Glos.* vi; religious houses, *Glos.* ii*
Textiles (Textile Industries, Textile Trades), *Bucks.* ii; *Derb.* ii; *Dur.* ii; *Hants* v; *Herts.* iv; *Lancs.* ii; *Oxon.* ii; *Som.* ii; *Staffs.* ii; *Suss.* ii; *Wilts.* iv; *Yorks.* ii; and Allied Trades (Miscellaneous Textile and Allied Industries), *Northants.* ii; *Surr.* ii; Mixed (Drabbet, Horsehair, Cocoa-Nut Fibre) and Ready-Made Clothing, *Suff.* ii; *and see* Cloth; Waterproofs; Wool; Worsted
Thame, *Oxon.* vii; Abbey, *Oxon.* ii; Hundred, *Oxon.* vii; *and see* Tax Assessments
Thames: Embankments in Kent, *Kent* i; Regattas, *see* Regattas
Thatcham, *Berks.* iii
Theale Hundred, *Berks.* iii
Theddingworth, *Leics.* v
Thele, *see* Stanstead St. Margaret's
Thelsford, Trinitarian Friars, *Warws.* ii
Therfield, *Herts.* iii
Thetford: religious houses, *Norf.* ii*; *Suff.* ii*; School, *Suff.* ii
Thetford (with Stretham), *Cambs.* iv
Theydon Bois, *Essex* iv
Theydon Garnon, *Essex* iv
Theydon Mount, *Essex* iv
Thicket Priory, *Yorks.* iii
Thirkleby, *Yorks. N.R.* ii
Thirsk, *Yorks. N.R.* ii
Thistleton, *Rut.* ii
Thoby Priory, *Essex* ii
Thompson College, *Norf.* ii
Thorley, *Hants* v
Thorley, *Herts.* iii
Thormanby, *Yorks. N.R.* ii
Thornborough, *Bucks.* iv
Thorney, *Cambs.* iv; Abbey, *Cambs.* ii
Thorney, West, *Suss.* iv
Thorngate Hundred, *Hants* iv
Thornhaugh, *Northants.* ii
Thornholme Priory, *Lincs.* ii
Thornton Family, *see* Genealogy
Thornton, *Bucks.* iv
Thornton (part of), *Lancs.* viii
Thornton, religious houses, *Lincs.* ii*
Thornton Dale, *Yorks. N.R.* ii
Thornton-le-Clay (in Foston), *Yorks. N.R.* ii
Thornton le Street, *Yorks. N.R.* i
Thornton Steward, *Yorks. N.R.* i
Thornton Watlass, *Yorks. N.R.* i
Thorpe, *Surr.* iii
Thorpe, Castle (in Hanslope), *Bucks.* iv
Thorpe Achurch, *Northants.* iii

Thorpe-by-Water (in Seaton), *Rut.* ii
Thorpe Malsor, Maunsell of, *see* Genealogy
Thrapston, *Northants.* iii; Hospital of St. Leonard, *Northants.* ii
Thread (Thread-Making), *see* Lace
Thremhall Priory, *Essex* ii
Throcking, *Herts.* iv; Elwes (Cary-Elwes) of, *see* Genealogy
Throckmorton (in Fladbury), *Worcs.* iii
Throwley Priory, *Kent* ii
Thruxton, *Hants* iv
Thundridge, *Herts.* iii
Thurgarton Priory, *Notts.* ii
Thurlaston (with Dunchurch), *Warws.* vi
Thurleigh, *Beds.* iii
Thurlow, Great, Hospital, *Suff.* ii
Thurnby, *Leics.* v
Thurning, *Hunts.* iii
Thurning, *Northants.* iii
Thursley, *Surr.* iii
Tibberton, *Worcs.* iii
Tibblestone Hundred, *Glos.* viii
Ticehurst, *Suss.* ix
Tichborne, *Hants* iii
Tickencote, *Rut.* ii
Tickford (or Newport Pagnel) Priory, *Bucks.* i
Tickhill, religious houses, *Yorks.* iii*
Tiddington (in Albury), *Oxon.* v
Tideswell Grammar School, *Derb.* ii
Tidmarsh, *Berks.* iii
Tidmington, *Worcs.* iii
Tidworth, South, *Hants* iv
Tilbrook, *Beds.* iii
Tilbrook, *Hunts.* iii
Tilbury, East, Hospital, *Essex* ii
Tilehurst, *Berks.* iii
Tiles, *Worcs.* ii; and Bricks, *Oxon.* ii; Tile-Works, Encaustic and Tesselated, *Salop.* i; *and see* Brick-Making; Pottery
Tilsworth, *Beds.* iii
Tilty Abbey, *Essex* ii
Timber, etc., *Glos.* ii
Timsbury, *Hants* iv
Tin-Mining, *Cornw.* i
Tingewick, *Bucks.* iv
Tingrith, *Beds.* iii
Tinplate and Allied Products, *Staffs.* ii
Tinwell, with Ingthorpe, *Rut.* ii
Tiptree Priory, *Essex* ii
Tirley, *Glos.* viii
Tisted, East and West, *Hants* iii*
Titchfield, *Hants* iii; Abbey, *Hants* ii; Hundred, *Hants* iii
Titchmarsh, *Northants.* iii
Titsey, *Surr.* iv
Tixover, *Rut.* ii
Tobacco, *Mdx.* ii; *Wilts.* iv
Tobacco Pipes (Clay Pipes, Pipe-Making), *Essex* ii; *Northants.* ii; *Salop.* i
Tockenham, *Wilts.* ix
Toddington, *Beds.* iii; Hospital of St. John Baptist, *Beds.* i
Todenham, *Glos.* vi
Toft Monks Priory, *Norf.* ii
Tolethorpe Hospital, *Rut.* i
Tonbridge Priory, *Kent* ii
Tonge Hospital, *see* Puckeshall Hospital
Tools, *Worcs.* ii; Edge-Tools, *Staffs.* ii
Tooting Graveney, *Surr.* iv
Tooting Priory, *Surr.* ii
Topcliffe, *Yorks. N.R.* ii
Torksey Priory, *Lincs.* ii
Tortington Priory, *Suss.* ii
Toseland, *Hunts.* ii; Hundred, *Hunts.* ii
Tottenham Grammar School, *Mdx.* i
Totteridge, *Herts.* iii
Totternhoe, *Beds.* iii

Towcester, religious houses, *Northants.* ii*
Towersey, *Bucks.* iv
Towns [Romano-British], *Kent* iii; *and see* Settlement Sites
Townships, *see* Parishes
Trade, *see* Communications
Trail Hounds, North Country, and Trails, *Cumb.* ii
Trainers, Famous, *see* Racing Celebrities
Training Establishments and Stud Farms, *Dors.* ii
Transport, *Yorks.* York
Tredington, *Glos.* viii
Tredington, with Armscote, Blackwell, Darlingscott, and Newbold on Stour, *Worcs.* iii
Trentham Priory, *Staffs.* iii
Treyford, *Suss.* iv
Trichoptera (Caddis-flies), *Cambs.* i; *Derb.* i; *Herts.* i; *Oxon.* i; *Staffs.* i; *Worcs.* i; and Neuroptera, *Hants* i; *Norf.* i; *Surr.* i; *Yorks.* i
Tring, with Long Marston, *Herts.* ii
Trotton, *Suss.* iv
Trowbridge, *Wilts.* vii
Tubney, *Berks.* iv
Tuckington, *see* Tufton
Tudor Period and the Civil War, *Cambs.* ii
Tufton (Tuckington), *Hants* iv
Tunstall, *Lancs.* viii; School, *Lancs.* ii
Tunstall, *Staffs.* viii
Tunstall Priory, *Lincs.* ii
Tunworth, *Hants* iv
Tupholme Abbey, *Lincs.* ii
Turbellaria, *Cambs.* i
Turner Family, *see* Genealogy
Turnpike Roads, *see* Roads
Turvey, *Beds.* iii
Turville, *Bucks.* iii
Turweston, *Bucks.* iv
Tusmore, *Oxon.* vi
Tutbury Priory, *Staffs.* iii
Tuxford: College, *Notts.* ii; Grammar School, *Notts.* ii
Twickenham, *Mdx.* iii
Twine Manufacture, *see* Rope
Twineham, *Suss.* vii
Twyford, *Hants* iii
Twyford, with Charndon and Poundon, *Bucks.* iv
Twyneham, Christchurch, Priory, *Hants* ii
Twywell, *Northants.* iii
Tydd St. Giles, *Cambs.* iv
Tyringham, with Filgrave, *Bucks.* iv
Tysoe, *Warws.* v
Tytherley, East, *Hants* iv
Tytherley, West, with Buckholt, *Hants* iv

Udimore, *Suss.* ix
Uffington, *Berks.* iv; White Horse at, *Berks.* i
Ufford, *Northants.* ii
Ufton, *Warws.* vi
Ufton Nervet, *Berks.* iii
Ullenhall, *Warws.* iii
Ulverscroft Priory, *Leics.* ii
Ulverston, *Lancs.* viii; Grammar School, *Lancs.* ii
Underditch Hundred, *Wilts.* vi
Upavon Priory, *Wilts.* iii
Upham, *Hants* iii
Upholland: religious houses, *Lancs.* ii*; School, *Lancs.* i
Upleatham, *Yorks. N.R.* ii
Uppingham, *Rut.* ii; Grammar School, *Rut.* i
Upsall-in-Cleveland, Hospital of St. Lawrence, *Yorks.* iii
Upton (in Blewbury), *Berks.* iii
Upton (in Dinton), *Bucks.* ii
Upton, *Hunts.* iii
Upton, *Northants.* ii
Upton-cum-Chalvey, *Bucks.* iii
Upton Grey, *Hants* iii
Upton Scudamore, *Wilts.* viii
Upton Snodsbury, *Worcs.* iv
Upton-upon-Severn, *Worcs.* iv

Upton Warren, *Worcs.* iii
Upwell (with Outwell), *Cambs.* iv
Upwood, *Hunts.* ii
Urswick, *Lancs.* viii; Grammar School, *Lancs.* ii

Vagrancy, *Cambs.* ii
Vaudey Abbey, *Lincs.* ii
Velvet, *see* Silk
Vent, The, *Oxon.* v
Verney Family, *see* Genealogy, Calvert
Vernhams Dean, *Hants* iv
Verulam, Earl of, *see* Genealogy, Grimston
Victoria County History: Committees, *Essex* iii–v, *Essex Bibl.*; *Leics.* iii–iv; *Oxon.* v–viii; *Staffs.* ii–v, viii; *Wilts.* i (1), ii–vi, viii–ix; *Yorks. E.R.* i; *Yorks. York*; Council, *Mdx.* i, iii; *and see* County Committees
Villages [Romano-British], *see* Settlement Sites
Villiers Family, *see* Genealogy
Vinegar-Making, *Essex* ii; Vinegar and British Wines, *Surr.* ii
Vine Hunt, *see* Hunts

Wadborough (in Pershore Holy Cross), *Worcs.* iv
Waddesdon, with Westcott and Woodham, *Bucks.* iv
Wadenhoe, *Northants.* iii
Wake Family, *see* Genealogy
Wakely (in Aspenden), *Herts.* iv
Walcot (in Pershore Holy Cross), *Worcs.* iv
Walcot Hospital, *Lincs.* ii
Walden, King's, *Herts.* iii
Walden, St. Paul's, *Herts.* ii
Walden Abbey, *Essex* ii
Walgrave, *Northants.* iv
Walkern, *Herts.* iii
Wallingford: Borough, *Berks.* iii; Grammar School, *Berks.* ii; religious houses, *Berks.* ii*
Wallington, *Herts.* iii
Wallington Hundred, *Surr.* iv
Wallingwells Priory, *Notts.* ii
Wallop, Nether and Over, *Hants* iv*
Walsgrave-on-Sowe, *Warws.* viii
Walsingham, religious houses, *Norf.* ii*
Walsoken Hospital, *Norf.* ii
Waltham, Bishop's, *Hants* iii; Hundred, *Hants* iii
Waltham, Little, Luckyn of, *see* Genealogy, Grimston
Waltham, North, *Hants* iv
Waltham, Up, *Suss.* iv
Waltham, White, *Berks.* iii
Waltham Holy Cross, *Essex* v; Abbey, *Essex* ii; Hundred, *Essex* v
Waltham St. Lawrence, *Berks.* iii
Walton, *Bucks.* iv
Walton (in Aylesbury), *Bucks.* iii
Walton (in Wellesbourne), *Warws.* v
Walton, Wood, *Hunts.* iii
Walton Cardiff, *Glos.* viii
Walton-on-Thames, *Surr.* iii
Walton on the Hill, *Lancs.* iii
Walton-on-the-Hill, *Surr.* iii
Wanborough, *Surr.* iii
Wanborough, *Wilts.* ix
Wandsworth, *Surr.* iv
Wangford Priory, *Suff.* ii
Wansford, *Northants.* ii
Wantage, *Berks.* iv; Grammar School, *Berks.* ii; Hundred, *Berks.* iv
Wappenbury and Eathorpe, *Warws.* vi
War-Rockets, Congreve, Manufacture of, *Essex* ii
Warbleton, *Suss.* ix
Warblington, with Emsworth, *Hants* iii
Warboys, *Hunts.* ii
Warden, Old, *Beds.* iii; Warden Abbey, *Beds.* i
Wardley, *Rut.* ii
Ware, *Herts.* iii; religious houses, *Herts.* iv*; schools, *Herts.* ii*
Wareham, religious houses, *Dors.* ii*

Waresley, *Hunts.* ii
Warfield, *Berks.* iii
Wargrave, *Berks.* iii; Hundred, *Berks.* iii
Warkton, *Northants.* iii
Warley Wigorn (in Halesowen), *Worcs.* iii
Warlingham, *Surr.* iv
Warminghurst Ballivate, *Suss.* ii
Warmington, *Northants.* iii
Warmington, *Warws.* v; Priory, *Warws.* ii
Warminster, *Wilts.* viii; Hundred, *Wilts.* viii
Warnborough, South, *Hants* iii
Warndon, *Worcs.* iii
Warnford, *Hants* iii
Warnham Staghounds, *see* Staghounds
Warrington, *Lancs.* iii; Boteler Grammar School, *Lancs.* ii; House of Austin Friars, *Lancs.* ii
Warrington (in Olney), *Bucks.* iv
Warter Priory, *Yorks.* iii
Warthill, *Yorks. N.R.* ii
Wartling, *Suss.* ix
Warton, *Lancs.* viii; School, *Lancs.* ii
Warwick: Borough, *Warws.* viii; Castle and Castle Estate, *Warws.* viii; religious houses, *Warws.* ii*; School, *Warws.* ii
Warwickshire, Hundreds of, *Warws.* iii
Washbourne, Great, *Glos.* vi
Washbourne, Little (in Overbury), *Worcs.* iii
Washingley, *Hunts.* iii
Wasing, *Berks.* iv
Wasperton, *Warws.* v
Wasps (Hymenoptera Aculeata), *see* Hymenoptera
Watch-Making, *Lancs.* ii; *and see* Clock- and Watch-Making
Water-Cress Growing, *Herts.* iv
Waterbeach Abbey, *Cambs.* ii
Waterperry, *Oxon.* v
Waterproofs, Ropes, and Other Textiles, *Glos.* ii
Waterstock, *Oxon.* vii
Watford, *Herts.* ii; Endowed Schools, *Herts.* ii
Wath, *Yorks. N.R.* i
Watlington, *Oxon.* viii
Watton-at-Stone, *Herts.* iii
Watton Priory, *Yorks.* iii
Wavendon, *Bucks.* iv
Waverley, *Surr.* ii; Abbey, *Surr.* ii
Weald, South, Hospital of Brook Street in, *Essex* ii
Weald Bassett, North, *Essex* iv
Wearmouth and Jarrow Monasteries, *Dur.* ii
Weddington, *Warws.* iv
Weedon (in Hardwick), *Bucks.* iii
Weedon Beck Priory, *Northants.* ii
Weedon Pinkney (Weedon Lois) Priory, *Northants.* ii
Weeke (Wyke), *Hants* iii
Weethley, *Warws.* iii
Welbeck Abbey, *Notts.* ii
Welbury, *Yorks. N.R.* ii
Welches Dam, *Cambs.* iv
Weld or Dyers' Weed Cultivation, *Essex* ii
Welford, *Berks.* iv
Welford-on-Avon, *Warws.* v
Welham, *Leics.* v
Well, *Yorks. N.R.* i; Hospital of St. Michael, *Yorks.* iii
Well Hall, *see* Welle
Welland, *Worcs.* iii
Welle (Well Hall) Priory, in Gayton, *Norf.* ii
Wellesbourne, with Walton, *Warws.* v
Wellingborough, *Northants.* iv
Wellington College, *Berks.* ii, (cricket), *Berks.* ii, (football), *Berks.* ii
Wellow, East, with Dunwood and Embley, *Hants* iv
Wellow Abbey, *see* Grimsby Abbey
Wells: religious houses, *Som.* ii*; schools, *Som.* ii*
Wells Subscription Harriers, *see* Harriers
Welwyn, *Herts.* iii
Wendlebury, *Oxon.* vi
Wendling Abbey, *Norf.* ii

INDEX OF TITLES OF ARTICLES

Wendover: Borough, *Bucks*. iii; Hospital of St. John Baptist, *Bucks*. i
Wenghale Priory, *Lincs*. ii
Wensley, *Yorks. N.R.* i
Wensleydale Foxhounds, *see* Foxhounds
Wentbridge Leper House, *Yorks*. iii
Wentworth, *Cambs*. iv
Wereham, Priory of St. Winwaloe, *Norf*. ii
Werhale Hospital, *Dur*. ii
West Somerset Hunt, *see* Hunts
Westbourne, *Suss*. iv; and Singleton Hundred, *Suss*. iv
Westbrook (in Boxford), *Berks*. iv
Westbury, *Bucks*. iv
Westbury, *Salop*. viii
Westbury, *Wilts*. viii; Hundred, *Wilts*. viii
Westbury-on-Trym College, *Glos*. ii
Westcote, *Glos*. vi
Westcott (in Waddesdon), *Bucks*. iv
Westerdale, *Yorks. N.R.* ii; Preceptory, *Yorks*. iii
Westfield, *Suss*. ix
Westham Hospital, *Suss*. ii
Westhampnett, *Suss*. iv
Westmeston, *Suss*. vii
Westmill, *Herts*. iii
Westminster, religious houses, *Lond*. i*
Westminster Hundred: Lower Division, *Glos*. viii; Upper Division, *Glos*. vi
Westmorland, Earl of, *see* Genealogy, Fane
Weston (Hants), *see* St. Mary Extra
Weston, *Herts*. iii
Weston, Edith, *Rut*. ii; Priory, *Rut*. i
Weston, Hail, *Hunts*. ii
Weston, Old, *Hunts*. iii
Weston, South, *Oxon*. viii
Weston Corbett, *Hants* iii
Weston Favell, *Northants*. iv
Weston Harriers, *see* Harriers
Weston-on-the-Green, *Oxon*. vi
Weston Patrick, *Hants* iv
Weston Turville, *Bucks*. ii
Weston under Lizard, *Staffs*. iv
Weston-under-Wetherley, *Warws*. vi
Weston Underwood, *Bucks*. iv
Weston-upon-Avon, with Milcote, *Warws*. v
Westoning, *Beds*. iii
Westover (in Wherwell), *Hants* iv
Westover Liberty, with Parishes of Holdenhurst and Bournemouth, *Hants* v
Westwood Abbey, *see* Lesnes Abbey
Westwood Park, *Worcs*. iii
Westwood Priory, *Worcs*. ii
Wetheral Priory, *Cumb*. ii
Wexham, *Bucks*. iii
Weybourne Priory, *Norf*. ii
Weybridge, *Surr*. iii
Weybridge Priory, *Norf*. ii
Weyhill, with Penton Grafton, *Hants* iv
Whaddon, *Wilts*. vii
Whaddon, with Nash, *Bucks*. iii
Whaddon Chase Hunt, *see* Hunts
Whalesbone Hundred, *Suss*. vii
Whalley, *Lancs*. vi; Abbey, *Lancs*. ii, vi; Grammar School, *Lancs*. ii
Whatcombe (in Fawley), *Berks*. iv
Whatcote, *Warws*. v
Whatlington, *Suss*. ix
Wheatfield, *Oxon*. viii
Wheathampstead, with Harpenden, *Herts*. ii
Wheatley, Old, and Coombe, *Oxon*. v
Wheatley and Littleworth, *Oxon*. v
Whelks, *see* Mollusca
Whenby, *Yorks. N.R.* ii
Wherwell: with Westover, *Hants* iv; Abbey, *Hants* ii; Hundred, *Hants* iv
Whichford, *Warws*. v
Whippet-Racing, *Lancs*. ii

Whippingham, *Hants* v
Whips [industry], *Northants*. ii
Whips, *see* Huntsmen
Whipsnade, *Beds*. iii
Whissendine, *Rut*. ii
Whiston, *Northants*. iv
Whistones (in Claines), *Worcs*. iii; Priory, *Worcs*. ii
Whitacre, Nether and Over, *Warws*. iv*
Whitby, *Yorks. N.R.* ii; religious houses, *Yorks*. iii*; Whitby Strand Liberty, *Yorks. N.R.* ii
Whitchurch, *Bucks*. iii
Whitchurch, *Hants* iv
Whitchurch, *Warws*. v
Whiting Manufacture, *Essex* ii
Whitley (in Reading Borough), *Berks*. iii
Whitley (with Pinley), *Warws*. viii; Preceptory, *Yorks*. iii
Whitmore Park (with Harnall), *Warws*. viii
Whitnash, *Warws*. vi
Whitsbury, *Hants* iv
Whittington, *Lancs*. viii
Whittington (in St. Peter), *Worcs*. iii
Whittlesey, *Cambs*. iv
Whitwell, *Hants* v
Whitwell, *Rut*. ii
Whoberley (with Asthill), *Warws*. viii
Whorlton, *Yorks. N.R.* ii
Whorwellsdown Hundred, *Wilts*. viii
Wibtoft, *Warws*. iv
Wichenford, *Worcs*. iii
Wick (in Pershore St. Andrew), *Worcs*. iv
Wicker Basket Industry, *see* Pavenham
Wickham, *Hants* iii
Wickhamford, *Worcs*. ii
Widford, *Herts*. iii
Widley, *Hants* iii
Widnes, Farnworth Grammar School, *Lancs*. ii
Wield, *Hants* iii
Wigan, *Lancs*. iv; Grammar School, *Lancs*. ii
Wigginton, *Herts*. ii
Wigginton, *Oxon*. ii
Wigginton, *Yorks. N.R.* ii
Wight, Isle of: Hunt, *see* Hunts; religious houses, *Hants* ii*
Wigsthorpe (in Lilford), *Northants*. iii
Wigton, Hospital of St. Leonard, *Cumb*. ii
Wilberfoss Priory, *Yorks*. iii
Wilbraham, Great, Preceptory, *Cambs*. ii
Wilburton, *Cambs*. iv
Wilby, *Northants*. iv
Wilcheswood [monastery], *Dors*. ii
Wild Fowling, *Cumb*. ii; *Essex* ii; *Glos*. ii; *Lincs*. ii; *Suff*. ii
Wilden, *Beds*. iii
Willen, *Bucks*. iv
Willenhall, *Warws*. viii
Willes Family, *see* Genealogy
Willey, *Warws*. vi; Isham of, *see* Genealogy
Willey Hundred, *Beds*. iii
Willian, *Herts*. iii
Willington, *Beds*. iii
Willoughby, *Warws*. vi
Willoughton, religious houses, *Lincs*. ii*
Willybrook Hundred, *Northants*. ii
Wilmington Priory, *Suss*. ii
Wilnecote, *Warws*. iv
Wilsford, *Wilts*. vi
Wilsford Priory, *Lincs*. ii
Wilshamstead, *Beds*. iii
Wilshere Family, *see* Genealogy
Wilton: Borough, *Wilts*. vi; religious houses, *Wilts*. iii*
Wimbledon, *Surr*. iv
Wimborne, religious houses, *Dors*. ii*
Wimington, *see* Wymington
Winchcombe, religious houses, *Glos*. ii*
Winchelsea, *Suss*. ix; religious houses, *Suss*. ii*
Winchendon, Lower (Nether) and Upper, *Bucks*. iv*
Winchester, *Hants* v; Cathedral, *Hants* v; College, *Hants* v; Hospital of St. Cross near, *Hants* ii; Hyde

INDEX OF TITLES OF ARTICLES

Abbey or New Minster by, *Hants* ii; Monastic Buildings, *Hants* v; other religious houses, *Hants* ii*
Winchester Survey, The, *Hants* i
Winchfield, *Hants* iv
Windham Hospital, *Suss.* ii
Windlesham, *Surr.* iii
Windrush, *Glos.* vi
Windsor: Royal Borough of, *Berks.* iii; religious houses, *Berks.* ii*
Windsor, Old, *Berks.* iii
Wine, *see* Cider; Vinegar
Wing, *Bucks.* iii; Priory, *Bucks.* i
Wing, *Rut.* ii
Wingfield, *Wilts.* vii
Wingfield (in Chalgrove), *Beds.* iii
Wingfield College, *Suff.* ii
Wingham College, *Kent* ii
Wingrave, *Bucks.* iii
Winkfield, *Berks.* iii
Winnall, *Hants* iii
Winslade, with Kempshott, *Hants* iv
Winslow, *Bucks.* iii
Winterbourne (in Chieveley), *Berks.* iv
Wintney Priory, *Hants* ii
Winwick, *Hunts.* iii
Winwick, *Lancs.* iv; School, *Lancs.* ii
Wirksworth Grammar School, *Derb.* ii
Wisbech, *Cambs.* iv; Grammar School, *Cambs.* ii; Hospital, *Cambs.* ii; Hundred, *Cambs.* iv; Wisbech St. Mary, *Cambs.* iv
Wishaw, *Warws.* iv
Wisley, *Surr.* iii
Wistow, *Hunts.* ii
Wistow, *Leics.* v
Witcham, *Cambs.* iv
Witchford, *Cambs.* iv; Hundreds, North and South, *Cambs.* iv*
Witchingham Priory, *Norf.* ii
Witham Priory, *Som.* ii
Witham, South, Preceptory, *Lincs.* ii
Withcote Hall, Palmer of, *see* Genealogy
Withybrook, *Warws.* vi
Withyham Priory, *Suss.* ii
Witley, *Surr.* iii
Witley, Great, *Worcs.* iv
Witley, Little (in Holt), *Worcs.* iii
Wittenham, Little and Long, *Berks.* iv*
Wittering, *Northants.* ii
Wittering, East and West, *Suss.* iv*
Witton, East, and West, *Yorks. N.R.* i*
Witton Gilbert, Hospital of St. Mary Magdalen, *Dur.* ii
Wivelsfield, *Suss.* vii
Wix Priory, *Essex* ii
Wixamtree Hundred, *Beds.* iii
Wixford, *Warws.* iii
Woburn, *Beds.* iii; Abbey, *Beds.* i, iii
Woking, *Surr.* iii; Hundred, *Surr.* iii
Wokingham, *Berks.* iii
Wold, *see* Old
Woldingham, *Surr.* iv
Wolfhamcote, *Warws.* vi
Wolford, *Warws.* v
Wollaston, *Northants.* iv
Wolston, *Warws.* vi; Priory, *Warws.* ii
Wolverhampton, religious houses, *Staffs.* iii*
Wolverley, *Worcs.* iii; Free Grammar School, *Worcs.* iv
Wolverton, *Bucks.* iv; County School, *Bucks.* ii
Wolverton, *Hants* iv
Wolverton, *Warws.* iii
Wolvey, *Warws.* vi
Wonersh, *Surr.* iii
Wonston, *Hants* iii
Wood-Carving, *see* Cabinet-Making
Woodard Schools, *Suss.* ii
Woodbridge Priory, *Suff.* ii
Woodburn, *Bucks.* iii

Woodcott, *Hants* iv
Wooden Ware and Chair-Making, *Bucks.* ii
Woodford, *Northants.* iii
Woodford, *Wilts.* vi
Woodham (in Waddesdon), *Bucks.* iv
Woodham Ferrers Priory, *see* Bicknacre Priory
Woodhay, East, *Hants* iv
Woodhay, West, *Berks.* iv
Woodhurst, *Hunts.* ii
Woodley (in Sonning), *Berks.* iii
Woodmancott, *Hants* iv
Woodmansterne, *Surr.* iv
Woodnewton, *Northants.* ii
Woodsfield (in Powick), *Worcs.* iv
Woodstock, religious houses, *Oxon.* ii*
Woodston, *Hunts.* iii
Wool, *Glos.* ii; *Notts.* ii; and Textiles, *Rut.* i; Woollen Cloth, The Old Draperies, *Suff.* ii; Woollen Industry, *Essex* ii; *Lancs.* ii; Woollen Industry before 1550, *Wilts.* iv; *and see* Cloth; Textiles
Woolbeding, *Suss.* iv
Woolcombing, *see* Draperies, New
Woolhampton, *Berks.* iii
Woollen Cloth, Industry, *see* Wool
Woolley, *Hunts.* iii
Woolley (in Chaddleworth), *Berks.* iv
Woolstaston, *Salop.* viii
Woolstone, *Glos.* viii
Woolstone, Great and Little, *Bucks.* iv*
Wooton St. Lawrence, *Hants* iv
Wootton, *Beds.* iii
Wootton, *Hants* v
Wootton, *Northants.* iv
Wootton, Leek, *Warws.* vi
Wootton Bassett, *Wilts.* ix; Hospital of St. John, *Wilts.* iii
Wootton Wawen, *Warws.* iii; Priory, *Warws.* ii
Worcester, *Worcs.* iv; religious houses, *Worcs.* ii*; schools, *Worcs.* iv*
Worcestershire Surveys, Early, *Worcs.* i
Worksop Priory, *Notts.* ii
Worldham, East and West, *Hants* ii*
Wormegay Priory, *Norf.* ii
Worminghall, *Bucks.* iv
Wormleighton, *Warws.* v
Wormley, *Herts.* iii
Worplesdon, *Surr.* iii
Worspring Priory, *Som.* ii
Worsted [industry], *Notts.* ii
Worth, *Suss.* vii
Worthy, Headbourne, *Hants* iv
Worthy, Kings, *Hants* iv
Worthy, Martyr, with Chilland, *Hants* iii
Worting, *Hants* iv
Wothorpe Priory, *Northants.* ii
Wotton, *Surr.* iii; Hundred, *Surr.* iii
Wotton-under-Edge, Crutched Friars, *Glos.* ii
Wotton Underwood, *Bucks.* iv
Woughton-on-the-Green, *Bucks.* iv
Wrandike Hundred, *Rut.* ii
Wrawby Hospital, *see* Glanford Bridge Hospital
Wraysbury, *see* Wyrardisbury
Wrestling, *Cumb.* ii; *Lancs.* ii
Wrestlingworth, *Beds.* ii
Writtle Hospital, *Essex* ii
Wroxall, *Warws.* iii; Priory, *Warws.* ii
Wroxton, *Oxon.* ix; Priory, *Oxon.* ii
Wycliffe, *Yorks. N.R.* i
Wycombe, High, *Bucks.* iii; schools, *Bucks.* ii*; religious houses, *Bucks.* i*
Wycombe Abbey School, *Bucks.* ii
Wyke, *see* Weeke
Wymering, with Cosham and Hilsea, *Hants* iii
Wymington (Wimington), *Beds.* iii
Wymondham, religious houses, *Norf.* ii*
Wymondley, Great (Much), *Herts.* iii
Wymondley, Little, *Herts.* iii; Priory, *Herts.* iv

INDEX OF TITLES OF ARTICLES

Wyrardisbury (Wraysbury), *Bucks*. iii
Wyresdale Abbey, *Lancs*. ii
Wyrley, Great, *Staffs*. v
Wytham, *Berks*. iv
Wyton, *Hunts*. ii

Xylonite, *Suff*. ii

Yachts, Pleasure, Building of, *Essex* ii
Yardley, *Worcs*. iii
Yardley Hastings, *Northants*. iv
Yarm, *Yorks. N.R.* ii; religious houses, *Yorks*. iii*
Yarmouth, *Hants* v
Yarmouth, religious houses, *Norf*. ii
Yarwell, *Northants*. ii
Yateley, *Hants* iv
Yattendon and Speenham, *Berks*. iv
Yaverland, *Hants* v
Yaxley, *Hunts*. iii
Yeast Industry, *Essex* ii
Yeaveley and Barrow Preceptory, *Derb*. ii
Yedingham Priory, *Yorks*. iii
Yelden, *Beds*. iii

Yelling, *Hunts*. ii
Yeovil: Almshouse, *Som*. ii; Grammar School, *Som*. ii
York: Bailiwick, *Yorks*. iii; Castle and the Old Baile, *Yorks. York*; Cathedral Church of St. Peter, *Yorks*. iii; City, *Yorks. York*; Minster and its Precincts, *Yorks. York*; Minster, Worship in, *Yorks. York*; Preceptory of Copmanthorpe with the Castle Mills, *Yorks*. iii; religious houses, *Yorks*. iii*; religious houses, sites and remains, *Yorks. York*
York and Ainsty Foxhounds, *see* Foxhounds
Yorkshire Preceptory, *Yorks*. iii
Young Family, *see* Genealogy
Younsmere Hundred, *Suss*. vii

Zetland, Lord, his Foxhounds, *see* Foxhounds
Zinc, *Derb*. ii; *Som*. ii
Zoology, *Beds*. i; *Berks*. i; *Bucks*. i; *Cambs*. i; *Cornw*. i; *Cumb*. i; *Derb*. i; *Devon* i; *Dur*. i; *Essex* i; *Herefs*. i; *Herts*. i; *Hunts*. i; *Kent* i; *Lancs*. i; *Leics*. i; *Norf*. i; *Northants*. i; *Notts*. i; *Oxon*. i; *Rut*. i; *Salop*. i; *Som*. i; *Staffs*. i; *Suff*. i; *Surr*. i; *Warws*. i; *Worcs*. i; *Yorks*. i; Marine, *Cornw*. i; *Devon* i; *Dur*. i; *Essex* i; *Hants* i; *Kent* i; *Lancs*. i; *Norf*. i; *Suff*. i; *Suss*. i; *Yorks*. i

INDEX OF AUTHORS

THE following index is of authors' and indexers' names that are printed in the tables of contents. Only limited attempts have been made to penetrate beyond those tables. Thus if a section of an article is attributed to someone in a footnote printed in the text the name of that person will not be found in the index. The titles or prefixes 'the Revd.', 'the Revd. Canon', etc., 'Sir', 'Prof.', and naval and military ranks in abbreviated form have been included in the index of authors if they ever appear in a table of contents. 'Dr.' has not been included, nor have 'Mrs.' and 'Miss' except where the forename is unknown and the title is necessary to show that the author is a woman, or where the use of 'Mrs.' with the husband's initials distinguishes those initials from her own.

An asterisk (*) has been placed against the number of a volume in which an author's name, in the foregoing lists of contents, is printed more than once.

Abbott, George Wyman, *Hunts.* i
Adams, Frederick C., *Hants* i; Lionel E., *Derb.* i; *Hants* i; *Northants.* i*
Adkins, William Ryland Dent, *Northants.* ii*
Alcock, Charles William, *Cumb.* ii; *Essex* ii; *Herts.* i; *Northants.* ii; *Surr.* ii*
Alexander, Boyd, *Kent* i; Nora, *Berks.* iii*–iv*; Wilfred Backhouse, *Oxon.* i
Alington, Charles E. A., *Beds.* ii
Allaway, Prof. Albert John, *Leics.* iii
Allen, John Romilly, *Derb.* i; *Hants* ii; *Norf.* ii; *Northants.* ii; *Worcs.* ii; William Bird, *Salop.* i
Allingham (*née* Brodie), Emily G., *Hants* iii; *Surr.* iii*, iv
Allison, Keith John, *Warws.* viii*; *Yorks. E.R.* i*; *Yorks. York*; R.A., *Cumb.* ii
Amphlett, John, *Worcs.* i*
Anderson, A. Whitford, *Herts.* ii*–iii*, iv; F., *Essex* ii; Robert, *Glos.* ii
Angas, Richard Lindsey, *Oxon.* ii
Arkell, William Joscelyn, *Oxon.* i
Armitage, Ella Sophia, *Yorks.* ii
Arnold, the Revd. Frederick Henry, *Suss.* i
Ashworth, Colin, *Leics.* iv; Prof. William, *Essex* v
Atkey, R. W., *Beds.* iii; *Mdx.* ii; *Yorks. N.R.* i*
Atkinson, Thomas Dinham, *Cambs.* iv
Aubrook, Edward W., *Oxon.* i
Auden, the Revd. Preb. Thomas, *Salop.* i
Austen, Ernest Edward, *Devon* i; *Surr.* i
Avery, John, *Essex* ii

Backhouse, James, *Yorks.* ii
Bagnall, James Eustace, *Staffs.* i; *Warws.* i; *Worcs.* i
Baker, the Revd. Eric Paul, *Oxon.* vi; Frederick James, *Kent* i; John Gilbert, *Yorks.* i; John Norman Leonard, *Oxon.* iii
Ball, Richard Francis, *Essex* ii*
Bankes, Eustace Ralph, *Hants* i; *Northants.* i
Barclay, E. N., *Cambs.* i
Barker, Eric Ernest, *Essex* iv*
Barnes, Patricia Mary, *Leics.* iv
Barran, Mary R., *Oxon.* vi–vii
Barrett, Charles Golding, *Beds.* i; *Bucks.* i; *Devon* i; *Hants* i; *Norf.* i*; *Surr.* i*
Barron, Oswald, *Herts. Fam.*
Barstow, Beatrice, *Yorks.* iii*
Bartlett, Mary, *Yorks. E.R.* i
Bates, the Revd. Edward Harbin, *Som.* i
Bateson, Mary, *Northants.* ii; *Worcs.* iii
Baugh, George Crombie, *Staffs.* ii, iii*
Bayford, Edwin Goldthorp, *Yorks.* i
Bayley, Kennet Champain, *Dur.* ii–iii
Beaumont, Alfred, *Surr.* i; George Frederick, *Essex* i
Beckinsale, Robert Percy, *Oxon.* vi*

Bedwell, Ernest Charles, *Cambs.* i
Beeby, William Hadden, *Surr.* i*
Bell, Henry Esmond, *Oxon.* v
Bellot, Prof. Hugh Hale, *Mdx.* i
Bembrose, H. Arnold, *Derb.* i
Benson, Richard de Gylpyn, *Salop.* i; Robert Bernard, *Cambs.* i; *Oxon.* i
Beresford, Maurice Warwick, *Essex* iv; *Wilts.* iv*
Beveridge, Catherine, *Beds.* iii*
Bevir, Joseph Louis, *Berks.* ii
Bezodis, Peter Albert, *Cambs.* iii
Bickley, Francis Lawrance, *Hants* iv*; *Herts. Fam.*
Biddell, Herman, *Suff.* ii
Bignell, George C., *Devon* i*
Bindoff, Prof. Stanley Thomas, *Wilts.* v
Binstead, the Revd. Charles Herbert, *Cumb.* i; *Herefs.* i; *Som.* i
Birch, Alan, *Staffs.* ii
Bird, Ruth, *Leics.* iv
Birkett, William, *Mdx.* ii; *Suss.* ii
Blake, Prof. John Frederick, *Notts.* i
Blakiston, the Revd. Herbert Edward Douglas, *Oxon.* iii; Hugh Noel, *Wilts.* iii
Blathwayt, the Revd. Francis Linley, *Som.* i; Lt.-Col. Linley, *Som.* i*
Bloe, John William, *Beds.* ii; *Berks.* iii, iv*; *Hants* iv; *Surr.* iii–iv; *Suss.* iii–iv, vii, ix*; *Warws.* iii–v; *Worcs.* iii*; *Yorks. N.R.* i*–ii*
Bloomfield, the Revd. Edwin Newson, *Suff.* i*; *Suss.* i*
Blount, Frances Riddell, *Oxon.* v*, vi–vii
Bolton, Diane Kay, *Mdx.* i; *Warws.* viii*; Herbert, *Lancs.* i; James Laurence, *Oxon.* ix
Bond, Doris M., *Warws.* iii*
Bonnett, Frank ('East Sussex'), *Hants* v; *Kent* i*; *Notts.* ii*; *Yorks.* ii*
Booth, Cynthia E., *Essex* iv
Borley, John Oliver, *Yorks.* i
Borradaile, Lancelot Alexander, *Cambs.* iii; Oswell Robert, *Essex* ii; *Suss.* ii
Boston, the Revd. Noel, *Warws.* iv
Bothamley, Charles Herbert, *Som.* ii
Boulenger, George Albert, *Hants* i; *Herts.* i; *Kent* i; *Northants.* i; *Som.* i; *Surr.* i
Bourne, James William, *Bucks.* ii; *Derb.* ii; *Glos.* ii; *Lincs.* ii; *Oxon.* ii; *Suss.* ii; *Worcs.* ii
Bouskell, Frank, *Leics.* i*; *Northants.* i
Bower, Benjamin A., *Kent* i; the Revd. Canon Richard, *Cumb.* ii
Bowles, Charles Eyre Bradshaw, *Derb.* ii
Bradby, Henry Christopher, *Warws.* ii
Bradford, Gladys, *see* Temperley
Bradley, Arthur Granville, *Northants.* ii; Cuthbert, *Lincs.* ii; *Rut.* i; *Suff.* ii; Ralph C., *Warws.* i

Bradshaw, Frederick, *Dur.* ii

Brakspear, Sir Harold, *Hants* iii–v; *Surr.* ii; *Suss.* ix; *Worcs.* iii*, iv; *Yorks. N.R.* i

Braun, Hugh Stanley, *Suss.* vii*

Briggs, Prof. Asa, *Warws.* vii*; Charles A., *Devon* i; *Surr.* i; Helen M., *Suss.* iv*; *Warws.* iv*; Nancy, *Essex* v; Thomas Henry, *Northants.* i; *Surr.* i*

Bright, Percy M., *Hants* i

Brindley, Harold Hulme, *Cambs.* i

Brinson, Major John George Samuel, *Essex* iii

Bristowe, William Syer, *Cambs.* i

Brocklebank, Harold, *Lancs.* ii

Brodie, Dorothy Margaret, *Cambs.* iii; Emily G., *see* Allingham

Brook, the Revd. Victor John Knight, *Oxon.* iii

Brooke, George Cyril, *Hunts.* ii

Brooking-Rowe, Joshua, *Devon* i

Brooks, Frederick William, *Yorks. E.R.* i

Brough, Frances, *Berks.* iv; *Hants* iii*–iv*

Brougham, Henry William, *Berks.* ii

Brown, Arthur F. J., *Essex* iv–v; *Essex Bibl.*; Lucy Margaret, *Yorks. E.R.* i; Mary Croom, *Suff.* ii; William E., *Wilts.* iv

Brownbill, John, *Dur.* iii*; *Hunts.* ii; *Lancs.* iii, iv*, v–viii; *Northants.* iii*

Browne, Montagu, *Leics.* i

Bryant, Margaret Elizabeth, *Mdx.* i

Bryden, Henry Anderson, *Derb.* ii*; *Suss.* ii*

Buckland, Jessie Hatch (Mrs. C. S. B. Buckland), *Hunts.* ii

Buckle, A. J., *Dors.* ii

Buckley, James Edward, *Wilts.* iv

Bucknall, Cedric, *Som.* i

Bucknill, John Alexander Strachey, *Surr.* i*

Buckton, George Bowdler, *Surr.* i

Bull, Frederick William, *Northants.* iii

Bullen, George Ebsworth, *Herts.* iv

Bullock-Webster, the Revd. George Russell, *Norf.* i; *Suff.* i

Burkitt, Miles Crawford, *Hunts.* i

Burley, Kevin Hubert, *Essex* iv

Burnard, Robert, *Devon* i

Burne, Sambrooke Arthur Higgins, *Staffs.* ii*, iv*–v*

Burr, Malcolm, *Hants* i; *Kent* i; *Surr.* i; *Suss.* i

Burrows, Christine Mary Elizabeth, *Oxon.* iii

Bury, John Patrick Tuer, *Cambs.* iii

Butcher, Emily Elizabeth, *Wilts.* v

Butler, Christina Violet, *Glos.* ii*; Edward A., *Kent* i; *Suss.* i*; the Revd. Pierce Armar ('Purbeck Pilgrim'), *Dors.* ii*; Ruth Florence, *Glos.* ii*; *Oxon.* iii

Butterfield, Prof. Herbert, *Cambs.* iii; W. C. J. Ruskin, *Suss.* i*

Calthrop, Charlotte Margaret, *Berks.* i; *Bucks.* iv*; *Northants.* iii*; *Rut.* ii*; *Surr.* iv*; *Yorks. N.R.* i*–ii*; Muriel M. C., *Dors.* ii*; *Lincs.* ii; *Worcs.* ii*

Cam, Prof. Helen Maud, *Cambs.* iii; *Northants.* iii

Campbell-Curtis, M., *Worcs.* iii*

Candler, Howard, *Rut.* i

Cantrill, Thomas Crosbee, *Salop.* i; *Warws.* i

Carlyle, Edward Irving, *Herefs.* i

Caröe, William Douglas, *Surr.* iv

Carpenter, the Revd. Harry James, *Oxon.* iii

Carr, Prof. John Wesley, *Notts.* i*

Carslaw, Ronald McGregor, *Cambs.* ii

Carter, William Fowler, *Warws.* i

Carus-Wilson, Prof. Eleanora Mary, *Wilts.* iv

Cavill, Reginald J. W., *Warws.* iv

Celoria, Francis Sergius Cajetan, *Mdx.* i

Chamberlain, Alexander Geoffrey, *Yorks. E.R.* i

Chambers, Charles Gore, *Beds.* ii; *Suss.* ix*

Champion, George Champion, *Kent* i; *Surr.* i

Chapman, Anne (or Annie) Beatrice Wallis, *Berks.* iv; *Notts.* ii; Prof. Sydney John, *Lancs.* ii*

Charbonnier, Henry J., *Som.* i

Charity Commission [informant], *Suss.* iv

Chasmore, Philip, *Suss.* ii

Chavasse, the Rt. Revd. Christopher Maude, *Oxon.* iii

Chawner, Ethel F., *Hants* i; *Surr.* i

Chaytor, the Revd. Henry John, *Lancs.* ii*

Cheetham, Frank Haliday, *Berks.* iv*; *Dur.* iii*; *Lancs.* iv–viii; *Northants.* iii*, iv; *Rut.* ii; *Worcs.* iv*; *Yorks. N.R.* ii*

Chettle, Henry Francis, *Wilts.* iii*, vii

Chew, Helena Mary, *Mdx.* i; *Wilts.* iii

Chibnall, Marjorie McCallum, *Mdx.* i; *Wilts.* iii

China, William Edward, *Oxon.* i

Chitty, Arthur John, *Kent* i

Christie (*née* Seebohm), Mabel Elizabeth, *Bucks.* ii; *Herts.* iii*; *Suss.* vii*, ix*

Christy, Miller, *Essex* i, ii*

Clapham, Alfred William, *Berks.* iv*; *Herts.* iii; *Surr.* iv; *Worcs.* iv*; *Yorks. N.R.* i*–ii*

Clark, Sir George Norman, *Oxon.* v*; Prof. James, *Cornw.* i*; John Grahame, *Cambs.* i; Philip L., *Staffs.* ii

Clarke, Celia Beatrice, *Warws.* viii*; David K., *Suss.* iii

Clinch, George, *Berks.* i–ii; *Bucks.* i; *Dur.* i; *Herefs.* i; *Kent* i; *Leics.* i; *Norf.* i; *Staffs.* i; *Suff.* i; *Surr.* i, iv; *Suss.* i*; *Warws.* i; *Yorks.* i

Clinker, Charles Ralph, *Wilts.* iv

Cobbold, Edgar Sterling, *Salop.* i*

Cockburn, James Swanston, *Mdx.* i*

Cocks, Alfred Heneage, *Berks.* i; *Bucks.* i–ii

Cole, Jaquetta Catherine, *Oxon.* v*

Collin, James E., *Cambs.* i

Collingwood, Robin George, *Cornw.* ii (5); William Gersham, *Cumb.* i; *Yorks.* ii

Collins, George Edwin, *Lincs.* ii*

Colvin, Howard Montagu, *Oxon.* iii, vi–vii

Cook, Charles Henry, *Berks.* i–ii; *Bucks.* i–ii; *Surr.* iii; Daniel, *Cambs.* ii; Theodore Andrea, *Bucks.* ii; *Oxon.* ii

Cooper, William, *Warws.* iii*, vi

Cope, John Hautenville, *Beds.* iii*; *Berks.* iii*

Cordley, Clifford, *Warws.* ii*

Cornford, Margaret E., *Dur.* ii; *Lond.* i*; *Surr.* iii*

Cornish, Charles John, *Berks.* i*, ii; *Cornw.* i*

Cossons, Arthur, *Wilts.* iv

Cowie, the Revd. Leonard Wallace, *Staffs.* iii; *Wilts.* iii; *Yorks. York*

Cowper, Henry Swainson, *Lancs.* ii

Cox, Anthony David Machell, *Oxon.* vi; the Revd. John Charles, *Beds.* ii; *Berks.* ii*; *Bucks.* ii; *Derb.* i, ii*; *Dors.* ii; *Dur.* ii; *Essex* ii; *Hants* ii; *Herts.* iv; *Kent* i; *Lincs.* ii; *Lond.* i*; *Mdx.* ii; *Norf.* ii*; *Northants.* ii*; *Notts.* i–ii; *Oxon.* ii; *Rut.* i; *Salop.* i; *Som.* ii; *Suff.* ii*; *Surr.* ii; *Warws.* ii*; *Yorks.* i

Craig, Margaret, *Yorks. York*

Craster, Sir (Herbert Henry) Edmund, *Oxon.* viii

Crawley, Charles William, *Cambs.* iii

Crick, Margaret Mary, *Dors.* ii*

Crippen, the Revd. Thomas George, *Lond.* i

Crittall, Christine Elizabeth, *Wilts.* iii*, iv, vi*–ix*

Crombie, the Revd. James Morrison, *Norf.* i

Crook, Barbara, *Suss.* iv

Croome, Arthur Capel Molyneux, *Berks.* ii*

Crossley, Alan, *Glos.* viii; *Oxon.* ix

Crossman, Alan F., *Herts.* i

Crowther-Beynon, Vernon Bryan, *Rut.* i

Cuming, Edward Walter Dirom, *Beds.* ii*; *Bucks.* ii*; *Derb.* ii*; *Essex* ii*; *Glos.* ii*; *Lincs.* ii; *Northants.* ii; *Oxon.* ii; *Suff.* ii*; *Surr.* ii; *Suss.* ii*; *Worcs.* ii

Cunningham, Joseph Thomas, *Cornw.* i; *Devon* i; *Suff.* i; Valerie, *Hunts.* iii; *Rut.* ii

Curtis, Mrs. M. J., *Worcs.* ii; Myra, *Berks.* iv*; *Bucks.* iv*; *Dur.* iii*; *Hants* iv; *Yorks. N.R.* i*–ii*

Curtler, William Henry Ricketts, *Hants* v; *Herefs.* i; *Lancs.* ii; *Notts.* ii; *Rut.* i; *Staffs.* i; *Warws.* ii

Cuttle, William Lindsell, *Cambs.* iii

Dale, Marian Kate, *Leics.* iv; *Northants.* iv*; *Wilts.* vi*

Dales, Sidney Phillips, *Warws.* vi*

Dannatt, Gwendoline H., *Oxon.* vi

Darby, Prof. Henry Clifford, *Cambs.* ii*; *Hunts.* iii

Darlington, Prof. Reginald Ralph, *Wilts.* ii*
Davey, Frederick Hamilton, *Cornw.* i*
Davies, the Revd. David John, *Yorks.* iii; the Revd. John Silvester, *Hants* iii; Katharine Llewelyn, *Staffs.* iv*
Davis, Ralph Henry Carless, *Oxon.* iii
Dawkins, William Boyd, *Hants* i; *Som.* i
Day, Frank H., *Cumb.* i
De Paravicini, Percy John, *Berks.* ii
De Villiers, Evangeline, Lady, *Oxon.* iii*, v*
Denholm-Young, Noel, *Oxon.* iii
Dewey, Henry, *Hunts.* i
Dibben, Alan Arthur, *Essex* iv
Dickens, Prof. Arthur Geoffrey, *Yorks. York*
Dickinson, the Revd. John Compton, *Cambs.* iii; *Staffs.* iii; Joycelyne Gledhill, *Oxon.* v*
Ditchfield, the Revd. Peter Hampson, *Berks.* i, ii*–iii*
Dixon, George B., *Northants.* i; Hugh Neville, *Hants* i; *Norf.* i; *Northants.* i
Dodd, B. Sturges, *Notts.* i
Dodds, Madeleine Hope, *Dur.* iii*
Donald, J. H., *Bucks.* i
Donaldson, Barbara, *see* Young
Donisthorpe, Horace St. John Kelly, *Cambs.* i; *Surr.* i
Dorling, the Revd. Edward Earle, *Beds.* ii–iii; *Berks.* ii–iv; *Bucks.* ii–iv; *Dors.* ii*; *Dur.* ii, iii*; *Hants* iii–iv, v*; *Herts.* ii*–iii*, iv, *Fam.*; *Hunts.* ii–iii; *Kent* i*; *Lancs.* ii*, iii–viii; *Mdx.* ii; *Northants.* ii–iv; *Notts.* ii; *Rut.* i–ii; *Som.* ii*; *Surr.* iii–iv; *Suss.* iii, vii, ix; *Warws.* ii*, iii–iv; *Worcs.* iii–iv; *Yorks.* ii*; *Yorks. N.R.* i–ii
Dormer-Harris, Mary, *Warws.* ii
Douglas, James, *Surr.* ii; Robert N., *Rut.* i
Douglas-Irvine, Helen, *Herts.* ii–iii, iv*; *Lond.* i; *Northants.* iii*; *Surr.* iv*; *Yorks. N.R.* ii
Downman, the Revd. Edward Andrews, *Herefs.* i; *Kent* i; *Northants.* ii; *Salop.* i
Drinkwater, the Revd. Charles Henry, *Salop.* i
Druce, George Claridge, *Beds.* i; *Berks.* i; *Bucks.* i; *Hunts.* i; *Northants.* i; *Oxon.* i
Drucker, Lucy, *Surr.* iv*
Duffield, John Elwes, *Oxon.* i
Duggan, Arthur Patrick, *Staffs.* iii
Dunning, Robert William, *Warws.* viii*; *Wilts.* ix
D'Urban, William S. M., *Devon* i
Durston, C. C., *Berks.* iii–iv; *Hants* v; *Mdx.* ii; *Surr.* iii; *Yorks. N.R.* i*, ii
Dutt, William Alfred, *Suff.* i
Dymond, Mary E., *Yorks. E.R.* i*; Thomas Southall, *Essex* ii

'East Sussex', *see* Bonnett
Eaton, the Revd. Alfred Edwin, *Derb.* i; *Staffs.* i*
Editorial Staff, *Warws.* viii*; *and see* Oxfordshire; Page, William; Staffordshire
Edwards, James, *Hants* i; *Norf.* i*; Kathleen, *Wilts.* iii*; Maud Frances, *Herts.* iii*–iv*; *Surr.* iv*
Elgar, H., *Kent* i
Elliman, E. George, *Herts.* i
Ellis, Colin Dare Bernard, *Leics.* iii; Dorothy M. B., *Cambs.* ii; Grace A., *Beds.* iii; *Bucks.* iii*–iv*; H. Willoughby, *Warws.* i*
Elrington, Christopher Robin, *Cambs.* iii; *Glos.* vi*, viii; *Warws.* vii*; *Wilts.* iv, vii
Elspeth, Sister, of the Community of All Saints, *see* Hodge, Elizabeth Anne
Elton, Charles Sutherland, *Oxon.* i
Emden, Alfred Brotherston, *Oxon.* iii
Erith, Edward J., *Essex* iv
Erskine, Audrey Mary, *Leics.* iv
Evans, Anne Katharine Babette, wife of Rupert Hambling, *Staffs.* iii*; Arthur Humble, *Cambs.* i; Sir John, *Herts.* i; Lewis, *Herts.* iv; Rupert Hambling, *Leics.* iv; *Staffs.* iii
Everitt, Nicholas, *Suff.* ii
Eversley, David Edward Charles, *Warws.* vii; *Wilts.* iv
Eyre, the Revd. William Leigh Williamson, *Hants* i

Fagan, Eileen H., *Suss.* vii*
Falconer, William, *Oxon.* i
Fallow, Thomas McCall, *Yorks.* iii*
Farr, Michael Walter, *Warws.* viii
Farrer, Joseph H., *Essex* iv; William, *Lancs.* i, ii*, iii, iv*, v–viii; *Yorks.* ii*
Fell-Smith, Charlotte, *Essex* ii*
Fenn, Charles, *Kent* i
Ferguson, Richard Saul, *Cumb.* i
Fetherston-Dilke, Beaumont Albany, *Warws.* iv
Field, the Revd. John Edward, *Berks.* iii*
Fisher, Harry, *Lancs.* i; *Leics.* i; the Revd. Canon John Lionel, *Essex* v*
Fishwick, J. Lacey, *Beds.* i
Fletcher, Frank, *Notts.* ii; *Rut.* i; Joseph E., *Worcs.* i*; Margery A., *Northants.* iv*; *Warws.* iii*; William H. B., *Hants* i*; *Suss.* i*
Foley, the Revd. Brian C. [informant], *Essex* iv
Forbes, Arthur Charles, *Dur.* ii; Henry Ogg, *Lancs.* i; Urquhart A., *Mdx.* ii*; *Rut.* i
Ford, James, *Oxon.* i
Forrest, Herbert Edward, *Salop.* i
Forster, Gordon Colin Fawcett, *Yorks. E.R.* i; *Yorks. York*
Fowler, Robert Copp, *Essex* ii*; *Kent* ii*; the Revd. Canon William Weeks, *Beds.* i; *Berks.* i; *Bucks.* i; *Devon* i; *Hants* i; *Herefs.* i*; *Kent* i; *Northants.* i; *Surr.* i; *Suss.* i
Fowler-Dixon, John Edwin, *Bucks.* ii; *Glos.* ii; *Lincs.* ii; *Suff.* ii
Fox, Cyril, *Hunts.* i; George Edward, *Hants* i; *Leics.* i; *Norf.* ii; *Suff.* i; Levi, *Warws.* iii*
Fox-Strangways, Charles Edward, *Leics.* i
Fripp, Mrs. Edward, *Dors.* ii; Madeleine C., *Dors.* ii
Fryer, Frederick Eustace Reade, *Suff.* ii; John Claude Fortescue, *Cambs.* i; P. H., *Northants.* ii

Galbraith, Georgina Rosalie, *Wilts.* iii*
Gale, Walter Keith Vernon, *Staffs.* ii*
Gallichan, Walter M., *Derb.* ii
Gambles, R. Moylan, *Cambs.* i
Gamester, Ernest Richard, *Essex Bibl.*
Gamlen, St. John Onslow, *Rut.* ii
Garbett, Henrietta L. Elizabeth, *Berks.* iv*; *Bucks.* iv*; *Dur.* iii; *Hants* iv; *Herts.* iv; *Lond.* i; *Surr.* iii*
Gard, Robin Martin, *Leics.* iv
Gardner, Willoughby, *Lancs.* ii; *Warws.*i
Garrod, Heathcote William, *Oxon.* iii
Garstang, John, *Lancs.* i; Walter, *Essex* i; *Hants* i; *Norf.* i
Garton, A. J., *Herts.* i
Gaskoin, Charles Jacinth Bellaire, *Cambs.* iii
Gaston, Alfred J., *Suss.* ii
Gaydon, Alexander Thomas, *Oxon.* vi; *Salop.* viii
Gee, the Very Revd. Henry, *Dur.* ii–iii
Geldart, Herbert D., *Norf.* i*
George, Thomas John, *Northants.* i, ii*
Gibbs, Arthur Ernest, *Bucks.* i; *Herts.* i
Gibson, Strickland, *Oxon.* iii; Walcot, *Staffs.*i
Gifford, Joyce, *Wilts.* i (1)
Gilbey, Col. Alfred, *Bucks.* i
Gilchrist, Douglas Alston, *Dur.* ii
Gill, Edwin Leonard, *Dur.* i*
Gillam, Stanley George, *Oxon.* iii*
Gilmour, John Scott Lennox, *Cambs.* iii
Giuseppi, Montague Spencer, *Surr.* ii
Glenny, William Wallis, *Essex* ii*
Goddard, Algernon Robertson, *Beds.* i
Godfrey, Walter Hindes, *Suss.* iii, vii*, ix
Godwin, Harry, *Cambs.* i
Goodchild, John George, *Cumb.* i
Gordon, Sir Home, *Bucks.* ii; *Derb.* ii; *Essex* ii; *Glos.* ii; *Herts.* i; *Kent* i; *Lancs.* ii; *Mdx.* ii; *Northants.* ii; *Notts.* ii; *Som.* ii; *Surr.* ii; *Suss.* ii; *Warws.* ii; *Worcs.* ii; *Yorks.* ii
Goschen, Diana Marjorie [informant], *Wilts.* vii
Goss, Herbert, *Devon* i; *Hants* i*; *Kent* i*; *Northants.* i*; *Surr.* i*; *Suss.* i*

Gotch, John Alfred, *Northants.* ii, iii*–iv*; *Rut.* ii*
Gould, Isaac Chalkley, *Dur.* i; *Essex* i*; *Herefs.* i; *Kent* i
Grabham, Oxley, *Yorks.* i
Grace, William Gilbert, junior, *Northants.* ii
Graham, Rose, *Glos.* ii; *Lincs.* ii*
Granger, Prof. Frank, *Notts.* i
Grant, Raymond Kenneth James, *Wilts.* iv
Greaves, Robert William, *Leics.* iv
Green-Price, Sir Richard, *Worcs.* ii
Greenslade, Michael Washington, *Staffs.* ii*–v*, viii*
Greenwell, the Revd. William, *Dur.* i
Grensted, the Revd. Prof. Laurence William, *Oxon.* i*
Greswell, the Revd. William Henry Parr, *Som.* ii
Grierson, Philip, *Cambs.* iii
Grimshaw, Percy H., *Yorks.* i
Grinsell, Leslie Valentine, *Wilts.* i (1)
Grundy, Annie R., *Beds.* iii*; *Hants* iii
Guest, William, *Oxon.* vii
Guy, the Revd. Ralph Courtenay, *Essex* ii

Hadfield, Ellis Charles Raymond, *Wilts.* iv
Haggar, Reginald G., *Staffs.* ii
Haines, Charles Reginald, *Rut.* i; Robert Markham, *Oxon.* v, vii*
Hale, John, *Oxon.* v
Hall, Alfred Daniel, *Herts.* ii; Ivan, *Yorks. E.R.* i
Hamilton, William P., *Salop.* i*
Hamm, Albert Harry, *Berks.* i*; *Oxon.* i*
Hampson, Ethel Mary, *Cambs.* ii*, iv
Hamson, John, *Beds.* i
Hannah, Ian Campbell, *Suss.* ix*
Hannam, Una Constance, *Staffs.* iii*
Harden, Donald Benjamin, *Oxon.* i
Harding, Ambrose, *Hunts.* i*; Walter Ambrose Heath, *Cambs.* i*
Hardy, William John, *Hants* ii
Harley, John, *Hants* v*
Harrington, Geoffrey, *Essex* iv
Harris, James Rendel, *Staffs.* ii
Harrison, William Jerome, *Cambs.* iii
Hartert, Ernst, *Bucks.* i
Hartland, Ethel M., *Hants* iii; *Worcs.* iii*
Hartley, Gilfrid W., *Cumb.* ii*
Hartshorne, Albert, *Northants.* i
Harvey, Barbara Fitzgerald, *Oxon.* vi*
Harwood, William Henry, *Essex* i
Hassall, William Owen, *Oxon.* iii, v*
Haverfield, Prof. Francis John, *Cornw.* ii (5); *Derb.* i; *Hants* i; *Kent* iii*; *Norf.* i; *Northants.* i; *Salop.* i; *Som.* i; *Surr.* iv; *Warws.* i; *Worcs.* i
Hawkes, Charles Francis Christopher, *Kent* iii
Hawtrey, Valentina, *Surr.* iii*, iv; *Worcs.* iv*
Haynes, Henrietta, *Berks.* iii*
Heath, Peter, *Staffs.* iii
Heinemann, Arthur B., *Som.* ii*
Hendy, Miss A. M., *Hants* iii*, iv
Herbert, Charles, *Essex* ii; *Northants.* ii; *Surr.* ii; *Worcs.* ii; Nicholas Martin, *Glos.* viii
Hervey, Lord John (d. 1902), *Suff.* i
Hewitt, Ethel M., *Hants* v*; *Herts.* iv; *Kent* iii; *Lincs.* ii; *Notts.* ii*; *Rut.* i; *Som.* ii*; *Suff.* ii; *Warws.* ii*
Hiern, William Philip, *Devon* i*
Hill, James Bastian, *Cornw.* i; Sir (James William) Francis, *Wilts.* vi
Hilton, Rodney Howard, *Leics.* ii
Hoare, Archer, *Glos.* ii
Hobby, Bertram Maurice, *Oxon.* i*
Hockaday, Job, *Cornw.* i
Hodge, Elizabeth Anne (Sister Elspeth of the Community of All Saints), *Beds.* i*; *Bucks.* i; *Hunts.* i*; *Leics.* i; *Lincs.* ii*; *Rut.* i*
Hodges, Charles Clement, *Dur.* i
Hodgett, Gerald Augustus John, *Wilts.* v
Hodgkin, Robert Howard, *Oxon.* iii
Hodgson, William, *Cumb.* i*
Hogg, V. W., *Leics.* iv

Holland, William, *Berks.* i*
Hollings, Marjory, *Berks.* iii*, iv; *Hants* iv*, v; *Hunts.* iii*; *Rut.* ii*; *Worcs.* iii*
Holmes, Edward Morell, *Beds.* i; *Cornw.* i; *Devon* i; *Hants* i; *Kent* i*; *Som.* i; *Surr.* i; George, *Cumb.* ii; John H., *Essex* iv*; the Revd. Chancellor Thomas Scott, *Som.* ii*; Thomas Vincent, *Kent* i
Homeshaw, Ernest James, *Staffs.* ii
Honeybourne, Marjorie Blanche, *Mdx.* i
Hook, Judith, *Oxon.* ix
Hope, Sir William Henry St. John, *Berks.* iii; *Hants* i, ii*; *Yorks. N.R.* i
Hopkinson, John, *Beds.* i; *Herts.* i*
Hoskins, William George, *Leics.* iii; *Wilts.* iv
Howard, Lady Mabel Harriet, *Cumb.* ii
Huband, the Revd. Hugo Richard, *Warws.* iii
Hubbard, Cyril Ernest Boyce, *Warws.* iv*–v*
Hudd, Alfred Edmund, *Som.* i
Huddleston, Edward, *Suff.* ii
Huddlestone, Dorothy, *Surr.* iv
Hull, Mark Reginald, *Essex* iii*; William, *Northants.* i
Hunt, Richard William, *Oxon.* iii
Hurst, Alexander Saxby, *Suss.* ii
Hurstfield, Joel, *Wilts.* v
Hutchings, Dennis W., *Essex* iii
Hyde, Prof. Francis Edwin, *Wilts.* v

Imms, Augustus Daniel, *Cambs.* i*
Ingram, Mallard Edward, *Yorks. E.R.* i; T. F., *Beds.* iii; *Yorks. N.R.* i*; Walter F., *Suss.* ii
Irvine, Lionel Herbert, *Leics.* iii

Jackson, Charles Herbert Newton, *Cambs.* i; Charles Kains, *Mdx.* ii
Jacob, Prof. Ernest Fraser, *Oxon.* iii
Jalland, Beatrice Mary Hamilton, *Oxon.* iii
James, Harold Arthur, *Warws.* vi–vii; Margery Kirkbride, *Wilts.* vi
Jamison, Catherine, *Berks.* iii*; *Bucks.* ii*, iii; *Hunts.* ii*–iii*; *Northants.* iii*; *Rut.* ii*; *Suss.* vii
Jeffery, Reginald Welbury, *Oxon.* ii
Jeffries Davies, Eliza, *Lond.* i*; Joyce, *Lond.* i*; *Northants.* ii
Jenkins, Hester Truex, *Oxon.* v*–vii*, viii–ix; John Gilbert, *Staffs.* ii*, iv, viii*; William Anthony, *Leics.* iv
Jenkinson (*née* Rickards), Alice Violet, *Beds.* ii*–iii*; *Bucks.* iii–iv*
Jenner, James Herbert A., *Suss.* i*
Jennings, Dorothy M., *Bucks.* iii*, iv
Jephcott, W. Ellery, *Staffs.* ii
Jessopp, the Revd. Canon Augustus, *Norf.* ii
Jessup, Ronald Frederick, *Kent* iii
Johnson, Ann Julia (*née* Kettle), wife of Douglas Anthony, *Staffs.* ii*, iii; Prof. Basil Leonard Clyde, *Staffs.* ii*; Charles, *Norf.* ii*; Douglas Anthony, *Staffs.* ii*–iii*
Johnston, Francis Raymond, *Mdx.* i; Philip Mainwaring, *Surr.* ii–iii, iv*; *Suss.* ii
Johnstone, Hilda, *Staffs.* iii; James, *Lancs.* i*, ii
Jones, Prof. Arnold Hugh Martin, *Oxon.* iii*; Freda Katharine, wife of Arnold Hugh Martin, *Cambs.* iii; *Oxon.* iii; George, *Worcs.* ii; Prof. Gwilym Peredur, *Oxon.* iii*; Marjorie, *Oxon.* vii*, viii–ix; Stanley Robert, *Glos.* viii; *Leics.* v; *Staffs.* iv–v; *Warws.* viii; W. Unite, *Warws.* iii; William Henry Samuel, *Cambs.* iii; William Thorpe, *Dur.* iii
Jourdain, the Revd. Francis Charles Robert, *Derb.* i*; *Staffs.* i*; Margaret, *Warws.* ii
Joy, Norman H., *Berks.* i
Jukes-Browne, Alfred John, *Rut.* i

Kaines-Smith, Solomon Charles, *Beds.* iii*; *Hants* v; *Herts.* iii*; *Lancs.* vi, viii*; *Surr.* iv*; *Yorks. N.R.* i
Keate, Edith Murray, *Beds.* ii; *Leics.* i; *Mdx.* ii; *Staffs.* i; *Surr.* iv
Kemp, Dorothy, *Suff.*

Kendall, John Murray, *Beds.* ii; *Bucks.* ii; *Hants* iv–v; *Herts.* ii*, iv; *Mdx.* ii; *Surr.* iii–iv; *Worcs.* iii*; *Yorks. N.R.* i; Prof. Percy Fry, *Yorks.* i

Kennedy, Frances, *Hants* iv*

Kerrich, Geoffrey John, *Cambs.* i; *Oxon.* i

Kerridge, Eric William Joseph, *Leics.* iv; *Wilts.* iv

Kettle, Ann Julia, *see* Johnson

Kiddle, David Frederick Arthur, *Mdx.* iii*

Killington, Frederick James, *Oxon.* i*

King, Heinz Peter Francis, *Mdx.* i*; James J. Francis Xavier, *Hants* i

Kingston, J. P., *Northants.* ii

Kirby, John Lavan, *Cambs.* iii; *Mdx.* i*; *Staffs.* iii* *Wilts.* iii*;

Kirke, Edith M., *Kent* iii

Kitchin, the Very Revd. George William, *Dur.* i

Knecht, Robert Jean, *Wilts.* vi

Knoop, Prof. Douglas, *Lancs.* ii*; *Oxon.* iii*

Knowles, Prof. the Revd. Michael Clive (in religion David), *Mdx.* i; Yalden H., *Surr.* ii

Lacaille, Armand Donald, *Mdx.* i

Ladds, Sydney Inskip, *Hunts.* i, ii*–iii*

Laffan, Robert George Dalrymple, *Cambs.* iii

Lamonby, William Farquharson, *Cumb.* ii

Lamplugh, George William, *Kent* i; *Surr.* i

Lancaster, Joan Cadogan, *Warws.* viii*

Lander, Mrs. J. H., *Derb.* ii*

Lane, Samuel Francis Beeke, *Beds.* ii; *Bucks.* ii; *Hants* iv–v; *Surr.* iv; *Worcs.* iii*; *Yorks. N.R.* i*

Langdon, Arthur Gregory, *Cornw.* i

Lapsley, Gaillard Thomas, *Dur.* i

Lascelles, the Hon. Gerald William, *Hants* i–ii, v

Latham, Percy Holland, *Herts.* i

Laughton, Gladys A., *Hants* iii*; Leonard George Carr, *Hants* v

Laver, Henry, *Essex* i*–ii*

Law, Alice, *Lancs.* ii*

Lawson, James Bazille, *Salop.* viii; John, *Yorks. E.R.* i

Lea, H. S. F., *Beds.* iii*

Leach, Arthur Francis, *Beds.* ii; *Berks.* ii; *Bucks.* ii; *Derb.* ii*; *Dur.* i; *Glos.* ii; *Hants* ii, v; *Herts.* ii; *Lancs.* ii*; *Lincs.* ii; *Northants.* ii; *Notts.* ii; *Som.* ii; *Suff.* ii; *Surr.* ii; *Suss.* ii; *Warws.* ii; *Worcs.* iv; *Yorks.* i

Leake, William Ralph Martin, *Surr.* ii

Lebour, George Alexander Louis, *Dur.* i

Ledger, Horace, *Essex* ii; *Suff.* ii

Lee, John Michael, *Leics.* v*

Leeds, Edward Thurlow, *Hunts.* i; *Oxon.* i*

Lees, Beatrice Adelaide, *Oxon.* ii; *Suff.* i

Legge, W. Heneage, *Suss.* ii

Leighton, Gerald Rowley, *Herefs.* i

Lethbridge, Thomas Charles, *Cambs.* i

Levett, Prof. Ada Elizabeth, *Suss.* iii

Lewis, George Randall, *Cornw.* i; *Glos.* ii; Richard Albert, *Wilts.* v

Ley, the Revd. Augustin, *Herefs.* i

Light (*née* Powell), Hilda M., *Hants* iv–v; *Worcs.* iii*

Lilford, Lord, *see* Powys

Lindsay, Miss B., *Herefs.* i; Jean Olivia, *Cambs.* iii

Linton, the Revd. William Richardson, *Derb.* i

Little, Andrew George, *Dors.* ii; *Kent* ii; *Lincs.* ii; *Oxon.* ii; *Worcs.* ii; *Yorks.* iii

Livett, the Revd. Canon Grenvile Mairis, *Kent* ii

Lloyd, Robert Wyllie, *Surr.* i

Lloyd-Baker, Henry Orde, *Glos.* ii

Lobel, Mary Doreen, *Oxon.* i, iii*–viii*, ix

Locke, Amy Audrey, *Hants* iii*, iv, v*; *Notts.* i; *Worcs.* ii*, iv

Lockwood, Herbert H., *Essex* v

Lodge, Eleanor Constance, *Berks.* ii

Long, Edward Tudor, *Cambs.* iv; *Suss.* ix*; Moira Hastings, *Oxon.* vi*

Longworth, Thomas James, *Glos.* ii

Louis, Prof. Henry, *Dur.* ii

Loukes, Harold, *Oxon.* v

Loveday, Alexander, *Oxon.* iii

Lovell, Charles E., *Bucks.* iii–iv

Lowe, Edwin Ernest, *Devon* i; John, *Norf.* i

Lowndes, Ashley Gordon, *Cambs.* i; *Oxon.* i

Lucas, William J., *Berks.* i; *Herefs.* i; *Kent* i; *Salop.* i; *Surr.* i*; *Suss.* i*

Lydekker, Richard, *Beds.* i; *Berks.* i; *Bucks.* i; *Cumb.* i; *Cornw.* i; *Derb.* i; *Devon* i; *Dur.* i; *Essex* i; *Hants* i; *Herefs.* i; *Herts.* i; *Hunts.* i; *Kent* i; *Lancs.* i; *Leics.* i; *Norf.* i; *Northants.* i; *Notts.* i; *Rut.* i; *Salop.* i; *Som.* i; *Staffs.* i; *Suff.* i; *Surr.* i; *Suss.* i; *Warws.* i; *Worcs.* i; *Yorks.* i

Lynam, Charles, *Staffs.* i; Edward, *Hunts.* iii

Mabbs, Alfred Walter, *Staffs.* v

McCann, the Very Revd. Philip Justin, *Oxon.* iii

Macdonald, Jean K., *Mdx.* i

McDonnell, Kevin George Thomas, *Mdx.* i

Mackay, Margaret L., *Yorks. N.R.* ii*

McKilliam, Annie M., *Hants* iv*; *Yorks. N.R.* ii

McKinley, Richard Alexander, *Leics.* ii*–v*

McLachlan, Robert, *Hants* i; *Kent* i; *Surr.* i

Maclagan, Michael, *Oxon.* iii

McLaren, Colin Andrew, *Yorks. E.R.* i*

MacMunn, Nora E., *Essex* ii

Macpherson, the Revd. Hugh Alexander, *Cumb.* i*

Magnus, Leonard Arthur, *Berks.* iii; *Surr.* iv*

Main, John Mackellar, *Cumb.* ii

Malden, Arthur Russell, *Hants* v; Henry Elliott, *Surr.* i, ii*, iii, iv*

Manfield, Muriel Rose, *Beds.* ii*–iii*; *Bucks.* iii*–iv*

Mann, Julia de Lacy, *Wilts.* iv

Mansfield, the Revd. Reginald, *Staffs.* iii–v

Markham, Christopher Alexander, *Northants.* ii*

Marr, Prof. John Edward, *Cambs.* i

Marriage, Wilson, *Essex* ii

Marriott, Charles John Bruce, *Dur.* ii; *Herts.* i; *Lancs.* ii; *Mdx.* ii*; *Warws.* ii; *Yorks.* ii

Marshall, the Revd. Edward Shearburn, *Kent* i*

Martin, Janet Douglas, *Leics.* iii, iv*–v*; *Oxon.* vi

Martineau, Alfred H., *Warws.* i; *Worcs.* i

Masefield, John Richard Beech, *Staffs.* i*

Mason, John Frederick Arthur, *Oxon.* ix; Richard, *Lincs.* ii

Massee, George, *Surr.* i

Massingberd, the Revd. William Oswald, *Lincs.* ii*

Mayall, Robert Hume Davidson, *Cambs.* iii

Mayfield, Arthur, *Suff.* i

Maynard, Mabel, *Yorks. N.R.* i*

Meade-Waldo, Edmund G. B., *Hants* i

Meads, William Edward, *Suss.* ix

Meek, Alexander, *Dur.* i

Meekings, Cecil Anthony Francis, *Cambs.* iii–iv

Melhuish, Miss S., *Lincs.* ii

Mellersh, William Lock, *Glos.* ii

Mellor, J. Vivien, *Mdx.* ii*; Jeffrey Duncan, *Mdx.* i

Melville, A. M., *Suss.* iii

Michell, Stephen, *Cornw.* i

Midgley, Laura Margaret, *Oxon.* i; *Staffs.* iv*–v*; *Suss.* vii*; *Warws.* iii*–iv*

Millais, John Guille, *Suss.* i

Millar, A. J., *Herts.* i

Miller, Edward, *Cambs.* ii–iv; *Yorks. York*; Eliza B., *Surr.* iii*–iv*

Minchin, George S., *Beds.* ii; *Berks.* ii; *Bucks.* ii; *Cambs.* ii; *Derb.* ii; *Dors.* ii; *Dur.* ii; *Essex* ii; *Glos.* ii; *Hants* v; *Herts.* ii; *Hunts.* ii; *Kent* ii; *Lancs.* ii; *Lincs.* ii; *Mdx.* ii; *Notts.* ii; *Oxon.* ii; *Rut.* i; *Som.* ii; *Staffs.* ii; *Suff.* i; *Surr.* iv; *Suss.* ii; *Warws.* ii; *Worcs.* iv; *Yorks.* iii

Minchinton, Prof. Walter Edward, *Staffs.* ii

Ministry of Housing and Local Government [informant], *Essex* iv*

Minns, Sir Ellis Hovell, *Cambs.* iii

Moffat, Miss S. E., *Rut.* i

Moger, Olive M., *Beds.* ii–iii; *Hants* iv*–v*; *Herts.* ii*; *Rut.* ii*; *Suss.* iv, vii*; *Warws.* iii*–iv*; *Worcs.* iii*–iv*

Molland, Ralph, *Wilts.* iv
Monckton, Horace Wollaston, *Berks.* i
Monington, Harold W., *Surr.* i
Monson, Augustus Debonnaire John, Baron Monson, *Lincs.* ii
Montgomerie, Duncan Hector, *Herts.* ii*; *Surr.* iv; *Worcs.* iv; *Yorks.* ii; *Yorks. N.R.* ii
Moore, Richard William, *Cumb.* ii
Morewood, Caroline C., *Yorks. N.R.* i*–ii*
Morey, George Edgar, *Suss.* vii
Morgan, Kathleen Mary, *Glos.* vi, viii; Paul, *Warws.* v
Morice, the Revd. Francis David, *Surr.* i*
Morley, Claude, *Suff.* i*; *Suss.* i
Morris, Ernest, *Leics.* iii; Margaret (formerly Saunders), *Wilts.* iv*, vi*
Morton, Kenneth, *Hants* i
Mountford, Arnold R., *Staffs.* ii
Muir, Prof. Ramsay, *Lancs.* iv
Murray, Herbert Willaume, *Surr.* i; the Revd. Richard Paget, *Som.* i*; the Revd. Robert Henry, *Hunts.* ii
Muscott, Bruce B., *Northants.* ii*

Nathan, Lt.-Col. Sir Frederick Lewis, *Essex* ii
Nattriss, J. B., *Yorks. E.R.* i
Naylor, Leonard George Richard, *Oxon.* vii*
Neilson, Prof. Nellie, *Kent* iii*
Nevill, Ralph, *Surr.* ii
Newnham, F. B., *Salop.* i*
Newton, John, *Yorks.* ii
Nicholson, Francis, *Cumb.* ii*
Nicol, William, *Cumb.* ii
Niemeyer, Annie Franziska Helena, *Herts.* iii–iv
Nisbet, John, *Cumb.* ii; *Essex* ii; *Glos.* ii; *Hants* ii; *Northants.* ii; *Surr.* ii; *Worcs.* ii
Nixon, Gilbert Edward James, *Oxon.* i
Noble, Heatley, *Berks.* i; the Revd. Canon William Mackreth, *Hunts.* ii
Norman, the Revd. Alfred Merle, *Dur.* i; J. Earl, *Herts.* i

O'Leary, John Gerard, *Essex* v
Omer-Cooper, Joseph, *Hunts.* i
O'Neil, Helen Evangeline, *Glos.* vi
Onslow, Major Hughes, *Rut.* i
Oppenheim, Michael, *Cornw.* i; *Dors.* ii; *Essex* ii; *Kent* ii; *Som.* ii; *Suff.* ii; *Suss.* ii
Oswald, Arthur, *Oxon.* iii
Otway-Ruthven, Jocelyn, *Cambs.* i
Owsley, John William [informant], *Beds.* ii–iii; *Berks.* iii–iv; *Bucks.* ii–iv; *Dur.* iii*; *Hants* iii–v; *Herts.* ii*, iii–iv; *Mdx.* ii; *Surr.* iv*; *Worcs.* iii–iv; *Yorks. N.R.* i–ii
Oxfordshire Editorial Staff, *Oxon.* v–vii, ix
Oxley, James Edwin, *Essex* v

Pafford, John Henry Pyle, *Wilts.* iv
Page, Frances Mary, *Cambs.* ii; William, *Beds.* ii–iii; *Berks.* i, iii–iv; *Bucks.* iii–iv; *Dur.* iii*; *Herts.* ii*, iii, iv*; *Hunts.* i, ii*, iii; *Leics.* i; *Northants.* ii, iii*, iv; *Rut.* ii*; *Staffs.* i; *Surr.* iii, iv*; *Suss.* iii*, ix*; *Worcs.* iii–iv; *Yorks. N.R.* i–ii; Staff of, *Suss.* ix
Paget, Major Thomas Guy Frederick, *Leics.* iii
Pantin, William Abel, *Oxon.* iii
Parker, Leslie Arthur, *Leics.* iii
Parris, Henry Walter, *Yorks. York*
Parry, Mary, *Warws.* vii
Parsloe, Charles Guy, *Hunts.* ii
Parsons, Margaret Agnes, *Wilts.* iii*
Part, Charles T., *Herts.* i
Paskin, Sir Jesse John, *Wilts.* iv
Patterson, Alfred Temple, *Leics.* iii
Peake, the Revd. Edward, *Hunts.* i, ii*; Harold John Edward, *Berks.* i, iv*
Pearce-Serocold, Oswald, *see* Serocold
Peckham, Walter Divie, *Suss.* iii–iv
Peers, Sir Charles Reed, *Beds.* ii*, iii; *Bucks.* ii; *Dur.* iii; *Hants* ii*–iii*, iv, v*; *Herts.* ii*; *Lancs.* iii–v; *Mdx.* ii*; *Northants.* ii; *Rut.* ii; *Surr.* ii*, iii–iv; *Worcs.* ii*, iii; *Yorks. N.R.* i*
Pelham, Reginald Arthur, *Warws.* vii
Perkin, Herbert, *Yorks.* ii
Perkins, E. W. [informant], *Northants.* iv; *Suss.* vii; *Warws.* iii–v; John Frederick, *Oxon.* i
Perry, Margaret, *Hants* iv*
Phillips, Charles William, *Cambs.* ii; E. Cambridge, *Herefs.* i; William, *Salop.* i*
Pickard-Cambridge, Frederick O., *Beds.* i; *Berks.* i; *Bucks.* i; *Cornw.* i; *Cumb.* i; *Derb.* i; *Devon* i; *Dur.* i; *Essex* i; *Hants* i; *Herts.* i; *Kent* i; *Lancs.* i; *Norf.* i; *Som.* i; *Staffs.* i; *Surr.* i; *Suss.* i; *Warws.* i; *Worcs.* i; the Revd. Octavius, *Cornw.* i; *Herefs.* i; *Lancs.* i; *Salop.* i; *Yorks.* i
Pidgeon, Dorothy A., *Leics.* iv
Pillans, E. B., *Worcs.* ii
Pinder, Thomas George, *Mdx.* i*
Plomer, Henry Robert, *Herts.* iv
Plowright, Charles Bagge, *Norf.* i
Plumb, John Harold, *Leics.* ii
Pocock, Reginald Innes, *Cumb.* i; *Essex* i; *Hants* i; *Norf.* i; *Som.* i; *Surr.* i
Poole, Edward Humphry Lane, *Wilts.* iv; Robert Henry John, *Dur.* i
Pope, Walter H., *Hants* v
Porritt, George T., *Yorks.* i*
Potter, the Revd. Michael Cressé, *Dur.* i
Potts, William, *Oxon.* ii
Powell, Avril Hayman, wife of William Raymond, *Essex* iii, v; Dorothy Letitia, *Bucks.* iii*–iv*; *Hunts.* ii*; *Surr.* iii*–iv*; Hilda M., *see* Light; William Raymond, *Essex* iv*–v*, *Bibl.*; *Wilts.* vii*
Powicke, Frederick Maurice, *Lancs.* ii
Powys, John, Baron Lilford, *Northants.* ii
Proby, Granville, *Hunts.* ii
Pugh, Clarence Woodburn, *Wilts.* iv*; Patricia, *Oxon.* vi; Ralph Bernard, *Warws.* viii; *Wilts.* iii, v*–vii*, viii; *Yorks. York*
'Purbeck Pilgrim', *see* Butler, the Revd. Pierce A.
Purvis, C. M., *Northants.* ii

Quekett, John, *Berks.* iii, iv*; *Bucks.* iii*–iv*; *Dur.* iii; *Hants* v; *Herts.* iii; *Surr.* iv; *Worcs.* iii*–iv*; *Yorks. N.R.* i*–ii*

Rackham, Harris, *Cambs.* iii
Radcliffe, J. B., *Dur.* ii
Radclyffe, Capt. Eustace, *Dors.* ii
Ragg, the Revd. Frederick William, *Beds.* i*; *Berks.* i; *Bucks.* i, iv; *Herts.* i; *Kent* iii
Rahbula, Ernest Alexander Rahles, *Beds.* iii; *Berks.* iii–iv; *Surr.* iv; *Worcs.* iii*, iv; *Yorks. N.R.* i
Rait, Sir Robert Sangster, *Oxon.* i
Ramm, Herman Gabriel, *Yorks. York*
Ramsay, John M., *Lond.* i; *Oxon.* i; *Rut.* i
Ramsden, Phyllis M., *Hunts.* iii
Randall, John, *Salop.* i; J. L., *Derb.* ii
Ransom, Arthur, *Beds.* ii*
Ransome, Mary Edith, *Wilts.* v, vi*
Raven, Alice, *Berks.* iii*–iv*; *Herts.* iii*–iv*; *Worcs.* iii
Ray, John E., *Suss.* ix*; Winifred M., *Surr.* iii*
Rea, Carleton, *Herefs.* i; *Worcs.* i*
Reader, Francis W., *Lond.* i
Reddan, Minnie, *Herts.* iv*; *Lond.* i*; *Yorks. N.R.* ii*
Redmayne, Prof. Richard Augustine Studdert, *Warws.* ii; *Worcs.* ii
Redstone, Lilian Jane, *Berks.* iii*; *Bucks.* iv; *Hants* iii*; *Herts.* iii*, iv; *Hunts.* ii*; *Surr.* iii*–iv*; *Worcs.* iii
Reeves, Marjorie Ethel, *Wilts.* iii
Reichel, the Revd. Oswald Joseph, *Devon* i
Reid, Charles John, *Herts.* i; Clement, *Hants* i; *Suss.* i; Eleanor J. B., *Herts.* iii*–iv*; Capt. Philip Savile Grey, *Hants* i; *Kent* i
Reynolds, Frederick, *Cumb.* ii; Susan Mary Grace, *Cambs.* iii; *Essex* iv; *Leics.* iii; *Mdx.* iii*; *Warws.* vii*

Richards, Owain Westmacott, *Oxon.* i
Richardson, Charles, *Surr.* ii; Linsdall, *Herefs.* i
Richmond, Prof. Ian Archibald, *Essex* iii
Rickards, Alice Violet, *see* Jenkinson
Rigby, George Reginald, *Staffs.* iv–v
Roach, John Peter Charles, *Cambs.* iii*
Roberts, Agnes Elizabeth, *Rut.* ii; Sir Sydney, *Cambs.* iii
Robertson, Alexander James R., *Beds.* ii; *Bucks.* ii; *Essex* ii; *Oxon.* ii; *Surr.* ii; *Suss.* ii
Robinson, Thomas, *Cumb.* ii
Robson, John E., *Dur.* i
Roebuck, William Denison, *Yorks.* i
Rogers, the Revd. John Francis, *Oxon.* iii; Kenneth Howard, *Wilts.* vi*, viii*, ix; the Revd. William Moyle, *Cornw.* i; *Devon* i*; *Hants* i; *Surr.* i; *Suss.* i
Rope, G. T., *Suff.* i*
Rose, Robert Barrie, *Mdx.* iii; *Warws.* vii*–viii*; *Yorks. York*
Ross, Alexander Michael, *Mdx.* i
Rothschild, the Hon. Walter, *Bucks.* i
Round, John Horace, *Beds.* i; *Berks.* i; *Bucks.* i; *Essex* i, ii*; *Hants* i; *Herefs.* i; *Herts.* i, *Fam.*; *Northants.* i; *Som.* i; *Surr.* i; *Suss.* i; *Warws.* i; *Worcs.* i
Rowe, Hurford, *Suss.* iii
Ruck-Keene, Capt. Harry Lancelot, *Oxon.* ii*
Rufford, Philip James, *Suss.* i
Ruggles-Brise, Archibald Weyland, *Essex* ii
Rushforth, Gordon McNeil, *Worcs.* iv
Russell, Ada, *Berks.* iv; *Hunts.* iii*; *Northants.* iv*; *Rut.* ii*; *Suss.* ix; *Yorks. N.R.* i*–ii*; Percy, *Leics.* iii*
Rye, Walter [informant], *Norf.* ii

Sabin, Charles W., *Kent* i
Salisbury, Edward, *Norf.* ii
Salmon, Charles Edgar, *Suff.* i
Salter, Frank Reyner, *Cambs.* iii; G. F., *Suss.* ii; the Revd. Herbert Edward, *Oxon.* ii*–iii*; John Henry, *Essex* ii
Saltman, Avrom, *Staffs.* iii*
Saltmarsh, John, *Cambs.* iii
Salzman, Louis Francis (formerly Salzmann), *Cambs.* i, ii*; *Cornw.* ii (8); *Herts.* iv; *Northants.* iv*; *Surr.* iii; *Suss.* i*–ii*, iv, ix*; *Warws.* ii, iii*–iv*, v–vii; *Yorks.* iii*; Peter Louis, *Suss.* ix; Rainald Russell, *Suss.* vii
Sandeman, Fraser, *Cumb.* ii
Sanderson, Lucy M., *Herts.* ii, iii*
Sandford, Kenneth Stuart, *Oxon.* i; Mary A. Wills, *Som.* ii
Saunders, Edward, *Hants* i*; *Kent* i; *Surr.* i*; *Suss.* i; James, *Beds.* i*; *Kent* i; Margaret, *see* Morris
Savill, Ethel, *Oxon.* vi–viii; Mary, *Oxon.* vi–vii
Savory, Hubert Newman, *Oxon.* i
Sawyer, Peter Hayes, *Oxon.* vii*
Scott, Richenda, *Wilts.* iv
Scroggs, Edith S., *Warws.* iii
Seebohm, Mabel Elizabeth, *see* Christie
Sellars, Colin W., *Yorks. York*
Sellers, Maud, *Dur.* ii; *Yorks.* ii*, iii
Senhouse, Humphrey P., *Cumb.* ii
Sergeant, Alice, *Berks.* ii
Serjeantson, the Revd. Robert Meyricke, *Northants.* ii*
Serocold, Oswald Pearce, *Bucks.* ii
Sewter, Albert Charles, *Leics.* iii
Sharp, Henry, *Lincs.* ii; Margaret, *Suss.* vii; William Ernest, *Lancs.* i
Shaw, William Arthur, *Lancs.* ii
Shenstone, James C., *Essex* i, ii*
Shillington, Violet Mary, *Hants* v
Shorrocks, Derek Martyn Marsh, *Essex* iv*
Shorter, Alfred H., *Wilts.* iv
Shrimpton, Colin, *Wilts.* ix*
Shrubsole, Octavius Albert, *Berks.* i
Sievers, Nowell, *Herts.* iv
Sigsworth, Eric M., *Yorks. York*
Sikes, Jeffrey Garrett, *Cambs.* iii
Simkins, Maud E., *Bucks.* iv*; *Herts.* ii; *Hunts.* ii*–iii*; *Kent* ii–iii; *Norf.* ii; *Northants.* iii*; *Rut.* ii*; *Worcs.* iv*

Simmons, Prof. Jack, *Leics.* iii; John Simon Gabriel, *Warws.* iv, v*; William Anker, *Berks.* ii
Skipton, H. S. Kennedy, *Glos.* ii*
Slade, Cecil Frederick, *Staffs.* iv*
Sladen, Frederick William Lambart, *Kent* i
Slater, Gilbert, *Kent* iii; the Revd. Henry Horrocks, *Northants.* i
Slatter, Mary Doreen, *Leics.* iv
Smith, Barbara M. D., *Warws.* vii; Bernard W., *Warws.* v; Clifford Thorpe, *Leics.* iii, iv*; J. R. [informant], *Hunts.* ii–iii; *Northants.* iii–iv; *Rut.* ii; *Suss.* iii, ix; John Thomas, *Warws.* vi*; Reginald Allender, *Beds.* i; *Berks.* i; *Bucks.* i; *Cornw.* i; *Devon* i; *Essex* i; *Hants* i; *Herts.* i; *Hunts.* i; *Kent* i; *Lond.* i*; *Norf.* i; *Northants.* i; *Notts.* i; *Rut.* i; *Som.* i; *Staffs.* i; *Suff.* i; *Surr.* i; *Suss.* i; *Warws.* i; *Worcs.* i; *Yorks.* ii; Sophie Shilleto, *Bucks.* ii; Worthington George, *Beds.* i
Snow, Edward Eric, *Leics.* iii
Solloway, the Revd. John, *Yorks.* iii*
Somerset, Henry Vere Fitzroy, *Oxon.* iii
Sorby, Henry Clifton, *Essex* i; *Kent* i; *Suff.* i
Southern, Ena Madeline Bowen, *Oxon.* iii; Richard William, *Oxon.* iii
Southwell, Thomas, *Norf.* i
Spalding, Philip Anthony, *Dors.* iii; *Leics.* v; *Staffs.* viii; *Wilts.* ii–iii, v–ix; *Warws.* viii
Spencer, Aubrey J., *Surr.* iv; Mildred, *Staffs.* i
Spilman, Anne (Nancy), *Bucks.* iv*; *Worcs.* iv*; *Yorks. N.R.* i*–ii*
Spokes, Peter Spencer, *Oxon.* iii
Sprules, Dorothy Winifred, *Surr.* iii*
Spurrell, Flaxman Charles John, *Kent* i
Staffordshire Editorial Staff, *Staffs.* iv–v
Stebbing, the Revd. Thomas Roscoe Rede, *Beds.* i; *Berks.* i; *Bucks.* i; *Cornw.* i; *Cumb.* i; *Derb.* i; *Devon* i; *Dur.* i; *Essex* i; *Hants* i; *Herefs.* i; *Herts.* i; *Hunts.* i; *Kent* i; *Lancs.* i; *Leics.* i; *Norf.* i; *Northants.* i; *Notts.* i; *Rut.* i; *Salop.* i; *Som.* i; *Staffs.* i; *Suff.* i; *Surr.* i; *Suss.* i; *Warws.* i; *Worcs.* i; *Yorks.* i
Steed, H. E., *Surr.* ii
Steel, William, *Cumb.* ii
Steele-Elliott, Jannion, *Beds.* i
Steele-Hutton, Elizabeth Peddie, *Suff.* ii; *Warws.* ii
Stenton, Prof. Frank Merry, *Derb.* i; *Hunts.* i; *Leics.* i; *Notts.* i; *Oxon.* i; *Rut.* i; *Worcs.* iv*
Stephens, Percy S. T., *Dur.* ii*; Rosemary, wife of William Brewer, *Warws.* vii; William Brewer, *Warws.* vii*–viii*
Stevenson, Janet Helen, *Wilts.* ix*; William Henry, *Notts.* i
Stokes, Ethel, *Essex* ii
Stone, Prof. Lawrence, *Oxon.* ix; *Wilts.* ii; Percy Goddard, *Hants* v*
Storer, George H., *Derb.* i; *Staffs.* i*
Sturge, William Allen, *Suff.* i
Styles, Dorothy, wife of Philip, *Staffs.* iii; *Warws.* iii; *Wilts.* iii*; Philip, *Warws.* iii*
'Sussex, East', *see* Bonnett, Frank
Sutherland, Carol Humphrey Vivian, *Oxon.* i; Lucy Stuart, *Oxon.* iii*
Symonds, James Frederick, *Herefs.* i

Tait, the Revd. Arthur James, *Surr.* ii; Prof. James, *Lancs.* ii*; *Surr.* i
Tanner, Mary E., *Mdx.* ii
Tansley, Prof. Arthur George, *Oxon.* i
Taylor, Prof. Arthur John, *Staffs.* ii; Audrey Mary, *Essex* iv*; E., *Oxon.* i; Margerie Venables, *Cornw.* ii (5); *Herts.* iv; *Hunts.* i; *Kent* iii*; *Oxon.* i*; *Salop.* i; *Worcs.* ii*; the Revd. Thomas, *Cornw.* i*, ii (8)
Temperley (*née* Bradford), Gladys, *Berks.* iii*; *Som.* ii
Templeman, Geoffrey, *Warws.* iv; *Wilts.* iii
Thirsk, Irene Joan, *Leics.* ii
Thomas, H. Dighton, *Cambs.* i; John, *Staffs.* ii*
Thompson, Prof. Alexander Hamilton, *Northants.* iii*; *Yorks.* iii*; Arthur R., *Beds.* i; Beeby, *Northants.* i–ii; Francis Michael Longstreth, *Wilts.* iv; M. Lawson, *Yorks.* i

Thunder, Clare, *Beds.* iii*
Tibbits, Edward George, *Warws.* iii*
Tildesley, Norman W., *Staffs.* ii
Tillott, Peter Muir, *Warws.* vii*; *Wilts.* vii*; *Yorks. E.R.* i; *Yorks. York*
Todd, Reginald Austen, *Devon* i
Tomes, Robert Fisher, *Warws.* i; *Worcs.* i
Tomlin, John Read le Brockton, *Derb.* i; *Staffs.* i
Tomlinson, Margaret, *Essex* iv–v; *Glos.* vi, viii; *Leics.* v; *Salop.* viii; *Staffs.* iv–v, viii*; *Warws.* vii*–viii*; *Wilts.* viii–ix
Tonkinson, Ernest, *Wilts.* iv*
Townsend, Frederick, *Hants* i
Toy, Sidney, *Bucks.* iii–iv; *Suss.* ix*; *Worcs.* iii*–iv*
Toynbee, Margaret Ruth, *Oxon.* iii, vi*
Trappes-Lomax, Brig. Thomas Byrnand, *Leics.* ii; *Wilts.* iii
Tregelles, George Fox, *Cornw.* i
Trenholme, Norman Maclaren, *Worcs.* ii
Trevor-Battye, Aubyn B. R., *Hants* i*
Tristram, the Revd. Henry Baker, *Dur.* i
Tuck, the Revd. Julian G., *Suff.* i
Tucker, Bernard William, *Oxon.* i
Turrell, Walter John, *Oxon.* ii
Tyson, John C., *Warws.* vii

Ullyott, Philip, *Cambs.* i
Underhill, Charles Hayward, *Staffs.* ii
Unwin, Prof. George, *Suff.* i–ii
Upcott, Katharine M., *Hants* iv*, v
Ussher, William Augustus Edmond, *Devon* i

Vellacott, Charles Henry, *Derb.* ii*; *Dors.* ii*; *Dur.* ii; *Glos.* ii*; *Hants* iv, v*; *Herts.* iv; *Lincs.* ii; *Northants.* ii; *Notts.* ii; *Som.* ii*; *Worcs.* ii*, iv; *Yorks.* ii*
Vine, A. C., *Suss.* i
Vipan, Capt. John Alexander Maylin, *Northants.* i

Waechter, John D'Arcy, *Mdx.* i
Wainwright, Colbran J., *Warws.* i*
Walker A. J. [informant], *Warws.* vi; Benjamin, *Warws.* iii–iv; Charles Edward, *Suss.* i; Eldred G. F., *Som.* ii; Comdr. James John, *Hants* i; *Oxon.* i; Ronald Francis, *Oxon.* v, vi*, ix
Wall, James Charles, *Devon* i; *Leics.* i; *Mdx.* ii; *Rut.* i; *Salop.* i; *Suff.* i
Walters, Henry Beauchamp, *Herefs.* i; *Herts.* iv; *Lond.* i; *Notts.* ii; *Rut.* i; *Suss.* ix; *Yorks.* ii
Ward, Gladys Amy, *Essex* iv; John, *Derb.* i*; the Revd. Percival, *Worcs.* ii; William Reginald, *Wilts.* v
Warrand, Duncan, *Herts. Fam.*
Warrener, William T., *Lincs.* ii
Waterhouse, Rachel Elizabeth, *Wilts.* v
Watkin, Dom (Christopher) Aelred (Paul), *Wilts.* iii
Watts, David George, *Warws.* vii*–viii*; *Wilts.* vi
Webb, Sydney, *Surr.* i*

Welch, Charles, *Mdx.* i
Wells, Henry Briant, *Cambs.* iv; *Oxon.* iii; *Warws.* vi; *Wilts.* vii
West, George Stephen, *Surr.* i; William, *Kent* i; *Surr.* i
Weston, Blanche Marion Percy, *Surr.* iii, iv*; *Yorks. N.R.* i*, ii
Westray, Robert, *Cumb.* ii
Wheeler, Robert Eric Mortimer, *Kent* iii*
While, George Hunt, *Warws.* vi*
Whitaker, Joseph, *Notts.* i
White, M. R. L., *Northants.* ii
Whiteman, Elizabeth Anne Osborn, *Wilts.* iii
Whiting, Wykeham Herbert, *Cambs.* i
Whitworth, the Revd. Richard Hisco, *Notts.* i
Wilkinson, William Henry, *Hants* i
Williams, C. Stanley D., *Beds.* iii*; Elizabeth Ann, *Dors.* iii*; James Eccles, *Yorks. E.R.* i
Willis-Bund, John William, *Glos.* ii; *Worcs.* i*–ii*
Willoughby-Osborne, Major Arthur, *Lancs.* ii*
Wilmot, Cicely, *Hants* iii; *Herts.* iii*
Wilson, the Revd. James, *Cumb.* i, ii*; O. Pauline, *Leics.* iv; R. S., *Cumb.* ii
Winbolt, Samuel Edward, *Suss.* iii
Windle, Bertram Coghill Alan, *Worcs.* i
Wingate, the Revd. William John, *Dur.* i
Winnington-Ingram, the Revd. Arthur Rogers, *Glos.* ii
Wise, Gwyneth A., *Warws.* iv*; Prof. Michael John, *Staffs.* ii
Witchell, Charles A., *Glos.* ii
Wolffe, Bertram Percy, *Oxon.* v*
Wood, James George, *Herefs.* i; John Henry, *Herefs.* i; Margaret Envys, *Suss.* iv*, vii*; Susan Meriel, *Oxon.* v*
Wood-Legh, Kathleen Louise, *Cambs.* ii
Woodgate, Giles Musgrave Gordon, *Cambs.* iv*; Walter Bradford, *Berks.* ii
Woodruff, Prof. William, *Wilts.* iv
Woods, John Aubin, *Yorks. E.R.* i
Woodward, Bernard Barham, *Beds.* i; *Berks.* i; *Bucks.* i; *Cornw.* i; *Cumb.* i; *Derb.* i; *Devon* i; *Dur.* i; *Essex* i; *Hants* i; *Herefs.* i; *Herts.* i; *Kent* i; *Lancs.* i; *Leics.* i; *Norf.* i; *Northants.* i; *Notts.* i; *Rut.* i; *Salop.* i; *Som.* i; *Staffs.* i; *Suff.* i; *Surr.* i; *Suss.* i; *Warws.* i; *Worcs.* i; *Yorks.* i; Horace Bolingbroke, *Bucks.* i; *Essex* i; *Hunts.* i; *Norf.* i; *Som.* i; *Suff.* i; *Worcs.* i
Wooldridge, Sidney William, *Mdx.* i
Worsley, Anne Victoria, *Essex* v*
Worthington, Edgar Barton, *Cambs.* i*
Wragge, Alfred, *Worcs.* iii*; Phyllis, *Dors.* ii; *Lincs.* ii; *Lond.* i; *Suss.* ii
Wright, Charles East, *Rut.* i
Wyld, Gillian Ruth, *Mdx.* iii*
Wymer, John J., *Mdx.* i
Wynter, Capt. Philip Henry Mascie, *Oxon.* ii

Yaxley, David Christopher, *Mdx.* i*
Yerbury, Col. John William, *Kent* i
Young (*née* Donaldson), Barbara, *Staffs.* iv, v*, viii*